Disease and Mortality
in Sub-Saharan Africa

Disease and Mortality in Sub-Saharan Africa

edited by
Richard G. Feachem
Dean T. Jamison

Published for The World Bank
Oxford University Press

Oxford University Press

OXFORD NEW YORK TORONTO DELHI CALCUTTA MADRAS
KARACHI PETALING JAYA SINGAPORE HONG KONG TOKYO
NAIROBI DAR ES SALAAM CAPE TOWN MELBOURNE
AUCKLAND
and associated companies in
BERLIN IBADAN

Manufactured in the United States of America
First printing June 1991

Library of Congress Cataloging-in-Publication Data

Disease and mortality in Sub-Saharan Africa / edited by Richard G.
 Feachem, Dean T. Jamison.
      p. cm.
   "Published for the World Bank."
   Includes bibliographical references.
   ISBN 0–19–520826–9
   1. Public health—Africa, Sub-Saharan. I. Feachem, Richard G.,
1947–   . II. Jamison, Dean. III. International Bank for
Reconstruction and Development.
RA552.S8D57   1991
362.1' 0967—dc20   91-11991
                                                    CIP

Foreword

A decade ago African delegates joined the representatives of other nations in endorsing the Alma Ata declaration, which committed all governments throughout the world to the common goal of achieving "Health for All" by the year 2000. It is widely acknowledged that this goal is ambitious, even for the well-established health services in industrial countries, which have access to powerful health technologies and abundant resources of money, health personnel, and institutions. For developing countries, particularly those in Sub-Saharan Africa, this goal is daunting. African governments have boldly tackled the challenge of improving the health status of their populations in the spirit of the Alma Ata declaration. Health care is receiving attention in the context of the overall development effort in the region. The concept of development has been broadened to include human resources, and health is now recognized as an important element of human welfare.

This book documents the significant changes in the health situation in Sub-Saharan Africa during the past few decades. Some of the advances resulted from specific interventions by the health services, but others reflect the impact of better nutrition, improvements in water supplies and other aspects of environmental sanitation, higher educational levels, and other non-medical changes. The limited data available suggest that progress has not been uniform throughout the region. The gains are more apparent in some countries than in others, and in some cases there may have been significant setbacks in recent years. It is not clear to what extent the downward trend results from the natural disasters, the social and political upheavals, or the economic crises that have plagued the region.

African governments face many obvious constraints in their pursuit of the goal of health for all. Despite the strong commitment to the implementation of the Alma Ata Declaration, the competing needs of other sectors limit the amount of resources allocated to health services. The situation is particularly difficult now in view of the economic crisis facing most Sub-Saharan countries. New plans must therefore be made realistically in the context of severe economic constraints. Better health must be achieved by developing programs that are more cost-effective rather than by increasing public spending on health services. Even the most advanced African countries need to do a lot more if they are to move decisively toward the achievement of health for all. All the nations of the region need to review their national health policies, to abandon old strategies that are not compatible with the new goals, to design programs based on new approaches, and to make rapid progress in the new directions.

Ideally, reform of the health services should be guided by good data about the health of the population as well as by the results of well-designed studies on innovative ways to deliver health care. Unfortunately, for most of the countries in the region health data may indicate broad patterns and general trends but are not detailed enough to form a basis for critical analyses and informed policy decisions. Ministries of health do not have up-to-date information about the health status of populations in different parts of the country. The absence of current, reliable information is perhaps the most serious handicap in developing and managing health services in the region; decisions are often based on intuition or on conclusions derived from experiences that have not been rigorously tested in the field.

The chapters in this book illustrate the enormous gaps in our knowledge about health and disease in Africa. Often, there are not sufficient data to permit calculation of the common indexes of community health on a national basis. In the absence of a system for registering births and deaths, national estimates of infant mortality and of child, maternal, and other death rates are based on extrapolations of data gathered from a few isolated studies. Some countries have collected more representative data from carefully designed sample surveys, but they cannot update the information regularly because of the cost and complexity of such projects. Although some effort is being made to strengthen national health information systems, for the time being policymakers must continue to rely on data that are limited in quality and quantity. For the future, the countries in the region should develop and strengthen their health information systems so that decisionmakers will have access to valid data as the basis for planning, implementing, and evaluating health care.

Meanwhile, it is useful to extract the maximum value from the limited data available. This book illustrates how useful, if not definitive, conclusions can be derived from the skillful analysis of incomplete and somewhat fragmentary data. The authors draw useful insights concerning the patterns of health and disease in the region from information pieced together from various sources. They have discerned interesting trends in the health status of populations, including important differences that require further research and analysis. They have described and evaluated some new programs, including innovative approaches to community diagnosis and health care delivery. They have also drawn attention to difficult and unresolved issues, such as the estimation of the mortality attributable to malaria.

Health care givers in Africa, especially decisionmakers, can make good use of the book as a reference manual that brings together in convenient form important facts about health in Africa. Some of the material has been published in scientific journals, but these are not easily accessible to officials at ministries of health.

The book provides universities and other training institutions with relevant materials for teaching and for developing research projects. The section on longitudinal studies on small populations will be particularly helpful. Few such studies have been carried out in Sub-Saharan Africa because they are difficult to manage and expensive to run and demand long-term commitments of funding and personnel. Apart from the valuable information gathered, these studies are useful models that should guide others in the design of research projects and public health programs. Any health worker who is seriously engaged in teaching, service, or research in Africa should be familiar with the classic studies that are conveniently summarized in this section—Pare-Taveta and Kilombero in Tanzania, Machakos in Kenya, Keneba in the Gambia, Malumfashi in Nigeria, and Danfa in Ghana.

This book sets an important part of the agenda of work for African health officials over the next decade. Perhaps its most important contribution would be to stimulate health care givers and research scientists in Africa to make urgent and strenuous efforts to increase the quantity and quality of health information. Priority should be given to developing and improving systems for collecting data about births and deaths on a national basis, to designing and carrying out epidemiological studies designed to elucidate the patterns of mortality and morbidity, and to identifying major risk factors. Simple alternative approaches to health care delivery should be tested through well-designed studies so that the results can provide useful guidance to health care givers and policymakers. All these initiatives will strengthen the scientific basis for making progress toward the goal of health for all by the year 2000.

Adetokunbo O. Lucas
Harvard School of Public Health

Contents

Contributors

Roy M. Anderson	Professor and Head, Department of Pure and Applied Biology, Imperial College of Science, Technology and Medicine, University of London
Ann Ashworth	Human Nutrition Unit, Department of Public Health and Policy, London School of Hygiene and Tropical Medicine
John G. C. Blacker	Centre for Population Studies, Department of Epidemiology and Population Sciences, London School of Hygiene and Tropical Medicine
Eduard R. Bos	Population and Human Resources Department, The World Bank
Andrew Bradley	Endemic Diseases Research Unit, Liverpool School of Tropical Medicine
David J. Bradley	Professor of Tropical Hygiene, Department of Epidemiology and Population Sciences, London School of Hygiene and Tropical Medicine
Alice Bradley-Moore	Medical Research Council Laboratories, Fajara, The Gambia
Eric Burnier	St. Francis Designated District Hospital, Ifakara, Tanzania
James Chin	Chief, Surveillance, Forecasting and Impact Assessment Unit, Global Programme on AIDS, World Health Organization, Geneva
Antoine Degremont	Professor and Director, Swiss Tropical Institute, Basel
Don De Savigny	International Development Research Centre, Ottawa
Elizabeth Dowler	Human Nutrition Unit, Department of Public Health and Policy, London School of Hygiene and Tropical Medicine
Richard G. Feachem	Principal Public Health Specialist, Population and Human Resources Department, The World Bank; currently Dean, London School of Hygiene and Tropical Medicine
Herbert Gilles	Liverpool School of Tropical Medicine
Wendy J. Graham	Maternal and Child Epidemiology Unit, Department of Epidemiology and Population Sciences, London School of Hygiene and Tropical Medicine
Brian Greenwood	Director, Medical Research Council Laboratories, Fajara, The Gambia
Christoph Hatz	Department of Public Health and Epidemiology, Swiss Tropical Institute, Basel
Althea Hill	Africa Technical Department, The World Bank
Michael S. R. Hutt	Emeritus Professor of Geographical Pathology, United Medical and Dental Schools of Guy's and St. Thomas's Hospitals, London
Dean T. Jamison	Chief, Population, Health, and Nutrition Division, Population and Human Resources Department, The World Bank; currently Professor, School of Public Health and Graduate School of Education, University of California, Los Angeles
Betty R. Kirkwood	Head, Maternal and Child Epidemiology Unit, Department of Epidemiology and Population Sciences, London School of Hygiene and Tropical Medicine

Adetokunbo O. Lucas	Professor of International Health, Harvard University
Sarah MacFarlane	Statistics and Epidemiology Unit, Liverpool School of Tropical Medicine
Charles Mayombana	Swiss Tropical Institute Field Laboratory, Ifakara, Tanzania
Ian A. McGregor	Visiting Professor, Department of Tropical Medicine and Infectious Diseases, Liverpool School of Tropical Medicine
Alexander S. Muller	Professor of Tropical Health, University of Amsterdam, and Director, Department of Tropical Hygiene, Royal Tropical Institute, Amsterdam
Janet Nassim	Population and Human Resources Department, The World Bank
Alfred K. Neumann	Professor and Director, Preventive Medicine Residency Program, and Associate Dean of Students, School of Public Health, University of California, Los Angeles
Samuel Ofosu-Amaah	Professor of Community Health, University of Ghana Medical School Accra; currently Senior Advisor, PHC, Bamako Initiative Management Unit, UNICEF
Laura C. Rodrigues	Communicable Disease Epidemiology Unit, Department of Epidemiology and Population Sciences, London School of Hygiene and Tropical Medicine
Frederick T. Sai	Senior Population Advisor, Population and Human Resources Department, The World Bank
Marcel Tanner	Head, Department of Public Health and Epidemiology, Swiss Tropical Institute, Basel
Eleuther Tarimo	Director, Division of Strengthening Health Services, World Health Organization, Geneva
Severio Tayari	District Health Office, Ifakara, Tanzania
Ian M. Timæus	Centre for Population Studies, Department of Epidemiology and Population Sciences, London School of Hygiene and Tropical Medicine
Andrew Tomkins	Department of Clinical Sciences, London School of Hygiene and Tropical Medicine; currently Professor and Head, Department of International Child Health, Institute of Child Health, University of London
Jeroen K. van Ginneken	Netherlands Interdisciplinary Demographic Institute, The Hague

Preface

To guide the development of its lending program and to inform its dialogue with governments, the World Bank from time to time reviews its sector policies. The last such review for the health sector was conducted in the late 1970s. It led to the Bank's decision, as stated in the 1980 *Health Sector Policy Paper,* to begin direct lending in the sector. A department was created to develop the Bank's lending program and to carry out analytical work in health, in addition to continuing the existing activities in population and nutrition. During the ten years ending in June 1990 the Bank committed more than $2.7 billion for 78 population, health, and nutrition projects, almost half of them in Africa.

This book marks the first step in a new review of health policy—a review that focuses specifically on Sub-Saharan Africa. Several factors make this exercise particularly timely:

- The concern that the economic downturn of the early 1980s may have adversely affected the health sector in Africa
- The need to evaluate the impact of the primary health care strategies—especially the key elements of immunization and oral rehydration—that were articulated at Alma Ata a decade ago and to draw lessons from their implementation
- The completion of a substantial body of epidemiological and demographic analyses, which provides a much improved empirical basis for assessing health conditions and recent health trends
- The concern that the global emergence of AIDS and its sharp impact in selected African foci have undermined development prospects in some countries
- The potential value of explicitly seeking lessons from the Bank's experience with health sector operations in Africa.

The chapters in this book were commissioned to address the third point—to assemble in one place lessons from the analyses of the epidemiological and demographic conditions that define the problems facing Africa's health systems. Although the original purpose of the book was to assist the Bank's policy review, we hope that a broader audience will find the contributions useful.

Early drafts of many of the papers included in this volume were presented for comment and discussion at a meeting in Tunbridge Wells, England, in November 1987. That meeting brought together prominent specialists from Africa and elsewhere, as well as several World Bank staff, to review the current state of knowledge on this subject. The shaping of the volume as a whole and of many of the specific papers in it has benefited greatly from critiques and comments by participants at that meeting. Those participating, in addition to many chapter authors, included Eliwo Akoto (Zaire), Fredrick Golladay (World Bank), Aklilu Habte (then with the World Bank, now with UNICEF), Ann Hamilton (World Bank), Ishrat Husain (World Bank), Dan Kaseje (Kenya), Marjorie Koblinsky (United States), Alan López (World Health Organization), Anthony Measham (World Bank), Fatma Mrisho (Tanzania), Ana Novoa (Mozambique), and Phillip Payne (United Kingdom). We are indebted to Lynne Davies of the London School of Hygiene and Tropical Medicine and Zarine Vania of the World Bank for their administrative and word processing support, to Maureen Depolo of the University of California, Los Angeles, for editorial assistance, and to Elizabeth Forsyth for copyediting the manuscript. Their hard work and good cheer greatly facilitated preparation of this volume.

Richard G. Feachem
Dean T. Jamison

Disease and Mortality
in Sub-Saharan Africa

Chapter 1

Changing Patterns of Disease and Mortality in Sub-Saharan Africa

Richard G. Feachem, Dean T. Jamison, and Eduard R. Bos

During the 1960s, at the time of independence for most African nations, inadequate data sharply limited the capacity of the new African governments to form an adequate picture of the demographic and epidemiological status of the populations for which they were responsible. An important achievement of many of these countries in the ensuing quarter century has been to inform themselves much more fully and comprehensively about characteristics of their populations that are important for efficient resource allocation in the health sector and in the economy more generally. Censuses, household surveys, and epidemiological studies have all contributed to strengthening the information base for public policy. This accumulation of analysis and experience makes it both timely and possible to formulate an (at least approximate) overview of demographic and epidemiological conditions for the continent as a whole, and the collection of chapters in this volume is a first attempt to assemble in one place the main conclusions of this now-extensive literature.[1] Although there are important limitations to its coverage—the epidemiology of several important parasitic diseases, for example, was beyond its mandate—this volume provides comprehensive reviews of current knowledge in most relevant areas. The papers in part I present available analyses of levels and trends in mortality; those in part II present analyses of the epidemiology of major groups of diseases; and those in part III present the distilled results of six of the major prospective studies of health in circumscribed rural areas of Africa that have been conducted since 1950.

Our first purpose in this chapter is to summarize, from the perspective of their implications for health policy, the main lessons learned from the other chapters about the levels, trends, and geographic distribution of mortality and morbidity and, whenever possible, to do so in terms of the specific diseases responsible. The underlying trends have, for the most part, been favorable—life expectancy, for example, in Sub-Saharan Africa is estimated to have increased from 43 years in 1965 to 51 years in 1988—but the geographic distribution of progress has been uneven, and concerns have arisen about the health impact of the economic downturn of the early 1980s. In reviewing the papers in this volume, which richly document these trends, we became acutely aware of the lack of adequate information on certain topics of importance to policy. Despite progress in the postindependence era, for some countries very little is known, and for all countries important gaps remain. For example, the distribution of the causes of adult morbidity and mortality throughout the region is poorly understood. Our second purpose, then, is to delineate the gaps in demographic and epidemiological information that are most pressing from the perspective of policy and to indicate the lessons that the studies reported in this volume convey for how these information gaps might best be filled.

The next section touches briefly on the relation between information and health policy. The third section discusses levels, trends, and correlates of mortality in Sub-Saharan Africa, followed by a section on specific diseases. The fifth section discusses the instruments used for acquiring the information reported and how the relevance and efficacy of the available instruments have improved in the past 10 to 15 years. This chapter concludes with policy implications of the volume's findings concerning patterns of mortality and morbidity and with suggestions on how best to improve that knowledge base in the future.

Demography, Epidemiology, and Health Policy

Many of the studies summarized in this volume apply and exemplify, in an African context, the range of new demographic and epidemiological methods that allow important and robust conclusions to be drawn from much less expensive data sets than was previously possible. These methodological advances enhance the empirical base for scholarly analysis and professional training and thereby contribute, in the long term, to improving health in Africa. The principal concern of this volume, and particularly of this chapter, however, is with the short-to-medium term. What are, or should be, the information needs of policymakers? How can available analyses and data best be presented to serve those needs? How can the methods of data collection and analysis that are now available improve the information base for policy?

Policymakers must address—implicitly, if not explicitly—questions of *whether* the health sector ought to be a priority concern, of *where* problems of differing types are most severe, of *which* conditions and diseases are placing the greatest burden on the population (and on the health care system), of *why* diseases occur (through quantification of risk factors), and of *how* most efficiently and effectively to prevent disease and manage those cases that do occur. Demographic and epidemiological analyses address, at least partially, the first four of these questions: whether? where? which? why? Information on *how* to respond to prevalent problems is best obtained through economic and operational analyses that are largely beyond the scope of this volume.

Improving health conditions is a national priority virtually everywhere. The policy questions of *whether*, and to what extent, the health sector should be a high priority of development policy in a particular country still remain, given competing needs. The whether question tends to receive two types of answer. The first type resides in health indicators alone. Are child mortality rates (relatively) high? Is life expectancy low? Are trends in these indicators favorable relative to what other countries in similar circumstances have been able to achieve? Part I of this volume contains chapters reviewing evidence on these matters from about 36 Sub-Saharan African countries. The data clearly indicate that levels of mortality in some countries are so adverse that the case for national concern is strong indeed. The second type of answer to whether the health sector should be a concern would lie in an assessment of the economic and broader consequences of the levels and types of mortality and morbidity that a country suffers. In principle, such assessments would provide more thorough answers to the question of whether, and by now a substantial economic literature examines the impact of specific

health investments on development in general and on development of human resources in particular. No such studies are included in this volume.

Important for efficient (and equitable) resource allocation is a good sense of *where* problems are occurring. Are they in province X or province Y? Are they in males? Do they particularly affect one economic or educational class? The types of surveys that provide information on the magnitude of aggregate problems to illuminate the whether question can also address the where question. The difficulty is obvious: the more fine-grained the desired answer to the question of where a problem is occurring, the larger the sample size, cost, and complexity of the survey that will be required to provide answers. Demographers and epidemiologists seek virtually unlimited detail; policymakers must balance detail against cost, timeliness, and the actual capacity to target interventions. The chapters in this volume, however, illustrate the feasibility of obtaining reasonably rich responses to the where questions, if policymakers so desire.

Information on *which* conditions figure most prominently in a country's profile of diseases is obviously of great importance in planning health services. The study of causes of mortality in childhood illustrates this point. As recently as 20 years ago, little was known specifically about the contribution of different conditions to the overall burden of under-five mortality; today far more is known, and the targeting of resources to and among interventions to reduce child mortality reflects this new knowledge. Even for child mortality, differences among African countries remain to be explained, and for adult mortality (and morbidity) the composition of causes is virtually unknown. As is the case for acquiring data on the geographic distribution of health problems, understanding the causes of adult mortality will require large samples and studies conducted with care and competence. Costs will be high, and quick-and-dirty approaches will be unlikely to yield much of value. The cost of usefulness may be substantial, and gathering data on causes of adult ill health may be attractive only for health systems with relatively sophisticated management capacity. In contrast to population-based assessments of the causes of mortality (or morbidity), it is relatively inexpensive to study the distribution of causes of illness among persons who seek treatment at or die in health facilities. This type of study is very useful, of course, in projecting demand on the facilities; it remains to be seen (in an African context) what insights into population problems such information from facilities can provide, although Hutt (see chapter 15, this volume) reviews facilities-based evidence that sheds much light on the nature of cancer and cardiovascular disease as health problems in Africa.

Finally, a set of questions asks *why* diseases occur; these questions concern the nature of the environmental and the behavioral risk factors that, in any given country or region, may be important contributors to the incidence of disease. Such understanding clearly underpins the design of preventive interventions, and, just as clearly, much relevant information is local. (One has only to reflect on the limited utility in Africa of much that has been learned in San Francisco about prevention of AIDS—acquired immune deficiency syndrome.) Chapters in this volume report only a few epidemiological investigations of risk factors in Africa; the paucity of relevant studies suggests an important domain for further research. That domain needs to be carefully defined, however, to take into account the substantial fraction of available etiologic epidemiology that has produced results transportable across national boundaries in Africa or, indeed, across continents.

The remaining sections of this chapter summarize the volume's findings and ask how well they address these policy questions. For those questions that have good answers in many countries, we attempt to draw lessons for policy. For those questions where answers are fragmentary or are limited to a few countries, we assess the feasibility (and desirability) of improving the quality of the answers that could be available in ten years.

Levels, Trends, and Correlates of Mortality

Mortality levels and their trends in the recent past provide the most fundamental and widely used measure of the health status of populations. Death is a readily defined state, and deaths from different causes may be aggregated (although debate continues about the desirability of alternative ways of aggregating deaths at different ages and grouping deaths from different causes). Neither of these characteristics holds for morbidity. Reducing childhood mortality and premature mortality more generally, together with increasing life expectancy, are universally accepted goals for public policy.

National mortality data are regarded as a yardstick for national development. A country with an improving mortality picture is seen, at least in one important sense, to be a successful country in developmental terms. Conversely, a country with a stagnating or worsening mortality picture is seen as failing even if other yardsticks of development, such as gross national product (GNP), are improving. Generally, however, experience has shown that economic performance and a decline in mortality follow similar trends, even though several countries show that it is possible for mortality rates to fall much more rapidly than could be accounted for by economic growth alone (Halstead *et al.*, 1985). In order to guide public policy and influence the nature of government intervention, national mortality levels need to be measured reliably on a regular basis. As Hill, Blacker, Timæus, and Graham (see chapters 3–6, this volume) show clearly, some countries in Sub-Saharan Africa have reasonably reliable and consistent estimates of childhood mortality, but many do not. No country in Sub-Saharan Africa is in a position to have regularly updated estimates of childhood mortality, and no country has adequate data on adult mortality.

In addition to national mortality data, regional estimates are also of value in pinpointing disadvantaged areas that may require specific measures and responses. Geography is not the only basis of mortality differentials, however, and data on mortality by gender, occupation, and socioeconomic status can assist greatly in understanding the determinants of mortality levels and in targeting government programs toward specific groups with specific needs. Although some data on regional variation in childhood mortality are presented by Hill and Blacker in chapters 3 and 4 of this volume, there is a general scarcity of data on mortality differentials of this type.

Mortality in Sub-Saharan Africa is high by world standards, and life expectancy is commensurately low. Table 1-1 presents comparative data (from World Bank data sources) on mortality, life expectancy, fertility, income, and education for major subregions of the world. It is clear that Sub-Saharan Africa, with a population of about 467 million in 1988, ranks last on each variable. Life expectancies at birth (51 years) and at ten years (53 years) are the lowest, and risk of death in childhood (17 percent) is the highest, by considerable margins. (The crude death rate—18.7 per thousand—is also very high, although the crude birth rate, which is about 47 per thousand, is sufficiently high to produce a staggering population growth rate of 2.8 percent.) The total fertility rate (6.6) is high by world standards, and secondary school enrollment is low (16 percent). None of this is perhaps surprising when one sees the disappointing economic data: GNP per capita is only 82 percent of that in Asia and 2 percent of that in industrial countries. GNP per capita has increased, on average, less than 1 percent per year since 1965, and in some countries it has declined.

Table 1-1. Indicators of Mortality, Fertility, Education, and Economic Performance in Sub-Saharan Africa and Other Regions.

| Region | Population, 1988 (millions) | GNP per capita | | Life expectancy and mortality, 1988[a] | | | Total fertility rate, 1988[b] | Secondary school enrollment, 1986[c] |
		Dollars, 1987	Average annual growth, 1965–87 (percent)	e(0)	e(10)	q(5)		
1. Sub-Saharan Africa	467	330	0.6	51	53	172	6.6	16
2. Latin America and the Caribbean	424	1,790	2.1	67	62	67	3.6	48
3. Middle East and North Africa	410	1,401[d]	2.8[d]	60	58	118	5.6	47
4. Asia	2,595	402	3.8	64	60	87	3.3	39
5. Industrial nonmarket economies	423	n.a.	n.a.	70	62	27	2.3	93
6. Industrial market economies	782	14,137	2.3	76	67	18	1.8	92
7. World	5,101	n.a.	n.a.	65	61	94	3.4	54

n.a. Not available.

Note: South Africa is in region 6; the boundary between regions 3 and 4 is at the Pakistan-India border; region 5 is the U.S.S.R. and all the countries of Eastern Europe; and Oceania (but not Australia and New Zealand which are in region 6) and China are in region 4.

a. Life expectancy at age zero, $e(0)$, is the number of years a newborn infant would live if he or she were subject to the overall pattern of mortality prevailing at the time, assuming this pattern remained unchanged.

Life expectancy at age 10, $e(10)$, is the number of years a person who has reached age 10 would live on average after exact age 10, assuming the prevailing pattern of mortality would remain unchanged.

Child mortality risk, $q(5)$, is the probability of dying before reaching exact age 5 and is expressed here per thousand.

b. Total fertility rate is the mean total number of children that a woman would bear were she to experience the current age-specific fertility rates.

c. Percentage of the school-age population enrolled.

d. Excludes Iran and Iraq.

Source: World Bank data.

Table 1-2 provides data on population, education, fertility, and economic performance for each country with a population of over 500,000 in Sub-Saharan Africa. The rich variety of experience and circumstance within the continent is revealed by these figures. GNP per capita ranges from $130 (Ethiopia) to $2,700 (Gabon), and the average annual change in GNP per capita since 1965 ranges from −2.7 percent (Uganda) to +8.9 percent (Botswana). Population size varies from 0.7 million (Swaziland) to over 100 million (Nigeria), and annual population growth rates over the past 23 years range from 1.5 percent (Mauritius) to 4.2 percent (Côte d'Ivoire). Fertility is uniformly high: all countries except Mauritius have total fertility rates of 5 or greater. Secondary school enrollment is generally below 30 percent and varies from 3 percent in Rwanda and Tanzania to 51 percent in Mauritius.

The comparative mortality and life expectancy data used in table 1-1 are estimates for 1988, and many are based on a complex web of assumptions and projections (Murray, 1987). In presenting the child and adult mortality data in chapters 3 and 5 of this volume, Hill and Timæus have restricted themselves to older data that were derived from censuses and surveys. Table 1-3 summarizes by country the child mortality analyses reported by Hill in chapter 3 and the adult life expectancy estimates presented by Timæus in chapter 5. Dramatic differences across countries clearly exist in the levels of both child and adult mortality; figure 1-1 illustrates these differences in the case of child mortality. Levels of child mortality risk in the 1970s varied from more than 30 percent to less than 15 percent. The rates of change of this risk between the mid-1950s and the mid-1970s ranged between a decline of more than 3 percent per year (Congo, Côte d'Ivoire) and an increase of 1 percent per year (Mozambique), as is illustrated in figure 1-2. Life expectancy at age 15 also varied greatly, from 56 years

Table 1-2. Indicators of Economic Performance, Population, Fertility, and Education in Sub-Saharan Africa

Country	GNP per capita		Population		Total fertility rate, 1987	Secondary school enrollment, 1986
	Dollars, 1987	Average annual growth, 1965–87 (percent)	Size, 1987 (thousands)	Average annual growth, 1965–87 (percent)		
Low-income economies						
Semiarid						
Chad	150	−2.0	5,267	2.2	5.9	6
Burkina Faso	190	1.6	8,312	2.3	6.5	6
Mali	210	n.a.	7,774	2.2	6.5	7
Gambia, The	220	1.2	797	3.1	6.5	12
Niger	260	−2.2	6,787	2.8	7.0	6
Somalia	290	−0.3	5,711	2.8	6.8	12
Other						
Ethiopia	130	0.1	44,786	2.5	6.5	12
Zaire	150	−2.4	32,604	2.9	6.1	n.a.
Malawi	160	1.4	7,905	3.2	7.6	4
Guinea-Bissau	160	−1.9	922	2.6	6.0	n.a.
Mozambique	170	n.a.	14,555	2.6	6.3	7
Tanzania	180	−0.4	23,870	3.4	7.0	3
Madagascar	210	−1.8	10,902	2.7	6.4	36
Burundi	250	1.6	4,990	2.1	6.8	4
Uganda	260	−2.7	15,666	3.0	6.9	n.a.
Togo	290	0.0	3,249	3.2	6.5	21
Sierra Leone	300	0.2	3,841	2.1	6.5	n.a.
Benin	310	0.2	4,313	2.8	6.5	16
Central African Republic	330	−0.3	2,720	2.0	5.8	13
Rwanda	330	1.6	6,434	3.3	8.0	3
Kenya	330	1.9	22,096	3.7	7.7	20
Sudan	330	−0.5	23,119	2.9	6.4	20
Ghana	390	−1.6	13,571	2.5	6.4	35
Senegal	520	−0.6	6,950	2.6	6.5	13
Guinea	n.a.	n.a.	6,479	2.0	6.2	12
Middle-income economies						
Oil importers						
Zambia	250	−2.1	7,213	3.1	6.8	19
Lesotho	370	4.7	1,639	2.5	5.8	22
Mauritania	440	−0.4	1,860	2.4	6.5	15
Liberia	450	−1.6	2,324	3.1	6.5	n.a.
Zimbabwe	580	0.9	9,044	3.3	5.9	46
Swaziland	700	2.4	712	3.0	n.a.	n.a.
Côte d'Ivoire	740	1.0	11,126	4.2	7.4	20
Botswana	1,050	8.9	1,135	3.5	5.0	31
Mauritius	1,490	3.2	1,038	1.5	2.1	51
Oil exporters						
Nigeria	370	1.1	106,638	2.7	6.5	n.a.
Congo	870	4.2	2,018	2.9	6.5	n.a.
Cameroon	970	3.8	10,859	2.8	6.5	23
Gabon	2,700	1.1	1,050	3.8	5.5	27
Angola	n.a.	n.a.	9,180	2.6	n.a.	13
Sub-Saharan Africa	330	0.6	452,820	2.9	6.6	16

n.a. Not available.

Note: See table 1-1 for definitions.

Source: World Bank socioeconomic data base.

Table 1-3. Survey-Based Estimates of Child and Adult Mortality in Sub-Saharan Africa

	Under-five mortality risk (percent)[a]			Life expectancy at age 15 (years)[a]	
Country	Early	More recent[b]	Average annual rate of change, 1955–75[c]	Early	More recent[b]
Low-income economies					
Semiarid					
Chad	31 (1959)				
Burkina Faso	42 (1948)	28 (1971)	−2.3		
Mali	37 (1956)				
Gambia, The	35 (1960)	34 (1968)		39 (1958)	52 (1978)
Niger	31 (1955)				
Somalia	24 (1967)	21 (1974)			
Other					
Ethiopia	24 (1958)	22 (1975)	−0.7		
Zaire	27 (1951)				
Malawi	37 (1958)	33 (1972)	−0.4		47 (1974)
Guinea-Bissau	30 (1944)				
Mozambique	26 (1936)	28 (1974)	1.0		
Tanzania	26 (1953)	22 (1973)	−0.9	48 (1961)	54 (1965)
Madagascar					
Burundi	26 (1959)	22 (1973)	−0.9		45 (1971)
Uganda	25 (1957)	20 (1964)		44 (1956)	54 (1965)
Togo	35 (1949)	23 (1968)			
Sierra Leone	39 (1962)	38 (1969)		34 (1956)	39 (1970)
Benin	36 (1948)	22 (1977)	−1.8	46 (1966)	47 (1970)
Central African Republic	36 (1948)	24 (1970)	−2.2		
Rwanda	27 (1956)	22 (1979)	−0.8		
Kenya	26 (1947)	15 (1975)	−2.2	48 (1956)	53 (1974)
Sudan	20 (1959)	19 (1965)		48 (1958)	56 (1975)
Ghana	37 (1935)	20 (1967)			47 (1969)
Senegal	37 (1946)	28 (1971)	−0.6	41 (1965)	50 (1978)
Guinea	38 (1950)				
Middle-income economies					
Oil importers					
Zambia	22 (1956)	17 (1970)			
Lesotho	21 (1956)	18 (1973)	−0.6	48 (1957)	47 (1976)
Mauritania				40 (1948)	52 (1975)
Liberia	32 (1957)	28 (1965)			46 (1971)
Zimbabwe	16 (1957)	14 (1978)	−0.6	53 (1970)	55 (1975)
Swaziland	24 (1951)	22 (1969)	−0.5		46 (1972)
Côte d'Ivoire	27 (1966)	21 (1974)	−3.1	39 (1962)	49 (1979)
Botswana	18 (1959)	12 (1977)	−2.3	51 (1961)	48 (1981)
Mauritius					
Oil exporters					
Nigeria	20 (1967)	17 (1978)	−1.8		
Congo	29 (1948)	15 (1969)	−3.5	48 (1960)	55 (1967)
Cameroon	29 (1955)	19 (1973)	−2.3	44 (1963)	52 (1975)
Gabon	25 (1956)				
Angola	36 (1935)				
Western Africa[d]	30 (1955)	20 (1975)	−2.0		
Eastern Africa[d]	24 (1955)	19 (1975)	−1.1		

a. Numbers in parentheses are years of reference.

b. "More recent" estimates refer to the most recent estimate that is post-1960. If there is no post-1960 estimate, the "more recent" column is left blank, and the figure used in the "early" column is the latest available.

c. Annual rate of change is calculated only where estimates are available from both the mid-1950s and the mid-1970s.

d. Estimates are weighted and interpolated. Definitions of western and eastern Africa are as in chapter 3, this volume; eastern Africa includes southern Africa.

Source: Under-five mortality risks are from Hill (chapter 3, this volume); adult life expectancy data are from Timæus (chapter 5, this volume).

Figure 1-1. Under-Five Mortality Risk in Sub-Saharan Africa, 1975

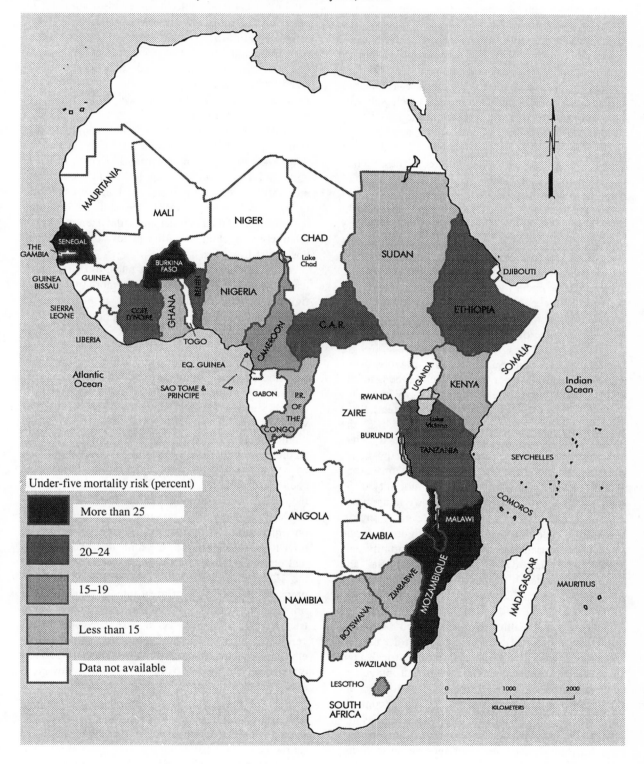

(Sudan) to 39 years (Sierra Leone).[2] The summaries for western Africa and for eastern (including southern) Africa at the bottom of table 1-3 show that western Africa's child mortality, which lagged behind that of eastern Africa in the 1950s, had substantially caught up by the mid-1970s. (This conclusion contrasts with that reached by Hill in chapter 3.) In most Sub-Saharan African countries, childhood mortality fell substantially over the two decades preceding the mid-1970s, and the same is true for adult mortality, except in some southern African countries (Botswana, Lesotho, and Zimbabwe; see chapter 5, this volume). These trends are encouraging and have been achieved despite generally poor economic performance.

The association between income and mortality in Sub-Saharan Africa is illustrated in figure 1-3, which plots the more reliable childhood mortality data against GNP per capita for 1964–69. There is a significant inverse relationship ($p = 0.007$) between the mortality risk of children under five and GNP per capita: the latter explains 27 percent of the variance of the former. More important, 73 percent of the variance is *not* explained, and a wide range of child mortality levels fall in the low GNP range (say, less than $400). Botswana, Congo, Kenya, Lesotho, and Sudan perform notably better than predicted by GNP per capita, whereas the Gambia, Malawi, and Sierra Leone perform notably worse. This has policy relevance and is also, at least potentially, a source of hope for countries such as Malawi. If all the points in figure 1-3 lay along or close to the line, economic growth would appear to be a prerequisite for reducing childhood mortality. In these circumstances, to achieve the much lower childhood mortality of its neighbor Zimbabwe, Malawi would have to approach Zimbabwe's much greater income level. There is, however, a wide scatter of points in figure 1-3, and much of the variance in the childhood mortality data remains unexplained by GNP per capita. Sai and Nassim, in chapter 2, further discuss the complicated interrelations among socioeconomic conditions, mortality, and fertility.

If all the good health performers shared a common cultural or ecological characteristic (if, for example, they were high-altitude, low-malaria countries), their improved performance could be largely attributable to this characteristic. However, the good performers are very diverse in ecological and cultural terms (contrast, for example, Kenya with Lesotho), which implies that government policy (not necessarily health policy) played a role, perhaps an important role, in lowering their childhood mortality. This in turn implies that Malawi could, with suitable policy reform, aspire to

the childhood mortality rates of Zimbabwe, even without, as is probable, a marked upturn in its economic fortunes over the next decade.

This is a limited example in the African context of the good-health-at-low-cost phenomenon reviewed by Halstead *et al.* (1985). Halstead and colleagues analyzed striking examples of low mortality with low GNP per capita in areas outside Africa: China, Costa Rica, Kerala State in India, and Sri Lanka. The African equivalent of this phenomenon is not so marked. For example, at or below Sri Lanka's 1986 GNP per capita ($400), the best African performer is Kenya, which in 1986 had a per capita GNP of $300 and a childhood mortality risk of 11.6 percent. Sri Lanka's childhood mortality risk in 1986 was 4.5 percent. Even though less spectacular than in other areas, the phenomenon of relatively low child mortality at low GNP per capita does exist in Africa.

Secondary school enrollment rates, too, are significantly associated with under-five mortality risk. In figure 1-4, the education variable accounts for 18 percent of the variance in the child mortality variable. The Gambia, Malawi, and Sierra Leone are strikingly poor performers for their educational levels.[3] Analysis with multiple independent variables did not add any significant relationships or insights. Modeling the variation by country in childhood and adult mortality, though outside the realm of this chapter, can be valuable, nonetheless, for clarifying the role of certain public policies in achieving low mortality. To be credible, the modeling of mortality variance must be based on reliable estimates of mortality. These have been scarce hitherto, but, as chapters 3 and 5 indicate, the situation is improving.

The data on mortality presented in chapters 3 and 5, on which table 1-3 and figures 1-3 and 1-4 are based, refer to periods ending in the mid- or late 1970s. No real data (that is, data not based on projections) from the 1980s were available when these chapters were prepared in 1987. It is of great interest, and potential importance to policy formulation, to know how countries have fared in the recent past. Have the trends continued downward? Have stagnating mortality levels continued to stagnate? What have been the effects on mortality in the 1980s of the economic downturn experienced by most Sub-Saharan African countries and of the climatic and military disasters faced by some? Perhaps most interesting, what has been the impact of the approaches to reducing childhood mortality, particularly immunization and oral rehydration, that were emphasized by African governments and development agencies in the 1980s?

Figure 1-2. Annual Decline in Under-five Mortality Risk Sub-Saharan Africa, 1955–1975.

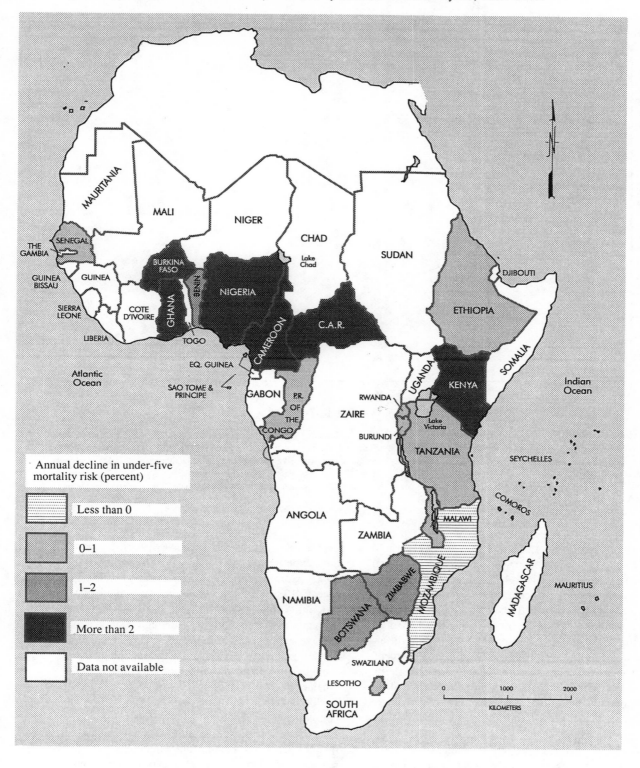

Figure 1-3. Under-Five Mortality Risk and GNP Per Capita in 27 Countries of Sub-Saharan Africa, 1964-79

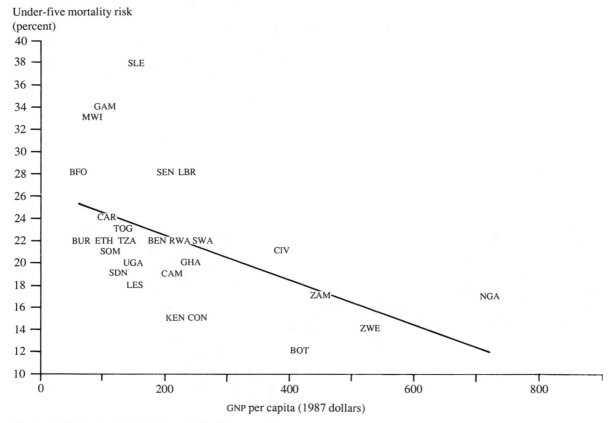

Note: BEN, Benin; BFO, Burkina Faso; BOT, Botswana; BUR, Burundi; CAM, Cameroon; CAR, Central African Republic; CIV, Côte d'Ivoire; CON, Congo; ETH, Ethiopia; GAM, the Gambia; GHA, Ghana; KEN, Kenya; LBR, Liberia; LES, Lesotho; MWI, Malawi; NGA, Nigeria; RWA, Rwanda; SDN, Sudan; SEN, Senegal; SLE, Sierra Leone; SOM, Somalia; SWA, Swaziland; TOG, Togo; TZA, Tanzania; UGA, Uganda; ZAM, Zambia; and ZWE, Zimbabwe.

The under-five mortality risk, $q(5)$, is regressed on GNP per capita, Y, for the same year as the mortality estimate. The regression equation is given by $q(5) = 26.6 - 0.27 \ (Y)$, with $p < 0.01$, $R^2 = 0.27$.

To answer these questions in part, we turn to analyses of quite recent surveys conducted in several African countries. Table 1-4 combines the results of analysis of data from recent surveys with those of older data presented in chapter 3 to create a picture of recent child mortality trends in nine Sub-Saharan African countries. For the nine countries, the absolute difference in the most recent estimates of $q(5)$ is 21 percent, ranging between Botswana with the lowest mortality and Mali with the highest.[4] Malawi, which had an exceptionally high child mortality level for southern Africa in the 1970s, appears to continue to be exceptional in the early 1980s, although more recent survey-based estimates are not available.

It has been suggested that, as a result of economic stagnation and imbalances and the consequent strin-

gent adjustment measures imposed, African countries have experienced deteriorating health conditions in the 1980s (Cornia *et al.*, 1987; Sanders and Davies, 1988; UNICEF, 1989). Of the countries represented in table 1-4, only Ghana presents a clear and consistent picture of increasing child mortality, although Nigeria appears to have experienced an annual increase in under-five mortality of about 0.6 percent between 1974 and 1985. Although the trend in child mortality in Nigeria and Ghana may be related to economic recession, it is unclear whether the increase in child mortality was a consequence of economic adjustments or of the deteriorating policies and conditions that necessitated them. Except for Ghana and Nigeria, all countries registered declines in under-five mortality when the average annual change in the late 1970s and early

Figure 1-4. Under-Five Mortality Risk and Secondary School Enrollment in 28 Countries of Sub-Saharan Africa, 1964–79

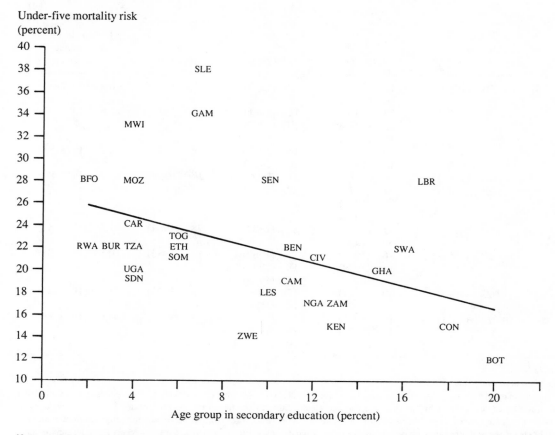

Note: MOZ, Mozambique; for other country abbreviations, see note to figure 1-3. The under-five mortality risk, $q(5)$, is regressed on secondary school enrollment, E, for the same year as the mortality estimate. The regression equation is given by $q(5) = 26.8 - 0.51\ (E)$, with $p < 0.01$, $R^2 = 0.18$.

1980s is considered. These declines were most pronounced for the southern African countries of Botswana and Zimbabwe, while the higher-mortality countries further north experienced slight to moderate declines. The finding that the economic downturn of the early 1980s had a relatively limited impact on mortality is consistent with the findings of the more global and long-term analysis by Hill and David (1989).

The persistence of wide differentials in child mortality in Sub-Saharan Africa, coupled with the marked declines at relatively low levels of mortality, implies that substantial inroads can be made in reducing the risk of child death in Sub-Saharan Africa. Much less is understood about the levels of and differentials in adult mortality in Sub-Saharan Africa. Ongoing World Bank analyses (Feachem *et al.*, forthcoming) suggest that the burden of adult mortality in the developing world is much higher than has generally been thought and that much of this mortality is preventable. Further understanding of the persistence of differentials in Africa may be gained by a greater understanding of the differences among countries in the cause structure of mortality. We now turn to the available information on the main causes of mortality and morbidity.

Causes of Mortality and Morbidity

All-cause mortality data, of the types presented by Hill, Blacker, and Timæus in chapters 3, 4, and 5, are useful as guides to policy, and their value is increased manyfold by information on cause. Nearly all premature deaths (deaths before old age) are due to specific causes or combinations of causes, be they breast cancer or involvement in a train accident or measles complicated by pneumonia. These causes have different

Table 1-4. Estimates of Under-Five Mortality Risk in Nine Sub-Saharan African Countries, 1960s–80s

Country	Under-five mortality risk (percent)[a]				Average annual rate of change (percent)
	Late 1960s and early 1970s	Mid-1970s	Early 1980s	Mid-1980s	
Botswana	15 (1970)	12 (1977)* 9 (1978)	8 (1980) 6 (1982)	7 (1984)	−6.9 (1977–84)
Burundi	22 (1970)*	22 (1976) 22 (1976)* 19 (1979)	19 (1981) 19 (1983)	17 (1985)	−2.6 (1977–85)
Ghana	20 (1967)*	15 (1977) 15 (1979)	16 (1982) 16 (1984)	18 (1985)	+2.2 (1978–85)
Liberia	28 (1966)*	28 (1971–75)	24 (1976–80)	22 (1981–86)	−2.2 (1972–82)
Malawi	33 (1973)*	27 (1975) 25 (1977) 26 (1979)	27 (1981)	n.a.	n.a.
Mali	n.a.	31 (1976) 30 (1978)	26 (1982)	28 (1984)	−1.3 (1977–84)
Nigeria	20 (1968)*	16 (1974)* 17 (1979)*	18 (1980) 18 (1982) 15 (1983)	17 (1985)	+0.55 (1974–85)
Togo	22 (1968)*	19 (1977)	17 (1980) 18 (1982)	16 (1986)	−1.7 (1977–86)
Zimbabwe	15 (1971)*	10 (1977) 14 (1978)*	10 (1980) 8 (1982) 10 (1984)	8 (1986)	−5.0 (1977–86)

n.a. Not available.

a. Numbers in parentheses are years of reference.

Source: All estimates marked with asterisks are taken·from tables 3A-22 and 3A-23. All other estimates are from Stephens (forthcoming) and, except for Malawi, are based on analyses of the Demographic and Health Surveys conducted by the Institute for Resource Development, Westinghouse. Malawi data are derived from the 1984 Family Formation Survey. Except for Nigeria, depicted trends are a result of comparing estimates of mortality from one or more nationally representative surveys and censuses. For Nigeria, data for 1980–85 are from the Demographic and Health Surveys for Ondo State and probably represent lower mortality than exists in the rest of the country. The estimates are taken to represent the lower bound of recent mortality for Nigeria. The method of analysis for all countries except Liberia was the Trussell variant of the Brass child survival technique. For Liberia data are from direct reports of complete maternity histories.

determinants and distributions, and their prevention and treatment require different governmental and private responses. Admittedly, some public policies, such as taxing tobacco products or improving female education, can affect mortality that is due to many causes and occurs in several age groups. However, most health sector policies (especially preventive policies) and some other areas of policy have effects that are disease specific and age specific. For example, rotavirus immunization would reduce mortality from one form of diarrhea in children under two years of age, and seat-belt legislation and enforcement would reduce mortality among certain categories of motor vehicle users. To design appropriate policies and evaluate their impact, governments need to know age-specific, cause-specific death rates and morbidity rates for at least a representative sample of the population. In addition, as Blacker points out in chapter 4, we are unlikely to explain or reduce the large ecological, ethnic, or socioeconomic differentials in mortality until we have broken down mortality by cause. Comprehensive cause-specific mortality and morbidity data are unavailable in Sub-Saharan African countries at the present time. Little is being done to rectify this situation, and we return later in this chapter to a consideration of the most pressing needs for new data collection initiatives.

Although comprehensive data on causes of mortality and morbidity are unavailable, this volume summarizes important suggestive studies. Concerning mortality in childhood, chapters in part II assemble data on mortality due to diarrhea (Kirkwood, chapter 9), acute respiratory diseases—ARI (Kirkwood, chapter 10), EPI (the World Health Organization's Expanded

Programme on Immunization) target diseases (Rodrigues, chapter 11), and malaria (Bradley, chapter 12). These data confirm the well-established belief that diarrhea, ARI, measles, and malaria are prominent causes of childhood death in Sub-Saharan Africa. This is further confirmed by childhood mortality data from longitudinal studies in Kenya (Muller and van Ginneken, chapter 18), Tanzania (Tanner *et al.*, chapter 19), the Gambia (McGregor, chapter 20), Nigeria (Tomkins *et al.*, chapter 21), and Ghana (Neumann *et al.*, chapter 22).

Concerning adult mortality, maternal mortality is reviewed by Graham in chapter 6, and data are presented on a variety of causes in Sierra Leone (chapter 5) and Kenya (chapters 5 and 18). Since none of this adds up to an overall picture of age-specific, cause-specific mortality in Sub-Saharan Africa, we also present recent estimations of the cause-specific mortality patterns in Africa (Bulatao and Stephens, forthcoming). These data, which are from numerous sources and are shown in table 1-5, represent a best guess at the cause-specific mortality pattern in Sub-Saharan Africa in 1985. The large proportion of deaths in all age groups (16–28 percent) that are lumped under other causes reflects the weakness of the data base and the caution that is required in interpreting it. The high proportion of deaths in all age groups that are attributed to infectious and parasitic causes, although generally declining with age, is striking. So too is the importance of perinatal death for infant mortality. Cancer and circulatory system diseases, especially the latter, increase in importance with age. Injuries are surprisingly unimportant, and the accuracy of these estimates is doubtful.

The major causes of mortality in various age groups in Sub-Saharan Africa are also important causes of morbidity. In addition, some important causes of morbidity do not feature prominently in the cause-specific mortality data because they have low case-fatality rates. Examples of such diseases in Africa include schistosomiasis, hookworm, and infections of the skin (see chapter 17, table 17-5, and chapter 19, table 19-1 and figures 19-6, 19-7, and 19-8).

It is not possible in a volume such as this to provide a comprehensive account of all the major diseases in Africa. In addition, while some causes of morbidity and mortality are copiously documented, others such as injuries are poorly described in the African setting. In part II a few selected diseases are treated in detail, and in chapter 7 Ofosu-Amaah provides some data on a number of conditions not described more fully in other chapters. In addition, the longitudinal studies reported in part III contain information on a number of health problems in particular settings. Below is a summary of some of the highlights of part II, followed by remarks concerning disease-specific priorities for both operations and research.

The high childhood mortality rates in Sub-Saharan Africa are caused largely by infectious diseases, particularly diarrhea, ARI, malaria, and measles (see table 1-5). The epidemiological evidence strongly suggests that these infections are more likely to be severe and to be fatal when they occur in children who are malnourished (see chapters 9–12). Without attempting a detailed analysis of the relationships between data on child mortality and child malnutrition at the national level, a superficial comparison between the mortality data reviewed by Hill (chapter 3) and the

Table 1-5. Distribution of Causes of Death within Age Group in Sub-Saharan Africa, 1985

Cause of death	Proportion of total deaths within the age category[a]						Total deaths	
	Less than 1	1–4	5–14	15–44	45–64	65 and older	Number (thousands)	Percent
Perinatal	30	0	0	0	0	0	672	9.3
Infectious and parasitic	45	71	62	53	28	19	3,403	47.2
Cancers	0.1	0.3	1	3	14	9	42	3.4
Circulatory system	1	2	6	12	34	41	909	12.6
Maternal	0	0	0	4	0.2	0	48	0.7
Injury	1	3	6	12	5	2	294	4.1
Other	23	24	24	16	18	28	1,635	22.7
Total	100	100	100	100	100	100	7,203	100.0

a. Ages are in years.
Source: Adapted from Bulatao and Stephens (forthcoming).

nutrition data reviewed by Ashworth and Dowler (chapter 8) is of interest. The worst performers in under-five mortality in the 1970s included Burkina Faso, the Gambia, Malawi, Mozambique, Senegal, and Sierra Leone (table 1-3). Moreover, the values for the prevalence rates of wasting, stunting, and underweight in these six countries are toward the upper end of the range of values, but not strikingly so. The only really striking finding is the very high rate of stunting in Malawi (figure 8-2). Malawi also has a significant public health problem of vitamin A deficiency. In addition to malnutrition, high levels of fertility put children (and their mothers) at increased risk of mortality; this point and the potential for intervention are discussed by Sai and Nassim in chapter 2.

The enormous progress made in the 1980s in understanding the epidemiology of diarrhea in Africa is well illustrated by Kirkwood in chapter 9. The typical African child less than five years old has five episodes of diarrhea per year, a 10 percent risk of having diarrhea on any given day, and a 14 percent risk of dying from an episode sufficiently severe that he or she must be brought to a health facility. That child also has a 5 percent risk of dying from diarrhea before reaching his or her fifth birthday. Diarrhea accounts for 25 percent of all illness in childhood and for 15 percent of childhood visits and admissions to health facilities. Of the five most commonly isolated viral and bacterial causes of childhood diarrhea, three had not been identified by medical science as recently as 1970. For one of these, rotavirus, a vaccine may be available soon for widespread application.

About ARI, the other dominant infectious cause of severe morbidity and mortality in childhood, we know much less. The typical child appears to have around ten episodes per year and a 25 percent chance of having an ARI on any particular day. ARI *may* be responsible for 30 percent of illness in children and for around 25 percent of visits and admissions by children to a health facility. The data collected between 1951 and 1978 in a rural hospital in the West Nile District of Uganda showed that pneumonia ranked third as a cause of hospital admission and second as a cause of hospital death, for both children and adults (Williams *et al.*, 1986). The risk of death from pneumonia before five years of age seems to lie in the range of 1.5–6 percent, and the childhood proportional mortality rate may be around 7 percent. Diseases of the respiratory system (mainly pneumonia) are the leading cause of death in all ages at Machakos, Kenya (chapter 18). Data on ARI in Sub-Saharan Africa remain seriously deficient. Only three estimates of the incidence rate of ARI were located (Kirkwood, chapter 10); for the majority of countries

in Sub-Saharan Africa there is no substantial information on these diseases, and information on adults is almost totally lacking. ARI must be one of the top priorities for increased scientific and operational endeavor during the 1990s.

The EPI target diseases have been a priority for most African countries in recent years, judging by the resources that have gone into developing and strengthening national EPI efforts. The typical African child has a risk of around 13 percent of dying from three important vaccine-preventable diseases: measles (8 percent), pertussis (4 percent), and neonatal tetanus (1 percent) (Rodrigues, chapter 11). There is also a substantial lifetime risk of death from tuberculosis; although data are inadequate, Murray *et al.* (forthcoming) have projected more than 500,000 deaths from tuberculosis in Africa in 1990 and have estimated that, on the basis of current trends, the number will increase by 50 percent in 25 years despite its decline in every other region of the world. Recent findings from the Gambia raise concern about the persistence of high childhood death rates despite high EPI coverage (Greenwood *et al.*, 1987a) and help to clarify the determinants of EPI compliance at the family level (Hanlon *et al.*, 1988). These subjects require further investigation, and the findings need to be incorporated into national vaccination policy.

As Bradley warns in chapter 12, and as is further amplified in chapters 17 and 19–22, malaria is a massive problem that appears to be worsening in much of Sub-Saharan Africa. The increase in malaria is attributed to the collapse (owing to managerial, institutional, and financial constraints) of the malaria control programs in many countries, together with the increasingly widespread resistance of malaria vectors to the available insecticides and of malaria parasites to the available chemoprophylactic and chemotherapeutic agents (Schapira, 1989). Bradley predicts that by 1992 all countries in Sub-Saharan Africa will have chloroquine-resistant *Plasmodium falciparum*, the most common and lethal of the malaria parasites. Data in this book show clearly that malaria is a major cause of morbidity and mortality in childhood, and a major cause of morbidity in adulthood, throughout much of Sub-Saharan Africa. This conclusion is reinforced by a recent study in the Gambia (Greenwood *et al.*, 1987b). Given this situation and the long period, perhaps ten years or more, before an effective malaria vaccine might become available for widespread application, malaria control deserves to be given a new sense of priority and urgency in both research and operational activity.

AIDS has rapidly risen to the top of the public health agenda of many countries in Sub-Saharan Africa as well as in other parts of the world. Two contributions to this volume deal with AIDS, and they indicate very clearly why AIDS has risen so rapidly to prominence as a health concern. In chapter 13 Chin summarizes data available to the World Health Organization (WHO) on the prevalence of human immunodeficiency virus (HIV) infection in Africa and provides estimates of the probable level of resulting mortality. The WHO estimation procedures suggest that by the end of 1990 a cumulative total of about 700,000 AIDS cases in adults and close to 400,000 in children had occurred; cases were assumed to result in death within a year of diagnosis. The WHO estimation procedures also suggest that about 5 million individuals in Sub-Saharan Africa were infected with HIV by the end of 1989; this accounts for about half the global total. These numbers take on their significance less from their size than from their rapid growth rates (400,000 new AIDS cases are expected to occur in 1992) and their high degree of geographic concentration (80 percent of infections are estimated to occur in 12 countries in central Africa). As in the industrial countries, AIDS in Africa occurs largely in cities; AIDS in Africa, unlike in the industrial countries, appears to be transmitted principally through heterosexual intercourse rather than homosexual intercourse or unsanitary practices with skin-piercing instruments. Mother-to-child transmission is also relatively more important in Africa, in part because adult females are as likely as males to carry the infection.

While chapter 13 deals with the current situation and short-term projections, Anderson provides an overview in chapter 14 of the methods and results of medium- to long-term modeling efforts that he and colleagues have undertaken concerning the demographic impact of the AIDS epidemic in Africa. With plausible values of his model's parameters, Anderson concludes that AIDS may over a period of many decades cause population decline in Africa. The economic and social consequences of this massive mortality can be expected to be extremely serious, particularly if, as preliminary data support, AIDS rates are especially high in the more educated and urbanized sections of the population.[5]

Part II of this volume includes seven condition-specific chapters: one on malnutrition, five on infectious diseases, and one on noninfectious diseases (Hutt, chapter 15, on cancer and cardiovascular disease).[6] In contrast to the situation in high-income countries, infection plays an important etiologic role even with cancer and cardiovascular disease in Sub-Saharan Africa. The genesis of a number of cancers that are very rare in Europe and North America, but of

substantial epidemiological significance in parts or all of Africa, appears to have an important viral involvement: the Epstein-Barr virus is implicated in both nasopharyngeal cancer and Burkitt's lymphoma; the human papilloma virus is implicated in cancer of the penis and the cervix, the latter being the most important malignancy in Sub-Saharan Africa; the hepatitis B virus is implicated in hepatocellular carcinoma; and HIV infection is implicated in a variant of Kaposi's sarcoma that is more aggressive than the variety endemic (but of obscure etiology) in much of Africa. In addition, a history of tropical skin ulcers seems to predispose to subsequent skin malignancy; parasitic infection from *Schistosoma haematobium* predisposes to bladder cancer; and malaria infection appears to be a cofactor in the etiology of Burkitt's lymphoma. Cancer in Africa appears, then, to be linked to high burdens of infection. A number of cancers responsible for much mortality in high-income countries—such as lung, breast, colorectal, and prostate cancer—are much less significant in Africa. As smoking becomes more prevalent and dietary patterns change, however, a higher incidence of these cancers is to be expected and, indeed, is being observed in a number of urban areas. Waterhouse *et al.* (1982) contains a compilation of data on cancer incidence in Africa, in the context of data from other continents.

Cardiovascular diseases in Africa can be usefully characterized as either traditional ones that have, presumably, afflicted African populations over sustained periods or as emerging ones that are only now becoming important in terms of age- and sex-specific incidence and mortality rates. Vaughan (1977) provides a valuable early review of the literature on these conditions in Sub-Saharan Africa, which Hutt updates and extends in chapter 15. Of traditional cardiovascular conditions, rheumatic heart disease emerges as important in studies conducted across much of Africa; typically more than 20 percent of cardiac patients suffer from this condition. Another 10–25 percent of patients also suffer from conditions that are relatively rare in the West—endomyocardial fibrosis, idiopathic cardiomegaly, and syphilitic heart disease. In high-income countries most cardiovascular disease has its origin in hypertension or atherosclerosis or both, with these two underlying conditions assuming quite different degrees of importance in different countries. Hutt clearly shows that hypertension (and its consequences in hypertensive heart disease and stroke) is already emerging as highly important in Sub-Saharan Africa despite evidence that as recently as 50 years ago hypertension was quite rare. In contrast to the rapidly emerging problems with hypertension, atherosclerotically induced conditions such as coronary artery disease remain quite rare in Africa, typically accounting for less than 1 percent of cardiac cases in hospitals. Again, as with cancers prominent in the West, coronary artery disease may be expected to emerge as a significant consequence of changing behavioral patterns unless appropriate preventive measures are initiated soon.

Cancer and cardiovascular disease are often neglected in discussions of health problems in Africa, yet these conditions already account for perhaps a sixth of all deaths and are projected to cause a much higher percentage within 25 years (Bulatao and Stephens, forthcoming; see also table 1-5). Attention to the epidemiology of these conditions, and to the design and implementation of low-cost approaches to prevention and case management, is clearly a growing need. Further discussion of issues associated with policy toward noninfectious diseases in developing countries may be found in Jamison and Mosley (forthcoming).

The preceding paragraphs highlighted some of the major conclusions of the authors of chapters 7–15 of part II of this book. There are several other diseases in Sub-Saharan Africa about which a great deal is known. Schistosomiasis is a good example. Other important diseases and health problems exist, however, about which not enough is known. These include low birth weight, neonatal death, injuries, liver disease, and maternal illness. In light of available knowledge, and

knowledge gaps, table 1-6 presents a tentative agenda for disease-specific priorities, both for operational emphasis and for research, that may be appropriate for Sub-Saharan African countries. We have deliberately tried to keep the list as short as possible in the belief that numerous priorities become no priorities. Items not listed are, by implication, given no plus marks. Research is emphasized where cost-effective interventions are not yet available; operations are emphasized where we already know enough to be effective; and both are emphasized where, even though we have a good basis for action, we urgently need to know more. Our purpose here is to highlight options and to draw attention to neglected issues. It is for each country to decide, on the basis of careful analysis of its health situation, what its operational priorities and research emphases should be.

Valuable experience has already been gained with country-specific (usually region-specific) assessments of health conditions and intervention priorities. Perhaps more than other continents, Africa has experience with a range of long-term focused studies of small-to-medium-size communities and their health problems. Part III of this volume contains papers summarizing six such efforts;[7] figure 1-5 shows the location of these efforts, and table 1-7 summarizes their objectives and main findings. Individually and collectively, they have added greatly to our knowledge of the causes of morbidity and mortality in different locales as well as the efficacy of a broad range of interventions.

Table 1-6. Recommended Operational and Research Priorities for Countries in Sub-Saharan Africa, by Type of Health Problem

Health problem	Operational priority	Research priority
Child health		
Malaria	++	++
Diarrhea	++	+
Acute respiratory infection	++	++
EPI diseases	++	+
Malnutrition	++	+
Neonatal health		+
AIDS		++
Injuries and violence		+
Adult health		
AIDS	++	++
Injuries and violence	+	++
Cancers		+
Cardiovascular disease		+
Tuberculosis	++	+
Maternal health	++	+

++ Top priority.
 + Secondary priority.

Figure 1-5. Location of Community-Based Studies in Sub-Saharan Africa.

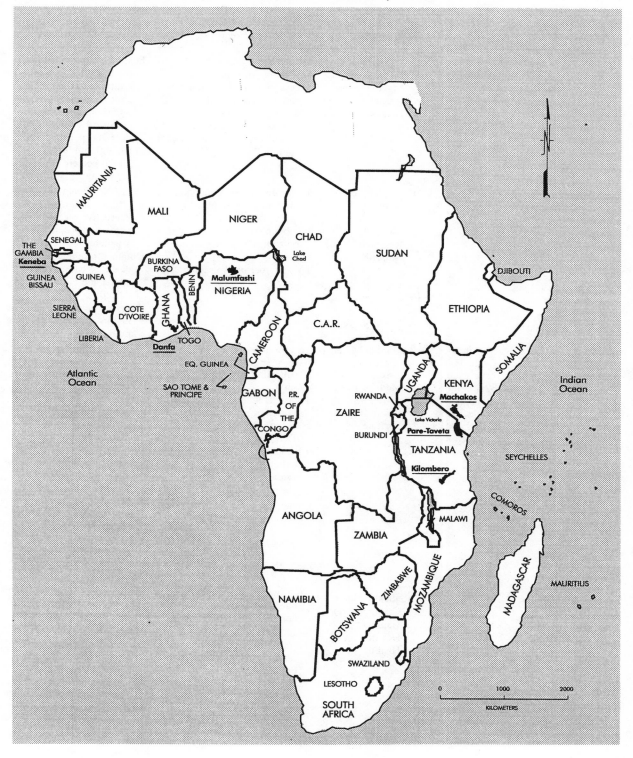

Table 1-7. Characteristics of Six Community Health Studies in Sub-Saharan Africa

Study and period of operation	Population covered	Institutions involved	Objectives	Selected outcomes
Pare-Taveta, Kenya and Tanzania, 1954–66 (chapter 17)	1,500 households	East Africa Institute for Malaria; Ross Institute, London[a]	To assess the public health importance of malaria under conditions of high transmission and (potentially) immune populations. To assess the efficacy of residual insecticides for malaria control	Residual insecticides dramatically reduced morbidity and infant and child mortality. The infant mortality rate dropped by 100 from over 200 per thousand; hemoglobin levels rose 10–20 percent depending on age
Machakos, Kenya, 1974–81 (chapter 18)	4,000 households	Royal Tropical Institute, Amsterdam; Medical Research Centre, Nairobi[b]	To obtain data on childhood morbidity, mortality, and malnutrition. To obtain data on pregnancy outcomes and their determinants. To study pertussis vaccine efficacy	Obtained valuable data on efficacy and timing of alternative measles and pertussis vaccine schedules. Obtained rare data on death by cause for adults and children in Africa. Assessed levels and risk factors for perinatal mortality
Kilombero, Tanzania, 1982–present (chapter 19 covers the period to 1987)	1,900 individuals surveyed 132,000 individuals reflected in routine data collection	Tanzanian Ministry of Health; Tanzanian Medical Research Institute; Swiss Tropical Institute	To improve primary health care by strengthening routine data collection and adding special surveys. To assess levels, trends, and causes of malnutrition, morbidity, and mortality in rural Tanzania. To implement and evaluate sanitation and health care interventions	Used household questionnaires, clinic records, and special surveys to yield similar results on much morbidity, but required special surveys to find malnutrition and eye disease. Integrated community health research with local health services to benefit both and provide a model for the sentinel district concept. Collected extensive local data on morbidity and malnutrition
Keneba, the Gambia, 1950–present (chapter 20 covers the period to 1975)	700–900 individuals	Medical Research Council (UK); Gambian Department of Health	To provide information on the nature and epidemiology of communicable diseases in rural areas. To relate infection to malnutrition, particularly protein deficiency	Documented high levels of communicable disease, particularly among children. Identified strong seasonality of disease and child mortality. Concluded that malnutrition resulted principally from infection. Assessed efficacy of some interventions

Table 1-7 (continued)

Study and period of operation	Population covered	Institutions involved	Objectives	Selected outcomes
Malumfashi, Nigeria, 1974–79 (chapter 21)	43,000 individuals	Faculty of Medicine, Ahmadu Bello University; Liverpool School of Tropical Medicine	To study malaria and its consequences for reducing immunity To study the impact of schistosomiasis in the community To study epidemiology and efficacy of intervention against meningococcal infections	Found that malaria's adverse consequences were often indirect; chemoprophylaxis was highly effective in improving hemoglobin levels in children Developed approaches to chemotherapy for meningococcal infection; assessed vaccine performance Combined studies with intervention to generate community good will and health awareness, but this was not exploited by service delivery system
Danfa, Ghana, 1969–79 (chapter 22)	4,000 individuals (core study group)	University of Ghana Medical School; University of California, Los Angeles	To assess cost-effectiveness of integrating family planning services with health services To conduct an epidemiological investigation of a rural Ghanaian community, including assessment of behavioral risk factors	Discovered that family planning was best delivered through health services Found that poliomyelitis was much more significant than had been thought Found that malaria chemoprophylaxis was effective but induced resistance Obtained substantial data on disability, morbidity, functional impairment, and risk factors

a. The East Africa Institute for Malaria has been merged into the Tanzanian Institute for Malaria and Vector-borne Diseases in Amani, Tanzania. The Ross Institute was a part of the London School of Hygiene and Tropical Medicine.

b. The Medical Research Centre, Nairobi, is now part of the Kenya Medical Research Institute.

Options for Acquiring Information

The preceding pages summarized this volume's analyses of epidemiological and demographic data relevant to health policy for Sub-Saharan Africa. These analyses have emerged from studies that require varying degrees of time, money, and sophistication and that, in some cases, reflect recent and substantial improvements in methods for both design and analysis. One important dimension of health policy concerns the extent to which ministries of health should invest in generating information relevant to policy and in developing the institutional capacity to process and use such information. This volume sheds light on this question by describing (albeit briefly) the main methods that have been used and by indicating the extent to which the methods have passed from research instruments to proven operational tools. This section draws together the main lessons concerning the options open to ministries and statistical offices; it concludes that several new and powerful approaches—use of indirect demographic methods, adoption of case-control epidemiological techniques, and, particularly, expanded use of sentinel districts and facilities—offer highly cost-effective ways for health ministries to meet an important part of their information needs.

Table 1-8. Study Designs Relevant to Answering Different Policy Questions

Policy questions	Cross-sectional studies		Prospective population studies		Routine data collection		
	Surveys	Censuses	Multiround or continuous	Sentinel districts	Vital records	Hospital records	Sentinel facilities
Whether levels and trends suggest priority	Yes	Yes	Yes	Yes	Potential	No	No
Where the problems are most acute	Yes	Potential	No	No	Potential	No	No
Which diseases are important	Limited	No	Limited	Yes	Potential	Yes[a]	Yes[a]
Why diseases occur (risk factors)	For some diseases	No	Yes	Yes	No	Yes[b]	Yes[b]
How prevention and case management should be approached	Limited	No	Yes	Yes	No	Potential	Potential

a. For planning facilities.
b. With case control methodologies.

Different instruments for generating data serve, of course, to answer different policy questions. Table 1-8 recapitulates the five classes of policy questions that were discussed earlier and lists broad approaches to generating data relevant to answering them: cross-sectional studies, prospective population studies, and routine data collection. The table draws on the lessons of the volume's chapters to indicate which approaches seem most promising for which data needs. The following subsections deal further with experience concerning the three broad approaches to data generation.

Cross-Sectional Surveys and Censuses

Cross-sectional analysis has long been the backbone of social science research. It provides snapshots of an entire population (in the case of censuses) or of a sample population, perhaps randomly selected and representative of a larger population (in the case of surveys). Although cross-sectional studies can provide longitudinal information through retrospective questions, they more typically produce static estimates. Causal analysis, such as that made possible in prospective studies by experimental design and the analysis of rates of change, is beyond their power.

Censuses cover an entire population and are therefore more suited than are surveys to answering the question of where problems are occurring, but only on a limited number of topics. Because it requires complete coverage of a population, a census needs to limit the variety of topics that it covers in order to maintain high quality and remain economical. Census-es usually achieve better response rates than surveys because of the public relations campaigns that attend them (Kish, 1987). Surveys, however, by virtue of their smaller sizes, can be designed to obtain more in-depth information from respondents. Cross-sectional surveys and censuses are useful in policymaking because, compared with prospective studies, they are relatively cheap and easy to conduct and their results can generally be made available more quickly.

As is shown in table 1-8, both surveys and censuses can indicate levels in the prevalence of health problems; censuses can do this better when prevalence is low or is restricted to certain locations. However, censuses often do not include the questions necessary to ascertain the prevalence of diseases. Surveys and censuses are well suited for studying the where question—in other words, for determining the distribution of ill health by locational, socioeconomic, or other criteria. Determining which diseases are most frequent, or important in some other way, requires collecting much information and would typically overburden a census. The which question can be addressed to some degree in a survey, but surveys do not allow the incidence or frequency of disease to be measured over time or the strong seasonal variability in the frequency of some communicable diseases to be understood. For risk-factor studies (the why question) surveys can be used selectively if they control adequately for confounding. In the same manner, they can be used to estimate the impact of an intervention on a specific disease (table 1-8).

One promising advance in survey methodology

comes from the use of indirect demographic methods to measure mortality rates in cross-sectional surveys. Indirect methods involve asking questions of specific categories of persons about the survival of specific categories of relatives. Questions are asked about survival of parents (the orphanhood method), of spouses (the widowhood method), of siblings (the sisterhood or brotherhood method), and of children. These methods were recently reviewed by Timæus and Graham (1989) and by Hill and David (1989). The sisterhood method was developed specifically to measure maternal mortality (Graham *et al.*, 1988a, 1988b). Questions about child survival have been modified into the preceding birth technique, which enables reliable estimates of the risk of death before the age of two to be obtained from very simple questions asked mothers during surveys or at health facilities (Aguirre and Hill, 1987; Brass and Macrae, 1985; Hill and David, 1989). Indirect methods are the source of much of the mortality data in chapters 3 and 5 of this volume. Advances in indirect methods are taking place in estimating cause-specific mortality (for example, maternal mortality) and specifying better the ages and time periods to which the mortality estimates refer. Indirect methods are a rapidly moving area of methodological and analytical development, and they hold the prospect for measuring mortality more frequently, with greater accuracy, and at lower cost in African countries.

Prospective Studies

Prospective studies differ from cross-sectional ones in that collection of data takes place at more than one point in time. These studies (also called follow-up, cohort, or panel studies) select a sample and follow the subjects forward in time. They allow, therefore, a dynamic analysis by providing information on changes in individuals and on the incidence of diseases. Diaries may be used by respondents to record events between rounds, thus providing accurate information on the timing of the events (as used, for example, in Nigeria; Huttly *et al.*, 1990). Dynamic analysis is not only more informative; it also allows easier testing of relationships, and standard errors of coefficients tend to be smaller, leading to better statistical inference (Tuma and Hannan, 1984). Recent advances in the methodology for analyzing data generated by prospective studies have greatly facilitated and stimulated their use.

Prospective studies can be designed as controlled intervention trials, in which the sample is divided, preferably at random, into groups that either do or do not receive a particular intervention. Repeated ob-

servations then provide information on the effects of the intervention. There are, however, both practical and ethical complications in treating human populations in this way, and quasi-experimental designs for estimating the impact of interventions are more commonly used (Briscoe *et al.*, 1986). The disadvantages of prospective studies are the high cost of following individuals through time, attrition owing to mobility and mortality, and considerable time before results become available. On occasion, reinterview laxity on the part of the interviewers and retest reactivity on the part of the respondents have created difficulty.

A particular form of prospective enquiry, now increasingly advocated, is the use of sentinel districts. As Tarimo (chapter 16) notes, the prospective studies of small areas that are summarized in part III can be viewed as precursors of the sentinel model, and the study at Ifakara in Tanzania comes very close to being one (Tanner *et al.*, chapter 19). A sentinel district is a selected geographic area corresponding to a unit of health services management. In Africa the appropriate unit would typically be a district. In this district special systems for recording morbidity, mortality, risk factors, and intervention coverage (for example, EPI) are put in place without disrupting the normal functioning of the district's health services. These measurement instruments provide a continuing source of information for district-level health management and, when passed on to the regional or national level, assist in the wider task of resource allocation and health sector planning. A country would wish initially to select several districts that are roughly representative of the diversity of culture and ecology of the country. As the systems of data collection are refined, all districts may adopt the simpler of these systems, while the sentinel districts are reserved for special enquiries, such as community-based intervention trials (Kirkwood and Morrow, 1989). Thus sentinel districts contribute to methodological development and are an important source of health data. Sentinel districts often contain sentinel facilities, which are discussed below under routine data collection. It seems probable that the development of the sentinel district concept will be one of the major advances in health data collection in Africa over the next decade (see chapters 15, 19, and 20 and Tanner, 1988).

Routine Data Collection

Vital statistics usually include live births, deaths, stillbirths, marriages, divorces, and adoptions. Some of this information will be of legal value only. To be of epidemiological and demographic value, further information on age, gender, and cause of death should be provided on death certificates, and births should be recorded by the age and parity of the mother. Additional information that is sometimes included on birth certificates is whether the birth took place in a hospital, whether a midwife or medical doctor was in attendance, the duration of the pregnancy, and the child's weight at birth. The usefulness of vital statistics for demographic analysis depends largely on the completeness of the register because the persons registered are not necessarily representative of the population. Indirect estimation techniques have been developed, however, that allow adult mortality and fertility to be estimated from incomplete vital registration systems when other data, such as a census or a fertility survey, are available (Brass, 1975; Timæus and Graham, 1989; United Nations, 1983).

Hospital records, if carefully and accurately kept, provide a picture of who uses health services and why, which aids planning and managing health services. Records do not provide a good picture of disease or death in the community because in most of Africa a large proportion of disease and death is never seen at a health facility and what is seen is unlikely to be representative. The careful analysis of 27 years of records at a hospital in West Nile District in Uganda showed schistosomiasis to be the leading cause of death in persons over ten years of age (Williams *et al.*, 1986). That this could be true for the community as a whole is not believable and illustrates the problem with interpreting hospital records. Hill and Graham (1988) provide a valuable discussion, in a West African context, of the limitations and potential for making greater use of data generated by routine record keeping. Hutt (in chapter 15) relies heavily on data from cancer registries and autopsy series that provide valuable insights into cancer and cardiovascular disease using quasi-routine records.

As Tarimo stresses in chapter 16, considerable interest is now focused on the sentinel facility. A sentinel facility, such as a clinic or hospital, is selected and its systems of recording data and undertaking analysis are upgraded beyond those that would be possible at all clinics or hospitals. Sentinel facilities may be located in sentinel districts, but need not be, and are selected to represent the diversity of culture, ecology, and type of health facility found in the country. These facilities can undertake several special forms of data collection and analysis. Most promising is the development of facility-based measurement of under-two child mortality risk using the preceding birth technique (Hill and David, 1989) and of the impact of immunization, water supply and sanitation,

and other interventions using ongoing case-control methods (Briscoe *et al.*, 1986; Cousens *et al.*, 1988a, 1988b; Mahmood *et al.*, 1989; Orenstein *et al.*, 1985; Rodrigues and Kirkwood, 1990; Smith, 1987; Smith *et al.*, 1984). These advances hold out the prospect of sentinel facilities that have microcomputers programmed with sophisticated but highly user-friendly software, undertaking continuous data entry and analysis of vaccine effectiveness and intervention impact in their catchment area.

Conclusions

The postindependence era has witnessed sustained, substantial reductions in mortality in Sub-Saharan Africa, although these reduction have been unevenly distributed over time and among and within countries. The same period has also witnessed the development of demographic and epidemiological techniques for assessing the magnitude, distribution, and cause of health problems; these new methods allow less expensive, simpler, and quicker approaches to gathering and presenting data, and they allow sharper evaluation of intervention efficacy. Their application in Africa, and the continued application of familiar methods, has led to an accumulation of knowledge sufficient to give a broad (if incomplete) overview of epidemiological and demographic trends and current conditions. This volume attempts, through a structured set of chapters, to provide such an overview. In so doing, it also provides a sense of the applicability in the African context of the range of epidemiological and demographic tools that are potentially important instruments of national health policy.

Our conclusions deal generally with the changing patterns of mortality and morbidity. First, even though progress in reducing mortality has been substantial, mortality and morbidity levels in Africa remain the highest in the world. The examples of some particularly successful countries (Botswana, Congo, Kenya, Sudan, and Zimbabwe) indicate that substantial progress in closing the health gap with other regions can proceed much more rapidly than increasing income growth. At the same time, periods of actual increase in under-five mortality rates in some countries (Ghana, Nigeria) and generally poor performance in others (the Gambia, Malawi, Sierra Leone) warn that continued progress is far from automatic.

Second, Africa shares much with other regions of the world in the prevalence of specific diseases and their distribution by age. Diarrheal disease, acute respiratory infection, malnutrition, and vaccine-preventable diseases are important causes of illness and death in children; maternal death and tuberculosis are important and preventable contributors to very high adult mortality rates. The technologies for dealing with these diseases have succeeded in parts of Africa (and even more completely elsewhere); this fact points to specific policy directions for countries wishing to emulate the success of Kenya or Zimbabwe. Although the broad patterns of disease in Africa are similar to those in other developing countries, even if the burdens are greater, there are two worrying exceptions: both malaria and AIDS are substantially more significant in many African locales than elsewhere. Rather less is known about how to address these two conditions effectively, and the rapid growth rate of HIV prevalence suggests that AIDS will have a substantial demographic impact on seriously affected countries by early in the next century.

Third, with the exception of a single chapter covering cancer and cardiovascular disease, this volume omits discussion of noncommunicable diseases and injuries (and, therefore, of most of the problems that afflict adults and the elderly). That omission may be justified, given the paucity of the literature. The existing literature simply does not deal with the probable current and certain future significance of these conditions. Epidemiological work on injury, cancer, cardiovascular disease, and other noncommunicable conditions in Africa is a high priority.

Fourth, although some countries do have mechanisms in place for assessing basic epidemiological and demographic conditions, many do not. Implementing minimal national packages to increase the data collection and analysis capacity of countries lacking such capacity is a key priority that would allow the formulation and implementation of more effective and efficient health sector policies.

Fifth, countries with existing epidemiological and demographic capacity are, typically, the first ones to address the broader range of health problems that results from initial success in controlling fertility and infectious disease. A larger capacity for gathering information, which would probably include a greatly expanded use of sentinel districts and of facility-based indirect and case-control techniques, will be a high priority for many of these countries.

Acknowledgments

The authors are indebted, for valuable comments on earlier drafts, to many of the other authors of chapters in this volume, as well as to O. Echeverri, A. R. Measham, and M. Phillips.

Notes

1. A recent volume on population policy in Sub-Saharan Africa (World Bank, 1986) provides a synopsis of available studies on fertility and its determinants and the implications for population policy of the findings of those studies.
2. These and other comments on Sudan in this chapter should be viewed cautiously because the data apply more to the north of the country than to the large and impoverished south.
3. For a recent review of education and education policies in Sub-Saharan Africa, and their relationship to development, see World Bank (1988). The links between education and mortality have been comprehensively reviewed by Cochrane et al. (1982) and Caldwell (1986).
4. Many of the data sets from which the child mortality estimates reported in tables 1-3 and 1-4 are drawn also lend themselves to analysis of levels of and differentials in fertility. Cochrane and Farid (1989) have undertaken such analyses, concluding that African fertility levels have a high base with relatively small differentials around it. (Asia has a low base and small differentials; Latin America a high base and large differentials.) It is tempting to draw a parallel between the patterns of fertility and of mortality.
5. De Zalduondo et al. (1989) provide an up-to-date account of issues surrounding AIDS in Africa along with extensive references to a substantial and rapidly growing literature. Over et al. (1988) have provided careful empirical documentation of the costs of AIDS (both direct and indirect) in two countries that have foci of high prevalence, Tanzania and Zaire; and Rowley et al. (n.d.) have used the long-term model described in chapter 14 to assess the economic and demographic effects of reducing the spread of HIV infection.
6. The geographic distribution of other noninfectious diseases, with particular reference to Africa, is discussed in Hutt and Burkitt (1985).
7. Examples of similar efforts outside Africa include those of Narangwal (India), Lampang (Thailand), Matlab (Bangladesh), and Framingham (United States). Important African examples not reviewed here include Kasongo in Zaire (Kasongo Project Team, 1983), a study of nutrition in Kenya (Neumann and Bwibe, 1987), anthropological and demographic studies that are ongoing in Tanzania and Botswana (Blurton-Jones, 1989), a community-based study emphasizing malaria control in Saradidi, Kenya (Kaseje and Spencer, 1989), and studies of child health in Addis Ababa, Ethiopia (Freij, 1977).

References

Aguirre, A. and Hill, A. G. (1987). *Childhood Mortality Estimates Using the Preceding Birth Technique: Some Applications and Extensions*. Centre for Population Studies Research Paper, no. 87-2. London: London School of Hygiene and Tropical Medicine.

Blurton-Jones, N. G. (1989). The costs of children and the adaptive scheduling of births: towards a sociobiological perspective on demography. In: *The Sociobiology of Sexual and Reproductive Strategies*, Ras, A. E., Vogel, C., and Voland, E. (editors), pp. 265–282. London and New York: Chapman and Hall.

Brass, W. (1975). *Methods for Estimating Fertility and Mortality from Limited and Defective Data.* Chapel Hill, N.C.: Carolina Population Center.

Brass, W. and Macrae, S. (1985). Childhood mortality estimated from reports on previous births given by mothers at the time of maternity. 1: preceding birth technique. *Asian and Pacific Census Forum*, 11 (2), 5–8.

Briscoe, J., Feachem, R. G., and Rahaman, M. (1986). *Evaluating Health Impact: Water Supply, Sanitation, Hygiene Education.* Ottawa: International Development Research Centre.

Bulatao, R. A., and Stephens, P. W. (forthcoming). Estimates and projections of mortality by cause: a global overview, 1970–2015. In: *Disease Control Priorities in Developing Countries,* Jamison, D. T. and Mosley, W. H. (editors). New York: Oxford University Press.

Caldwell, J. C. (1986). Routes to low mortality in poor countries. *Population and Development*, 12, 171–220.

Cochrane, S. H. and Farid, S. M. (1989). *Fertility in Sub-Saharan Africa: Analysis and Explanation.* World Bank Discussion Paper, no. 43. Washington, D.C.

Cochrane, S. H., Leslie, J., and O'Hara, D. (1982). Parental education and child health: intracountry evidence. *Health Policy and Education*, 2, 213–250.

Cornia, G. A., Jolly, R., and Stewart, F., editors. (1987). *Adjustment with a Human Face: Protecting the Vulnerable and Promoting Growth.* Oxford: Clarendon Press.

Cousens, S. N., Feachem, R. G., Kirkwood, B. R., Mertens, T. E., and Smith, P. G. (1988a). *Case-Control Studies of Childhood Diarrhoea. Pt. 1: Minimizing Bias.* Diarrhoeal Diseases Control Programme Document, no. CDD/EDP/88.2. Geneva: World Health Organization.

———. (1988b). *Case-Control Studies of Childhood Diarrhoea. Pt. 2: Sample Size.* Diarrhoeal Diseases Control Programme Document, no. CCD/EDP/88.3. Geneva: World Health Organization.

de Zalduondo, B. O., Msamanga, G. I., and Chen, L. C. (1989). AIDS in Africa: unity and contrasts in the global pandemic. *Daedalus*, 118, 165–204.

Feachem, R. G., Kjellstrom, T., Murray, C., Over, M., and Phillips, M. A., editors (forthcoming). *The Health of Adults in the Developing World.* New York: Oxford University Press.

Freij, L. (1977). Exploring child health and its ecology. The Kirkas Study in Addis Ababa, an evaluation of procedures in the measurement of acute morbidity and a search for causal structure. *Acta Pediatrica Scandanavica*, 67 (supplement), 1–180.

Graham, W., Brass, W., and Snow, R. W. (1988a). Estimating maternal mortality in developing countries. *Lancet*, 1, 416–417.

———. (1988b). *Indirect Estimation of Maternal Mortality: The Sisterhood Method.* Centre for Population Studies Research Paper, no. 88-1. London: London School of Hygiene and Tropical Medicine.

Greenwood, B. M., Greenwood, A. M., Bradley, A. K., Tulloch, S., Hayes, R., and Oldfield, F. S. J. (1987a). Deaths in infancy and early childhood in a well-vaccinated, rural, West African population. *Annals of Tropical Pediatrics*, 2, 91–99.

Greenwood, B. M., Bradley, A. K., Greenwood, A. M., Byass, P., Jammeh, K., Marsh, K., Tulloch, S., Oldfield, F. S. J., and Hayes, R. (1987b). Mortality and morbidity from malaria among children in a rural area of the Gambia, West Africa. *Transactions of the Royal Society of Tropical Medicine and Hygiene*, 81, 478–486.

Halstead, S. B., Walsh, J. A., and Warren, K. S., editors. (1985). *Good Health at Low Cost.* New York: Rockefeller Foundation.

Hanlon, P., Byass, P., Yamuah, M., Hayes, R., Bennett, S., and M'Boge, B. H. (1988). Factors influencing vaccination compliance in peri-urban Gambian children. *Journal of Tropical Medicine and Hygiene*, 91, 29–33.

Hill, A. G. and David, P. H. (1989). Monitoring changes in child mortality: new methods for use in developing countries. *Health Policy and Planning*, 3, 214–226.

Hill, A. G. and Graham, W. J. (1988). *West African Sources of Health and Mortality Information: A Comparative Review.* Technical Study, no. 58e. Ottawa, Canada: International Development Research Centre.

Hill, Kenneth. (1989). Demographic response to economic shock. Washington, D.C.: World Bank, World Development Report Office.

Hutt, M. S. R. and Burkitt, D. P. (1985). *The Geography of Noninfectious Disease.* Oxford: Oxford University Press.

Huttly, S. R. A., Blum, D., Kirkwood, B. R., Emeh, R. N., Okeke, N., Ajala, M., Smith, G. S., Carson, D. C., Dosunmu-Ogunbi, O., and Feachem, R. G. (1990). The Imo State (Nigeria) drinking water supply and sanitation project. 2: impact on dracunculiasis, diarrhoea and nutritional status. *Transactions of the Royal Society of Tropical Medicine and Hygiene*, 84, 316–321.

Jamison, D. T. and Mosley, W. H. (forthcoming). Selecting disease control priorities in developing countries. In: *Disease Control Priorities in Developing Countries,* Jamison, D. T. and Mosley, W. H. (editors). New York: Oxford University Press.

Kaseje, D. C. O. and Spencer, H. (1989). The Saradidi, Kenya, Rural Health Development Programme. *Annals of Tropical Medicine and Parasitology*, 81 (supplement 1), 1–12.

Kasongo Project Team. (1983). The Kasongo Project. *World Health Forum*, 4, 41–45.

Kirkwood, B. R. and Morrow, R. H. (1989). Community-based intervention trials. *Journal of Biosocial Science*, 10 (supplement), 79–86.

Kish, L. (1987). *Statistical Design for Research.* New York: John Wiley and Sons.

Mahmood, D. A., Feachem, R. G., and Huttly, S. R. A. (1989). Infant feeding and risk of severe diarrhoea in Basrah city, Iraq: a case-control study. *Bulletin of the World Health Organization*, 67, 701–706.

Murray, C. (1987). A critical review of international mortality data. *Social Science and Medicine,* 25, 773–781.

Murray, C., Styblo, K., and Rouillon, A. (forthcoming). Tuberculosis. In: *Disease Control Priorities in Developing Countries,* Jamison, D. T. and Mosley, W. H. (editors). New York: Oxford University Press.

Neumann, C. and Bwibe, N. (1987). *The Collaborative Research Support Program on Food Intake and Human Function, Kenya Project, Final Report.* Nairobi and Los Angeles: University of Nairobi, Faculty of Medicine, and UCLA School of Public Health.

Orenstein, W. A., Bernier, R. H., Dondero, T. J., Hinman, A. R., Marks, J. S., Bart, K. J., and Sirotkin, B. (1985). Field evaluation of vaccine efficacy. *Bulletin of the World Health Organization,* 63, 1055–1068.

Over, M., Bertozzi, S., Chin, J., N'Galy, B., and Nyanurye-kung'e, K. (1988). The direct and indirect cost of HIV infections in developing countries: the cases of Zaire and Tanzania. In: *The Global Impact of AIDS,* Fleming, A.F., *et al.* (editors)., pp 123–135. New York: Alan R. Liss, Inc.

Rodrigues, L. and Kirkwood, B. (1990). Case-control designs in the study of common diseases: updates on the demise of the rare disease assumption, and the choice of sampling scheme for controls. *International Journal of Epidemiology,* 19, 205–213.

Rowley, J. T., Anderson, R. M., and Ng, T. W. (n.d.). Reducing the spread of HIV infection in Sub-Saharan Africa: some demographic and economic implications. London: Imperial College, Parasite Epidemiology Research Group.

Sanders, D. and Davies, R. (1988). Economic adjustment and current trends in child survival: the case of Zimbabwe. *Health Policy and Planning,* 3, 195–204.

Schapira, A. (1989). Chloroquine resistant malaria in Africa: the challenge to health services. *Health Policy and Planning,* 4, 17–28.

Smith, P. G. (1987). Evaluating interventions against tropical diseases. *International Journal of Epidemiology,* 16, 159–166.

Smith, P. G., Rodrigues, L. C., and Fine, P. E. M. (1984). Assessment of the protective efficacy of vaccines against common diseases using case-control and cohort studies. *International Journal of Epidemiology,* 13, 87–93.

Stephens, P. W. (forthcoming). Recent estimates of childhood mortality change in Sub-Saharan Africa.

Tanner, M. (1988). District-level data collection and use. Paper prepared for the Independent International Commission on Health Research for Development. Boston, Mass.: Harvard University, School of Public Health.

Timæus, I. and Graham, W. (1989). Measuring adult mortality in developing countries: a review and assessment of methods. Policy, Planning, and Research Working Paper Series, no. 20. Washington, D.C.: World Bank, Policy, Planning, and Research Department.

Tuma, N. B. and Hannan, M. T. (1984). *Social Dynamics.* New York: Academic Press.

United Nations. (1983). *Manual X. Indirect Techniques for Demographic Estimation.* New York.

UNICEF. (1989). *The State of the World's Children, 1989.* New York: Oxford University Press.

Vaughan, J. P. (1977). A brief review of cardiovascular disease in Africa. *Transactions of the Royal Society of Tropical Medicine and Hygiene,* 71, 226–231.

Waterhouse, J. A. W., Shanmugaratnam, K., Muir, C. S., and Powell, J., editors. (1982). *Cancer Incidence in Five Continents.* Vol. 4. IARC Publication no. 42. Lyon, France: International Agency for Research on Cancer.

Williams, E. H., Hayes, R. J., and Smith, P. G. (1986). Admissions to a rural hospital in the West Nile District of Uganda over a 27 year period. *Journal of Tropical Medicine and Hygiene,* 89, 193–211.

World Bank. (1986). *Population Growth and Policies in Sub-Saharan Africa.* A World Bank Policy Study. Washington, D.C.

———. (1988). *Education in Sub-Saharan Africa: Policies for Adjustment, Revitalization, and Expansion.* A World Bank Policy Study. Washington, D.C.

Part I
The Patterns of Mortality

Chapter 2

Mortality in Sub-Saharan Africa: An Overview

Frederick T. Sai and Janet Nassim

Mortality levels and trends are strongly influenced by the level and course of socioeconomic development. So accepted is this fact that mortality indicators such as infant mortality rates and life expectancy at birth are commonly used as social indicators of development. Not only does the level of socioeconomic development directly affect expenditures on health; standards of living in general, nutrition, education, and housing, for example, also determine health status. Most governments in Africa see mortality reduction as an important objective of government and have joined the global effort, given impetus by the Alma Ata Conference in 1978, to achieve Health for All by the Year 2000. To meet these objectives health planners need information on which to base policies and programs: they need information on the extent of mortality in their countries and its causes, both pathological and social, and on the interventions most likely to prove effective. The following four chapters of part I draw together what is currently known about the levels, trends, and patterns of mortality in Sub-Saharan Africa. Although this comparative review is the main focus, another extremely important theme is the limitations of currently available data. This leads to useful discussions of the demographic techniques that can help overcome these limitations and to suggestions of the critical information gaps that need to be filled in order to plan interventions.

Chapters 3 and 4 examine infant and child mortality. In chapter 3 Hill presents a comparative analysis of levels of mortality among children under five in the late 1970s and, where possible, of trends since the 1940s. Later data were not available when chapter 3 was written, although some are presented in table 1-4. The censuses and surveys conducted in most countries in Sub-Saharan Africa in the 1970s provide the most recent published information allowing comparison across the region. In chapter 4 Blacker explores the factors that might help to account for the considerable geographic differences in infant and child mortality both between and within countries. He considers both the different hazards present under different ecological conditions and the means available for preventing and treating these risks to health and life. In chapters 5 and 6 Timæus and Graham examine adult mortality: Timæus presents an overview, and Graham specifically examines maternal mortality. Timæus considers differentials by country, gender, and cause, while Graham finds it all but impossible to make comparisons since the lack of adequate statistical infrastructure makes distinguishing patterns due to risk from those due to data deficiencies difficult.

Main Findings

The first finding is that levels of mortality are higher, on average, in Sub-Saharan Africa than in other developing regions of the world. Levels of mortality among children are such that 20 percent die before they reach the age of five. Young people aged 15 have on average less than 50 years of life remaining, which is lower than life expectancy at 15 in most developing countries. Women in Africa face two to three times the risk of dying in childbirth as women in Asia. Yet there is great heterogeneity within the region: the mortality levels in some countries compare favorably with those in individual countries of other developing regions.

With notable exceptions, the differences between countries in Sub-Saharan Africa fit a pattern. The second major finding is that there is a rough gradient that crosses from northwest to southeast, with higher levels of infant, young child, and adult mortality in western than in eastern or southern Africa. The picture for maternal mortality is complicated by the fact that the level of fertility affects the number of maternal deaths. Although the risk of death in each pregnancy is higher in western than in eastern Africa, higher fertility levels mean that a woman in the east faces a lifetime risk of maternal death similar to that in the west.

Rapid population growth in the region is frequently ascribed to declining mortality not yet matched by declining fertility. One of the most heartening findings presented by Hill is that under-five mortality has indeed been reduced since the 1940s in the vast majority of countries for which data are available. The exceptions are largely countries ravaged by war and civil unrest. The situation of adult mortality seems more mixed. Timæus concludes that while mortality in western Africa in the late 1970s had declined considerably from the very high levels of the 1950s, mortality in eastern African countries, while lower to begin with, had apparently not improved over the period. This finding gives cause for concern.

Differences among groups in the incidence of disease and mortality often provide clues to their determinants. Several interesting differences emerge from these chapters: the geographic pattern noted above; age differences (of particular note, the finding that the countries with the lowest levels of under-five mortality are not necessarily those with the lowest levels of adult mortality); differences in the relative importance of various causes of death; and gender differences. In many developing countries in other regions high maternal mortality results in lower life expectancy for women. No such difference exists in Sub-Saharan Africa, and other causes must also be taking a large toll on men. Blacker and Timæus, in particular, discuss the possible determinants of the above differentials and reach two main conclusions: we need to begin by establishing the principal causes of morbidity and mortality, and explanations in terms of particular socioeconomic indicators or the availability of health services are unlikely to be correct. Instead, as Timæus puts it, "the pattern is probably determined by the interaction of disease ecology with the physical environment on the one hand and broad aspects of culture and social structure on the other."

Implications for Health Planning

The second major purpose of part I is to discuss the sources of data, their coverage of the population, the completeness of the mortality information they provide, and the reliability of that information. The most obvious need is for more current information. No country in Africa has a system of vital registration that provides national coverage and reliable data on mortality. This is one area where increased donor support might make a valuable contribution to developing planning capability. In the absence of registration data, national estimates are derived from censuses and surveys. In several countries examined by Timæus, however, the most up-to-date sources on levels of adult mortality were from the 1960s. The most reliable data on which Hill could base cross-country comparisons were derived mainly from censuses and surveys in the 1970s. Such comparisons can give important insight into the reason for differing mortality levels and rates of decline, but their value would obviously be enhanced if they could take into account more recent developments.

More is known about child mortality than about adult mortality, mainly because attention has been given to developing indirect measures that can be applied to census data. However, Timæus and Graham report progress with analogous measures of adult mortality and specifically with measures of maternal mortality. These estimates are based on census and survey questions that ask respondents about the death of their parents during their own childhood or of their sisters as a result of pregnancy. In the absence of vital registration systems, incorporating a few standard questions that would allow mortality to be estimated in these ways could yield invaluable information. Indirect methods of estimating child mortality are a powerful demographic tool, as may be the newer orphanhood and sisterhood methods of estimating adult and maternal mortality whose early development is described here. One valuable aspect of this section is that it draws attention to the feasibility and utility of such questions and techniques.

The fact that questions on the number of surviving children, parents, and sisters yield more reliable information than direct questions on the death of household members indicates how sensitive, or how subject to recall bias, such questions are. In calling for more data, therefore, survey designers should bear in mind three questions. First, what does the information mean to the informant, and what is his or her perception of why it is required? For example, any implication of blame will lead to underreporting. Second, what does the information mean to the person collecting it? Unless local people or health personnel have a stake in the data collection process (because, for example, they see it as a tool in community-level planning), deficiencies can be expected. Third, is the information gathered so that it is amenable to standardized classification and grouping by age? Only standardized information will be of use to health planners.

How can we encourage these developments? The improvements that are taking place in establishing better links between the primary health services and the communities they serve should help bring community leaders into data-collecting arrangements. Regulations that run counter to traditional community beliefs or practices must be reviewed. For example, instead of insisting that deaths be registered at a distant administrative office before burial, health authorities and the communities could agree on acceptable burial sites and let village elders sign the initial certificate of death. We should be able to make people understand that the reasons for registration are to identify and prevent or improve the conditions that cause most risk to the health of themselves and their families. Sanction approaches are not appropriate at present. Ministries of health need to examine their reporting requirements and enable their departments of statistics to work better with data collectors in the field. They should work better with health staff at the periphery and also help them to understand the purposes for which the data are being collected. As first steps, the use of standard definitions and classifications should be encouraged. The utility of the data already being collected could be much improved by such relatively simple measures. Perhaps it would be possible to use maternal mortality as a test case and the data collection, findings, and plans for services as a community education exercise.

From the point of view of health policy and planning, this lack of data divided into standard age groups and into standard classifications of cause of death is the most important deficiency in the data currently available. Ability to break down mortality into its components is basic to understanding the determinants of levels, trends, and differentials and, therefore, to planning appropriate interventions. In many countries of Sub-Saharan Africa the main source of population-based data on age at death and cause of death is small area surveys, such as those reported in part III of this volume. Although there are difficulties in extrapolating the cause of death structure of a small area to a country as a whole, an indirect benefit of such surveys is often their spillover effect: the impact that being the focus of attention has on the community.

The other main source of data on cause of death is hospital records. Again, many sources of bias make hospital statistics an insecure foundation on which to base estimates of causes of death in the population as a whole. Only in the specific setting can one judge whether and how the data distort the level and pattern of mortality in that area.

Although many questions remain to be answered,

two crucial points stand out. First, interventions cannot wait until we have perfect data. Second, these chapters are themselves testament to how far understanding has advanced in the past ten to fifteen years. Studies revealing the extent of infant and child mortality have helped to focus attention and programs on young children and their mothers. More recently, the realization that women in Sub-Saharan Africa run a lifetime risk of dying in pregnancy of roughly 1 in 20, as against 1 in just under 10,000 in northern Europe, has galvanized the health community into action. Unfortunately, as Graham points out, "the information needed to push a health problem to the forefront of attention is often quite different, in quality and quantity, from that required to implement action." Yet the material gathered here does suggest some ways to proceed.

First, Blacker, Timæus, and Graham (chapters 4, 5, and 6) agree that relatively few causes of death account for the majority of child, adult, and maternal deaths. Furthermore, several of the major threats to children also account for one-quarter to one-third of the deaths of adults: infectious diseases, respiratory infections, and diarrheal diseases. A number of health problems do affect adults disproportionately: cardiovascular disease, respiratory tuberculosis, and accidents and violence. Ways to reduce the incidence and severity of many of these diseases are already known (for example, immunization, improvements in water supply and sanitation, and better nutrition). In addition, the feasibility of intervention against a disease may be as important a consideration in planning services as is the size of the contribution of that cause to overall mortality. Similarly, interventions can only be directed effectively against the known causes of death. Although deaths from unknown causes form a large proportion of adult deaths, it is important to proceed against known diseases while continuing to search for understanding of the unknown. The toll of adult lives taken by accidents and violence is best reduced by preventive measures. A first step might be to disaggregate this important category of death into deaths from interpersonal violence and deaths due to accidents, which are further separated into accidents in the home, accidents at the place of work, and accidents on the street.

Death is the end result of a complex web of factors. Working backwards from the point of death, one can see that case management of the illness, and the technology and services available to the patient, make a difference, as does the likelihood of contracting a disease (the degree of exposure to risk). With regard to many infectious diseases, this risk can be reduced by immunization campaigns and by controlling the vectors of disease and their routes of transmission. Resistance to disease is also important, and nutritional status is a vital factor in determining an individual's vulnerability to infection and the severity of the attack. To some extent these factors are under individual control: education seems to improve the ability of the individual to protect himself and to use services sensibly. However, many of the other factors influencing health are outside individual control and depend on community provision and the level of socioeconomic development. Our understanding of the role of these various factors would be greatly advanced by development of a coherent analytical framework.

The need for such a framework was first elaborated by Mosley and Chen (1984). In the field of fertility analysis the development of a proximate determinants framework has proved an invaluable tool for policy development (Bongaarts, 1978). The framework allows not only for elucidation of the variables through which social and economic factors influence fertility but also for measurement of their effect. Mortality is a much more complex phenomenon than fertility, being not a single outcome but the product of many causes of death. Nevertheless, Mosley and Chen propose a set of biological mechanisms (the proximate determinants) through which, and only through which, social and economic factors can influence mortality, in this case child mortality. There have been several attempts to build on or modify this framework (Nag, 1988), and much empirical investigation needs to be done before it can be said with confidence how, for example, education influences mortality. Yet the effort is extremely worthwhile. The development of such a framework could help direct attention to gaps in the data and to the issues of relevance to policymakers. It might also make it possible to estimate the mortality-reducing effect of a particular intervention and to evaluate the efficacy of one intervention compared with another. It is all the more important, therefore, to heed the call of authors who request more information on causes of death and age at death.

Broad Policy Issues

The contributions to this volume combine insights from the field of demography and the field of health, and the data have implications for both health policy and population policy. A major implication of the trends in the data presented here is that exceptions to the general picture of declining mortality occur in conditions of war and where socioeconomic progress is lacking. The declining economic situation in much of Sub-Saharan Africa in the 1980s must therefore give rise to concern. According to World Bank figures, GNP per capita is declining in 13 of the 32 countries for which information is available (World Bank, 1988). In conditions of economic austerity, how can scarce resources best be used?

Some of the problems facing policymakers have been raised above, in particular the balance to be struck between preventive and clinical services. A related and very important point is that interventions that reduce mortality may or may not improve health. Thus, a person may be saved from death but left with his or her health permanently impaired. Or improvements in mortality as a result of health services may coexist with high levels of generally poor health status. This may, for example, have occurred in Zimbabwe after independence; there, child mortality has declined as a result of the health care drive, but high levels of child undernutrition, associated with declining real incomes, remain (Sanders and Davies, 1988).

Other choices facing health policymakers concern the priority given to different age groups or to men and women. While attention to the needs of adults in their working years might seem to benefit the economy, mortality levels in the society as a whole will be influenced the most by reductions in infant and child mortality. Reductions in infant and child mortality affect, at least in the short term, population growth rates exactly as would an increase in fertility. Policymakers therefore need to be aware of the rapid adjustment efforts that must be made to accommodate short-term increases in the rate of population growth, even if the goal and expectation are for long-term decline.

At the aggregate level, high rates of population growth can undermine socioeconomic advances. It has already been noted that per capita income growth has been negligible or has even declined in many African countries in the 1980s. Although low returns on investment are perhaps the chief reason for this stagnation, accelerating rates of population growth are an important factor. This constrains a government's ability to devote resources to health. It is important to recognize the declines in child mortality made in many African countries since independence, but the fact that one in five children still do not live to see their fifth birthday is a tragedy. Furthermore, satisfaction with the declines must be tempered by concern that in many countries high fertility is resulting in an increase in the absolute number of deaths of children under five (UNICEF, 1985, 1988).

The whole question of the relationship between fertility and mortality at different levels and rates of socioeconomic development is extremely complex. While advances in medical technology and understanding have succeeded in bringing death rates down, among young children at least, and to some extent among adults, there is some evidence that mortality levels have not as yet reached the threshold level necessary to induce fertility change. The argument is that where life expectancy at birth is under 50, mainly as a result of high infant and child mortality, parents' actual family size generally falls short of desired family size. As mortality conditions improve but child loss remains common, parents begin to make conscious reproductive decisions, such as adopting an insurance strategy of having more children than they might ideally want. The response to continued improvement in mortality is to adopt a replacement strategy, such as having a child only after losing another. In Sub-Saharan Africa life expectancy is below 50 in half the 32 countries for which data are given in *World Development Report 1988* (World Bank, 1988). It is over 55 in only five of them. Efforts to bring down mortality are therefore a crucial component of efforts to bring about fertility change. Until they are successful, however, high fertility imperils the very socioeconomic improvements on which declining mortality depends.

At the individual level, high fertility is a factor in the high risk to mothers and children in Africa. Perhaps this is most apparent with regard to maternal mortality. A reduction in fertility would obviously result in a commensurate reduction in maternal mortality, since only pregnant and postpartum women are at risk of maternal death. As Graham points out in chapter 6, the relatively low obstetric risk of women in eastern Africa is nullified by their high fertility. To the extent that reductions in fertility are also associated with a safer pattern of childbearing, with fewer births at very low and high ages and fewer at very high parities, the health benefits of reducing the number of births are enhanced. With regard to infant and child mortality, the results from the few countries in Sub-Saharan Africa that participated in the World Fertility Survey showed a strong relationship between child spacing and mortality. There were higher risks both to the newborn infant and to the preceding sibling where the interval between their births was less than two years.

High fertility is itself, therefore, a major area toward which preventive action can be directed. The maternal factors of age, parity, and birth interval are one group of mechanisms identified by Mosley and Chen (1984)

as important proximate determinants of child mortality, and the same is obviously true for maternal mortality. Family planning is one of the preventive measures most frequently suggested, but, as Graham points out in chapter 6, its potential for reducing maternal deaths, compared with that of health services, is still being debated. Its influence on infant and child mortality is also controversial, with opinions divided about whether its effects are direct or indirect (Trussell *et al.*, 1988). Here, perhaps, is a good example of how useful an analytical framework might be. The contribution of interventions such as family planning or nutrition, which have a relatively slight impact on a single cause of mortality and yet have multiple benefits, might be evaluated better in such a context.

For far too long, we African health planners and experts have used statements such as "there are no data" or "the data are not dependable" to defend planning by hunch. Yet we have done very little to improve the gathering of data, especially data on adult morbidity and mortality. The effort to control infant and childhood mortality, spearheaded by UNICEF, has helped to generate more information on infants and young children. The time has come for us to make a greater effort to understand mortality in general. The studies in the first part of this book draw together most of what is known about mortality levels, trends, and differentials in Sub-Saharan Africa and about the contribution of specific diseases. In so doing, it directs attention to the great deal that is not known. Current work at the World Bank and elsewhere will help fill some of these gaps in our understanding of the cause structure of mortality, and of adult mortality in particular. Much of the comparative analysis presented here, however, is new. It represents significant progress in our understanding of mortality in Sub-Saharan Africa and helps to build momentum for further advances in knowledge and action.

References

Bongaarts, J. (1978). A framework for analyzing the proximate determinants of fertility. *Population and Development Review,* 4 (1), 105–132.

Mosley, W. H. and Chen, L. C. (1984). An analytical framework for the study of child survival in developing countries. *Population and Development Review,* 10 (supplement), 25–45.

Nag, M. (1988). A framework for the study of proximate determinants of infant mortality in less developed countries. In: *Infant Mortality in India. Differentials and Determinants,* Jain, A. K. and Visaria, P. (editors). London: Sage Publications.

Sanders, D. and Davies, R. (1988). The economy, the health sector and child health in Zimbabwe since independence. *Social Science and Medicine*, 27 (7), 723–731.

Trussell, T. J., Potter, J. E., and Bongaarts, J. (1988). Does family planning reduce infant mortality? *Population and Development Review,* 14 (1), 171–195.

UNICEF. (1985). *The State of the World's Children, 1985.* New York: Oxford University Press.

————. (1988). *The State of the World's Children, 1988.* New York: Oxford University Press.

World Bank. (1988). *World Development Report 1988.* New York: Oxford University Press.

Chapter 3

Infant and Child Mortality: Levels, Trends, and Data Deficiencies

Althea Hill

This paper presents a broad, comparative outline of levels, patterns, and trends of childhood mortality in Sub-Saharan mainland Africa from the late 1940s to the late 1970s. The mainstay of the analysis is information on child survival collected in population censuses and demographic surveys. (Details are given in the methodological appendix to this chapter; for a general discussion of methodology, see chapter 4 as well.) Methods of analysis were standardized as much as possible in order to focus on the overall pattern of differentials in mortality levels and trends. Thus the estimates presented may not be the best that could be obtained for any one country with the aid of more refined methodology and country-specific information from other sources. It is hoped, however, that the broad picture is substantially correct and will suggest and support further investigation into the determinants of childhood mortality in Africa.

Sources of Data

Africa is rich in data on child survival as reported retrospectively by mothers in censuses and surveys.[1] Such data are available at the national level for almost all Sub-Saharan African mainland countries for at least one period (the exceptions being Equatorial Guinea, Mauritania,[2] Namibia, and South Africa, which have none), and for the majority for at least two. However, two major gaps in the data should be borne in mind:

- Few countries have yet published data collected in the 1980s. Because data on child survival yield reliable estimates of childhood mortality only up to two or three years prior to their collection, the analysis of trends can be carried only up to the late 1970s. Therefore the effect of the economic and climatic shocks of the early 1980s (recessions, debt crises, and droughts) cannot yet be studied.

- Data for periods of social and political turmoil, or open war, are also scarce; hence, the effects of such disturbances cannot yet be traced with confidence.

The measure of childhood mortality used is the proportion of children dying before the age of five years. (UNICEF has christened this measure the under-five mortality rate.) Demographers often neglect the infant mortality rate, traditional and familiar to non-demographers though it is, for two reasons:

- It cannot be measured reliably with the Brass child-survival estimation methodology used here, which is heavily dependent on the model of age patterns of mortality in early childhood that is incorporated in the estimation procedure. The proportion of children dying in the first five years of life is a much more robust measure.

- More important, in much of Africa child mortality after the first year of life is high, sometimes as high as or higher than mortality in infancy (see the methodological appendix). Focusing exclusively on infant mortality therefore makes no sense from either the analytical or the policy and program standpoint.

Childhood Mortality in Sub-Saharan Africa

The picture of continental trends in the mortality of children under five is displayed in figure 3-1 and of those in western and eastern Africa in figures 3-2 and 3-3.[3] Four general features are at once obvious and striking:

- Declines in childhood mortality since World War II in most countries where data are available
- Much variation among countries in the type of decline
- Much variation among countries in the level of mortality

38   *Althea Hill*

Figure 3-1. Risk of Dying before Age Five, Sub-Saharan Africa, 1926–80

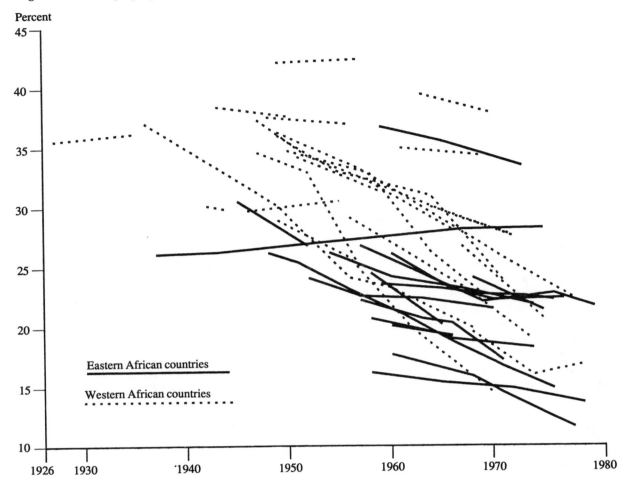

• A marked overall difference in mortality levels between eastern and western Africa.

There are also three interesting exceptions to these general patterns:

• A few countries with static or rising mortality (notably Angola, Ethiopia, Mozambique, Niger, Nigeria, and Rwanda)
• A few West African countries whose mortality has fallen to eastern African levels (Cameroon, Congo, and Ghana)
• One eastern African country with a West African level of mortality, which is high even by western African standards (Malawi).

We will briefly describe first the four major features of the continental pattern and then the three types of outlier. We will end by summarizing the position of Africa with respect to that of other parts of the developing world.

Major Features of Childhood Mortality Patterns

OVERALL MORTALITY DECLINES. Childhood mortality appears to have declined somewhat between the end of World War II and 1980 in the vast majority of African countries for which postwar data exist. The overall magnitude of the fall can be summarized by noting that in many African countries during the 1950s 30 to 40 percent of children died before reaching the age of five years, whereas in very few did less than 22 percent die. By the mid-1970s, however, very few African countries lost more than 27 percent of their children before age five, and many lost less than 22 percent. This represents a major postwar achievement in African development.

VARIATION IN DECLINES. The declines were not uniform, however, and varied greatly in size, timing, and

Figure 3-2. Risk of Dying before Age Five, Western Africa, 1926–80

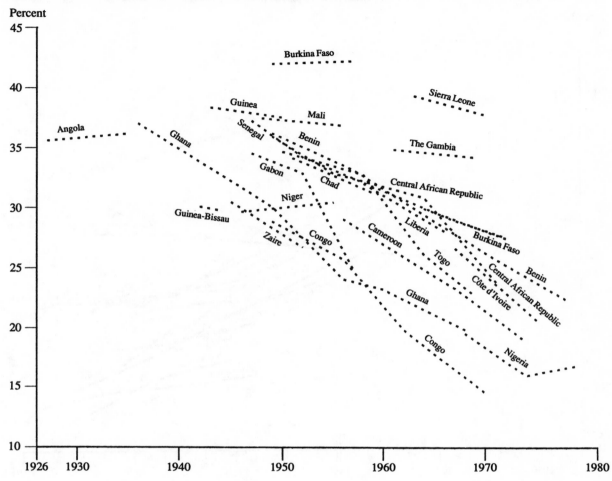

pace even when the methodological difficulties of dating retrospective child survival data are taken into account. In some countries, the fall in mortality has been dramatic. The percentage of children dying before their fifth birthday almost halved in Ghana over the 30 years between the late 1930s and late 1960s (from 37 to 20 percent), in Congo over the 20 years between the late 1940s and late 1960s (from 29 to 15 percent), and in Kenya over the 25 years between the late 1940s and early 1970s (from 26 to 15 percent). In other countries the declines were much more gradual. In Swaziland, for example, the percentage of children dying by age five only fell from 24 to 21.5 percent between 1950 and 1970; in Lesotho, from 21 to 18 percent between the mid-1950s and mid-1970s; and in Sierra Leone, from 39.5 to 38 percent over the decade of the 1960s. Indeed, in a few countries, such as Guinea and Mali (all with data available only for one

early period), the observed decline was even smaller: 1 percent or less over the period of observation. The decline in most countries, however, ranged somewhere between these two extremes.

VARIATION IN MORTALITY LEVELS. The variations in mortality levels in Africa are striking in all periods for which data exist, even though the range narrowed somewhat during the post–World War II period. In the late 1950s, for example, the proportion of children dying before age five ranged rather evenly between 16 and over 40 percent, corresponding roughly to a difference of 20 to 25 years in life expectancy (30–35 years compared with 50–55 years). Even by the late 1970s the proportion still ranged from 12 to 33 percent, although that of most countries did not exceed 27 percent.

Figure 3-3. Risk of Dying before Age Five, Eastern Africa, 1926–80

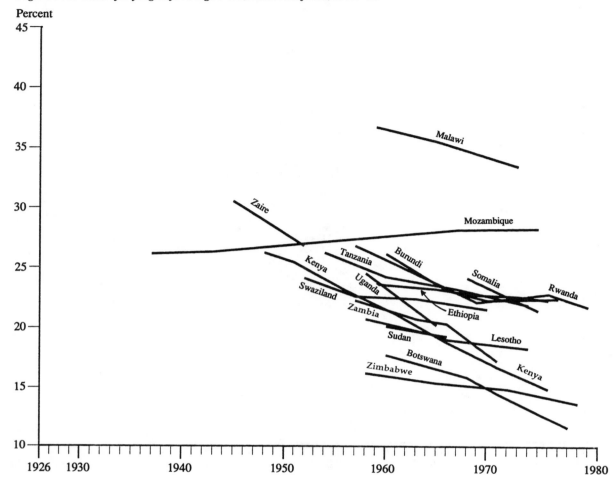

Percent

DIFFERENTIALS BETWEEN EAST AND WEST AFRICA. Beyond doubt, a marked and consistent differential exists between the childhood mortality levels of eastern and western Africa. That differential existed throughout the postwar period but has narrowed in more recent times. Childhood mortality has generally been much severer in western than in eastern Africa, with a rough gradient crossing the continent from northwest to southeast. The highest levels of childhood mortality are recorded in West and Sahelian Africa, the next highest in central Africa, the next to the lowest in East Africa, and the lowest in southern Africa.[4] Thus, in the 1950s, between 30 and 40 percent of children died before the age of five in most of West and Sahelian Africa, between 25 and 30 percent in central and East Africa, and between 15 and 25 percent in southern Africa. By the 1970s, 22 to 30 percent of the children under five were dying throughout much of West and

Sahelian Africa, compared with 20 to 22 percent in central and East Africa and 12 to 20 percent in southern Africa.

Exceptions to the Pattern

STATIC OR RISING MORTALITY. Six cases of persistent stagnation or increases in mortality are shown in figures 3-1–3-3: Angola, Ethiopia, Mozambique, Niger, Nigeria, and Rwanda. To these we may add Sudan, for reasons to be shown later (see the methodological appendix to this chapter).

For Angola and Niger the only data set that is available covers an early period and shows a slight rise in mortality. In the case of Angola further uncertainty is created by the quality of Portuguese data collection in Africa, which was generally very poor.[5] The uncertainties in the case of Nigeria, which are discussed in the methodological appendix, include the existence of only one data set. Thus attaching too much importance to these three trends is probably unwise.

For Ethiopia, Mozambique, Rwanda, and Sudan, two or more data sets exist (though in Sudan these only cover the north for a recent time period), and the trends must be taken more seriously. The data for Mozambique (which was also a Portuguese colony) are very unreliable and inconsistent. The trend shown in figures 3-1 and 3-2 was obtained by discarding the results of the 1970 census, which, unlike the censuses of 1950 and 1980, was taken at a time of widespread civil war, when government access to much of the country was severely limited. Therefore, different trends can be derived by selecting different data. Thus the inference that childhood mortality did not fall overall in Mozambique between the late 1930s and the late 1970s, though likely given the lack of socioeconomic development and the festering civil war of the period 1950–1975, cannot be taken as firmly established.

The case of Sudan is also unclear. The data are incomplete, of obviously poor quality, and inconsistent for levels of mortality in the north. The most prudent inference is that childhood mortality did not change greatly between the mid-1950s and mid-1970s; as in Mozambique this period coincides with a long-drawn-out and expensive civil war. However, doubts will remain at least until the child survival data from the 1983 census become available.

The case of Ethiopia is fairly straightforward. The data are consistent and appear to be reasonably accurate. Pending data from the 1984 census,[6] the picture of long-term, near-stagnant rates between the mid-1950s and mid-1970s must be accepted. Again, this stagnation coincides with a protracted and expensive civil war and a general lack of progress in socioeconomic development.

The case of Rwanda, while complex, has been clarified recently by direct evidence from maternity histories on trends in child survival. Though doubts must remain over the exact levels of mortality and the timing of trends, the overall picture clearly shows a decline in childhood mortality during the 1950s, followed by a plateau and a rise between the early 1960s and mid-1970s and a recovery in the late 1970s. Again, these trends appear to be a somewhat lagged response to the country's history of rapid development in the 1950s, civil turmoil and interrupted development in the 1960s, and resumed socioeconomic progress in the 1970s.[7]

To summarize, then, these four cases of stagnating or rising childhood mortality, taken individually, are subject to doubts or reservations. Taken together, however, they suggest that the evolution of childhood mortality may be very sensitive to sociopolitical instability, which is often accompanied by interrupted or stagnating socioeconomic development. Recent data are lacking for most African countries in periods of such upheaval, but the almost universal postwar declines in mortality observed in countries at peace may be absent in times of severe instability. This topic deserves further investigation by demographers and others.

CROSSOVER FROM WESTERN TO EASTERN MORTALITY LEVELS. Figures 3-1 and 3-2 show, against the general background of higher mortality in western Africa and lower mortality in eastern Africa, three western African countries whose rapid declines in mortality have brought them down from their initial western levels to levels that place them unequivocally within the eastern group. These countries are Cameroon, Congo, and Ghana. Nigeria is not included, since the quality of its data is so uncertain; Nigeria would, in fact, always have fallen within the eastern range if its directly reported child survival data were to be accepted.

The data from Ghana and Congo, discussed in detail in the methodological appendix, pose some difficulties of reconciliation and interpretation. According to the most plausible interpretation, however, these two countries boasted the lowest childhood mortality in western Africa at the start of the post–World War II period and then experienced (or continued to experience) dramatic declines throughout the 1950s and 1960s. By 1970 both had plunged well inside the eastern range; Ghanaian childhood mortality was comparable to that of contemporary Uganda and Zambia, while Congolese childhood mortality had actually reached the very low level of contemporary Botswana and Zimbabwe. Trends since 1970 cannot be measured for Congo until the 1984 census results become available. For Ghana, the picture is unclear: some leveling of the decline in mortality has probably taken place, although still within the eastern range.

The interesting question is whether the childhood mortality levels of these two countries have always been unusual or whether they simply declined earlier and more steeply than those of the rest of western Africa. Very early data are not available for Congo, but data for Ghana in the 1930s indicate mortality levels then that approached the severe levels of mortality characteristic of western Africa in the late 1940s. Perhaps Congo and Ghana were exceptional not because they had a natural initial advantage in health conditions but because they began their modern mortality decline earlier. Ghana developed modern economic and social services unusually early and Congo inherited a high degree of urbanization from the colonial government as a result of the development of the Congo railway.

Cameroon is a more recent and less spectacular case. Again, childhood mortality in the mid-1950s was comparatively low for western Africa and fell rapidly to within the eastern range by the mid-1970s. The same factors as operated in Ghana and Congo, namely rapid economic and educational development and rather heavy urbanization, may have been responsible for the crossover in Cameroon as well.

Finally, several other West African countries (Benin, Central African Republic, Côte d'Ivoire, Gabon, and Togo) appear to have been heading for a crossover at the last observed point in time. By 1975 Côte d'Ivoire actually passed the eastern countries with the highest mortality. Once again, rapid economic development and heavy urbanization were probably important factors.

A WESTERN MORTALITY LEVEL IN EASTERN AFRICA. In East and southern Africa, Malawi stands out as an exception to the general rule of relatively low childhood mortality.[8] The proportions of children dead before the age of five in the late 1950s and early 1970s (37 and 33 percent, respectively) are not only far above contemporary ranges in eastern Africa but among the highest even in contemporary western Africa. No single, obvious characteristic of Malawi can explain this anomaly.[9] The country has experienced political stability and good GNP growth over the past few decades and appears broadly similar to the rest of East and southern Africa in climate, culture, and epidemiology.

Childhood Mortality in Africa and the Rest of the Developing World

How does the childhood mortality of Sub-Saharan Africa compare with that of the rest of the developing world? It is often taken for granted that Africa is a continent of uniquely severe mortality. Given the evidence presented above, this assumption must be accepted as generally true, for two reasons:

• Africa contains several countries with the severest peacetime childhood mortality in the world, notably the Gambia, Malawi, Sierra Leone, and probably a few others in western Africa. Only Afghanistan has approached these levels nationally and in peacetime in recent decades.[10]

• Africa still possesses very few countries with the moderately low mortality common in much of East and Southeast Asia, Central and South America, and the Middle East. (Moreover, one of those countries, South Africa, achieved its low national level partly as a result of the European level of childhood mortality enjoyed by its large population of non-black minorities.)

It is equally important to emphasize that many African countries do not have exceptionally high childhood mortality. Much of East and southern Africa, as well as a few countries in West Africa, compares well with many parts of the Indian subcontinent, with Indonesia, and with several countries in Latin America, North Africa, and the Middle East. It is misleading, therefore, to portray Africa as a homogeneous continent whose mortality is uniformly higher than that of the rest of the world or to conclude that improvements in health conditions are necessarily more difficult to achieve in Africa than elsewhere.

Conclusions

The results presented above highlight two dominant characteristics of childhood mortality in Africa: a general but uneven postwar progress and an enormous heterogeneity of levels and trends among countries. In this chapter only national estimates were considered, but heterogeneity within countries is just as striking. Figures 3-4 and 3-5 display the proportions of children dead by age five in the districts of Zaire in the early 1950s (data were taken from the 1955–57 Demographic Inquiry) and for provinces of Zambia in the mid-1960s (from the 1969 census); the proportions range from 15 to 38 percent in Zaire and from 13 to 29 percent in Zambia.

Little is known of the determinants underlying these patterns of heterogeneity. Few systematic, integrated studies of the regional differentials within countries have been done, let alone of differentials between countries or between cultural or ecological groupings that straddle national boundaries. Such studies would help to elucidate the determinants of childhood mortality in Africa and thus assist in attempts to improve child survival still further. These important mortality differentials, and their possible relationships to socioeconomic, cultural, and ecological variables, are discussed further in chapter 4.

Methodological Appendix

The basic technique employed in this analysis was the Trussell variant of the Brass child survival method, as described in the United Nations' *Manual X* (for details

Figure 3-4. Under-Five Mortality Risk, Zaire, by District, 1950–53

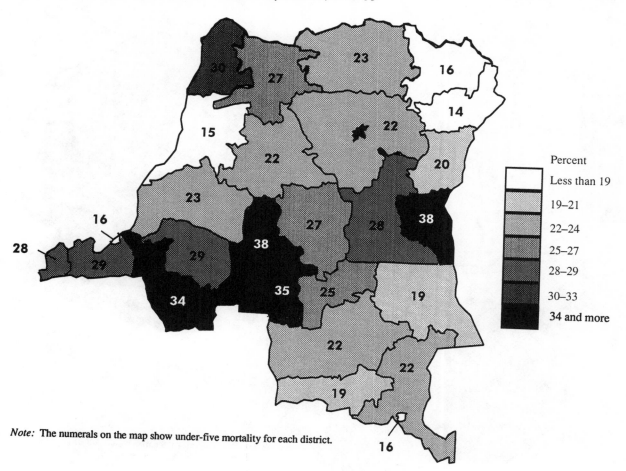

Percent

Less than 19

19–21

22–24

25–27

28–29

30–33

34 and more

Note: The numerals on the map show under-five mortality for each district.

of this variant, see United Nations, 1983). It was applied, using the AFEMOPC computer program, to all available sets of child survival data, including subnational information.[11] The resulting retrospective dated series of survival probabilities, expressed as matching levels in Coale-Demeny model life tables, were graphed and evaluated for consistency and regularity, both within each data set and between data sets collected at different times. Data from other sources, such as direct reports of child survival from World Fertility Survey (WFS) maternity histories or direct observations from longitudinal or multiround surveys, were also used for evaluation at this stage. Anomalous data sets and ones that were obviously of very poor quality were excluded from further analysis, as was all information collected from mothers under the age of 20, which is generally considered highly unreliable.[12] The results from the national series that seemed good enough to use were then crudely summarized to make

intercountry comparisons easier. This was normally done by selecting the Coale-Demeny model family that gave the most consistent results for each country. Then, for each data set, two averages were taken of the values of $q5$ (the proportion of children dying before age five) that correspond to the levels in the model family that were estimated from the proportions of dead reported by each age group of women. The first average is of the age groups 20–24, 25–29, and 30–34, and the second average is of the age groups 35–39, 40–44, and 45–49. These two averages were then dated by averaging dates of reference for the two groups.

Tables 3A-16 and 3A-17 give details of the summarized estimates for all countries, including notes on the sources of the data sets, an assessment of the overall quality of each data set, and any variant of the normal procedure described above. Further country-specific details are available from the author.

Figure 3-5. Under-Five Mortality Risk, Zambia, by Province, Mid-1960s

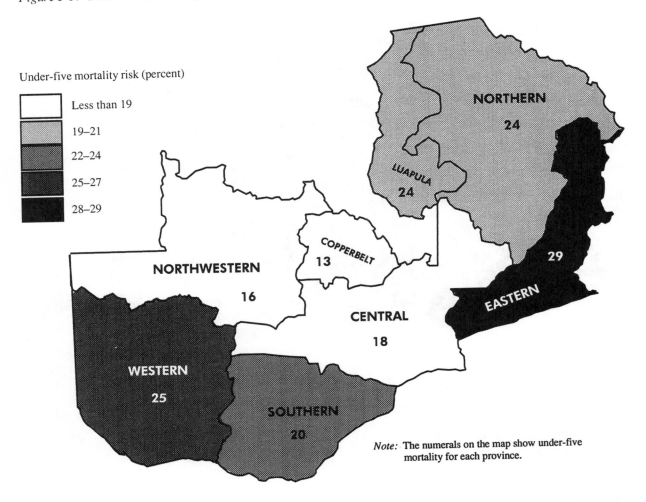

Under-five mortality risk (percent)

Less than 19
19–21
22–24
25–27
28–29

NORTHERN 24

LUAPULA 24

COPPERBELT 13

NORTHWESTERN 16

CENTRAL 18

EASTERN 29

WESTERN 25

SOUTHERN 20

Note: The numerals on the map show under-five mortality for each province.

Clearly, the methodology outlined above depends heavily on the quality of the base data, the validity of the analytical techniques employed, and the considerable degree of judgment required for selecting data points for the final summarized trend lines. The following examples of the treatment of data for various countries will be detailed below:

• Four examples of consistent data that present no real problems in summarization or interpretation (Benin, Botswana, Central African Republic, and Zimbabwe)
• Four examples of multiple data sets with difficulties of interpretation stemming from doubtful consistency or varying quality (Burkina Faso, Congo, Ghana, and Nigeria)
• One example where more refined methodology, based on information from small-scale surveys,

produces different results from the standard *Manual X* technique (Senegal).

Consistent Data for Zimbabwe, Benin, Botswana, and Central African Republic

Tables 3A-1–3A-4 and figures 3A-1–3A-4 show the results of a standard *Manual X* analysis of child survival data for these four countries, expressed in terms of $q5$ values.

The data from Zimbabwe and Botswana are clearly of very good quality: they are generally smooth and internally consistent (when the best-fitting model is chosen), and they reflect the high level of education in their populations.[13] The data from Benin and from the Central African Republic, the latter using an early subnational data set as a national proxy because it covered a large proportion of a rather homogeneous population, are rougher, but still acceptably consistent overall. None presents any real problem with interpretation and summarization.

Multiple and Difficult Data Sets

GHANA. Data for Ghana are shown in tables 3A-5 and 3A-6 and figure 3A-5. Although the overall picture clearly shows a substantial decline in mortality over time, the data are very rough in parts (notably for younger women in 1948 and older women in 1960) and the 1979–80 WFS information is seriously inconsistent in level with the data from the 1948, 1960, and 1970 censuses. (Data from the 1968 demographic survey were never published in full, and the few estimates that were published are inconsistent with the census data.) It is possible that the WFS sample of women overrepresented women of higher education and income, who therefore reported lower childhood mortality (15 percent of the sample households could not be relocated for individual interviews, and many were thought to consist of mobile construction workers and their families). For those reasons the WFS results were not used nor were the incomplete data from 1968. In summarizing the points from the three censuses, the 1948 data for younger women were not used.

BURKINA FASO. Data for Burkina Faso, shown in tables 3A-7 and figure 3A-6, present a puzzling picture. Information from both the 1960–61 demographic survey (which was only slightly compromised by only covering rural areas since the urban sector was tiny at that date) and the 1976 postcensus survey appears to be of good quality; that is, reasonably smooth and internally coherent. Yet the two data sets are mutually quite inconsistent, imply radically different levels of childhood mortality, and show little trend over time. According to the 1960–61 data, for example, over 40 percent of children were dying before age five at the end of the 1950s, but according to the 1976 data only around 30 percent were dying before age five at the beginning of the 1960s. The difference amounts to the equivalent of 8–10 years of life expectancy. Reconciling these two data sets is impossible, as is preferring one to the other on the basis of the consistency and quality of its internal data. Both have therefore been presented, in more or less standard summary, in table 3A-23 and figures 3-1 and 3-2. In either case, of course, Burkina Faso still remains among the countries with the highest mortality in contemporary Africa.

CONGO. Data for Congo are shown in table 3A-8 and figure 3A-7. In some ways the overall picture of the Congo resembles that of Burkina Faso, in that the rural levels of mortality for the 1950s, collected in the 1960 survey, are spectacularly higher than those for the late 1960s, collected in the 1974 census. In this case, however, the two data sets can be reconciled by the weighting of the urban sector, which in Congo was already important in 1960, and by the clear decline shown in the 1974 (and 1960) data. The quality of the 1974 data is still rough enough to leave residual doubt, which, it is hoped, will be resolved when the 1984 census data become available. At present, however, the overall trend appears acceptable.

NIGERIA. Data for Nigeria, shown in tables 3A-9 and 3A-10 and figure 3A-8, are very unsatisfactory. The 1971–73 data are exceptionally poor, showing fantastic declines over the space of a few years and extreme irregularities. To weight them for a national estimate would also be difficult, given the uncertainty over Nigerian population figures. These data were not used. The WFS data from 1981–82 also present problems. The child survival data show a decline in childhood mortality during the late 1960s and early 1970s (before the oil boom and during the civil war) followed by a marked rise in the late 1970s (during the oil boom). This trend is implausible in itself and may be the result of data errors (the proportions dead are lower for women aged 30–34 than for women aged 25–29, for example). The overall level of mortality reported in the WFS data is also extremely low for all periods, making Nigeria the country with the lowest mortality in West Africa around 1950 and one of the lowest at every point thereafter. This does not agree with small-scale data from Nigeria or with the results of the 1965–66 National Demographic Survey (which did not, unfortunately, collect child survival data). Thus, although the WFS child survival estimates are used here, they must be regarded with scepticism because they are derived from a single data set of doubtful quality.

Refinements of Standardized Child Survival Analysis

SENEGAL. Senegal, unlike most countries in Sub-Saharan Africa, possesses a great deal of good-quality data on the age pattern of mortality in childhood. These data were drawn from small-scale intensive surveys, most of which were multiround or longitudinal in design. Together with similar survey results from a decades-old longitudinal study in a Gambian village (described in full in chapter 20, this volume), these data demonstrate the existence of an age pattern of mortality in childhood very different from the patterns shown in the Coale-Demeny model life tables used in the Trussell variant. Levels of mortality in the second and third years of life are much higher than in the classical European pattern embodied in the Coale-Demeny models or indeed in those that prevail in most of the developing world for which such data exist. The risk of dying between the first and fifth birthdays may actually equal or exceed the risk of dying in infancy. When child survival data are analyzed using a model life table that incorporates this pattern, the results for Senegal are rather different from those obtained using a standard Trussell analysis, as is shown in tables 3A-11 and 3A-12 and figure 3A-9.[14] The data are still very rough in either case, but the tailormade analysis produces a much more coherent trend over the entire 1940–75 period.

The use of a similar model life table might improve estimation procedures in other countries in the region. Unfortunately, our knowledge of the age patterns of mortality in childhood across Africa is still too limited to permit use of such tailormade models in comparative analyses. Use of the Senegalese mortality pattern could be justified for Senegal and the Gambia and conceivably also for a few West African countries that appear to have similar patterns (for example, Benin, Burkina Faso, and Ghana[15]). However, in most African countries (particularly in eastern Africa) little or no data exist on age patterns of mortality in childhood, or the information that does exist shows a much attenuated or different pattern.[16] At the extreme, for example, WFS

data from maternity histories show a pattern for Lesotho very similar to the classic European patterns of heavy mortality in infancy relative to that in the next four years. It is unfortunate that retrospective determination of age at death is too unreliable in most African countries to allow WFS maternity history and other survey material on recent deaths to be used with confidence. At present, therefore, a standard analysis must be applied for comparative purposes to all countries, including Senegal. To minimize the difficulties of assigning the correct trend in Senegal, only points from older women in both data sets have been used.

Exceptions and Anomalies in the Comparative Results

As discussed in the main text, there are three types of exception to the general pattern of the overall results:

- Countries with static or rising mortality (Ethiopia, Mozambique, Rwanda, and Sudan)
- Western African countries whose mortality has fallen to East African levels (Cameroon, Congo, and Ghana)
- One eastern African country with a West African mortality level (Malawi).

The base data for these cases (excluding Congo and Ghana, which have already been discussed) are given in tables 3A-13–3A-21 and shown in figures 3A-10–3A-15. Tables 3A-22 and 3A-23 present summary data for Sub-Saharan Africa, by region and subregion.

The appendix tables and figures begin on the following page. Notes and references follow table 3A-23.

Table 3A-1. Zimbabwe: Child Survival Analysis Results from the 1969 and 1982 Censuses

Data source	Coale-Demeny North model		Coale-Demeny South model	
	Reference date	Equivalent value of q5	Reference date	Equivalent value of q5
1969 census	1954.83	0.1634	1953.95	0.1853
	1957.72	0.1641	1957.09	0.1810
	1960.41	0.1596	1959.97	0.1718
	1962.91	0.1554	1962.64	0.1613
	1965.14	0.1528	1965.03	0.1520
	1967.01	0.1606	1967.00	0.1515
1982 census	1968.28	0.1513	1967.42	0.1726
	1971.18	0.1467	1970.56	0.1624
	1973.85	0.1426	1973.43	0.1540
	1976.33	0.1399	1976.07	0.1449
	1978.53	0.1352	1978.43	0.1338
	1980.37	0.1340	1980.36	0.1246

Note: q5 is the proportion of children dying before age five, also known as the under-five mortality rate.
Source: For 1969, Rhodesia (n.d.), 11; for 1982, Zimbabwe (1985), table VII.2, 168.

Figure 3A-1. Risk of Dying before Age Five, Zimbabwe: 1969 and 1982 Censuses

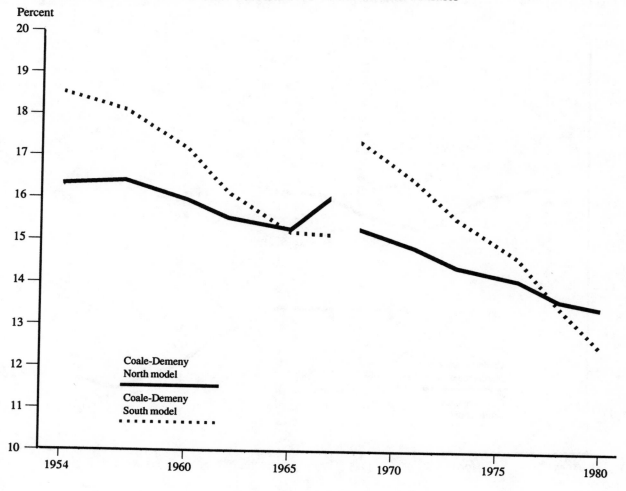

Table 3A-2. Botswana: Child Survival Analysis Results from the 1971 and 1981 Censuses

Data source	Coale-Demeny North model		Coale-Demeny South model	
	Reference date	Equivalent value of q5	Reference date	Equivalent value of q5
1971 census	1956.77	0.1637	1955.85	0.1862
	1959.73	0.1613	1959.05	0.1786
	1962.59	0.1530	1962.13	0.1654
	1965.28	0.1568	1965.01	0.1628
	1967.66	0.1617	1967.55	0.1606
	1969.60	0.1623	1969.60	0.1525
1981 census	1966.51	0.1341	1965.58	0.1550
	1969.42	0.1346	1968.73	0.1505
	1972.22	0.1276	1971.74	0.1391
	1974.87	0.1205	1974.58	0.1257
	1977.26	0.1149	1977.13	0.1138
	1979.26	0.1176	1979.25	0.1085

Source: For 1971, Botswana (1972), tables 17.1 and 17.2, 162, 175; for 1982, Botswana (1983), table 26.

Figure 3A-2. Risk of Dying before Age Five, Botswana: 1971 and 1981 Censuses

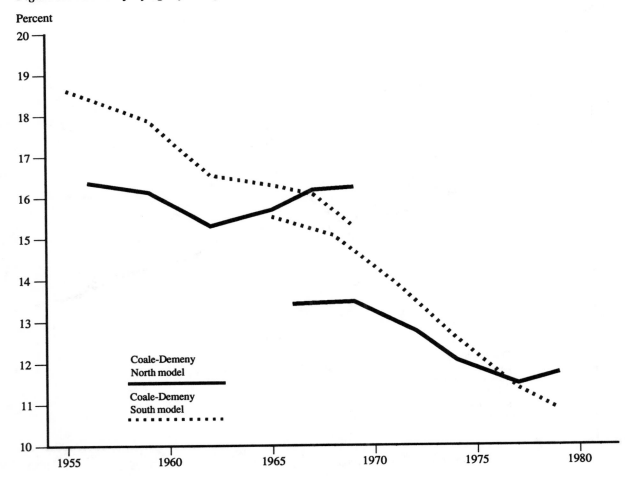

Table 3A-3. Benin: Child Survival Analysis Results from the 1961 and 1981–82 Demographic Surveys

Data source	Coale-Demeny North model		Coale-Demeny South model	
	Reference date	Equivalent value of q5	Reference date	Equivalent value of q5
1961 survey	1946.78	0.3411	1945.89	0.3675
	1949.57	0.3493	1948.94	0.3712
	1952.15	0.3329	1951.70	0.3503
	1954.57	0.3338	1954.28	0.3485
	1956.80	0.3227	1956.65	0.3306
	1958.75	0.3189	1958.72	0.3181
1981–82 survey	1968.07	0.2351	1967.22	0.2591
	1970.92	0.2531	1970.32	0.2727
	1973.51	0.2284	1973.09	0.2429
	1975.90	0.2321	1975.65	0.2408
	1978.06	0.1982	1977.94	0.1985
	1979.89	0.2395	1979.88	0.2319

Source: For 1961, Benin (1964), tables IV-1-8 and IV-2-2, 262, 266; for 1982, Benin (1983), table 16, 25.

Figure 3A-3. Risk of Dying before Age Five, Benin: 1961 and 1962 Surveys

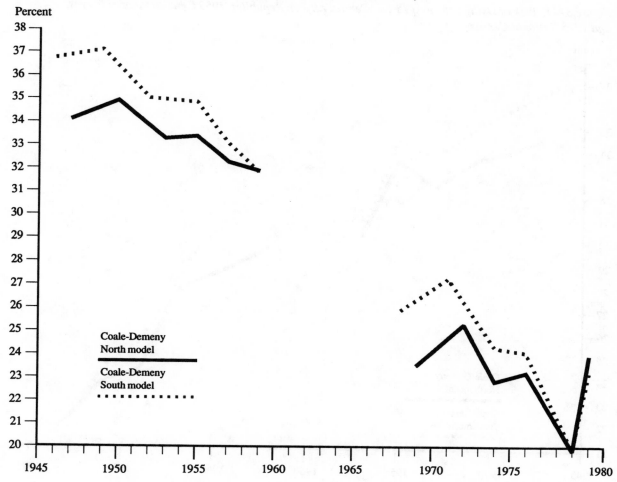

Table 3A-4. Central African Republic: Child Survival Analysis Results from the 1959 Centre-Oubangi Survey and 1975 Census

Data source	Coale-Demeny North model		Coale-Demeny South model	
	Reference date	Equivalent value of q5	Reference date	Equivalent value of q5
1959 Centre-Oubangi survey	1946.02	0.3468	1945.25	0.3707
	1948.69	0.3396	1948.17	0.3583
	1950.89	0.3352	1950.52	0.3498
	1952.89	0.3243	1952.63	0.3372
	1954.78	0.3355	1954.63	0.3450
	1956.52	0.3022	1956.47	0.3033
1975 census	1961.07	0.2977	1960.19	0.3230
	1963.76	0.2892	1963.14	0.3099
	1966.20	0.2787	1965.74	0.2955
	1968.50	0.2439	1968.18	0.2558
	1970.67	0.2390	1970.49	0.2449
	1972.65	0.2214	1972.61	0.2165

Source: For 1959, Brass *et al.* (1968), tables 7-3E and 7.5E, 427, 428; for 1975, Central African Republic (1980), tables 29 and 30, 87, 90.

*Figure 3A-4. **Risk of Dying before Age Five, Central African Republic: 1959 Centre-Oubangi Survey and 1975 National Census***

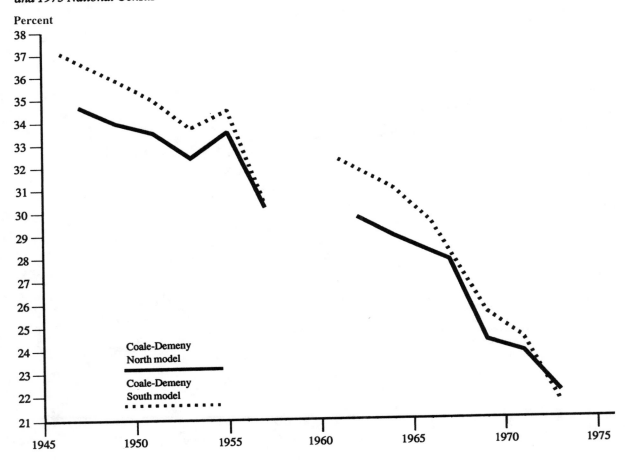

Table 3A-5. Ghana: Child Survival Analysis Results from the Supplementary Enquiries to the Censuses of 1948, 1960, and 1970 and the 1979–80 Fertility Survey

Data source	Coale-Demeny North model		Coale-Demeny South model	
	Reference date	*Equivalent value of q5*	*Reference date*	*Equivalent value of q5*
1948 census	1934.00	0.3555	1933.21	0.3800
supplementary	1936.64	0.3422	1936.10	0.3624
enquiry	1938.84	0.3543	1938.45	0.3700
	1940.86	0.3321	1940.58	0.3467
	1942.80	0.2915	1942.63	0.3004
	1944.61	0.2483	1944.56	0.2460
1960 census	1945.99	0.2632	1945.14	0.2876
supplementary	1948.75	0.3242	1948.16	0.3446
enquiry	1951.22	0.2541	1950.80	0.2693
	1953.52	0.2453	1953.24	0.2555
	1955.63	0.2391	1955.49	0.2426
	1957.50	0.2310	1957.47	0.2247
1970 census	1957.02	0.2196	1956.14	0.2436
supplementary	1959.91	0.2141	1959.28	0.2333
enquiry	1962.61	0.2076	1962.17	0.2219
	1965.13	0.2082	1964.86	0.2162
	1967.38	0.1981	1967.26	0.1982
	1969.27	0.1918	1969.26	0.1826
1979–80 fertility	1964.98	0.1488	1964.09	0.1702
survey,	1967.87	0.1369	1967.22	0.1524
individuals	1970.58	0.1232	1970.13	0.1341
	1973.11	0.1280	1972.84	0.1331
	1975.38	0.1254	1975.27	0.1242
	1977.30	0.1507	1977.29	0.1417

Source: For 1948, Ghana (1950), table 30, 396; for 1960, Gaisie (1969), tables 4A and 6, 30, 33; for 1971, Ramachandran (1979), 6, 7; for 1979-80, Owusu (1984), tables 13 and 21.

Table 3A-6. Ghana: Directly Reported Child Survival from Maternity Histories, 1979–80 Fertility Survey

Date of reference	Value of q5
1949–54	0.211
1954–59	0.171
1959–64	0.143
1964–69	0.144
1969–74	0.117

Source: Owusu (1984), table 23.

Figure 3A-5. Risk of Dying before Age Five, Ghana: 1948, 1960, and 1970 Censuses and 1979–80 Fertility Survey

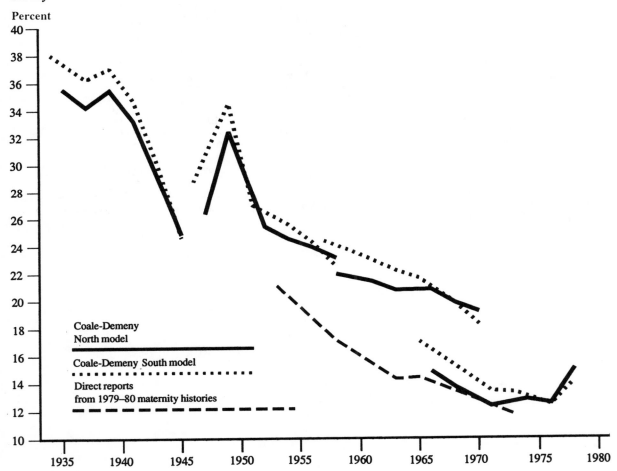

Table 3A-7. Burkina Faso: Child Survival Analysis Results from the 1960–61 Rural Survey, 1961 Ouagadougou Survey, and 1976 Postcensal Survey

Data source	Coale-Demeny North model		Coale-Demeny South model	
	Reference date	Equivalent value of q5	Reference date	Equivalent value of q5
Rural survey 1960–61	1946.36	0.3933	1945.47	0.4204
	1949.22	0.4063	1948.59	0.4288
	1951.90	0.4060	1951.45	0.4238
	1954.39	0.4025	1954.12	0.4185
	1956.64	0.4210	1956.52	0.4311
	1958.55	0.4307	1958.53	0.4346
Ouagadougou survey, 1961	1947.99	0.2561	1947.22	0.2790
	1950.55	0.2591	1950.04	0.2771
	1952.61	0.2588	1952.23	0.2732
	1954.49	0.2618	1954.21	0.2736
	1956.33	0.2279	1956.15	0.2342
	1958.12	0.1900	1958.06	0.1864
1976 postcensal survey	1961.61	0.2856	1960.74	0.3108
	1964.44	0.2804	1963.81	0.3010
	1967.04	0.2718	1966.59	0.2878
	1969.46	0.2754	1969.18	0.2868
	1971.67	0.2687	1971.54	0.2728
	1973.58	0.2700	1973.56	0.2650

Source: For the 1960–61 rural survey and the 1976 postcensal survey, Burkina Faso (1981), table 3.5, 12; for the Ouagadougou 1961 survey, Burkina Faso (n.d.), tables 43 and 46, 46, 49.

Figure 3A-6. Risk of Dying before Age Five, Burkina Faso: 1960–61 Rural Survey, 1961 Ouagadougou Survey, and 1976 Postcensal Survey

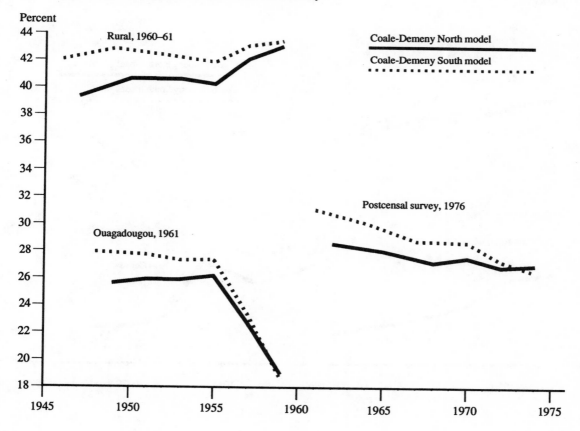

Table 3A-8. Congo: Child Survival Analysis Results from the 1960–61 Rural Survey, 1961 Brazzaville Survey, and 1974 Census

Data source	Coale-Demeny North model		Coale-Demeny South model	
	Reference date	*Equivalent value of q5*	*Reference date*	*Equivalent value of q5*
Rural survey 1960–61	1945.87	0.2956	1944.97	0.3213
	1948.65	0.2921	1947.99	0.3133
	1951.22	0.2802	1950.75	0.2973
	1953.66	0.2827	1953.35	0.2959
	1955.92	0.2772	1955.76	0.2838
	1957.92	0.2691	1957.88	0.2656
1961 Brazzaville survey	1946.43	0.1793	1945.50	0.2026
	1949.15	0.1737	1948.47	0.1919
	1951.72	0.1562	1951.21	0.1696
	1954.19	0.1473	1953.84	0.1552
	1956.51	0.1431	1956.33	0.1455
	1958.62	0.1391	1958.58	0.1322
1974 census	1959.69	0.1848	1958.83	0.2076
	1962.51	0.1720	1961.91	0.1890
	1965.08	0.1876	1964.65	0.2011
	1967.46	0.1499	1967.19	0.1559
	1969.63	0.1440	1969.50	0.1438
	1971.50	0.1435	1971.48	0.1350

Source: For the 1960–61 rural survey, Congo (1965a), table 25, 127; for the 1961 Brazzaville survey, Congo (1965b), tables 1,000 and 1,001, 97; for the 1974 census, Congo (1978), table 38, 97.

Figure 3A-7. Risk of Dying before Age Five, Congo: 1960–71 Rural Survey, 1961 Brazzaville Survey, and 1974 National Census

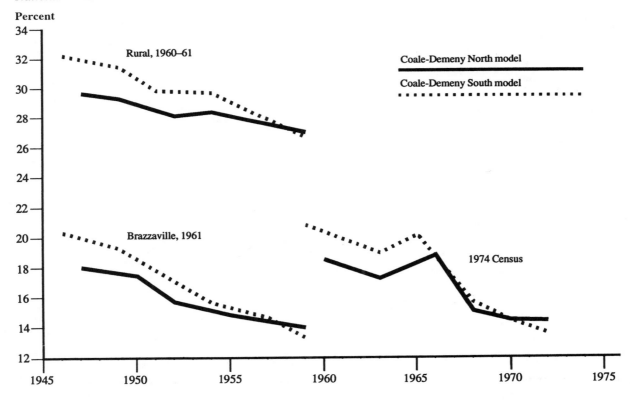

Table 3A-9. Nigeria: Child Survival Analysis Results from the 1971–73 Demographic Survey and 1981–82 Fertility Survey

Data source	Coale-Demeny North model		Coale-Demeny South model	
	Reference date	Equivalent value of q5	Reference date	Equivalent value of q5
1971–73 survey, South Western region	1960.50	0.2779	1960.00	0.2967
	1962.89	0.3051	1962.67	0.3172
	1964.23	0.2322	1964.08	0.2416
	1965.24	0.2224	1965.08	0.2288
	1966.32	0.1657	1966.17	0.1681
	1967.53	0.1236	1967.46	0.1193
1971–73 survey, Eastern region	1960.63	0.2203	1960.02	0.2407
	1963.13	0.1772	1962.80	0.1911
	1964.82	0.2119	1964.58	0.2227
	1966.22	0.2042	1966.02	0.2109
	1967.62	0.1769	1967.47	0.1794
	1969.03	0.1000	1968.97	0.0946
1971–73 survey, Northern region	1958.49	0.2235	1957.69	0.2463
	1960.93	0.2021	1960.38	0.2195
	1962.88	0.1810	1962.45	0.1945
	1964.72	0.1892	1964.38	0.1999
	1966.61	0.1216	1966.37	0.1255
	1968.55	0.1024	1968.47	0.0991
1981–82 fertility survey, individual survey	1966.92	0.1729	1965.97	0.1961
	1969.81	0.1778	1969.10	0.1964
	1972.63	0.1570	1972.12	0.1703
	1975.31	0.1427	1975.00	0.1492
	1977.74	0.1596	1977.60	0.1601
	1979.80	0.1876	1979.78	0.1787

Source: For 1971–73, Ojelade (1979); for 1981–82, Nigeria (1984), table 5.17, 89.

Table 3A-10. Nigeria: Directly Reported Child Survival from Maternity Histories, 1981–82 Fertility Survey

Date of reference	Value of q5
1947–52	0.266
1952–57	0.249
1957–62	0.210
1962–67	0.190
1967–72	0.177
1972–77	0.152

Source: Nigeria (n.d.), table 31.

Figure 3A-8. Risk of Dying before Age Five, Nigeria: 1971–73 Demographic Survey and 1981–82 Fertility Survey

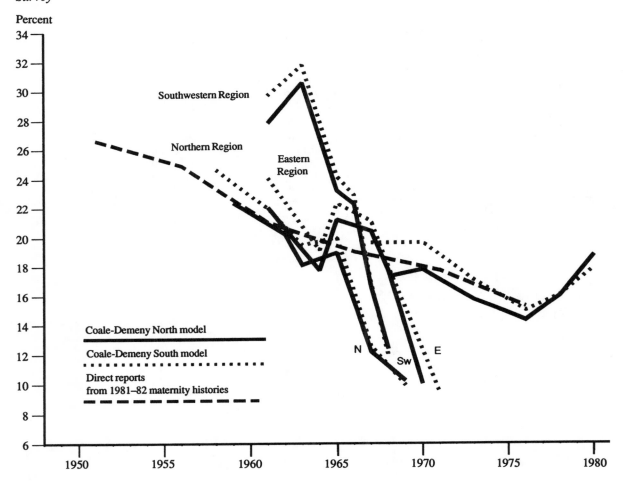

Table 3A-11. Senegal: Child Survival Analysis Results from the 1960 Survey and 1978 Fertility Survey

Data source	Coale-Demeny North model		Coale-Demeny South model		Ewbank "Senegal" model	
	Reference date	Equivalent value of q5	Reference date	Equivalent value of q5	Reference date	Equivalent value of q5
1960 survey	1945.58	0.3472	1944.71	0.3733	1941.60	0.386
	1948.33	0.3513	1947.71	0.3728	1945.60	0.385
	1950.83	0.3300	1950.38	0.3471	1948.80	0.360
	1953.17	0.3243	1952.88	0.3389	1951.50	0.353
	1955.35	0.2984	1955.19	0.3061	1954.10	0.328
	1957.29	0.2881	1957.25	0.2865	1956.50	0.327
1978 survey	1965.98	0.2548	1965.28	0.2769	1959.60	0.237
	1968.75	0.2865	1968.31	0.3034	1963.60	0.299
	1970.97	0.2751	1970.68	0.2872	1966.80	0.287
	1972.91	0.2583	1972.72	0.2656	1969.50	0.266
	1974.66	0.2736	1974.56	0.2754	1972.10	0.281
	1976.18	0.2735	1976.16	0.2689	1974.50	0.281

Source: For 1960, United Nations (1986), table 7, 494; for 1978, Senegal (n.d.), vol. 1, table 5.1, 62, and vol. 2, tables 22.1 and 3.3.1, 107, 183.

Table 3A-12. Senegal: Directly Reported Child Survival from Maternity Histories, 1978 Survey

Date of reference	Value of q5
1950–54	0.292
1955–59	0.277
1960–64	0.282
1965–69	0.284
1970–74	0.264
1975–77	0.167

Note: The averages of the annual figures for the proportion of children dying before the age of five were calculated for the periods specified.
Source: Douglas Ewbank, Population Studies Center, University of Pennsylvania, unpublished paper on the demography of Senegal commissioned by the World Bank in 1985.

Figure 3A-9. Risk of Dying before Age Five, Senegal: 1960 and 1978 Surveys

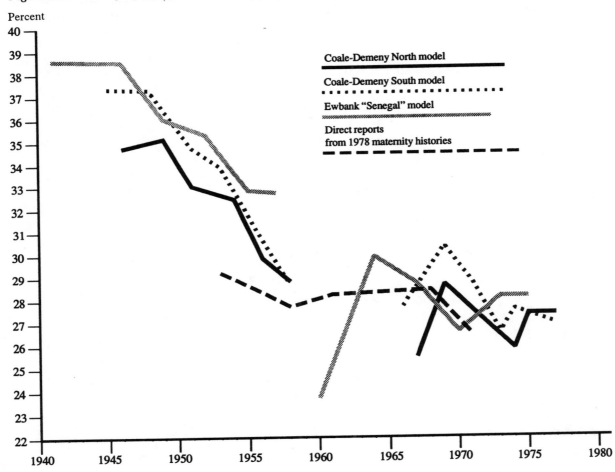

Table 3A-13. Mozambique: Child Survival Analysis Results from the 1950, 1970, and 1980 Censuses

Data source	Coale-Demeny North model		Coale-Demeny South model	
	Reference date	Equivalent value of q5	Reference date	Equivalent value of q5
1950 census	1935.98	0.2410	1935.10	0.2655
	1938.88	0.2360	1938.25	0.2557
	1941.58	0.2434	1941.14	0.2586
	1944.08	0.2575	1943.82	0.2672
	1946.33	0.2878	1946.21	0.2908
	1948.20	0.3403	1948.19	0.3379
1970 census	1955.39	0.2146	1954.44	0.2394
	1958.27	0.2072	1957.57	0.2273
	1961.09	0.2024	1960.59	0.2179
	1963.78	0.2050	1963.47	0.2143
	1966.21	0.2135	1966.07	0.2150
	1968.26	0.2463	1968.25	0.2389
1980 census	1964.86	0.2532	1963.89	0.2794
	1967.69	0.2596	1966.97	0.2819
	1970.48	0.2636	1969.96	0.2818
	1973.17	0.2689	1972.83	0.2826
	1975.64	0.2746	1975.48	0.2810
	1977.78	0.2954	1977.75	0.2929

Source: Mozambique (n.d.).

Figure 3A-10. Risk of Dying before Age Five, Mozambique: 1950, 1970, and 1980 Censuses

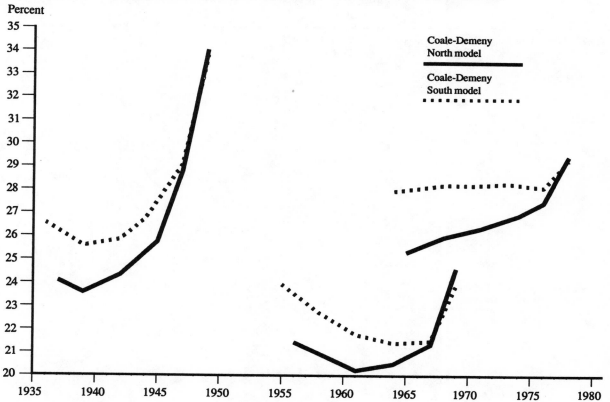

Table 3A-14. Sudan: Child Survival Analysis Results from the 1973 Census and 1979 Fertility Survey

Data source	Coale-Demeny North model		Coale-Demeny South model	
	Reference date	Equivalent value of q5	Reference date	Equivalent value of q5
1973 census, national	1958.22	0.2016	1957.31	0.2256
	1961.09	0.2009	1960.42	0.2203
	1963.82	0.1886	1963.35	0.2030
	1966.40	0.1966	1966.10	0.2051
	1968.73	0.2036	1968.60	0.2048
	1970.72	0.2310	1970.70	0.2230
1973 census, Northern Sudan	1958.52	0.1807	1957.63	0.2036
	1961.38	0.1815	1960.73	0.1997
	1964.04	0.1675	1963.59	0.1804
	1966.54	0.1701	1966.26	0.1771
	1968.80	0.1713	1968.67	0.1717
	1970.73	0.1946	1970.71	0.1859
1979 fertility survey, household survey	1965.15	0.1303	1964.32	0.1502
	1968.07	0.1529	1967.48	0.1687
	1970.72	0.1386	1970.32	0.1493
	1973.13	0.1534	1972.90	0.1584
	1975.26	0.1502	1975.17	0.1486
	1977.01	0.1782	1977.01	0.1685
1979 fertility survey, individual survey	1964.53	0.1380	1963.64	0.1588
	1967.49	0.1360	1966.84	0.1516
	1970.30	0.1369	1969.86	0.1482
	1972.92	0.1381	1972.66	0.1430
	1975.22	0.1348	1975.12	0.1328
	1977.10	0.2178	1977.10	0.2075

Source: For 1973, Sudan (n.d.), unpublished tables; for 1979, Sudan (1982), table 6.1, 66.

Table 3A-15. *Sudan: Directly Reported Child Survival from Maternity Histories, 1979 Fertility Survey*

Date of reference	Value of q5
1960–64	0.151
1965–69	0.140
1969–74	0.135
1975–79	0.153

Source: Sudan (1982), vol. 1, table 6.4, 68.

Figure 3A-11. **Risk of Dying before Age Five, Sudan: 1973 National Census and 1979 Fertility Survey for Northern Sudan**

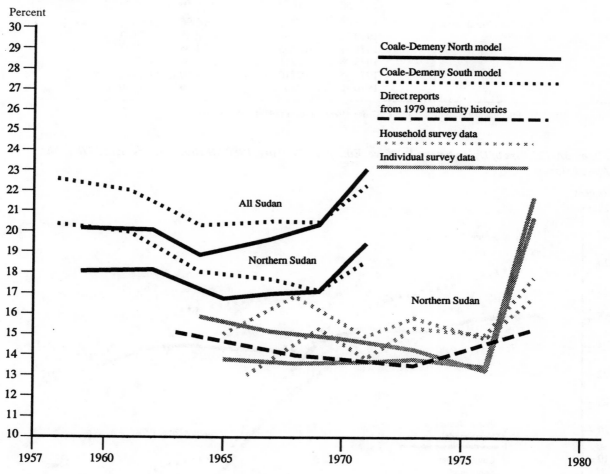

Table 3A-16. Ethiopia: Child Survival Analysis Results from the 1970 and 1980–81 Rural Demographic Surveys and 1978 Addis Ababa Demographic Survey

Data source	Coale-Demeny North model		Coale-Demeny South model	
	Reference date	Equivalent value of q5	Reference date	Equivalent value of q5
1970 rural survey	1955.56	0.2434	1954.70	0.2676
	1958.33	0.2393	1957.72	0.2591
	1960.84	0.2346	1960.40	0.2497
	1963.17	0.2358	1962.89	0.2458
	1965.32	0.2311	1965.18	0.2342
	1967.22	0.2135	1967.19	0.2063
1978 Addis Ababa survey	1964.81	0.2253	1963.99	0.2486
	1967.72	0.2077	1967.15	0.2257
	1970.33	0.1786	1969.95	0.1906
	1972.70	0.1807	1972.48	0.1863
	1974.78	0.1791	1974.70	0.1776
	1976.50	0.1832	1976.50	0.1735
1980–81 rural survey	1966.69	0.2277	1965.96	0.2497
	1969.32	0.2281	1968.85	0.2454
	1971.41	0.2293	1971.08	0.2421
	1973.28	0.2281	1973.04	0.2366
	1975.05	0.2216	1974.90	0.2249
	1976.70	0.2302	1976.66	0.2260

Source: For 1970, Ethiopia (1974), vol. 1, table 1, 87; for 1978, Ethiopia (1979), table 34, 63.

Figure 3A-12. Risk of Dying before Age Five, Ethiopia: 1970 and 1980–81 Rural Surveys and 1978 Addis Ababa Survey

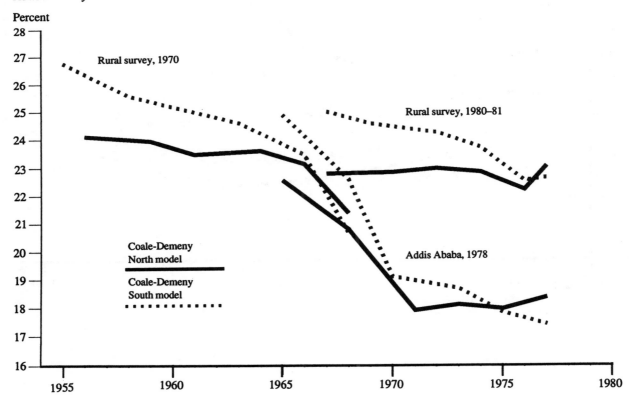

Table 3A-17. Rwanda: Child Survival Analysis Results from the 1970 Survey, 1978 Census, and 1983 Survey

Data source	Coale-Demeny North model		Coale-Demeny South model	
	Reference date	*Equivalent value of q5*	*Reference date*	*Equivalent value of q5*
1970 survey	1957.06	0.2445	1956.24	0.2681
	1960.01	0.2093	1959.45	0.2271
	1962.67	0.1820	1962.30	0.1940
	1965.07	0.1795	1964.86	0.1847
	1967.17	0.1776	1967.10	0.1754
	1968.86	0.1914	1968.86	0.1810
1978 census	1965.56	0.2069	1964.81	0.2291
	1968.49	0.2037	1967.99	0.2205
	1971.02	0.2129	1970.70	0.2248
	1973.25	0.2221	1973.07	0.2275
	1975.19	0.2343	1975.13	0.2321
	1976.75	0.2380	1976.75	0.2284
1983 survey	1970.36	0.2096	1969.57	0.2322
	1973.30	0.2037	1972.76	0.2210
	1975.89	0.2031	1975.54	0.2155
	1978.22	0.2125	1978.02	0.2184
	1980.24	0.2179	1980.17	0.2157
	1981.89	0.2382	1981.89	0.2287

Source: For 1970, United Nations (1986), tables 4-6, 4-7, and 7, 106, 108, 494; for 1978, Rwanda (n.d.a), vol. 3, tables 22 and 25, 7, 82; for 1983, Rwanda (n.d.b), tables 5.13 and 47, 108, 176.

Table 3A-18. Rwanda: Directly Reported Child Survival from Maternity Histories, 1983 Survey

	Date of reference	Value of q5
	1948.8–1953.8	0.2641
	1953.8–1958.8	0.2868
	1958.8–1963.8	0.2344
	1963.8–1968.8	0.2177
	1968.8–1973.8	0.2279
	1973.8–1978.8	0.2466
	1978.8–1983.8	0.1954

Source: Rwanda (n.d.b), table 5.3, 155.

Figure 3A-13. Risk of Dying before Age Five, Rwanda: 1970 and 1983 Surveys and 1978 Census

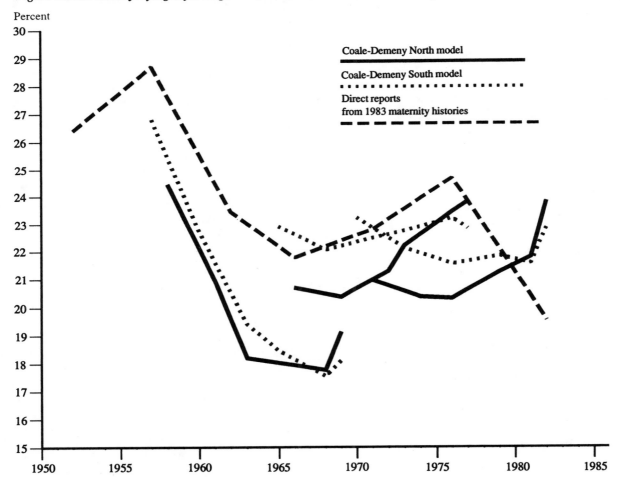

Table 3A-19. Cameroon: Child Survival Analysis Results from the 1978 Fertility Survey

Data source	Coale-Demeny North model		Coale-Demeny South model	
	Reference date	Equivalent value of q5	Reference date	Equivalent value of q5
Household survey	1963.76	0.2384	1962.89	0.2626
	1966.50	0.2349	1965.89	0.2544
	1968.98	0.2318	1968.54	0.2471
	1971.30	0.2129	1971.01	0.2225
	1973.46	0.1987	1973.31	0.2015
	1975.39	0.1847	1975.36	0.1778
Individual survey	1964.04	0.2216	1963.19	0.2452
	1966.83	0.2149	1966.23	0.2335
	1969.35	0.2090	1968.92	0.2231
	1971.68	0.1990	1971.40	0.2071
	1973.81	0.1909	1973.68	0.1922
	1975.67	0.1768	1975.65	0.1689

Source: Cameroon (1983), vol. 1, table 6.1, 92.

Table 3A-20. Cameroon: Directly Reported Child Survival from Maternity Histories, 1978 Fertility Survey

Date of reference	Value of q5
1953–58	0.2910
1958–63	0.2407
1963–68	0.2425
1968–73	0.1938
1973–78	0.1950

Source: Cameroon (1983), vol. 1, table 6.3, 94.

Figure 3A-14. Risk of Dying before Age Five, Cameroon: 1978 Fertility Survey

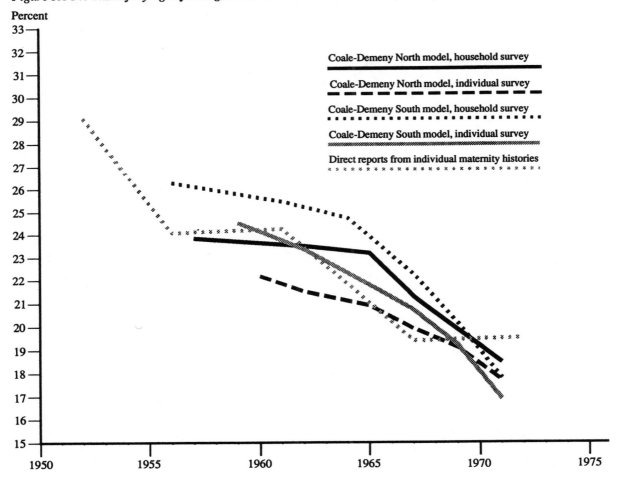

Table 3A-21. *Malawi: Child Survival Analysis Results from the 1970–72 Survey and 1977 Census*

Data source	Coale-Demeny North model		Coale-Demeny South model	
	Reference date	Equivalent value of q5	Reference date	Equivalent value of q5
1970–72 population change survey	1955.93	0.3400	1955.08	0.3656
	1958.80	0.3443	1958.20	0.3655
	1961.43	0.3536	1961.01	0.3696
	1963.84	0.3392	1963.59	0.3515
	1966.01	0.3740	1965.90	0.3804
	1967.83	0.4188	1967.81	0.4214
1977 census	1963.07	0.3184	1962.20	0.3441
	1965.87	0.3236	1965.25	0.3453
	1968.44	0.3273	1967.99	0.3442
	1970.85	0.3271	1970.56	0.3411
	1973.05	0.3258	1972.91	0.3334
	1974.97	0.3280	1974.95	0.3276

Source: For 1970–72, Malawi (1973), table 7, 65; for 1977, Malawi (1980), tables 2.2.1 and 2.2.2, 102, 105.

Figure 3A-15. **Risk of Dying before Age Five, Malawi: 1970–72 Survey and 1977 Census**

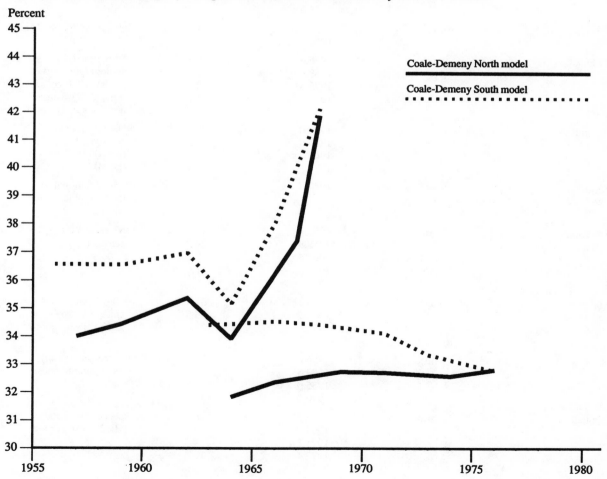

Table 3A-22. Summary Estimates of Childhood Mortality over Time, Eastern Africa

Subregion and country	Coale-Demeny model used	Date of reference	Estimated value of q5 (percent)	Sources and quality of data[a]
Horn of Africa				
Sudan[b]	North	1959.7	20.1	1973 census (poor)
		1965.1	19.3	
Ethiopia[c]	North	1958.2	23.6	1970 rural demographic
		1964.3	23.2	survey (good);
		1968.0	22.7	1978 Addis Ababa
		1972.4	22.6	demographic survey
		1975.9	22.3	(fair); 1980–81 rural
				demographic survey
				(good)
Somalia[d]	North	1967.9	24.1	1980 national
		1974.3	21.4	population survey
East and central Africa				
Kenya[e]	North	1947.5	26.2	1962 census (good);
		1950.0	25.4	1969 census (good);
		1955.0	23.1	1979 census (good)
		1960.0	21.1	
		1965.0	18.8	
		1970.0	16.7	
		1975.0	14.9	
Uganda	North	1957.1	24.5	1969 census (fair)
		1964.7	20.2	
Rwanda[f]	South	1956.2	26.8	1970 national
		1968.0	22.1	demographic survey
		1975.8	22.8	(poor); 1978 census
		1979.1	21.7	(fair); 1983 national
				fertility survey (fair)
Burundi	North	1959.0	26.1	1970–71 national
		1965.5	23.1	demographic survey
		1969.5	22.3	(good); 1979 census
		1976.5	22.4	(good)
Zaire[g]	South	1944.4	30.5	1955–57 national
				demographic survey
				(fair)
Tanzania[h]	North	1953.4	26.2	1967 census (fair); 1978
		1958.9	24.2	census (?)
		1966.5	23.2	
		1973.0	21.9	
Zambezi countries				
Malawi[i]	South	1958.1	36.7	1970–71 population
		1964.2	35.5	change survey (poor);
		1972.8	33.4	1977 census (good)
Zambia[j]	North	1956.0	22.3	1969 census (good);
		1962.5	20.7	1974 sample census
		1965.0	20.3	(fair)
		1970.0	17.2	
Zimbabwe[k]	North	1957.5	16.2	1969 census (good);
		1964.0	15.4	1982 census (good)
		1971.1	14.7	
		1978.4	13.6	

Table 3A-22 (continued)

Subregion and country	Coale-Demeny model used	Date of reference	Estimated value of q5 (percent)	Sources and quality of data[a]
Mozambique[l]	South	1936.7	26.1	1950 census (poor); 1980 census (fair)
		1942.5	26.3	
		1966.9	28.1	
		1974.2	28.2	
Southern Africa				
Botswana[m]	South	1959.0	17.7	1971 census (good); 1981 census (good)
		1967.4	15.9	
		1970.2	14.5	
		1977.0	11.6	
Swaziland[n]	South	1951.7	24.1	1966 census (good); 1976 census (good)
		1959.1	22.6	
		1962.8	22.4	
		1969.7	21.5	
Lesotho[o]	West	1956.9	20.7	1968–69 demographic survey (good); 1977 fertility survey (poor)
		1964.7	19.4	
		1965.1	19.0	
		1973.0	18.3	

a. Quality refers to the regularity and consistency of the results. Single data sets are never labeled better than fair since no external checks of consistency can be made.

b. *Sudan*: To reflect the trend in the base data better, three averages of two points only were taken.

c. *Ethiopia*: To reflect trends in base data better, three averages of two points each were taken from 1980–81 rural data. National averages were estimated by weighting rural values by 0.89, Addis Ababa values by 0.03, and other urban centers (assumed to be midway between Addis Ababa and rural values) by 0.08, following the 1984 census distribution of population. These same weightings were maintained at earlier periods for convenience. Since mortality appeared to approach rural levels and thus to have little impact on national values. Addis Ababa values for the 1950s were also assumed to be the same as in the 1960s and again to have little potential impact on national values.

d. *Somalia*: 1975 census data were examined but not used because they were not available for the nomadic half of the population. The value for women aged 20–24 was not used because it was extremely high and out of line with other values. Averages of the next three points were taken, as were those of the last two.

e. *Kenya*: Values were taken from an analysis of child survival reported by K. H. Hill in an unpublished paper prepared for the National Academy of Sciences Committee on Population and Demography in 1981. Data from national surveys in 1977 and 1978 were examined but were not used because they were out of line with census results.

f. *Rwanda*: Points from child survival data were chosen to correspond best with the trend from direct maternity history reports given the serious inconsistencies in child survival data. The values chosen were for women aged 45–49 in 1970, 40–44 in 1978, 20–24 in 1978, and an average of age groups 20–24 and 25–29 in 1983.

g. *Zaire*: Since data were tabulated only for age groups 35–44 and 45–54, the last point was not used and an average of the values for 35–39 and 40–44 (which were estimated from exactly the same raw values of children ever born and since dead) was taken.

h. *Tanzania*: Some uncertainty exists over the correct national figures for 1978 (no national aggregations were done for the census tabulations). Two separate aggregations, done at the U.S. Bureau of the Census and at the Population Studies Center, University of Pennsylvania, gave differing results. The aggregations of the former were highly consistent with the 1967 data but irregular; those of the latter were less consistent but smoother. The Pennsylvania aggregation was used here. To smooth the series, only the data for the four oldest age groups in 1967 were used, with two averages of 2 points. The point for women aged 20–24 in 1978 was also excluded, with an average of women aged 25–34 taken instead.

i. *Malawi*: To smooth the transition between the highly irregular 1970 data and the smooth 1977 data, points for the mid-1960s are the average of 1970 values for women aged 25–29 and 30–34 years and of 1977 values for women aged 40–44 and 45–49. For details of the full analysis see Hill (1986). The 1984 family formation survey results have not yet been released and could not be used.

j. *Zambia*: Standard procedure was followed. For details of the full analysis see Hill (1985).

k. *Zimbabwe*: Because of a slight anomaly in the value for women aged 20–24 in 1969 (it was too high), only the average of ages 25–29 and 30–34 was taken for the 1969 data series. Data from the 1984 reproductive health survey could not be used because they were published in insufficient detail (only one decimal point was given for children ever born).

l. *Mozambique*: Data for women aged 20–29 from 1950 were not used because they were evidently poor. Two points were taken from the averages for women aged 30–34 and 35–39 and for women aged 40–44 and 45–49. Data for women aged 20–24 in 1980 were not used because they were anomalous (too high); instead the last point was taken from the average of women aged 25–29 and 30–34. Data from the 1970 census were not used because they were grossly out of line (lower) with the 1950 and 1980 data and because the enumeration may have been incomplete due to widespread insurrection (as indicated by intercensal growth rates).

(Notes continue on the following page.)

Table 3A-22 (continued)

m. *Botswana*: To smooth the transition between the series, 1981 data from women aged 45–49 were not used; instead, the average for women aged 35–49 and 40–44 were used.

n. *Swaziland*: In both data sets the values for women aged 20–24 years were anomalously high (possibly because of late marriage and hence a high proportion of first births) and were therefore not used. Averages of women aged 25–39 and 40–49 were taken instead.

o. *Lesotho*: Data from the 1971–73 demographic survey and the 1976 census were not used because they gave results far out of line with the 1968–69 demographic survey and the 1977 fertility survey and with each other.

Table 3A-23. Summary Estimates of Childhood Mortality over Time, Western Africa

Subregion and country	Coale-Demeny model used	Date of reference	Estimated value of q5 (percent)	Sources and quality of data[a]
Sahel				
Mali	South	1947.9	37.5	1960–61 demographic
		1955.7	36.9	survey (fair)
Niger	South	1945.9	29.7	1959 national
		1954.6	30.5	demographic survey (fair)
Chad	South	1950.4	34.2	1964 national
		1958.8	31.3	demographic survey (fair)
Senegal[b]	South	1946.2	37.3	1960 national
		1951.6	34.3	demographic survey
		1966.8	29.0	(poor); 1978
		1971.7	27.6	fertility survey (poor)
Gambia, The	South	1960.6	34.9	1973 census (fair)
		1968.1	34.3	
Burkina Faso[c]	South	1948.5	42.1	1960–61 rural
		1956.4	42.3	demographic survey(?);
		1963.7	30.0	1961 Ouagadougou
		1971.4	27.5	demographic survey(?); 1976 postcensal survey(?)
Guinea-Bissau[d]	South	1941.4	30.1	1950 census (poor)
		1943.9	29.8	
Coastal strip				
Guinea	South	1942.2	38.4	1955 national
		1949.7	37.6	demographic survey (fair)
Sierra Leone	South	1962.2	39.4	1974 census (fair)
		1969.4	37.8	
Liberia[e]	South	1957.3	32.1	1970–71 population
		1965.6	28.1	growth survey (fair)
Côte d'Ivoire[f]	South	1966.5	26.7	1978–79 national
		1974.3	20.7	multiround demographic survey (good)
Ghana[g]	South	1935.9	37.1	1948 census, S.E. (poor);
		1948.0	30.1	1960 census, S.E. (fair);
		1955.4	24.1	1970 census, S.E.
		1959.2	23.3	(good)
		1967.1	19.9	
Togo[h]	South	1949.9	34.7	1961 national
		1957.2	32.8	demographic survey
		1963.5	26.2	(fair); 1971 national
		1968.0	22.7	demographic survey (fair)
Benin	South	1948.8	36.3	1961 national
		1956.6	33.2	demographic survey
		1970.2	25.8	(good); 1981 fertility
		1977.8	22.4	survey (poor)

(Table continues on the following page.)

Table 3A-23 (continued)

Subregion and country	Coale-Demeny model used	Date of reference	Estimated value of q5 (percent)	Sources and quality of data[a]
Central and western countries				
Nigeria[i]	South	1967.5	19.6	1981–82 fertility
		1973.6	16.0	survey, individual
		1978.7	16.9	survey (poor?)
Cameroon[j]	South	1955.9	29.1	1978 fertility survey
		1966.1	23.4	(fair)
		1973.6	18.9	
Central African Republic	South	1948.0	36.0	1959 demographic survey of Centre-Oubangi (fair); 1975 census (fair)
		1954.6	32.9	
		1963.0	30.9	
		1970.4	23.9	
Gabon[k]	South	1946.3	34.6	1960 national demographic survey (poor)
		1951.5	32.9	
		1956.1	24.9	
Congo[l]	South	1948.0	28.9	1960–61 rural demographic survey (good); 1961 Brazzaville demographic survey (good); 1974 census (fair)
		1955.8	25.8	
		1961.8	19.9	
		1969.4	14.5	
Angola[m]	South	1926.4	35.6	1940 census (fair)
		1934.8	36.2	

a. Quality refers to the regularity and consistency of the results. Single data sets are never labeled better than fair since no external checks of consistency can be made.

b. *Senegal*: To smooth the very irregular series and conform as much as possible to the Ewbank analysis and the directly reported data, only data from the four oldest age groups of women in 1960 and 1978 were used. They were divided into two averages, for ages 30–34 and 35–39, and for ages 40–44 and 45–49.

c. *Burkina Faso*: The quality of both survey and census data is problematic; both are internally smooth and regular (which would merit a rating of fair or good), but they are utterly inconsistent with each other. Two separate trend lines were used, since there is no internal basis for preferring one data set to the other. National estimates from 1960–61 data were obtained by weighting rural and Ouagadougou values by 0.976 and 0.024, respectively; the assumption was made that the only other town, Bobo Dioulasso (which together with Ouagadougou accounted for the estimated 2.4 percent urban share of the population at that date) had levels of childhood mortality similar to those of Ouagadougou.

d. *Guinea-Bissau*: Owing to exceptionally poor and erratic data, points for women aged 45–49, 20–24, and 25–29 were not used (all much lower values than the rest). The remaining four values were grouped in two averages of two points each.

e. *Liberia*: Child survival data, collected in both 1970 and 1971, gave somewhat different levels and trends. Data from 1971 showed generally higher mortality than did those from 1970, except for the youngest women, but showed mortality falling in recent years, unlike 1970, which showed it rising. The levels and trends are difficult to interpret. (The cholera epidemic in 1971 would not have affected 1970 data at all and would have affected 1971 only to a minor degree. Its effects are not consistent with the differential in trends.) An average of the two sets of data was taken. 1974 census data were not used because although the data from the oldest women were close to the 1970–71 level, they showed a fantastic decline for the youngest women. Probably errors stemming from the imputation programs used for processing the census data are responsible.

f. *Côte d'Ivoire*: The point for women aged 30–34 from the 1978–79 survey was omitted because of obvious errors in the raw numbers (mortality was far too high). The average taken was of points for women aged 20–24 and 25–29 only. Child survival data from the 1980–81 survey were not used because they were inconsistent with both 1978–79 and its own direct maternity history reports (which were very consistent with 1978–79).

g. *Ghana*: The three points for the younger women in 1948 were not used.

h. *Togo*: Points for the two oldest age groups in 1971 were omitted in order to smooth the transition between the two series; averages were taken of women aged 20–24 and 25–29 and for women aged 30–34 and 35–39.

(Notes continue on the following page.)

Table 3A-23 (continued)

i. Nigeria: The Coale-Demeny South model was used because it was closest to the direct reports of child survival. Three averages of two points each were used to reflect the trend of the base data.

j. Cameroon: Child survival data collected in the individual survey were used rather than the household survey data even though not on very strong grounds. The Coale-Demeny South model was selected because it fit the directly reported trend best. The earliest point from the direct data was also used since no indirect estimates reached that far back.

k. Gabon: Because of a very jerky, step-wise trend, averages were done in three pairs.

l. Congo: National estimates from 1960–61 data were obtained by weighting values from each survey by the 1960 distribution of total population (16.1 percent was in Brazzaville, 8.4 percent in Pointe-Noire, 75.5 percent in the rest of the country covered by the rural survey). The not very important assumption made was that Pointe-Noire childhood mortality levels were similar to the national average.

m. Angola: Because of anomalously high values for women aged 20–24, this point was omitted and an average of two points for the 25–29 and 30–34 age groups only was used.

Notes

1. A list of the data sets examined and used for each country is available from the author, together with printouts and graphs.

The terms western Africa and eastern Africa refer to the World Bank's operational groupings. The line between the two groups runs north-south along the western borders of Sudan, Uganda, Rwanda, Burundi, Tanzania, and Zambia and then westward along the northern border of Namibia. The terms East Africa and West Africa correspond to common usage; East Africa consists of Uganda, Kenya, and Tanzania, and West Africa refers to the group of coastal countries running from Senegal through Nigeria.

2. In Mauritania the demographic survey of 1965 excluded urban areas without, as in other countries, collecting in a separate operation comparable urban data that could be combined with rural data, whereas the 1981 survey excluded the nomad population.

3. Note that trends in Burkina Faso are represented by two lines, which are far apart. The difficulties in interpreting the data that created this pattern are discussed in the methodological appendix.

4. South Africa and Namibia are not included in this analysis because they lack child survival data—indeed any large-scale survey or census demographic data. Their vital registration is complete for the nonblack population, but not for the black population. Nevertheless, the incomplete evidence available indicates that the mortality of the black population of South Africa conforms to this general gradient, resembling somewhat that of its neighbor Lesotho. The national level is, of course, the lowest in Africa because the large white, Asian, and coloured minorities enjoy European levels of childhood mortality.

5. See Brass *et al.* (1968) for details of Portuguese methods, including censuses by assembly with much child survival data gathered secondhand.

6. Census results for Addis Ababa have already been published but cannot be used here since they do not include full raw data on child survival.

7. Rwanda's "twin" country of Burundi had a somewhat similar response: a decline in the 1950s followed by only slow improvement in the 1960s and a plateau in the 1970s. This trend can be linked to a history of rapid development in the 1950s, followed by civil unrest in the 1960s that culminated in civil war and slowed development in the early 1970s. For more detail, see Hill (1983).

8. Mozambique also now falls within the western range but only because its lack of decline occurred against the background of significant declines in mortality elsewhere; by contrast, Malawi had apparently always been far outside the eastern range.

9. Moreover the neighboring areas of Mozambique, Tanzania, and Zambia also show exceptionally high childhood mortality. In the ethnically and culturally similar Eastern province of Zambia, for example, nearly 30 percent of children died before the age of five in the mid-1960s, compared with around 20 percent for Zambia as a whole. For further details, see figure 3-5, Hill (1985), and Hill (1986).

10. See, for crude comparisons, the tables of mortality indicators in World Bank (1988) and UNICEF (1987).

11. The AFEMOPC computer program was developed by K. H. Hill to apply the Brass P/F ratio and child survival methods using the methodology recommended in the United Nations' *Manual X*. An earlier mainframe version was published in Zlotnik (1981).

12. See United Nations (1983) for a discussion of these methodological problems.

13. For Zimbabwe only data from the 1969 and 1982 censuses were available at the time of this analysis. The data from the 1984 Reproductive Health Survey were not used because they were published in insufficient detail (they only reported to one decimal average children ever born and children surviving).

14. From an unpublished paper by Douglas Ewbank, Population Studies Center, University of Pennsylvania, on the demography of Senegal, commissioned by the World Bank in 1985.

15. See the longitudinal study conducted by Jain (n.d.) in the western region of Ghana.

16. This is the case with data on reported deaths from the 1960 national demographic surveys in Guinea, North Cameroon, and parts of the Central African Republic. See Brass *et al.* (1968).

References

Benin. (1964). *Enquête demographique au Dahomey, 1961. Résultats définitifs.* Paris: INSEE.

———. (1983). *Enquête fécondité au Benin. Rapport préliminaire,* WFS/RP. Cotonou.

Botswana. Central Statistical Office. (1972). *Report on the Population Census, 1971.* Gaborone.

———. (1983). *1981 Population and Housing Census: Administrative/Technical Report and National Statistical Tables,* C50. Gaborone.

Brass, W., Coale, A. J., Demeny, P., Heisel, D. R., Lorimer, F., Romanuik, A., and van de Walle, E. (1968). *The Demography of Tropical Africa.* Princeton, N.J.: Princeton University Press.

Burkina Faso. (n.d.). *Recensement démographique, Ouagadougou, 1961–62. Résultats définitifs.* Paris: INSEE.

Burkina Faso. Institut National de la Statistique et de la Démographie. (1981). Dossier Technique, no. 4. *Morbidité et mortalité en Haute-Volta: 1960–76.* Ouagadougou.

Cameroon. (1983) *Enquête national sur la fécondité du Cameroun, 1978: Rapport principal.* Vol. 1: *Analyse des principaux résultats.* Yaoundé.

Central African Republic. Bureau Central du Recensement, Direction General de la Statistique. (1980). *Résultats globaux, tableaux de synthèse.* Bangui.

Congo. (1965a). *Enquête démographique, République du Congo, 1960–61. Résultats définitifs.* Paris: INSEE.

———. (1965b). *Recensement de Brazzaville, 1961. Résultats définitifs.* Paris: INSEE.

Congo. Centre National de la Statistique et des Etudes Economiques. (1978). *Recensement général de la population du Congo, 1974.* Vol. 4: *Tableaux statistiques détaillés.* Brazzaville.

Ethiopia. Central Statistical Office. (1974). *Results of the National Sample Survey, Second Round.* Vol. 1: *The Demography of Ethiopia.* Addis Ababa.

———. (1979). *Report on the Analysis of the Addis Ababa Demographic Survey, September 1978.* Statistical Bulletin, no. 22. Addis Ababa.

Gaisie, S. K. (1969). *Estimation of Vital Rates for Ghana: Population Studies.* March.

Ghana. (1950). *The Gold Coast: Census of Population, 1948. Report and Tables.* Accra.

Hill, A. (1983). The demographic situation in Burundi. PHN Technical Note, no. Dem-3. Washington, D.C.: World Bank, Population, Health, and Nutrition Division.

———. (1985). The demography of Zambia. PHN Technical Note, no. 85-9. Washington, D.C.: World Bank, Population, Health, and Nutrition Division.

———. (1986). The demography of Malawi. PHN Technical Note, no. 86-20. Washington, D.C.: World Bank, Population, Health, and Nutrition Division.

Jain, S. K. (n.d.). *The Longitudinal Mortality and Fertility Survey in the Western Region of Ghana.* Canberra: Australia National University, Department of Demography.

Malawi. National Statistical Office. (1973). *Malawi Population Change Survey, 1970–72.* Zomba.

———. (1980). *Malawi Population Census, 1977: Final Report.* Vol. 1. Zomba.

Mozambique. Ministry of Statistics. (n.d.) Mortalidad. Annex to: *1980 Census Report.* Maputo: Departamento de Demographia, Direccão Nacional de Estatica.

Nigeria. (1984). *The Nigeria Fertility Survey, 1981/82: Principal Report.* Vol. 1. Lagos: NPC/WFS.

———. (n.d.). *Evaluation of the Nigeria Fertility Survey, 1981–82.* WFS Scientific Report. Accra: ISI/WFS.

Ojelade, M. A. (1979). *A Comparative Demographic Account of South-Western, Eastern, and Northern Nigeria (1971–73): Evidence from a Sample Survey.* Philadelphia: University of Pennsylvania.

Owusu, J. Y. (1984). *Evaluation of the Ghana Fertility Survey.* WFS Scientific Report. Accra: ISI/WFS.

Ramachandran, K. V. (1979). Fertility and mortality levels, patterns, and trends in some anglophone African countries. Paper prepared for the ECA expert group meeting on fertility and mortality levels, patterns, and trends in Africa and their policy implications, Monrovia, Liberia, November–December.

Rhodesia. Central Statistical Office. (n.d.). *Report of the Census of Population, 1969.* Salisbury.

Rwanda. (n.d.a). *République rwandaise: Recensement général de la population et de l'habitat, 1978. Résultats définitifs.* Vol. 3. Kigali: Office National de la Population.

———. (n.d.b). *Rwanda 1983. Enquête national sur la fécondité.* Vol. 1. *Analyse des résultats.* Kigali: Office National de la Population.

Senegal. (n.d.) *Enquête senegalaise sur la fécondité: Rapport national d'analyse.* 2 vols. Dakar.

Sudan Department of Statistics. (n.d.). *The Sudan Population Census, 1973.* Khartoum.

———. (1982). *The Sudan Fertility Survey, 1979: Principal Report.* Vol. 1. Khartoum: WFS/ISI, Department of Statistics.

UNICEF. (1987). *The State of the World's Children, 1987.* New York: Oxford University Press.

United Nations. (1983). *Manual X. Indirect Techniques for Demographic Estimation.* E.83.XIII.2. New York.

———. (1986). *Demographic Yearbook, Special Issue 1979. Historical Supplement.* New York.

World Bank. (1988). *World Development Report 1988.* New York: Oxford University Press.

Zimbabwe. Central Statistical Office. (1985). *Advance Report of the Ten Percent Sample Report, 1982 Census.* Harare.

Zlotnik, H. (1981). *Computer Program for Demographic Estimation: A User's Guide.* Washington, D.C.: National Academy Press.

Chapter 4

Infant and Child Mortality: Development, Environment, and Custom

John G. C. Blacker

This chapter gives a demographer's overview of what we know about the current levels and trends in infant and child mortality in the countries of Sub-Saharan Africa. Any such study immediately reveals large differentials among the mortality rates in these countries. This chapter also suggests some of the principal factors that help to explain these differentials. In making this review, I have drawn heavily from the papers presented at the International Union for the Scientific Study of Population (IUSSP) Seminar on Mortality and Society in Sub-Saharan Africa that was held in Yaoundé, Cameroon, in October 1987.

Data Sources

No country on the continent of Africa south of the Sahara has a system of vital registration capable of producing valid indices of infant and child mortality at the national level. Where they do exist, such systems of civil registration are generally confined to urban areas or to relatively small parts of the rural population that cannot be regarded as representative of the rest of the country. Thus all our mortality estimates are based on census and survey data, which may be conveniently divided into three categories.

Indirect Estimates

The first are indirect estimates of infant and child mortality derived by asking women about the number of children ever born and classifying their answers as children still living and children who are dead. The estimates are termed indirect because they are not based on information about the ages of the living children or the ages at death of those who died. All we have is information on the ages of the mothers. Clearly, the older the mothers, the older, on average, will be their children. The precise nature of this relationship was first established by Brass in the early 1960s (Brass

et al., 1968), and though variations have been composed on this theme (Sullivan, 1972; Trussell, 1975; Preston and Palloni, 1978; United Nations, 1983), their results differ only trivially from those obtained by using the original Brass technique.

Since most infant and childhood deaths take place in the first two years of life, the older the mothers, the farther in the past will the deaths, on average, have occurred. If mortality is changing, the proportion of children dying in each age group of mothers will represent a different level of mortality. Thus by relating each mortality estimate to a model life table, it is possible to reconstruct trends over time. The method of time location was first devised by Feeney in the 1970s (Feeney, 1976; Feeney, 1980), though again several modifications of the procedure have been devised (Coale and Trussell, 1978; United Nations, 1983; Brass, 1985). When the requisite data have been collected in two or more censuses or surveys, the consistency of the implied trends provides a powerful test of the validity of both the data and the estimation procedures. In this respect there is wide variation among African countries: in some, such as Kenya, the consistency is remarkable; in others, such as Burkina Faso, wide discrepancies surface in the estimates derived from different surveys, which suggests that at least some of the data must be seriously biased.

The indirect estimates provide by far the most plentiful source of information on mortality in Sub-Saharan Africa and were the basis of the analysis of continental trends reported in chapter 3. Few countries have data that were collected after 1980 and that have been, at the time of writing, processed and analyzed; none have any after 1983. Because the mortality estimates generally refer to time periods preceding the actual date of the census or survey by several years, all estimates of mortality for the 1980s have generally been based on extrapolation of trends reconstructed for the 1960s and 1970s. Thus persons who wish to examine the effect on infant and child mortality of events such as the Sahelian famines of the mid-1980s, the recent epidemic of AIDS in eastern and central Africa, or the general economic depression that affected most African countries in the 1980s will have to wait until the results of the 1990 round of censuses become available.

Direct Estimates

Our second category of data sources consists of the direct estimates of mortality calculated from birth histories in which all the women surveyed are asked to give the date of birth of each of their children and, if they have died, the date or age of death. At the time of writing, the only countries in Sub-Saharan Africa where such data have been obtained from nationally representative samples were those that had participated in the World Fertility Survey (WFS): Benin, Côte d'Ivoire, Ghana, Kenya, Lesotho, Mauritania, Nigeria, Senegal, and Sudan. Similar data are now being collected by the Demographic and Health Surveys, so that the countries participating in these surveys will again be able to calculate direct estimates of child mortality. Although they do not have to rely on the more uncertain assumptions that have to be made when using the indirect techniques, such estimates are nevertheless subject to their own particular kind of errors and biases. These include the selective omission of children who die shortly after birth and the misreporting of dates of birth and ages at death. The latter errors often consist of rounding ages to multiples of six or twelve months, which results in a general upward bias in the ages reported. In this case the infant mortality rate would be underreported while that of toddlers would be correspondingly inflated (Blacker *et al.*, 1985).

Longitudinal Surveys

The third source of mortality data consists of the longitudinal surveys of the type described in part III of this book. Since the births and deaths are recorded more or less as they occur, these data do not suffer from the biases and dating errors that afflict birth history surveys. Longitudinal surveys have other drawbacks: the numbers involved are often uncomfortably small, and the areas covered have invariably been purposively selected and cannot be regarded as representative of the countries as a whole. However, in many cases they provide valuable insights into features such as the age patterns of mortality, the causes of death, or the patterns of seasonal fluctuations.

Geographic Differentials

Two recent comprehensive studies have reviewed the available published data of the types described above for all the countries of Sub-Saharan Africa. The first was by Althea Hill of the World Bank, the results of which are summarized in chapter 3 of this book. The second study was undertaken by the Population Division of the United Nations with funding provided by UNICEF (United Nations, 1988); its objective was not only to analyze existing data but also to reconstruct trends in infant and child mortality since 1950 for all countries of the world and to project the trends up to the year 2025. The latter part of the exercise unavoidably involved the use of subjective judgment and speculation. Both studies suggest the two broad conclusions set out in chapter 3, which, at the risk of repetition, are summarized again here.

First, the great majority of African countries experienced appreciable declines in child mortality during the past twenty years. The rates of decline vary considerably, however, and in a few countries mortality appears to have been virtually static or even rising. These include Angola, Ethiopia, Mozambique, Niger, Nigeria, and Rwanda.

Second, there are enormous variations in the levels of mortality among African countries, and mortality is generally much higher in West Africa than in East and southern Africa. Once again, important exceptions are apparent on both sides of the continent: in West Africa mortality is relatively low in Cameroon, Congo, and Ghana; in East Africa, mortality is exceptionally high in Malawi and in neighboring Mozambique. Farther north the high mortality of the Sahelian countries of West Africa appears to be carried across the continent into Ethiopia, Somalia, and Sudan. These geographic variations are further illustrated by the map shown in figure 4-1, which is based on the United Nations figures for the 1975–80 quinquennium. As noted above, this is the most recent period for which hard data are available; the figures for the 1980s would be based almost entirely on extrapolated trends from the 1960s and 1970s. Overall, the United Nations estimates of mortality in the first five years of life range from 115 per 1,000 live births in Botswana to 335 in Mali and Sierra Leone.

The national averages portrayed in this map often conceal substantial variations within countries. Two examples are given in chapter 3: Zaire in the early 1950s and Zambia in the mid-1960s both had child-

Figure 4-1. Geographic Variations in Under-Five Mortality Rates in Africa, 1975–80

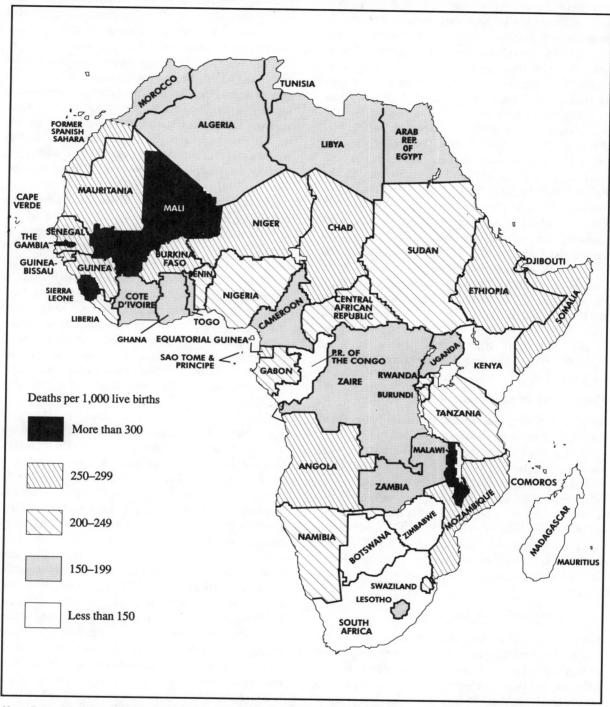

Note: Proportions of children who die in the first five years of life for every 1,000 live births.
Source: United Nations (1988).

hood mortality levels varying by a ratio of more than 2 between the districts or provinces with the highest and the lowest levels. Such variation can be found in countries at both ends of the spectrum. In Botswana the 1971 census showed levels of infant and child mortality that were twice as high in Ngamiland as in the South-East District, and in Kenya the 1979 census showed ratios of 4 or 5 to 1 in the levels of under-five mortality between districts with the highest and the lowest levels of mortality (Blacker *et al.*, 1987; Williams, 1987). At the other end of the scale, localized surveys conducted in Mali in 1981–82 revealed prodigious levels of mortality among the Fulani people living in the Central Niger River Delta, where over half the children were dying in the first five years of life (van den Eerenbeemt, 1985). This mortality was substantially higher than that found among the Fulani living in other parts of Mali and showed little change from the mortality levels in the Central Niger River Delta that were revealed by a survey conducted in the late 1950s. It surpasses even the levels found in Keneba, the Gambia, in the 1950s and 1960s (see chapter 20), and if one wished to identify the area of Africa with, in normal times, the highest mortality, the Central Niger River Delta would be a strong contender.

Factors Affecting Geographic Differentials

Why, it may be asked, should mortality be so much higher in some parts of Africa than in others, and in particular why should it be higher in West Africa than in East and southern Africa? How have infant and child mortality been reduced substantially in some countries while remaining static or even rising in others? No definitive answers exist to these questions given the present state of our knowledge, but it is nevertheless possible to suggest important factors while warning that these constitute unproven hypotheses and that in most cases important exceptions seem to disprove the rules.

Level of Socioeconomic Development

The first and most obvious factor to be examined is the general level of socioeconomic development. Infant and child mortality are frequently regarded as indices reflecting the degree of poverty and deprivation of a population. Thus the mortality in the first few years of life may be expected to fall as a country's general level of living rises. A simple index of such development is the proportion of women who have been to school. Indeed, as a determinant of infant and child mortality, female education is more than an index of socio-economic status. The United Nations study of factors affecting mortality in 15 developing countries, using both bivariate and multivariate analysis, concluded that "taking these economic variables one at a time neglects their combined effect and can lead to an underestimate of their importance in strategies for improving health. But the results suggest that even the sum of direct mortality effects of doubling everyone's income, providing every household with a flush lavatory and piped water, and turning every agricultural labourer into a professional/white-collar worker would be less than the direct effect of providing ten years of schooling for each woman" (United Nations, 1985, p. 289).

The universal tendency is, of course, for wealthier people to be better educated than the rest of the population. How much of the apparent influence of education on child mortality is due to the fact that education is a proxy for income and the health-giving benefits resulting from it, and how much may be attributed to education itself? Numerous attempts have been made to disentangle these factors, and Cleland and van Ginneken (1989), in reviewing those studies, have concluded that "the economic advantages associated with education (income, water and latrine facilities, clothing, housing quality, etc.) account for about one-half of the overall education-mortality association." (p. 20).

Table 4-1 shows for select countries of East and West Africa the proportions of women in each age group who have no schooling. There is a clear contrast between the figures for the high-mortality countries of West Africa (the Gambia, Mali, and Sierra Leone), where the vast majority of women have no schooling, and those for the low-mortality countries of East and southern Africa (Botswana, Kenya, and Zimbabwe), where less than half of the women in the peak childbearing ages have never been to school. Furthermore, a conspicuous feature of the low-mortality countries, particularly Kenya, is that the proportions of women with no schooling drop rapidly with age, reflecting substantial increases in the primary school enrollment ratios over the past 30 or 40 years. These changes clearly correlate with the reductions in child mortality achieved in these countries and contrast with the situation in the three West African countries where improvements in both female education and in child mortality have been much more modest.

Table 4-1 also presents figures for two countries, Ghana and Malawi, that constitute exceptions to the general patterns of East-West mortality differentials. The figures for Ghana are from the 1970 census, so

Table 4-1. Percentages of Females in Each Age Group Who Have Never Been to School, Selected African Countries

Age group (years)	Sierra Leone, 1974	Mali, 1976	The Gambia, 1983	Ghana, 1970	Kenya, 1979	Botswana, 1981	Zimbabwe, 1982	Malawi, 1977
15–19	78.8	84.8	75.1	42.2	22.9	19.9	11.1	46.0
20–24	85.3	88.8	81.8	66.8	38.8	32.3		54.0
25–29	89.2	95.4	86.1	81.3	49.9	36.7		57.1
30–34	94.5	97.4	88.4		62.7	38.1	33.8[a]	61.3
35–39	95.5	97.8	89.5	90.8	72.1	45.9		67.1
40–44	95.0	98.6	91.6		79.0	50.5		69.7
45–49	95.3	98.9	91.2		82.9	53.9		73.9

a. For women age 20 and older.

Source: For Botswana, Kenya, Malawi, Mali, and Zimbabwe, census reports; for Ghana and Sierra Leone, personal communication; and for the Gambia, unpublished tabulations.

when they are compared with those for Kenya and Botswana, the ages of each cohort should be increased approximately ten years: thus the proportion with no schooling in the 15–19 age group in Ghana should be compared with those in the 25–29 age group in Kenya and Botswana. On this basis, the levels of education achieved in Ghana are clearly much more closely akin to those of the low-mortality countries on the other side of the continent than to those of the other West African countries shown in the table. This fact may partially explain why mortality is lower in Ghana than in most of the rest of West Africa. The case of Malawi, however, is much more puzzling because the proportions of women under the age of 30 who have no schooling, though somewhat higher than in the other countries of East Africa, are in no way as low as those in the Gambia, Mali, or Sierra Leone. Thus lack of female education cannot explain the extraordinarily high levels of infant and child mortality in Malawi.

Education — or any single index of socioeconomic status, for that matter—cannot account for everything, and several of the Yaoundé papers cast doubts on the preeminence of education as a determinant of infant and child mortality. Akoto and Tabutin (1987) in their multivariate analysis of WFS data from Kenya and Cameroon showed that the effect of the parents' education was subsidiary to that of ethnicity and region of residence. Mbacké and van de Walle (1987), also using multivariate analysis with data from the 1981–84 IFORD survey of the town Bobo Dioulasso in Burkina Faso, concluded that "the first surprise in our results is the poor performance of maternal education as an explanatory variable, once additional factors such as the quality of housing, income, and the use of services

have been included in the regressions" (p. 15). Antoine and Diouf (1987) from their analysis of a survey done in 1986 in Pikine (a rapidly growing suburb of Dakar) showed that a lack of basic facilities, such as piped water and maternal and child health (MCH) clinics, as well as the behavior of individuals were important factors keeping mortality at high levels in certain quarters. Ngatchou and van der Pol (1987), using data from a survey of infant and child mortality in Yaoundé to elucidate the causal mechanisms that link education and child mortality, found that in some circumstances education increased rather than decreased mortality, particularly when it resulted in a reduction in breast-feeding.

Figure 4-2 shows the relationship between mortality in the first five years of life and the education of the mother in Kenya and Sierra Leone. In both countries mortality falls steeply as education rises, but in each educational category the mortality is two to three times higher in Sierra Leone than in Kenya. Thus the mortality of children borne by mothers with secondary schooling in Sierra Leone is marginally higher than that of children borne by mothers with no schooling in Kenya. We must therefore conclude that, over and above the differences in socioeconomic development, basic environmental factors contribute to the mortality differentials between West and East Africa.

Environmental Factors

The first obvious environmental factor is altitude and its relationship, through temperature and humidity, with malaria. In West Africa not only the countries of the coastal belt but also the inland countries of the Sahel lie at altitudes of under 500 meters; only a few

*Figure 4-2. Under-Five Mortality Rates,
Sierra Leone (1974) and Kenya (1979),
by Mother's Education*

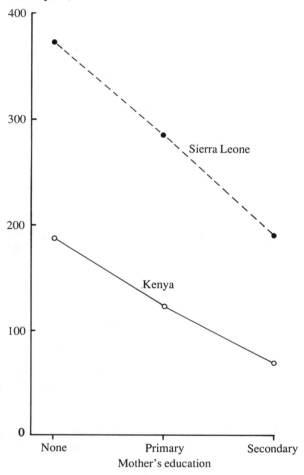

Source: For Kenya, Kenya (n.d.), vol. 2; for Sierra Leone, Okoye (1980).

The second important environmental factor that has been linked to mortality differentials is that East Africa has two rainy seasons during the year and West Africa has only one (Rowland, 1979). Thus data from Keneba in the Gambia (chapter 20, this volume) show important seasonal variations in infant and child mortality. Death rates peak in the period between August and January owing to a combination of factors: the increased prevalence of malaria coincides with the onset of the rains; food shortages occur as stocks from the previous year's crop become exhausted; the water supply created by the rains becomes polluted; and standards of child care are lowered because women do heavy agricultural work during the planting season (Rowland *et al.*, 1981). Likewise in Mali, van den Eerenbeemt (1985) found significant seasonal fluctuations in child mortality among the Fulani, and Hilderbrand (1985) showed how seasonal stress affects nutritional intake and weight loss, though the patterns vary for pastoralists and agriculturalists.

In contrast, the data from Machakos, Kenya (chapter 17, this volume), which has two rainy seasons during the year, showed no significant seasonal fluctuations. Williams (1987) found a marked seasonal pattern of infant and child mortality in Siaya District in Kenya, but a pattern completely different from that found in the Gambia: deaths peaked in June and July (that is, the months immediately following the long rains). Williams attributes this to measles and pneumonia, which, for reasons not fully elucidated, appear to be more prevalent in many parts of Africa during the dry season (Sutton, 1981; Tomkins, 1981; Goetz, 1981). Likewise, Fargues and Nassour (1987), in studying the seasonal variations in mortality in Bamako, found that deaths from measles peak sharply in April, which in Mali is the hottest time of the year and at the end of the dry season. Gaigbe Togbe (1987) also found that in Yaoundé deaths from measles were at a maximum in March, again the hottest month of the year since it comes at the end of the dry season and the beginning of the short rains. Yaoundé has a bimodal pattern of rainfall similar to that found in East Africa. Indeed the pronouncedly unimodal pattern is characteristic primarily of the extreme western bulge of Africa and of the Sahel. Many of the countries around the Gulf of Guinea have a bimodal pattern, which would seem to support our general hypothesis since countries such as Cameroon, Congo, and Ghana have relatively low mortality. On the other hand, the countries of southern and southeastern Africa, notably Botswana and Zimbabwe, have the lowest mortality of all Sub-Saharan Africa and but one rainy season in the year. These

isolated areas, such as the Jos Plateau in Nigeria, the mountain ranges of the South Sahara, or the Adamaoua Massif in Cameroon, rise to altitudes of over 1,000 meters. In contrast, in East Africa (Kenya, Uganda, Tanzania, Zambia, and Zimbabwe) the majority of the population lives at altitudes of over 1,000 meters. The relationship between altitude and malaria is well established (Bagster Wilson, 1949; Russell *et al.*, 1963); malaria is still a serious problem in many parts of East Africa over 1,000 meters (around Lake Victoria, for example) but rarely reaches the holoendemic levels found in West Africa.

again would appear to be the exceptions that disprove the rule.

A third environmental factor that has been invoked to explain the East-West differential is that the population in West Africa tends to live in large clustered villages, whereas in East Africa it lives in scattered dwellings where each family has its hut on its own holding (Rowland, 1979). The clustering in West Africa is conducive to high mortality because it facilitates the spread of epidemic diseases such as measles and respiratory infections, leads to the pollution of water supplies, and results in a lower standard of child care (women walk long distances to work in the fields and often leave their children behind).

The importance of crowding as a factor in the spread of infectious disease has recently been highlighted by work in Guinea-Bissau. Aaby (1987) found that case-fatality rates for measles were significantly higher among those who caught measles from other members of the same household than among those who contracted the disease outside the house. The differential remained even when the data were standardized by age. He concluded that crowding within the household, resulting in intensive exposure and a larger dose of the infective virus, was a major determinant of measles mortality. The role of crowding in the conglomeration of households is less clear. Aaby found higher measles mortality in rural than in urban areas. In urban areas measles was more or less continuously endemic; in rural villages, on the other hand, the intervals between epidemics were longer: "In endemic situations there is a high likelihood that other siblings are already immune when measles is introduced into the household. With an increasing inter-epidemic interval, more individuals in a household are likely to be susceptible simultaneously; this would tend to increase the risk of multiple cases and intensive exposure." But he also suggests that large compounds may be a risk factor in measles mortality, and one factor that might help explain why measles mortality is higher in West than in East Africa is that "settlement patterns tend to be more dispersed in East Africa whereas West Africa often has large, dense villages" (p. 20). Throughout most of the developing world, mortality levels tend to be lower in urban than in rural areas. This differential has generally been explained by the higher educational levels and the more and better health services and amenities, such as clean water supplies, of the urban population. In the absence of factors of this type, urban mortality can often exceed rural mortality, as was the case in Britain in the nineteenth and early twentieth centuries. Thus Woods (1987) has estimated that the expectation of life at birth in England and Wales in the first half of the nineteenth century was more than ten years greater in rural than in urban areas.

However, the hypothesis that crowding, both within households and of dwelling clusters, can explain the geographic variations in child mortality in Africa requires much investigation. The pattern of scattered settlement generally said to characterize East Africa is typical of much of Kenya and Uganda (and Tanzania before the government embarked on its policy of villagization), but is by no means universally found farther south. Thus in Botswana much of the population lives in large villages, while in Sierra Leone the majority of the population lives in hamlets that are so small as scarcely to merit the term village. Kandeh (1987) investigated whether the community and compound structure influenced mortality and was unable to demonstrate any relationship between mortality on the one hand and the size of the settlement or household on the other.

A Framework for Research

The factors offered to account for the massive differentials in infant and child mortality in Africa are at best only of partial applicability. Some may apply in parts of the continent but are clearly irrelevant and inappropriate elsewhere.

The level of infant and child mortality in any population is the result of the interaction between hazards present in the environment and the ability of the population to defend itself against those hazards. The defenses (which include methods of both prevention and treatment) may be divided into those provided by the government or the community, such as mass spraying for mosquitoes or providing treated water, and those utilized by individuals, such as boiling drinking water or washing hands after defecation. Sometimes the measures provided by the government require the collaboration of individuals, as in the case of immunization. The ability of the individuals to defend themselves and the members of their households depends, first, on whether they have the necessary *knowledge* of how to defend themselves (which is why education is of such crucial importance), and, second, on whether they have the necessary *weapons*. In some cases the weapons may simply not be available (for example, the local dispensary has run out of antimalarial drugs); in others they may be available only to those who can afford them.

Most of the studies that have sought to elucidate the determinants and correlates of mortality differentials, both among and within countries, have concentrated on the factors that are likely to determine the defenses employed, such as income, education, or the provision of or access to health services. In contrast, relatively little attention has been paid to the factors that determine whether or not a particular health hazard may be present in the environment. As a result, such studies, most of which have used some form of multivariate analysis, have generally left a large part of the variance unexplained or identified factors such as "region" or "ethnicity" that effectively tell us nothing. To throw further light on these associations, the relationships between the ecology of the areas concerned and the etiology of the major causes of infant and child deaths must be clarified.

Causes of Infant and Child Mortality

Fortunately, the causes of infant and child mortality are relatively few in number: malaria, diarrhea, acute respiratory infections (including pertussis), measles, malnutrition, tetanus, and other neonatal causes account for the great majority of deaths in the first five years of life (Boerma, 1986). Low birth weight, though not a direct cause of death, should be included in this discussion because it is such an important risk factor in neonatal mortality.

Mosley and Chen (1984) in their exposition of the proximate determinants of child mortality list climate, soil, rainfall, temperature, altitude, and seasonality as ecological factors. To these we may add the slope of the terrain, population density, and crowding within households. Establishing the effect, if any, these factors have on the major childhood killers would enable us to generate more specific hypotheses about the environmental determinants of child mortality in particular ecological settings.

MALARIA. The effect of altitude and temperature on the prevalence of malaria has already been discussed. The relative abundance of breeding sites for mosquitoes is also clearly influenced by the timing of rainfall and the slope of the terrain. If rainfall is highly seasonal and the breeding sites are dry most of the year, malaria will be seasonally epidemic, but where the breeding sites are permanent, either because the dry season is too short for them to dry up or because there are perennial swamps or lakes, malaria remains endemic. Population density is also an important factor in malaria transmission, and since population density and rainfall are, for obvious reasons, highly correlated, the effects of the climatic factors are further reinforced. On the other hand, crowding within households seems unlikely to be a major factor in malaria transmission, though the evidence on this point is inconclusive.

DIARRHEA. The ecological factors that tend to promote malaria are also conducive to diarrhea, or at least to bacterial diarrhea. Contamination of weaning foods and water supplies by enteric bacteria increases with the level of temperature, humidity, and rainfall; flies, which may be important transmission vectors, breed more readily at high temperatures; water supplies are more liable to become polluted when they pass through areas of high population density and when they come from stagnant or sluggish sources. On the other hand, diarrhea attributed to rotavirus is more prevalent in the cooler season. Since all the bacterial and viral agents of diarrhea can be transmitted by personal contact, crowding within households must constitute a risk factor in diarrheal mortality. These issues are discussed further in chapter 9.

RESPIRATORY INFECTIONS. Respiratory infections, particularly colds, influenza, bronchitis, and pneumonia, are more prevalent in cold conditions. Transmission is facilitated when people huddle for warmth at night or light smoky fires in poorly ventilated dwellings. Thus crowding within households could be expected to play the same role in respiratory infections as in measles. Overall population density could also be a risk factor facilitating transmission, particularly of diseases such as influenza where one episode does not confer lasting immunity. Chapter 10 provides more detailed information on acute respiratory infections.

MEASLES. Epidemics of measles generally occur during the dry season, but whether this season coincides with the hot or the cool time of year varies by region in Africa. This does not mean, however, that temperature and humidity are important risk factors in measles mortality. In the absence of immunization, almost all children can be expected to contract measles at some stage, whether they live in hot or cold, wet or dry, environments. What we are looking for are the determinants of case fatality. The opinions on this subject are far from unanimous. Aaby (1987) identified crowding within households as an important factor, which he believes works through the dose of the infection. Reves (1985) suggested that the age at infection, also influenced by crowding, is an important determinant. Yet others have advanced the view that morbidity from other causes, such as malaria, diarrhea, and malnutrition, that debilitate the child and suppress the immune system also constitute major risk factors.

If this is true, the environmental conditions that promote these other diseases should also be seen as determinants of measles mortality. The epidemiology of measles is discussed further in chapter 11.

MALNUTRITION. The same argument can be used for malnutrition, at least insofar as this is measured by anthropometric indices such as height-for-age, weight-for-height, upper-arm circumference, or skin-fold thickness. These overt signs of faltering growth may be the result of chronic infections, particularly diarrhea, as much as of dietary deficiencies. But environmental factors such as temperature, rainfall, and fertility of the soil may also determine the staple diets and weaning foods of the population. In this respect it is perhaps ironic that in the more arid, less fertile areas inhabited by pastoral peoples, children will normally be weaned onto milk, which has greater nutritional value than many of the porridges made from grain or root crops grown by agricultural peoples in more fertile areas. The possibilities for contamination and subsequent infection may operate in the reverse direction, however, and the evidence to answer whether faltering growth is more or less prevalent among pastoral than among agricultural peoples is inconclusive. Vitamin A deficiency, a potentially important factor in child mortality (Serdula, 1987), is more common in dry areas where green leafy vegetables are scarce. The distribution of malnutrition in Africa is discussed further in chapter 8.

LOW BIRTH WEIGHT. The interaction of environment, infection, malnutrition, and mortality may also operate through the mechanism of low birth weight. In particular, chronic or episodic illnesses in a pregnant mother retard the intrauterine growth of the fetus so that the newborn infant is at a much greater risk from the major causes of neonatal mortality. Such illnesses may include malaria, hookworm, and other parasitic diseases, most of which are prevalent in hot and wet environments (Brabin, 1983; McGregor *et al.*, 1983; MacLeod, 1988). Weight loss in the mother due to a combination of periodic food shortages and heavy agricultural work, consequent on the seasonality of the rainfall, has also been shown to cause low birth weight (Prentice *et al.*, 1987).

TETANUS. The other major cause of neonatal mortality that we need to consider is tetanus. The prevalence of this disease varies greatly in different parts of Africa. In some countries, such as Lesotho, it appears to be almost unknown (Timæus, 1984); in others, most notably Sierra Leone, it accounts for between one-quarter and one-third of all infant deaths (Kandeh and Dow, 1987). The ecological factors determining its prevalence are far from clear. In general tetanus is thought to be more prevalent in areas with warm, humid climates and fertile soils (Bytchenko, 1966; Stanfield and Galazka, 1984), and to be notably absent in high, mountainous, and arid areas such as Ladakh and the highland regions of Tibet (Ball *et al.*, 1987; Seaman, personal communication). But other relationships are not so clear. There is conflicting evidence as to whether the incidence of tetanus is greater in the wet or the dry season; some researchers have found that the presence of large animals is a risk factor, others have found no such relationship; and the prevalence of the disease can vary dramatically from village to village (Leroy and Garenne, 1987; Retel-Laurentin and Benoit, 1976). Thomas (1987) has shown that variations in the prevalence of tetanus in different parts of Sierra Leone cannot be explained either by differences in immunization coverage or by differing obstetric practices among traditional birth attendants. The major factor must be the relative presence or absence of *Clostridium* spores in the environment, which in turn must be influenced by ecological factors as yet to be elucidated. Tetanus is further discussed in chapter 11.

"Ethnicity" has been sometimes identified as an important variable associated with child mortality. In some cases this relationship may be explained by the fact that the type of country inhabited by certain ethnic groups tends to be either healthy or unhealthy, for the reasons suggested above. But it is also possible that customs might strengthen or weaken a group's defenses against environmental hazards. A preliminary checklist of such practices would include the following:

- Obstetric methods used by traditional birth attendants, especially the type of dressing put on the umbilical stump
- Traditions affecting the duration of breast-feeding, including that of full, unsupplemented breast-feeding and the appropriate period before breast-feeding should cease altogether
- Type and nutritional value of the weaning foods generally given to infants and the methods of their preparation, particularly their susceptibility to bacterial contamination
- Traditional diets and food avoidances likely to affect the nutritional status of pregnant and breast-feeding mothers and hence the birth weight of their children and their own ability to breast-feed adequately

- Other traditional practices, particularly postpartum abstinence, likely to affect birth spacing
- Traditional treatments and remedies prescribed for childhood sicknesses, particularly diarrhea, with particular reference to whether or not fluids are withdrawn, and other practices likely to aggravate the condition and weaken the child, such as giving enemas of chillies, scarification, uvulectomies, or extracting milk teeth
- Traditional practices relating to sanitation and the disposal of human excrement
- Modes of living that affect crowding (whether, for example, the wives and children in polygamous households live in the same dwelling or are housed separately)

It would be possible to prolong this list indefinitely, but the foregoing will at least demonstrate that numerous aspects of behavior which are unrelated to socioeconomic status and development can nevertheless have an important influence on child survival. Among the mechanisms by which ethnicity may influence child mortality, genetic elements should also be considered. The most obvious of these is the sickle-cell trait, which protects against malaria but also contributes to infant mortality through sickle-cell anemia.

Conclusions

Most attempts to explain the massive differentials that exist in infant and child mortality among communities in Africa have concentrated on the apparent effects of a few somewhat crude indices of socioeconomic development. However, quantifying the contribution of these variables by the use of either bivariate or multivariate analysis has generally found them to explain only a relatively small proportion of the total variance. Even where certain variables, such as maternal education, are significantly correlated with mortality, the exact causal mechanisms have yet to be elucidated (Cleland and van Ginneken, 1989). Relatively little attention has been paid to the hazards to health that may be present in the environment or to the ways in which traditional practices may either provide the people with a valid defense against these hazards or open the door to their incursion.

To throw further light on this question, it is necessary to determine first the principal causes of morbidity and mortality. Cause-specific mortality rates are the product of incidence and case fatality, and until these elements are quantified, the search for determinants is likely to have only limited success. A classic example of this is provided by the case of Sierra Leone.

Kandeh and Dow (1987) showed that the district variations in infant and child mortality in Sierra Leone cannot be explained by variations in the provision of health services, in the endemicity of malaria, in maternal education, or in a host of other socio-economic factors. They also show that the leading cause of infant death is tetanus, and, as we have observed, the incidence of this disease tends to vary from place to place in an anomalous way that can only be attributed to poorly understood environmental factors. Until the contribution that tetanus makes to mortality in each district has been quantified and eliminated, the significance of variables likely to operate through other causes of death cannot be properly assessed.

The crudeness and inadequacy of the data for assessing even the overall levels and trends in infant and child mortality on a national basis make specifying age- and cause-specific mortality rates a tall order. It is in this respect, however, that relatively small-scale, in-depth surveys and surveillance systems, such as those described in part III, can make their most valuable contribution to our knowledge of African mortality.

References

Aaby, P. (1987). Overcrowding: a major determinant of variations in measles mortality in Africa. Paper presented at the IUSSP seminar on mortality and society in Sub-Saharan Africa, Yaoundé, Cameroon, 19–23 October.

Akoto, E. and Tabutin, D. (1987). Inégalités socio-économiques en matière de mortalité en Afrique au sud du Sahara. Paper presented at the IUSSP seminar on mortality and society in Sub-Saharan Africa, Yaoundé, Cameroon, 19–23 October.

Antonie, P. and Diouf, P. D. (1987). Urbanisation, scolarisation, et mortalité des enfants. Paper presented at the IUSSP seminar on mortality and society in Sub-Saharan Africa, Yaoundé, Cameroon, 19–23 October.

Bagster Wilson, D. (1949). Malaria incidence in Central and South Africa. In: *Malariology,* Boyd, M. E. (editor), vol. 2, pp. 800–809. Philadelphia and London: W. B. Saunders Company.

Ball, K., Elford, J., and Seaman, J. (1987). Tetanus and altitude. *Lancet,* 1, 801.

Blacker, J., Hill, A. G., and Timæus, I. (1985). Age patterns of mortality in Africa: an examination of recent evidence. *International Population Conference, Florence,* vol. 2, pp. 287–298.

Blacker, J., Mukiza-Gapere, J., Kibet, M., Airey, P., and Werner, L. (1987). Mortality differentials in Kenya. Paper presented at the IUSSP seminar on mortality and society in Sub-Saharan Africa, Yaoundé, Cameroon, 19–23 October.

Boerma, Ties. (1986). Monitoring and evaluation of health interventions: age- and cause-specific mortality and morbidity in childhood. Paper presented at the International Epidemiologist Association conference, Nairobi, Kenya.

Brabin, B. J. (1983). An analysis of malaria in pregnancy in Africa. *Bulletin of the World Health Organization*, 61, 1005–1016.

Brass, W. (1985). *Advances in Methods for Estimating Fertility and Mortality from Limited and Defective Data*. London: Centre for Population Studies.

Brass, W., Coale, A. J., Demeny, P., Heisel, D. R., Lorimer, F., Romaniuk, A., and van de Walle, E. (1968). *The Demography of Tropical Africa*. Princeton, N.J.: Princeton University Press.

Bytchenko, B. (1966). Geographical distribution of tetanus in the world, 1951–60: a review of the problem. *Bulletin of the World Health Organization*, 34 (1), 71–104.

Chambers, R., Longhurst, R., and Pacey, A., editors. (1981). *Seasonal Dimensions to Rural Poverty*. London: Frances Pinter, Ltd.

Cleland, J. and van Ginneken, J. (1989). Maternal schooling and childhood mortality. In: *Health Interventions and Mortality Change in Developing Countries,* Hill, A. G. and Roberts, D. F. (editors). Cambridge, England: Parkes Foundation.

Coale, A. J. and Trussell, T. J. (1978). Estimating the time to which Brass estimates apply. Appendix to: Fine-tuning Brass-type mortality estimates with data on ages of surviving children, Preston, S. H. and Palloni, A. *Population Bulletin of the United Nations*, 10, 87–89.

Fargues, P. and Nassour, O. (1987). Les saisons de la mortalité urbaine en Afrique. Paper presented at the IUSSP seminar on mortality and society in Sub-Saharan Africa, Yaoundé, Cameroon, 19–23 October.

Feeney, G. (1976). Estimating infant mortality rates from child survivorship data by age of mother. *Asia and Pacific Census Newsletter*, 3 (2), 15–16.

————. (1980). Estimating infant mortality trends from child survivorship data. *Population Studies*, 34 (1), 109–128.

Gaigbe Togbe, V. (1987). Saisonnalité et causes de décès infantiles à Yaoundé. Paper presented at the seminar on mortality and society in Sub-Saharan Africa, Yaoundé, Cameroon, 19–23 October.

Goetz, J. P. (1981). A study of childhood disease in Tanzania. In: *Seasonal Dimensions to Rural Poverty,* Chambers, R. *et al.* (editors), pp. 18–186. London: Frances Pinter, Ltd.

Hilderbrand, K. (1985). Assessing the components of seasonal stress amongst Fulani of the Seno-Mango, Central Mali. In: *Population, Health, and Nutrition in the Sahel,* Hill, A. G. (editor). London: KPI Ltd.

Kandeh, H. B. S. (1987). Child mortality differentials in Sierra Leone: influence of community and compound structure. Paper presented at the IUSSP seminar on mortality and society in Sub-Saharan Africa, Yaoundé, Cameroon, 19–23 October.

Kandeh, H. B. S. and Dow, T. (1987). Infant and child

mortality in Sierra Leone, 1987: a project report. Ford-Rockefeller Population and Development Policy Research Programme.

Kenya. (n.d.) *1979 Population Census*. Vol. 2: *Analytical Report*. Nairobi: Central Bureau of Statistics.

Leroy, O. and Garenne, M. (1987). Les deux jours les plus dangereux de la vie: une étude de tétanos néonatal au Senegal (Niakhar). Paper presented at the IUSSP seminar on mortality and society in Sub-Saharan Africa, Yaoundé, Cameroon, 19–23 October.

MacLeod, C. L., editor. (1988). *Parasitic Infections in Pregnancy and the Newborn*. Oxford: Oxford University Press.

Mbacké, C. and van de Walle, E. (1987). Socio-economic factors and access to health services as determinants of child mortality. Paper presented at the IUSSP seminar on mortality and society in Sub-Saharan Africa, Yaoundé, Cameroon, 19–23 October.

McGregor, I. A., Wilson, M. E., and Billewicz, W. Z. (1983). Malaria infection of the placenta in The Gambia, West Africa: its incidence and relationship to stillbirth, birthweight, and placental weight. *Transactions of the Royal Society of Tropical Medicine and Hygiene*, 77, 232–244.

Mosley, W. H. and Chen, L. C. (1984). An analytical framework for the study of child survival in developing countries. *Population and Development Review*, 10 (supplement), 25–45.

Ngatchou, R. D. and van der Pol, H. (1987). Niveau d'instruction de la mère et mortalité infantile: une évaluation critique. Paper presented at the IUSSP seminar on mortality and society in Sub-Saharan Africa, Yaoundé, Cameroon, 19–23 October.

Okoye, C. S. (1980). *Mortality Levels and Differentials in Sierra Leone*. Vol. 2: *Census Analysis*. Freetown: Central Statistics Office.

Prentice, A. M., Cole, P. J., Foord, F. A., Lamb, W. H., and Whitehead, R. G. (1987). Increased birthweight after pre-natal dietary supplementation of rural African women. *American Journal of Clinical Nutrition*, 46, 912–925.

Preston, S. H. and Palloni, A. (1978). Fine-tuning Brass-type mortality estimates with data on ages of surviving children. *Population Bulletin of the United Nations*, 10, 72–87.

Retel-Laurentin, A. and Benoit, D. (1976). Infant mortality and birth intervals. *Population Studies*, 30 (20), 279–293.

Reves, R. (1985). Declining fertility in England and Wales as a major cause of the twentieth century decline in mortality: the role of changing family size and age structure in infectious disease and mortality in infancy. *American Journal of Epidemiology*, 122, 112–126.

Rowland, M. G. M. (1979). Dietary and environmental factors in child mortality in The Gambia and Uganda. Paper presented at a conference on the medical aspects of African demography, Cambridge, England.

Rowland, M. G. M. *et al.* (1981). Seasonality and the growth of infants in a Gambian village. In: *Seasonal Dimen-*

sions to Rural Poverty, Chambers, R. *et al.* (editors), pp. 164–175. London: Frances Pinter, Ltd.

Russell, P. F., West, L. S., Maxwell, R. D., and MacDonald, G. (1963). *Practical Malariology.* 2d ed. London: Oxford University Press.

Serdula, Mary. (1987). Diet, malnutrition, and mortality in Sub-Saharan Africa. Paper presented at the seminar on mortality and society in Sub-Saharan Africa, Yaoundé, Cameroon, 19–23 October.

Stanfield, J. P. and Galazka, A. (1984). Neonatal tetanus in the world today. *Bulletin of the World Health Organization,* 62, 647–669.

Sullivan, J. M. (1972). Models for the estimation of the probability of dying between birth and exact ages of early childhood. *Population Studies,* 26 (1), 79–97.

Sutton, R. N. P. (1981). Respiratory diseases. In: *Seasonal Dimensions to Rural Poverty,* Chambers, R. *et al.* (editors), pp. 112–114. London: Frances Pinter, Ltd.

Thomas, Armand C. (1987). Levels and causes of infant and child mortality in Sierra Leone. Ph.D. diss., University of London.

Timæus, I. (1984). *Mortality in Lesotho: A Study of Levels, Trends, and Differentials Based on Retrospective Survey Data.* WFS Scientific Report, no. 59. Voorburg, Netherlands.

Tomkins, A. (1981). Seasonal health problems in the Zaria Region. In: *Seasonal Dimensions to Rural Poverty,* Chambers, R. *et al.* (editors), pp. 177–181. London: Frances Pinter, Ltd.

Trussell, T. J. (1975). A re-estimation of the multiplying factors for the Brass technique for determining childhood survivorship rates. *Population Studies,* 29 (1), 97–107.

United Nations. (1983). *Manual X. Indirect Techniques for Demographic Estimation.* ST/ESA/SER.A/81. New York.

———. (1985). *Socio-Economic Differentials in Child Mortality in Developing Countries.* ST/ESA/SER.A/97. New York.

———. (1988). *Mortality of Children under Five: World Estimates and Projections, 1950–2025.* ST/ESA/SER.A/105. New York.

van den Eerenbeemt, M-L. (1985). A demographic profile of the Fulani of Central Mali with special emphasis on infant and child mortality. In: *Population, Health, and Nutrition in the Sahel.,* Hill, A. G. (editor). London: KPI, Ltd.

Williams, G. W. (1987). Disease and inequalities in infant and child mortality in rural Kenya. Paper presented at the IUSSP seminar on mortality and society in Sub-Saharan Africa, Yaoundé, Cameroon, 19–23 October.

Woods, R. (1987). The effects of population redistribution on the level of mortality in 19th century England and Wales. *Journal of Economic History,* 45 (3), 645–651.

Chapter 5

Adult Mortality: Levels, Trends, and Data Sources

Ian M. Timæus

In Sub-Saharan Africa the death of adults before they reach old age remains a major health problem. At current levels of mortality the proportion of Africans age 15 who can expect to die before age 60 ranges from around 20 percent to over 50 percent. Despite its high level in Sub-Saharan Africa, adult mortality is a public health issue that has received much less attention than infant and child mortality. A summary of some of the factors underlying this neglect constitutes a useful introduction to this chapter.

Both explicitly and implicitly, because the provision of primary health care has been given high priority in recent years, research attention and health care expenditure have been directed toward the problems of child health. The first consideration of importance is that a large proportion of all serious ill health and deaths occurs among young children. Disease incidence and mortality rates among children are an order of magnitude higher than those among young adults. In addition, high levels of fertility mean that in most of Africa, some 45 percent of the population are below the age of 15. While these facts are of major practical significance, the adoption of a lifetime perspective on the chances of ill health and death suggests a rather different picture. The probability that a person born in Africa will die between the ages of 15 and 60 is broadly similar to the probability that he or she will die in childhood. Moreover, the social and economic consequences of the deaths of young adults are particularly serious. Such deaths represent the loss of experienced and productive members of the labor force, and the great majority produce a widowed spouse. In a typical African population about 175 children less than 15 years old will be orphaned for every 100 women age 15 to 59 who die. Among the most vulnerable groups, serious illness of the principal breadwinner can set off a cycle of increasing privation

and ill health that may result in the extinction of the whole family.

A second reason why attention is concentrated on child health is that the great majority of deaths in childhood occur from a limited number of infectious diseases. Diarrhea, acute respiratory infections (ARI), malaria, measles, and neonatal tetanus figure prominently. Most deaths from such causes are readily preventable. In contrast, the health problems of adults are both more diverse and, to some extent, more intractable. Again this view needs to be qualified. Diarrhea, ARI, and malaria are common illnesses among adults as well as children. Moreover, although it may be difficult to identify single interventions that would have the massive impact on adult mortality that many believe oral rehydration therapy and immunization programs can have on child mortality, a substantial proportion of adult deaths arises from a limited range of diseases that could be treated by a basic, but effective, health care system. Indeed it can be argued that the achievements of countries such as China, Costa Rica, and Sri Lanka, which have attained good health at low cost (Halstead *et al.*, 1985), have been as impressive in the field of adult mortality as in that of child mortality.

A third reason for the lack of research into public health issues relating to adult mortality and morbidity is the relative difficulty of obtaining population-based measures relevant to the health problems of adults. Because the incidence of disease and death is much lower among adults than children, large-scale studies are required to obtain samples of events large enough for statistical analysis. Moreover, while data about dead children can readily be collected from their parents, identifying a respondent who can supply useful information about dead adults is more difficult. Yet, in part, such difficulties reflect the priorities of planners and researchers. Investigations that focus on child health are unlikely to provide optimal vehicles for studying adult health. Routinely collected registration and facility-based data are often neglected because they yield incomplete statistics on children's health. In some instances, however, they can provide a representative picture of the patterns of disease and death affecting adults.

Sources of Data

Before reviewing the available information on adult health and mortality in Africa, this chapter will describe the sources from which such data can be obtained and the limitations of the scope and quality of the statistics that are presented in the following sections. On the basis of this assessment, some suggestions will be ventured concerning priorities for data collection.

In almost all of Sub-Saharan Africa the registration of vital events, and in particular of deaths, is far too incomplete for data derived from the registration system to be useful for demographic estimation. The majority of deaths occur outside the framework of the official health care system, and legal and administrative exigencies, such as the requirement that a death certificate be produced before a corpse can be disposed of, fail to operate. Despite their limitations, vital registration statistics do have unexploited potential for the study of adult mortality. The registration of adult deaths is typically more complete than that of deaths of young children. Techniques exist for evaluating the completeness of reports of adult deaths that, in favorable conditions, can be used to adjust the data (see, for example, United Nations, 1983). With a few exceptions, national death registration statistics in Sub-Saharan Africa are far too incomplete for researchers to consider applying such methods. In some countries coverage is much better in certain areas, such as major cities, than elsewhere. Moreover, particularly in cities, death statistics collected by the authority responsible for issuing burial permits may be more complete than those derived from the civil registration system (Hill and Kaufmann, 1987). Although the impact of migration on the age structure of the populations of small areas renders many methods of evaluating and adjusting death statistics inappropriate, useful results have been obtained by approaches based on model life tables and the age distribution of reported deaths (Courbage and Fargues, 1979; Fargues and Nassour, 1987).

Apart from civil registration systems, the major source of routine statistics on adult mortality and morbidity is the health care system. In most of Sub-Saharan Africa such statistics are of limited utility. By definition they refer only to the limited portion of the population that is in contact with the health services. Often they are further restricted to data on hospital inpatients. Thus health service statistics are not only incomplete but subject to numerous selection biases when treated as data on the health problems of the entire population. In addition, in many countries the persons responsible for making statistical returns are overwhelmed by the demands put on them, which leads to delays and inaccuracies in the production of tables. Simpler reporting systems are needed that encompass primary health care as well as hospital-based services and that can rapidly and reliably produce a few key indicators to be fed back into the planning and monitoring processes (Graham, 1986).

The inadequacy of routinely collected administrative statistics on adult mortality in Sub-Saharan Africa means that most of the data available on the subject have been collected in ad hoc enquiries. Unfortunately, the retrospective questions concerning adult deaths that are asked in censuses and surveys have been less successful than the equivalent questions about child mortality. The conceptually most straightforward approach, which is to ask household heads about deaths in their households in the past 12 or 24 months, has performed particularly badly. The 1981 census of Botswana is the only census to yield data complete enough to analyze. Even in several carefully conducted surveys that took place under the World Fertility Survey (WFS) umbrella, this approach provided useful information in only one country, Lesotho. One or two further successes include some of the early surveys conducted in francophone Africa, which were particularly meticulous. The enquiry in Guinea, for example, adopted exhaustive measures, such as combing the bush for freshly dug graves, to ensure that deaths were reported completely.

Another problem with this approach is that estimating adult mortality precisely requires a large sample of perhaps 20,000 households (Blacker and Scott, 1974). In general, the approach cannot be recommended.

An alternative source of information on adult mortality consists of longitudinal studies. In a Sub-Saharan African context these can be divided fairly clearly into two groups. First are national multiround surveys designed to estimate demographic rates, such as those conducted in the early 1970s in Burundi, Liberia, and Malawi or more recently in Côte d'Ivoire and Senegal. Second are the more intensive studies of smaller, geographically localized populations.

Multiround surveys greatly reduce the reference period errors and omissions that vitiate retrospective questions about recent deaths. In these surveys data are collected about deaths in previously enumerated households during the intervals between rounds of the survey. Unfortunately, such surveys are complex and expensive operations. Information has to be collected on a large sample of households in order to measure mortality levels precisely using one or two years' data; enquiries that are large enough to permit differentials in adult mortality to be studied are prohibitively expensive. Moreover, tracing and reinterviewing households after an interval of several months is difficult, and loss to follow-up is almost always a major problem. While many multiround surveys eventually produce plausible results, others collapse because of problems encountered during fieldwork and data processing.

The value of the data on adult mortality that have been collected in in-depth population laboratory studies conducted in Africa is variable. Some studies devoted great efforts to collecting accurate information on adult ages and deaths and yielded extremely useful information (Pison and Langaney, 1985). On the other hand, the data collected in Malumfashi were clearly deficient (see chapter 21 and Bradley *et al.*, 1982), and the level of adult mortality recorded in Machakos was so light as to seem implausible (see chapter 18 and van Ginneken *et al.*, 1984). Measuring adult mortality was only a subsidiary objective of these studies. Many prospective epidemiological investigations concentrate entirely on child health, and most longitudinal studies conducted in Africa cover too small a population to allow the health problems of adults to be investigated in any detail. For example, the life tables that are available for Ngayokheme (Cantrelle *et al.*, 1986), Bandafassi (Pison and Langaney, 1985), and Keneba (see chapter 20 and Billewicz and McGregor, 1981) are based on deaths recorded during a period of more than a decade.

Adult mortality can also be estimated from the age distributions of two successive censuses using a variety of methods based on intercensal survival and growth (see, for example, United Nations, 1983). The high level of migration among countries and the poor reporting of age make the application of such techniques problematic in Africa. On the whole, analyses based on the changes that occurred between the 1970 round of censuses and the less sophisticated population counts that occurred previously did not prove very fruitful. Estimates based on the 1970 and 1980 round of censuses may be more reliable. One possible

strategy is to use an intercensal projection to assess the plausibility of fertility and mortality estimates derived from retrospective questions.

A second approach that can be used to collect information retrospectively about adult mortality is to ask questions about the survival of close relatives, parents in particular, but also spouses, and to estimate mortality from these data using models of demographic relationships (see, for example, United Nations, 1983). The questions on widowhood have not been used widely in Africa. In the wfs surveys they did not perform particularly well, and they cannot be recommended for use in national censuses. On occasion, however, plausible estimates of male mortality have been obtained from questions asking women about the survival of their first husband, and the approach may be worth pursuing in surveys for which estimating adult mortality is a major objective (Timæus, 1987b).

Much more experience has been gained in the use of questions about orphanhood. There are theoretical reasons to expect the approach to underestimate somewhat the level of adult mortality (Palloni *et al.*, 1984). Comparisons with other sources of estimates tend to confirm this view. In some applications, however, the orphanhood method has performed as well as much more expensive ways of collecting data (Blacker, 1977). Orphanhood-based estimates of adult mortality in 12 Sub-Saharan African countries are presented in figures 5-1, 5-2, and 5-3.[1] These estimates were made by reanalyzing data contained in census reports and wfs household survey data files, using methods developed for measuring long-term trends in mortality (Brass and Bamgboye, 1981).

One particular concern about the orphanhood technique is the adoption effect, that is, the underreporting of orphanhood by respondents who lost their parents at young ages but whose replies refer to their foster parents or stepparents. The impact of the adoption effect is greatest on estimates based on the reports of young respondents, and this problem may underlie the implausibly steep declines in the level of adult mortality and the inconsistency of successive series of orphanhood estimates observed in several East African countries (see figure 5-2 and the discussions in Timæus, 1986, and Blacker and Mukiza-Gapere, 1988). The mortality estimates for such countries are based, where possible, on the reports of adults. It is reasonable to suppose that the impact of the adoption effect on reporting about mothers is larger than its impact on reporting about fathers. This probably underlies the tendency for orphanhood data collected

Figure 5-1. Life Expectancy at Age 15, Selected Countries of West Africa, Estimated from Orphanhood Data, 1945–80

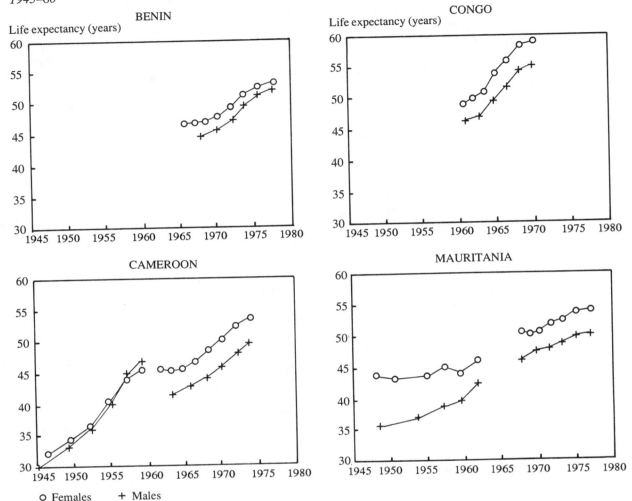

o Females   + Males

in Africa to indicate steeper declines in the level of adult female, than of adult male, mortality (see, for example, Kenya in figure 5-2 or Botswana and Zimbabwe in figure 5-3). Nevertheless, recent assessments emphasize the major contribution made by orphanhood-based estimates to our knowledge of adult mortality in Sub-Saharan Africa (Blacker and Mukiza-Gapere, 1988). The consistency of successive series of orphanhood data and of orphanhood-based and other estimates in countries such as Cameroon, Lesotho, Mauritania, and Sudan is impressive and suggests that, in at least these countries, the questions have worked well.

Use of questions about orphanhood can therefore be recommended. Their value is greatly enhanced once

two sets of data are available for a single country and their consistency can be compared. Recent methodological advances that take full advantage of this (Timæus, 1986) and that define the period of exposure to risk much more closely (Chackiel and Orellana, 1985) should lead to increasing returns from the collection of orphanhood data. It is unfortunate that these questions have not been asked in all the Demographic and Health Surveys conducted in Africa.

Mortality Levels

Considering the sources of data clearly reveals how little is known about adult mortality in Sub-Saharan Africa. In broad terms it is possible to indicate the levels of infant and child mortality prevailing across

Figure 5-2. *Life Expectancy at Age 15, Selected Countries of East Africa, Estimated from Orphanhood Data, 1945–80*

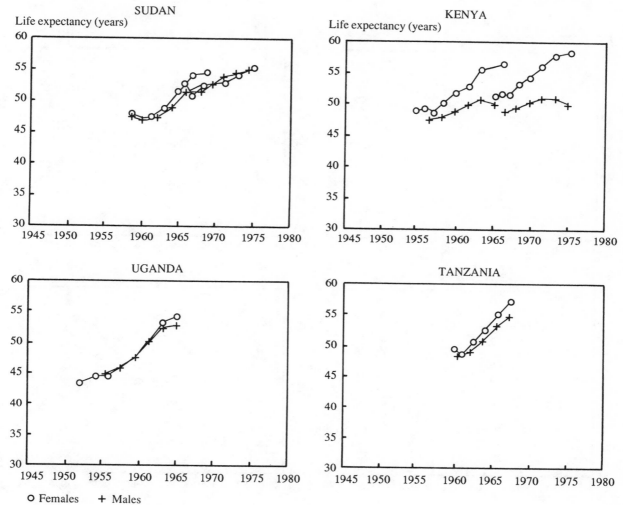

O Females   + Males

the continent and the pattern of decline in early-age mortality since the 1950s (see, for example, chapter 3 and United Nations, 1988). To do the same for adult mortality is impossible even though the available data suggest significant patterns that deserve further investigation.

Table 5-1 presents estimates of the expectation of life at age 15 in 16 Sub-Saharan African countries during the 1970s and during 1964–69 in another five countries for which no more recent information is available.[2] Unfortunately, well-founded national estimates cannot be made for some populous countries such as Ethiopia and Nigeria. Most of the measures were obtained from data on orphanhood or from multiround survey data. With the exception of western

Zaire, the orphanhood-based estimates were calculated by fitting a regression line to the analyses shown in figures 5-1, 5-2, and 5-3 (together with the comparable data for the Gambia and Sierra Leone), excluding any discrepant estimates derived from the oldest and youngest respondents. The table also includes measures of the per capita GNP in 1983 U.S. dollars for the date of the mortality data. These measures are based on World Bank figures for 1983 and on the average rate of growth in per capita GNP over the period 1965–83 (World Bank, 1986).

The life chances of adults in Sub-Saharan Africa are very heterogeneous. In the 1970s life expectancy at age 15 ranged from under 40 years in Sierra Leone to more than 55 years in the northern half of the Sudan.

Figure 5-3. Life Expectancy at Age 15, Selected Countries of Southern Africa, Estimated from Orphanhood Data, 1945–80

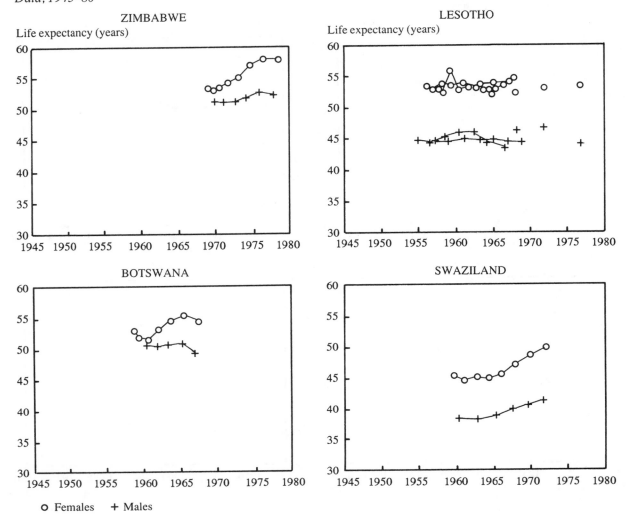

o Females   + Males

All the available sources of data for Africa tend to understate adult mortality; despite this, in half the countries for which estimates are presented, life expectancy at age 15 remained well under 50 years during the 1970s. This accords with evidence, shown in table 5-2, from some of the smaller, more intensive longitudinal studies that have been conducted in West Africa. In contrast, in most of the developing world life expectancy at age 15 is at least 50 years, and some middle-income countries now have levels of adult mortality within the range found in the developed world (Feachem *et al.*, 1989).

National estimates of adult mortality obscure considerable differentials within countries. In Kenya life expectancy at age 15 ranges from around 45 years to

57 years in different districts (Blacker *et al.*, 1987). This range is nearly as large as that existing between countries. The surveys conducted in West Zaire in the mid-1970s found that the same measure varied between 40.9 years in the less developed districts and 47.4 years in Bas Zaire (Université Catholique de Louvain, 1978). To take one example of differences in adult mortality among socioeconomic groups, detailed analysis of data collected in the Lesotho Fertility Survey suggests that the parents of respondents with secondary schooling can expect to live about six years longer than those of respondents without formal schooling (Timæus, 1984).

Despite the measure's lack of specificity and the existence of important exceptions, the level of mor-

Table 5-1. Life Expectancy at Age 15 (e$_{15}$), Sub-Saharan Africa, Various Years

Country	Date	Life expectancy at age 15			Per capita GNP (dollars)	Method of estimation
		Males	Females	Both sexes		
Senegal	1978	48.9	51.5	50.0	451	Multiround survey
Gambia, The	1978	51.3	53.4	52.4	271	Orphanhood
Sierra Leone	1970	38.0	39.7	38.9	286	Orphanhood
Liberia	1971	44.3	46.9	45.6	436	Multiround survey
Côte d'Ivoire	1978–79	48.1	49.0	48.6	679	Multiround survey
Ghana	1968–69	45.5	47.5	46.5	422	Sample registration
Benin	1970	46.2	48.3	47.3	255	Orphanhood
Cameroon	1975	50.5	54.2	52.4	663	Orphanhood
Congo	1967	53.0	57.1	55.1	709	Orphanhood
Zaire (west)	1964	—	—	42.8	218	Orphanhood
Burundi	1970–71	43.1	46.2	44.6	185	Multiround survey
Mauritania	1975	49.6	53.3	51.5	469	Orphanhood
Sudan (north)	1975	55.9	55.6	55.7	361	Orphanhood
Uganda	1965	53.4	53.8	53.6	495	Orphanhood
Kenya	1974	49.5	55.9	52.7	277	Intercensal orphanhood
Tanzania	1965	52.8	54.4	53.6	204	Orphanhood
Malawi	1971	48.4	45.4	46.9	162	Multiround survey
Zimbabwe	1975	52.3	57.0	54.6	657	Orphanhood
Botswana	1981	44.9	51.4	48.2	750	Retrospective reports
Lesotho	1976	42.3	52.4	47.4	300	Retrospective reports
Swaziland	1972	41.8	49.3	45.6	656	Orphanhood

Source: For Senegal, Cantrelle *et al.* (1986); for the Gambia, Blacker and Mukiza-Gapere (1988); for Sierra Leone, Okoye (1980); for Liberia, World Health Organization (1986); for Côte d'Ivoire, Ahonzo *et al.* (1984); for Ghana, Gaisie (1976); for Benin, Benin (n.d.); for Cameroon and north Sudan, WFS household survey data tapes; for Congo, Congo (1978); for Zaire, Université Catholique de Louvain (1978); for Burundi, Condé *et al.* (1980); for Mauritania, Timæus (1987a); for Uganda, Uganda (1976); for Kenya, Ph.D. dissertation in progress, courtesy of J. Mukiza-Gapere; for Tanzania, Tanzania (n.d.); for Malawi, Malawi (1973); for Zimbabwe, Zimbabwe (1985); for Botswana, Botswana (1983); for Lesotho, Timæus (1984); and for Swaziland, Swaziland (1980).

tality in a country tends to be related to the overall standard of living. On a global scale the relationship between life expectancy at birth and per capita GNP has been carefully documented and explored by Preston (1976, 1986). At first sight, the data on adult mortality in Africa presented in table 5-1 show no such relationship. It is also readily apparent, however, that the median expectation of life at age 15 in West and central African countries is about six years lower than that in East Africa. In figure 5-4 the estimates of life expectancy at age 15 are taken from table 5-1 and plotted against per capita GNP, for the nations of West and East Africa, and of southern Africa. Although the points are erratic, all the East African countries have lower levels of adult mortality than West or southern African countries with similar per capita national incomes. The low life expectancies found in the small sample of southern African countries are partly accounted for by their high levels of male mortality. Even on the basis of female mortality, however, this

region (which perhaps should also include Malawi) does less well than East Africa.

Although the reliability of some of the mortality estimates for particular countries is questionable, the overall pattern they suggest is likely to be significant. Regression lines fitted to the points for West Africa and East Africa in figure 5-4, with didactic rather than prescriptive intent, confirm that adult mortality tends to be lower in high-income countries. They also indicate that, on average, at any given level of per capita GNP, 15-year-olds in West or central Africa will die about five years earlier than 15-year-olds in the Sahel or East Africa. West Africa's particularly adverse levels of child mortality have been recognized for some time; this evidence reveals that the mortality of its adults is also unusually severe. Given the wide range of countries considered here, straightforward explanations of this pattern in terms of particular socioeconomic indicators or the availability of health services are unlikely to succeed. Instead the pattern is

Table 5-2. Life Expectancy at Age 15 (e₁₅), Selected Longitudinal Studies

Study area	Dates	e_{15}	Source
Ngayokheme, Senegal	1963–81	48.4	Cantrelle *et al.* (1986)
Bandafassi, Senegal	1970–83	42.7	Pison and Langaney (1985)
Keneba, The Gambia	1951–75	45.3	Billewicz and McGregor (1981)
Cape Coast, Ghana	1974–77	46.9	Jain (1982)

Figure 5-4. Life Expectancy at Age 15 and Per Capita Gross National Product, Sub-Saharan Africa, by Region

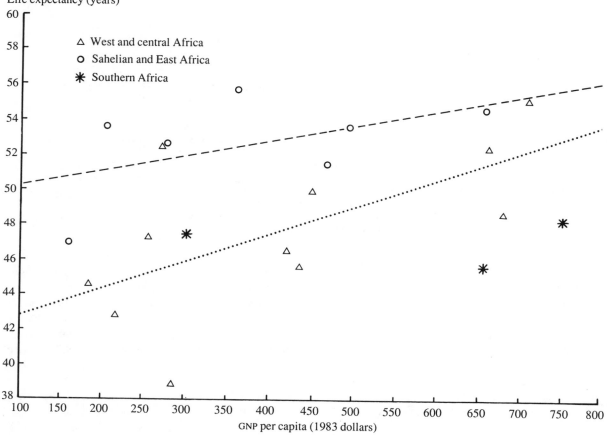

probably determined by the interaction of disease ecology with the physical environment on the one hand and broad aspects of culture and social structure on the other.

Mortality Trends

Rapid reductions in the death rates of adults have been achieved by many West and central African countries during the postwar period, which suggests that the relatively high level of mortality characteristic of these regions was at one time even more pronounced. The surveys conducted in francophone Africa between the mid-1950s and mid-1960s produced the bulk of the information on adult mortality available for that period. Although varying in quality, many of their results seem plausible (Condé *et al.*, 1980). In some instances the levels of adult mortality are very high. For example, surveys conducted in Guinea in 1954–55 and Chad in 1963–64 yielded life expectancies at age 15 of around 30 years. Whether the persistence of such elevated levels of adult mortality into the second half of this century was widespread is unclear. The surveys in Burkina Faso, Côte d'Ivoire, and Togo in the early 1960s estimated the expectation of life at age 15 to be about 40 years. Orphanhood data collected in West Cameroon also indicate very high levels of mortality in the 1940s but suggest that considerable advances had already been made ten years later (see figure 5-1). The early orphanhood-based estimates for Mauritania reveal a broadly similar picture (see figure 5-1 and Timæus, 1987a).

In much of West Africa the level of adult mortality continued to improve rapidly in the 1960s and 1970s. In Côte d'Ivoire the 1978–79 multiround survey found that the life expectancy at age 15 had risen to nearly 49 years from an estimated 38 years in 1961–62. In Senegal a series of multiround surveys indicated that it had risen from 41 to 50 years between 1965 and 1978 (Cantrelle *et al.*, 1986). According to orphanhood-based estimates, life expectancy at age 15 increased about seven years in Benin and Cameroon during the decade centered on 1973 and perhaps by even more in Congo during the 1960s; in the Gambia life expectancy at age 15, only 39 years in the mid-1950s, had reached 52 years in 1978 (Blacker and Mukiza-Gapere, 1988). By the 1970s life expectancy at age 15 in the countries just mentioned was probably only marginally lower than one would expect in an East African country with a similar level of income. Most countries that lowered their adult mortality had relatively strong economies by African standards; Benin and the Gambia, however,

seem to have reduced adult mortality to a moderate level despite remaining very poor.[3] Moreover, even in a high-mortality country like Sierra Leone, life expectancy at age 15 apparently rose about five years between the mid-1950s and 1970.

Orphanhood data for two Sahelian countries, Mauritania and the Sudan, also indicate rapid reductions in the level of adult mortality between the mid-1960s and mid-1970s (see figures 5-1 and 5-2). Although mortality was already lower in both countries than in most of the West African countries cited, life expectancy at age 15 probably increased more than five years in the decade before 1975.

The history of mortality decline in East and southern Africa has been rather different from that in the west of the continent. For a fairly large sample of countries, adult mortality in the late 1950s can be estimated from the 1970 round of censuses using reports from older respondents about the survival of their parents (see figures 5-2 and 5-3). None of these populations exhibits the very high mortality found in some West African countries at that time. Except in Swaziland, the expectation of life at age 15 was between 45 and 50 years.

It seems unlikely that the initial advantage enjoyed by these regions of Africa was followed by declines in their levels of adult mortality. In some cases the evidence is unequivocal: the mortality of adults did not fall to any significant extent in Lesotho between the mid-1950s and 1977 (see figure 5-3 and Timæus, 1984). In Kenya the two sets of estimates of adult female mortality are inconsistent, while those of adult male mortality agree that a very modest decline in mortality took place (see figure 5-2). If, as is argued in the previous section, data on the survival of mothers are more biased by the adoption effect than those on the survival of fathers, the data on adult male mortality are probably more reliable for indicating overall trends in adult mortality. Successive series of orphanhood data for Malawi exhibit inconsistencies similar to those for Kenya and offer little evidence of mortality decline (Timæus, 1986). Based on the estimates for males, the life expectancy of adults does not appear to have improved in Botswana or Zimbabwe, although some advances may have occurred in Swaziland (see figure 5-3). The estimates for Uganda and Tanzania are more difficult to assess. The information that survives from the 1980 census of Uganda suggests that earlier estimates exaggerated the degree of mortality decline (Mukiza-Gapere, personal communication) and that life expectancy at age 15 could not have reached 55 years in either country by the late 1960s.

Age and Gender Patterns of Mortality

The overall pattern of adult mortality can be compared with what we know about child mortality in Sub-Saharan Africa. The review by Hill (chapter 3, this volume) of data on child mortality concludes:

> Beyond doubt, a marked and consistent differential exists between the childhood mortality levels of eastern and western Africa. That differential existed throughout the postwar period, but has narrowed in more recent times. Childhood mortality has generally been much severer in western than in eastern Africa, with a rough gradient crossing the continent from northwest to southeast.

To some extent this generalization also holds for adults. West Africa appears to be distinguished by relatively heavy mortality at all ages and East Africa by relatively light mortality. The overall association between the levels of child and adult mortality does not, however, hold throughout Africa. In the southern African countries considered here, heavy adult mortality is combined with low levels of childhood mortality. The two Sahelian countries exhibit the opposite pattern. Furthermore, Blacker *et al.* (1985) demonstrate that the relative levels of early-age and adult mortality can vary markedly even among neighboring populations. In addition, postwar trends in adult and early-age mortality have been very different in a number of countries. For example, Sudan and Mauritania have experienced rapid declines in adult mortality in recent years, but there has been little reduction in levels of infant and child mortality in either country (see chapter 3 and Rutstein, 1984). In contrast, childhood mortality in Kenya has fallen rapidly compared with a modest improvement in its level of adult mortality.

The topic of gender differentials in the level of adult mortality deserves particular mention. In most of Sub-Saharan Africa such differentials are modest, and given the uncertainties in the methods of estimating adult mortality, no significance should be attached to small variations in their size. In table 5-1 only the multiround survey data for Malawi suggest that adult women experience appreciably higher levels of mortality than adult men. Estimates for Malawi based on changes in the proportions of respondents who were orphaned between the 1971 survey and the 1977 census suggest a similar conclusion (Timæus, 1986), which may mean that this population is genuinely anomalous. A much more striking feature of the estimates in table 5-1 is the very large differential in the level of adult mortality by gender in southern

African countries, Lesotho and Swaziland, in particular, where adult male mortality is exceptionally high. This is almost certainly related to the role that labor migration to South Africa plays in the economy of southern Africa and to the "epidemic" of tuberculosis originating in the mining industry (de Beer, 1984).

Ill Health and Causes of Death

Despite increasing interest in using health interview surveys to collect information about patterns of ill health in Africa, only a few published surveys consider the health problems of adults. What is perhaps most striking about the findings that are available is that many of the common forms of adult sickness in Africa are also common in the West (for example, Belcher *et al.*, 1976; Nchinda, 1977). They include respiratory tract infections, lower back pain, toothaches, various forms of physical injury, and acute diarrhea. Many of these health problems neither require nor are easily subject to effective medical intervention. A more distinctive feature of the pattern of adult disease in Sub-Saharan Africa is the importance of a wide range of parasitic infections. The prevalence of these diseases can vary markedly over a small geographic area, making generalizations about the impact of particular problems difficult. Even if they are seldom fatal for young adults, parasitic infections often impose major demands on the health services. For example, a study conducted in a rural hospital in Uganda found hookworm and schistosomiasis to be the main causes of hospital admission among patients aged ten years and over (Williams *et al.*, 1986).

Community-based studies of causes of death are particularly important because they provide information about patterns of life-threatening disease. Unfortunately, several of the investigations that used the fairly complete death reporting available for some urban areas focus on child mortality (for example, Adegbola and Chojnacka, 1984; Cantrelle *et al.*, 1986). Statistics on young adults from two particularly useful studies are presented in table 5-3. Those on Sierra Leone were obtained from death registration data that yield a plausible overall estimate of the level of adult mortality (Wurie, 1979). The majority of the deaths, 69 percent, were medically certified, and although dominated by Freetown, the area covered included rural dwellers. The Machakos data came from a longitudinal study of a rural population in Kenya, described in chapter 18. The level of adult mortality yielded by the study was very low, which can be ascribed to age exaggeration by persons over 45 rather than to omission of deaths (Omondi-Odhiambo *et al.*,

Table 5-3. Causes of Death for Ages 15–44, West Sierra Leone and Machakos, Kenya
(percent, unless otherwise specified)

Cause of death[a]	West Sierra Leone	Machakos, Kenya	Preston's estimates[b]
Respiratory tuberculosis	7.6	14.4	27.5
Other infectious and parasitic diseases	14.1	20.7	10.8
Neoplasms	1.2	7.2	3.5
Cardiovascular disease	8.2	2.7	9.5
Influenza, pneumonia, bronchitis	12.7	3.6	8.9
Diarrhea, gastritis, enteritis	4.5	1.8	2.3
Diabetes, ulcers, liver disease	6.0	6.3	3.6
Maternal mortality	5.1	3.6	3.5
Accidents and violence	8.0	23.4	12.1
Others and unknown	32.6	16.2	18.4
Total	100.0	100.0	100.0
Number of deaths	2,242	111	—

— Not applicable.

a. For detailed definitions see Preston (1976).

b. Calculated from cause-specific death rates estimated by Preston (1976) for life expectancies of 45–55 years using data on 42 populations and applied to a Princeton South stable population model, level 15, GRR = 3.0.

Source: For Sierra Leone, Wurrie (1979); for Machakos, Omondi-Odhiambo *et al.* (1987).

1990). The number of deaths is very small, but only broad features of the distribution of causes of death are considered here. To facilitate interpretation, these statistics have been related to a standard pattern of causes of death derived by Preston (1976) from historical data on European and Latin American populations with levels of overall life expectancy comparable to those prevailing in Africa today.

In broad outline, the pattern of causes of adult death in Sub-Saharan Africa is similar to that found in other high-mortality populations. The infectious diseases (with notable exceptions such as measles), respiratory infections, and diarrheal diseases that are major causes of death in childhood also account for one-quarter to one-third of the deaths of young adults. In addition, a number of health problems that have a disproportionate impact on adults figure prominently, notably, cardiovascular disease, respiratory tuberculosis, and accidents and violence. This is confirmed by studies in Bamako, Mali (Fargues and Nassour, 1987), eastern Ghana (Grosse, 1980), and Lagos, Nigeria (Ayeni, 1980).

In both Sierra Leone and Machakos the contribution of tuberculosis to adult mortality is far lower than it was in Europe or Latin America when they had levels of mortality similar to those of Africa today. (Nevertheless, tuberculosis remains a major cause of death.) In Ghana tuberculosis accounted for 10 percent of deaths at ages 15 to 44 (Grosse, 1980), while in Lagos

in 1977 it accounted for only 5 percent of deaths in this age group (Ayeni, 1980). Moreover, a study that covered the whole of Kenya and adopted a variety of methods to assess the importance of tuberculosis as a cause of death (Ewbank *et al.*, 1986) concluded that it was probably about one-half as common as would be anticipated on the basis of Preston's estimates. Two explanations of this pattern are probably important. First, although tuberculosis became a major health problem where mining and other economic developments during the colonial period brought large numbers of workers together in poor living conditions, the disease was never as prevalent in the rural populations of Sub-Saharan Africa as in the more urbanized societies on which Preston's figures are based. Second, Sub-Saharan Africa has benefited from medical advances in the prevention and treatment of this disease. For example, Ewbank *et al.* (1986) suggest that the declining importance of tuberculosis as a cause of death in Kenya since the early 1960s is attributable solely to the progress of the BCG immunization program.

A second broad category of adult deaths that the data from Sierra Leone and elsewhere suggest may be relatively uncommon in Sub-Saharan Africa is deaths from cancer. Cancer mortality may merely be particularly subject to underreporting. Whether or not this is so, some of the types of cancer that are most common in Africa differ from those characteristic of other regions of the world. Lung cancer and cancer of the intestines and rectum remain relatively rare, but liver cancer and cancer of the esophagus are much more significant health problems in Africa than in Europe or the Americas.

By definition, if tuberculosis and neoplasms are relatively uncommon causes of death in Sub-Saharan Africa, other diseases must be responsible for the region's persistently high levels of adult mortality. The data in table 5-3 suggest that infectious diseases, including malaria, are particularly significant. In addition both West Sierra Leone and Kenya exhibit high proportions of deaths in Preston's category of certain chronic diseases, which include various forms of liver disease. Cirrhosis of the liver caused 8 percent and hepatitis caused 4 percent of all deaths in the age group 15 to 44 in the Ghana study (Grosse, 1980). Fargues and Nassour's (1987) study of Bamako is even more striking: various forms of liver disease, considered together, represent the leading cause of death at ages 15 to 59 and were responsible for 13 percent of male and 8 percent of female deaths in this age group. They calculate that liver disease is responsible for the loss of more years of life above age 20 than any other disease.

Conclusions

This chapter considered, in turn, the collection of data on the health of adults in Sub-Saharan Africa, what is known about trends and differentials in adult mortality across the continent, and the patterns of adult disease and, in particular, causes of death in Africa. This concluding section attempts, briefly, to link these aspects of the discussion and to identify areas in which research is needed if we are to develop a more integrated understanding of adult health in this region of the world.

One theme of this chapter has been the primitive state of knowledge about adult health in Sub-Saharan Africa. This weakness is particularly serious because Africa is characterized by elevated levels of adult as well as of child mortality compared with much of the developing world. In much of the continent, adult mortality rates appear to be stagnating at relatively high levels, which emphasizes the importance of gaining a better understanding of adult health.

To extrapolate adult mortality rates from data on children can be very misleading. Genuine information on adult mortality is needed to formulate policy, but has only been collected in a minority of Sub-Saharan African countries. Recommendations about priorities for data collection are difficult to make except in the context of a particular country. Moreover, measures

that rationalize and improve routine reporting on the health of adults can only be proposed in relation to equivalent measures that provide more policy-relevant data about children. Nevertheless, two specific suggestions can be made. First, administrative statistics that include data on causes of death are recorded in a number of localities for a substantial proportion of young adult deaths. Although most are collected in urban areas, detailed analyses of a number of such sources of data, using standardized definitions and methods, could provide a much better picture of patterns of adult ill health across Sub-Saharan Africa. Second, to improve both national health sector planning and our understanding of adult mortality generally, priority needs to be given to producing district-level estimates of adult mortality. Detailed studies of Kenya (Blacker et al., 1987; Ewbank et al., 1986) have begun to reveal the gains that can be made using such an approach. Although problems are sometimes encountered in their analysis, incorporating questions about orphanhood in national censuses and large-scale surveys is the only cost-effective way of achieving this aim. Even where other sources of national estimates are available, including the orphanhood questions in censuses and producing tabulations and analyses for small administrative areas and different socioeconomic groups would be worthwhile.

Interpreting the data on adult mortality in Sub-Saharan Africa is perhaps premature at this time. The findings presented here probably underestimate mortality levels in particular countries by a substantial amount. They may be more reliable, however, as an indication of general patterns in adult mortality across the continent. The evidence that rapid declines in the level of adult mortality have been concentrated in the western part of Sub-Saharan Africa is fairly clear. So is the evidence that adult mortality remains higher in West and southern Africa than elsewhere in the continent. Very little is known about the differences and changes in the total burden of sickness borne by adults that must underlie such diverse experience. A better understanding of such issues could produce better strategies for health intervention. Information about patterns of causes of death would also yield insights. The key to a fuller understanding, however, must lie in detailed studies of the social and biological dynamics of adult ill health. Thus the case could be made for conducting a limited number of explicitly comparative, prospective studies of health and disease on a large enough scale to encompass the health problems of adults as well as those of children.

Finally, despite our ignorance, it is clear that

effective interventions exist against many of the serious health problems of adults in Sub-Saharan Africa. Tuberculosis, for example, is an important cause of adult death against which substantial progress has already been made. Most maternal deaths can be prevented by basic obstetric services (Fathalla, 1985). Improvements in sanitation would make inroads into a wide range of diseases. Moreover, many deaths from accidents and violence are clearly avoidable, including the massive number of deaths from traffic accidents in cities such as Lagos (Ayeni, 1980). The main obstacles to improving adult health in Sub-Saharan Africa are neither technical nor lack of information on the problems to be tackled. They are economic, political, and managerial.

Acknowledgments

The mortality estimates presented here for Cameroon and Sudan are taken from an unpublished study of data collected using the WFS household schedule mortality module. It was conducted by John Blacker, Rogelio Fernández, and myself with partial funding from the International Statistical Institute. I would like to thank Althea Hill, Jackson Mukiza-Gapere, and Mary Yamuah for providing me with data on Botswana, Congo, Kenya, and the Gambia.

Notes

1. Estimates obtained from retrospective questions about deaths in the household are also shown for Lesotho.
2. Table 5-1 contains estimates for the bulk of the countries for which well-founded measures exist of the level of adult mortality. It is not, however, exhaustive and is restricted to sources available in London.
3. The estimates shown for Benin in figure 5-1 could be biased by the adoption effect, but they are consistent with what is known about child mortality, which has been falling rapidly in the southern half of the country (Hill, chapter 3, this volume).

References

Adegbola, O. and Chojnacka, H. (1984). Causes of death in Lagos: structure and change. *African Journal of Medicine and Medical Sciences*, 13, 71–83.

Ahonzo, E., Barrere, B., and Kopylov, P. (1984). *Population de la Côte d'Ivoire*. Abidjan: Ministère de l'Economie et des Finances.

Ayeni, O. (1980). Causes of mortality in an African city. *African Journal of Medicine and Medical Sciences*, 9, 139–149.

Belcher, D. W., Wurapa, F. K., Neumann, A. K., and Lourie, I. M. (1976). A household morbidity survey in rural Africa. *International Journal of Epidemiology*, 5, 113–120.

Benin. Bureau Central de Recensement. (n.d.). *Enquête sur la fécondité au Benin*. Cotonou.

Billewicz, W. Z. and McGregor, I. A. (1981). The demography of two West African (Gambian) villages, 1951–75. *Journal of Biosocial Science*, 13, 219–243.

Blacker, J. G. C. (1977). The estimation of adult mortality in Africa from data on orphanhood. *Population Studies*, 31, 107–128.

Blacker, J. and Mukiza-Gapere, J. (1988). The indirect measurement of adult mortality in Africa: results and prospects. In: *African Population Conference, Dakar 1988*, vol. 2, pp. 3.2.23–3.2.38. Liège: International Union for the Scientific Study of Population.

Blacker, J. G. C. and Scott, C. S. (1974). *Manual on Demographic Sample Surveys in Africa*. New York: UNECA-UNESCO.

Blacker, J. G. C., Hill, A. G., and Timæus, I. (1985). Age patterns of mortality in Africa: an examination of recent evidence. In: *International Population Conference, Florence 1985*, vol. 2, pp. 287–298. Liège: International Union for the Scientific Study of Population.

Blacker, J., Mukiza-Gapere, J., Kibet, M., Airey, P., and Werner, L. (1987). Mortality differentials in Kenya. Paper presented at the IUSSP seminar on mortality and society in Sub-Saharan Africa, Yaoundé, Cameroon, 19–23 October.

Botswana. Central Statistics Office. (1983). *1981 Population and Housing Census: Administrative/Technical Report and National Statistical Tables*. Gaborone: Government Printer.

Bradley, A. K., MacFarlane, S. B. J., Moody, J. B., Gilles, H. M., Blacker, J. G. C., and Musa, B. D. (1982). Malumfashi Endemic Diseases Research Project. 20: demographic findings: mortality. *Annals of Tropical Medicine and Parasitology*, 76, 393–404.

Brass, W., and Bamgboye, E. (1981). *The Time Location of Reports of Survivorship: Estimates for Maternal and Paternal Orphanhood and the Ever-widowed*. Centre for Population Studies Working Paper, no. 81-1. London: London School of Hygiene and Tropical Medicine.

Cantrelle, P., Diop, I. L., Garenne, M., Gueye, M., and Sadio, A. (1986). The profile of mortality and its determinants in Senegal, 1960–1980. In: *Determinants of Mortality Change and Differentials in Developing Countries*. E.85.XIII.4, pp. 86–116. New York: United Nations.

Chackiel, J. and Orellana, H. (1985). Adult female mortality trends from retrospective questions about maternal orphanhood included in census and surveys. In: *International Population Conference: Florence 1985*, vol. 4, pp. 39–51. Liège: International Union for the Scientific Study of Population.

Condé, J., Fleury-Brousse, M., and Waltisperger, D. (1980). *Mortality in Developing Countries*. Paris: Organisation for Economic Co-operation and Development.

Congo. Centre National de la Statistique et des Etudes Economiques. (1978). *Recensement général de la population du Congo, 1974*. Vol. 4. Brazzaville.

Courbage, Y. and Fargues, P. (1979). A method for deriving

mortality estimates from incomplete vital statistics. *Population Studies,* 33, 165–180.

de Beer, C. (1984). *The South African Disease.* London: CIIR.

Ewbank, D., Henin, R., and Kekovole, J. (1986). An integration of demographic and epidemiologic research on mortality in Kenya. In: *Determinants of Mortality Change and Differentials in Developing Countries.* E.85.XIII.4, pp. 33–85. New York: United Nations.

Fargues, P. and Nassour, O. (1987). Les saisons et la mortalité urbaine en Afrique. Paper presented at the IUSSP seminar on mortality and society in Sub-Saharan Africa, Yaoundé, Cameroon, 19–23 October.

Fathalla, M. F. (1985). *The Causes of Maternal Death: A Global Review.* Geneva: World Health Organization.

Feachem, R. G., Graham, W. G., and Timæus, I. M. (1989). Identifying health problems and health research priorities in developing countries. *Journal of Tropical Medicine and Hygiene,* 92, 133–191.

Gaisie, S. K. (1976). *Estimating Ghanaian Fertility, Mortality, and Age Structure.* Population Studies, no. 5. Legon: University of Ghana.

Graham, W. J. (1986). *Health Status Indicators in Developing Countries.* London: Commonwealth Secretariat.

Grosse, R. N. (1980). Interrelation between health and population: observations derived from field experience. *Social Science and Medicine,* 14C, 99–120.

Halstead, S. B., Walsh, J. A., and Warren, K. S. (1985). *Good Health at Low Cost.* New York: Rockefeller Foundation.

Hill, A. G. and Kaufmann, G. L. (1987). *A Review of Materials and Methods for the Study of Infant and Child Mortality in Africa.* CPS Research Paper, no. 87-1. London: London School of Hygiene and Tropical Medicine.

Jain, S. K. (1982). Mortality in Ghana: evidence from the Cape Coast project data. *Population Studies,* 36, 271–289.

Malawi. National Statistical Office. (1973). *Malawi Population Change Survey, February 1970–January 1972.* Zomba: Government Printer.

Nchinda, T. C. (1977). A household study of illness prevalence and health care performances in a rural district of Cameroon. *International Journal of Epidemiology,* 6, 235–241.

Okoye, C. S. (1980). *Mortality Levels and Differentials in Sierra Leone.* Vol. 2: *Census Analysis.* Freetown: Central Statistics Office.

Omondi-Odhiambo, van Ginneken, J. K., and Voorhoeve, A. M. (1990). Mortality by cause of death in a rural area of Machakos District, Kenya, in 1975–1978. *Journal of Biosocial Science,* 22, 63–75.

Palloni, A., Massagli, M., and Marcotte, J. (1984). Estimating adult mortality with maternal orphanhood data: analysis of sensitivity of the techniques. *Population Studies,* 38, 255–280.

Pison, G. and Langaney, A. (1985). The level and age pattern of mortality in Bandafassi (eastern Senegal): results from a small-scale and intensive multi-round survey. *Population Studies,* 39, 387–405.

Preston, S. H. (1976). *Mortality Patterns in National Populations.* New York: Academic Press.

———. (1986). Mortality and development revisited. *Population Bulletin of the United Nations,* 18, 34–40.

Rutstein, S. O. (1984). *Infant and Child Mortality: Levels, Trends, and Demographic Differentials.* WFS Comparative Studies, no. 43. Voorburg, Netherlands: International Statistical Institute.

Swaziland. Central Statistical Office. (1980). *Report on the 1976 Swaziland Population Census.* Vol. 2. Mbabane.

Tanzania. Bureau of Statistics. (n.d.) *1973 National Demographic Survey of Tanzania.* Vol. 1. Dar es Salaam.

Timæus, I. (1984). *Mortality in Lesotho: A Study of Levels, Trends, and Differentials Based on Retrospective Survey Data.* WFS Scientific Report, no. 59. Voorburg, Netherlands: International Statistical Institute.

———. (1986). An assessment of methods for estimating adult mortality from two sets of data on maternal orphanhood. *Demography,* 23, 435–449.

———. (1987a). Adult mortality in Mauritania. Appendix to: *Evaluation de l'enquête nationale mauritanienne sur la fécondité.* WFS Scientific Report, no. 83. Voorburg, Netherlands: International Statistical Institute.

———. (1987b). Estimation of fertility and mortality from WFS household surveys. In: *The World Fertility Survey: An Assessment,* Cleland, J. and Scott, C. (editors), pp. 93–128. Oxford: Oxford University Press.

Uganda. Ministry of Planning and Economic Development. (1976). *Report on the 1969 Population Census.* Vol. 4. Kampala.

United Nations. (1983). *Manual X. Indirect Techniques for Demographic Estimation.* E.83.XIII.2. New York.

———. (1988). *Mortality of Children under Age Five: World Estimates and Projections, 1950–2025.* E.88.XIII.4. New York.

Université Catholique de Louvain. (1978). *Synthèse des études démographiques de l'ouest du Zaire, 1974–1977.* Louvain-la-Neuve.

van Ginneken, J. K., Muller, A. S., Voorhoeve, A. M., and Omondi-Odhiambo. (1984). Demographic characteristics of a rural area in Kenya in 1974–80. *Journal of Biosocial Science,* 16, 411–423.

Williams, E. H., Hayes, R. J., and Smith, P. G. (1986). Admissions to a rural hospital in the West Nile District of Uganda over a 27 year period. *Journal of Tropical Medicine and Hygiene,* 89, 193–211.

World Bank. (1986). *Population Growth and Policies in Sub-Saharan Africa.* A World Bank Policy Study. Washington, D.C.

World Health Organization. (1986). *World Health Statistics Annual, 1986.* Geneva.

Wurie, F. (1979). Analysis of mortality by cause of death for the western area in Sierra Leone, 1972–1975. M.Sc. thesis, London School of Hygiene and Tropical Medicine.

Zimbabwe. Central Statistics Office. (1985). *Main Demographic Features of the Population of Zimbabwe.* Harare.

Chapter 6

Maternal Mortality: Levels, Trends, and Data Deficiencies

Wendy J. Graham

Safe motherhood has recently joined the list of goals to be met by developing countries. This late awareness of unsafe motherhood is surprising given the historical evidence of the high mortality risks of childbearing in Europe during the nineteenth century. Comparisons have long been made between the current levels of infant and child mortality in developing countries and the historical levels in developed countries. However, the analogy between the estimated level of maternal mortality for, say, Sub-Saharan Africa now and for England and Wales a century ago has only recently been drawn, evoking a wave of international concern and activity. The affront that maternal mortality poses to global issues of equality—to Health for All by the Year 2000—is considerable. While the gap between child mortality in developing and developed countries has narrowed significantly over the past 50 years, measures of pregnancy-related mortality show wider international disparities than any other statistics of public health (Mahler, 1987). Maternal mortality is now seen as an indicator not only of socioeconomic development but also of sexual equality, since pregnancy-related deaths are being regarded as one more example of the neglect of the needs and rights of women in developing countries (Germain, 1987). Lack of information is both a cause and an effect of the more general neglect of maternal mortality. Data deficiencies impose major constraints on the programs being launched to reduce the number of pregnancy-related deaths and on the value of using maternal mortality to measure the progress of developing countries. The current picture is an incomplete jigsaw puzzle. This chapter attempts to put together the pieces for Sub-Saharan Africa.

A number of recent studies provide an overview of maternal mortality in developing countries; for example, Kwast (1988), Royston and Lopez (1987), and Weston (1986). Similarly, several others review the policy, programmatic, and operational issues faced in the Call to Action on maternal mortality; for example, Herz and Measham (1987), Maine *et al.* (1986), and Winikoff and Sullivan (1987). Comparatively few articles, however, specifically address questions about measurement and data sources; for example, Fortney (1987), Grubb *et al.* (1988), and Graham and Airey (1987). Fewer still focus on the overall situation in Sub-Saharan Africa; for example, Boerma (1987b) and Wallace (1984). This chapter combines discussion of issues of measurement with a regional focus and describes the levels, trends, and differentials in maternal mortality revealed by existing sources for Sub-Saharan Africa. It does not deal specifically with program options or describe the data sources in general. Since pregnancy-related mortality is a component of adult mortality, chapter 4 may be consulted for a general description of data sources. This discussion concentrates on the issues of specific relevance to maternal mortality.

Measurement and Data Sources

The recent literature demonstrates some ambiguity in defining the term maternal mortality. Some researchers regard it as a category of mortality comparable to adolescent, infant, or child mortality and define it essentially as a stage in the life cycle—here, the reproductive period. Alternatively, others regard maternal mortality as a cause of death. This chapter interprets it as a generic term for pathogenic causes, such as a ruptured uterus or postpartum hemorrhage. These different interpretations have implications for assessing the availability of information and the approaches available for measuring rates. Thus although particular sources may give a reasonably complete picture of maternal mortality overall, they may inaccurately assign maternal mortality to specific pathogenic causes. Similarly, recent advances in estimating levels of all-cause maternal mortality in the community do not extend yet to providing cause-specific estimates. Such observations can also be applied to subcategories of adult mortality.

Certain causes of death, broad or pathogenic, are easier to detect through routine sources, such as vital registration or household enquiries, than others. The accuracy and extent of reporting depend on a combination of the circumstances of death (sudden, violent, place, time-lapsed), respondent factors (sensitivity, relationship to deceased, memory, motivation), diagnosis (medical, lay, underlying, contributory), and incidence (age and gender specificity, geographic factors, temporal patterns) (Graham and Brass, 1988). These factors will obviously vary by cause of death. An appreciation of their influence on the reporting of maternal mortality is an important prerequisite to reviewing the data sources and profile for Sub-Saharan Africa.

According to the World Health Organization's (1977) International Classification of Diseases (ICD-9), "A maternal death is defined as the death of a woman while pregnant or within 42 days of termination of pregnancy, irrespective of the duration and the site of the pregnancy, from any cause related to or aggravated by the pregnancy or its management, but not from accidental or incidental causes." This is essentially a time-of-death definition, acknowledging the occurrence of death before or after the natural or premature end to a pregnancy (Royston and Lopez, 1987). Thus pregnancy-related deaths can in fact occur in women who are no longer pregnant.

The ICD definition highlights three key aspects of the measurement of maternal mortality. First, the group of women exposed to risk includes both pregnant women and women in the reproductive age group. The distinction between the two is reflected in the two conventional measures of maternal mortality: the maternal mortality ratio (maternal deaths per 100,000 live births) and the maternal mortality rate (maternal deaths per 10,000 women in the reproductive age group). Neither measure adequately reflects the two components of the probability of a woman dying of pregnancy-related causes: the probability of becoming pregnant and the probability of dying as a result of pregnancy (Graham and Airey, 1987). The second issue raised by the ICD definition is the inclusion of maternal deaths regardless of the gestational age of the associated pregnancy. Unfortunately, it is widely accepted that often neither the woman herself nor her

relatives acknowledge or indeed recognize pregnancies during the first trimester. Thus pregnancy-related deaths in this interval are almost universally underreported. This is particularly likely in the case of deaths arising from the complications of illicitly induced abortions. In addition to the potential for omissions in early pregnancy, the use of a 42-day cutoff point may also exclude some maternal deaths (Walker *et al.*, 1986). The third feature of the ICD definition relevant to measuring maternal mortality is the need to discount accidental or incidental causes during the specified interval, from pregnancy to 42 days postpartum. Pregnancy-related pathogenic causes can be divided into two major groups: direct obstetric deaths related specifically to the pregnant state and its management and indirect obstetric deaths due to preexisting conditions that were aggravated by pregnancy. The ratio between direct, indirect, and incidental causes depends on the level of maternal mortality. The higher this level, the lower the percentage contribution made by incidental causes to deaths of women during the reproductive period (World Health Organization, 1987).

The extent to which these three aspects of the measurement of maternal mortality can be adequately addressed varies according to the source of information. The countries of Sub-Saharan Africa do not differ significantly from other developing nations in the range of sources that exist but rather in their generally lower levels of coverage, completeness, and reliability.[1] The three main sources of data are vital registration, health service statistics, and population-based enquiries.

Vital Registration Data

The general characteristics and inadequacies of vital registration in Sub-Saharan Africa have been discussed in detail elsewhere (Makannah, 1984) and in chapters 3, 4, and 5 of this volume. In theory, period-specific maternal mortality ratios can be calculated using data from vital registration alone, the numerator being registered maternal deaths and the denominator registered live births. This is generally preferable to measures based on numerator and denominator information from different sources, but the potential still exists for inconsistencies that can produce considerable, but often unquantifiable, biases in the estimates. Overall, births are more likely to be registered than deaths, but in many Sub-Saharan countries with high levels of infant mortality, births failing to survive the neonatal period can be seriously underreported. Moreover, strictly speaking, the correct denominator for expressing the obstetric risk of maternal death is total pregnancies, a measure that is rarely obtainable. Where the level of induced abortion is low, live births underestimate the number of pregnancies by about 10 percent (World Health Organization, 1986a). It may be unsatisfactory, however, to continue to assume this low level in Sub-Saharan Africa (Coeytaux, 1988). If the degree of underreporting of maternal deaths is approximately similar to that of live births, the resulting maternal mortality ratio may give a reasonable population-based estimate. Although procedures exist for gauging and adjusting for underreporting of deaths from all causes, their suitability for adjusting broad cause-specific mortality is unknown.

In Sub-Saharan Africa vital registration typically covers less than one-tenth of the national population (Tietze, 1977), predominantly in the more privileged urban areas of the country. Combined with low levels of completeness, these low levels of coverage seriously limit the value of data from vital registration for studying maternal deaths. Mauritius provides a notable exception among the Sub-Saharan countries for the completeness and coverage of its vital statistics and the long time period over which these data have been gathered. This country gives a rare insight into trends in maternal mortality in a developing country (Mauritius, 1981). Elsewhere on the African continent the high levels of underreporting of maternal deaths by the vital registration system arise from two main sources: failure to register deaths and misclassification of causes of death. In the absence of incentives to register deaths, such as the need for a burial certificate, many social, religious, and emotional reasons explain why maternal deaths go unregistered. The absence of a responsible relative, as for example with unmarried women, feelings of culpability by relatives, and the desire to disguise an abortion-related death can all lead to underreporting (Royston and Lopez, 1987). Moreover, statistics on the proportion of particular causes of death that are not registered are rare for developing countries and are often little more than speculation. In Niger, for example, controversy over the relative completeness of data on births and deaths makes the claim that two-thirds of maternal deaths are unreported difficult to prove or to refute (Gray, 1984; Thuriaux and Lamotte, 1984).

In situations where vital registration is reasonably complete, generally regarded as above 60 percent (Preston, 1984), maternal deaths may still be underreported because the cause is misclassified. This is the major source of bias in estimates from developed countries. In the United States, for example, about 27 percent of deaths attributable to direct or indirect pregnancy-related causes are not coded as such (Rubin *et al.*, 1981). In developing countries the potential level of misclassification can be gauged by examining the proportion of deaths to women in the reproductive period that are assigned to the category symptoms and ill-defined causes. In Wurie's (1979) study in Sierra Leone, for example, just over one-third of the female deaths at age 15–44 were attributed to "others and unknown."

An alternative method for assessing the extent of misclassification, which is commonly used in developed countries (United Kingdom, 1979), is record reviews. This involves comparing the cause recorded on the official death certificate and that assigned by an independent information source, usually a health service record, for a sample of deaths in a particular period and population. Owing largely to the absence of a reliable independent source, this method is rarely feasible in Sub-Saharan Africa. Although outside this region of Africa, Egypt provides a unique example of the verification of official statistics using data from the Reproductive Age Mortality Survey (RAMOS) conducted in 1981–83 in the governorate of Menoufia. A recent comparison by Grubb *et al.* (1988) found that data from registered death certificates reported less than one-third of the maternal deaths identified by RAMOS, and this occurred in an area where the completeness of reporting all deaths after the first year of life was officially estimated to be 96 percent.

Health Services Data

This source of information refers to maternal deaths at fixed health facilities, in the case of Sub-Saharan Africa, primarily at hospitals. Although, strictly speaking, deaths occurring at lower-level facilities, such as clinics or health posts, should be included under health service statistics, they tend to be omitted. This is due largely to general inefficiencies in the administrative system of reporting and aggregating data and possibly also to concern that blame may be attached to easily identifiable health personnel. In parts of the developing world that have effective referral networks, it may be assumed that hospitals report the vast majority of maternal deaths, thus making lower levels in the health service less important as sources of information. This is not a realistic assumption in Sub-Saharan Africa, as is shown below. Reasonably efficient reporting systems based on primary health workers provide an additional and valuable routine source of community-based data in some developing countries (World Health Organization, 1988). However, this is still relatively rare among the Sub-Saharan countries (Hill and Graham, 1988).

The major consideration in using and interpreting hospital-based estimates is the question of selectivity, which can be discussed in terms of geographic, socioeconomic, or obstetric differentials. In the context of Sub-Saharan Africa, only a small but unknown proportion of all women at risk, whether defined as pregnant women or women in the reproductive age range, have access to and use hospitals. In addition, these women tend to overrepresent both high-risk referred or emergency cases and comparatively low-risk pregnancies of the richer socioeconomic groups (Graham and Airey, 1987). It is therefore difficult to identify the catchment population of the hospital in order to calculate rates or to claim that the estimates have any relevance beyond the population of women using a particular hospital. Similarly, problems may arise from the lack of an appropriate denominator for deriving maternal mortality ratios. Hospital deliveries are commonly used in conjunction with hospital maternal deaths, often without specifying whether they include only live births or fetal deaths as well. Despite these reservations, the absence of hospital-based studies would create an enormous gap in the overall and regional picture for Sub-Saharan Africa. These studies offer certain advantages over vital registration and population-based enquiries: they provide higher-quality cause-specific information and a better indication of the proportion of maternal deaths associated with induced abortions.

The problems arising from the selectivity of hospital data can be partially addressed by disaggregation. Distinguishing between major referral centers and district-level hospitals, for example, helps explain widely different estimates of maternal mortality. Kwast (1988) is thus able to explain the difference between a maternal mortality ratio of 442 per 100,000 live births in all health facilities in Addis Ababa and 1,268 in the Black Lion Hospital by taking into account the latter's role as the major referral center for high-risk pregnancies and obstetric emergencies. A similar case can be made for separating deaths associated with booked deliveries from unbooked, or emergency, deliveries. Aggarwal (1980), for instance, points out that emergency referrals from district and provincial facilities in Kenya to the Kenyatta National Hospital in Nairobi constituted only 3 percent of the total deliveries at that institution but accounted for 59 percent of the maternal deaths. Distinguishing between booked and unbooked pregnancy-related deaths also tends to control for socioeconomic factors, since

women fall into the unbooked category because they had no contact with antenatal services, which, in turn, is often linked with low levels of education and high levels of poverty (Harrison, 1985; Mhango *et al.*, 1986).

Useful insights into the selectivity of hospital-based estimates can also be gained by considering the rate at which an institution's statistics cover births. Assuming that high coverage of births equates with high coverage of maternal deaths, then the rate of births can be used to indicate the rate of maternal deaths (Boerma, 1987b). Of course, this raises the perennial problem of the correct denominator, since not all pregnancy-related deaths are linked to a delivery. Moreover, calculating the institutional coverage of births depends on the availability of reliable figures for all births. If all deliveries with professional assistance take place in health facilities, the institutional coverage would be, on average, about 34 percent of all births (Royston and Ferguson, 1985). This figure is likely to show a pattern of selectivity similar to that of hospital-based estimates of maternal mortality.

Population-Based Data

The third source of information on maternal mortality in Sub-Saharan Africa is population-based enquiries. It is also the rarest. Population-based data may be gathered retrospectively or prospectively, and estimates may be derived using direct or indirect techniques. In addition to the drawbacks of each approach, which were described in chapter 5, a number of other considerations are peculiar to estimating maternal mortality. Most population-based enquiries use interviewers who have no medical knowledge and thus are unsuitable for gathering information on pathogenic causes. Experimentation with lay reporters using simple diagnostic algorithms is still at an early stage. The time-of-death definition of maternal mortality at least provides a simple means of asking questions about deaths due to this broad cause. Similar surrogates for cause may exist for ascertaining other types of adult deaths in the community.

Retrospective surveys enquiring about deaths in the household over a recent fixed interval and prospective enquiries identifying deaths between rounds of a survey or through continuous surveillance both face problems with the number of observations. On a period-specific basis, maternal deaths are rare compared with, say, infant deaths. Thus in West Africa, for example, an estimated ratio of 7 maternal deaths per 1,000 live births compares favorably with infant mortality rates generally in excess of 100. This comparison does not allow for the number of times a woman is exposed to the risk of maternal death during her reproductive life and is therefore inappropriate for the purposes of allocating resources (Graham and Airey, 1987). Still, for purposes of collecting data, a large number of observational units needs to be studied in order to yield stable estimates. Kwast's (1988) survey in Addis Ababa, for example, interviewed more than 32,000 households and discovered that 45 maternal deaths had occurred in the two years prior to the interview. Similarly, Greenwood *et al.*'s (1987) one-year prospective study of 672 pregnant women in the Gambia identified 15 maternal deaths, and the Machakos study in Kenya (chapter 18, and Voorhoeve *et al.*, 1984) yielded only 4. Such small numbers of deaths preclude the investigation of key differentials and are likely to fluctuate widely over time.

A further problem with population-based enquiries using direct estimation is the simple omission of events. As mentioned previously, respondents withhold information on maternal deaths for social, cultural, religious, and emotional reasons. Close relatives, though intuitively the most suitable informants, may in fact be the least reliable (El-Ghamry *et al.*, 1984). An equally serious problem arises when the reporting unit is dissolved following the death of one of its key members, the mother. Thus, for example, the high levels of loss to follow-up encountered by the IFORD multiround surveys in West Africa (van de Walle, 1974) may have been due, in part, to the break-up of households following adult deaths. Similarly, surveys enquiring about deaths during a recent fixed interval may seriously underestimate maternal deaths when the same residential group no longer exists.

The sisterhood method, a recent development in the population-based estimation of maternal mortality, overcomes some of the problems raised above (Graham and Brass, 1988). As a new addition to the array of indirect techniques discussed in chapter 5, the method is at an early stage in its evolution. The results of the initial field trials have been described as encouraging by independent assessors (Arretx, 1988). As a comparatively simple and low-cost technique, it is particularly suited to situations in which the conventional sources of information are inadequate and are unlikely to improve dramatically in the foreseeable future. The sisterhood method provides a means of deriving indicators of maternal mortality from censuses and surveys that ask adult respondents whether any of their adult sisters have died from pregnancy-related causes (Graham *et al.*, 1989). Estimates of lifetime risk are calculated that provide an indication of the two essential components of the probability of maternal death. If the numbers of sisters reported in each respondent age group are large enough, both age-specific estimates and time trends may be examined. Since the method maximizes the number of reported woman-years of exposure to risk by asking each respondent about all of his or her sisters who reached reproductive age, reasonably stable estimates may be calculated based on relatively small samples of respondents. If a single estimate of maternal mortality is required, interviews with about 3,000–6,000 adults will be necessary, depending on the expected level of maternal mortality (Graham and Brass, 1988). Since the time that has passed since the reported deaths occurred will, on average, increase as the age of the respondent increases, a procedure was also devised for locating the estimates in time. The number of years prior to data collection to which the estimates refer ranges from about 5 years for the reports of respondents aged 15–19 to 35 years for those aged 60–65.

The first field trial of the sisterhood method was carried out in the Gambia in 1987 (Graham *et al.*, 1988). The population studied fell within the Farafenni surveillance area of the British Medical Research Council (MRC). The estimates derived from the sisterhood method, based on 2,163 adults interviewed in five days, compare favorably with those produced by the intensive prospective studies of the MRC (Billewicz and McGregor, 1981). Additional field investigations and methodological refinements to the method are under way or planned, which include the addition of simple questions on the place and pathogenic cause of death. Estimates using information on the sisters of adult respondents interviewed at fixed health facilities will be compared with those obtained from population-based surveys. Finally, techniques are being developed to derive current estimates of maternal mortality based on the sisterhood method.

The three major sources of information on maternal mortality discussed above yield widely different estimates for the Sub-Saharan countries. Although no single source is entirely satisfactory and multiple sources are essential (World Health Organization, 1986a), an urgent need also exists to reconcile disparate estimates and to produce information of value to the programs being launched to reduce the number of pregnancy-related deaths. An assessment is needed of the extent to which biases in the coverage, as opposed to the completeness, of the various information sources and in the denominators used, result in large but real differences in the level of maternal mortality. Policymakers and planners urgently require guidance in handling both the wide range of information available from different sources and for different populations and the huge variations in the estimates. The jigsaw puzzle of maternal mortality in Sub-Saharan Africa has many ill-fitting as well as missing pieces.

Levels of Maternal Mortality

The level of maternal mortality may be examined on four scales: global, regional, national, and subnational. A similar range of data deficiencies is faced on each of these scales, but the extent to which the pattern observed may be largely artifactual tends to increase as one moves from the global to the subnational scale.

The absolute value of global figures on the annual number and ratio of maternal deaths to live births must be regarded with caution; the relative picture may, however, be less distorted. Data from the World Health Organization (Royston and Lopez, 1987) suggest that about 126,000 maternal deaths occurred in Sub-Saharan Africa in 1983. In absolute numbers, this compares favorably with the 308,000 in Asia, but not with the 6,000 in all developed countries taken together. Relating these figures to the number of live births, and thus to obstetric risk, changes the picture, with ratios of 640, 420, and 30 maternal deaths per 100,000 live births, respectively, for these world regions. Thus Sub-Saharan Africa has an estimated 18 percent of the world's births but 30 percent of its maternal deaths (World Health Organization, 1986b). Even these comparisons based on obstetric risk do not, however, convey the overwhelming disadvantage of women in Sub-Saharan Africa as regards the probability of maternal death. To reveal this disadvantage, allowance needs to be made not only for the risk of death once pregnant but also for the probability of pregnancy. Comparatively high fertility combines with comparatively high obstetric risks in the Sub-Saharan African countries. Table 6-1, adapted from Herz and Measham (1987), shows the pattern of lifetime risk of maternal death and the level of fertility in selected regions of the world. Thus for Sub-Saharan Africa as a whole, a woman has a 1 in 21 chance of dying of pregnancy-related causes during her reproductive life, compared with 1 in 54 in Asia and 1 in 2,089 in Europe. Although these summary figures hide enormous regional variations among the countries of Asia and Europe, for Sub-Saharan Africa the lifetime risk remains high in all areas.

Table 6-1 also displays the level of maternal mortality on a regional scale. For Sub-Saharan Africa the pattern resembles that described in chapter 5 for all adult mortality. Levels are highest in West Africa

when expressed as the maternal mortality ratio. The low ranking of southern Africa may be explained by the inclusion of South Africa. The lifetime risk in East Africa is the next lowest, ranking equal with West Africa. Conversely, central Africa has a marginally lower lifetime risk, but a higher maternal mortality ratio, than East Africa. These patterns largely reflect variations in the level of fertility. The two measures, the maternal mortality ratio and the lifetime risk, however, assume constant risks throughout the reproductive period; the extent to which this is a valid assumption will be discussed later.

Comparisons between the level of maternal mortality on a national scale encounter serious problems with the coverage, completeness, and quality of data. The situation is compounded by variations in the definition used for maternal deaths in published figures and by the failure to indicate the categories included or excluded. Thus, for example, the ICD 42-day cutoff point may or may not be observed. Deaths during pregnancy, childbirth, or the puerperium due to incidental causes may be included or excluded. In particular, there is considerable variation in the way maternal deaths due to complications from induced abortion or ectopic pregnancy are dealt with in official statistics and selected studies. Moreover, as mentioned previously, it is essential that comparisons between estimates from different countries allow for the source of information. The crucial issue is that, apart from Mauritius, none of the countries of Sub-Saharan Africa has what may be regarded as national estimates of maternal mortality that are based on data for all areas and subgroups of the population. The figures quoted in the literature reflect any data that are available in the country and should not be regarded as nationally representative.

Boerma (1987c) has attempted to overcome some of these constraints and to draw national comparisons. Using an estimate of the all-cause mortality rate for women aged 15–49 derived from model life tables and an estimate of the average general fertility rate for Sub-Saharan Africa (214 per 1,000), that study calculated the maternal mortality ratio for each country. These estimates range from 827 maternal deaths per 100,000 live births for Chad to 217 for Kenya; the overall average is 460. Although the crudeness of the estimation procedure can be criticized on a number of grounds, the fundamental problem is the lack of independent information with which to evaluate Boerma's figures. Thus, the imprecision of mortality estimates based on model life tables is well known, and the use of a general fertility rate averaged across

Table 6-1. Indicators of Maternal Mortality and Fertility for Selected World Regions, 1975–84

Region	Maternal mortality ratio (MMR)[a]	Total fertility rate	Lifetime risk of maternal death[b]
Africa	640	6.3	1 in 21
North	500	6.0	1 in 28
Sub-Saharan Africa	655	6.1	1 in 21
East	660	6.8	1 in 19
Middle	690	6.1	1 in 20
West	700	6.4	1 in 19
South	570	5.2	1 in 29
Asia	420	3.7	1 in 54
East	55	2.1	1 in 722
Southeast	420	4.5	1 in 44
Middle	650	4.9	1 in 26
Southwest	420	5.8	1 in 34
Europe	21	1.9	1 in 2,089
Northern	5	1.8	1 in 9,850
Western	15	1.7	1 in 3,268
Southern	19	1.8	1 in 2,437
Eastern	44	2.0	1 in 947
World	390	3.7	1 in 58

a. Maternal deaths per 100,000 live births.

b. Calculated as $1 - [(1 - MMR)^{(1.2\,TFR)}]$, where the maternal mortality ratio (MMR) is expressed as a decimal and the total fertility rate (TFR) is adjusted by 1.2 to allow for pregnancies not ending in live births. The risk is expressed as odds.

Source: Adapted from Herz and Measham (1987).

Sub-Saharan Africa will undoubtedly differentially bias the estimates for different countries. Mauritius is the only country claiming to have national estimates, and its ratio for 1975–79 was 117 maternal deaths per 100,000 live births. Unfortunately Boerma did not include this country in his analysis.

Data from other parts of the African continent examine the level of maternal mortality on the subnational scale. Table 6-2 indicates the range of subnational estimates of the maternal mortality ratio available for Sub-Saharan countries in the past 15 years. It is difficult and probably pointless to discern any distinct patterns. Comparing, for example, estimates from referral hospitals for different countries reveals a huge variation, which possibly says more about hospital catchment areas, health service utilization, and the quality and availability of emergency obstetric care than about differences in the risk of childbearing. Examining patterns of maternal mortality is not directly comparable to examining geographic patterns in the incidence of particular diseases. Thus rural-urban differences in the maternal mortality ratio may reflect not higher rural levels of obstetrical problems or exposure to risk factors but differences in the uptake and availability of maternity services. Maternal mortality ratios in referral hospitals dealing with predominantly urban populations may in fact be higher than in regional hospitals covering both rural and urban communities, as seen in table 6-2 for Tanzania. Some authors have attributed such an observation to rural-urban differences in the frequency of induced abortions (Kwast, 1988). An alternative explanation is the more efficient and timely reporting of maternal deaths in towns and cities. At present, none of the countries in Sub-Saharan Africa has a sufficiently adequate statistical infrastructure to enable geographic patterns caused by data deficiencies to be disentangled from patterns due to risk.

Finally, the level of maternal mortality can be examined for its contribution to all female mortality in the reproductive period. This has recently been investigated by Boerma (1987a). The necessary data are, however, very limited in the case of Sub-Saharan Africa. The potential for examining proportionate mortality ratios and, indeed, case-fatality ratios among matched groups of women attending hospitals has yet to be fully exploited. Royston and Lopez (1987) suggest that the proportion of adult female deaths due to pregnancy-related causes for all developing countries is in the range of one-quarter to one-third. This is supported by a population-based figure of 29 percent for a rural area of the Gambia (Lamb *et al.*, 1984); the

Table 6-2. Maternal Mortality Ratio Estimated from Various Data Sources for Selected Sub-Saharan African Countries, 1950s–1980s

Country	Maternal mortality ratio, by data source[a]			Number of deaths	Year	Location[b]	Reference
	Referral hospital	Regional hospital	Population-based survey				
Ethiopia	1,268	—	—	89	1982–83	Urban	1
	—	442	—	182	1981–83	Urban	1
	—	—	566	45	1981–83	Urban	1
Gambia, The	—	—	1,050	12	1951–75	Rural	2
	—	—	1,005	91	1975[c]	Rural	3
	—	—	2,362	15	1982–83	Rural	4
Ghana	230	—	—	11	1981–82	Urban	5
Guinea-Bissau	—	—	473	6	1982–84	Rural	6
Kenya	511	—	—	17	1977	Urban	7
	—	—	86	4	1975–78	Rural	8
Malawi	—	263	—	112	1977	Urban	9
Mali	11	—	—	1	1979–80	Urban	5
Mauritius	—	—	117[d]	136	1975–79	Rural/urban	10
Niger	519[e]	—	—	374	1980	Rural/urban	11
Nigeria	1,047	—	—	238	1976–79	Urban	12
	634	—	—	141	1976–77	Urban	13
Sierra Leone	140	—	—	8	1980–81	Urban	5
Tanzania	680	—	—	85	1983–84	Urban	14
	—	253	—	89	1983	Urban	15
Uganda	377	—	—	256	1971–80	Urban	16
Zambia	118	—	—	60	1982–83	Urban	17
Zimbabwe	122	—	—	39	1987	Urban	18

— Not applicable.

Note: The maternal mortality ratio is the number of maternal deaths per 100,000 live births.

a. The distinction between referral and regional hospitals is not necessarily the same in all countries, but generally the former represents a higher level in the health facilities hierarchy.

b. Denotes where the data were collected rather than the population covered. (For example, regional hospitals tend to be located in urban areas but to cover a rural and an urban catchment area.)

c. Retrospective estimate based on the sisterhood method and referring to about 12 years prior to data collection.

d. Based on vital statistics.

e. All health facilities.

Source: The key for the reference column is as follows: 1, Kwast (1988); 2, Billewicz and McGregor (1981); 3, Graham *et al.* (1988); 4, Greenwood *et al.* (1987); 5, Wallace (1984); 6, Aaby (1987); 7, Aggarwal (1980); 8, Voorhoeve *et al.* (1984); 9, Bullough (1981); 10, Mauritius (1981); 11, Thuriaux and Lamotte (1984); 12, Harrison (1985); 13, Caffrey (1979); 14, Justesen (1985); 15, Price (1984); 16, Zake (1982); 17, Mhango *et al.* (1986); 18, Ashworth (1988).

Machakos study (chapter 18, this volume, and Voorhoeve *et al.*, 1984), in contrast, estimates 11 percent, which seems surprisingly low given the high levels of fertility in Kenya. Evidence from developed countries strongly suggests that the contribution made by pregnancy-related causes to all deaths of women in the reproductive age range declines as the level of all-cause mortality falls (Tietze, 1977). This has been attributed largely to the combined role of falling fertility and a decreasing number of exposures to pregnancy-related death; to improvements in the general standard of living, which affect the overall health status of women; and to advances in medical technol-ogy and the availability of maternity care to deal with high-risk pregnancies and obstetric emergencies. Support for similar temporal trends in Sub-Saharan Africa is largely circumstantial.

Trends in Maternal Mortality

The two components of the probability of maternal death—the probability of becoming pregnant and that of dying from pregnancy-related causes once pregnant—can contribute independently to a decline in maternal mortality. Thus it is possible for the maternal mortality rate (maternal deaths to women in the reproductive period) to decline without a decrease in the maternal mortality ratio. A fall in fertility will automatically translate into a fall in the number of maternal deaths, since fewer women will be exposed to the risks of pregnancy in a given period; this does not necessarily imply that the level of obstetric risk, expressed by the maternal mortality ratio, will also fall (Winikoff and Sullivan, 1987). To achieve the latter requires either a shift in the structure of fertility, such that certain women avoid pregnancy and other women avoid pregnancy at certain periods in their reproductive life, or an improvement in the availability and utilization of maternity services. The greatest impact is likely to be attained through a combination of both.

The evidence that fertility has fallen in certain countries of Sub-Saharan Africa (Frank, 1987) may be cause for speculation about the likelihood of a fall in the maternal mortality rate and in the lifetime risk of maternal death. However, the picture is complicated by the confounding effect of socioeconomic differentials in fertility and maternal mortality. More information is needed on how an observed fall in fertility is distributed among subgroups of women in order to gauge the likelihood and extent of a trend in maternal mortality. A similar argument applies to the numerous speculations about the potential impact of family planning services on reducing maternal mortality (Maine *et al.*, 1985; Trussell and Pebley, 1984; Winikoff and Sullivan, 1987).

Chapter 5 offered some evidence of a fall in all-cause female adult mortality in certain countries of Sub-Saharan Africa. These countries do not seem to coincide with the countries experiencing apparent falls in fertility. In Kenya, for example, despite some inconsistency in the timing of the increase, an improvement is discernible in female life expectancy at age 15. Nonetheless, the level of fertility in Kenya continues to be among the highest in Sub-Saharan Africa. In Uganda, by contrast, the possibility of increasing female life expectancy may tie in with evidence from two studies, quoted in Kwast (1988), that a 72 percent reduction took place in the maternal mortality ratio between the early 1950s and the late 1960s. Similarly, the national estimates for Mauritius show a steady decline from 349 maternal deaths per 100,000 live births in 1949–53 to 103 in 1985, except for a minor fluctuation between 1970–74 (Mauritius, 1981; Royston and Lopez, 1987).

Causes and Correlates of Maternal Mortality

Reviews of individual cases of pregnancy-related deaths have helped to distinguish four main tiers of

contributory factors: pathogenic causes, health service factors, reproductive factors, and socioeconomic factors (Kwast, 1987; World Health Organization, 1986a). This categorization is useful for discussing maternal mortality as an aggregate phenomenon.

Pathogenic Causes

Most of the information on medically defined causes of maternal death in Sub-Saharan Africa is derived, not surprisingly, from hospital-based studies. As mentioned earlier, only a small and selective fraction of registered deaths are medically certified, and the collection of causes in population-based enquiries using lay interviewers has yet to be fully explored, although intuitively it seems problematic. Hospital data show clear patterns of the principal direct causes of maternal death. Ranking these in importance is complicated, however, by misclassification biases and by the inclusion or exclusion of abortion-related deaths.

The situation is further aggravated by differences in the extent to which the International Classification of Diseases is followed. Thus both obstructed labor and uterine rupture are used selectively but often refer to the same condition, while sepsis and hemorrhage that are complications from induced abortion may be coded without reference to abortion or as complications of induced abortion. It is, therefore, not possible to state confidently that apparently similar patterns of pathogenic cause do not simply reflect the deficiencies and misclassification biases of the data.

Table 6-3 presents information on pathogenic causes from four hospital studies. Hemorrhage, sepsis, toxemia, uterine rupture, and complications from induced abortion together are responsible for about half to three-quarters of the maternal deaths in the hospitals studied, although their relative contributions vary somewhat. This pattern, which has been found in other regions of the developing world, may be an artifact of misclassification biases. For indirect causes of maternal mortality, there is a diverse range of conditions, including pneumonia, tuberculosis, cerebral malaria, and diarrheal diseases, which together make up the substantial "other" category in table 6-3. Many of the indirect causes may be linked with depressed cell-mediated immunity in pregnancy (Weinberg, 1984). Overall, viral hepatitis (hepatic coma or infective hepatitis) and anemia seem to be the most frequently cited indirect causes of maternal death in Sub-Saharan Africa. Both of these conditions can be linked with poor nutritional status, especially protein deficiency, and represent diseases of poverty (Kwast

Table 6-3. Distribution of Pathogenic Causes of Maternal Deaths, from Selected Studies in Sub-Saharan Africa
(percent, unless otherwise specified)

Country	Data source	Number of deaths	Direct cause						Indirect cause			
			Hemorrhage	Sepsis	Toxemia	Uterine rupture[a]	Induced abortion	Other	Hepatic coma[b]	Anemia	Other	Unknown
Ethiopia	Referral and city hospital	100	7	13	4	15	26	5	18	0	10	2
Nigeria	Referral hospital	141	10	9	9	9	0	32	7	0	16	9
Tanzania	Referral hospital	239	9	14	18	7	12	18	<1	12	7	2
Zambia	Referral hospital	60	17	15	20	0	23	5	2	3	15	0

a. Includes obstructed labor.
b. Includes viral and infective hepatitis.
Source: For Ethiopia, Kwast (1988); for Nigeria, Caffrey (1979); for Tanzania, Mtimavalye et al. (1980); and for Zambia, Mhango et al. (1986).

and Stevens, 1987; Ojo and Savage, 1974). Their prevalence is likely to be underreported, since few studies are able to handle multiple causes of death; yet they undoubtedly contribute to many fatalities that are classified otherwise. Harrison (1985), for example, noted anemia as a major underlying factor in deaths coded as hemorrhage.

Health Service Factors

Following a tradition established in confidential enquiries of maternal deaths in developed countries, such as England and Wales (United Kingdom, 1979), it has become fashionable to consider the proportion of maternal deaths that are preventable with appropriate health care (World Health Organization, 1986a; Mhango *et al.*, 1986). The claim that well over three-quarters of all maternal deaths are avoidable has attracted international attention (Mahler, 1987). The distinction between the availability and utilization of maternity care is useful, although it is sometimes used as a means of distributing blame between the health services and personnel and the deceased woman. The correlation between maternal mortality and the uptake of antenatal care has been shown in numerous studies. For example, the ratio of maternal deaths per 100,000 live births for persons who do and do not attend hospitals was found in hospital-based studies to be, respectively, 285 and 2,706 in midwest Nigeria (Hartfield, 1980) and 160 and 1,090 in Addis Ababa (Frost, 1984). Contact with antenatal services, when available, provides a basis for both preventive action in the case of pregnancies defined as high risk and curative care in the case of morbidity during pregnancy. Thus, so-called booked deliveries are essentially derived from antenatal care patients; inasmuch as a proportion of these are booked because problems are expected during delivery, comparing maternal mortality among booked and unbooked cases may in fact be confounded. Essex and Everett (1977) found in Tanzania, for example, that 80 percent of high-risk mothers could be identified during their first antenatal visit. Other authors emphasize the converse, namely that 15–20 percent of women will develop fatal complications that could not have been predicted in any number of antenatal visits (Maine *et al.*, 1986).

The low sensitivity and specificity of the indicators for screening are the subject of continuing research (Fortney and Whitehorne, 1982). The failure to predict life-threatening complications places added emphasis on improving the quality and availability of emergency obstetric services (Winikoff, 1986). Studies considering the contribution of inadequacies in these services

tend to distinguish between deficient medical management and lack of equipment and supplies (World Health Organization, 1986a). Mhango *et al.* (1986), for example, found that 52 and 2 percent, respectively, of the 60 maternal deaths in a Lusaka teaching hospital were attributable to these two deficiencies.

Reproductive Factors

Reproductive factors refer to the known demographic risk factors associated with pregnancy-related death, primarily maternal age and parity. A fairly extensive literature examines the independent and combined effects of these variables on maternal mortality, which can be summarized in the phrase "too early, too late, too many, too close" (Population Reports, 1984). Thus pregnancies at ages below 20 or above 34 years and at parity four or above are generally seen as high risk and the subject of targeting for both ante- and intrapartum care and the preventive strategies of family planning. The debate on the limited impact of this targeting given the large proportion of all pregnancies that do not fall into these categories has been raised elsewhere (Graham and Airey, 1987; Winikoff and Sullivan, 1987). First pregnancies, obviously one of the major factors associated with elevated mortality, cannot be tackled by family planning.

Most of the reliable evidence on the role of maternal age and parity comes from outside Sub-Saharan Africa and, indeed, from historical studies of developed country populations. The essential constraint of this information is that it contains insufficient numbers of maternal deaths to produce age- and parity-specific estimates, as seen in table 6-2. Thus, for example, considerable importance has been attached to Chen *et al.*'s (1974) study in Bangladesh, which is based on only 119 deaths and whose disaggregated figures warrant little confidence. The sample size requirements for looking at age, parity, and the combination of age and parity effects run into the several thousands and thus are most likely to be met by hospital- rather than population-based studies. The demographic selection factors in hospital-based studies, mentioned earlier, tend to coincide with the age and parity distribution of maternal mortality and illustrate the interaction between health service factors, reproductive factors, and data sources.

Table 6-4 presents the age and parity distribution of maternal deaths that was revealed by three urban hospital-based studies in Sub-Saharan Africa: Addis Ababa (Kwast, 1988), Nairobi (Makokha, 1980), and Lusaka (Mhango *et al.*, 1986). The table also raises a

Table 6-4. Maternal Deaths, by Age and Parity
(percent, for distribution of maternal deaths)

Ethiopia

Country and data source	Number or ratio	Age group						Parity[a]				
		<15	15–19	20–24	25–29	30–34	35+	0	1	2–3	4+	Unknown
Referral and city hospital												
Maternal deaths	100	1	18	23	24	18	16	31	16	25	26	2
Maternal mortality ratio[b]	983	n.a.	n.a.	n.a.	n.a.	n.a.	n.a.	n.a.	n.a.	n.a.	n.a.	n.a.
Population based												
Maternal deaths	45	0	18	31	22	13	16	16	24	20	40	0
Maternal mortality ratio[c]	566	n.a.	1,322	737	423	291	428	—[c]	814	321	361	0

Kenya

Country and data source	Number or ratio	Age group						Parity[a]			
		Unknown	15–20	21–25	26–30	31–35	36+	0	1–3	4+	Unknown
Referral hospital											
Maternal deaths	99	18	26	25	19	8	3	28	29	32	10
Maternal mortality ratio[b]	483	n.a.	n.a.	n.a.	n.a.	n.a.	n.a.	n.a.	n.a.	n.a.	n.a.

Zambia

Country and data source	Number or ratio	Age group				Parity[a]		
		Unknown	15–24	25–34	35+	0	1–4	5+
Referral hospital								
Maternal deaths	60	5	47	27	22	23	40	37
Maternal mortality ratio	118	n.a.	90	94	512	112	85	228

n.a. Not available.
a. Number of children previously born alive to a woman. Parity 0 refers to women who die undelivered during a first pregnancy.
b. The number of maternal deaths per 100,000 live births.
c. For parity, the ratio is expressed as deaths among undelivered nulliparous women to 100,000 deliveries to nulliparous women.
Source: For Ethiopia, Kwast (1988); for Kenya, Makokha (1980); and for Zambia, Mhango et al. (1986).

data collection and presentation problem, since standard age and parity groupings are rarely used. Moreover, a good case can be made for using a finer division for the under-20 age group since the 15–19 age group encompasses women with widely different risks. Age and parity, of course, are closely linked, with birth interval a confounding factor. Unfortunately, few studies from Sub-Saharan Africa enable their independent effects to be assessed. Nortman (1974) has examined the evidence from other developing countries and suggests that the effect of age is particularly significant for indirect obstetric deaths, while parity plays a proportionally greater part in explaining direct causes, such as toxemia and ruptured uterus. This ties in with evidence of a maternal depletion syndrome that is related to high parity and implicated in maternal deaths (Graham and Danso-Manu, 1988).

Socioeconomic Factors

Socioeconomic factors are closely associated with the reproductive variables discussed above. Thus, for example, a period effect is observed in the link between high maternal age, low educational status, and maternal mortality. Similarly, high-parity women, often with short birth intervals, predominate in the lower socioeconomic groups of many Sub-Saharan countries (Kwast, 1988; Harrison, 1985). Women with little or no education tend to be underrepresented in populations using antenatal care services or seeking professional assistance at delivery; as a consequence, they form a large proportion of the unbooked hospital deliveries that end in maternal deaths. Socioeconomic factors are also related to specific pathogenic causes, partly through the intermediary of age and parity. Cultural influences leading to an early age at first pregnancy, as for example in northern Nigeria (Harrison, 1985), contribute to problems of cephalopelvic disproportion, ruptured uterus, and hemorrhage. Deaths arising from the complications of induced abortion, on the other hand, are associated with the extremes of socioeconomic status and educational level (Coeytaux, 1988).

The four tiers in the etiology of pregnancy-related deaths represent overlapping pieces of the puzzle of maternal mortality in Sub-Saharan Africa. Socioeconomic influences appear to operate through proximate determinants of reproductive and health service factors to influence the pathogenic causes. The limitations of existing data and sources of information prevent the refinement and quantification of these paths of association.

Conclusions

The field of public health provides many examples of problems that are rapidly elevated to the level of priorities on the basis of limited information. Although this progression is triggered by a huge and diverse range of factors, an emotional component is often detectable. Such is the case with maternal mortality in developing countries. Here the rise to fame has many of the elements necessary to arouse international sentiment and sympathy; maternal mortality can be used as an indicator of a massive national division between rich and poor, of sexual inequalities in health risks and rights, of avoidable deaths, and of family tragedies with serious implications for the health and survival of the thousands of small children who lose their mothers every year. The information needed to push a health problem to the forefront of attention is often quite different, in quality and quantity, from that required to implement action. Of course, in the context of developing countries the reality of imperfect statistical infrastructure must be accepted with pragmatism. Delaying the initiation of programs and expenditures until perfect data are available would be to condemn to death thousands of women and their children. Lack of information was an accepted excuse for the comparative neglect of maternal deaths in the past. Now that the attention of the international community has been alerted, however, existing sources have become the basis for multimillion-dollar projects, in spite of obvious deficiencies in the data. Acknowledging the possibilities and limitations of these sources for decisionmaking may help to avoid disappointing results similar to those achieved by the child survival "revolution." Measurement-related research efforts should thus form an essential complement to the operational activities currently being emphasized.

This chapter has described the levels, trends, and differentials in maternal mortality in Sub-Saharan Africa. The importance of the accompanying critique of the nature and quality of existing data cannot be overemphasized. A cursory inspection of reports on maternal mortality in this part of the developing world over the past twenty years may create the illusion of a complete picture. What in fact exists is the outline of a jigsaw puzzle with ill-fitting as well as missing pieces. Comparisons within and between countries are virtually impossible given the huge variations among studies in the coverage of maternal deaths, the classification of pathogenic causes, the reference dates, the style of data presentation, and the details provided on methodology. The extent to which massive differences in the estimates of maternal mortality reflect patterns of risk rather than patterns of data deficiencies cannot be stated with confidence. Given the comparatively small proportion of women who have access to and use health facilities in Sub-Saharan Africa, the need for population-based sources of information on maternal mortality is obvious. Possibilities for meeting this need are being developed using indirect methods of estimation. Opportunities for quantifying the selection biases in health services data, however, remain to be explored. Methodological developments in measuring maternal mortality in Sub-Saharan Africa should be balanced by efforts to bridge the even larger gap in knowledge on maternal morbidity. Deaths averted is likely to prove as unsatisfactory an indicator and goal for the "M" as for the "C" in MCH (maternal and child health) programs.

Acknowledgments

I would like to thank my close colleagues, Oona Campbell and Ian Timæus, for commenting on an earlier draft, and Professor William Brass for supporting and encouraging my interest in maternal mortality.

Note

1. Completeness refers to the extent to which all relevant vital events are reported; coverage is the extent to which the entire population of a country falls within the vital registration system.

References

Aaby, P. (1987). Personal communication cited in Boerma, J. T. (1987c), Maternal mortality in Sub-Saharan Africa: levels, causes, and interventions. Paper presented at the IUSSP seminar on mortality and society in Sub-Saharan Africa, Yaoundé, Cameroon, 19–23 October.

Aggarwal, V. P. (1980). Obstetric emergency referrals to Kenyatta National Hospital. *East African Medical Journal*, 58, 25–36.

Arretx, C. (1988). Seminar on collection and processing of demographic data in Latin America, Santiago, May 23–27, 1988. *International Union for the Scientific Study of Populations Newsletter*, 33, 35–42.

Ashworth, F. (1988). *Maternal mortality report, 1987.* Unpublished report, no. 19.2.88. Harare: Greater Harare Maternity Unit.

Billewicz, W. Z. and McGregor, I. A. (1981). The demography of two West African (Gambian) villages, 1951–75. *Journal of Biosocial Science*, 13, 219–240.

Boerma, J. T. (1987a). Levels of maternal mortality in developing countries. *Studies in Family Planning*, 18 (4), 213–221.

———. (1987b). The magnitude of the maternal mortality problem in Sub-Saharan Africa. *Social Science and Medicine*, 24 (6), 551–558.

———. (1987c). Maternal mortality in Sub-Saharan Africa: levels, causes, and interventions. Paper presented at the IUSSP seminar on mortality and society in Sub-Saharan Africa, Yaoundé, Cameroon, 19–23 October.

Bullough, C. H. W. (1981). Analysis of maternal deaths in the central region of Malawi. *East African Medical Journal*, 58, 25–36.

Caffrey, K. T. (1979). Maternal mortality: a continuing challenge in tropical practice. A report from Kaduna, northern Nigeria. *East African Medical Journal*, 56, 274–277.

Chen, L. C., Gesche, M. C., Ahmed, S., Chowdhury, A. I., and Mosley, W. H. (1974). Maternal mortality in rural Bangladesh. *Studies in Family Planning*, 5, 334–341.

Coeytaux, F. M. (1988). Induced abortion in sub-Saharan Africa: what we do and do not know. *Studies in Family Planning*, 19 (3), 186–190.

El-Ghamry, A., Hussein, M., El-Sherbini, A. S., El-Khantawi, A. F., and Hamoud, T. I. (1984). The feasibility of getting information about maternal mortality from the husband. *Bulletin of the High Institute of Public Affairs*, 14, 195–223.

Essex, B. J. and Everett, V. J. (1977). Use of action-oriented record card for ante-natal screening. *Tropical Doctor*, 7, 134–138.

Fortney, J. A. (1987). The importance of family planning in reducing maternal mortality. *Studies in Family Planning*, 18 (2), 109–114.

Fortney, J. A. and Whitehorne, E. W. (1982). The development of an index of high-risk pregnancy. *American Journal of Obstetrics and Gynecology*, 143, 501–508.

Frank, O. (1987). The demand for fertility control in sub-Saharan Africa. *Studies in Family Planning*, 18 (4), 181–201.

Frost, O. (1984). Maternal and perinatal deaths in Addis Ababa hospital, 1980. *Ethiopian Medical Journal*, 22, 143–146.

Germain, A. (1987). Reproductive health and dignity: choices by Third World women. Technical background paper prepared for the international conference on better health for women and children through family planning, Nairobi, 5–9 October.

Graham, W. and Airey, P. (1987). Measuring maternal mortality: sense and sensitivity. *Health Policy and Planning*, 2 (4), 323–333.

Graham, W. and Brass, W. (1988). Field performance of the sisterhood method for measuring maternal mortality. Paper presented at the IUSSP/CELADE seminar on the collection and processing of demographic data in Latin America, Santiago, 23–27 May.

Graham, W. J. and Danso-Manu, M. (1988). Maternal depletion and maternal mortality: the missing link. Paper presented at the IUSSP African population conference, Dakar, 7–12 November.

Graham, W., Brass, W., and Snow, R. W. (1988). *Indirect Estimation of Maternal Mortality: The Sisterhood Method.* Centre for Population Studies Research Paper, no. 88-1. London: London School of Hygiene and Tropical Medicine.

———. (1989). Estimating maternal mortality: the sisterhood method. *Studies in Family Planning*, 20 (3), 125–135.

Gray, R. H. (1984). Maternal mortality in developing countries [letter]. *International Journal of Epidemiology*, 13, 337.

Greenwood, A. M., Greenwood, B. M., Bradley, A. K., Williams, K., Shenton, F., Tulloch, S., Byass, P., and Oldfield, F. S. J. (1987). A prospective survey of the outcome of pregnancy in a rural area of the Gambia. *Bulletin of the World Health Organization*, 65 (5), 635–643.

Grubb, G. S., Fortney, J. A., Saleh, S., Gadalla, S., el-Baz, A., Feldblum, P., and Rogers, S. M. (1988). A comparison of two cause-of-death classification systems for deaths among women of reproductive age in Menoufia, Egypt. *International Journal of Epidemiology*, 17 (2), 201–207.

Harrison, K. A. (1985). Child-bearing, health, and social priorities: a survey of 22,774 consecutive hospital births in Zaria, northern Nigeria. *British Journal of Obstetrics and Gynaecology*, 92 (supplement 5).

Hartfield, V. J. (1980). Maternal mortality in Nigeria compared with earlier international experience. *International Journal of Gynecology and Obstetrics*, 18, 70–75.

Herz, B. and Measham, A. R. (1987). The safe motherhood initiative: proposals for action. Background paper prepared for the safe motherhood conference, Nairobi, 10–13 February.

Hill, A. G. and Graham, W. J. (1988). *West African Sources of Health and Mortality Information: A Comparative Review*. Technical Study, no. 58e. Ottawa: International Development Research Centre.

Justesen, A. (1985). An analysis of maternal mortality in Muhumbili Medical Centre, Dar es Salaam, July 1984. *Journal of Obstetrics and Gynaecology of East and Central Africa*, 4, 5–8.

Kwast, B. E. (1987). Roads to maternal death: case histories. Informal paper prepared for the safe motherhood conference, Nairobi, 10–13 February.

———. (1988). *Unsafe Motherhood: A Monumental Challenge*. Netherlands.

Kwast, B. E. and Stevens, J. A. (1987). Viral hepatitis as a major cause of maternal mortality. *International Journal of Gynecology and Obstetrics*, 25, 99–106.

Lamb, W. H., Lamb, C. H. W., Foord, F. A., and Whitehead, R. G. (1984). Changes in maternal and child mortality rates in three isolated Gambian villages over ten years. *Lancet*, 2, 912–914.

Mahler, H. (1987). The Safe Motherhood Initiative: a call to action. *Lancet*, 1, 268–70.

Maine, D., McNamara, R., Wray, J., Farah, A.-A., and Wallace, M. (1985). Effects of fertility change on maternal and child survival: prospects for Sub-Saharan Africa. PHN Technical Note, no. 85-15. Washington, D.C.: World Bank, Population, Health, and Nutrition Division.

Maine, D., Rosenfield, A., Wallace, M., Kimball, A. M., Kwast, B., Papiernik, E., and White, S. (1986). Prevention of maternal mortality in developing countries. Background paper prepared for the safe motherhood conference, Nairobi, 10–13 February.

Makannah, T. J. (1984). Methods and problems of civil registration practices and vital statistics collection in Africa. In: *Improving Civil Registration*, Linder, F. E. and Moriyama, I. (editors). Bethesda, Md.: International Institute for Vital Registration and Statistics.

Makokha, A. E. (1980). Maternal mortality: Kenyatta National Hospital, 1972–1977. *East African Medical Journal*, 57 (7), 451–460.

Mauritius. Ministry of Health. (1981). *Vital and Health Statistics of the Island of Mauritius, 1980*. Port Louis: Ministry of Health, Statistics Division.

Mhango, C., Rochat, R., and Arkutu, A. (1986). Reproductive mortality in Lusaka, Zambia, 1982–1983. *Studies in Family Planning*, 17 (5), 243–251.

Mtimavalye, L. A. R., Lisasi, D., and Ntuyabaliwe, W. K. (1980). Maternal mortality in Dar es Salaam, Tanzania, 1974–1977. *East African Medical Journal*, 57 (2), 111–117.

Nortman, D. (1974). Parental age as a factor in pregnancy outcome and child development. Reports on Population and Family Planning, no. 16. New York: Population Council.

Ojo, O. A. and Savage, V. Y. (1974). A ten year review of maternal mortality rates in University College, Ibadan, Nigeria. *American Journal of Obstetrics and Gynecology*, 118, 517–522.

Population Reports. (1984). *Healthier Mothers and Children through Family Planning*. Series J, no. 27. Baltimore, Md.: Johns Hopkins University.

Preston, S. H. (1984). Use of direct and indirect techniques for estimating the completeness of death registration systems. In: *Data Bases for Mortality Measurement*. New York: United Nations.

Price, T. G. (1984). Preliminary report on maternal deaths in the southern highlands of Tanzania in 1981. *Journal of Obstetrics and Gynaecology of East and Central Africa*, 3, 103–110.

Royston, E. and Ferguson, J. (1985). The coverage of maternity care: a critical review of available information. *World Health Statistics Quarterly*, 38, 267–288.

Royston, E. and Lopez, A. D. (1987). On the assessment of maternal mortality. *World Health Statistics Quarterly*, 40, 214–224.

Rubin, G., McCarthy, B., Shelton, J., Rochat, R. W., and Terry, J. (1981). The risk of childbearing re-evaluated. *American Journal of Public Health*, 71, 712–716.

Thuriaux, M. C. and Lamotte, J. M. (1984). Maternal mortality in developing countries: a note on the choice of denominator [letter]. *International Journal of Epidemiology*, 13, 246–247.

Tietze, C. (1977). Maternal mortality, excluding abortion mortality. *World Health Statistics Report*, 30, 312–339.

Trussell, T. J. and Pebley, A. R. (1984). The potential impact of changes in fertility on infant, child, and maternal mortality. *Studies in Family Planning*, 15 (6), 253–266.

United Kingdom. Department of Health and Social Security. (1979). *Report on the Confidential Enquiries into Maternal Deaths in England and Wales 1973–75.* Report on Health and Social Security Subjects, no. 14. London: HMSO.

van de Walle, E. (1974). The role of multi-round surveys in the strategy of demographic research. In: *Population in African Development*, vol. 1, pp. 301–308. Cantrelle, P. (editor). Liège: Ordina.

Voorhoeve, A. M., Muller, A. S., and W'Oigo, H. (1984). The outcome of pregnancy. In: *Maternal and Child Health in Rural Kenya: An Epidemiological Study.* van Ginneken, J. K. and Muller, A. S. (editors). London: Croom Helm.

Walker, G. J. A., Ashley, D. E. C., McCaw, A. M., and Bernard, G. W. (1986). Maternal mortality in Jamaica. *Lancet*, 1, 456–458.

Wallace, S. (1984). Maternal mortality. In: *Reproductive Health in Africa: Issues and Options.* Janowitz, B. *et al.* (editors). Research Triangle Park, N.C.: Family Health International.

Weinberg, E. D. (1984). Pregnancy-associated depression of cell-mediated immunity. *Reviews of Infectious Diseases*, 6 (6), 814–831.

Weston, L. (1986). Reducing maternal deaths in developing countries. PHN Technical Note, no. 86-10. Washington, D.C.: World Bank, Population, Health, and Nutrition Division.

Winikoff, B. (1986). Medical services to save mothers' lives: feasible approaches to reducing maternal mortality. Background paper prepared for the safe motherhood conference, Nairobi, 10–13 February.

Winikoff, B. and Sullivan, M. (1987). Assessing the role of family planning in reducing maternal mortality. *Studies in Family Planning*, 18 (3), 128–143.

World Health Organization. (1977). *Manual of the International Statistical Classification of Diseases, Injuries, and Causes of Death.* Geneva.

———. (1986a). Maternal mortality: helping women off the road to death. *WHO Chronicle*, 40, 175–183.

———. (1986b). *Maternal Mortality Rates: A Tabulation of Available Information*, 2d ed. WHO/FHE/86.3. Geneva.

———. (1987). Measuring maternal mortality. WHO/FHE/SMC/87.1. Paper presented at the safe motherhood conference, Nairobi, 10–13 February.

———. (1988). Information support to health system development and management. *World Health Statistics Quarterly*, 41 (1).

Wurie, F. (1979). Analysis of mortality by cause of death for the western area in Sierra Leone, 1972–1975. M.S. thesis, London School of Hygiene and Tropical Medicine.

Zake, E. Z. (1982). A ten-year review of maternal mortality in an upcountry regional and referral general hospital. *Singapore Journal of Obstetrics and Gynaecology*, 13, 55–59.

Part II
Specific Diseases and Conditions

Chapter 7

Disease in Sub-Saharan Africa: An Overview

Samuel Ofosu-Amaah

The health status of the people of Sub-Saharan Africa has been improving, especially over the past 30 years, but still lags behind that of all other major regions of the world (UNICEF, 1988). A relatively high prevalence of infective and parasitic disease remains, and patients commonly have multiple pathologies and florid clinical expressions of disease to a degree not seen elsewhere. The observation of Kimble (1960) that "the rural African lives in thraldom to sickness" is still accurate. The disease burden is heavy whether measured by life expectancy, "days of useful life lost" (Ghana Health Assessment Project Team, 1981), or inability to perform normal daily functions (Danfa Project, 1979).

Infective and parasitic diseases are the most important causes of morbidity, and although they have the most serious impact on young children, these diseases also cause the deaths of adolescents and adults in Africa more often than in other regions of the world. The chapters in this part deal with some of the most urgent infective and parasitic diseases, such as malaria, diarrheal diseases, acute respiratory infections, the target diseases of the World Health Organization's Expanded Programme on Immunization (EPI), and AIDS, as well as with the underlying problem of malnutrition. The final chapter in this part discusses cancer and cardiovascular disease. The authors of these chapters provide comprehensive, up-to-date accounts of the current literature on these subjects.

Malaria

Malaria remains one of the most difficult epidemiological, pharmacological, and immunological challenges in the region. Its influence on practically every aspect of life in many African countries has been profound and sustained over the centuries, and malaria remains a major cause of morbidity and mortality. Moreover,

the epidemiological situation appears to be changing for the worse in many countries. The vectorial capacity of *Anopheles gambiae* and *Anopheles funestus* remains undiminished, and the resistance of these vectors to insecticides and of the parasites to drugs has increased. This crisis has to be addressed, particularly by African scientists and public health officials, whose interest in practically every facet of the problem of malaria must be revived. Unfortunately the shortage of African malariologists and technicians is acute, and concerted malaria control activities have all but ceased in many countries.

Diarrhea

Diarrheal diseases are among the most important causes of morbidity and mortality in young children in Sub-Saharan Africa, and the case-fatality rate for children hospitalized with acute dehydrating diarrhea can be as high as 19 percent. The dysenteries, typhoid, and other salmonella infections occur in all age groups but have received much less attention than diarrheal diseases in children. El Tor cholera has become established in the region in the past 20 years. An additional burden, especially in young children, is intestinal parasitic infection, especially with ascaris and hookworm.

The importance of personal and food hygiene, effective excreta disposal, and safe water supply in preventing diarrhea and other intestinal infections needs to be constantly emphasized, as does the protective effect of breast-feeding, which fortunately is widely prevalent in the region.

Acute Respiratory Infections

Acute respiratory infections (ARI), together with diarrhea, cause about half of all deaths of children under five years of age in many countries. Until recently, it was assumed that, serious as these diseases were, their management was beyond the means of village-level health workers. Now it is hoped that appropriate antibiotic therapy, in the hands of trained community health workers, will achieve in the management of pneumonia what oral rehydration salts have contributed to the management of dehydration. This particular advance in the management of ARI stems from the belated recognition that in Africa pneumonia in young children is mainly due to bacterial causes, such as *Streptococcus pneumoniae* and *Haemophilus influenzae*, and could therefore be treated with antibiotics.

More epidemiological work needs to be carried out, however, not only to define more clearly the associated factors and the extent of ARI and related conditions, but also to monitor changes in the etiologic agents as antimicrobial drugs become more prescribed. The role that viral agents, pollutants, and irritants play in ARI needs further investigation as well.

The Expanded Programme on Immunization (EPI)

The six diseases of the Expanded Programme on Immunization continue to cause serious child morbidity and mortality in Africa and require further epidemiological work. Aaby *et al.* (1981) have started an interesting debate on the epidemiology of severe measles. The situation with both pertussis and diphtheria remains confusing since not much epidemiological investigation has been conducted on these diseases. The prevalence of tuberculosis is also higher in Africa than in other regions and could be worsening because of rapidly increasing urbanization, the spread of HIV infection, and a decline in the resources being directed to diagnosis and control.

Surveys in several African countries have clearly indicated a higher than expected incidence of neonatal tetanus, and more attention is being paid to immunizing women with tetanus toxoid.

Since the pioneering work in Ghana reported in chapter 22, many surveys have fully established the extent of lameness and other disabilities caused by poliomyelitis in Africa. Although the focus should remain on immunization, since the percentage of area provided with the polio vaccine is still low compared with that of other continents, too little attention has been directed to the unfortunate children who are disabled by poliomyelitis. Rehabilitative surgery and other measures, which were pioneered in Uganda in the 1960s (Huckstep, 1970), should receive more attention.

Since the Expanded Programme on Immunization is one of the best-supported programs in public health care in Africa, significant improvements have been made in the program's cold chain and logistics, and large numbers of health workers in Africa have been trained for the program. Political commitment to universal childhood immunization is very high, and several countries, with the help of UNICEF, the World Health Organization, and external donors, have achieved high coverage rates.

The Gambia stands out as having consistently achieved 80 percent coverage in children under two years of age with measles, DPT-3, BCG, polio-3, and even yellow fever vaccine. Many African countries have added yellow fever vaccine to their immunization program, and the Gambia is experimenting with the hepatitis B vaccine.

The incidence of measles, pertussis, and neonatal tetanus has been reduced to very low levels in the Gambia. If other countries also maintain high coverage rates, the epidemiology of these diseases could change significantly. All countries need to establish effective surveillance systems to monitor the expected changes and to maintain vigilance. With among the highest birth rates in the world, Sub-Saharan Africa has an ever increasing pool of children susceptible to measles, pertussis, and neonatal tetanus.

AIDS

Chin, in chapter 13, provides up-to-date WHO estimates of the burden of HIV infections and AIDS cases in Africa. In chapter 14 Anderson demonstrates elegantly the likely demographic effect on Africa of the HIV infection, which significantly adds to the burden of a region already beleaguered by disease. The methods of analysis being developed promise to increase interest in the field of mathematical epidemiology and to indicate to policymakers alternative ways of thinking about serious health problems.

Malnutrition

Malnutrition is highlighted in chapter 8 as well as in the other chapters in this section. Despite the paucity of good data, what is known about malnutrition underlines the great deficits in African nutrition and its attendant sequelae. The prevalence of wasting is estimated to be 9 percent, with rather wide confidence intervals. A large percentage of children who survive early infancy with the protective nutritional shield of breast milk go through a period of growth stagnation that is exacerbated by numerous episodes of infection at a critical period of their lives. The median prevalence of stunting is 40 percent, which clearly indicates the nutritional burden placed on African children. This burden should not be seen merely as a lack of protein and energy, but also as a deficit of micronutrients: iron, vitamin A, vitamin C, and the B group of vitamins. Protein-energy malnutrition as well as micronutrient deficiencies are also prevalent in adults.

Nutritional anemia is widespread and becomes critical in pregnant women because maternal health care in Africa is inadequate. Endemic goiter caused by dietary deficiencies or substances that interfere with the metabolism of thyroxine is recognized as an important problem in many areas of Africa. More investigation needs to be carried out to define this problem fully and to seek low-cost control measures. The current interest in micronutrient deficiencies highlights new ways of looking at old problems. A few cases of xerophthalmia in children indicate widespread vitamin A deficiency in the community, and an opportunity is lost when all attention is focused on the serious clinical cases. This epidemiological truism also holds for goiters and iodine deficiency.

Also of great significance is the seasonality of malnutrition, whose regular cycle moves from moderate inadequacy to serious nutrient deprivation, particularly in the Sahel. This cycle has significant implications for health.

Other Health Problems

Many of the other important endemic and epidemic diseases that are highly prevalent in Africa have been largely controlled in other regions of the world. An estimated 3.5 million cases of leprosy exist in Africa, with 8 out of 1,000 persons contracting the disease. By contrast, in Southeast Asia, with an estimated 5.6 million cases, approximately 4 out of 1,000 persons have leprosy. Meningococcal meningitis epidemics continue to afflict the Sahelian belt, as do yellow fever epidemics, despite the availability of vaccines. Diseases such as dracunculiasis, schistosomiasis, and onchocerciasis persist, and yaws is now resurgent.

Infective and parasitic diseases are also linked to the etiologies of rheumatic heart disease, hypertension, diabetes, and cancers such as hepatocellular carcinoma, Burkitt's lymphoma, and Kaposi's sarcoma. Sickle-cell disease and the other hemoglobinopathies are another example in which selective pressures, in this case from malaria, have caused profound genetic change. Infective disease can be intergenerational, leading to acute disease in newborns, to congenital disability, and to the premature delivery of low-birth-weight infants.

A disturbing sight in any African town is the large number of people of all ages with deformities and other physical handicaps. Moreover, an estimated six million persons in Africa are blind. These conditions may be congenital or acquired from infections or accidents, and appropriate care may not be available. Injuries from traffic accidents have increased rapidly with the use of motor vehicles in Africa.

So important and pervasive are infectious and parasitic diseases and malnutrition as causes of death in Africa that other causes become relatively insignificant. That is not to imply that diseases of the cardiovascular, renal, endocrine, and other systems, malignant neoplasms, psychiatric disorders, and congenital and genetic diseases do not burden African populations. The need for more information on these conditions is highlighted in chapter 1.

Conclusions

The contributions in part II of this volume call attention to the insufficiency of data and the weakness of surveillance and other health information systems in Africa. Health workers and policymakers need to use the data already in hand, which would help define the information that needs to be collected. Much of the current information is from special studies, usually instigated by external interests. Whether expedient or not, these surveys ought not to undermine or replace the development of viable health information and surveillance systems. The fragmented and inadequate methods for collecting health information and the lack of trained nationals in these fields are serious constraints on the development of effective health systems for reducing morbidity and mortality in Sub-Saharan Africa.

References

Aaby, P., Bukh, J., Lisse, I. M., and Smits, A. J. (1981). Measles vaccination and child mortality [letter]. *Lancet*, 2 (8237), 93.

Danfa Project. (1979). *Final Report*. Accra and Los Angeles: University of Ghana and UCLA.

Ghana Health Assessment Project Team. (1981). A quantitative method of assessing the health impact of different diseases in less developed countries. *International Journal of Epidemiology*, 10 (1), 73–80.

Huckstep, R. L. (1970). Poliomyelitis in Uganda. *Physiotherapy*, 56 (8), 347–353.

Kimble, G. H. T. (1960). *Tropical Africa*. Vol. 2. New York: Twentieth Century Fund.

UNICEF. (1988). *Statistics on Children in UNICEF-Assisted Countries*. New York.

Chapter 8

Child Malnutrition

Ann Ashworth and Elizabeth Dowler

The indicators for assessing the nutritional status of populations may be categorized as either input indicators, such as food availability and dietary adequacy, or outcome indicators, such as physical and clinical manifestations of deficiency. In this paper we examine the outcome indicators. We focus on the anthropometric indicators of childhood malnutrition, but also report the prevalence of vitamin A deficiency, iodine deficiency, and anemia. These four conditions have far-reaching consequences for both individuals and households, including impaired growth, increased risk of mortality and morbidity, lowered economic potential, and physical and mental handicaps. Ideally we would have included other anthropometric indicators whose consequences are known to be adverse, such as maternal weight and height or birth weight, but such data are limited in Sub-Saharan Africa.

Anthropometric Indicators

Anthropometry is the most commonly used tool for assessing the nutritional status of populations as well as for monitoring the health and growth of individual children. For either task the anthropometric measurement is compared with a reference median and expressed as a percentile or a percentage of the median, or as a standard deviation score (Z score). The recommended international reference data were developed by the National Center for Health Statistics (NCHS), and individuals who fall below certain commonly accepted cutoff points are regarded as malnourished to varying degrees (World Health Organization, 1978). To some extent, these cutoff points correspond to points below which increased risks of mortality have been observed. The problems associated with expressing anthropometric measurements as percentiles and percent-of-median and the historical and technical considerations of the reference data are fully discussed

by Waterlow *et al.* (1977), Keller and Fillmore (1983), and Dibley *et al.* (1987a). In essence, percentiles have limited practical application in developing countries, since the majority of poor children are below the lowest percentile of the reference population. The percent-of-median, though commonly used, is also limited because it does not take into account variations in the width of the distributions at different ages and across indicators. These limitations can be overcome, however, by expressing anthropometric indicators as deviations from the reference median. Recently Dibley *et al.* (1987b) discussed the problems pertaining to the NCHS reference data.

The most frequently used anthropometric indices of childhood malnutrition are weight-for-age, weight-for-height, and height-for-age. A low weight-for-age signifies a deficit in total body mass, that is, an underweight child. A low weight-for-age can arise when a child is short (stunted), thin (wasted), or both. For some purposes distinguishing between stunting and wasting is necessary (Waterlow, 1978; WHO Working Group, 1986).

A low weight-for-height signifies a wasted child with a deficit of tissue and fat mass compared with the amount expected in a normal, healthy child of the same height or length. A low weight-for-height is the result of weight loss or diminished weight gain and is frequently caused by an acute, severe inadequacy in energy intake due to illness, poor weaning practices, or food shortage. It may have a rapid onset and can be reversed just as rapidly. The prevalence of wasting is therefore said to approximate the incidence of the process causing the weight deficit (WHO Working Group, 1986).

A low height-for-age signifies a stunted child and is the result of retarded linear growth. Its etiology is not fully understood, and it may or may not be associated with wasting. The opportunity for catch-up in linear growth seems to be limited in poor environments, and stunting often persists into adulthood (Martorell, 1985; Ashworth and Millward, 1986). Thus the prevalence of stunting cannot in any way be equated with the incidence of its causal factor(s). The prevalence of stunting may, perhaps, measure overall social deprivation.

Data Sources

Weight-for-age, weight-for-height, and height-for-age can be measured by occasional national or local surveys, by ongoing household surveys, or by primary health care growth-monitoring programs. In this chapter we use national surveys wherever possible, although few countries have purposive nationally representative sample surveys (Cameroon, Ethiopia, Kenya, Lesotho, Liberia, Malawi, Nigeria, Senegal, Sierra Leone, Swaziland, and Togo; Botswana has national clinic data). To facilitate intercountry comparisons we selected surveys in which the prevalence data are available in a standardized form and are disaggregated by age, and in which 2.0 standard deviations below the NCHS reference median (−2SD) has been used as the cutoff for low weight-for-age, weight-for-height, and height-for-age. In the majority of these national surveys the prevalences were already based on −2SD as the cutoff point; in some, the original raw data were reanalyzed using the standard format by the WHO Nutrition Unit, while in others, the reported prevalences were converted to −2SD without recourse to the raw data (World Health Organization, 1987).

The only source of trend data for most Sub-Saharan countries is weight-for-age data from growth-monitoring programs. These aggregated data are often collected from an unknown and varying sample of children and must therefore be interpreted with caution. Changes in the policy for admitting children to a growth-monitoring program may, for example, invalidate using the data for deducing national trends.

Results

Prevalence of Underweight Children

Figure 8-1 shows the prevalence of low weight-for-age among preschool children in nine national surveys. Although the surveys span 22 years and were conducted during different seasons, a characteristic pattern emerges: the prevalence of underweight peaks in children 12–23 months of age.

Prevalence of Stunted and Wasted Children

Figure 8-2 shows the prevalence of low height-for-age and low weight-for-height among preschool children in 12 national surveys. A remarkable tenfold difference exists in the prevalence of stunting and wasting among children 24 months of age and older. Furthermore, whereas the prevalence of wasting characteristically peaks at 12–23 months, the prevalence of stunting does not peak consistently. The median prevalence of stunting remains at approximately 40 percent among children between the ages of 12 and 59 months (see table 8-1). In contrast the median prevalence of wasting beyond 36 months is not substantially different from that expected in the reference population (3 and 2.3 percent, respectively). Of the 12 countries considered, only Botswana and Ethiopia have a prevalence of wasting among children aged 36–59 months that is substantially higher than expected. Both countries were experiencing drought and food access problems when the surveys were undertaken. The lack of correlation between wasting and stunting supports the hypothesis that the two conditions have different etiologies.

Stunted and Wasted Children by Economic Grouping

We used the World Bank's economic groupings for this analysis, and only prevalence data collected within the past decade. As the aim was to contrast the groups, we included local, district, and regional standardized prevalence data when no national data existed. Figure 8-3 shows that at 12 to 23 months, children in low-income arid countries have the lowest median prevalence of stunting but the highest prevalence of wasting. This changes by 48 to 59 months of age, when children of all economic categories have a lower prevalence of wasting than they do at 12 to 23 months; the decline in the low-income, nonarid countries is proportionately greater. Only the middle-income oil-exporting countries show a substantial fall in the prevalence of stunting in children 48–59 months of age. Very few oil-exporting countries were represented in the data, however, and the results must be interpreted with caution. Data for individual countries are given in tables 8-2 and 8-3.

Prevalence Data from Elsewhere

Table 8-4 presents data for the countries that were excluded from tables 8-2 and 8-3 either because the children's ages were unknown or the data were not in a standardized format (different cutoffs or aggregated

Figure 8-1. Prevalence of Underweight Preschool Children in Nine Countries of Sub-Saharan Africa

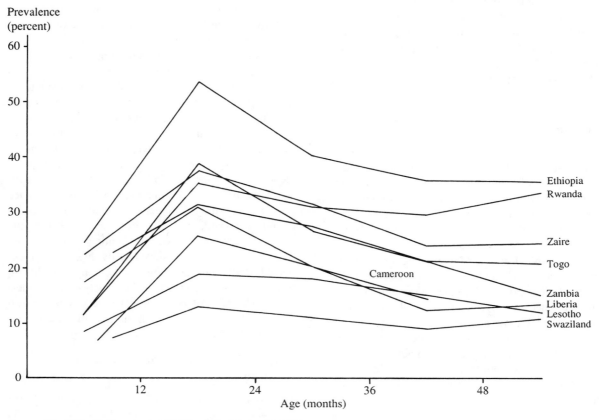

Source: World Health Organization (1987) and Serdula *et al.* (1987a).

age groups). Not unexpectedly, the drought-affected countries have a high prevalence of wasting, and the magnitude varies with the degree of destitution and the extent of emergency relief.

There have, of course, always been periods of crop or pasture failure throughout the Sahel and many other parts of Africa. Most societies have evolved coping strategies, with varying degrees of success. In recent years, however, the capacity to adapt has seemed to diminish, either because rapid changes in the environment have overwhelmed the traditional responses or because the potential responses are no longer appropriate or feasible.

Trends in the Prevalence of Malnutrition

As mentioned briefly, little can be deduced about national trends because the limited amount of information available is largely confined to clinic data from growth-monitoring programs. Nonetheless, the early 1980s were clearly critical years for much of Africa, as problems with food availability and economic stability were caused or exacerbated by drought. In several countries (for example, Botswana, Lesotho, and Ghana) the prevalence of preschool malnutrition seems to have increased as droughts, the country's economic position, or both, worsened (United Nations, 1987).

Table 8-1. Median Prevalences of Underweight, Stunted, and Wasted Children in National Surveys
(percent)

Age (months)	Underweight	Stunted	Wasted
0–11	11	24	4
12–23	31	42	9
24–35	27	40	4
36–47	21	42	3
48–59	18	39	3

Source: Figures 8-1 and 8-2.

Figure 8-2. Prevalence of Stunted and Wasted Preschool Children in 12 Countries of Sub-Saharan Africa

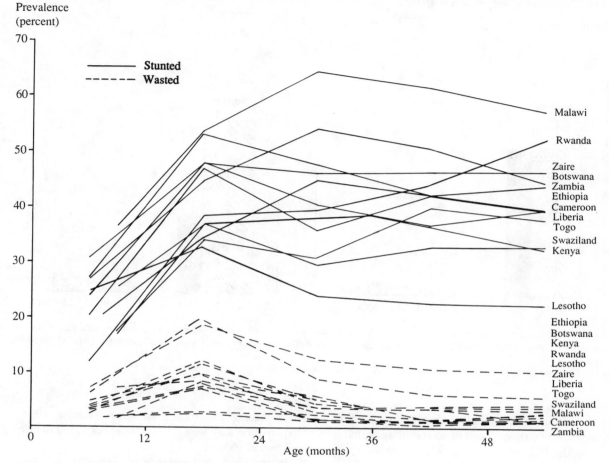

Source: World Health Organization (1987) and Serdula *et al.* (1987a).

GENDER DIFFERENCES. In general, few surveys give data disaggregated by gender. Only Malawi, Lesotho, and Swaziland report apparently significant differences, most of which occur in wasting in boys 6–23 months of age, perhaps because girls remain closer to their mothers, while young boys are expected to be more independent.

URBAN-RURAL DIFFERENCES. Table 8-5 shows urban and periurban and rural data, which were collected in average postharvest months, for Malawi (UNICEF and Cornell Surveillance Program, 1984). The prevalence of underweight children in rural areas was higher than that in urban areas, which is fairly consistent with the findings in countries with comparable data (Cameroon, Lesotho, Sierra Leone, and Zimbabwe). Urban communities, however, are arguably less homogeneous than rural areas, and children living in urban squatter settlements, possibly outside government registration systems and therefore outside national sampling frames, might have a poorer nutritional status than rural children. No data on squatter children were found for any country.

SEASONAL DIFFERENCES. In Malawi wasting is more prevalent in preharvest than in postharvest seasons, but the prevalence of stunting remains stable throughout the year (see table 8-6). The same is true for other national data sets (Lesotho, 1977; Sierra Leone, 1978). More detailed knowledge of the livelihood zones of individual countries, particularly the balance between agriculture and pastoralism, is needed to interpret these seasonal differences. For example, there is some evidence that in good years people in pastoral com-

Figure 8-3. Prevalence of Stunted and Wasted Children Aged 12–23 Months and 48–59 Months, Selected Countries of Sub-Saharan Africa

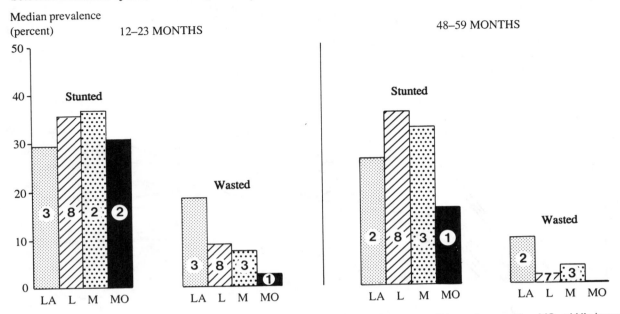

Note: LA, low-income semiarid countries; L, other low-income countries; M, middle-income oil-importing countries; MO, middle-income oil-exporting countries. The numerals inside the bars indicate the number of countries surveyed. For the specific countries included, see tables 8-2 and 8-3.
Source: For all countries except Swaziland, World Health Organization (1987); for Swaziland, Serdula et al. (1987a).

munities do not experience the dramatic wet-season weight losses that have been observed in agricultural communities (Chambers *et al.*, 1981). Furthermore in fair or poor years pastoralists tend to lose weight at a different time of year (the end of the dry season) than people engaged primarily in agriculture (Loutan and Lamotte, 1984; Hilderbrand *et al.*, 1985). In the Gambia the adverse effects that the wet season has on child growth are less pronounced in urban than in rural areas (Tomkins *et al.*, 1986).

SOCIOECONOMIC FACTORS. Evaluating malnutrition in particular socioeconomic groups focuses on households rather than individuals and raises the question of why particular livelihood systems are more at risk than others in a given circumstance. While malnutrition may be rooted in poverty, assuming a simple linear relationship between household income and the prevalence of malnutrition would be misleading. For example, in a longitudinal study of child growth in Machakos, Kenya, although poor nutritional status tended to occur more frequently among the very poor and less frequently among the most well-off, between these extremes no association existed between house-

hold income and nutritional status (Kenya, 1984). Explanation may well lie in differences in intrahousehold relationships.

In the southern highlands of Tanzania, Jakobsen (1987) found a U-shaped relationship between material wealth and nutritional status (see figure 8-4), with subsistence farmers and the economic elite having the lowest prevalence of underweight children (32 and 36 percent, respectively). In contrast, families cultivating cash crops (mainly pyrethrum and tea) had a high prevalence of underweight children (58 percent). Cash cropping can result in poor nutritional status in children for a number of reasons, many of which have to do with the allocation of resources, decisionmaking, and monetary control within the household. Cash cropping may actually reduce food production by diverting labor and (often the best) land into cash rather than subsistence crops, and financial and food resources away from women. Cash crops, unlike food crops, are more likely to be controlled by men, and increased monetarization tends to increase male cash-in-hand, especially lump-sum cash. This may produce expenditure patterns that are dominated by so-called male preferences, which may not include household

Table 8-2. Prevalence of Wasted, Stunted, and Underweight Children Aged 12–23 Months in 17 Sub-Saharan African Countries

Country	Number	Type of survey	Wasted	Stunted	Underweight	Date of survey	World Bank designation
Botswana	11,262E	National (clinic data)	19.2E	44.8E	n.a.	1979–81	M
Burkina Faso	2,189	Local (Mossi)	18.2	29.2	39.2	1973–82	LA
Burundi	90E	District (Ruyaga)	4.1	52.3	35.2	1979 (December)	L
Cameroon	400E	National (urban and rural)	2.4E	34.8E	25.5E	1977–78	MO
Ethiopia	556	National	18.7	53.1	53.8	1982	L
Gabon	218	Regional (Lambarene)	n.a.	26.6	22.0	1984 (February–April)	MO
Gambia, The	222E	Local (Bakau, urban)	9.7	18.9	19.0	1982 (February and September)	LA
Ghana	858E	Local (Accra, urban)	27.8E	31.2E	35.6E	1978–80	L
Kenya	783E	National	8.4	36.8	n.a.	1978–79 (November–January)	L
Lesotho	1,559	National	7.4	32.8	18.7	1981 (January)	M
Malawi	1,000E	National	8.0	53.9	n.a.	1982 (March)	L
Niger	499	Local (Niancy, Filingue, Ouallam)	23.7	32.3	49.1	1980 (June–August)	LA
Senegal	77	Regional (Casamance)	19.8E	n.a.	n.a.	1979	L
Swaziland	953	National (Rural)	2.5	36.5	13.0	1983–84 (September–January)	M
Togo	1,328	National	9.4	34.0	31.5	1977	L
Uganda	157	Local (Lira, Apac, Soroti, Kumi)	2.5	26.7	19.1	1985 (April–May)	L
Zaire	7,470	District (Kasongo)	n.a.	28.2	21.6	1983	L

n.a. Not available.

Note: Wasted, stunted, and underweight are defined as 2.0 standard deviations below the National Center for Health Statistics reference median. LA, low-income, semiarid; L, low-income, other; M, middle-income oil importer; MO, middle-income oil exporter; E, estimated.

Source: Data were compiled from World Health Organization (1987) for all countries except Swaziland, for which data were estimated from the graph in Serdula *et al.* (1987a).

Figure 8-4. Prevalence of Underweight Children, by Family Livelihood

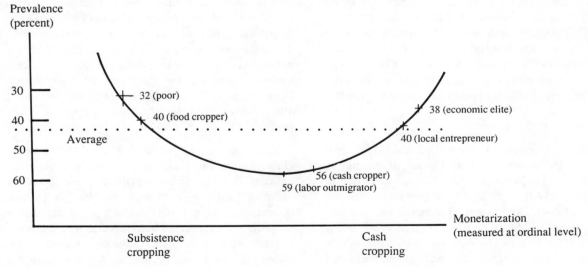

Source: Jakobsen (1987).

Table 8-3. Prevalence of Wasted, Stunted, and Underweight Children Aged 48–59 Months in 14 Sub-Saharan African Countries

Country	Number	Type of survey	Wasted	Stunted	Underweight	Date of survey	World Bank designation
			\<_Prevalence (percent)_\>				
Botswana	11,262E	National (clinic data)	5.5E	44.8E	n.a.	1979–81	M
Burkina Faso	470	Local (Mossi)	7.0	28.1	28.9	1973–82	LA
Burundi	90E	District (Ruyaga)	1.1	60.7	31.8	1979 (December)	L
Ethiopia	774	National	9.9	39.5	35.3	1982	L
Gabon	139	Regional (Lambarene)	n.a.	15.8	13.7	1984 (February–April)	MO
Ghana	858E	Local (Accra, urban)	21.5E	34.1E	27.8E	1978–80	L
Kenya	783E	National	4.1	32.2	n.a.	1978–79	L
Lesotho	669	National	3.1	22.3	12.0	1981 (January)	M
Malawi	1,000E	National	0.7	57.4	n.a.	1982 (March)	L
Niger	430	Local (Niancy, Filingue, Ouallam)	11.7	24.4	28.0	1980 (June–August)	LA
Swaziland	707	National (rural)	1.0	32.5	10.5	1983–84 (September–January)	M
Togo	1,008	National	1.8	37.5	21.1	1977	L
Uganda	94	Local (Lira, Apac, Soroti, Kumi)	0.0	31.9	11.7	1985 (April–May)	L
Zaire	5,677	District (Kasongo)	n.a.	28.8	17.7	1983	L

n.a. Not available.

Note: For definitions, see note to table 8-2.

Source: Data were compiled from World Health Organization (1987) for all countries except Swaziland, for which data were estimated from the graph in Serdula *et al.* (1987a).

food or children's welfare (Trenchard, 1987). A high prevalence of underweight children (59 percent) was also found in families where adult males were absent for part of the year. In these circumstances the input of male labor to domestic agriculture, such as clearing new land and maintaining irrigation systems, is often disrupted, and women have commensurately greater work burdens and less time for child care (Jakobsen, 1987). Similarly, severe malnutrition has been reported in highly fertile areas of Kenya where cash crops (sugar cane and tea) are grown (Kenya, 1984). Jakobsen (1987) concludes that, at least in the short term, there appears to be a tradeoff between nutritional well-being and efforts to promote economic growth.

Nutritional Deficiencies

VITAMIN A DEFICIENCY. Figure 8-5 shows the geographic distribution of clinical signs of vitamin A deficiency. The most severely affected countries in Sub-Saharan Africa are Benin, Burkino Faso, Ethiopia, Mali, Malawi, Mauritania, Tanzania, and Zambia (DeMaeyer, 1986). Vitamin A deficiency is often associated with measles and most commonly affects young children. Severe cases result in blindness and

death. Recent studies also suggest a close association between vitamin A deficiency and increased mortality and morbidity from respiratory and gastrointestinal infections.

ANEMIA. DeMaeyer and Adiels-Tegman (1985) have reviewed the prevalence data on anemia in 28 countries in Sub-Saharan Africa. Most of the data relate to pregnant women and young children, of whom 63 and 56 percent, respectively, were estimated to be anemic. The main cause of anemia is iron deficiency, which is not necessarily related to a dietary deficiency. Recent studies suggest that iron deficiency adversely affects brain function, school achievement (Soemantri *et al.*, 1985; Addy, 1986), and the immune response (Dallman, 1987).

IODINE DEFICIENCY. Iodine deficiency disorders include goiters and endemic cretinism (characterized by deaf-mutism, mental impairment, and defective growth). Goiter is a frequent problem in eastern, central, and southern Africa, and a goiter prevalence exceeding 40 percent has been reported for Cameroon, Central African Republic, Ethiopia, Kenya, Mali, Nigeria, Sierra Leone, Tanzania, Zaire, and Zambia

Table 8-4. Prevalence of Wasted, Stunted, and Underweight Children Aged 12–23 Months in 14 Sub-Saharan African Countries

Country	Number and age range	Type of survey	Wasted	Stunted	Underweight	Date of survey
			Prevalence (percent)			
Cape Verde	772	9 islands	n.a.	n.a.	28.5[a]	1977
Chad (drought affected)	3,464 (6–47 months)	Southern Chad	22.3[a]	n.a.	n.a.	1984–85
Congo	92	Villages on plateau	n.a.	n.a.	42.4[a]	1976–77
Guinea-Bissau	573	National	n.a.	n.a.	32.6[a]	1978–80
Madagascar	47	4 villages	n.a.	n.a.	57.4[a]	1974
Mali (drought affected)	n.a. (small)	National and local	17.5[a]	56.5[a]		1977–78
	n.a. (0–59 months)		8–26.5[a]	n.a.	n.a.	1985 (February–October)
Mauritania (drought affected)	(0–59 months)	River region	n.a.	n.a.	52.0[a]	1986–87
Mauritius	118	National	n.a.	n.a.	19.5[b]	1983
	2,400 households (0–59 months)	National	16.2[b]	21.5[b]	23.9[b]	1985
	129 estimated (12–35 months)	MCH center	n.a.	n.a.	24.4[b]	1982
Mozambique	1,086	Tete province	8.9[a]	n.a.	n.a.	1985
Niger (drought affected)	618	Provincial	25.6[a]	n.a.	n.a.	1986 (November–December)
	n.a. (0–47 months)	Camp populations	n.a.	n.a.	28–34[a]	1985
Nigeria	1,280 (0–59 months)	National (urban)	21.1[b]	n.a.	n.a.	1983–84
	499 (0–59 months)	National (rural)	21.4[b]	n.a.	n.a.	1983–84
Rwanda	169	Southern district (Gikongoro)	4.0[a]	27.0[a]	n.a.	1974
	193	Eastern district (Kibungo)	n.a.	31.1[a]	n.a.	1980
Sierra Leone	392 estimated	National	25.6[b]	35.5[b]	35.3[b]	1974–75
	1,177	National	4.0[a]	28.0[a]	38.5[a]	1977–78
Zimbabwe	1,787	Provincial (Bindura)	11.8[b]	29.6[b]	22.6[b]	1980–82

n.a. Not available. The statistics for stunting and underweight were measured, but not reported.

Note: In surveys where ages were not known or not measured, a height approximation was used to delineate children in a given age range.

a. Defined using a cutoff point of 80 percent of weight-for-height, 80 percent of weight-for-age, or 90 percent of height-for-age.

b. Defined using a cutoff point of 2.0 standard deviations below the National Center for Health Statistics reference median.

Source: Data for Cape Verde, Congo, Guinea-Bissau, Madagascar, Mauritius (1983), and Rwanda were taken from Keller and Fillmore (1983); data for Mauritius (1982), Niger (1986), Nigeria, and Sierra Leone from the World Health Organization (1987); data for Chad, Mauritania, and Niger (1985) from UNOEOA (1986); for Mali from Mondot-Bernard *et al.* (1980) and Lefevre (1986); for Mauritius (1985) from Mauritius and UNICEF (1987); for Mozambique from unpublished UNICEF data; for Sierra Leone (1977) from Sierra Leone (1978); and for Zimbabwe from Zimbabwe and UNICEF (1985).

(International Council for Control of Iodine Deficiency Disorders, 1985; Benmiloud *et al.*, 1986).

Discussion

We have briefly described the anthropometric indicators that are most commonly used for assessing the prevalence of malnutrition in children. We have not examined causation, nor have we dealt with the relation between the degree of deficit in an indicator and the risk of undesirable consequences such as mortality or morbidity.

National data from 12 Sub-Saharan African countries show that wasting reaches a peak in children between the ages of 12 to 23 months, with a median

Table 8-5. Prevalence of Underweight Children in Rural and Urban Malawi, June–August 1983
(percent)

Age (months)	Urban and periurban		Rural	
	Percent	Sample size	Percent	Sample size
0–11	38	2,273	45	5,199
12–23	50	1,096	54	3,468
24–35	45	312	49	1,246
36–47	45	128	38	394

Note: Underweight is defined using a cutoff point of 80 percent of weight-for-age.
Source: UNICEF and Cornell Nutritional Surveillance Program (1984).

prevalence of 9 percent, and that the prevalence of wasting beyond 35 months of age is low, except in drought-affected countries. In contrast the median prevalence of stunting at 12–23 months is 42 percent, with little subsequent change. These findings have implications for future data collection. First, data should not be aggregated for all preschool children, since nutritional risk is not uniform in children 0 to 5 years of age, and age-specific anthropometric data are required. Second, weight-for-age is of limited usefulness, since it fails to distinguish between children who are wasted and those who are stunted. In Sub-Saharan countries not affected by drought, low weight-for-age in children over 35 months of age is invariably due to poor growth in the first two years of life. Little opportunity appears to exist for children to catch up in linear growth, except possibly in the more affluent oil-exporting countries.

Dibley *et al.* (1987b) consider the abrupt and uniform fall in the prevalence of wasting to be spurious and the result of the disjunction in the reference curves at 24–35 months. Disjunction also applies to height-for-age, however, and since there is no uniform fall in

the prevalence of stunting, we consider that the peak in wasting is not artifactual. Such a peak is consistent with difficulties encountered during the weaning period, such as low intakes of nutrients and high levels of morbidity.

Few conclusions can be drawn about trends except that nutritional status is obviously worsening in countries afflicted by famine. One approach to overcoming the paucity of data is to predict the prevalence of malnutrition from the per capita energy intake and the mortality rate of 1-to-4-year-olds using an equation based on data from 22 developing countries throughout the world (Haaga *et al.*, 1985). Estimating per capita energy intake is unreliable, however, in countries where a major proportion of the food is produced and consumed locally. Nevertheless, such estimates have been used by the United Nations Sub-Committee on Nutrition to support their recent statement on the status of world nutrition (United Nations, 1987).

Although few countries in Sub-Saharan Africa have purposive nationally representative sample surveys, we do not necessarily recommend that governments and external agencies invest further in large-scale

Table 8-6. Prevalence of Underweight, Stunted, and Wasted Children in Malawi, October 1980–December 1981

Characteristic	Postharvest		Preharvest	
	Percent	Sample size	Percent	Sample size
Underweight	27.4	4,988	35.6	2,780
Stunted	56.4	4,433	56.3	2,471
Wasted	1.5	4,433	2.8	2,471

Note: Underweight is defined using a cutoff point of 80 percent of weight-for-age; stunting is defined using a cutoff point of −2 SD of height-for-age; and wasting is defined using a cutoff point of −2SD of weight-for-height.
Source: UNICEF and Cornell Nutritional Surveillance Program (1984).

Figure 8-5. Distribution of Vitamin A Deficiency in Africa, 1984

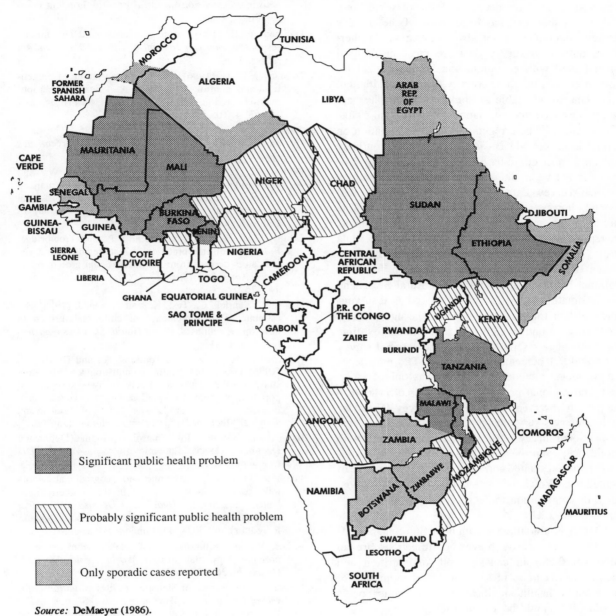

Significant public health problem

Probably significant public health problem

Only sporadic cases reported

Source: **DeMaeyer (1986).**

surveys. In our view, data should only be collected if they will be used for decisionmaking of some kind. The use, if any, that has been made of the surveys already undertaken is not always apparent. Furthermore, nutritional survey data are most meaningful when linked with economic and agroecological information from the same country or region. Although such data are available in some countries, they are rarely integrated into evaluations of nutritional status.

In countries where regular national information on malnutrition prevalence is needed, data routinely collected from clinic-based growth monitoring programs might be an alternative to costly and complex national survey data. The feasibility of this will depend, however, on the reliability of the routine measurements and the degree to which clinic attenders are representative of the population as a whole. Serdula *et al.* (1987b) have compared estimates of the prevalence of underweight preschool children from the National Nutrition Status Survey of Rural Swaziland with estimates obtained from the clinic-based surveillance system for the same period. The age-adjusted prevalence of underweight children among first-time clinic attenders resembled that of the national survey (10.1 and 9.4 percent, respectively). The prevalence among repeat attenders, however, was only 4.4 percent, and regional prevalences did not correspond to the pattern observed in the national survey. Therefore each country's surveillance data should be validated by a national survey before clinic data can be used with confidence; even then, clinic data that do not distinguish between stunted and wasted children would be of limited use. Whichever national data system is envisaged, its contribution to decision-making should be a prime raison d'être.

Anemia is ubiquitous throughout Sub-Saharan Africa but is not easily prevented. Infections are an important factor in causing both malnutrition and anemia. Deficiencies of vitamin A and iodine are of great public health significance; their eradication is feasible and should be a high priority.

References

Addy, D. P. (1986). Happiness is: iron. *British Medical Journal*, 292, 969–970.

Ashworth, A. and Millward, D. J. M. (1986). Catch-up growth in children. *Nutrition Reviews*, 44, 157–163.

Benmiloud, M., Bachtarzi-Sahnoun, H., Chauoki, M. L., and Maoni, R. (1986). Prevalence et aspects du goitre en Afrique. In: *Les malnutritions dans les pays du Tiers-Monde*, Lemonnier, D. and Ingenbleek, Y. (editors), vol. 136, pp. 373–386. Paris: Colloque INSERM.

Chambers, R., Longhurst, R., and Pacey, A., editors. (1981). *Seasonal Dimensions to Rural Poverty*. London: Frances Pinter, Ltd.

Dallman, P. R. (1987). Iron deficiency and the immune response. *American Journal of Clinical Nutrition*, 46, 329–334.

DeMaeyer, E. M. (1986). The WHO programme of prevention and control of vitamin A deficiency, xerophthalmia, and nutritional blindness. *Nutrition and Health*, 4, 105–112.

DeMaeyer, E. and Adiels-Tegman, M. (1985). The prevalence of anaemia in the world. *World Health Statistics Quarterly*, 38, 302–316.

Dibley, M. J., Goldsby, J. B., Staehling, N. W., and Trowbridge, F. L. (1987a). Development of normalized curves for the international growth reference: historical and technical considerations. *American Journal of Clinical Nutrition*, 46, 736–748.

Dibley, M. J., Staehling, N., Nieburg, P., and Trowbridge, F. L. (1987b). Interpretation of Z-score anthropometric indicators derived from the international growth reference. *American Journal of Clinical Nutrition*, 46, 749–762.

Haaga, J., Kenrick, C., Test, K., and Mason, J. (1985). An estimate of the prevalence of child malnutrition in developing countries. *World Health Statistics Quarterly*, 38, 331–347.

Hilderbrand, K., Thiam, A., Tomkins, A., and Dowler, E. (1985). Food, work, health and nutrition: a comparative study of the seasonal effects in two agropastoral populations from the Malian Gurma. Unpublished report to ODA. London: London School of Hygiene and Tropical Medicine, Department of Human Nutrition.

International Council for Control of Iodine Deficiency Disorders. (1985). Endemic goitre in Africa. *IDD Newsletter*, 1, 11–12.

Jakobsen, O. (1987). Economic and geographical factors influencing child malnutrition in the southern highlands, Tanzania. In: *Health and Disease in Tropical Africa: Geographical and Medical Viewpoints*, Akhtar, R. (editor), pp. 203–244. London: Harwood.

Keller, W. and Fillmore, C. M. (1983). Prevalence of protein-energy malnutrition. *World Health Statistics Quarterly*, 36, 129–167.

Kenya. Central Bureau of Statistics. (1984). *Situation Analysis of Children and Women in Kenya. Section 4. The Well-being of Children*, pp. 77–80. Nairobi: Central Bureau of Statistics and UNICEF.

LeFevre, D. (1986). *Analyse de la situation nutritionelle au Mali et perspectives*. Vol. 3. *Synthèse*. Bamako: CEE/CESA.

Lesotho. (1977). *The Kingdom of Lesotho National Nutrition Survey*. Washington, D.C.: Agency for International Development, Office of Nutrition, Development Support Bureau.

Loutan, L. and Lamotte, J. M. (1984). Seasonal variations in nutrition among a group of nomadic pastoralists in Niger. *Lancet*, 1, 945–947.

Martorell, R. (1985). Child growth retardation: a discussion of its causes and its relationship to health. In: *Nutritional Adaptation in Man*, Blaxter, K. and Waterlow, J. C. (editors), pp. 13–29. London: John Libbey.

Mauritius Ministry of Health and UNICEF. (1987). *Mauritius Nutrition Survey*. Port Louis.

Mondot-Bernard, J., Monjour, L., and Karam, M. (1980). *Satisfaction of Food Requirements and Agricultural Development in Mali. Vol. 2. Results of Medical and Nutritional Surveys*. Paris: Organisation for Economic Co-operation and Development.

Serdula, M. K., Aphane, J. M., Kunene, P. F., Gama, D. M., Staehling, N., Peck, R., Seward, J., Sullivan, B., and Trowbridge, F. L. (1987a). Acute and chronic under-nutrition in Swaziland. *Journal of Tropical Pediatrics*, 33, 35–42.

Serdula, M. K., Herman, D., Williamson, D. F., Binkin, N. J., Aph, J. M., and Trowbridge, F. (1987b). Validity of clinic-based nutritional surveillance for prevalence estimation of undernutrition. *Bulletin of the World Health Organization*, 65, 529–533.

Sierra Leone. (1978). *Sierra Leone National Nutrition Survey*. Washington, D.C.: Agency for International Development, Office of Nutrition, Development Support Bureau.

Soemantri, A. G., Pollitt, E., and Kim, I. (1985). Iron deficiency anaemia and educational achievement. *American Journal of Clinical Nutrition*, 42, 1221–1228.

Tomkins, A. M., Dunn, D. T., Hayes, R. J., and Bradley, A. K. (1986). Seasonal variations in the nutritional status of urban Gambian children. *British Journal of Nutrition*, 56, 533–543.

Trenchard, E. (1987). Rural women's work in sub-Saharan Africa and the implications for nutrition. In: *Geography of Gender in the Third World*, Momsen, J. H. and Townsend, J. (editors), pp. 153–172. London: Hutchinson.

United Nations. (1987). First report on the world nutrition situation. A report compiled for the 13th session of the ACC sub-committee on nutrition, Washington, D.C., 2–6 March. Rome: Food and Agriculture Organization.

UNICEF and Cornell Nutritional Surveillance Program. (1984). *Report on Botswana Workshop on Clinic-Based Nutritional Surveillance Systems and Integrated Data Bases*, vol. 7, no. 1. New York: UNICEF.

UNOEOA. (1986). *Special Report on the Emergency Situation in Africa: Review of 1985 and 1986 Emergency Needs*. New York: United Nations Office for Emergency Operations in Africa.

Waterlow, J. C. (1978). Observations on the assessment of protein-energy malnutrition with special reference to stunting. *Courier*, 28, 455–460.

Waterlow, J. C., Buzina, R., Keller, W., Lane, J. M., Nichaman, M. Z., and Tanner, J. M. (1977). The presentation and use of height and weight data for comparing the nutritional status of groups of children under the age of 10 years. *Bulletin of the World Health Organization*, 55, 489–498.

World Health Organization. (1978). *A Growth Chart for International Use in Maternal and Child Care: Guidelines for Primary Health Care Personnel*. Geneva.

———. (1987). Nutrition: global surveillance through anthropometric measurements. Part 2: Prevalence of wasting and stunting in the African region. *Weekly Epidemiological Record*, 62, 45–50.

WHO Working Group. (1986). Use and interpretation of anthropometric indicators of nutritional status. *Bulletin of the World Health Organization*, 64, 929–941.

Zimbabwe and UNICEF (1985). *Women and Children in Zimbabwe: A Situation Analysis*. Harare.

Chapter 9

Diarrhea

Betty R. Kirkwood

Diarrheal diseases are widely recognized as a major cause of morbidity and mortality in Sub-Saharan Africa. However, the exact magnitude of the problem and how it compares with that in the rest of the developing world is not generally known. This chapter reviews the current state of knowledge about the patterns and determinants of diarrheal disease in Sub-Saharan Africa. Attention is paid to the type of data sources available and their relative advantages and disadvantages. Data deficiencies requiring more research are highlighted.

When Snyder and Merson (1982) reviewed the magnitude of the global problem of acute diarrheal disease, they applied strict selection criteria. They only included longitudinal, prospective, community-based studies of stable populations with low migration rates in which frequent surveillance was carried out for at least a year. Twenty-two studies met these criteria, three of which were from Sub-Saharan Africa. Applying the same criteria, with the further restriction that the studies had to have been conducted after 1970, yielded six studies from Sub-Saharan Africa, with three estimates of mortality rates and five estimates of morbidity rates.

The aim of this review is to present as complete a picture as possible and to cover as many countries as possible. The objective is to assess the importance of diarrhea, describe its epidemiology, and estimate its incidence and mortality rates. Furthermore, epidemiological thinking has changed in recent years, and the value of designs other than comprehensive longitudinal studies has become more widely appreciated. For these reasons, no selection criteria were applied, and results from both cross-sectional and longitudinal community studies, as well as analyses of routine statistics, were included.

Data Sources

A computer search using the MEDLINE data base was made of the scientific literature from 1977 to October 1987 to locate all papers containing information, however minimal, on diarrheal morbidity and mortality in Sub-Saharan Africa. Some papers appearing after this date and some in press were included as well. No restrictions were imposed on the type of study, the data source, or the features of the design. Thirty-five studies from 16 countries were identified and categorized as shown in table 9-1. Results were obtained from 16 community studies, 12 longitudinal and 4 cross-sectional, and from 19 analyses of routine statistics, 12 based on health facility records and 7 on registered deaths.

Table 9-1. Data Sources on Diarrhea, Sub-Saharan Africa

Type of study	Number of studies	Number of countries covered
Community studies		
Longitudinal	12	10
Cross-sectional	4	4
Analyses of routine statistics		
Health facility records	12	7
Registered deaths	7	4
Total published information	35	16
WHO/CDD morbidity, mortality, and treatment surveys	67	22
WHO/CDD data from national diarrhea control programs (NCDDP)	7	5
Overall total	109	33

In addition, the Diarrhoeal Diseases Control Programme (CDD) at the World Health Organization (WHO) gave access to information of two kinds. The first was a compilation of results from 67 cross-sectional morbidity, mortality, and treatment surveys carried out in 22 countries using standard CDD methodology. This was by far the largest data source and provided some information on both morbidity and mortality. Results from the three WHO/CDD surveys carried out in Cameroon also appeared in the scientific literature (Merlin *et al.*, 1986). The second source of information was seven sets of data collected by national diarrheal diseases control programs (NCDDP) in five countries.

The grand total was 109 studies carried out in 33 countries, as shown in table 9-2. Information was not located for six countries, but both morbidity and mortality data were found for 26. The quantity and quality of information varied greatly, however, and was rarely representative of the country as a whole. For example, the only information available for Zimbabwe was the percentage of outpatient attendances due to diarrhea in Harare City and Matebeleland South. In contrast, Nigeria had 20 WHO/CDD morbidity surveys, 1 additional cross-sectional study, 2 longitudinal studies, 3 analyses of hospital statistics, and 2 analyses of registered deaths. Yet even these did not give a complete picture of either diarrheal morbidity or mortality in Nigeria. All of the WHO/CDD Nigerian surveys were conducted in urban areas, and only one study (Huttly *et al.*, 1987) looked at a range of possible risk factors. This study was also unusual because it was not restricted to children less than five years old but collected data on the prevalence of diarrhea over the whole range of ages, including adulthood.

Measures of Morbidity and Mortality

The data sources contained a variety of measures of diarrheal morbidity and mortality. These varied according to the type of study design, as shown in table 9-3. In brief, measures of incidence, prevalence, and the percentage of all episodes of illness require community-based surveys, which most accurately reflect the morbidity burden to the community. Percentages of outpatient attendances and of admissions are based on health facility records and tend to reflect more severe episodes of disease. In general, they are not representative of the community as a whole because the availability, accessibility, and use of health services vary among subgroups of the population.

The diarrheal mortality rate (that is, the annual number of diarrhea-associated deaths that occur for

Table 9-2. Availability of Data on Morbidity and Mortality from Diarrhea, by Country and Data Source

Country	Morbidity	Mortality
Angola	0	1R
Benin	0	0
Botswana	1W	0
Burkina Faso	1L	0
Burundi	1W	1W
Cameroon	3W	3W
Central African Republic	1W	1W
Chad	3W	2W
Congo	2W	2W
Côte d'Ivoire	2W	2W
Ethiopia	14W, 1L, 1N	14W, 1N
Gabon	1W	1W
Gambia, The	2L	0
Ghana	1C, 1H	0
Guinea	2W	1W
Guinea-Bissau	1W	1W
Kenya	1W, 1L, 1H	1L, 2R
Lesotho	1H, 1N	1H
Liberia	0	0
Madagascar	0	0
Malawi	1L	1L
Mali	4W	2W
Mauritania	1W	1W
Mauritius	0	0
Mozambique	2W	2W
Niger	1N	1N
Nigeria	20W, 2L, 1C, 1H	1L, 3H, 2R
Rwanda	1W	1W
Senegal	1C	1C, 1L, 2R
Sierra Leone	1W, 1L	1W, 1L
Somalia	0	1C
Sudan	1W	1W, 1L
Swaziland	0	0
Tanzania	1W, 1H, 2N	1L
Togo	0	0
Uganda	1H	1H
Zaire	2W	2W
Zambia	2W, 1H	2W, 2H
Zimbabwe	2N	0

Note: C, cross-sectional study; H, health facility records; L, longitudinal study; N, NCDDP data; R, registered deaths; and W, WHO/CDD survey.

every 1,000 persons) can be estimated either from census data and vital statistics registration systems or from community-based surveys. The percentage of deaths attributable to diarrhea can be estimated with each of the study designs, although the accuracy and representativeness of the estimates may vary. The

Table 9-3. Measures of Morbidity and Mortality from Diarrhea, by Type of Study Design

| Measure | Community surveys | | | Health facility records | Registered deaths | NCDDP data |
	Longitudinal	WHO/CDD	Cross-sectional			
Morbidity						
Episodes per person per year	*	(*)	(*)			
Prevalence or short-term incidence	*	*	*			*
Percentage of all illness episodes	*		*			*
Percentage of health facility attendances or admissions				*		*
Mortality						
Case-fatality rate	*			*		
Percentage of all deaths	*	*	*	*	*	*
Deaths per 1,000 persons per year	*	*			*	

* Estimated directly.
(*) Calculated.

case-fatality rate (that is, the proportion of episodes of diarrhea that lead to death) can be either measured in a longitudinal community study or based on data from health facility admissions. Estimates based on admissions will be considerably higher than those measured in a community survey, since they reflect the risk of death from relatively severe diarrheal episodes.

Longitudinal Studies

Well-conducted longitudinal studies potentially yield the most detailed and accurate information. They are the only way to obtain direct estimates of the incidence of illness and of deaths due to diarrheal diseases. They are, however, expensive, time-consuming, and logistically complex, both to carry out and to analyze. For this reason they tend to be limited in number.

Ten major longitudinal studies have been carried out in Sub-Saharan Africa since the beginning of 1970; they have various design features and use different outcome measures, which are summarized in table 9-4. One study covered all ages, and one covered children up to 12 years of age, but the majority concentrated on children younger than five years. Three studies restricted attention still further by concentrating on the weaning period, when children are at greatest risk (Rowland, 1986); one studied children in their first year of life, and two studied them in their first three years, excluding the first six months, which precede weaning.

The study in the Machakos District of Kenya, which is described in chapter 18, was a large-scale, rural, longitudinal, population-based project covering almost 4,000 households. It obtained accurate data on the

major causes of childhood, maternal, and perinatal morbidity and mortality, including acute diarrheal disease, with the aim of improving maternal and child health in the area. For the first three years of the study, information on diarrheal morbidity was collected only for children reported as ill. The procedure was changed for the last year of the study, when diarrheal information was collected for all children. This led to a fivefold increase in incidence rates, indicating that mothers in this community often did not consider diarrhea an illness. Incidence results from the final year only were included here.

Two studies, in Chingale, Malawi, and in Imo State, Nigeria, were carried out as part of larger studies evaluating water supply and sanitation projects. The data for Bagamoyo, Tanzania, were collected as part of an evaluation of a primary health care approach to preventing deaths caused by acute respiratory infections.

The longitudinal study in Imo State was accompanied by larger cross-sectional surveys on the whole population. The Malawi study used methodology similar to that employed ten years earlier by a Swedish team in the Kirkos study in Ethiopia. Both studies placed particular emphasis on social and environmental determinants of disease, as did the study carried out by Pickering in the Gambia (Pickering *et al.*, 1987). The other Gambian study attempted to explore the relations between weaning practices, growth, and diarrheal morbidity.

The studies from the Malumfashi area of northern Nigeria formed part of the series of epidemiological and demographic studies described in chapter 21.

Although the majority were concerned with malaria and chemoprophylaxis in early childhood, urinary schistosomiasis, and meningococcal infections, two also yielded information on the epidemiology of diarrhea. One was a small longitudinal study investigating the influence of preexisting malnutrition on the incidence and severity of diarrhea (Tomkins, 1981); the other analyzed data on cause of death that were collected from a population base of 26,100 over a period of one year (Bradley and Gilles, 1984).

Information on diarrheal mortality during childhood was also collected in a major in-depth demographic study carried out from the end of 1962 to 1981 in Ngayokheme, a rural area in the Sine-Saloum region of Senegal. Approximately 5,000 persons of all ages were interviewed each year, but cause-specific results are only available for young children.

The main focus of the study in Burkina Faso was to investigate the importance and epidemiology of acute respiratory infections (ARI), but data collection was not restricted to ARI. Each week information was obtained about episodes of diarrhea and fever, as well as cough and auricular and nasal discharge, and each month the children were visited by a physician. Unfortunately, detailed analyses of the weekly data on diarrhea have not yet been reported. The monthly data yielded estimates of the average daily prevalence and the percentage of episodes of illness associated with diarrhea.

Two longitudinal surveys were also carried out in Sierra Leone (World Health Organization, 1981) and the Sudan (Callum, 1983) as part of an interregional ad hoc survey program organized by the Division of Health Statistics at the World Health Organization. These two surveys were not included in table 9-3, since studying diarrheal diseases was not among their major objectives. The published results are limited, comprising information on the percentage of childhood deaths due to diarrhea in both countries and of childhood episodes of illness due to diarrhea in Sierra Leone.

WHO/CDD Cross-Sectional Surveys

The Diarrhoeal Diseases Control Programme (CDD) of the World Health Organization developed and produced a manual describing a standard household survey methodology for gathering community-based information on diarrheal morbidity, mortality, and treatment practices for children less than five years old (World Health Organization, 1986). Such information was intended for national programs seeking to assess the extent of diarrheal disease in order to determine priorities for health care, evaluate the current status of

a control program, and establish a baseline against which to measure changes. The first such household surveys were carried out in 1981 and the first in Sub-Saharan Africa in 1982. By the end of 1987 a total of 276 surveys had been carried out in 60 countries (World Health Organization, 1988), and 67 of these were conducted in 22 countries of Sub-Saharan Africa (table 9-2 and the appendix to this chapter).

The use of longitudinal studies on a large scale is both unrealistic and inappropriate. The methodology employed in these studies was purposely quick, cheap, and easy to carry out and straightforward to analyze. Large sample sizes were readily accommodated, and the surveys were cross-sectional in nature and used a cluster-sampling technique. The majority of countries used the minimum number of 30 clusters recommended, although a few studied more. The sample size depended on the exact objectives of the survey and on the likely values for the outcome measures. In Sub-Saharan Africa the number of children selected varied between approximately 1,000 and 10,000.

DIARRHEAL MORBIDITY. The manual recommends studying diarrheal morbidity by collecting information about episodes of diarrhea that started during the two-week period prior to the survey (including the day of the survey). This measures the diarrheal incidence rate for two weeks, which can be multiplied by 26 to estimate the annual incidence of diarrhea, expressed as the number of diarrheal episodes per child per year. In order to avoid small numbers, the two-week incidence is usually presented as a percentage (that is, as the number of episodes per 100 children).

Two complications occur. First, mothers may have difficulty remembering exactly when an episode of diarrhea began. It may be better simply to ask whether a child has had diarrhea or not at any time during the past two weeks. This question gives an estimate of the two-week prevalence, rather than the incidence, of diarrhea. This prevalence can, however, be converted to incidence when the average duration of diarrheal episodes is known or can be assumed.

Second, in many countries diarrheal morbidity is not constant throughout the year, and the two-week period covered by the survey will not be representative of the entire year; strong seasonal variation may occur, as figure 9-1 illustrates for Lesotho (Feachem *et al.*, 1978). The WHO/CDD manual suggests an adjustment that takes these variations into account. Using the most recent and complete data from either surveillance systems or a selection of health facilities, an estimate is made of the proportion of the annual number of

Table 9-4. Design Features of Major Longitudinal Studies of Diarrhea in Sub-Saharan Africa

Location	Date	Sample size	Age	Length of follow-up	Frequency of visits	Type of data	Outcome measures	References
Bana, Burkina Faso	July–Sept. 1983 Jan.–March 1984	151	Less than 5 years	3 months rainy, 3 months dry season	Monthly	Current illness	Average daily prevalence, percentage of illness episodes	Lang et al. (1986)
Kirkos, Ethiopia	March 1972–March 1973	749	Less than 12 years	1 year	Biweekly	Current illness	Average daily prevalence	Freij and Wall (1977)
	Feb.–March 1975	216	Less than 12 years	60 days	Daily	Current illness	Episodes per child, percentage of illness episodes	
Bakau, The Gambia	March 1981–Feb. 1984	126	Less than 1 year	Birth to 1 year	Weekly	Recall	Episodes per child per year, average daily prevalence	Goh-Rowland et al. (1985); Rowland et al. (1986)
	July–Oct. 1984	244	6–35 months	15 weeks	Weekly	Recall	Episodes per child, average daily prevalence	Pickering et al. (1987)
Machakos, Kenya	June 1974–June 1977	3,899 (average)	Less than 5 years	Variable	Biweekly	Recall	Average two-week incidence, deaths per 1,000 per year, percentage of all deaths	Leeuwenburg et al. (1984); Omondi-Odhiambo et al. (1984)
Chingale, Malawi	Feb. 1983–March 1984 Sept. 1984–Sept. 1985	637 (average)	Less than 5 years	Variable	Biweekly	Current illness	Average daily prevalence, deaths per 1,000 per year, percentage of all deaths	Lindskog (1987)
Malumfashi, Nigeria	April–June 1979	343	6–35 months	3 months	Weekly	Recall	Episodes per child	Tomkins (1981)
Imo State, Nigeria	Nov. 1977–Oct. 1978	26,100	All	1 year	Monthly	Recall	Percentage of all deaths	Bradley and Gilles (1984)
	Nov. 1982–June 1986	454 (average)	Less than 5 years	Variable	Biweekly	Daily diaries	Episodes per child per year	Blum et al. (1990)
Ngayokheme, Senegal	Dec. 1962–April 1981	620 (average)	Less than 5 years	Variable	Yearly	Recall	Deaths per 1,000 per year, percentage of all deaths	Cantrelle et al. (1986)
Bagamoyo, Tanzania	June 1983–Sept. 1985	17,570 (average)	Less than 5 years	Variable	Yearly	Recall	Deaths per 1,000 per year, percentage of all deaths	Mtango and Neuvians (1986)

Figure 9-1. Monthly Incidence of Diarrhea, Lesotho, 1971–75

Number
of reported episodes

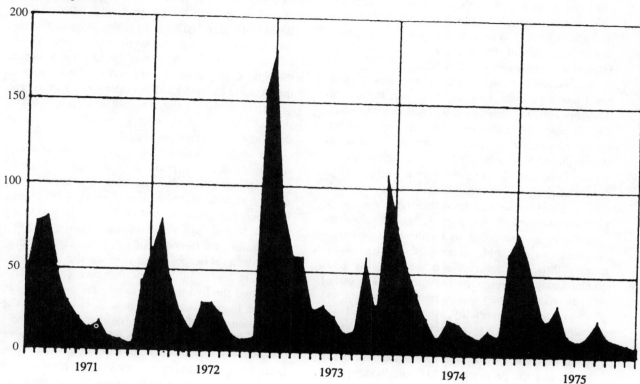

Source: Feachem *et al.* (1978).

diarrheal episodes that are likely to occur in the two-week period covered by the survey. The two-week incidence is then divided by this proportion, termed the seasonality adjustment factor, to give an annual incidence rate. If there were no seasonal variation, the adjustment factor would equal 1/26.

This adjustment was employed in many of the surveys (see the appendix). It is, of course, based on many assumptions. In particular it assumes that the seasonal variation in diarrheal cases seen at health facilities directly reflects the seasonal variation in incidence experienced by the community. This should be true for the incidence of severe diarrhea, provided that access, which can be disrupted by heavy rains, and health-seeking behaviors, which can vary if the amount of time available for child care fluctuates with the time devoted to agricultural activities, remain the same throughout the year. It is less likely to be true for the incidence of all diarrheal episodes, since seasonal

variations tend to be related to differences in the etiology of diarrhea: the bacterial diarrheas peak in the hot wet months, and rotavirus diarrhea peaks in the colder months. Data from Bangladesh suggest that the severity of an episode depends on its etiology. In a one-year study conducted in a village in rural Bangladesh, Black *et al.* (1981) found that children less than two years old with diarrhea and isolated rotavirus or enterotoxigenic *Escherichia coli* were more likely to be dehydrated than children with diarrhea associated with other pathogens (44 and 14 percent, respectively, compared with 5 percent) and were more likely to be taken to a health facility (30 and 5 percent, respectively, compared with 2 percent).

An annual estimate derived from a single cross-sectional survey is at best a rough estimate and must be interpreted with care. Nevertheless it can indicate the general magnitude of the problem and is easier to assimilate than a two-week incidence.

DIARRHEAL MORTALITY. Since mortality is rarer than illness, estimating mortality requires larger sample sizes and more resources than estimating morbidity. The manual suggests collecting mortality data if diarrhea is known to be a major cause of childhood death, say, one of the top five causes, or if no information exists on causes of death.

The CDD surveys estimated three measures of childhood mortality over the preceding year: the overall mortality rate, the diarrhea-associated mortality rate, and the proportion of deaths associated with diarrhea. Family members were asked to recall childhood deaths that occurred during the 12 months preceding the survey. Care was taken to minimize the likelihood that particular groups of childhood deaths were missed; in some cultures babies that die within days or weeks of birth are purposefully forgotten. Using a local events calendar is recommended to fix the time period as accurately as possible. Accomplishing this is extremely difficult, however, and the mortality rates obtained may contain many inaccuracies. The use of alternative indirect methods of estimating overall and diarrhea-associated mortality, which it is hoped will prove more accurate, is therefore being explored by the CDD program and the London School of Hygiene and Tropical Medicine (World Health Organization, 1988).

Estimating the proportion of all childhood deaths associated with diarrhea faces the same issues, regardless of whether direct or indirect methods are used to estimate mortality rates. The estimate relies on correctly identifying the symptoms associated with a death, which has inherent problems of misclassification and is likely to be less accurate the longer the amount of time that has elapsed since the death.

Other Cross-Sectional Surveys

Four other cross-sectional surveys were reviewed, from Ghana (Danfa Project, 1979), Nigeria (Huttly *et al.*, 1987), Senegal (Fontaine *et al.*, 1984), and Somalia (Aden and Birk, 1981), that have very different designs and objectives.

The cross-sectional study in Ghana covered approximately 4,000 persons of all ages and produced estimates of the prevalence of diarrhea over the two weeks preceding the study. It was carried out in 1972 as a small part of the Danfa Comprehensive Rural Health and Family Planning Project, which is described in chapter 22.

The objective of the study in Imo State, Nigeria, was to evaluate a water supply and sanitation project. The longitudinal component of this study has already been mentioned (see table 9-4). In addition large cross-

sectional surveys were carried out twice a year, once during the dry season and once during the wet. The data presented here were collected by baseline studies carried out in 1983 that covered about 5,000 persons. Because they showed similar epidemiological patterns, the results for the two seasons were combined to yield average estimates of the prevalence of diarrhea during the eight days preceding the interview (two weeks in the local Ibo calendar) and its putative risk factors. The investigators also estimated annual incidence, based on the eight-day prevalence rates, by assuming an average duration of four days per episode.

The study in Senegal was a rapid cross-sectional survey carried out prior to launching a national program against diarrheal diseases. It collected minimal information on the extent of diarrhea in children less than five years old and on the way it was being treated. In five days, the investigators surveyed 1,083 households in a crowded suburb of Dakar and measured the prevalence of diarrhea on the day of the survey in 1,940 children less than five years of age. Forty-two children had died during the previous year, and the likely cause of death was ascertained. The population resisted discussing deaths, and the authors of that study consider the number of deaths to be considerably underestimated. This should not, however, have affected the representativeness of the cause-of-death data, and only data on the percentage of deaths due to diarrhea, and its prominence, were used here. Mortality rates were not included.

The study in Somalia was conducted to discover the principal causes of death of infants and young children, including stillbirths and abortions, as part of a strategy to improve the effectiveness of the maternal and child health (MCH) services. Between April and November 1977, 852 mothers were interviewed about their obstetric history. They had delivered 3,774 children, 932 of whom had died, most (94 percent) before their fifth birthday. The cause of death was ascertained for 913 of these deaths. No time limit was placed on the recall period, and some of the deaths had taken place more than five years before. Thus the data are likely to be of varying reliability.

Analyses of Health Facility Records

Although the most complete picture of the disease experience of a community is undoubtedly obtained from carefully conducted community studies, routinely collected health facility records also provide a useful and readily accessible source of information. The percentage of attendances and admissions for diarrhea indicates the relative importance of diarrhea as a cause of severe morbidity, while the percentage of deaths indicates its position as a major cause of mortality.

It must be realized, however, that health facility records are not representative of the disease burden in the community. Many persons with diarrhea do not seek medical attention for a variety of reasons. They may consider the episode to be too mild, prefer traditional practitioners, lack access to appropriate facilities, or have financial or time constraints. Attendances tend to be drawn from certain subsections of the community and to represent the most severe episodes. Similarly, the deaths that occur in hospitals tend to represent only a small proportion of all deaths. For example, the 338 childhood deaths that were recorded in hospitals in Lesotho in 1974 account for less than one-fifteenth of the minimum number of 7,000 childhood deaths calculated from community-based estimates of the crude birth rate and under-five death rate (Feachem *et al.*, 1978). Thus hospital records are not appropriate for estimating incidence rates or mortality rates.

Seven analyses of attendances, admissions, or both have been reported in the literature since 1977 for the following countries: Ghana (Danfa Project, 1979), Kenya (Mutanda, 1980), Lesotho (Feachem *et al.*, 1978), Nigeria (Osuhor and Etta, 1980), Tanzania (Tanner *et al.*, 1987), Uganda (Williams *et al.*, 1986), and Zambia (Balint and Anand, 1979). The data sets are of varying size. At one extreme is the analysis of 30,129 admissions recorded from July 1951 to August 1978 in a small mission hospital in a rural area of the West Nile District of Uganda; at the other is the analysis of 399 attendances recorded during two months at a clinic for children under five in Zaria, Nigeria.

Two studies, those from Uganda and Zambia, also looked at diarrhea as a cause of hospital deaths. The analyses of admissions and deaths were combined to estimate the case-fatality rates occurring in the hospitals studied; that is, the probability that a child admitted with diarrhea will die from it.

Five additional studies reported causes of hospital deaths, one from Lesotho (Feachem *et al.*, 1978), three from Nigeria (Alakija, 1981; Adeyokunnu *et al.*, 1980; Hunpono-Wusu, 1976), and one from Zambia (Watts and Chintu, 1983).

Analyses of Registered Deaths

The usefulness of the registration systems that do exist is often restricted by substantial underregistration. Moreover, errors occur in the reported age of death,

many entries record the age as not known, standard definitions and classifications may not be used, and clear rules may not govern which of multiple illnesses should be recorded as the cause of death. The variation in the quality and quantity of information from different areas of the country is likely to be considerable (Black, 1984). These problems of inaccuracies in reported age and cause of death also apply to analyses of health facility records.

Mauritius is the only country in Sub-Saharan Africa for which cause-specific mortality rates are reported in the *World Health Statistics Annual*, but no category corresponds directly to diarrheal diseases. The only national diarrhea-specific mortality rates and percentage cause of death reported in the United Nations 1979 *Demographic Yearbook* are for Angola and Kenya (United Nations, 1979), and those are several years out of date (1972 and 1970, respectively) and not available by age group.

In 1981 the United Nations and the World Health Organization initiated a series of case studies of mortality determinants in five developing countries. Two Sub-Saharan African countries were selected, Kenya and Senegal, together with Bangladesh, Guatemala, and Sri Lanka. The Kenya study included analyses of deaths reported to the registrar general in 1977 for 24 of the country's 41 districts and gave estimates of the percentage of deaths due to diarrhea and of the diarrhea-specific mortality rates among children less than five years old (Ewbank *et al.*, 1986). The latter rates were adjusted to allow for the considerable underreporting present in this registration system. All districts with more than 20 percent coverage were included, as were a few districts to ensure regional representation. The maximum coverage for infant and child deaths was estimated to be 73 percent, and the coverage rate exceeded 50 percent in just four districts. In addition, the quality of the cause-of-death data was variable: in one district with a coverage of 64 percent, for example, only 7 percent of the death certificates were medically certified. Median values of the district estimates were used in this review.

Relevant data from the Senegal study include results from the Ngayokheme longitudinal study, described above, plus two sets of cause-of-death data based on analyses of deaths registered from 1973–80 in the cities of Dakar and Saint-Louis (Cantrelle *et al.*, 1986).

In addition, two reports analyze deaths recorded by the vital statistics registration system of Lagos City, Nigeria. The first, by Ayeni (1980), is based on data for 1977 and compares the leading causes of death with those in other areas of the world. The second analysis, by Adegbola and Chojnacka (1984), looks at the changing structure of the causes of death between 1965 and 1975. This review included only the results for 1977, which were the most recent at the time of this writing. The Lagos system appears to be 60 percent complete and to be better than that of any other city in Nigeria (Ayeni, 1980). In 1977, 17 percent of death certificates showed ill-defined causes, which is below the 25 percent limit set by the World Health Organization for acceptability of death certification (Ayeni, 1980).

NCDDP Data

The national diarrheal disease control programs report seven sets of data. Ethiopia has national figures on the percentages of childhood outpatient attendances, of childhood admissions, and of all deaths attributed to diarrhea; Niger has national estimates of the percentages of childhood episodes of illness and of all deaths due to diarrhea. The two sets of health facility data from Tanzania and the two from Zimbabwe are more restricted and more localized. Finally, one community-based estimate of childhood prevalence was reviewed for Lesotho.

Childhood Morbidity

The compilation of results in table 9-5 confirms that diarrheal diseases are a major cause of childhood morbidity in Sub-Saharan Africa. The average child is likely to experience as many as 4.9 episodes of diarrhea a year and to have diarrhea 9.7 percent of the time, or 35 days each year. The burden on the health facilities is high. On average, diarrhea is responsible for 25 percent of all episodes of childhood illness, 14.0 percent of outpatient attendances, and 15.7 percent of hospital admissions, which can reach 40 percent.

Incidence

The overall median incidence of diarrhea is estimated to be 4.9 episodes per year for a child less than five years old (table 9-5). There is, however, considerable variation, with estimates from the 73 studies carried out in 23 countries ranging from 1.6 to 9.9 episodes per child per year (see figure 9-2). Only three values (4.1 percent) are below the median global incidence rate of 2.2 episodes per child per year, which was estimated by Snyder and Merson (1982) in their review. Four values (5.5 percent) are above 9.0 episodes, and a sizable proportion (18 values, or 24.7 percent) are above six episodes per child per year.

As much variation exists between countries as within a country, and there are no obvious differences between urban and rural settings (see the appendix). The estimates from the 20 WHO/CDD surveys carried out in 20 urban areas of Nigeria during September 1986 range from 2.0 to 9.9 episodes per child per year and vary as much as the data set as a whole.

The incidence estimates in the 67 WHO/CDD surveys were calculated from two-week prevalence or incidence data. As discussed earlier, such estimates are very dependent on the time of year chosen for the survey, particularly whether it was conducted during the peak or the low season. Five of the other estimates were from longitudinal studies, but only two covered all seasons of the year; the other three were carried out over periods of just a few months (table 9-4). Two of these studies also restricted attention to either the first year of life or the first three years, age groups that are at particularly high risk. The final estimate from the study in Imo State, Nigeria, was based on two cross-sectional surveys carried out in two different seasons, wet and dry (Huttly *et al.*, 1987).

The estimates of incidence may therefore be biased upwards, particularly given the usual (and indeed advisable) practice of carrying out surveys during the peak transmission season. It seems unlikely, however, that this is the case or that methodological issues explain much of the observed variation. First, just over half the WHO/CDD surveys employed some sort of seasonal adjustment in the calculation (see the appendix) and half did not; yet the amounts of variation within these two sets are similar, as are the sizes of the estimates obtained. Second, just as much variation is seen in the 20 studies in Nigeria that were carried out within a month of each other as in the data set as a whole.

Age- and Gender-Specific Rates

A few studies present results in sufficient age detail to examine variations in diarrheal morbidity rates over the first five years of life. Figure 9-3 presents as yet unpublished results from the longitudinal component of the study in Imo State, Nigeria, which followed an average of 454 children for four years. Daily diarrheal information was obtained from diaries completed by the mothers (Blum *et al.*, 1990). The incidence rates were clearly highest for children 6–11 months and 1 year of age, the time of the traditional weaning period. This pattern resembles that found in many other studies, although the exact shape and timing of the peak varies. In the Machakos study in Kenya the peak

Table 9-5. Diarrheal Morbidity Results for Children Aged 0–4

Results and type of study	Median	Minimum	Maximum	Number of studies	Number of countries covered
Episodes per child per year					
WHO/CDD surveys	4.8	1.6	9.9	67	22
Other surveys	7.1	3.6	9.7	6	3
Overall	4.9	1.6	9.9	73	23
Two-week prevalence or incidence					
WHO/CDD surveys	16.7	7.4	38.1	67	22
Other surveys	10.5	7.0	34.0	3	3
Overall	16.6	7.0	38.1	70	24
Eight-day prevalence	23.4	—	—	1	1
Daily prevalence	9.7	4.5	16.0	6	5
Percentage of all illness episodes	25.0	9.3	41.8	5	5
Percentage of health facility					
Attendances	14.0	8.9	23.4	7	6
Admissions	15.7	5.6	38.4	6	6

occurred among infants 6–11 months of age (Leeuwenburg *et al.*, 1984), with 1-year-olds and infants from birth to 5 months of age at similar risk.

A surprising finding in the study of Imo State is the excessive diarrhea among young males compared with females. This gender difference is also apparent in both the wet and dry season cross-sectional surveys (Huttly *et al.*, 1987). The only other study to examine this issue found a slight but insignificant excess of episodes among males: 2.9 compared with 2.7 episodes over a 15-week period in urban Gambia (Pickering *et al.*, 1987).

Severity

Four longitudinal studies give information on the duration of diarrheal episodes (Blum *et al.*, 1990; Freij and Wall, 1977; Pickering *et al.*, 1987; Goh-Rowland *et al.*, 1985), reporting median values between four and five days. Pickering *et al.* (1987) found a trend of decreasing mean duration of episodes with increasing age among their cohort of Gambian children less than 3 years of age. Freij and Wall (1977) found a similar trend over the first 12 years of life in the Kirkos study in Ethiopia; the median duration decreased from 5.7 days among children less than 2 years old, to 3.8 days among those age 2–4, to 3.4 days among those age 5–11.

Between 2 and 11 percent of episodes were found to persist for more than two weeks, and thus to be at particular risk of leading to severe nutritional disorders

Figure 9-2. Distribution of 73 Estimates of Incidence of Diarrheal Episodes per Child per Year

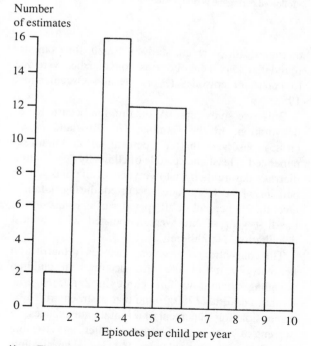

Note: These estimates of the overall incidence of diarrhea in children under five years of age are from 73 studies carried out in 23 countries.

Figure 9-3. Incidence of Diarrhea in Children, Imo State, Nigeria, November 1982–June 1986

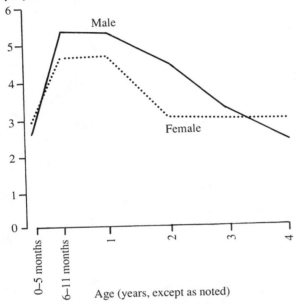

Note: The incidence is based on an average of 454 children followed during the period of study.

or even death. A recent study in Brazil, for example, found that 35 percent of deaths from diarrhea were due to persistent episodes (World Health Organization, 1988).

Only one study reported data on the occurrence of dehydration. In the Gambia, Goh-Rowland *et al.* (1985) observed that 17 percent of children experienced at least one episode of clinically dehydrating diarrhea during their first two years of life and that 76 percent of such episodes occurred during infancy. Overall, 2.9 percent of all episodes of diarrhea during the first year of life were associated with clinical dehydration. No children died.

The concentration of severe episodes of diarrhea in the early years of life also occurred in children attending a child welfare clinic in Zaria, Nigeria. Osuhor and Etta (1980) found that gastroenteritis was responsible for 18 percent of all infant attendances, 14 percent of attendances among children age 1–2 but only 3 percent among those age 3–4. The absolute number of clinic attendances was also considerably lower for the 3–4 age group, one-quarter to one-fifth of those for the younger age groups.

Diarrhea is also a frequent complication of measles and has a high associated case-fatality rate (Feachem and Koblinsky, 1983). Unpublished results from the longitudinal component of the study in Nigeria's Imo State show that over 70 percent of measles episodes had an associated episode of diarrhea; that is, an episode of diarrhea occurring during the period from one week before the onset of the measles rash to six months after. Overall, measles accounted for 5.1 percent of all episodes of diarrhea among children under five. This is almost the same as the figure of 6.1 percent that was observed over 20 years earlier in another study in Nigeria (Morley *et al.*, 1963).

Morbidity at Older Ages

The vast majority of studies focus on children during their first five years of life; few consider older children or adults. The cross-sectional surveys carried out in Imo State, Nigeria, provide the only data that give a detailed picture of diarrhea morbidity rates over the whole range of ages (Huttly *et al.*, 1987). The results are summarized in figure 9-4.

Diarrhea was associated with up to 66 percent of all illnesses in young children and with about 20 percent of illnesses in adults. The prevalence rates peaked in the 6–11 month and 1 year age groups and then decreased through the remainder of childhood. They reached their lowest level during adolescence and early adulthood. From then on they gradually increased so that the rates in old age were approximately twice as high as those in early adulthood. The male excess of diarrheal morbidity in early childhood was statistically significant (P < 0.01). This trend reversed in adulthood, when the prevalence rates for females were consistently higher than those for males (P < 0.001).

Overall the diarrheal morbidity rates among the adults observed in this study were three to five times lower than those found among children in the high-risk weaning period. Similar differentials were found in the Danfa cross-sectional survey (Danfa Project, 1979) and in data on hospital admissions from Lesotho (Feachem *et al.*, 1978) and Uganda (Williams *et al.*, 1986). Nevertheless, diarrhea affected a sizable proportion of the adult population in Imo State, Nigeria, and accounted for one-fifth of all adult illnesses.

Childhood Mortality

The compilation of results in table 9-6 clearly shows diarrhea to be a major cause of childhood mortality. This was apparent in all types of data sources, community-based studies, analyses of hospital admissions, and registered deaths. All 14 studies that

Figure 9-4. Diarrheal Morbidity, Imo State, Nigeria, 1983

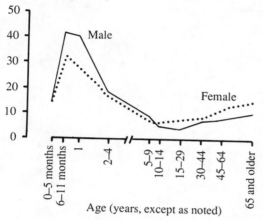

Prevalence (percent)

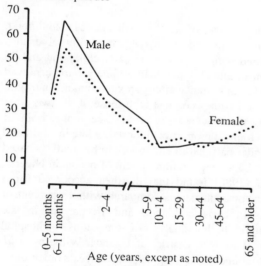

Diarrhea as percentage of all illness episodes

Age (years, except as noted)

Note: The recall period for the prevalence of diarrhea was eight days. These are the average results from surveys conducted in the wet and dry seasons. The sample size was 5,170.

assessed the relative importance of diseases placed diarrhea among the top three causes of death.

Diarrheal Mortality Rate

The annual number of diarrhea-associated deaths for every 1,000 children is the best measure of the mortality risk to children in the community from diarrhea. It is, however, extremely difficult to determine. The most reliable way is through large-scale community studies with regular surveillance, pref-

erably every month (Snyder and Merson, 1982), although regular surveillance and attendant health care can lead to reduced estimates. Only 2 of the 45 estimates satisfied these criteria; those from the Machakos study in Kenya (Omondi-Odhiambo *et al.*, 1984) and the Chingale study in Malawi (Lindskog, 1987). These estimates were 3.4 and 18.0 diarrhea deaths per 1,000 children per year. The other two longitudinal estimates were based on yearly recall. That from the Bagamoyo study in Tanzania equaled 4.9 deaths per 1,000 children per year (Mtango and Neuvians, 1986) and that from the Ngayokheme study in Senegal equaled 21.8 deaths (Cantrelle *et al.*, 1986). The estimate based on registered deaths from 23 districts in Kenya was 3.6 (Ewbank *et al.*, 1986), which resembles the estimate from the Machakos study.

The other 40 estimates of diarrhea mortality rates were obtained from WHO/CDD cross-sectional surveys. They varied considerably, ranging from 1.3 to 76.8 deaths per 1,000 children per year. The median was 11.8 deaths. As previously discussed, the mortality estimates from these surveys are likely to contain many inaccuracies, largely caused by problems in fixing the time period. They should therefore be interpreted with caution.

Proportional Mortality Rate

Fifty-nine surveys estimated the proportional mortality rate; that is, the percentage of childhood deaths that are attributed to diarrhea. Estimates from the 40 WHO/CDD surveys ranged from 13.2 to 70.4 percent, while those from the 19 other types of studies ranged from 4.0 to 46.0 percent (see table 9-6). The median value of 45 percent derived from the WHO/CDD surveys was higher than all but 1 of the 19 estimates from the other studies. This suggests that the WHO/CDD methodology may have produced inflated estimates of the proportional diarrheal mortality rate, possibly because it specifically focused on diarrhea as a cause of death rather than on a variety of different causes, as the majority of other studies did.

Case-Fatality Rate

Three hospital studies reported case-fatality rates for diarrhea (Balint and Anand, 1979; Feachem *et al.*, 1978; Williams *et al.*, 1986). They estimated that 11–19 percent of children admitted with diarrhea die from it. In their community-based study of Machakos, Kenya, Omondi-Odhiambo *et al.* (1984) estimated that 0.1 percent (that is, 1 in 1,000) of all childhood diarrheal episodes end in death. This is considerably lower than the hospital-based estimates, as would be

Table 9-6. Diarrheal Mortality Results for Children Aged 0–4

Results and type of study	Median	Minimum	Maximum	Number of studies	Number of countries covered
Rank as cause of death	2	3	1	14	11
Deaths per 1,000 per year					
WHO/CDD surveys	11.8	1.3	76.8	40	18
Other surveys	4.9	3.4	21.8	5	4
Overall	11.0	1.3	76.8	45	22
Percentage of all deaths					
WHO/CDD surveys	45.0	13.2	70.4	40	18
Longitudinal	20.0	14.2	46.0	7	7
Cross-sectional	22.0	4.0	26.2	3	3
Health facility records	28.7	9.1	34.8	5	4
Registered deaths	11.5	7.7	12.7	4	3
Overall	37.7	4.0	70.4	59	28
Case-fatality rate					
Community study	0.1	—	—	1	1
Health facility records	14.2	11.0	19.4	3	3

expected, since it was based on all diarrheal episodes occurring in the community and not just on those severe enough to lead to hospital admission.

Age-Specific Rates

Six studies presented proportional diarrheal mortality rates in narrower age groups, as summarized in table 9-7. The majority found a peak in infants 1–11 months old, and all studies found considerably lower rates during the neonatal period. In the Machakos study in Kenya Omondi-Odhiambo *et al.* (1984) found that just over three-quarters of childhood deaths from diarrhea occurred during infancy and that the diarrheal mortality rate was eleven times higher among infants than among children age 1–4 years (10.9 compared with 1.0 diarrhea deaths per 1,000 children per year).

Mortality at Older Ages

Childhood deaths account for a large proportion of all deaths in developing countries. In the community-based surveillance study carried out in the Malumfashi area of Nigeria, for example, 61 percent of all deaths occurred among children less than five years old (Bradley and Gilles, 1984). It is not surprising, therefore, that research has focused on childhood mortality and that little information is available for older age groups. The exceptions, such as the Malumfashi study, which covered all ages, are few. Although overall mortality rates in Malumfashi were highest in early childhood, the proportional diarrheal mortality rates were fairly constant, and diarrhea remained an

important cause of death at all ages. In adulthood, diarrhea accounted for about 21 percent of deaths, compared with 24 percent in early childhood and 28 percent in late childhood. In all age groups it ranked second in importance after pyrexia of unknown origin.

These findings contrast with those of the two other studies that covered the whole age range, both of which found a proportional mortality rate in adulthood just under half that in childhood. In his analysis based on the Lagos registration system of deaths in Nigeria, Ayeni (1980) found that diarrhea accounted for 5 percent of adult deaths compared with 13 percent of deaths in early childhood and 10 percent in late childhood. In their analysis of admissions to a hospital in the West Nile District of Uganda, Williams *et al.* (1986) found that among persons ten years old or older 3.8 percent of deaths were due to diarrhea, compared with 9.1 percent of deaths among those less than ten years old.

Etiology

The etiology of diarrhea was investigated in only one of the studies reviewed. In their study in the Gambia covering the first two years of life, Goh-Rowland *et al.* (1985) isolated bacterial and viral pathogens from 27.5 percent of the stools collected during diarrheal episodes and from 19.0 percent of the stools collected during control periods. Enterotoxigenic *Escherichia coli*, with an isolation rate of 9.9 percent compared with 5.9 percent during control periods, was the most common pathogen associated with diarrhea. Next was

Table 9-7. Percentage of Deaths due to Diarrhea, by Age, Children Aged 0–4

Location	Date	Less than 1 week	1–3 weeks	0–3 weeks	1–11 months	1–4 years	Reference
				Age			
Machakos, Kenya	1975–78			2.9	39.6	13.6	Omondi-Odhiambo *et al.* (1984)
Nigeria							
Ibadan	1969–73			3.7	17.7	24.1	Adeyokunnu *et al.* (1980)
Lagos	1967	0.4	4.2		22.5	12.7	Adegbola and Chojnacka (1984)
Lagos	1977	1.0	5.5		31.9	13.7	Ayeni (1980)
Mogadishu, Somalia	1977			8.8	33.2	29.0	Aden and Birk (1981)
Northern Sudan	1975–76			36	52	46	Callum (1983)

Note: Empty cells are the result of differences in the age groups studied.

rotavirus, which was associated with 5.8 percent of diarrheal episodes and 1.4 percent of control periods. *Campylobacter jejuni* also had a relatively high isolation rate but occurred more frequently during control periods than during episodes of illness (6.9 and 4.3 percent, respectively).

In addition, 23 studies were identified which specifically studied the etiology of diarrhea. One community-based study was from Ghana (Addy and Aikins-Bekoe, 1986), and one was from Liberia (Højlying *et al.*, 1986). The remainder were hospital based. These included one study from the Central African Republic (Georges *et al.*, 1984); four from Ethiopia (Ashenafi and Gedebou, 1985; Muhe *et al.*, 1986; Stintzing *et al.*, 1981; Thoren *et al.*, 1982); one from Gabon (Sitbon *et al.*, 1985); one from the Gambia (Billingham, 1981); three from Kenya (Hansen *et al.*, 1978; Mutanda *et al.*, 1984; Wamola, 1980); six from Nigeria (Abiodun *et al.*, 1984; Akinterinwa and Paul, 1982; Yakubu and Sathiakumar, 1985; Offor and Wemambu, 1982; Dosunmu-Ogunbi *et al.*, 1983; Olusanya *et al.*, 1983); three from Rwanda (Bogaerts *et al.*, 1984; De Mol and Bosmans, 1978; De Mol *et al.*, 1984); one from Zaire (De Mol *et al.*, 1983); and one from Zambia (Patel *et al.*, 1982).

Thus data were available from 24 etiological studies carried out in 11 countries. These by no means form a homogeneous set: 3 were community-based studies, and the other 21 were hospital based. Nine studies had comparison results from control groups. The age ranges covered varied from the first 18 months of life to the whole span of ages, which may have affected the resulting isolation rates. For example, rotavirus infec-

tions occur primarily during the first two years of life because older children and adults have generally acquired resistance to them (Black, 1984). Furthermore, some studies investigated a range of possible pathogens, while others focused on a single pathogen, which produced varying numbers of results for each pathogen (table 9-8).

Although some caution is necessary in interpreting the results, clear patterns do emerge. The predominant organisms discovered were rotavirus, *Campylobacter jejuni*, enterotoxigenic *Escherichia coli* (ETEC), enteropathogenic *E. coli* (EPEC), and *Cryptosporidium* spp., and their importance was confirmed by control data. Where available, the control isolation rates were lower than those for patients with diarrhea with the exception of the *Campylobacter jejuni* result from the community-based Gambian study. In his review Black (1984) identified the first four pathogens on this list; *Campylobacter* was a new addition at that time. Relatively few data are available for *Cryptosporidium* spp., which emerged since Black's review as an important cause of diarrhea. In a study of its epidemiology in Liberia, Højlying *et al.* (1986) found that the prevalence of *Cryptosporidium* spp. decreased with age and was highest during the first two years of life. Notable risk factors were bottle feeding and crowding, and its presence was restricted to non-Muslim households.

Salmonella, *Shigella*, and *Giardia lamblia* were also significant causes of diarrheal disease. In general the most commonly isolated *Shigella* serogroup was *S. flexneri*. Two major outbreaks of dysentery have occurred in Sub-Saharan Africa in recent years. The

Table 9-8. Frequency of Isolation of Etiologic Agents

Pathogen	Episodes per child per year			Number of studies	Number of countries covered
	Median	Minimum	Maximum		
Campylobacter jejuni	10.8	2.0	16.1	10	6
Cryptosporidium	8.4	3.0	12.9	5	3
Ent. histolytica	1.7	1.0	14.8	7	6
EPEC	7.0	0.4	19.0	11	7
ETEC	9.4	1.2	13.5	6	6
Giardia lamblia	4.6	1.0	26.1	8	7
Rotavirus	19.8	3.4	49.0	8	6
Salmonella	4.2	1.2	15.0	17	8
Shigella	4.6	0.0	32.4	18	7

first, an extensive outbreak caused by *S. dysenteriae* type 1, started in Central Africa in 1979 and involved over the next two or three years much of Zaire as well as Rwanda and Burundi (Malengreau *et al.*, 1983; Ebright *et al.*, 1984). The second was a national epidemic caused by all four serogroups, which occurred in Tanzania in 1981–82 (Mhalu *et al.*, 1984).

Other Determinants of Disease

Information on risk factors associated with diarrhea in Sub-Saharan Africa is relatively scarce. Three studies looked at a range of social and environmental factors, Pickering's (1985) study in the Gambia, the Kirkos study in Ethiopia (Freij and Wall, 1977), and the Imo State cross-sectional surveys in Nigeria (Huttly *et al.*, 1987). A few others focused on particular issues, such as the relationships between diarrhea and growth or the impact of improved water supplies and sanitation facilities. The Imo State study is the only one that investigated risk factors for adult as well as childhood morbidity.

In her study in urban Gambia Pickering (1985) surprisingly found no significant associations between diarrheal morbidity and 36 factors, although some of these, such as the lack of a standpipe in the compound, the lack of a flush toilet, the lack of a refrigerator, and living in traditional housing, were related to the risk of chronic malnutrition, as assessed by low height-for-age. In the same urban area, Rowland *et al.* (1988) found that diarrheal diseases contributed significantly to faltering weight and were estimated to explain half of the observed deficit. In Nigeria, Tomkins (1981) investigated this relationship between growth and diarrhea the other way around. He found that low weight-for-age, low height-for-age, and low weight-for-height had no effect on the incidence of diarrhea

but that all three were associated with increased duration of diarrhea.

In Ethiopia De Sole *et al.* (1987) found that children with vitamin A deficiency were twice as likely to have suffered a severe episode of diarrhea in the preceding year as nondeficient children. They were not able to investigate within their data set which, if either, was more likely to be causal. Limited evidence from elsewhere in the world, Indonesia in particular, suggests that vitamin A deficiency predisposes persons to increased risk of diarrheal illness and predisposes preschool children to an increased risk of death (Feachem, 1987).

In their cross-sectional study in Nigeria Huttly *et al.* (1987) also found no association between diarrhea and education or occupation; they did, however, find that poor housing, an unclean domestic environment, use of nonpurified water, and lack of soap were all associated with increased risk of diarrhea. Inexplicably, they found that pregnant women seemed to be at particularly low risk. They also found that exclusive breast-feeding conferred considerable protection on infants during the first few months of life. Children less than three months old who were not breast-fed at all were 10.2 times more likely to have had diarrhea during the two weeks prior to the survey than children of the same age who were breast-fed exclusively. Those who were breast-fed some of the time were 3.3 times more likely to have had diarrhea than those who were breast-fed exclusively. In the Gambia early weaning was associated with a slight increase in diarrheal morbidity and an increased risk of persistent diarrhea, but these findings were not statistically significant (Rowland *et al.*, 1986). Another study of weaning-age children in the Gambia found no increased risk of morbidity associated with contaminated food and water; in fact, the levels of contamination were so high that it was difficult to understand why some children did not have more diarrhea (Lloyd-Evans *et al.*, 1984).

In their analysis of the Kirkos study in Ethiopia Freij and Wall (1977, 1979) investigated the associations among 18 individual and household characteristics and the average daily prevalence of diarrhea using multivariate THAID (Theta-Automatic Interaction Detector) analysis. Poor housing, crowded conditions, low income, poor nutritional status, inadequate water supply, inadequate sanitation, and low water consumption emerged as the main risk factors. These results, together with those from the Imo State project, suggest the importance of promoting personal and domestic hygiene, particularly in the context of water supply and sanitation projects.

The Imo State project also measured the impact of improved water supply and sanitation facilities, which were introduced into three of the five villages studied. The other two villages acted as control groups. An impact on diarrheal morbidity was found in limited subgroups of the population only. Morbidity rates in young children seemed to be associated with water availability more than with water quantity (Huttly *et al.*, 1990). The Chingale project in Malawi based its evaluation on a comparison of data collected one year before and one year after the introduction of a piped water supply. Although total morbidity rates were reduced in households using the new supply, no impact on diarrheal diseases was seen (Lindskog, 1987). Such evaluations are fraught with methodological difficulties (Blum and Feachem, 1983). The first of a new generation of studies using the case-control approach suggested by Briscoe *et al.* (1986) was recently completed in the Zomba District of Malawi (Young and Briscoe, 1988). That study compared the water and sanitation facilities used by children who attended clinics because of acute diarrhea with those used by a control group, who went to the clinic because of diseases unrelated to water. During the warm, rainy season, improved water and sanitation facilities were associated with a 20 percent reduction in the risk of attending a clinic for diarrhea, although this did not quite reach statistical significance.

Control Programs

Thirty-four of the 39 countries in Sub-Saharan Africa have operational diarrheal disease control programs, and another 3 (Burkina Faso, Gabon, and Guinea-Bissau) have plans for such programs. The two exceptions are Guinea and Mauritius (World Health Organization, 1988). The control programs are based largely on a case-management strategy that emphasizes increasing the usage rate of oral rehydration therapy (ORT). ORT includes oral rehydration salts (ORS), salt-and-sugar solutions (SSS), and recommended home fluids (RHF), such as rice water, cereal-based gruels, soups, and teas. Salt-and-sugar solutions are becoming increasingly unattractive, because of problems associated with preparing them correctly and because sugar is unavailable in many countries. Three other strategies are also being progressively introduced: improved nutrition, especially breast-feeding and appropriate weaning, use of safe water, and good personal and domestic hygiene (World Health Organization, 1988).

By the end of 1988 ten countries in Sub-Saharan Africa produced ORS locally. At the end of 1987 approximately 38 percent of the population of Sub-Saharan Africa had access to someone who was trained to use ORS and who received adequate supplies of it. It is also estimated that 12 percent of diarrheal episodes in children under five years of age were being treated with ORS and that appropriate ORT (including ORS) was administered in 19 percent of the episodes (World Health Organization, 1989). Although they have more than doubled since 1985, these rates are still substantially lower than those in other regions of the world (table 9-9). There is, of course, considerable variation among countries. In Guinea and Guinea-Bissau the ORT usage rate was only 1 percent, whereas it was 68 percent in Lesotho and 59 percent in Zambia.

A recent study carried out by Mozambique's Ministry of Health (1988) highlighted the gap that exists between promoting the use of ORT in a clinic setting and successfully implementing its use in the home. ORT was advised in 83 percent of 218 cases observed in four health facilities. Of these, ORS was prescribed in 72 percent, and home-based ORS was advocated in the remaining 28 percent. The investigators managed to follow up 59 episodes at home: 87 percent of the mothers said they had given ORS as recommended, 84 percent of whom correctly described how to prepare it. However, only 44 percent of the mothers had the liter container necessary for preparing ORS, and only 37 percent had a solution at the time of the interview. Half of the children had received less than 500 ml, which is too small a quantity to have had a substantial effect on the outcome of the episode, and 10 percent had received virtually none, since the mothers had mistakenly administered one teaspoonful three times a day. The results of this evaluation were used to design more appropriate health education at the clinic and

Table 9-9. Median Rates of ORS Access, ORS Use, and ORT Use for Children Aged 0–4, by Region, 1987
(percent)

Region	ORS		ORT use rate
	Access rate	Use rate	
Americas	62.1	24.0	39.0
Eastern Mediterranean	69.1	26.7	39.8
Southeast Asia	64.0	18.3	28.5
Sub-Saharan Africa	38.3	12.1	19.2
Western Pacific	57.5	14.6	34.4
Total	58.1	18.9	30.2

Note: ORS, oral rehydration salts; ORT, oral rehydration therapy.

improved training materials and methods for health workers.

Comparison with Other Regions of the World

Table 9-10 presents the results from 276 WHO/CDD surveys of developing countries that are contained in the *Sixth Programme Report* of the Diarrhoeal Diseases Control Programme (World Health Organization, 1988). (The median values in this table were calculated using median values for countries where more than one survey has been conducted rather than individual values, as was done in tables 9-5 and 9-6. This explains the slight discrepancies. Given as much within- as between-country variation, both approaches are valid.)

The median number of episodes per child per year estimated for Sub-Saharan Africa is considerably higher than that for the Eastern Mediterranean, Southeast Asia, and Western Pacific regions. It is similar to that for the Americas, which is based, however, on relatively few surveys. The top of the range is also considerably higher than that for Southeast Asia and the Western Pacific. This contrasts with the earlier findings of Snyder and Merson (1982), who found that for most age groups the median incidence of diarrhea was higher in Asia than in Africa or Latin America. Their results were based on a very few studies, however, and there was a wide (and not very different) range of incidences within each region.

Table 9-10 does not show such striking differences in the proportional mortality rates. The median percentages of deaths associated with diarrhea, and their ranges, are similar for Sub-Saharan Africa, the Americas, and the Eastern Mediterranean. The median percentages are somewhat lower, and the ranges are

considerably lower, in the Southeast Asia and Western Pacific regions.

As previously discussed, the data on mortality rates collected in these surveys are likely to contain many inaccuracies, and the exact values obtained must be treated with caution. Despite these cautions, which apply equally to all 276 surveys, a clear pattern emerges: both the overall childhood mortality rate and the diarrhea-associated mortality rate are higher in Sub-Saharan Africa than in any other region of the world.

Conclusions

The data reviewed here leave no doubt that diarrhea is a major cause of childhood morbidity and mortality in Sub-Saharan Africa. In fact, morbidity and mortality rates in Africa may be higher than in any other part of the world. Nevertheless, there are many gaps in our knowledge. Information regarding adults is notably lacking. In terms of absolute numbers of deaths, the greatest burden of diarrheal mortality is certainly in early childhood, and in public health terms this deserves the greatest concern. However, diarrhea may also be a significant cause of morbidity in adulthood, which may have associated adverse economic consequences. This area clearly warrants more attention. The other notable gap is the paucity of data for assessing trends over time. This gap needs to be remedied urgently.

The WHO/CDD surveys provide by far the major source of data. They are an extremely valuable planning resource. Because they apply the same methodology on a large scale, comparisons can easily be made. However, they suffer from two drawbacks.

Table 9-10. *Morbidity and Mortality Results for Children Aged 0–4 from 276 Surveys Using WHO/CDD Methodology, 1981–87*

Region	Surveys conducted	Countries covered	Episodes per child per year			Percentage of deaths associated with diarrhea		
			Median	Minimum	Maximum	Median	Minimum	Maximum
Americas	12	8	4.9	0.8	10.4	35.2	16.6	60.0
Eastern Mediterranean	47	10	2.7	2.0	10.7	39.1	20.0	63.3
Southeast Asia	96	9	2.7	1.5	5.4	28.3	0.0	48.0
Sub-Saharan Africa	67	22	4.4	1.6	9.9	37.7	15.1	65.2
Western Pacific	54	11	2.4	1.1	5.6	29.0	0.0	43.9
Total	276	60	3.3	0.8	10.7	35.8	0.0	65.2

Note: The median rates were calculated using median values, rather than individual values, for countries where more than one survey had been conducted.

First, by their very nature, they collect a minimal amount of information, which does not detail the epidemiology of diarrhea. Second, the variations within a single country at a given point in time are as great as those between different countries at different times. Repeat surveys and the collection of additional explanatory data on known risk factors are needed to assess whether this within-country variation is real or simply reflects an imprecise method. Also needed is an assessment of the amount of variation to be expected over time. The observed variation must be better understood before this methodology can be confidently used for detecting short- and medium-term trends over time and for assessing the impact of interventions.

Acknowledgments

I would like to express my appreciation to the Diarrhoeal Diseases Control Programme for giving me access to the results from the WHO/CDD surveys. I would also like to thank Lynne Davies and Jacqui Wright for much appreciated help in compiling and typing the references.

Appendix

The appendix, Survey Results for WHO/CDD Morbidity, Mortality, and Treatment of Disease in Sub-Saharan Africa, 1981–87, begins on the following page.

Appendix. Survey Results for WHO/CDD Morbidity, Mortality, and Treatment of Diarrhea in Sub-Saharan Africa, 1981–87

Country and sample data	Urban or rural	Date	Sample size	Incidence — Two-week Rate[a]	Incidence — Two-week 2 × s.e.	Incidence — Annual Rate[b]	Incidence — Annual 2 × s.e.	Mortality — All causes Rate[c]	Mortality — All causes 2 × s.e.	Mortality — Diarrhea-associated Rate[c]	Mortality — Diarrhea-associated 2 × s.e.	Percentage of deaths associated with diarrhea Rate[a]	Percentage 2 × s.e.
Botswana, national		Aug/86	4,351	8.2		3.8*		10.8		1.5		15.1	5.8
Burundi, Muramvya	Rural	May/84	10,147	7.4	1.6	1.6*		51.0	14.0	7.7	2.4		
Cameroon													
Centre-Sud Province	Rural	Oct/83	10,099	17.6	2.3	3.6*		40.1	6.0	23.0	4.0	57.3	5.8
Douala	Urban	Nov/83	10,245	12.7	1.2	3.1*		24.5	4.6	12.1	2.9	49.4	6.8
Mora Secteur,	Rural	Mar/84	6,889	23.0	4.2	7.6*		75.9	16.3	32.4	8.4	42.6	7.7
Mayo Sava	Urban	Nov/83	6,584	23.4	2.3	6.1	0.6	28.6	6.6	14.7	3.8	51.6	4.5
Central African Republic													
Chad													
Mayo Kebbi	Rural	Apr/87	2,184	33.0	3.1	8.0*		109.1	25.6	76.8	19.3	70.4	5.4
N'Djamena	Urban	Dec/83	6,443	28.1		7.8*		55.0		33.0		60.0	
N'Djamena	Urban	Dec/85	2,852	29.6		8.2*							
Congo													
Brazzaville	Urban	Mar/84	6,834	16.6	1.8	5.9*		18.9	5.5	9.1	4.2	48.1	15.5
Pointe-Noire	Urban	Mar/85	7,007	20.1	3.1	7.1*		41.0	11.6	25.7	7.6	62.7	7.8
Côte d'Ivoire													
Bouaki	Urban	Feb/82	2,808	10.4	1.9	4.1*		26.4	9.6	8.9	5.7	33.8	10.8
Korhogo	Urban	Feb/82	2,758	9.2	1.9	3.6*		23.9	9.4	9.4	5.9	39.4	11.8
Ethiopia													
Addis Ababa	Urban	Dec/84	2,986	16.7	2.5	3.4*		10.7	4.5	4.7	2.8	43.8	18.3
Addis Ababa	Urban	Jul/84	3,015	15.2	2.4	2.8*		21.9	12.8	10.0	6.5	45.5	12.3
Arssi region	Rural	May/84	3,014	19.2	2.7	4.9*		28.5	8.5	12.6	5.1	44.2	9.9
Arssi region		Apr/86	3,013	15.7		4.1	1.5	22.0		11.0		47.0	
Asmara, Eritrea region	Urban	Jul/84	3,020	26.2	5.4	4.8*		69.5	49.7	28.8	17.6	41.4	12.7
Deir Seir and Nazareth	Urban	Dec/83	3,021	11.5		2.3*		34.4	2.5	18.5		53.8	
Gondar	Urban	Jan/85	3,014	5.4	2.7	4.8*		5.3		1.3	1.3	25.0	21.6
Gondar	Urban	Aug/84	3,011	23.0	5.1	6.7*		32.5	14.4	15.3	4.7	46.9	16.8
Haran	Urban	Jan/85	3,009	18.4	4.0	5.7*		15.6	5.0	8.3	3.8	53.2	16.2
Keffa	Urban	Jan/85	3,000	16.2	2.0	5.0*		12.7	4.6	7.7	3.4	60.5	17.6

Ethiopia (*continued*)												
Selected rural areas												
Shoa	Rural	Oct/84	3,011	16.2	3.7	3.6*	17.6	5.9	4.0	2.5	22.6	12.4
Sidamo	Urban	Jan/85	3,011	16.7	2.6	5.2*	36.5	13.1	16.9	6.2	46.4	9.0
Wollo	Urban	Jan/85	3,015	15.7	3.3	4.9*	11.6	6.0	7.0	4.2	60.0	21.9
Gabon, Libreville	Urban	Jan/85	3,029	10.7	2.8	3.3*	9.6	4.5	2.3	1.8	24.1	16.5
Guinea	Urban	Jan/84	6,807	20.2	2.9	4.4*	22.8	6.2	10.1	2.8	44.5	11.2
Conakry	Urban	Jun/84	2,740	24.2	3.3	5.1*	28.1	10.3	10.6	8.2	37.7	18.7
Conakry	Urban	May/86	2,080	13.2		3.5						
Guinea-Bissau	Urban	Aug/82	2,736	20.8		5.7*	45.7		16.8		36.8	
Kenya, national	Urban	Sep/87	2,185	13.6		4.0						
Mali												
Bamako	Urban	Sep/82	2,714	36.6		7.6*	28.3		15.7		55.4	
Bamako	Urban	Sep/86	1,079	19.9		3.8*						
Kati		Aug/85	1,052	16.5	3.2	4.3*						
Lake area Niger valley	Rural	Feb/85	3,028	15.3	3.7	6.1*	13.9	4.8	8.9	3.8	64.3	15.2
Mauritania, Nouakchott	Urban	Aug/83	2,719	37.7	4.2	9.9*	56.3	17.4	34.2	11.0	60.8	8.5
Mozambique												
Beira	Urban	Jul/85	4,547	24.4		6.3	37.8		15.0		39.5	
Quelimane	Urban	Feb/86	4,626	11.0		3.0	30.0		4.1		13.2	
Nigeria												
Abeokuta	Urban	Sep/86		11.3		2.8						
Akure	Urban	Sep/86		12.0		3.1						
Bauchi	Urban	Sep/86		24.2		6.2						
Calabar	Urban	Sep/86		12.0		3.1						
Chanchaga	Urban	Sep/86		20.8		5.4						
Enugu	Urban	Sep/86		10.7		2.8						
Ibadan	Urban	Sep/86		13.8		3.6						
Ilorin	Urban	Sep/86		9.0		2.3						
Jos	Urban	Sep/86		19.0		4.9						
Kaduna	Urban	Sep/86		17.3		4.5						
Kano	Urban	Sep/86		32.0		8.3						
Lagos	Urban	Sep/86		9.8		2.5						
Maiduguri	Urban	Sep/86		31.7		8.2						
Makurdi	Urban	Sep/86		20.8		5.4						
Oredo	Urban	Sep/86		9.4		2.4						
Owerri	Urban	Sep/86		11.7		3.0						

(Table continues on the following page.)

153

Appendix (continued)

Country and sample data	Urban or rural	Date	Sample size	Incidence — Two-week Rate[a]	2 × s.e.	Incidence — Annual Rate[b]	2 × s.e.	Mortality — All causes Rate[c]	2 × s.e.	Mortality — Diarrhea-associated Rate[c]	2 × s.e.	Percentage of deaths associated with diarrhea Rate[a]	2 × s.e.
Nigeria (continued)													
Owo	Urban	Sep/86		7.6		2.0							
Port Harcourt	Urban	Sep/86		15.8		4.1							
Sokoto	Urban	Sep/86		38.1		9.9							
Yola	Urban	Sep/86		36.5		9.5							
Rwanda, 30 sectors	Rural	Nov/82	3,109	10.6		6.6*		44.1		8.3		19.0	
Sierra Leone, Freetown	Urban	Sep/87	10,140	13.9	1.8	3.2*	0.4	49.0	9.0	15.0	3.8	30.8	5.0
Sudan, El Obeid	Urban and rural	Oct/87	2,518	21.7	2.2	5.6	0.6	71.1	12.5	44.9	10.2	63.1	7.2
Tanzania, national	Rural	May/86	1,765	19.4		5.1							
Zaire													
Bandundu region	Rural	Jun/85	4,830	10.5	1.9	1.7*		70.8	15.3	22.2	7.8	31.3	8.5
Kinshasa	Urban	Jul/83	2,997	18.5	2.7	2.8*		42.7	9.7	17.4	5.8	40.6	10.2
Zambia													
National	Urban	Sep/86	8,498	27.2		7.1	0.8	15.0	0.4	8.0	0.2	55.5	9.3
National	Rural	Sep/86	7,845	22.7		5.9	0.6	22.0	4.0	8.0	2.0	35.5	8.3

*Adjusted for seasonal variation in the incidence of diarrhea.
Note: Blank cells indicate no data. 2 × s.e., 2 standard errors.
a. Percent.
b. Episodes per child per year.
c. Deaths per 1,000 children per year.

References

Abiodun, Ph. O., Imuekemhe, S. O., and Salami, C. E. (1984). Bacterial agents in diarrhoeal diseases of childhood. *Tropical Gastroenterology*, 5, 181–186.

Addy, P. and Aikins-Bekoe, P. (1986). Cryptosporidiosis in diarrhoeal children in Kumasi, Ghana. *Lancet*, 1, 735.

Adegbola, O. and Chojnacka, H. (1984). Causes of death in Lagos: structure and change. *African Journal of Medicine and Medical Sciences*, 13, 71–83.

Aden, A. and Birk, S. (1981). A study of child mortality in Mogadishu, Somalia. *Journal of Tropical Pediatrics*, 27, 279–284.

Adeyokunnu, A. A., Taiwo, O., and Antia, A. U. (1980). Childhood mortality among 22,255 consecutive admissions in the University College Hospital, Ibadan. *Nigerian Journal of Paediatrics*, 7, 7–15.

Akinterinwa, M. O. and Paul, M. O. (1982). Bacteriological investigations of infantile gastroenteritis in Ife, Nigeria. *Journal of Tropical Medicine and Hygiene*, 85, 139–141.

Alakija, W. (1981). Prevention of childhood mortality in Nigeria by use of medical auxiliaries. *Tropical Doctor*, 11, 118–120.

Ashenafi, M. and Gedebou, M. (1985). *Salmonella* and *Shigella* in adult diarrhoea in Addis Ababa—prevalence and antibiograms. *Transactions of the Royal Society of Tropical Medicine and Hygiene*, 79, 719–721.

Ayeni, O. (1980). Causes of mortality in an African city. *African Journal of Medicine and Medical Sciences*, 9, 139–149.

Balint, O. and Anand, K. (1979). Infectious and parasitic diseases in Zambian children. *Tropical Doctor*, 9, 99–103.

Billingham, J. D. (1981). *Campylobacter* enteritis in the Gambia. *Transactions of the Royal Society of Tropical Medicine and Hygiene*, 75, 641–644.

Black, R. E. (1984). Diarrhoeal diseases and child morbidity and mortality. *Population and Development Review*, 10 (supplement), 141–161.

Black, R. E., Merson, M. H., Huq, I., Alim, A. R. M. A., and Yunus, Md. (1981). Incidence and severity of rotavirus and *Escherichia coli* diarrhoea in rural Bangladesh. *Lancet*, 1, 141–142.

Blum, D., and Feachem, R. G. (1983). Measuring the health impact of water supply and sanitation investments on diarrhoeal diseases: problems of methodology. *International Journal of Epidemiology*, 12, 357–365.

Blum, D., Emeh, R. N., Huttly, S. R. A., Dosunmu-Ogunbi, O., Okeke, R. N., Ajala, M., Okoro, J. I., Akujobi, C., Kirkwood, B. R., and Feachem, R. G. (1990). The Imo State (Nigeria) Drinking Water Supply and Sanitation Project. 1: description of the project, evaluation methods, and impact on intervening variables. *Transactions of the Royal Society of Tropical Medicine and Hygiene*, 84, 309–315.

Bogaerts, J., Lepage, P., Rouvroy, D., and Vandepitte, J. (1984). *Cryptosporidium* spp., a frequent cause of diarrhea in central Africa. *Journal of Clinical Microbiology*, 20, 874–876.

Bradley, A. K. and Gilles, H. M. (1984). Malumfashi Endemic Diseases Research Project. 21: pointers to causes of death in the Malumfashi area, northern Nigeria. *Annals of Tropical Medicine and Parasitology*, 78, 265–271.

Briscoe, J., Feachem, R. G., and Rahaman, M. M. (1986). *Evaluating Health Impact: Water Supply, Sanitation, Hygiene Education*. Ottawa: International Development Research Centre.

Callum, C. (1983). Results of an ad hoc survey on infant and child mortality in Sudan: a summary report. *WHO Statistics Quarterly*, 36, 80–99.

Cantrelle, P., Diop, I. L., Garenne, M., Gueye, M., and Sadio, A. (1986). The profile of mortality and its determinants in Senegal, 1960–1980. In: *Determinants of Mortality Change and Differentials in Developing Countries*. E.85.XIII.4, pp. 86–116. New York: United Nations.

Danfa Project. (1979). *Final Report*. Accra and Los Angeles: University of Ghana and UCLA.

De Mol, P. and Bosmans, E. (1978). *Campylobacter* enteritis in central Africa. *Lancet*, 1, 604.

De Mol, P., Brasseur, D., Hemelhof, W., Tshimpaka Kalala, Butzler, J.-P., and Vis, H. L. (1983). Enteropathogenic agents in children with diarrhoea in rural Zaire. *Lancet*, 1, 516–518.

De Mol, P., Mukashema, S., Bogaerts, J., Hemelhof, W., and Butzler, J.-P. (1984). *Cryptosporidium* related to measles diarrhoea in Rwanda. *Lancet*, 2, 42–43.

De Sole, G., Belay, Y., and Zegeye, B. (1987). Vitamin A deficiency in southern Ethiopia. *American Journal of Clinical Nutrition*, 45, 780–784.

Dosunmu-Ogunbi, O., Coker, A. O., Agbonlaor, D. E., Solanke, S. O., and Uzoma, K. C. (1983). Local pattern of acute enteric bacterial infections in man—Lagos, Nigeria. *Developments in Biological Standardizations*, 53, 277–283.

Ebright, J. R., Moore, E. C., Sanborn, W. R., Schaberg, D., Kyle, J., and Ishida, K. (1984). Epidemic shiga bacillus dysentery in central Africa. *American Journal of Tropical Medicine and Hygiene*, 33, 1192–1197.

Ewbank, D., Henin, R., and Kekovole, J. (1986). An integration of demographic and epidemiologic research on mortality in Kenya. In: *Determinants of Mortality Change and Differentials in Developing Countries*. E.85.XIII.4, pp. 33–85. New York: United Nations.

Feachem, R. G. (1987). Vitamin A deficiency and diarrhoea: a review of interrelationships and their implications for the control of xerophthalmia and diarrhoea. *Tropical Diseases Bulletin*, 84 (3).

Feachem, R. G. and Koblinsky, M. A. (1983). Interventions for the control of diarrhoeal diseases among young children: measles immunisation. *Bulletin of the World Health Organization*, 61, 641–652.

Feachem, R. G., Burns, E., Cairncross, S., Cronin, A., Cross, P., Curtis, D., Khalid Khan, M., Lamb, D., and Southall, H. (1978). *Water, Health, and Development: An Interdisciplinary Evaluation*. London: Tri-Med Books.

Fontaine, O., Diop, B., Beau, J. P., Briend, A., and Ndiaye, M. (1984). La diarrhée infantile au Sénégal: enquête épidémiologique dans un faubourg de Dakar. *Médecine tropicale*, 44, 27–31.

Freij, L. and Wall, S. (1977). Exploring child health and its ecology: the Kirkos study in Addis Ababa. *Acta Paediatrica Scandinavica*, 267 (supplement).

———. (1979). Quantity and variation in morbidity: THAID-analysis of the occurrence of gastroenteritis among Ethiopian children. *International Journal of Epidemiology*, 8, 313–325.

Georges, M. C., Wachsmuth, I. K., Meunier, D. M. V., Nebout, N., Didier, F., Siopathis, M. R., and Georges, A. J. (1984). Parasitic bacterial, and viral enteric pathogens associated with diarrhea in the Central African Republic. *Journal of Clinical Microbiology*, 19, 571–575.

Goh-Rowland, S. G. J., Lloyd-Evans, N., Williams, K., and Rowland, M. G. M. (1985). The etiology of diarrhoea studied in the community in young urban Gambian children. *Journal of Diarrhoeal Diseases Research*, 3, 7–13.

Hansen, D. P., Kaminsky, R. G., Bagg, L. R., Kapikian, A. Z., Slack, R. C. B., and Sack, D. A. (1978). New and old agents in diarrhoea: a prospective study of an indigenous adult African population. *American Journal of Tropical Medicine and Hygiene*, 23, 609–615.

Højlying, N., Mølbak, K., and Jepsen, S. (1986). *Cryptosporidium* spp., a frequent cause of diarrhea in Liberian children. *Journal of Clinical Microbiology*, 23, 1109–1113.

Hunpono-Wusu, O. O. (1976). Disorders which shorten life among Nigerians: a study of mortality patterns in the age group 15–44 years in Kaduna, Nigeria. *Tropical and Geographical Medicine*, 28, 343–348.

Huttly, S. R. A., Blum, D., Kirkwood, B. R., Emeh, R. N., and Feachem, R. G. (1987). The epidemiology of acute diarrhoea in a rural community in Imo State, Nigeria. *Transactions of the Royal Society of Tropical Medicine and Hygiene*, 81, 865–870.

Huttly, S. R. A., Blum, D., Kirkwood, B. R., Emeh, R. N., Okeke, N., Ajala, M., Smith, G. S., Carson, D. C., Dosunmu-Ogunbi, O., and Feachem, R. G. (1990). The Imo State (Nigeria) Drinking Water Supply and Sanitation Project. 2: impact on dracunculiasis, diarrhea, and nutritional status. *Transactions of the Royal Society of Tropical Medicine and Hygiene*, 84, 316–321.

Lang, T., Lafaix, C., Fassin, D., Arnaut, I., Salmon, B., Baudon, D., and Ezekiel, J. (1986). Acute respiratory infections: a longitudinal study of 151 children in Burkina Faso. *International Journal of Epidemiology*, 15, 553–561.

Leeuwenburg, J., Gemert, W., Muller, A. S., and Patel, S. C. (1984). The incidence of diarrhoeal disease. In: *Maternal and Child Health in Rural Kenya: An Epidemiological Study*, van Ginneken, J. K., and Muller, A. S. (editors). London and Sydney: Croom Helm.

Lindskog, U. (1987). *Child Health and Household Water Supply: An Intervention Study from Malawi*. Linköping University Medical Dissertations, no. 259. Linköping, Sweden: Linköping University.

Lloyd-Evans, N., Pickering, H. A., Goh, S. G. J., and Rowland, M. G. M. (1984). Food and water hygiene and diarrhoea in young Gambian children: a limited case control study. *Transactions of the Royal Society of Tropical Medicine and Hygiene*, 78, 209–211.

Malengreau, M., Molima-Kaba, Gillieux, M., de Feyter, M., Kyele-Duibone, and Mukolo-Ndjolo. (1983). Outbreak of *Shigella* dysentery in eastern Zaire, 1980–1982. *Annales de la Société Belge de Médecine Tropicale*, 63, 59–67.

Merlin, M., Roure, C., Kollo, B., Sicard, J. M., Josse, R., Kesseng-Maben, G., and Kouka-Bemba, D. (1986). Évaluation de la morbidité, de la mortalité et des conduites thérapeutiques relatives aux maladies diarrhéiques chez les jeunes enfants au Cameroun. *Médecine tropicale*, 46, 355–358.

Mhalu, F. S., Moshi, W. K., and Mbaga, I. (1984). A bacillary dysentery epidemic in Dar es Salaam, Tanzania. *Journal of Diarrhoeal Diseases Research*, 2, 217–222.

Morley, D. C., Woodland, M., and Martin, W. (1963). Measles in Nigerian children. *Journal of Hygiene*, 61, 115–135.

Mozambique Ministry of Health and Eduardo Mondiane University Faculty of Medicine. (1988). *Journal of Tropical Medicine and Hygiene*, 91, 61–66.

Mtango, F. D. E. and Neuvians, D. (1986). Acute respiratory infections in children under five years. Central project in Bagameyo District, Tanzania. *Transactions of the Royal Society of Tropical Medicine and Hygiene*, 80, 851–858.

Muhe, L., Fredrikzon, B., and Habte, D. (1986). Clinical profile of rotavirus enteritis in Ethiopian children. *Ethiopian Medical Journal*, 24, 1–6.

Mutanda, L. N. (1980). Epidemiology of acute gastroenteritis in early childhood in Kenya. 1: incidence in hospitals. *Journal of Tropical Pediatrics*, 26, 172–176.

Mutanda, L. N., Kinoti, S. N., Gemert, W., and Lichenga, E. O. (1984). Age distribution and seasonal pattern of rotavirus infection in children in Kenya. *Journal of Diarrhoeal Diseases Research*, 2, 147–150.

Offor, E. and Wemambu, S. N. C. (1982). Bacterial profile of diarrhoeal disease in Benin City. *Public Health London*, 96, 211–215.

Olusanya, O., Adebayo, J. O., and Williams, B. (1983). *Campylobacter jejuni* as a bacterial cause of diarrhoea in Ile-Ife, Nigeria. *Journal of Hygiene Cambridge*, 91, 77–80.

Omondi-Odhiambo, Voorhoeve, A. M., and van Ginneken, J. K. (1984). Age-specific infant and childhood mortality and causes of death. In: *Maternal and Child Health in Rural Kenya: An Epidemiological Study*, van Ginneken, J. K. and Muller, A. S (editors). London and Sydney: Croom Helm.

Osuhor, P. C. and Etta, K. M. (1980). Morbidity patterns amongst children in a semi-urban community in northern Nigeria. *Journal of Tropical Pediatrics*, 26, 99–103.

Patel, I. U., Bhushan, V., Chintu, C., and Bathirunathan, N. (1982). Bacteriological study of diarrhoea in children at University Teaching Hospital, Lusaka, Zambia. *East African Medical Journal*, 59, 793–797.

Pickering, H. (1985). Social and environmental factors associated with diarrhoea and growth in young children: child health in urban Africa. *Social Science and Medicine*, 21, 121–127.

Pickering, H., Hayes, R. J., Tomkins, A. M., Carson, D., and Dunn, D. T. (1987). Alternative measures of diarrhoeal morbidity and their association with social and environmental factors in urban children in the Gambia. *Transactions of the Royal Society of Tropical Medicine and Hygiene*, 81, 853–859.

Rowland, M. G. M. (1986). The weanling's dilemma: are we making progress? *Acta Paediatrica Scandinavica*, 323 (supplement), 33–42.

Rowland, M. G. M., Goh-Rowland, S. G. J., and Dunn, D. T. (1986). The relation between weaning practices and patterns of morbidity from diarrhoea: an urban Gambian case study. In: *Diarrhoea and Malnutrition in Childhood*, Walker-Smith, J. A. and McNeish, A. S. (editors), pp. 7–13. London: Butterworth's.

Rowland, G. M., Goh-Rowland, S. G. J., and Cole, T. J. (1988). The impact of infection on the growth of children from 0 to 2 years in an urban West African community. *American Journal of Clinical Nutrition*, 47, 134–138.

Sitbon, M., Lecerf, A., Garin, Y., and Ivonoff, B. (1985). Rotavirus prevalence and relationships with climatological factors in Gabon, Africa. *Journal of Medical Virology*, 16, 177–182.

Snyder, J. D. and Merson M. H. (1982). The magnitude of the global problem of acute diarrhoeal disease: a review of active surveillance data. *Bulletin of the World Health Organization*, 60, 605–613.

Stintzing, G., Back, E., Tufvessor, B., Johnson, T., Wadström, T., and Habte, D. (1981). Seasonal fluctuations in the occurrence of enterotoxigenic bacteria and rotavirus in paediatric diarrhoea in Addis Ababa. *Bulletin of the World Health Organization*, 59, 67–73.

Tanner, M., Degremont, A., de Savigny, D., Freyvogel, T. A., Mayombana, Ch., and Tayari, S. (1987). Longitudinal study on the health status of children in Kikwawila village, Tanzania: study area and design. *Acta Tropica*, 44, 119–136.

Thoren, A., Stintzing, G., Tufvesson, B., Walder, M., and Habte, D. (1982). Aetiology and clinical features of severe infantile diarrhoea in Addis Ababa, Ethiopia. *Journal of Tropical Pediatrics*, 28, 127–131.

Tomkins, A. M. (1981). Nutritional status and severity of diarrhoea among pre-school children in rural Nigeria. *Lancet*, 1, 860–862.

United Nations. (1979). *Demographic Yearbook*. New York: United Nations.

Wamola, I. A. (1980). Bacterial stool pathogens in Kenyatta National Hospital. *East African Medical Journal*, 57, 867–871.

Watts, T. and Chintu, C. (1983). Child deaths in Lusaka. *Medical Journal of Zambia*, 17, 39–45.

Williams, E. H., Hayes, R. J., and Smith, P. G. (1986). Admissions to a rural hospital in the West Nile District of Uganda over a 27 year period. *Journal of Tropical Medicine and Hygiene*, 89, 193–211.

World Health Organization. (1981). Summary of the ad hoc survey on infant and early childhood mortality in Sierra Leone. *World Health Organization Statistics Quarterly*, 34, 220–238.

———. (1986). *Diarrhoea Morbidity, Mortality, and Treatment Practices—Household Survey Manual*. Document CDD/SER/86.2, Geneva.

———. (1987). *World Health Statistics Annual, 1987*. Geneva.

———. (1988). *Sixth Programme Report, 1986–1987. Programme for Control of Diarrhoeal Diseases*. Document WHO/CDD/88.28. Geneva.

———. (1989). *Interim Programme Report, 1988. Programme for Control of Diarrhoeal Diseases*. Document WHO/CDD/89.31. Geneva.

Yakubu, A. M. and Sathiakumar, N. (1985). Chronic diarrhoea in Nigerian children. *Journal of Diarrhoeal Diseases Research*, 3, 145–148.

Young, B. and Briscoe, J. (1988). A case-control study of the effect of environmental sanitation on diarrhoea morbidity in Malawi. *Journal of Epidemiology and Community Health*, 42, 83–88.

Chapter 10

Acute Respiratory Infections

Betty R. Kirkwood

Acute respiratory infections (ARI) are one of the leading causes of morbidity and mortality throughout the developing world. Young children and the elderly are at the most risk (Bulla and Hitze, 1978), and an estimated 15 million children die every year before their fifth birthday. One-third of these deaths are from ARI, the majority of which are caused by bacterial pneumonia (Shann *et al.*, 1984). The magnitude of deaths from these infections is similar to that of deaths from diarrhea (Snyder and Merson, 1982).

Other parallels can be drawn between ARI and diarrhea. Both are a common feature of life throughout the developed as well as the developing world, and the average child experiences several episodes of each a year (Pio *et al.*, 1985; Snyder and Merson, 1982). In the developed world, however, they rarely pose a threat; most episodes are mild and self-limiting, and severe episodes receive prompt and effective treatment. Both ARI and diarrhea are diseases of poverty, aggravated by malnutrition, and associated with poor and crowded housing, poor hygiene, failure to breastfeed, low levels of health care, and, in the case of ARI, air pollution. Both are caused by a variety of different etiologic agents.

This chapter reviews what is known about the patterns and determinants of ARI in Sub-Saharan Africa. The structure is the same as that used in chapter 9 to review diarrheal diseases. Several studies provided information about both respiratory and diarrheal diseases; these are described in both chapters, as are relevant comments on methodology. Although it produced some repetition, this approach eliminated the need to reference chapter 9 frequently.

Data Sources

A computer search using the MEDLINE data base was made of the scientific literature from 1975 to October 1987. The Acute Respiratory Infections Control Programme (ARI) at the World Health Organization (WHO) was visited, and their collection of papers consulted. Finally, past issues of the *World Health Statistics Annuals* and the United Nations *Demographic Yearbooks* were searched back to 1970. All results pertaining to 1970 or later were included. No restrictions were imposed on the type of study, the data source, or the features of the design. Forty-two studies were identified and were categorized as shown in table 10-1. Results were obtained from 12 community studies, 11 longitudinal and 1 cross-sectional, and from 30 analyses of routine statistics, 18 based on health facility records and 12 on registered deaths.

All of these studies were carried out in only 21 countries, as shown in table 10-2; that is, in just over half of the 39 countries comprising Sub-Saharan Africa. The quality and quantity of information presented in them are often minimal. In the Gambia, for example, mortality information is restricted to the case-fatality rate of pneumonia among 207 patients admitted to one hospital in a relatively privileged urban area, where medical care is easily accessible

Table 10-1. Summary of Data Sources

Type of study	Number of studies	Number of countries covered
Community studies		
Longitudinal	11	10
Cross-sectional	1	1
Analyses of routine statistics		
Health facility records	18	10
Registered deaths	12	7
Total	42	21

Table 10-2. Availability of Data on Acute Respiratory Infections, by Country and Type of Data Source

Country	Morbidity	Mortality
Angola	None	2R
Benin	None	None
Botswana	None	None
Burkina Faso	1L, 1H	None
Burundi	None	None
Cameroon	None	None
Central African Republic	None	None
Chad	None	None
Congo	None	None
Côte d'Ivoire	None	None
Ethiopia	1L	None
Gabon	None	None
Gambia, The	1L	1H
Ghana	1H	1H
Guinea	None	None
Guinea-Bissau	None	1R
Kenya	1L, 1H	1L, 2H, 3R
Liberia	None	None
Lesotho	None	None
Madagascar	None	None
Malawi	1L	1L
Mali	None	None
Mauritania	None	None
Mauritius	None	1R
Mozambique	None	1R
Niger	None	None
Nigeria	1H	1L, 3H, 2R
Rwanda	1H	1H
Senegal	None	1L, 2R
Sierra Leone	1L	1L
Somalia	None	1C
Sudan	None	1L
Swaziland	None	None
Tanzania	None	1L
Togo	None	None
Uganda	1H	1H
Zaire	None	1H
Zambia	1H	4H
Zimbabwe	None	1H

Note: L, longitudinal study; C, cross-sectional survey; H, health facility records; and R, registered deaths.

(Wall *et al.*, 1986); thus it is unlikely to be representative of the majority of the country. Estimates of the magnitude and relative importance of acute respiratory infections as a cause of death are only available for 15 countries; that is, for less than 40 percent of the region. Information on ARI morbidity is equally scarce; only 11 countries, less than 30 percent of the region, are represented.

Defining ARI

ARI are a complex of many conditions, with a variety of clinical manifestations, caused by a large number of etiologic agents. They can be subdivided into acute upper (including middle) respiratory infections (AURI) and acute lower respiratory infections (ALRI), which refer to conditions affecting the respiratory tract below the epiglottis. AURI include the common cold, acute otitis media, pharyngitis and tonsillitis, croup, tracheo-bronchitis, and acute epiglottitis (Berman and McIntosh, 1986). Episodes are usually mild and self-limiting; they rarely lead to death. ALRI comprise pneumonia and bronchiolitis. These syndromes may involve tachypnea, cough, nasal flaring, retractions, wheezing, rales, and cyanosis. Pneumonia is the most important cause of death. It is a common complication of measles and pertussis (see chapter 11), particularly among malnourished children (Pio *et al.*, 1986).

The data sources reviewed contain a variety of definitions and measures of ARI morbidity and mortality. These will be described in the context of the individual studies.

Longitudinal Studies

Well-conducted longitudinal studies potentially yield the most detailed and accurate information. They are the only way to obtain direct estimates of the incidence of episodes and of deaths due to respiratory diseases. They are, however, expensive, time-consuming, and logistically complex, both to carry out and to analyze. For this reason they tend to be limited in number.

Eight major longitudinal studies have been carried out in Sub-Saharan Africa since the beginning of 1970 (see table 10-3). These studies vary considerably in sample size, length of follow-up, frequency of visits, type of data collected, and outcome measures used.

Two studies, in Burkina Faso and Tanzania, focused primarily on acute respiratory infections. The study in Burkina Faso was designed to assess the importance of ARI as a source of morbidity and to determine the factors influencing its incidence, in order to plan appropriate control strategies. Every week information was obtained about episodes of cough, auricular and nasal discharge, diarrhea, and fever, and each month the children were visited by a physician. Upper and lower respiratory infections were recorded separately. The study took place during three months in the rainy season and three months in the dry season. Estimates from the two seasons were combined to give an annual estimate based on the assumption that a year comprises six months of rainy season and six months of dry.

Table 10-3. *Design Features of Major Longitudinal Studies on Acute Respiratory Infections*

Location	Date	Sample size	Age (in years)	Length of follow-up	Frequency of visits	Type of data	Outcome measure(s)	Reference(s)
Bana, Burkina Faso	July–Sept. 1983 Jan.–March 1984	151	Less than 5	3 months in rainy season and 3 months in dry season	Weekly Monthly	Recall Current illness	Episodes per child Average daily prevalence; percentage of illness episodes	Lang et al. (1986)
Kirkos, Ethiopia	March 1972–March 1973	749	Less than 12	1 year	Biweekly	Current illness	Average daily prevalence	Freij and Wall (1977)
	Feb.–March 1975	216	Less than 12	60 days	Daily	Current illness	Episodes per child; percentage of illness episodes	
Bakau, The Gambia	March 1981–Feb. 1984	126	Less than 2	Birth to 2 years	Monthly	Recall	Average daily prevalence	Rowland et al. (1988)
Machakos, Kenya	June 1974 –June 1977	3,899 (average)	Less than 5	Variable	Biweekly	Recall	Deaths per 1,000 per year; percentage of all deaths	Omondi-Odhiambo et al. (1984)
Chingale, Malawi	Feb. 1983–March 1984 Sept. 1984–Sept. 1985	637 (average)	Less than 5	Variable	Biweekly	Current illness	Average daily prevalence; deaths per 1,000 per year; percentage of all deaths	Lindskog (1987)
Malumfashi, Nigeria	Nov. 1977 –Oct. 1978	26,100	All	1 year	Monthly	Recall	Percentage of all deaths	Bradley and Gilles (1984)
Ngayokheme, Senegal	Dec. 1962–April 1981	620 (average)	Less than 5	Variable	Yearly	Recall	Deaths per 1,000 per year; percentage of all deaths	Cantrelle et al. (1986)
Bagamoyo, Tanzania	June 1983–Sept. 1985	17,570 (average)	Less than 5	Variable	Yearly	Recall	Deaths per 1,000 per year; percentage of all deaths	Mtango and Neuvians (1986)

The study in Bagamoyo District, Tanzania, was an intervention study to evaluate the effectiveness of a case-management strategy in preventing deaths caused by ARI. Deaths were identified by an annual census; a registration system using village health workers backed up by medical assistants to obtain verbal autopsies was abandoned because it failed to register 50 percent of all deaths. Mortality rates were compared between eight subdistricts that were chosen for intervention and eight that acted as controls.

This was one of ten similar intervention studies initiated with WHO support between 1983 and 1985. Two others were in Sub-Saharan Africa, one in Somalia and one in the Maragua area of Kenya. Both were discontinued after baseline information was collected. In Somalia the investigators had problems gathering reliable information. In Kenya the baseline infant mortality rate was too low to permit investigators to measure an impact (World Health Organization, 1988b), but related activities continue. An investigation in Maragua of the etiology and epidemiology of ARI, sponsored by the U.S. National Academy of Sciences (BOSTID), is under way. This two-year longitudinal study covers 470 children less than five years of age. The results of an indoor air pollution study, the first of the HEAL (Human Exposure Assessment Location) projects, are available (World Health Organization, 1987b) and include data on ARI incidence collected over 42 weeks from 71 children. Although the data were included in this review, no study details are available; therefore, this project is not included in table 10-3.

In all the other studies ARI was just one aspect of a more general concern with the causes of morbidity or mortality or both. The study undertaken in the Machakos District of Kenya, described in detail in chapter 18, was a large-scale rural longitudinal population-based project covering almost 4,000 households. Set up to obtain accurate data on the major causes of childhood, maternal, and perinatal morbidity and mortality, the study's eventual aim was to improve maternal and child health in the area. Almost 4,000 children were visited every two weeks for four years. Although data were collected on both ARI morbidity and mortality, results for morbidity have not been published.

The study from the Malumfashi area of northern Nigeria was one of the series of epidemiological and demographic studies described in chapter 21. The majority of those studies were concerned with malaria and chemoprophylaxis in early childhood, urinary schistosomiasis, and meningococcal infections. This study collected cause of death data from a population

base of 26,100 over a period of one year. Classification was based on lay reporting, and the main respiratory category used was cough.

Information on ARI mortality during childhood is also available in a major in-depth demographic study carried out from the end of 1962 to 1981 in Ngayokheme, a rural area in the Sine-Saloum region of Senegal. Data were collected yearly from a population base of approximately 5,000 persons. Although all ages were covered, cause-specific results were only available for young children. Classification of death was based on symptoms and causes according to the child's family; respiratory diseases included cough, tuberculosis, chest pain, cold, influenza, whooping cough, and difficulty in breathing.

The study in the Chingale area of Malawi was designed primarily to assess the health impact of an improved water supply, but was also concerned more generally with child health. Data were collected every two weeks for one year before intervention and one year after intervention, using a methodology similar to that employed ten years earlier by a Swedish team in the Kirkos study in Ethiopia. Both studies placed particular emphasis on social and environmental determinants of disease. In the Chingale study a respiratory tract infection was recorded if the child had one or more of the following: serious or purulent nasal discharge, cough, breathing difficulties, or otitis media. In the Kirkos study the corresponding symptoms comprised sore throat, cough, and breathing difficulty.

The study in Bakau Township in the Gambia investigated the interrelationships among weaning practices, growth, and morbidity. Newborns were recruited for the study at a government health center and followed from birth until their second birthday. They were examined monthly at routine clinics, where they were weighed and measured and their illnesses noted. Upper and lower respiratory infections were recorded separately. In addition, weekly household visits were carried out during infancy to collect data on diarrheal incidence and feeding practices.

Reports were also found of two longitudinal surveys carried out in Sierra Leone (World Health Organization, 1981) and the Sudan (Callum, 1983) as part of an interregional ad hoc survey program organized by the Division of Health Statistics at WHO. These two surveys are not included in table 10-3, since respiratory diseases were not their major focus. Both studies collected information on the percentage of childhood deaths due to pneumonia. The study from Sierra Leone also estimated the percentage of childhood illness episodes due to ARI.

Cross-Sectional Surveys

Only one cross-sectional survey was reviewed. Part of a strategy to improve the effectiveness of Somalia's maternal and child health (MCH) services, this study was conducted to find out the principal causes of death of infants and young children (Aden and Birk, 1981). Between April and November 1977, 852 mothers were interviewed. Of their children, 932 had died, most (94 percent) before their fifth birthday. The cause of death was ascertained for 913 of those deaths, some of which had occurred more than five years previously. Thus the data are likely to be of varying reliability.

Analyses of Health Facility Records

Although the most complete picture of the disease experience of a community is undoubtedly obtained from carefully conducted community studies, routinely collected health facility records may also provide a useful and readily accessible source of information. The percentage of attendances and admissions due to respiratory diseases indicates their relative importance as a cause of severe morbidity, while the percentage of deaths indicates that ARI is a major cause of mortality.

Health facility records are not, however, representative of the disease burden in the community. Many ill persons do not seek medical attention because they consider the episode to be too mild, prefer traditional practitioners, lack access to appropriate facilities, or have financial or time constraints. Thus attendances tend to be drawn from a particular subsection of the community and to represent the most severe episodes. Similarly, deaths that occur in hospitals tend to represent only a small proportion of all deaths. Feachem *et al.* (1978) estimated, for example, that less than one-fifteenth of childhood deaths in Lesotho occurred in hospitals. Hospital records are not appropriate, therefore, for estimating incidence rates or mortality rates.

ATTENDANCES AND ADMISSIONS. Six analyses of attendances or admissions or both have been reported in the literature since 1975 for the following countries: Burkina Faso (Lang *et al.*, 1986), Ghana (Danfa Project, 1979), Kenya (Wafula *et al.*, 1984), Nigeria (Osuhor and Etta, 1980), Uganda (Williams *et al.*, 1986), and Zambia (Balint and Anand, 1979). The data sets are of varying size. At one extreme is the analysis of 30,129 admissions recorded from July 1951 to August 1978 in a small mission hospital in a rural area of the West Nile District of Uganda. At the other is the analysis of 399 attendances recorded during two months at a clinic for children under five in Zaria, Nigeria.

DEATHS. Three studies, from Kenya, Uganda, and Zambia, also reported on pneumonia as a cause of hospital deaths. Five additional reports were found, one from Ghana (Pobee, 1976), three from Nigeria (Alakija, 1981; Adeyokunnu *et al.*, 1980; Hunpono-Wusu, 1976), and one from Zambia (Watts and Chintu, 1983).

CASE-FATALITY RATES. In the studies from Uganda (Williams *et al.*, 1986) and Zambia (Balint and Anand, 1979) the analyses of admissions and deaths were combined to give an estimate of the case-fatality rates occurring in hospitals; that is, the probability that a child admitted to a hospital with pneumonia will die from it. A further seven estimates of case-fatality rates based entirely on admissions for pneumonia were found from the Gambia (Wall *et al.*, 1986), Kenya (Slack *et al.*, 1976), Rwanda (Lepage *et al.*, 1981), Zaire (Ngalikpima, 1983), Zambia (Allen, 1984; El-Amin, 1978), and Zimbabwe (Collings and Martin, 1985).

Analyses of Registered Deaths

Mauritius is the only country whose cause-specific mortality rates are currently reported in the *World Health Statistics Annual*. This information provides estimates of the pneumonia-specific mortality rate and of the percentage of all deaths attributable to pneumonia, subdivided by age group. National estimates for Angola, Kenya, and Mozambique were found in the United Nations 1979 *Demographic Yearbook* (United Nations, 1979), but the information was out of date, referring to 1972, 1970, and 1974, respectively, and was not available by age group. Age-specific estimates of proportional mortality rates were found, however, for Angola (1973) and for Guinea-Bissau (1970) in the United Nations 1974 *Demographic Yearbook*. A more recent national estimate of the percentage of deaths due to pneumonia in Kenya in 1980 is in the paper by Wafula *et al.* (1984), but again this information is not subdivided by age.

The usefulness of the registration systems that do exist is often restricted by substantial underregistration. Moreover errors occur in the reported age of death, many entries give the age as not known, standard definitions and classifications may not be used, and clear rules may not govern which of multiple illnesses should be recorded as the cause of death. The variation in the quality and quantity of information from different areas of the country is likely to be considerable (Black, 1984). These problems of inaccuracies in reported age and cause of death also apply to analyses of health facility records.

Two reports analyzed registered deaths recorded by the vital statistics registration system of Lagos City, Nigeria. The first, by Ayeni (1980), is based on data for 1977. The second, by Adegbola and Chojnacka (1984), looks at the changing structure of the causes of death between 1965 and 1975. This review included only the results for 1977, which were the most recent. The Lagos registration system appears to be 60 percent complete and better than that of any other city in Nigeria (Ayeni, 1980). In 1977, 17 percent of death certificates showed ill-defined causes, which was below the 25 percent limit set by the World Health Organization for acceptability of death certification (Ayeni, 1980).

In 1981 the United Nations and WHO initiated a series of case studies of mortality determinants in five developing countries. Two Sub-Saharan African countries were selected, Kenya and Senegal, together with Bangladesh, Guatemala, and Sri Lanka. Estimates of the percentage of deaths due to respiratory causes in Kenya and of the respiratory-specific mortality rate among children less than five years of age were available from deaths reported to the registrar general in 1977 for 23 of the country's 41 districts (Ewbank *et al.*, 1986). The latter rates were adjusted to allow for the considerable underreporting present in this registration system. All districts with more than 20 percent coverage were included, as were a few districts to ensure regional representation. The maximum coverage for infant and child deaths was estimated at 73 percent, and the coverage rate exceeded 50 percent in just four districts. In addition, the quality of the cause-of-death data was variable: in one district with a coverage of 64 percent, for example, only 7 percent of the death certificates were medically certified. Median values of the district estimates were used in this review.

Relevant data from the Senegal study include results from the Ngayokheme longitudinal study, described above, plus two sets of cause-of-death data, based on analyses of deaths registered from 1973–80 in the cities of Dakar and Saint-Louis (Cantrelle *et al.*, 1986).

Morbidity

In all, 13 data sources provide information on ARI morbidity during early childhood (table 10-2). Because the type of study and choice of outcome differ, however, considerably fewer than 13 estimates are available for each index (see table 10-4).

All three estimates of incidence are high, as are three of the four estimates of average daily prevalence, which suggests that it is by no means uncommon for a child to have respiratory symptoms about 25 percent of the time and to experience as many as 8–13 episodes of ARI a year. The highest estimates of both incidence and prevalence were found in the Bana study in Burkina Faso (Lang *et al.*, 1986), and the lowest in the Kirkos study in Ethiopia (Freij and Wall, 1977), whose prevalence estimate is considerably lower than that of the other studies.

Two community studies recorded upper and lower respiratory infections separately. In the Bana study in Burkina Faso, just over half (7.5) of the estimated 13.2 ARI episodes per child per year were attributed to lower respiratory conditions, defined as cough with abnormalities observed during chest auscultation or pneumonia (Lang *et al.*, 1986). In contrast, Rowland *et al.* (1988) classified respiratory infections in the Gambia

Table 10-4. ARI Morbidity Results in Early Childhood

Result and country	Estimate	Age range (years)
Episodes per child per year		
Ethiopia	7.6	<5
Kenya	9.2	<5
Burkina Faso	13.2	<5
Daily prevalence		
Ethiopia	6.9	<5
Malawi	25.0	<5
The Gambia	27.8	<2
Burkina Faso	30.8	<5
Percentage of all illness episodes		
Sierra Leone	25.1	<5
Ethiopia	36.3	<5
Burkina Faso	66.0	<5
Percentage of health facility attendances		
Ghana	17.0	<5
Nigeria	25.1	<5
Burkina Faso	41.0	<5
Percentage of health facility admissions		
Uganda	8.6	<10
Rwanda	16.7	<2
Zambia	32.7	Children[a]
Kenya	41.7	Pediatric[a]

a. Exact ranges are not given in the studies.

as lower only 16 percent of the time; in this case lower respiratory infections referred to pneumonia and bronchitis. They found that lower, but not upper, respiratory infections contributed significantly to weight faltering and were responsible for one-quarter of the observed deficit at one year of age.

All the studies found respiratory infections to be responsible for a large proportion of childhood morbidity and to consume a considerable proportion of health care resources. ARI were estimated to explain between 25 and 66 percent of all episodes of illness, between 17 and 41 percent of health facility attendances, and between 9 and 42 percent of hospital admissions.

Different studies found different age-specific patterns of ARI morbidity, as illustrated in figure 10-1. The average daily prevalence peaked during the second and third years of life in both Burkina Faso (Lang *et al.*, 1986) and Kirkos, Ethiopia (Freij and Wall, 1977), although the peak was not as pronounced in Kirkos as in Burkina Faso, the levels of morbidity being generally considerably lower. The Kirkos study, which covered children up to 12 years of age, also showed a continuing, but less rapid, decline in levels after five

years of age. An intensive substudy in Kirkos found a similar decline in the incidence rates of ARI. In that study, 216 children were visited daily for 60 days, and the estimated rates fell gradually from 7.9 episodes per child per year during the first two years of life to 1.7 episodes between 8 and 11 years of age. A slight decline was also seen in the median duration of an episode, which decreased from 5.3 days among children less than 2 years old, to 4.9 days among children 2–4 years old, to 4.6 days among children between the ages of 5 and 11.

In contrast, the studies in Chingale, Malawi (Lindskog, 1987), and Bakau, the Gambia (Rowland *et al.*, 1988), found peak prevalences during infancy, followed by rapid declines. In their analysis of attendances at a child welfare clinic in Zaria, Nigeria, Osuhor and Etta (1980) also found that the absolute number of attendances due to respiratory diseases was highest during infancy and declined dramatically over the next four years of age. This was also true for the total number of attendances. However, although the proportion of attendances due to respiratory infections (28 percent) was also highest during infancy, it did not decline sharply thereafter, but remained at about 21–22 percent until five years of age. This is in contrast to attendances for diarrhea at this clinic, which were minimal once children reached their third year of life.

Only three studies considered children older than five or adults. The Kirkos study, which examined children up to 12 years old, found that morbidity rates declined with age. Such a trend was not clear from the other two studies that considered older age groups.

In their analyses of admissions to a small rural hospital in Uganda, Williams *et al.* (1986) subdivided the data into two age groups, one corresponding to children, defined as less than ten years old, and adults, defined as ten years old or more. They found that twice as many adults as children had been admitted. About one-fifth of the adult admissions were obstetric admissions among females who were largely healthy. They were excluded from the denominator in considering the role of ARI in morbidity. In both groups ARI ranked third in importance as a cause of admission to the hospital, accounting for 8.6 percent of admissions among children and 7.2 percent of admissions among adults.

ARI were also an important cause of clinic attendance at all ages in the Danfa project area of Ghana. They accounted for 14 percent of attendances over all age groups, ranking second only to malaria, compared with 17 percent of attendances among children less than five years old (Danfa Project, 1979).

Figure 10-1. Daily Prevalence of Acute Respiratory Infections in Four Countries of Sub-Saharan Africa

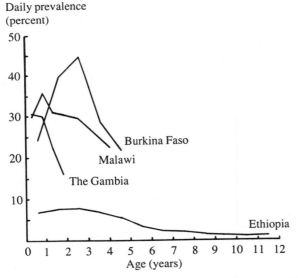

Daily prevalence
(percent)

Source: For Burkina Faso, Lang *et al.* (1986); for Ethiopia, Freij and Wall (1977); for the Gambia, Rowland *et al.* (1988); and for Malawi, Lindskog (1987).

Mortality

The majority of data sets refer to deaths due to pneumonia. Although these do not include all deaths due to ARI, the estimates can be used because the vast majority of ARI deaths are from pneumonia. Thus in Kenya, Ewbank *et al.* (1986) found that 90 percent of childhood inpatient respiratory deaths were ascribed to pneumonia, 4 percent to acute respiratory infection, and 4 percent to bronchitis or asthma; pneumonia appeared on the certificates of 89 percent of registered respiratory deaths. The same is true for Mauritius, where in 1986 pneumonia accounted for 89 percent of all ARI registered deaths (World Health Organization, 1987c).

Pneumonia is clearly a major cause of mortality at all ages. National figures from registration data place pneumonia as the second cause of death for all age groups in Angola, Kenya, and Mauritius; that is, in three of the five countries for which figures are available (United Nations, 1979; Wafula *et al.*, 1984). The exceptions are Guinea-Bissau where it was sixth overall and Mozambique where it did not appear on the list of top-ten important causes (United Nations, 1974, 1979). In addition, 5 of the 13 community and hospital studies that assessed its relative importance as a cause of childhood death placed pneumonia as the leading cause; three placed it second; and none placed it below fifth (table 10-5).

Pneumonia Mortality Rates

ARI-specific mortality rates give the best measure of the mortality risk in a community due to ARI. They are extremely difficult to measure, needing accurate regis-tration systems with high coverage rates or large-scale community studies with regular surveillance. Only one data source, registered deaths in Mauritius (World Health Organization, 1987c), provided age-specific mortality rates over the entire age range. In Mauritius infants and the elderly are the most vulnerable. Similar patterns were seen for males and females, although the rates were generally slightly less for females than for males. The number of pneumonia deaths per 1,000 persons per year peaked in infancy, fell sharply over the next four years, remained low during late childhood and early adulthood, increased slowly in mid-adulthood, and then rose sharply beginning at about 65 years of age to reach its highest level in old age. This age pattern is similar to that described by Bulla and Hitze (1978) in their global review of ARI.

Five other estimates of pneumonia mortality rates are available for children less than five years old. The six estimates are summarized in table 10-5, which also includes the other measures of childhood mortality. The lowest of these estimates, 0.3 deaths per 1,000 per year, was based on data from the vital registration system of Mauritius (World Health Organization, 1987a). The estimates from the two longitudinal studies that employed frequent surveillance were close in value and also relatively low. The estimate from the Chingale study in Malawi was 3.2 deaths per 1,000 per year (Lindskog, 1987) and that from the Machakos study in Kenya was 3.4 deaths (Omondi-Odhiambo *et al.*, 1984). The other estimate for Kenya, which was based on registration data from 23 districts, was considerably higher: 9.0 deaths per 1,000 per year (Ewbank *et al.*, 1986). This discrepancy did not occur in the diarrhea mortality rates of these two Kenyan studies, which were in close agreement (3.4 and 3.6

Table 10-5. Mortality due to Pneumonia in Early Childhood

	Episodes per child per year			Number of studies	Number of countries
Results and type of study	*Median*	*Minimum*	*Maximum*		
Rank as cause of death	2	5	1	13	10
Deaths per 1,000 per year	6.2	0.3	12.0	6	5
Percentage of all deaths					
Longitudinal	7.6	1.3	35.1	7	7
Cross-sectional	7.5	—	—	1	1
Health facility records	22.0	11.9	48.7	5	4
Registered deaths	7.5	2.0	28.0	7	6
Overall	11.7	1.3	48.7	20	13
Case-fatality rate	17.9	10.3	20.5	5	5

— Not applicable.

deaths per 1,000 per year, respectively). The two highest estimates of pneumonia mortality were derived from the two longitudinal studies with infrequent follow-up. Both the Ngayokheme study in Senegal (Cantrelle *et al.*, 1986) and the Bagamoyo study in Tanzania (Mtango and Neuvians, 1986) used yearly recall to yield estimates of 10.6 and 12.0 pneumonia deaths per 1,000 children per year, respectively.

Proportional Mortality Rates

Twenty estimates are available of the proportional mortality rate from childhood pneumonia; that is, the percentage of deaths among children less than five years of age that are due to pneumonia. These estimates, which were based on data from 13 countries, are summarized in table 10-5, where they are subdivided by type of study design. Estimates ranged from 1.3 to 48.7 percent of all deaths. The majority of estimates, 18 of the 20, were 6 percent or more, and over half were above 10 percent. The estimates from the community studies and from the analyses of registered deaths covered very similar ranges, and their median values were almost identical. The estimates based on analyses of hospital deaths, in contrast, were considerably higher in general. This suggests that the estimates based on hospital deaths may be biased upwards. This could arise from selection bias if children with pneumonia are more likely to seek advice from health services or are more likely than children with other complaints to be admitted. Pneumonia deaths would then be overrepresented in hospital studies compared with community studies.

Pneumonia also accounted for a high percentage of deaths for all ages. Seven of nine estimates covering the whole age range were above 6 percent, and five were above 10 percent. The majority of studies showed lower proportional mortality rates for adults than for children. Detailed age-specific rates were available from the registration systems of Angola, Guinea-Bissau, and Mauritius (United Nations, 1974, 1979), as shown in table 10-6. All three showed a peak in proportional mortality rates among children 1–4 and 5–14 years of age. The actual pneumonia mortality rates for Mauritius, in contrast, peaked in infancy and old age; the difference probably reflects relatively fewer deaths due to other causes from 1–14 years of age, which increased the prominence of pneumonia as an important cause of death in this age range. Similarly, all three data sets showed slightly higher proportional mortality rates for females than for males, whereas in Mauritius the number of deaths per 1,000 persons per year was higher for males than for females.

Case-Fatality Rates

Studies from Rwanda (Lepage *et al.*, 1981), Uganda (Williams *et al.*, 1986), Zaire (Ngalikpima, 1983), Zambia (Balint and Anand, 1979), and Zimbabwe (Collings and Martin, 1985) estimate that between 10 and 20 percent of children admitted to hospitals with pneumonia die from it (table 10-5). All of the studies that covered a wide age range found a decrease in risk with an increase in age. In Zaire Ngalikpima (1983) observed a case-fatality rate of 21.1 percent among infants, 19.8 percent among children 1–4 years of age, and a sharp decrease to 8.4 percent among children at least 5 years old. In Uganda Williams *et al.* (1986) found a rate of 3.9 percent among persons ten years old or more, almost one-fifth of the 19.7 percent observed among younger persons. In Rwanda Lepage *et al.* (1981) found that the risk was halved among children 2–15 years of age compared with children in the first two years of life (8.5 and 17.8 percent, respectively).

Lepage *et al.* (1981) also found a twofold increase in risk of death among children less than two years of age who had been weaned compared with those being breast-fed at the time of admission (27.5 compared with 13.4 percent). In Zimbabwe Collings and Martin (1985) found malnourished infants less than six months old to be in the highest risk category. Their case-fatality rate was 38.5 percent compared with a general rate of 10.3 percent for children less than three years old.

Table 10-6. Percentage of Deaths due to Pneumonia, by Age and Gender

Country	Date	\multicolumn{6}{c}{Age (years)}	Gender	
		0	1–4	5–14	15–44	45–64	65 and older	Males	Females
Angola	1973	8.2	15.2	13.0	6.5	5.3	3.5	7.9	9.5
Guinea-Bissau	1970	5.0	8.9	20.9	5.8	3.2	2.3	5.3	7.0
Mauritius	1986	3.5	13.1	8.4	2.8	2.1	4.0	3.2	3.7

The three studies that were confined to adults found case-fatality rates of about 2–4 percent, which are considerably lower than the rates observed in children. Two of these were from Zambia (Allen, 1984; El-Amin, 1978), and one was from Kenya (Slack *et al.*, 1976). Finally, one study from the Gambia gave a rate of 5 percent for all ages combined (Wall *et al.*, 1986).

Etiology

Most persons dying from respiratory infections in developing countries have bacterial pneumonia. The bacterial infection may be a primary invasion or a secondary invasion of the respiratory tract following a viral infection (Pio *et al.*, 1985). Studies suggest that children with bacterial pneumonia may be as much as 2.5 times more likely to die than children with other types of pneumonia (Shann, 1986). This is not true in developed countries, where viruses predominate, but it resembles the pattern that existed before the antibiotic era (Shann, 1986).

Table 10-7 summarizes the main results from seven studies of the etiology of pneumonia that investigated bacteria. All seven were hospital based. Four reported case-fatality rates; these were the studies of adults in Kenya (Slack *et al.*, 1976) and Zambia (Allen, 1984) and of pneumonia patients of all ages in the Gambia (Wall *et al.*, 1986) and Zaire (Ngalikpima, 1983). The three additional studies were from Ahmadu Bello University Teaching Hospital in Zaria, Nigeria. Silverman *et al.* (1977) studied pediatric admissions, Diallo *et al.* (1979) investigated malnourished children, and Macfarlane *et al.* (1979) examined adults. These three studies were not included in the summaries of data sources in tables 10-1 and 10-2 since they gave no information on the magnitude of ARI morbidity or mortality.

Bacteria were present in the cultures of at least 40 percent of the patients in each of the seven studies. In four, the isolation rate was 65 percent or more. Penicillin treatment failed to improve the infections of 54 (10.8 percent) of the 502 adult patients studied in Zambia (Allen, 1984) or those of 7 (6.7 percent) of the 105 adult patients in Kenya (Slack *et al.*, 1976). Overall, *Streptococcus pneumoniae* predominated, followed by hemolytic *Streptococcus* and *Hemophilus influenzae*. *Staphylococcus aureus*, *Klebsiella pneumoniae*, *Escherichia coli*, *Pseudomonas aeruginosa*, and *Proteus* spp. featured strongly in some series. El-Amin (1978) also found the same organisms in adults admitted with bacterial pneumonia in Zambia. In addition, many other bacteria were occasionally isolated: *Acinetobacter* spp., *Aspergillus* spp., *Bacteroides* spp., *Branhamella catarrhalis*, *Candida* spp., *Citrobacter* spp., *Diphtheroides* spp., *Entamoeba histolytica*, *Enterobacter* spp., *Flavobacterium*, *Flora commensal*, *Peptococcus*, *Providentia*, *Salmonella*, *Sarcina* spp., *Serratia marcescens*, and *Staphylococcus epidermidis*, among others.

Greenwood *et al.* (1980) found that type 1 was the predominant serotype of *Streptococcus pneumoniae* in West Africa, followed by types 3 and 5, a very different pattern from that seen in Europe and the United States. Such information is vital for developing pneumococcal vaccines that contain appropriate selections of antigens for developing countries.

Wall *et al.* (1986) investigated differences in etiology according to the age of the patient. They found that *S. pneumoniae* was the most frequent cause of ARI,

Table 10-7. Frequency of Isolation of Bacterial Agents Associated with Pneumonia

	Isolation rate (percent)			Studies conducted	Countries covered
Etiologic agent	*Median*	*Minimum*	*Maximum*		
Escherichia coli	2.3	0.4	8.0	4	3
Hemolytic *Streptococcus*	9.1	1.5	10.7	3	2
Hemophilus influenzae	5.3	0.0	20.3	4	3
Klebsiella pneumoniae	2.6	0.0	6.3	4	3
Proteus spp.	2.2	—	—	1	1
Pseudomonas aeruginosa	7.0	—	—	1	1
Staphylococcus aureus	1.6	1.0	14.3	7	5
Streptococcus pneumoniae	37.7	1.8	53.1	7	5
All	64.9	42.1	79.5	7	5

— Not applicable.

irrespective of age but that its isolation rate was slightly higher among persons at least ten years old than among younger persons (62 percent compared with 51 percent). *H. influenzae* was also an important cause in children but not in adolescents or adults. It was isolated in 14 of 51 cases of pneumonia in children less than ten years old, but in only 1 of 13 cases in older children.

Omer *et al.* (1985) also found that bacteria were an important cause of sore throats among outpatients attending a hospital in the Sudan but that the etiologic profile was different. The overall isolation rate from 164 specimens was 51.0 percent. The predominate pathogens were *Streptococcus pyogenes* (24.7 percent) and *Streptococcus faecalis* (8.1 percent).

Two studies looked at the viral etiology of severe ARI. In Kenya, Mutie *et al.* (1976) investigated 41 children less than two years old who were admitted with bronchiolitis or bronchopneumonia. They found evidence of infection with respiratory syncytial virus (RSV) in 16 cases (39.0 percent) and of parainfluenza virus in 3 cases (7.3 percent). In addition, adenovirus, cytomegalovirus, ECHO virus, and rhinovirus were each associated with one case. In their study of upper and lower ARI among inpatients and outpatients less than three years old in Uganda, Sobeslavsky *et al.* (1977) also found that RSV and parainfluenza viruses were the most important viral pathogens, being associated with 17 and 9 percent of the cases, respectively, and causing both upper and lower respiratory infections. No seasonal variation was seen. Adenoviruses, influenza virus, coxsackievirus, and ECHO virus, though present, were less important. Overall, viruses were identified in just over one-third of the cases.

Sobeslavsky *et al.* (1977) also investigated mycoplasma infections, which, unlike viruses, were not found to play a role in respiratory infections. Comparable isolation rates were found in children with respiratory infections and in a control group of children with kwashiorkor (20 and 18 percent, respectively). *Mycoplasma pneumoniae* was not detected among the respiratory cases, and was isolated from only one symptomless child in the control group. However, Macfarlane *et al.* (1979) found evidence of *M. pneumoniae* infection in 12 adult patients with pneumonia (16 percent), and in half of these it was associated with a pneumococcal infection. They suggest that *M. pneumoniae* infections may render the lung vulnerable to subsequent bacterial infection and therefore be an important prognostic factor in the development of pneumonia.

Other Determinants of Disease

Three community studies look at risk factors for ARI morbidity: the Bana study in Burkina Faso (Lang *et al.*, 1986), the Kirkos study in Ethiopia (Freij and Wall, 1977), and the Maragua study in Kenya (World Health Organization, 1987b).

Bana is a small rural village, typical of many Burkinabe villages. It is far from a town and several kilometers from a health center. Chronic malnutrition and high birth rank emerged as the main risk factors in the longitudinal study of 151 children (Lang *et al.*, 1986). Children with an arm circumference less than 13.5 cm suffered more episodes of both upper and lower respiratory infections and were ill for a greater proportion of the year than were children with a larger arm circumference. Increasing the duration of illness was the strongest effect, which suggests that chronic malnutrition was also lengthening the episodes of illness. Both effects were more pronounced in the dry than in the wet season.

An excess of ARI in the dry season was also noted in two hospital studies of adult pneumonia in Nigeria (Macfarlane *et al.*, 1979) and Zambia (Allen, 1984). In Nigeria, the admission rates for acute pneumonia were twice as high at the end of the dry season as in the middle of the rainy season. Both papers suggest that this may be due to low humidity, which dries nasal secretion and impairs defense mechanisms by reducing local immunoglobulin A (IgA) activity. Allen (1984) also suggests that a deterioration in nutritional status due to food scarcity at the end of the dry season might reduce resistance to bacterial infection. In contrast, Williams *et al.* (1986) notes that admissions for pneumonia in rural Uganda were more common from July to November, the relatively cool and wet time of year.

In the Bana study, the nutritional effect was confined to low arm circumference. Lang *et al.* (1986) found no association between low weight-for-age or low weight-for-height with increased ARI morbidity. Other nonsignificant factors were possession of a luxury item (moped, bicycle, radio), knowledge of health care, household size, or hemoglobin status.

A detailed study of the etiology and epidemiology of ARI is currently under way in the Maragua area of rural Kenya. Results are available from an indoor air pollution study carried out in conjunction with it (World Health Organization, 1987b). This was the first of the WHO program of HEAL (Human Exposure Assessment Location) projects, which are being conducted in a variety of settings to assess the impact on health of indoor air pollution caused by biomass fuel combustion. In Maragua almost all families cook with wood, usually inside the house (only 42 percent of homes have separate kitchens). Cooking takes place in the morning, afternoon, and evening. Lighting is provided by kerosene lamps. Levels of air pollutants were found to be homogeneously high in the 36 households studied and 20 times higher than levels caused by cigarette smoke in Dutch homes. It is therefore not surprising that no relationship was found between air pollution and incidence of ARI among young children in these households. Similarly high levels of air pollution were found in the second HEAL project in the Basse area of the Gambia (World Health Organization, 1987a).

The third study of risk factors was conducted in Kirkos, an area of Addis Ababa that represents the poor socioeconomic and environmental conditions in which many people in that large city live (Freij and Wall, 1977). Factors showing some association with increased ARI morbidity included having more than one child below five years of age, a mother less than 30 years old, a single parent, an illiterate father, an inadequate water supply, and poor housing, represented by a dirt floor. Muslims and the Amhara and Oromo ethnic groups were at lower risk than other groups. Income, crowding (number of persons per room; living area per person), inadequate sanitation, low water consumption, and low weight-for-age showed little or no association with ARI morbidity.

Finally, in a case-control study in Ethiopia De Sole *et al.* (1987) found that children with vitamin A deficiency were twice as likely to have suffered a severe episode of respiratory infection in the preceding year as nondeficient children. Their data set did not allow them to investigate which, if either, was more likely to be causal. Limited evidence from elsewhere in the world, in particular Indonesia and India, suggests that a deficiency of vitamin A predisposes persons to increased risk of respiratory illness and preschool children to increased risk of death (Mamdani and Ross, 1988).

ARI Control

In 1983 the World Health Organization initiated a series of intervention studies to evaluate a case-management strategy for controlling ARI. That strategy emphasizes early detection of ALRI and appropriate antibiotic treatment at the level of primary health care (World Health Organization, 1988b). One of these

intervention studies was successfully completed in the Bagamoyo District of Tanzania (Mtango and Neuvians, 1986). All households with young children were visited every six to eight weeks by village health workers (VHWs) who taught mothers to recognize the signs and symptoms of pneumonia and to seek treatment promptly. The VHWs immediately treated all cases of pneumonia detected during these visits with oral Cotrimoxazole and referred severe cases to the next level of care. Training courses on ARI management were also given to health center and dispensary staff.

The program started in June 1983 in 9 of the 18 villages in the district. The other 9 villages acted as controls during the first year; the program was expanded to the whole district in June 1984. Yearly census surveys of all births and deaths were carried out in August 1984 and September 1985, covering an average of 17,570 children less than five years old.

The results are summarized in table 10-8. The 1984 survey in the control villages gave estimates of preintervention mortality levels in the district, which are used as the baseline for all comparisons. The 1984 survey in the intervention villages and the 1985 survey in the control villages gave estimates of mortality during the first year of intervention. Finally, the 1985 survey in the intervention villages measured mortality during the second year of intervention.

During the two years of the study, immunization coverage improved, nutritional education was carried out, and malaria and diarrhea disease control activities were progressively implemented as part of primary health care. The impact of these intervention activities can be assessed by comparing the 1985 survey results in the intervention villages with the 1984 survey results in the control villages. Childhood mortality was reduced by 27.2 percent, but this reduction was not specific to pneumonia deaths. The pneumonia-specific mortality rate declined 30.1 percent over two years and accounted for only 39.4 percent of the overall reduction of deaths. The mortality rate due to diarrhea decreased 55.9 percent and that due to malaria, 19.3 percent.

The Bagamoyo ARI case management intervention did not employ active case finding. In practice, the VHWs were supplied irregularly with antibiotics, and most cases of pneumonia were sent to the dispensary for treatment. The reduction in mortality was lower than that achieved in similar studies that did employ active case management and did deliver antibiotic treatment in the community. The survey results for 1986 showed a 44.4 percent reduction in the pneumo-

Table 10-8. Mortality Rates among Children under Five, from the ARI Control Project, Bagamoyo District, Tanzania, 1984–85

Cause of death	Control villages		Intervention villages		Percentage reduction over two years
	1984 (0)	1985 (1)	1984 (1)	1985 (2)	
Diarrhea	6.1	4.4	6.0	3.0	55.9
Malaria	8.3	9.8	6.2	6.7	19.3
Pneumonia	14.3	12.2	11.6	10.0	30.1
All	40.1	35.0	32.4	29.2	27.2

Note: The number of years in which intervention activities took place are given in parentheses. Mortality rates are the number of deaths per 1,000 children per year.

Source: Mtango and Neuvians (1986).

nia mortality rate over four years (World Health Organization, 1988b).

At the end of 1987, national ARI control programs had been implemented in only two Sub-Saharan African countries, Tanzania and Zimbabwe, and technical guidelines and plans of operations had been drafted in Malawi and Zimbabwe (World Health Organization, 1988a).

Conclusions

Severe data deficiencies exist. Only three estimates of ARI incidence and six estimates of the pneumonia mortality rate were found for the entire region. Eighteen of the 39 countries comprising Sub-Saharan Africa are not represented at all, and in many others the available information is minimal. The majority of studies focus on young children: information on older children and adults is notably lacking. No information is available to assess trends over time.

Nevertheless, the data reviewed leave no doubt that acute respiratory infections are a major source of morbidity and mortality in Sub-Saharan Africa. In fact, the rates in this part of Africa may be higher than in any other region of the world. In a recent review of the magnitude of the problem of ARI, Pio et al. (1985) found that, on average, an urban child suffers between five and eight episodes of ARI each year and a rural child suffers between one and three. The three estimates of incidence available for Sub-Saharan Africa do not support their conclusion. The lowest estimate of 7.6 episodes per child per year was observed in the Kirkos study, which was conducted in the city of Addis Ababa, Ethiopia (Freij and Wall, 1977). The two other estimates, both from rural settings, were considerably higher. The incidence in the Maragua study in Kenya was 9.2 episodes per child per year (World Health

Organization, 1987b), and that in the Bana study in Burkina Faso was 13.2 episodes (Lang et al., 1986). Pio et al. (1985) featured the Kirkos estimate in their review; the two rural estimates were reported later. These results suggest that the incidence of ARI may be higher in Sub-Saharan Africa than elsewhere in the world and that the rural population is affected as much as the urban one.

Major initiatives are needed to remedy the severe data deficiencies that exist. The ARI program at the World Health Organization is building on the experience of the diarrheal diseases control program in collecting information through cross-sectional surveys (see chapter 9 of this volume). Because of the similarity in the magnitude of ARI and diarrhea and in the target group for each, efforts are being made to organize joint ARI and diarrhea surveys. Nine such surveys had taken place by the end of 1987, but none in Africa (World Health Organization, 1988a). This cross-sectional methodology still requires attention, as was discussed in the context of diarrheal diseases in chapter 9. Developmental work is also required in defining a case of ARI and pneumonia as either a direct or indirect cause of death (World Health Organization, 1988a).

Acknowledgments

I would like to thank Lynne Davies and Jacqui Wright for their much appreciated help in compiling and typing the references.

References

Adegbola, O. and Chojnacka, H. (1984). Causes of death in Lagos: structure and change. African Journal of Medicine and Medical Sciences, 13, 71–83.
Aden, A. and Birk, S. (1981). A study of child mortality in

Mogadishu, Somalia. *Journal of Tropical Pediatrics*, 27, 279–284.

Adeyokunnu, A. A., Taiwo, O., and Antia, A. U. (1980). Childhood mortality among 22,255 consecutive admissions in the University College Hospital, Ibadan. *Nigerian Journal of Paediatrics*, 7, 7–15.

Alakija, W. (1981). Prevention of childhood mortality in Nigeria by use of medical auxiliaries. *Tropical Doctor*, 11, 118–120.

Allen, S. C. (1984). Lobar pneumonia in Northern Zambia: clinical study of 502 adult patients. *Thorax*, 39, 612–616.

Ayeni, O. (1980). Causes of mortality in an African city. *African Journal of Medicine and Medical Sciences*, 9, 139–149.

Balint, O. and Anand, K. (1979). Infectious and parasitic diseases in Zambian children. *Tropical Doctor*, 9, 99–103.

Berman, S. and McIntosh, K. (1986). Acute respiratory infections. In: *Strategies for Primary Health Care*, Walsh, J. A. and Warren, K. S. (editors), pp. 29–46. Chicago: University of Chicago Press.

Black, R. E. (1984). Diarrhoeal diseases and child morbidity and mortality. *Population and Development Review*, 10 (supplement), 141–161.

Bradley, A. K. and Gilles, H. M. (1984). Malumfashi Endemic Diseases Research Project. 21: pointers to causes of death in the Malumfashi area, northern Nigeria. *Annals of Tropical Medicine and Parasitology*, 78, 265–271.

Bulla, A. and Hitze, K. L. (1978). Acute respiratory infections: a review. *Bulletin of the World Health Organization*, 56, 481–498.

Callum, C. (1983). Results of an ad hoc survey on infant and child mortality in Sudan: a summary report. *WHO Statistics Quarterly*, 36, 80–99.

Cantrelle, P., Diop, I. L., Garenne, M., Gueye, M., and Sadio, A. (1986). The profile of mortality and its determinants in Senegal, 1960–1980. In: *Determinants of Mortality Change and Differentials in Developing Countries*. E.85.XIII.4, pp. 86–116. New York: United Nations.

Cherian, T., John, T. J., Simoes, E., Steinhoff, M. C., and John, M. (1988). Evaluation of simple clinical signs for the diagnosis of acute lower respiratory tract infection. *Lancet*, 2, 125–128.

Collings, D. A. and Martin, K. S. (1985). A retrospective analysis of childhood pneumonia in a district hospital. *Central African Journal of Medicine*, 31, 152–156.

Danfa Project. (1979). *Final Report*. Accra and Los Angeles: University of Ghana and UCLA.

De Sole, G., Belay, Y., and Zegeye, B. (1987). Vitamin A deficiency in southern Ethiopia. *American Journal of Clinical Nutrition*, 45, 780–784.

Diallo, A. A., Silverman, M., and Egler, L. J. (1979). Bacteriology of lung puncture aspirates in malnourished children in Zaria. *Nigerian Medical Journal*, 9, 421–423.

El-Amin, A. M. (1978). Bacterial pneumonias in the rural society of Solwezi District of the North-Western Province of Zambia. *Medical Journal of Zambia*, 12, 42–45.

Ewbank, D., Henin, R., and Kekovole, J. (1986). An integration of demographic and epidemiologic research on mortality in Kenya. In: *Determinants of Mortality Change and Differentials in Developing Countries*. E.85.XIII.4, pp. 33–85. New York: United Nations.

Feachem, R. G., Burns, E., Cairncross, S., Cronin, A., Cross, P., Curtis, D., Khalid Khan, M., Lamb, D., and Southall, H. (1978). *Water, Health, and Development: An Interdisciplinary Evaluation*. London: Tri-Med Books.

Freij, L. and Wall, S. (1977). Exploring child health and its ecology: the Kirkos study in Addis Ababa. *Acta Paediatrica Scandinavica*, 267 (supplement), 1–180.

Greenwood, B. M., Hassan-King, M., Onyemelukwe, G., Macfarlane, J. T., Tubbs, H. R., Tugwell, P. J., Whittle, H. C., Denis, F., Chiron, J. P., M'Boup, S., Triau, R., Cadoz, M., and Diop Mar, I. (1980). Pneumococcal serotypes in West Africa. *Lancet*, 1, 360.

Hunpono-Wusu, O. O. (1976). Disorders which shorten life among Nigerians: a study of mortality patterns in the age group 15–44 years in Kaduna, Nigeria. *Tropical and Geographical Medicine*, 28, 343–348.

Lang, T., Lafaix, C., Fassin, D., Arnaut, I., Salmon, B., Baudon, D., and Ezekiel, J. (1986). Acute respiratory infections: a longitudinal study of 151 children in Burkina-Faso. *International Journal of Epidemiology*, 15, 553–561.

Leowski, J. (1986). Mortality from acute respiratory infections in children under 5 years of age: global estimates. *World Health Statistics Quarterly*, 39, 138–144.

Lepage, P., Munyakazi, C., and Hennart, P. (1981). Breast-feeding and hospital mortality in children in Rwanda. *Lancet*, 2, 409–411.

Lindskog, U. (1987). *Child Health and Household Water Supply: An Intervention Study from Malawi*. Linköping University Medical Dissertations, no. 259. Linköping, Sweden: Linköping University.

Macfarlane, J. T., Adegboye, D. S., and Warrell, M. J. (1979). Mycoplasma pneumoniae and the aetiology of lobar pneumonia in northern Nigeria. *Thorax*, 34, 713–719.

Mamdami, M. and Ross, D. A. (1988). *Vitamin A Supplementation and Child Survival: Magic Bullet or False Hope?* EPC Publication, no. 19. London: Evaluation and Planning Centre for Health Care.

Mtango, F. D. E. and Neuvians, D. (1986). Acute respiratory infections in children under five years. Central project in Bagameyo District, Tanzania. *Transactions of the Royal Society of Tropical Medicine and Hygiene*, 80, 851–858.

Mutie, D. M., Metselaar, D., Hillman, E. S., and McDonald, K. (1976). Isolation of respiratory syncytial virus from patients with lower respiratory tract infections in a paediatric observation ward in Kenya. *East African Medical Journal*, 53, 320–325.

Ngalikpima, V. F. (1983). Review of respiratory infections in a developing country. *European Journal of Respiratory Diseases*, 64, 481–486.

Omer, E-F. E., Hadi, A. E. G. E., and Sakhi, E. S. E. (1985). Bacteriology of sore throats in a Sudanese population. *Journal of Tropical Medicine and Hygiene*, 88, 337–341.

Omondi-Odhiambo, Voorhoeve, A. M., and van Ginneken, J. K. (1984). Age-specific infant and childhood mortality and causes of death. In: *Maternal and Child Health in Rural Kenya: An Epidemiological Study*, van Ginneken, J. K. and Muller, A. S. (editors). London and Sydney: Croom Helm.

Osuhor, P. C. and Etta, K. M. (1980). Morbidity patterns amongst children in a semi-urban community in northern Nigeria. *Journal of Tropical Pediatrics*, 26, 99–103.

Pio, A., Leowski, J., and ten Dam, H. G. (1985). The magnitude of the problem of acute respiratory infection. In: *Acute Respiratory Infections in Childhood*, Douglas, R. M. and Kerby-Eaton, E. (editors). Adelaide, Australia: University of Adelaide.

Pobee, J. O. M. (1976). A review of the causes of death in adult medical wards of Korle Bu Teaching Hospital, Accra, Ghana. *African Journal of Medicine and Medical Science*, 5, 79–85.

Rowland, M. G. M., Goh-Rowland, S. G. J., and Cole, T. J. (1988). The impact of infection on the growth of children from 0 to 2 years in an urban West African community. *American Journal of Clinical Nutrition*, 47, 134–138.

Shann, F. (1986). Etiology of severe pneumonia in children in developing countries. *Pediatric Infectious Disease*, 5, 247–252.

Shann, F., Gratten, M., Germer, S., Linnemann, V., Hazlett, D., and Payne, R. (1984). Aetiology of pneumonia in children in Goroka Hospital, Papua New Guinea. *Lancet*, 2, 537–541.

Silverman, M., Stratton, D., Diallo, A., and Egler, L. J. (1977). Diagnosis of acute bacterial pneumonia in Nigerian children. *Archives of Disease in Childhood*, 52, 925–931.

Slack, R. C. B., Stewart, J. D., Lewis, C. L. H., Cameron, D. I., Carvalho, G. R., Mangalji, Z., Lowry, P. R., and Wanjala, S. (1976). Acute pneumonias in adults in Nairobi. *East African Medical Journal*, 53, 480–483.

Snyder, J. D. and Merson, M. H. (1982). The magnitude of the global problem of acute diarrhoeal disease: a review of active surveillance data. *Bulletin of the World Health Organization*, 60, 605–613.

Sobeslavsky, O., Sebikari, S. R. K., Harland, P. S. E. G., Skrtic, N., Fayinka, O. A., and Soneji, A. D. (1977). The viral etiology of acute respiratory infections in children in Uganda. *Bulletin of the World Health Organization*, 55, 625–631.

United Nations. (1974). *Demographic Yearbook*. New York.

———. (1979). *Demographic Yearbook*. New York.

Wafula, E. M., Tukei, P. M., Bell, T. M., Nzanze, H., Pamba, A., Ndinya-Achola, J. O., Hazlett, D. T. G., and Ademba, G. R. (1984). How should primary health workers diagnose and treat acute respiratory infections (ARI)? *East African Medical Journal*, 61, 736–744.

Wall, R. A., Corrah, P. T., Mabey, D. C. W., and Greenwood, B. M. (1986). The etiology of lobar pneumonia in the Gambia. *Bulletin of the World Health Organization*, 64, 553–558.

Watts, T. and Chintu, C. (1983). Child deaths in Lusaka. *Medical Journal of Zambia*, 17, 39–45.

Williams, E. H., Hayes, R. J., and Smith, P. G. (1986). Admissions to a rural hospital in the West Nile District of Uganda over a 27 year period. *Journal of Tropical Medicine and Hygiene*, 89, 193–211.

World Health Organization. (1981). Summary of the ad hoc survey on infant and early childhood mortality in Sierra Leone. *WHO Statistics Quarterly*, 34, 220–238.

———. (1987a). *Indoor Air Quality in the Basse Area, the Gambia*. Document WHO/RSD/87.34. Geneva.

———. (1987b). *Indoor Air Pollution Study, Maragua Area, Kenya*. Document WHO/RSD/87.32. Geneva.

———. (1987c). *World Health Statistics Annual*. Geneva.

———. (1988a). *1987 Programme Report*. Document WHO/ARI/88.1. Geneva.

———. (1988b). *Case Management of Acute Respiratory Infections in Children: Intervention Studies*. Document WHO/ARI/88.2. Geneva.

Chapter 11

EPI Target Diseases: Measles, Tetanus, Polio, Tuberculosis, Pertussis, and Diphtheria

Laura C. Rodrigues

This chapter reviews special features of the epidemiology, public health importance, and strategies for control of measles, neonatal tetanus, pertussis, tuberculosis, polio, and diphtheria in Sub-Saharan Africa. These six diseases are grouped together because they can be prevented by vaccination and were selected as target diseases by the Expanded Programme on Immunization (EPI) of the World Health Organization (WHO). Next the state of the EPI in the 1980s is examined and areas of research proposed.

Data on these six EPI diseases in Africa are scarce and of variable quality. The World Health Organization supported standardized prevalence surveys of tuberculosis in the 1960s, paralytic polio in the late 1970s, and neonatal tetanus in the 1980s. Those surveys provided much useful information and have made clear the amount of undernotification of these diseases in Africa. Other useful sources of information are localized surveys (sometimes based on hospital data) and population laboratories.

Although these six diseases are extremely undernotified (Commey and Richardson, 1984), rough, conservative estimates were made for this chapter of their incidence and mortality in an average Sub-Saharan African population that has not been vaccinated. These estimates are based on median incidences of each disease in selected studies in Africa and are presented in table 11-1. EPI target diseases are associated with the deaths of 17 percent of all children, the majority of those in childhood. According to these estimates, 1 percent of all children in Africa die of neonatal tetanus, 9 percent of measles, 4 percent of pertussis, and 3 percent of tuberculosis; 0.6 percent develop paralytic polio, and the same percentage develop diphtheria, of which 20 percent die. I return to these estimates when discussing each disease.

Vaccination can be a powerful tool in the control of some of these diseases. In Sub-Saharan Africa as a whole vaccine uptake was still low in 1986: only 20 percent of African children had received, by the end of their first year of life, a complete course of vaccination

Table 11-1. *Lifelong Cumulative Incidence of and Mortality from the EPI Target Diseases in a Hypothetical Unvaccinated Cohort of 10,000 African Children*
(number)

Disease	Cases	Deaths
Diphtheria	60	12
Measles	9,500	850
Neonatal tetanus	110	100
Pertussis	7,000	430
Polio	64	5
Tuberculosis	1,200	320
Total	17,934	1,716

Source: The median for tetanus was taken from EPI surveys in Africa (Keja *et al.*, 1986); the median mortality for measles from Williams and Hull (1983), Aaby *et al.* (1986), and Commey and Richardson (1984); the median for pertussis from Voorhoeve *et al.* (1977); the median for polio from EPI surveys in Africa (Bernier, 1984); the median for tuberculosis from WHO surveys in Africa (Roelsgaard *et al.*, 1964), and the median for diphtheria from Heyworth and Ropp (1973).

against the six EPI diseases (EPI, 1987b). On the other hand, vaccination is not a panacea; data from the Gambia suggest that high levels of mortality can persist even in the presence of high vaccine coverage (Greenwood *et al.*, 1987).

Measles

Measles is a highly infectious viral disease. Serological surveys and studies of epidemics have established that generally, in the absence of vaccination and with the exception of isolated communities, nearly everyone contracts measles (Black, 1976). It is the biggest killer among the EPI target diseases. The EPI global advisory group calculated that measles causes two million deaths every year in the developing world, excluding China (EPI, 1985).

The epidemiology of measles in Africa has been studied or reviewed by several authors: Gans *et al.* (1961), Cobban (1963), Gupta and Singh (1975), Ofosu-Amaah (1983b), Morley *et al.* (1963), Morley (1973, 1985), and Aaby *et al.* (1984a, 1984b, 1984c, 1986).

In Sub-Saharan Africa, most unvaccinated children will acquire measles before their fifth birthday, and the median age of infection is around 24 months in well-populated settlements and a little later in rural communities (Ofosu-Amaah, 1983b). Figure 11-1 presents the age distribution of cases of measles in England and Wales and in a selection of African countries.

Mortality from all causes increases for several months after measles. Williams and Hull (1983) found

a case-fatality rate of 5 percent during the acute phase of the disease and 15 percent during the following nine months. The most common complications of measles are pneumonia, diarrhea, otitis, and malnutrition (Commey and Richardson, 1984; Williams and Hull, 1983; Debroise and Satge, 1967).

Puffer and Serrano (1973) found that in Latin America many deaths from measles were attributed to complications of measles, not to the disease itself. The result was underreporting. The same probably occurs in Africa. Ofosu-Amaah (1983b) estimated that in African countries measles may contribute to 10 percent of deaths in children less than five years of age.

High case-fatality rates were prevalent in Europe in the nineteenth century and are common in the developing world today (Morley *et al.*, 1963). Table 11-2 presents estimated case-fatality rates for measles in six African countries, in Glasgow at the beginning of the twentieth century, and in England and Wales in 1961.

It is not clear how poverty increases the severity of measles, but early age of infection, malnutrition, crowding (which leads to higher intensity of exposure), lack of access to medical care, and increased exposure to other diseases have been suggested as contributing factors.

The age at which measles is contracted influences

Figure 11-1. Age Distribution of Measles in the United Kingdom and Selected Countries of Sub-Saharan Africa, Various Years

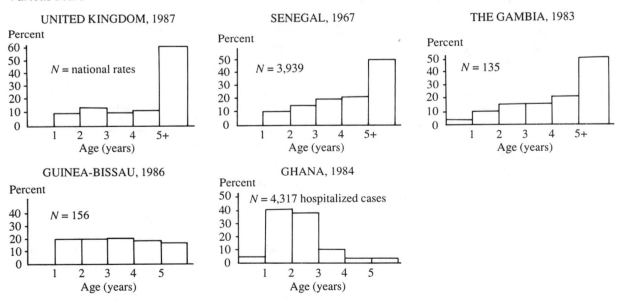

Source: For the Gambia, Williams and Hull (1983); for Ghana, Commey and Richardson (1984); for Guinea-Bissau, Aaby *et al.* (1986); for Senegal, Debroise and Satge (1967); for United Kingdom, Notifications, OPCS.

Table 11-2. Case-Fatality Rates for Measles, Selected Sites

Site	Year	Number of cases studied	Case-fatality rate	Reference
Burkina Faso	1963–64	5,701	3	Meyer (1965)
England and Wales	1961	764,000	0.02	Babbot et al. (1963)
Gambia, The	1981	135	5–15	Williams and Hull (1983)
Ghana	1973–81	4,317	17	Commey and Richardson (1984)
Guinea-Bissau	1980–82	161	9–14	Aaby et al. (1986)
Nigeria	1963	n.a.	3–5	Cobban (1963)
	1963	n.a.	7	Morley et al. (1963)
Scotland (Glasgow)	1908	22,000	5	Chalmers (1930)
Sierra Leone	1963	n.a.	15–30	Avery (1963)

n.a. Not available.

Note: The case-fatality rate is the number of deaths per 100 cases.

the severity of the case. Case-fatality rates decrease with age, except for the first six months, when most children are still protected by maternal antibodies. Table 11-3 presents case-fatality rates for measles by age group for three of the African studies mentioned in table 11-2. Case-fatality rates range from 20 to 78 percent for children between 6 and 12 months old and from 2 to 10 percent for children 4 years old or more.

The mechanism behind the associations among the severity of measles, undernutrition, and crowding is not well established. It is commonly accepted that measles in undernourished children is more severe. (Morley, 1985; Ofosu-Amaah, 1983b; Cantrelle, 1965). This association may not be causal but may reflect the association between undernutrition and crowding. Crowding leads to increased severity by heightening the intensity of exposure. Aaby *et al.* (1984a, 1984b, 1984c) found in community studies in Guinea-Bissau that severity was associated with the number of children in a household and that secondary cases were more severe than primary ones. Within primary or secondary cases, however, severity and nutritional status were not associated.

For the hypothetical African population presented in table 11-1, we used an incidence of measles of 100 percent for children who survived the first year of life and a case-fatality rate of 9 percent (which is the median between the highest and the lowest rates in the African studies presented in table 11-2).

What measures of control are available? In Europe and the United States measles mortality decreased as the standard of living and housing improved, even before the introduction of vaccines. In Africa today the main control activity is vaccination. Measles vaccine can be very effective, but it is sensitive to heat and is not very protective when given to children under nine months of age, who are protected by maternal antibodies. Vaccination not only protects the vaccinated

Table 11-3. Case-Fatality Rates for Measles by Age Group, Selected African Countries

Age (months)	The Gambia Case-fatality rate	The Gambia Number of cases	Guinea-Bissau Case-fatality rate	Guinea-Bissau Number of cases	Ghana Case-fatality rate	Ghana Number of cases
0–5	0	2	0	3	16	181
6–12	78	9	34	29	20	1,764
13–24	22	18			17	1,690
25–36	18	17	10	63	13	419
37–48	13	13	10	29	10	137
More than 48	4	66	10	32	2	126

Note: The case-fatality rate is the number of deaths per 100 cases.

Source: For the Gambia, Williams and Hull (1983); for Guinea-Bissau, Aaby *et al.* (1986); and for Ghana, Commey and Richardson (1984).

child; it also decreases the amount of transmission in the community, increases herd immunity, postpones the average age at which the disease is contracted, and protects unvaccinated children. Vaccinated cases are milder, and Aaby *et al.* (1986) found lower case-fatality rates among vaccinated children. Morley (1985) suggests that "measles immunization is likely to be the most [cost-]effective of all measures that . . . the health services [can] embark on."

The first attempts to control measles in Africa followed the discovery of a live attenuated vaccine in 1966 and relied heavily on vaccination campaigns (Osofu-Amaah, 1983b). The transmission of measles was in fact interrupted for a period of years in the Gambia (Foege, 1971). It soon became clear, however, that the impact of campaigns not supported by a routine health care program is short-lived. Efforts now concentrate on implementing a primary health care system offering routine vaccination.

Measles vaccination is one of the few measures that reduce overall infant mortality (in Zaire Kasongo Project Team, 1981; in Guinea-Bissau Aaby *et al.*, 1984b; and in Bangladesh EPI, 1987a, and Clemens *et al.*, 1988). Some controversy surrounds the permanency of this reduction. Hendrikse (1975) and the Kasongo Project Team (1981) suggest that this reduction is followed by a compensatory increase in mortality, in which weak, undernourished children protected against fatal measles by vaccination die of other diseases. Critics of this position argue that there is no compensatory mortality because vaccination prevents not only the deaths directly attributable to measles but also the weakness and undernutrition that leave measles survivors vulnerable to other diseases (EPI, 1987b; Aaby *et al.*, 1986; Clemens *et al.*, 1988).

Independent of which view is correct, economic development will reduce measles mortality in Africa, as it did in Europe and the United States, and an efficient measles vaccination program will lighten considerably the disease burden on African children and decrease (temporarily or permanently) childhood mortality.

The challenges involved in implementing an efficient routine vaccination program for measles in Sub-Saharan Africa are familiar: to provide primary health care to a scattered population, to keep the vaccine protected from the heat (cold chain), and to make vaccination accessible and acceptable to the population. These challenges will be examined further in the last section of this chapter.

EPI and UNICEF (EPI, 1987c) have recommended that vitamin A supplements be given to all children with measles and all children in areas with a high incidence of measles. Their aim is to prevent the blindness caused by measles-triggered vitamin A deficiency.

A new vaccine (EZ) able to induce immunity at early ages is being tested. Further research is necessary into the associations among crowding, malnutrition, and severity and into the impact of measles vaccination on mortality. Operational research into how best to improve the cold chain and extend vaccine uptake is still necessary.

Neonatal Tetanus

Tetanus is a major cause of avoidable mortality in Africa. It is estimated that one million babies die every year of neonatal tetanus in the developing world (Keja *et al.*, 1986). Stanfield and Galazka (1984) estimated that 150,000 neonatal deaths from tetanus occur in Africa each year.

Adult tetanus is also an important cause of mortality in Africa. Haddock (1985) estimated one adult death for every nine neonatal deaths from tetanus. Adult tetanus in Africa is mostly an occupational disease of workers on the land (Stanfield and Galazka, 1984). Vaccination is as efficient against adult as against neonatal tetanus, but as yet no program exists for controlling adult tetanus in Africa. Neither adult tetanus nor adult tuberculosis is a target disease of the EPI. Few studies look at controlling tetanus in adults (Kessel, 1984) or consider the duration of immunity and the logistics of vaccinating or revaccinating adults. There is a clear need to look further at the epidemiology and control of tetanus that is not neonatal in Africa.

Neonatal tetanus is usually caused by unsterile birth practices, mainly when the cord is handled or dressed. It has practically disappeared from countries where the health care system provides hygienic conditions for all deliveries and all umbilical cord dressings. In the United States neonatal tetanus mortality decreased from 64 per 100,000 births in the 1900s to 1 per 100,000 births in the 1960s (LaForce *et al.*, 1969).

Undernotification of neonatal tetanus is a major problem in the developing world. The EPI estimated that in the developing countries only 2–5 percent of neonatal tetanus cases are routinely recorded (EPI, 1982a). The very young age of death is partially responsible for the extent of undernotification: deaths may occur before the birth is registered or before the child is officially "introduced" to society. This is particularly true in societies that do not name the child until its survival is certain or where newborn infants are buried without ceremony (Robertson *et al.*, 1985).

Neonatal tetanus, more than the other EPI diseases, is typical in the absence of health care, and therefore of notification.

In the past decade the Expanded Programme on Immunization encouraged countries to undertake retrospective surveys to estimate the level of neonatal tetanus mortality. The suggested standard protocol consisted of asking a random selection of women who had delivered in the past 7 months if their baby had died and how (Stanfield and Galazka, 1984). The use of cluster samples and a sample size of 2,000 mothers was suggested. Early surveys in Africa found mortality rates for neonatal tetanus in the range of 40 to 70 deaths per 1,000 live births; recent surveys found lower values, usually below 20 per 1,000 live births. Table 11-4 lists the results of surveys in 17 African countries.

For the hypothetical African population in table 11-1, the median incidence of 11 deaths per 1,000 live births was chosen from table 11-4, with a 90 percent case-fatality rate.

Tetanus toxoid given to a mother during pregnancy protects her newborn child against tetanus (Schofield *et al.*, 1961); two doses are highly protective (Newell *et al.*, 1966). Vaccinating all women of childbearing age is an effective strategy (Black *et al.*, 1980). An alternative strategy for controlling neonatal tetanus, which led to its disappearance in most industrial developed countries, is to improve the conditions of antenatal care and delivery. This has been attempted in Africa by training traditional birth attendants (World Health Organization, 1986). Rahman (1982) compared these two interventions with a nonintervention group and found that neonatal tetanus was reduced by 76.7 percent in the babies delivered by trained midwives and by 93.3 percent in the children of immunized mothers. The overall neonatal mortality was lower in the first group, however, because training the birth

Table 11-4. Neonatal Tetanus Mortality Rate as Measured by Community Surveys in Africa

Country and year	Source	Number of live births	Mortality rate All causes	Tetanus
Burundi, 1984	4	3,099	n.a.	8
Cameroon				
1982	4	2,102	n.a.	7
1984	4	2,118	n.a.	8
Côte d'Ivoire, 1982	4	2,324	34	18
Ethiopia, 1983	3	2,010	8	5
Gambia, The				
1944–53	1	n.a.	53	43
1980[a]	1	224	84	9
1980[a]	3	4,976	n.a.	11
Kenya				
1984	4	2,132	16	11
1985	4	6,566	16	11
Malawi, 1982[b]	4	2,081	29	12
Senegal, 1955	2	n.a.	n.a.	80
Sierra Leone				
1979–80[a]	2	403	305	72
1981[a]	2	262	172	11
Somalia, 1981[b]	2	5,781	91	21
Sudan, 1981[b]	3	9,632	29	9
Togo, 1984	4	4,996	11	6
Uganda, 1984	4	525	38	15
Zaire, 1984[b]	4	3,836	12	1
Zimbabwe, 1983[b]	4	4,106	10	4

n.a. Not available.
Note: The mortality rate is the number of deaths per 1,000 live births.
a. Before and after introducing a program of vaccinating pregnant women.
b. Nationwide surveys.
Source: Key to source column is as follows: 1, MacGregor (1953) as quoted by Robertson *et al.* (1985); 2, quoted in World Health Organization (1986); 3, quoted in EPI (1987c); and 4, quoted by Keja *et al.* (1984).

attendants reduced other causes of mortality. The results of the trial, presented in table 11-5, suggest the need to combine the two strategies.

The control of neonatal tetanus shows that vaccination programs work best when integrated with the development of a primary health care system and the improvement of living conditions. As EPI (1982b) states, "The control of tetanus and other diseases in the EPI programme gives an opportunity to forge ahead with the development of primary care in developing countries."

The research priorities for neonatal tetanus in Africa are mostly operational and concentrate on defining the best ways to plan, implement, and monitor the impact of control activities.

Poliomyelitis

Paralytic polio is the most serious clinical manifestation of poliovirus infection. Poliovirus infection is very common in the developing world and, as with measles, virtually all children who are not vaccinated will acquire it.

Not all polio infections lead to paralysis. The ratio of paralysis to infection ranges from 140 to 600 infections for each paralytic case (Schonberger *et al.*, 1981). It is lower in the first six months of life, when the child has maternal antibodies. The transmission is mainly fecal-oral and is facilitated by unsanitary and crowded living conditions (Ofosu-Amaah, 1983a). Serological surveys suggest that most children in Africa will acquire poliovirus *infection* before the age of four (Domok, 1985). Ofosu-Amaah (1983a) found that 90.8 percent of the *paralysis* in Ghana was acquired during the first four years of life.

The importance of paralytic polio was systematically underestimated in Africa—as in the rest of the developing world—during the 1960s and 1970s, when the regular use of polio vaccine almost eliminated the disease in the economically developed world. At that time the belief was that being infected with polio during early childhood, a pattern typical in the developing world, led to a very low ratio of paralysis to infection and that the prevalence of residual paralytic polio was therefore low in the developing world (Nathanson and Martin, 1979).

The work of Ofosu-Amaah *et al.* (1977) and Nicholas *et al.* (1977) corrected this misconception. They attempted to quantify the extent of residual poliomyelitis paralysis of the lower limb through what has come to be known as the lameness survey in Ghana. They discovered that the prevalence, and the estimated incidence, of lameness in the developing world was as high as or higher than that in the economically developed countries during epidemic years and that the ratio of paralysis to infection did not increase substantially with age after the first six months of life.

Table 11-5. Neonatal Mortality Rates in One Nonintervention Group and Two Intervention Groups

Group and indicator	Number of births	Cause of death				
		Tetanus	Birth injury	Respiratory distress or infection	Other	All causes
Nonintervention group	998					
Number of deaths		24	13	29	19	85
Mortality rate		24	13	29	19	85
Women delivered by a trained birth attendant	713					
Number of deaths		4	3	6	4	17
Mortality rate		5.6	4.2	8.4	5.6	23.8
Percentage reduction		77	68	71	70	72
Women vaccinated with tetanus toxoid	771					
Number of deaths		1	9	17	3	30
Mortality rate		1.3	11.7	22.1	3.9	38.9
Percentage reduction		93	10	24	79	54

Note: The neonatal mortality rate is the number of deaths in the first month per 1,000 live births.
Source: Calculated from Rahman (1982).

The first lameness surveys consisted of a questionnaire asking schoolteachers how many students they taught and what proportion had lower limb lameness. The protocol was adapted by the World Health Organization (EPI, 1977), and standardizations were suggested (Bernier, 1983, 1984). Since those first surveys more than 15 surveys have been undertaken in Africa (their results are summarized in table 11-6). The prevalence of lameness they uncovered ranges from 0.7 to 13.2 per 1,000 children. These are almost certainly underestimates because they include only surviving children (although paralytic polio has a case fatality rate of around 10 percent) and sometimes only children still able to attend school. Since most cases in Africa occur before children reach four years of age, some researchers have suggested that dividing the prevalence by 5 (LaForce *et al.*, 1980) or by 3 or 4 (Bernier, 1984) can produce estimates of the average annual incidence during the first years of life. For the hypothetical African population in table 11-1, the median prevalence of 6.4 per 1,000 (from table 11-6) yields an annual incidence of 0.16 percent during the first four years of life.

The measures that control polio include improvements in the standards of hygiene (including availability of clean water, sanitation, and less crowded living conditions) and vaccination.

Oral poliovirus vaccine (OPV) is a preparation of three types of attenuated viruses. It is very protective in the economically developed countries but less so in Africa, possibly because other viral infections are present in the intestine (Montefiore *et al.*, 1963;

Table 11-6. Prevalence of Paralytic Polio from Lameness Surveys in African Children

Country and year	Location	Type of population	Case-finding method	Age group (years)	Number of children surveyed	Prevalence
Cameroon						
1979	Yaoundé	Urban	House to house	5–11	9,391	8.2
1979	Bamenda	Semirural	House to house	5–11	8,503	5.5
1979	Eseka	Rural	House to house	5–11	6,307	9.6
Côte d'Ivoire						
1979	Abidjan	Urban	School	6–11	10,847	7.9
1979	Abengourou	Rural	School and catchment area	5–14	6,180	8.3
1979	Ferke	Semirural	School and catchment area	8–12	5,717	12.0
1979	Dobou	Rural	School	6–12	4,168	8.0
Gambia, The, 1979	Bantul area	Urban	School	8–19	15,033	4.7
Ghana						
1974	Danfa	Rural	School and catchment area	6–15	7,347	7.5
1974	National	Urban and rural	School	6–15	74,609	5.8
Kenya, 1979	Machakos District	Rural	House to house	5–14	6,800	0.7
Madagascar, 1981	Toliary	Urban	School	6–10	6,810	3.5
Malawi, 1979	National	Urban and rural	House to house	0–15	17,580	6.5
Niger						
1981	Niamey	Urban	School	5–14	6,972	13.2
1981	Niamey Department	Rural	School and catchment area	5–14	23,600	6.4
Nigeria, 1980	Lagos State	Urban and rural	School	6–14	20,000	2.4
Sierra Leone[a]	Freetown and South Province	Urban and rural	House to house	5–15	n.a.	3.9
Somalia, 1982	13 districts	Urban and rural	School	5–13	12,938	10.0
Swaziland, 1979	5 sites	Urban	House to house	0–10	6,000	3.2

n.a. Not available

Note: Prevalence is measured as the number of cases of lameness attributed to polio for every 1,000 children.

a. Date unknown.

Source: Bernier (1984).

Bottiger *et al.*, 1981). John *et al.* (1980) found that a scheme of five or more doses overcomes the problem of low seroconversion rates in tropical settings. OPV is the recommended vaccine for countries with high incidence because it is easy to administer and spreads in the community, immunizing those to whom it is transmitted.

The strategy of simultaneously vaccinating an entire region with OPV has had a great impact in Brazil and Cuba (Sabin, 1980, 1981). Its logistic viability in many countries in Africa is problematic, however (Ofosu-Amaah, 1983a). As with the campaigns promoting measles vaccination, the impact of this strategy depends on backing the routine vaccination program with primary health care.

Substantial progress has been made in controlling polio in Africa as well as elsewhere. Researchers with the EPI assumed that undernotification is constant with time and place, which allowed them to look at the geographic distribution and time trends in the incidence of paralytic polio. Sub-Saharan Africa and South Asia have the highest incidence rates, and the number of notified cases began to decrease around 1980 in Africa and the world as a whole (EPI, 1987a). The increase in the levels of vaccination and the decrease in the notified cases of polio, which figure 11-2 illustrates for three African countries, are based on notifications and sentinel surveillance (EPI, 1987c). The EPI believes that this trend reflects a real fall in the number of cases, which is the result of vaccination and improved sanitation (EPI, 1987a, 1987c). The progress in controlling polio worldwide is so great that the 41st World Health Assembly pledged to eradicate polio throughout the world by the year 2000 (World Health Organization, 1988). Improving the quality of data is essential for monitoring and evaluating the progress properly. The recommended research is operational: determining the best ways to plan, implement, and monitor the impact of control programs.

Tuberculosis

Tuberculosis infection does not always lead to disease. The disease has many clinical manifestations, but only the open, smear-positive cases are infective and capable of being transmitted. Infection can be identified by a skin test, and Styblo and Rouillon (1981) estimate that of 1,000 infections, 25–30 progress to smear-positive cases and another 25–30 to closed forms (such as meningitis and osteomyelitis).

Tuberculosis was not introduced in Sub-Saharan Africa until the nineteenth century (Budd, 1867, quoted in Roelsgaard *et al.*, 1964). It soon became, as

Figure 11-2. Poliomyelitis Cases and Vaccine Coverage of Children Age 12–23 Months in Three African Countries, 1974–82

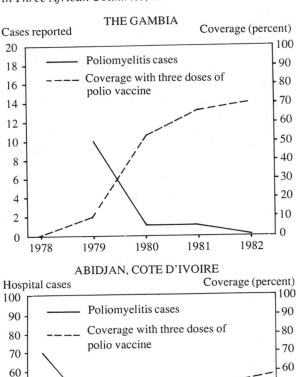

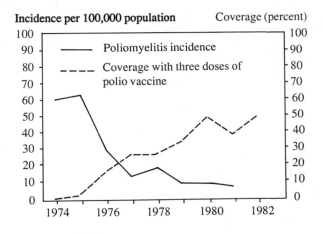

Source: EPI (1987c).

it is now, a major source of morbidity and mortality. Styblo and Rouillon (1981) estimate an incidence of smear-positive cases ranging between 1 and 4.5 per 1,000 persons per year in Africa, with a case-fatality rate of 50 percent in untreated cases. It is a disease of adults: 87 percent of all notified cases in Kenya and 80 percent in Tanzania are in persons at least 14 years of age (Tanzania/British Medical Research Council, 1985).

During the 1950s and 1960s the World Health Organization carried out a series of tuberculosis surveys in African countries. Those surveys estimated the prevalence of infection and smear-positive disease in a random sample of the population. The prevalence of smear-positive cases that those surveys found in 12 African countries is given in table 11-7. The range of prevalence is from 0 to 10 cases per 1,000 persons, with the median being 3.7 per 1,000. Although those surveys are 25 years old, Bleiker and Styblo (1978) suggest that their results are still valid because the levels of tuberculosis infection have not decreased in Africa since then.

For the hypothetical African population in table 11-1, the median prevalence given in table 11-7 was

used to estimate the life-long incidence of tuberculosis. To achieve this median prevalence the cohort will have 1.6 smear-positive cases per 1,000 persons per year, a life-long risk of developing smear-positive tuberculosis of 63 per 1,000, and a life-long risk of developing any form of tuberculosis of 126 per 1,000.

The incidence of tuberculosis increases with poverty. The decline in the incidence of tuberculosis in Europe started before the introduction of specific chemotherapy or vaccination and is usually attributed to improvements in the standard of living (Citron, 1988).

Strategies for control include protecting individuals through vaccination and interrupting transmission through case finding and treatment. The vaccine against tuberculosis, BCG, is controversial: the protection found in trials ranges from negative to 90 percent (Fine, 1988). Since a large random control trial in India (Tuberculosis Prevention Trial, 1980) reported no protection, many observational studies have looked at local efficacy. BCG has been used extensively in Sub-Saharan Africa, but its local protective effect against tuberculosis has not been evaluated randomly (Fillastre, 1986). Two recent observational studies in

Table 11-7. Prevalence of Smear-Positive Tuberculosis, Selected African Countries

Country	Persons examined	Positive cases	Prevalence
Botswana	2,103	19	9.0
Gambia, The			
Urban	581	0	0.0
Rural	1,151	1	0.9
Ghana			
Urban	410	2	4.9
Rural	1,661	8	4.8
Kenya			
Urban	8,066	6	0.7
Rural	4,957	32	6.5
Lesotho	2,162	11	5.2
Liberia			
Urban	974	1	1.0
Rural	2,176	3	1.4
Sierra Leone			
Urban	1,053	1	1.0
Rural	2,125	3	1.4
Swaziland	1,547	16	10.3
Tanzania	2,177	8	3.7
Uganda	4,014	13	3.2
Zanzibar			
Urban	1,134	11	9.7
Rural	2,093	8	3.8

Note: Prevalence is measured as the number of smear-positive cases of tuberculosis for every 1,000 persons.
Source: Roelsgaard *et al.* (1964).

Sub-Saharan Africa found 66 percent protection in Cameroon (Blin *et al.*, 1986) and 62 percent in Togo (Tidjani *et al.*, 1986).

For a long time BCG has been suspected of also protecting vaccinated persons against leprosy (Doull *et al.*, 1957; Noordeen, 1986). A longitudinal study in Uganda estimated an overall protection against leprosy of 81 percent (Stanley *et al.*, 1981). Two observational studies in Malawi found protections of 40 and 35 percent (Fine *et al.*, 1986), and studies in south India and Burma found lower, but significantly higher than zero, protective efficacies (Fine, 1988). In fact, BCG may offer better protection against leprosy than against tuberculosis (Fine, 1985). Assuming it is effective in Africa, BCG should be looked at as a means of protecting individual children and young adults from tuberculosis and its sequelae rather than as a tool for interrupting transmission. BCG vaccination prevents mainly the closed forms of the disease and has minimal impact on transmission (Grzybowski *et al.*, 1976).

Case finding and treatment are the most important components of a tuberculosis control program (Styblo, 1983; Sutherland, 1988; Fox, 1988). Most current research on tuberculosis in Africa focuses on how to increase case finding and how to ensure that a high proportion of detected cases are cured. As with other diseases, the quality of notification must be improved as well.

Pertussis

Pertussis is a common disease. The EPI (1985) estimates that 60 million cases and between 0.5 million and 1 million deaths occur in the world every year. It is very infectious, with a secondary attack rate as high as 90 percent. Incidence is consistently described as higher in girls than in boys (Armengaud *et al.*, 1960a; Morley *et al.*, 1966; Voorhoeve *et al.*, 1977). The case-fatality rate is estimated to be 1 percent, but it is three times higher in the first year of life (EPI, 1985; Voorhoeve *et al.*, 1977). According to hospital studies the main complications associated with high mortality in Africa are pneumonia, encephalitis, and malnutrition (Armengaud *et al.*, 1960a). Pertussis is difficult to diagnose: there is no good laboratory diagnostic test, and the clinical features are not typical during the first year of life. Most studies of pertussis rely on a system of scores, classifying cases from probable to certain. Official notification of pertussis is probably even more incomplete than that of measles; more or less the same number of cases of the two diseases can be expected in children, but many more cases of measles are reported (World Health Organization, 1976).

The best community follow-up study of pertussis in Africa, the Machakos Project (Voorhoeve *et al.*, 1977; Muller *et al.*, 1984), is reported in chapter 18 of this book. It studied the epidemiology of pertussis in two African communities in a rural area of Kenya. Most of the information used in this section comes from Machakos.

Two community studies of pertussis in Kenya and Nigeria suggest that the mean age of incidence in Africa is very low and the case-fatality rate is high (Morley, 1985; Voorhoeve *et al.*, 1977). The age distribution of cases from hospital studies is biased because pertussis in young children is generally more severe than in older children and adults and only the severest cases show up at hospitals. The age distribution of cases and deaths in the Machakos community is shown in table 11-8. The incidence was 17 percent during the first year of life, and the cumulative incidence was 93 percent at 14 years; that is, 93 percent of the children had pertussis before their 15th birthday. Moreover, 80 percent of all cases occurred before the child's sixth birthday. Morley *et al.* (1966) found a lower median age of incidence in Western Nigeria, which Voorhoeve *et al.* (1977) suggest is due to the higher contact among children of different households in Nigeria than in Kenya.

Case-fatality rates also depend on early treatment and the incidence of other diseases (Morley, 1985). Table 11-8, based on 12 deaths only, shows case-fatality rates by age at Machakos: 3.2 percent for children less than 12 months old, 1.3 percent for children 1 to 5 years old, and 0 for children 5 years of age or older.

Applying rates from the Machakos study to the hypothetical unvaccinated African population in table 11-1 yields the following statistics: 92.9 percent of all children have pertussis at some time: 16 percent during their first year of life, with a 3 percent case-fatality rate; 54 percent in the following four years, with a 1.3 percent case-fatality rate; and the remaining 23 percent at older ages, with no deaths.

The severity of pertussis does not appear to be associated with undernutrition, but pertussis may contribute to subsequent development of undernutrition (EPI, 1985).

Pertussis incidence and mortality decreased in the economically developed countries before the introduction of vaccination. The pertussis vaccine is slightly controversial because its efficacy is variable (estimated to range from 60 to 90 percent; EPI, 1985) and it can cause some very rare, very serious side effects (Miller, 1981). Mortality associated with vaccination, how-

Table 11-8. Pertussis in a Rural Area in Kenya

A. Estimated Age Distribution and Age-Specific Incidence

Age (years)	Child-years at risk	Cases	Incidence per 1,000	Cumulative incidence per 1,000	Pertussis cases as percentage of cases in all ages
Less than 1	1,035	165	159	159	17.3
1	1,020	107	105	264	11.3
2	991	133	134	398	14.0
3	798	133	167	565	14.0
4	848	116	137	702	12.2
5	880	109	124	826	11.4
6	861	69	80	906	7.2
7–14	5,308	120	23	929	12.6

B. Deaths, Case-Fatality Rate, Mortality, and Proportion of All Deaths, by Age

Age (years)	Number of deaths	Case-fatality rate	Mortality per 100,000	Pertussis deaths as percentage of all deaths
Less than 1	5	3.2	512	3.6
1	2	1.3	132	2.5
2	2	1.5	201	6.5
3	1	0.8	125	5.6
4	2	1.7	235	14.3
5 and older	0	0	0	0

Note: Incidence is measured as the number of cases of pertussis per 1,000 persons in a given age group per year. Cumulative incidence builds on the cases in the younger age groups to yield the number of cases per 1,000 persons up to and including a given age group. Mortality is measured as deaths per 1,000 persons.

Source: Modified from Voorhoeve *et al.* (1977).

ever, is negligible compared with that caused by the disease itself. The Expanded Programme on Immunization, while welcoming the research on a new acellular vaccine that is potentially more potent and less toxic, insists that the vaccine now available provides an efficient tool for controlling pertussis (EPI, 1985).

Because the case-fatality rate is very high during the first year of life and maternal immunity is not transferred to the child, children should be completely vaccinated at a very young age. Efficient control measures therefore include *early* vaccination and the identification of secondary cases among young siblings of children diagnosed with pertussis.

Areas requiring further attention include establishing the level of incidence in most countries; clarifying the role of crowding and social space in early incidence of the disease; studying the interaction of pertussis with nutrition, measles, and other respiratory diseases; and conducting operational research into how to improve early vaccine uptake.

Diphtheria

Of all the EPI target diseases, diphtheria is the least studied in Africa. The epidemiological picture is still tentative. In most countries almost everyone has acquired immunity, the carrier rate is extremely high, and the incidence of throat disease seems to be very low. The most accepted explanation is that the presence of widespread subclinical infection—probably cutaneous—leads to immunity.

No reliable source of community data on the incidence of diphtheria in Africa is available. Most studies are hospital based or case series, but the small number of cases in these suggests that very few diphtheria cases are diagnosed. Heyworth and Ropp (1973) suggest an annual incidence of 6 cases per 1,000 persons during the first five years of life in the Gambia. The incidence levels may be higher in northern Africa and in some Muslim countries such as Senegal (Muyembe *et al.*, 1972) and Madagascar (Saugrain, 1955). According to Salih *et al.* (1985)

Table 11-9. Diphtheria: Carrier Rate, Immunity, Incidence, and Mortality, Selected Countries of Sub-Saharan Africa

Indicator	The Gambia, 1973	Nigeria 1934	Nigeria 1961	Rwanda, 1937	Senegal, 1960	Uganda, 1970	Zaire 1937	Zaire 1972	Zaire 1980
Number surveyed	n.a.	1,959	2,000	400	n.a.	294	124	918	n.a.
Carrier rate (percent)									
Age 0–10	n.a.	n.a.	7[a]	n.a.	n.a.	n.a.	n.a.	9	n.a.
Age 10 or older	n.a.	n.a.	n.a.	n.a.	n.a.	n.a.	n.a.	6	n.a.
Immunity (Schick-negative) rate (percent)									
Age 1–5	n.a.	n.a.	n.a.	n.a.	n.a.	n.a.	n.a.	70	n.a.
Age 5–10	n.a.	n.a.	46	n.a.	n.a.	n.a.	78	100	n.a.
Age 10 or older	n.a.	98	n.a.	100	n.a.	n.a.	96	100	n.a.
Cases of diphtheria	9	n.a.	12	n.a.	53	13	n.a.	n.a.	28
Incidence (per 100,000 population)	n.a.	n.a.	n.a.	n.a.	n.a.	66[b]	n.a.	3[c]	n.a.
Deaths from diphtheria	1	n.a.	2	n.a.	13	5	n.a.	n.a.	8
Case-fatality rate (percent)	11	n.a.	16	n.a.	25	38	n.a.	n.a.	29

n.a. Not available.

a. Percentage of 500 children with sore throats.

b. Measured as the number of notified cases per 100,000 population.

c. In 1–5 age group.

Source: For the Gambia, Bezjak and Farsey. (1970b); for Nigeria, see Ikejiani (1961); for Rwanda, Neujean (1937); for Senegal, Armengaud *et al.* (1960b); for Uganda, Bwibo (1969); for Zaire 1937, Ramon and Nellis (1934); for Zaire 1972, see Muyembe *et al.* (1972); for Zaire 1980, Muganga *et al.* (1980).

diphtheria is one of the most important childhood diseases in the Sudan, and there have been isolated reports of epidemics (for example, Salih *et al.*, 1985; Bwibo, 1969).

The case-fatality rate of persons diagnosed with diphtheria is extremely high in Africa for a disease that need not lead to death if treated properly. Table 11-9 shows case-fatality rates from hospital studies in five African countries that range from 11 to 38 percent.

Diphtheria's causal agent, *Corynebacterium diphtheriae*, is widely disseminated in Africa (see, for example, Neujean, 1937). The Schick test (injecting diphtheria toxin into the skin) can identify immunity to diphtheria. Table 11-9 also presents the results of studies that used the Schick test in three African countries to screen healthy populations over 40 years. The lowest proportion of immunity found among teenagers or adults was 96 percent. Immunity is almost universal at birth, decreases around six months of age with the loss of maternal antibodies, and then increases with age.

More recently the rate of carriership has been estimated by culturing nose and throat swabs collected from healthy persons. The prevalence of the carrier state ranges from 6 to 9 percent—that is, ten times higher than the rate found in the United Kingdom in the 1920s, when the incidence of the disease was very high (Medical Research Council, 1923, quoted in Bezjak and Farsey, 1970a).

Most hypotheses put forward to explain the peculiar epidemiological features of diphtheria in Africa accept the low incidence of the disease and propose that some manner of subclinical infection leads to immunity (Ikejiani, 1961; Bwibo, 1969; Bezjak and Farsey, 1970a, 1970b; Muyembe *et al.*, 1972; Heyworth and Ropp, 1973). These peculiarities include cutaneous infections that cause mild disease and immunity, low toxicity of *Corynebacterium* in Africa, and living conditions that lead to low infective doses and cause mild, unrecognized disease.

It has also been suggested that the real incidence of diphtheria is higher than detected and that some of the upper respiratory tract infections treated in Africa are in fact diphtheria (Armengaud *et al.*, 1960b).

For the hypothetical African population in table 11-1, the mortality rate found in the Gambia (Heyworth and Ropp, 1973) of 6 deaths per 1,000 persons per year in the first five years of life yielded a case-fatality rate of 20 percent.

Independent of the mechanism responsible for the special epidemiological features of diphtheria in Sub-Saharan Africa, an efficient vaccination program must be kept going. Africa is changing very fast, and, given the high carriership rate, a change in the factors that keep diphtheria incidence low and immunity high may quickly increase the incidence of the disease (Bwibo, 1969).

Recommended research includes seeking a better understanding of the epidemiology of diphtheria in Africa, including why the case-fatality rate is so high; estimating the true levels of incidence and fatality; and exploring the possibility of geographic variation.

The EPI in Africa in the 1980s

Of all the WHO regions, Africa has the lowest vaccine uptake: in 1985 less than 20 percent of all children had received their complete vaccination before reaching their first birthday. Figure 11-3 presents the level of uptake for each vaccine by WHO region (EPI, 1986). Although virtually all countries in the region have implemented a vaccination program, many programs are restricted to a few areas or sometimes to a single city. In 1985, of the 45 countries in the region, only 22 implemented a vaccination program throughout the country (EPI, 1986). Strategies to accelerate the increase in vaccine coverage include combining mobile teams, outreach methods, and routine fixed posts (EPI, 1986, 1987a, 1987b, 1987c). Of the 33 African countries that reviewed their EPI program in 1985–86, 20 set up specific committees to launch an acceleration plan.

The lack of training for management of the cold chain has constrained vaccination programs in Africa in the past. UNICEF and WHO have made great steps toward identifying, testing, and evaluating new equipment and toward organizing training courses for maintaining and repairing equipment. Operational research into the cold chain and sterilization tech-

Figure 11-3. Immunization Coverage of Infants under 12 Months Old, by WHO Region, August 1986

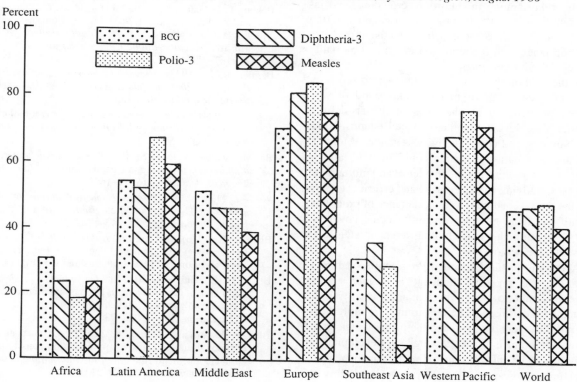

Source: EPI (1986).

niques is ongoing and a priority of the EPI. The region is making good progress in upgrading the management skills of its health personnel. In the first ten years after EPI was implemented in 1977, more than 26,000 senior, mid-, and peripheral-level personnel in Africa were trained in logistics, the cold chain, refrigerator repair, and other subjects (EPI, 1986).

Some research has been conducted on the factors associated with lack of compliance or low vaccine uptake, at the level both of families and of services (Hanlon *et al.*, 1988; Cutts *et al.*, 1989).

Good data on incidence and mortality are essential to planning health care and disease control programs. Levels of infections not yet targeted by the EPI need to be determined, since other vaccines (and indeed other interventions) can be added to the six basic EPI vaccines. In several African countries yellow fever and meningitis, and now hepatitis B in the Gambia, already form part of the EPI program. Rotavirus vaccination may be added in the next five years. The possibility of adding vitamin A and iodine supplementation to the program should also be explored (EPI, 1987c).

It is necessary to clarify further the epidemiological features of measles, pertussis, and diphtheria in Africa; the interplay among malnutrition, crowding, and infection; the role of the EPI target diseases in triggering respiratory infections and diarrhea; and the importance and permanence of the reduction in general mortality associated with vaccination.

In the field of operational research there is scope for further development of methods and standard simplified protocols along the lines of the EPI-defined protocols for vaccine uptake, neonatal tetanus, lameness surveys, and cost-effectiveness studies. Monitoring and evaluating programs could include, among other things, monitoring the incidence and mortality of diseases; studying vaccine uptake and efficacy; exploring the reasons behind the nonacceptance of programs; identifying local groups with low vaccine coverage; and evaluating the impact of different strategies to expand vaccine coverage.

According to the Expanded Programme on Immunization, "the pressing challenge is to increase the coverage, and to do so in a manner that can be sustained indefinitely. The constraints are more managerial than technological, and the primary concern of the EPI program is to use research on developmental activities as an integral part of routine management, directing it towards solving practical problems of implementation, to measure impact and to reduce the cost of the programme" (EPI, 1987c).

References

Aaby, P., Bukh, J., Lisse, I. M., and Smits, A. J. (1984a). Measles vaccination and reduction in child mortality: a community study from Guinea-Bissau. *Journal of Infections*, 8, 13–21.

———. (1984b). Overcrowding and intensive exposure as determinants of measles mortality. *American Journal of Epidemiology*, 120 (1), 49–63.

Aaby, P., Bukh, J., Lisse, I. M., Smits, A. J., Gomes, J., Fernandes, M. A., Indi, F., and Soares, M. (1984c). Determinants of measles mortality in a rural area in Guinea-Bissau. *Journal of Tropical Pediatrics*, 30, 164–168.

Aaby, P., Bukh, J., Leerhoy, J., Lisse, I. M., Mordhorst, C. H., and Pedersen, I.R. (1986). Vaccinated children get milder measles infection: a community study from Guinea-Bissau. *Journal of Infectious Diseases*, 154 (5), 858–863.

Armengaud, M., Frament, V., and Biran, D. (1960a). Considération sur la coqueluche en milieu africain. *Médecine d'Afrique Noir*, 24, 520.

———. (1960b). La diphtérie en milieu africain. *Médecine d'Afrique Noir*, 24, 515–519.

Avery, T. L. (1963). The analysis over eight years of children admitted with measles to a hospital in Sierra Leone, West Africa. *West African Medical Journal*, 12, 61–63.

Babbot, F. I., Galbraith, N. S., McDonalds, J. C., Shaw, A., and Zuckerman, A. J. (1963). Deaths from measles in England and Wales in 1961. *Monthly Bulletin of the Ministry of Health Public Health Laboratory Services*, 22, 167–175.

Bernier, R. H. (1983). *Prevalence Survey Techniques for Paralytic Polio: An Update*. EPI/GAG 83/WP10. Geneva: World Health Organization.

———. (1984). Some observations on poliomyelitis lameness surveys. *Review of Infectious Diseases*, 6 (supplement 2), S371–S375.

Bezjak, V. and Farsey, S. J. (1970a). *Corynebacterium diphtheriae* carriership in Ugandan children. *Journal of Tropical Pediatrics*, 16, 12–16.

———. (1970b). *Corynebacterium diphtheriae* in skin lesions in Ugandan children. *Bulletin of the World Health Organization*, 43, 643–650.

Black, F. L. (1976). Measles. In: *Viral Infections of Humans: Epidemiology and Control*, Evans, A. S. (editor). New York and London: Plenum Publishing Corporation.

Black, R. E., Huber, D. H., and Curling, G. T. (1980). Reduction of neonatal tetanus by mass immunization of nonpregnant women. *Bulletin of the World Health Organization*, 58 (6), 927–930.

Bleiker, M. A. and Styblo, K. (1978). Le taux annuel d'infection tuberculeuse et son évolution dans le pays en développement. *Bulletin of the International Union against Tuberculosis*, 53 (4), 313–316.

Blin, P., Delolme, H. G., Heyraud, J. D., Charpak, V., and Sentilhes, L. (1986). Evaluation of the protective effect of BCG vaccination by a case control study in Yaoundé, Cameroon. *Tubercle*, 67 (4), 283–288.

Bottiger, M., Litinov, S., Assaad, F., Lundbeck, H., Heller, L., and Beausoleil, E. G. (1981). Antibodies against poliomyelitis and measles viruses in immunized and unimmunized children, Ghana, 1976–78. *Bulletin of the World Health Organization*, 59 (5), 729–736.

Budd, W. (1867). Memorandum on the nature and the mode of propagation of phthisis. *Lancet*, 2, 451–452.

Bwibo, N. O. (1969). Diphtheria in African children. *Journal of Tropical Pediatrics*, 15, 15–17.

Cantrelle, P. A. (1965). Mortality and morbidity of measles in francophone West Africa. *Archiv für die Gesamte Virusforschung*, 167, 34–45.

Chalmers, A. K. (1930). *The Health of Glasgow, 1818–1925*. Glasgow: Bell and Bain.

Citron, K. M. (1988). Control and prevention of tuberculosis in Bulain. *British Medical Bulletin*, 44 (3), 704–716.

Clemens, J. D., Bonita, F. S., Chakraborty, J., Chowdhnury, S., Malla, R., Mohammed, A., Zimicki, S., and Wojty-niak, B. (1988). Measles vaccination and childhood mortality in rural Bangladesh. *American Journal of Epidemiology*, 128 (6), 1330–1339.

Cobban, K. (1963). Measles in Nigerian children. *West African Medical Journal*, 12, 18–23.

Commey, J. O. and Richardson, J. E. (1984). Measles in Ghana, 1973–1982. *Annals of Tropical Pediatrics*, 4, 189–194.

Cutts, F., Rodrigues, L., Colombo, S., and Bennet, S. (1989). Evaluation of factors influencing vaccine uptake in Mozambique. *International Journal of Epidemiology*, 18, 427–433.

Debroise, A. S. I. and Satge, P. (1967). La rougeole en zone rurale. *L'enfant en milieu tropicale*, 38, 20–36.

Domok, I. (1985). Enterovirus infections: poliomyelitis. In: *The Epidemiology and the Community Control of Disease in Warm Climate Countries*, Robinson, D. (editor). London: Churchill Livingstone.

Doull, J. A., Guinto, R. S., and Mabalay, M. C. (1957). Effect of BCG vaccination, lepromin testing, and natural causes in inducing reactivity to lepromin and tuber-culin. *International Journal of Leprosy*, 25, 13–37.

EPI (1977). Survey for residual poliomyelitis paralysis. *Weekly Epidemiological Record*, 52, 269–271.

———. (1982a). Neonatal tetanus mortality survey in Sudan. *Weekly Epidemiological Record*, 57, 205–207.

———. (1982b). Prevention of neonatal tetanus. *Weekly Epidemiological Record*, 57 (18), 137–142.

———. (1982c). The use of survey data to supplement disease surveillance. *Weekly Epidemiological Record*, 57 (47), 361–362.

———. (1985). *Report of the Expanded Programme on Immunization Global Advisory Group Meeting*. WHO mimeographed document, WHO/EPI/GEN/85/1.

———. (1986). *Report of the Expanded Programme on Immunization Global Advisory Group Meeting*. WHO mimeographed document, WHO/EPI/GEN/87/1.

———. (1987a). Poliomyelitis in 1985. *Weekly Epidemio-logical Record*, 62, 281–288.

———. (1987b). Report of the Expanded Programme on Immunization global advisory group meeting: a synop-sis. *Weekly Epidemiological Record*, 62, 5–12.

———. (1987c). The World Health Organization's Ex-panded Programme of Immunization: a global over-view. *World Health Statistics Quarterly*, 38, 231–252.

Fillastre, C. (1986). Efficacité du BCG en milieu tropical. Études en cours en Afrique. *Developments in Biolog-ical Standardization*, 58 (part A), 281–285.

Fine, P. E. (1985). The role of BCG in the control of leprosy. *Ethiopian Medical Journal*, 23 (40), 179–191.

———. (1988). BCG vaccination against tuberculosis and leprosy. *British Medical Bulletin*, 44 (3), 691–703.

Fine, P. E., Ponnighaus, J. M., Maine, N., Clarkson, J. A. and Bliss, L. (1986). Protective efficacy of BCG against leprosy in northern Malawi. *Lancet*, 2 (8505), 499–502.

Foege, W. H. (1971). Measles vaccination in Africa. In: *Proceedings of the Pan American Health Organization Conference on the Application of Vaccines against Viral, Rickettsial, and Bacterial Diseases in Man*. Scientific Publications, no. 226. Washington, D.C.: Pan American Health Organization.

Fox, W. (1988). Tuberculosis case finding and treatment programme in developing countries. *British Medical Bulletin*, 44 (3), 717–738.

Gans, B., Macnamara, F. N., Morley, D. C., Thomson, S. W., and Watt, A. (1961). Some observations in the epidemiology of measles in West Africa. *West African Medical Journal*, 10, 253–262.

Greenwood, B. M., Greenwood, A. M., Bradley, A. K., Tulloch, S., Hayes, R., and Oldfield, F. S. J. (1987). Deaths in infancy and early childhood in a well-vaccinated rural West African population. *Annals of Tropical Pediatrics*, 2, 91–99.

Grzybowski, S., Styblo, K., and Dorken, E. (1976). Tuber-culosis in Eskimos. *Tubercle*, 57 (supplement), S1–S58.

Gupta, B. M. and Singh, M. (1975). Mortality and morbidity patterns in measles in Tanga District, Tanzania. *Trop-ical Geographical Medicine*, 27 (4), 383–386.

Haddock, D. R. (1985). Tetanus. In: *The Epidemiology and the Community Control of Disease in Warm Climate Countries*, Robinson, D. (editor), 2d ed. London: Churchill Livingstone.

Hanlon, P., Byass, P., Yamuah, M., Hayes, R., Bennet, S., and M'Boga, B. H. (1988). Factors influencing vacci-nation compliance in peri-urban Gambian children. *Journal of Tropical Medicine and Hygiene*, 91, 29–33.

Hendrikse, R. G. (1975). Problems of future measles vaccination in developing countries. *Transactions of the Royal Society of Tropical Medicine and Hygiene*, 69 (2), 31–32.

Heyworth, B. and Ropp, M. (1973). Diphtheria in the Gambia. *Journal of Tropical Medicine and Hygiene*, 76, 61–78.

Hull, H. F. and Williams, P. F. (1980). Neonatal tetanus in North Bank division. *Ministry of Health Report, The Gambia*.

Ikejiani, O. (1961). Immunity against diphtheria among Nigerian children. *West African Medical Journal*, 10, 272–277.

John, T. J., Joseph, A., and Vijayarathnam, P. (1980). A better system for polio vaccination in developing countries? *British Medical Journal*, 281 (6239), 542.

Kasongo Project Team. (1981). Influence of measles vaccination on survival pattern of 7–35 months old children in Kasongo, Zaire. *Lancet*, 1, 764–767.

Keja, K., Chan, C., Brenner, E., and Henderson, R. (1986). Effectiveness of the Expanded Programme of Immunization. *World Health Statistics Quarterly*, 39, 161–170.

Kessel, E. (1984). Strategies for the control of neonatal tetanus. *Journal of Tropical Pediatrics*, 30 (3), 145–149.

LaForce, F. M., Dowel, S. Y., and Bennet, J. V. (1969). Tetanus in the United States (1965–69). *New England Journal of Medicine*, 280, 569–574.

LaForce, F. M., Lichnevski, M. S., Keja, J., and Henderson, R. H. (1980). Clinical survey techniques to estimate prevalence and annual incidence of poliomyelitis in developing countries. *Bulletin of the World Health Organization*, 58 (4), 609–620.

McGregor, I. A. (1953). Medical Research Council data on prospective study of pregnancies, 1949–53. London: Medical Research Council.

Medical Research Council. (1923). Diphtheria. London.

Meyer, H. M. (1965). Mass vaccination against measles in Upper Volta. *Archiv für die Gesamte Virusforschung*, 16, 243–245.

Miller, D. L. (1981). Pertussis immunization and serious neurological disease in children. *British Medical Journal*, 282, 1595–1599.

Montefiore, D., Jamieson, M. F., Collard, P., and Jolly, H. (1963). Trial of type 1 oral poliomyelitis vaccine (Sabin) in Nigerian children. *British Medical Journal*, 1, 1569–1572.

Morley, D. C. (1973). *Pediatrics Priorities in the Developing World*. London: Butterworth's.

———. (1985). Measles and whooping cough. In: *The Epidemiology and the Community Control of Disease in Warm Climate Countries*, Robinson, D. (editor), 2d ed. London: Churchill Livingstone.

Morley, D. C., Woodland, M., and Martin, W. (1963). Measles in Nigerian children: a study of the disease in West Africa and its manifestations in England and other countries during different epochs. *Journal of Hygiene*, 61, 115–135.

———. (1966). Whooping cough in Nigerian children. *Tropical and Geographical Medicine*, 18, 169–182.

Muganga, N., Omanga, U., and Mbensa, M. (1980). La diphtérie: prevalence, manifestation cliniques et complication en milieu urbain de Kinshasa, Zaire. *Annales de la Société Belge de Médecine Tropicale*, 60, 307–312.

Muller, A. S., Leeuwenburg, J., and Voorhoeve, A. M. (1984). Pertussis in a rural area of Kenya: epidemiology and results of a vaccine trial. *Bulletin of the World Health Organization*, 62 (6), 899–908.

Muyembe, D. J., Gatti, F., Spaepen, J., and Vandepitte, J. (1972). L'épidémiologie de la diphtérie en République du Zaire: le rôle de l'infection cutanée. *Annales de la Société Belge de Médecine Tropicale*, 52 (2), 141–152.

Nathanson, N. and Martin, J. R. (1979). The epidemiology of poliomyelitis: enigmas surrounding its appearance, epidemicity, and disappearance. *American Journal of Epidemiology*, 110 (6), 672–692.

Neujean, G. (1937). Recherche de la réaction de Schick chez les indigènes de la région de Kitega. *Annales de la Société Belge de Médecine Tropicale*, 17, 351–352.

Newell, K. W., Lehmann, A. D., Leblanc, D. R., and Osorio, N. G. (1966). The use of toxoid for the prevention of tetanus neonatorum: final report of a double blind controlled field trial. *Bulletin of the World Health Organization*, 35, 863–871.

Nicholas, D. D., Kratzer, J. H., Ofosu-Amaah, S., and Belcher, D. W. (1977). Is poliomyelitis a serious problem in developing countries? The Danfa experience. *British Medical Journal*, 1, 1009–1012.

Noordeen, S. K. (1986). BCG vaccination in leprosy. *Developments in Biological Standardization*, 58 (part A), 287–292.

Ofosu-Amaah, S. (1983a). The challenge of poliomyelitis in tropical Africa. *Reviews of Infectious Diseases*, 6 (supplement 2), S318–S320.

———. (1983b). The control of measles in tropical Africa: a review of past and present efforts. *Reviews of Infectious Diseases*, 5 (3), 546–553.

Ofosu-Amaah, S., Kratzer, J. H., and Nicholas, D. D. (1977). Is poliomyelitis a serious problem in developing countries? Lameness in Ghanaian schools. *British Medical Journal*, 1, 1012–1014.

Puffer, R. R. and Serrano, C. V. (1973). *Características de la mortalidad en la niñez*. Publicación scientífica, no. 262. Washington, D.C.: Organización Panamericana de la Salud.

Rahman, S. (1982). The effect of traditional birth attendants and tetanus toxoid in reduction of neonatal tetanus mortality. *Journal of Tropical Pediatrics*, 28 (4), 163–165.

Ramon, G. and Nellis, P. (1934). Immunité antidiphtérique chez le noir du congo belge. *Annales de la Société Belge de Médecine Tropicale*, 14, 457–467.

Robertson, R. L., Foster, S. O., Hull, H. F., and Williams, P. J. (1985). Cost effectiveness of immunization in the Gambia. *Journal of Tropical Medicine and Hygiene*, 88, 343–351.

Roelsgaard, E., Iversen, E., and Blocher, C. (1964). Tuberculosis in tropical Africa. *Bulletin of the World Health Organization*, 30, 459–518.

Sabin, A. B. (1980). Vaccination against poliomyelitis in economically underdeveloped countries. *Bulletin of the World Health Organization*, 58, 141–157.

———. (1981). Paralytic poliomyelitis: old dogmas and new perspectives. *Review of Infectious Diseases*, 3, 543–564.

Salih, M. A., El Hakeem, F., Suliman, G. I., Hassan, H., and El Khatim, A. S. (1985). An epidemiological study of the 1978 outbreak of diphtheria in Khartoum province. *Journal of Tropical Pediatrics*, 31, 812.

Saugrain, J. (1955). Un cas de diphtérie cutanée. *Médecine tropicale*, 15, 215–216.

Schofield, F. D., Tucker, V. M., and Westbrook, G. R. (1961). Neonatal tetanus in New Guinea: effect of active immunization in pregnancy. *British Medical Journal*, 2, 78–79.

Schonberger, L. B., Thaung, U., Daw, K. M. K., Than, S., Ma, O. K., and Bergman, D. (1981). The epidemiology of poliomyelitis in Burma, 1963–79. In: *Proceedings of the International Symposium on Reassessment of Inactivated Poliomyelitis Vaccine. Developments in Biological Standardization*, 47, 283–292.

Stanfield, J. P. and Galazka, A. (1984). Neonatal tetanus in the world today. *Bulletin of the World Health Organization*, 62 (4), 647–669.

Stanley, S. J., Howland, C., Stone, M. M., and Sutherland, I. (1981). BCG vaccination of children against leprosy in Uganda: final results. *Journal of Hygiene*, 87 (2), 233–248.

Styblo, K. (1983). The epidemiological situation of tuberculosis and the impact of control measures. *Bulletin of the International Union against Tuberculosis*, 58, 179–186.

Styblo, K. and Rouillon, A. (1981). Estimated global incidence of smear positive pulmonary tuberculosis. Unreliability of officially reported figures on tuberculosis. *Bulletin of the International Union against Tuberculosis*, 56 (3), 129–138.

Sutherland, I. (1988). Research into the control of tuberculosis and leprosy in the community. *British Medical Bulletin*, 44 (3), 523–527.

Tanzania/British Medical Research Council. (1985). Tuberculosis in Tanzania: a national survey of newly notified cases. *Tubercle*, 66, 161–178.

Tidjani, O., Amedome, A., and Ten Dan, H. G. (1986). The protective effect of BCG vaccination of the newborn against childhood tuberculosis in an African community. *Tubercle*, 67 (4), 269–281.

Tuberculosis Prevention Trial, Madras. (1980). *Indian Journal of Medical Research*, 72 (supplement), 1–74.

Voorhoeve, A. M., Muller, A. S., Shulpen, T. W. I., Manetje, W., and van Rens, M. (1977). Machakos project studies. The epidemiology of pertussis. *Tropical and Geographical Medicine*, 30 (1), 125–139.

Williams, P. J. and Hull, F. H. (1983). Status of measles in the Gambia, 1981. *Reviews of Infectious Diseases*, 5 (3), 391–394.

World Health Organization. (1976). *World Health Statistics Report*, 29, 416.

———. (1986). *The Potential of the Traditional Birth Attendant*, Maglacas, A. M. and Simmons, J. (editors). WHO Offset Publication, no. 95.

———. (1988). Global eradication of poliomyelitis by the year 2000. *Weekly Epidemiological Report*, 63, 161–162.

Chapter 12

Malaria

David J. Bradley

Malaria transmission reaches higher levels in Sub-Saharan Africa than anywhere else in the world, although it approaches these levels in parts of Papua New Guinea. The reasons for this depend on the African mosquito vectors of malaria, *Anopheles gambiae* and *An. funestus*, and can be understood in terms of the basic case reproduction rate (BCRR) of malaria, a convenient measure of transmission. The BCRR is the mean number of new cases of malaria to which one case will directly give rise after passing once through the vector mosquitoes under conditions of zero immunity in the human population. Thus with a BCRR of 5, 1 case will give rise to 5 cases in the next generation and 25 in the succeeding generation of cases; the spread will continue, with more and more people becoming infected. Conversely, should the BCRR fall below 1, the disease will tend to die out gradually. The goal of malaria transmission control may therefore be formulated as keeping the BCRR below 1. In an endemic malaria situation, the supply of uninfected individuals who are susceptible will be limited and immunity will play a role. Thus the criteria for directly observing the BCRR will not be met, but may be calculated by observing mosquito biology. Three characteristics of the female anopheline mosquito largely determine the BCRR: the density of mosquitoes, their man-biting habit, and their longevity.

Mosquito density is conveniently measured as the number of female mosquitoes per human inhabitant of an area. Malaria transmission is proportional to mosquito density, as might be expected. However, the impact of changes in the man-biting habit and longevity on malaria transmission is greater. The man-biting habit is the chance that a given female mosquito will feed on man on any one day. Mosquitoes may feed as often as alternate days, and if all their meals were on man, their man-biting habit would be 0.5. The man-

biting habit of a mosquito that feeds every third day and feeds on man for only 20 percent of those meals (the rest are on domestic stock) would be $0.33 \times 0.2 = 0.066$, or less than that of the other species by a factor of 7.6. However, since transmission is proportional to the square of the man-biting habit because it takes two bites to transmit malaria—one to infect the mosquito and one to infect man again—the second mosquito is 57 times less effective as a malaria vector. Mosquito longevity affects malaria transmission even more. It takes time for the parasite to develop within the female anopheline. The minimum time is temperature dependent, but even in the hot tropics at least ten days must elapse between the bite that infects the mosquito with malaria and the first time the mosquito can pass on the infection. Mosquitoes are often quite short-lived, with a steady daily mortality of 5–25 percent of the population, so few of the mosquitoes that catch malaria survive to pass it on. A really long-lived species can, however, be extremely effective at passing on the infection. Incidentally, the dramatic efficacy of residual insecticides such as DDT in controlling malaria lies in their ability to render the walls of houses toxic to mosquitoes. The main vectors tend to rest on the walls of houses each time they feed, and the chance of repeated exposure to insecticide means that adult mosquitoes have a greatly reduced chance of survival into a relatively "old age" for a vector. In this sense, "geriatric" mosquitoes are responsible for malaria transmission.

So, for effective malaria transmission, a mosquito species needs to be long-lived and have a high man-biting habit. Both of the vector species complexes largely responsible for African malaria transmission feed preferentially on people, feed frequently, and are long-lived in nature. In particular, the key members of the *An. gambiae* complex, *An. gambiae* and *An.*

arabiensis, are particularly long-lived and are the world's most efficient malaria vectors. *An. funestus* also appears very high in any table of vectorial capacity for malaria. Although any value for the basic case reproduction rate of malaria in excess of 1 will allow the infection to spread, in parts of Asia values of 3 and 5 are not uncommon in malarious areas. In Sub-Saharan Africa *An. gambiae* and *An. funestus* lead to values for the BCRR in excess of 1,000. There is therefore in many parts of Africa a vast excess of capacity for malaria transmission above that required to maintain endemicity.

This very high BCRR is responsible for the key features of malaria in much of Africa: first, transmission is extremely hard to control effectively since it has to be reduced dramatically (perhaps a thousandfold) before the infection dies out; second, everyone tends to become infected at an extremely early age, and exposures to infection are usual in the first year of life; and third, because the level of transmission is high, the natural variations in the determinants of transmission from one year to the next never reduce the BCRR to close to 1 so that malaria is always highly endemic, a situation called stable malaria because it varies so little. Malaria epidemics are unknown in much of the continent: in other words, "Africa is too unhealthy for epidemics"!

The chief determinant of malaria epidemiology is thus the pattern of acquired immunity to human malaria. If this immunity did not occur, the inhabitants of many parts of Africa would have malaria parasitemia every day of their lives. The pattern of infection under the extreme case of stable perennial transmission, called holoendemic malaria (table 12-2), is described below. This picture is modified by seasonal changes in the availability of surface water and humidity in much of Africa to give seasonally stable malaria. At the extreme limits of either aridity or altitude that affect the temperature for developing parasites in the mosquito, the limits of transmission are reached, with the BCRR varying above and below 1. Epidemics are the result. These processes will be outlined, and then the malaria picture seen in different parts of Sub-Saharan Africa will be classified into four broad categories. Their implications for morbidity and mortality are set out in general terms prior to discussing quantitative data on the extent of mortality.

Natural History of Malaria Infection

The epidemic situation is relatively easy to understand. Transmission of malaria begins when the ability of the anophelines to spread malaria changes (due to changes in their density, man-biting, or longevity) or when a case or cases of malarial infection are introduced into an already suitable environment for transmission. People who are not immune get bitten in increasing numbers by infective mosquitoes and suffer classical unmodified attacks of clinical malaria with severe intermittent fevers. Their attacks get worse, usually occurring every other day in the *Plasmodium vivax* infections, which are common initially, and on alternate days but more irregularly in cases of *P. falciparum*. The latter cases increase later in the epidemic but produce more severe disease and a mortality of 5–10 percent in persons remaining untreated. Such epidemics, though rare in Africa, may involve much of the population; the devastation caused before suitable chemotherapy was available has been graphically described for the Punjab (Christophers, 1911) and Sri Lanka. Comparable epidemics in their effects can affect migrants who move from uninfected highland areas to malarious lowland zones in search of work. This phenomenon, which has been called "malaria of the tropical aggregation of labor," has been significant in parts of southern Africa and in Ethiopia. As documented by Prothero (1965), it prevented parts of Asia from being settled and caused great mortality there. In recent years, however, chemotherapy and other measures have prevented mortality and reduced morbidity in the majority of planned population movements in Africa.

As the level of transmission in an area rises and time passes, an increasing proportion of the inhabitants will become infected, usually more than once. The first attack will have the morbidity and risk of death described above in the absence of treatment. Subsequent attacks in the survivors will be modified by the effects of gradually acquired, but incomplete, immunity. The duration and severity of illness will decrease, and the risk of death falls markedly. Persons who already have parasites circulating in their systems will often receive infective bites, and a complex pattern of superinfections may be built up. Children will usually be parasitemic for many years. The gradually increasing immunity first decreases the severity of the disease, then reduces the number of parasites in the blood and eventually reduces them to zero or at least below the level of detection on microscopy. But this process requires the whole of childhood to achieve, even under intense transmission. A further process is also at work. Only some stages of malaria parasites in the blood, the gametocytes, are infective to mosquitoes. Immunity to the production of this stage, and to its infectivity, is acquired very early and more rapidly than immunity to the other blood stages, so that under conditions of intense transmission, gametocytes are confined to extremely young children, and malaria is largely transmitted by this small segment of the population. The additional feature of intense transmission that is relevant to our concerns with immunity is the malaria antibodies that are passed from the immune mother to her child across the placenta and in breast milk. This does not completely prevent malaria in babies (see table 12-1), but may modify the severity of the attacks and substantially reduce mortality, so that in some communities the fatal outcome of malaria is more often seen after the first few months of life. The overall consequence of these processes for the pattern of infection in a community subject to intense malaria transmission, largely unmodified by chemotherapy, is best seen in Ugandan studies (Davidson and Draper, 1953; Davidson, 1955) as in table 12-1.

The Ugandan pattern is characteristic of the most intense perennial transmission. Under these circumstances of highly stable malaria, persons may receive an average in excess of one infective bite daily. Before the concept of "stability" was formulated, the epidemiological situation was described in terms of the proportion of children 5–9 years of age with enlarged spleens (the "spleen rate"), which resembled the parasite rate. Lesser degrees of endemicity were also defined by the spleen rate (table 12-2). The features of stable malaria, so typically seen in Sub-Saharan Africa, are set out in table 12-3. Although unstable epidemic malaria is much less frequent in Africa, its features are contrasted in that table.

The African vectors of malaria are very widely distributed within the continent. Both key members of the *An. gambiae* complex (*An. gambiae* sensu stricto and *An. arabiensis*) breed in sunlit temporary pools of water, even transient locations such as rainwater in a hoofprint, so that they are found during the wet season from the Sahel to the tropical rain forest. They also flourish in flooded rice fields soon after planting. Thus transmission is continuous where rainfall or irrigation provide standing water at all seasons. However, the savanna and the Sahel have a significant period without shallow surface water bodies for mosquito breeding. Nevertheless, transmission is regular and intense for part of the year, and the result is seasonally stable malaria, since the transmission-free period is not long enough for immunity to wane substantially. Where the rainfall becomes so scanty and unreliable that adequate anopheline habitats are only available some years, the malaria becomes unstable, as it does at the altitudinal limits of transmission. These features are used in the next section to categorize malarious areas of Africa. *An. funestus* prefers more long-lived bodies of water, including the periphery of perennial pools where emergent vegetation provides some shading from the sun. It colonizes flooded rice fields later than *An. gambiae*, which does not wait for the growing rice plants to provide shade.

Categories of African Malaria

Although Sub-Saharan Africa is remarkable for the intensity of malarial transmission throughout most of the subcontinent, some variants of the pattern are ecologically determined. Since Boyd's *Malariology* (Wilson, 1949) malariologists have recognized four

Table 12-1. Pattern of Parasitemia in Holoendemic Malaria, Lango, Uganda

Age	Parasites (percent)	Schizonts (thousands per cubic millimeter)	Gametocytes (percent)	Percentage with more than 100 gametocytes per cubic millimeter
2 weeks–3 months	66	7	41	13
4–5 months	83	15	44	3
6–8 months	90	13	51	2
9–11 months	99	13	44	3
12–17 months	98	10	44	2
18–23 months	98	11	36	2
24 months–4 years	97	5	35	0
5–9 years	94	2	28	1
10–14 years	88	1	15	0
15 years and older	31	0.1	5	0

Source: Davidson and Draper (1953).

Table 12-2. Traditional Terminology for Levels of Malaria Endemicity

Term	Spleen rate in children (percent)
Hypoendemic	Less than 10
Mesoendemic	11–50
Hyperendemic	51–75, more than 25 in adults
Holoendemic	More than 75, low in adults

main ecological zones of malarial transmission, refined by Carnevale *et al.* (1984) and set out in table 12-4. In the areas formerly occupied by tropical forest the transmission is continuous and intense: individuals receive hundreds of infective bites each year. Toward the savanna zones transmission is seasonal, but individuals still receive a hundred inoculations annually. The transmission period exceeds six months each year, and in both zones children are infected very early in life and attain substantial immunity by the end of childhood.

Malaria morbidity is mainly a feature of infancy and may account for 30–35 percent of the cases in persons seeking health care at rural dispensaries. It is spread evenly through the year in the forest zone and may account for between 10 and 80 percent of childhood fevers in the savanna zone. Some data suggest that mortality may reach its peak in the savanna, where malaria may be combined with malnutrition, maternal overwork, and lack of drugs in the season of maximal transmission.

In the Sahelian zone, the transmission season falls with increasing aridity to two or three months a year, so that each person receives a few bites each year and acquires only limited immunity, even as an adult. Seasonal fluctuations in the parasite rate affect persons of all ages and malarial intensity may vary markedly between years.

The final type of malaria, which is erratic, unpredictable, and epidemic, occurs at the edge of transmission, in hilly areas and among people who live just above the regular limit of transmission. It also occurs in southern regions that approach the temperature limits for transmission and in arid regions that are too close to being desert for regular transmission. Acquired immunity is absent, and the clinical consequences of infection are severe and affect all ages during epidemic spread.

Carnevale and Vaugelade (1987) draw attention to two situations with malaria that do not fit well into the above categorization. In the coastal zone, *An. melas* of the *An. gambiae* complex inhabits brackish water but is a less good vector. In urban areas malaria is also untidy and varies greatly among cities, and within cities, from 0 to over 50 infective bites annually. The introduction of irrigation and other related water resource developments sometimes transform the seasonal Sahelian malaria into perennial transmission but do not always do so.

Malarial Transmission and Community Impact

The relation between the transmission of malaria and its disease effects on the community has been the subject of some of the most vehement controversy in tropical health. This controversy centered on the

Table 12-3. Major Differences between Stable and Unstable Malaria

Characteristics	Unstable	Stable
Basic case reproduction rate	Relatively low, variable	High
Endemicity	Usually low	Usually high
Epidemics	Likely	Not seen except in migrants
Seasonal changes	Marked	Fall only in cold or dry season
Predominant parasite	*P. vivax*	*P. falciparum*
Incidence changes	Uneven and large	Small and only seasonal
Immunity of population	Variable	High
Clinical effects greatest in	All ages	Young children
Determinants		
Mosquito life	Short	Long
Man-biting habit	Low	High
Suitable climate	Short periods	Long periods
Anopheline density for transmission	High	Low is sufficient
Control	Feasible	Extremely difficult

Table 12-4. Categories of African Malaria

Characteristic	1	2	3	4
Ecological type	Former forest	Savanna	Sahel	High altitude
Transmission pattern	Intense and perennial	Intense and seasonal	Short season	Irregular
Mean annual number of infective bites per person	In the 100s	Approximately 100	Approximately 10	Rare
Duration of the transmission season	12 months a year	6–8 months	2–3 months	Nil except in epidemics
Parasite and spleen rates	Scarcely vary	Seasonal variation	Seasonal variation	Great variation between years
Acquired immunity	Very high even by 5 years of age	Very high by 10 years of age	Limited	Negligible

problems of African holoendemic malaria—the effects of epidemics have been relatively unequivocal—and the conflict was probably heightened by the underlying differences of philosophy between two schools of thought. The conflict in 1950 was over the advisability of attempting to eradicate malaria in Sub-Saharan Africa; that subject was superseded when it was subsequently shown in the field that eradicating malaria from parts of Africa was technically impossible. The discussions of desirability then became academic. One view, most thoroughly propounded by Wilson *et al.* (1950), was that an equilibrium is reached between parasites and the human community under conditions of holoendemic malaria. Its proponents were impressed by the limited morbidity and lack of mortality among indigenous adults, conscious of the difficulty of interrupting transmission with residual insecticides, and fearful of the increased lethality that might follow unsuccessful attempts to control the disease. Their philosophy (not stated as such) could be represented as not interfering with a naturally established equilibrium and had conservationist implications. By contrast, their opponents—led by Macdonald, whose 1951 paper is a model of forensic logic, Russell, and Soper—were convinced of the need to vanquish malaria, were confirmed interventionists, and had a strong commitment to eradication, well founded, in the case of Soper, in experience in Brazil and Egypt. Their philosophy was well aware of the price in infant deaths that had been paid to achieve equilibrium by adult life. Macdonald, in particular, had been immensely impressed by the fall in infant mortality in Freetown, Sierra Leone, that followed larviciding operations (Macdonald and Chowdhuri, 1926), as he had worked there. The interventionists won the day at

the Kampala African Malaria Conference in 1950, and Macdonald's influence lay behind the field research projects that attempted to stop transmission in Africa and provided much of the best evidence of malaria's impact on mortality.

In rural clinics, even those where microscopy is available, separating fevers due to malaria from those merely accompanied by parasitemia is not feasible. This problem of diagnosis means that routine reporting is not a source of reliable data. Nevertheless, information from numerous routine sources, particularly from West Africa, shows "malaria" to be one of the major clinical problems. In Sierra Leone malaria accounted for 18–35 percent of 11 common specific diagnoses in young children at an outpatient clinic. It was the most common cause of both admission to and death in a hospital in northwest Uganda, although it occupied a much less prominent position in the diagnoses of adult patients. In pediatric health care facilities throughout tropical Africa the three predominant causes of ill health recorded are respiratory infections, diarrheal diseases, and malaria. Their precise order of importance depends, however, on the region, the age category, and the type of health care facility being studied.

More sophisticated approaches to the overall burden of ill health have been used. In Ghana, for example, malaria was the chief cause of lost days of healthy life, an aggregate measure of the consequences of mortality, illness, and disability (Ghana Health Assessment Project Team, 1981). Malaria was responsible for 10.2 percent of all healthy life lost from disease, or 33 days per person per year, though much of this was due to deaths from malaria in infancy. Where attempts were made to transform this loss fairly directly into economic loss, the ranking of diseases by importance was affected by the discount rate applied to handling future values. Malaria remained the leading cause of loss when the discount rates were 0 and 5 percent but fell to fifth place when the rate was 10 percent.

The interactive ill-effects of malarial mortality have been discussed above. The interaction of malaria with other diseases in causing ill health that does not cause death has been extensively studied experimentally, but there are little relevant or good data from fieldwork. Studies have investigated the possible immunosuppressive interference of malaria with the efficacy of childhood immunizations. In studies from northern Nigeria one group of children was kept (relatively incompletely) on antimalarials while a control group, unless ill, was not. The resulting interference was negligible except in the conversion rate to meningococcal A or C vaccine, which was reduced 43 percent in the children exposed to malaria compared with those on prophylaxis (see chapter 21 of this volume). Such interactive morbidity is complex and subtle, and its potential importance cannot be calculated at this time.

Scale of Malarial Mortality

Mortality due to a disease such as malaria can be measured in three ways: from clinical records of the cause of death, from observing the rise in mortality during malaria epidemics, and by determining the fall in mortality when malaria is brought under control. Molineaux (1985) reviews some examples of the consequences of malaria control and adds a fourth method of assessing malarial mortality: calculating the mortality necessary to maintain the observed level of the sickling gene in a balanced polymorphism.

The scarcity of postmortem series in Africa and, more seriously, the extreme bias introduced because they only derive from tertiary care facilities and very rarely include young children and infants means that what is usually viewed as the best possible source of accurate data is not useful for assessing malarial mortality in Africa. Clinical records of cause of death are equally unsatisfactory in most of Africa, as most people die outside hospital; moreover, since malaria is a treatable condition, only persons who are exceedingly ill are likely to be admitted to the hospital for treatment. Add to this the scarcity of pediatric beds in many hospitals, and it is clear that the information on death certificates is a poor guide to what is happening in the community. Nevertheless malaria is the most common cause of both admissions to, and deaths of children under five years of age in, a Ugandan

community hospital (Williams *et al.*, 1986). Epidemic malaria is rare in Africa, and the only relevant data come from the outside the continent, where the great epidemics of *falciparum* malaria in the Punjab and Sri Lanka led to dramatic changes in mortality. In Sri Lanka the quarterly crude death rate at the height of the epidemic rose by a factor of 3.4, implying that 2.5 times more people died of malaria than of all other causes combined during that period. The Sri Lankan data on vital rates are sufficiently good to have been used in numerous, and controversial, analyses of the impact of malaria, which Molineaux (1985) discusses critically. Perhaps the most informative picture of that impact comes from comparing the least and the most malarious districts over a period of time that includes the introduction of malaria control. This comparison suggests that the crude death rate in the highly malarious districts was consistently double that in the other districts, although their death rates were identical after malaria control was introduced.

The best African data on malarial mortality were collected by local field research projects attempting to stop malarial transmission. These projects usually employed residual insecticides, although recent projects have increasingly relied on chemotherapy and chemoprophylaxis. Of particular interest are the projects that continued to observe malarial mortality even after abandoning attempts to control transmission. All of these projects are research scale because interrupting transmission on a national scale has not been feasible in Sub-Saharan Africa. The exceptions have been small islands; areas at the edge of transmission because of their temperature, which is determined by their high altitude or proximity to the southern limits of transmission; or arid areas at the northern limits of transmission. None of these areas is representative of the African situation in general.

Three major field projects have used residual insecticides to lower the transmission of malaria drastically over substantial, but research-scale, patches of Africa. The Pare-Taveta scheme described in chapter 17 was the earliest (spraying began in 1955) and in broad design the most elegant major field project. The intervention ceased after several years, and the degree of reversion could be observed. Unfortunately emphasis was originally placed on research in areas other than infant mortality, a hiatus took place in collecting the demographic data, and the long-term demography was subsequently carried out in a slightly different but more detailed way. The study looked carefully at morbidity, blood hemoglobin levels, and anthropometry as well as mortality. The striking findings about growth and morbidity were the apparent absence of malarial effect. Malaria was, however, clearly important in producing a substantial and widespread reduction of the hemoglobin level.

The mortality data, initially covering a limited population (2,000 people to start) showed substantial year-to-year variation but a clear and large fall in 1956, the first full year of spraying. Mortality remained low until 1958, when the spraying stopped. After the spraying ceased and demographic data collection was resumed on a larger scale (1962–66), a small rise occurred in the mortality of infants and adults over 40 years of age, and the death rates of children 1–4 years of age reverted toward their previous high rates. It should be noted that, first, malaria transmission only gradually resumed after the spraying ceased and had not reached its former level even by 1966. Second, concern had been felt about stopping the spraying, and a deliberate attempt was made to make antimalarials available to the population. Efforts were made to prevent a complete reversion of vital rates to their former levels. Other changes in socioeconomic progress were taking place, and drought also complicated the situation. Nevertheless, the immediate, precipitous fall in death rates, especially in infants and young children, that followed the spraying is very striking. In particular, the infant mortality rate fell from a level of 165–260 prior to spraying to 78–132 after, which amounts to cutting the infant mortality rate in half. The mortality rate of young children 1–4 years of age was also halved, although the level was of course much smaller than that of the infant mortality rate. The decrease in the deaths of older people was less dramatic.

A similar study that took place nearly 20 years later in the Kisumu area of Kenya, to the northeast of Victoria Nyanza, used Fenitrothion to achieve a 96 percent reduction in malarial transmission. This reduction was accompanied by a 40 percent fall in the infant mortality rate, from 157 to 93 deaths per 1,000. The malarial effect was greatest in infants between three and ten months of age (Payne et al., 1976).

The third study, the best documented and executed of the three, took place from 1971 to 1973 in the Garki area of northern Nigeria, a region with intense seasonal malarial transmission. Intervention was by residual insecticide spraying with propoxur, backed up by mass administration of the drug in part of the area. The combination reduced transmission substantially. Infants were not given drugs unless and until they were found to be infected (Molineaux and Gramiccia, 1980; Molineaux, 1985). The most dramatic findings were a large fall in the infant mortality rate, from 255 in the last baseline year to 55 in the first control year and 102 in the second. The infant mortality rate in comparable unprotected villages was greater by 80 and 90 deaths per 1,000 in the two intervention years. The death rate of children 1–4 years of age was less than half that in unprotected villages, as was the crude death rate. Moreover, in the absence of protection the seasonal parallel between the infant mortality rate (IMR) and the rate at which infants tested positive for parasites was close: the IMR was about 10 percent of this rate of incidence measure. Under protection, the IMR both fell and lost its seasonal peaks.

In Senegal, the first of three chemotherapy and chemoprophylaxis trials (Garenne et al., 1985) showed a marked fall in the mortality of children 6–35 months of age (which halved the rate) but no effect on that of those younger or older. Moreover, although the diagnosis "fever and malaria" fell dramatically as the stated cause of death, this fall was rather precisely balanced by a rise in the "miscellaneous or not known" category for other causes of death. This led Carnevale and Vaugelade (1987) to doubt the effect of these trials on mortality.

Subsequent studies in the Congo at Kinkala and in Burkina Faso at Bobo Dioulassou (see Baudon et al., 1984) showed little effect of intense chemoprophylaxis and chemotherapy on mortality. The results of these studies are difficult to reconcile with the weight of other evidence, except on some of the hypotheses considered below.

The gene for sickle cell anemia, when present in homozygous SS form, is effectively lethal before reproduction. For this gene to be maintained in the population, the heterozygous AS form must have a selective advantage over the normal homozygous AA. It is believed that this advantage consists of a relative protection against the lethal effects of falciparum malaria. If the relatively conservative assumption be made that all AS individuals have a zero death rate from malaria, it is possible to calculate the minimum malaria mortality of the AA group, and thus of the whole population, needed to maintain the S gene at an observed equilibrium frequency. The sickling gene is very prevalent in parts of Sub-Saharan Africa and may reach a prevalence of 40 percent sickle cell trait carriers. In East Africa the prevalence is commonly 18 percent of the prevalence of sickle cell trait (AS), or an S gene frequency of 10 percent. Assuming this level and complete loss of sicklers before puberty, an excess mortality of the order of 100 deaths from malaria per 1,000 persons is required in persons with the AA genotype, or an excess of approximately 81 deaths per 1,000 persons in the overall population. In other words, if, by puberty, the total cumulative mortality in the population is of the order of 300 per 1,000, over one-quarter of this mortality would be due to malaria if the gene frequency is to be maintained in equilibrium. If any of the AS die of malaria, the proportion of malaria deaths would need to be greater.

An incidental consequence of the way in which a proportional mortality of genes maintains the gene frequencies in balance is that where the nonspecific infant mortality is high, a lower mortality from malaria per 1,000 live births is needed to maintain the same gene frequency. To maintain the 10 percent sickle cell gene frequency (or the 18 percent sickle cell trait) requires a mortality of 90 deaths per 1,000 where malaria is the only cause of death, 81 deaths at a nonmalarial mortality of 100 before puberty, and 72 at a nonmalarial mortality of 200.

In general, where the proportion of hemoglobin A haplotypes is A and of hemoglobin S haplotypes is S ($S = 1 - A$), the proportion of heterozygous sickle cell trait carriers is $2AS$, and the proportional mortality before death from malaria, or before reaching puberty, is M, then mortality from malaria is $AS(1 - M)$ and mortality of AA genotype from malaria is $[S(1 - M)]/A$. To maintain 32 percent heterozygosity in a population with 200 premature deaths from causes other than malaria per 1,000 persons requires a malarial mortality of 128 per 1,000, and 200 per 1,000 AA individuals, or doubles the mortality in the AA group.

Table 12-5 shows, calculated on the above simplify-

ing assumptions, the total and malarial mortality needed to maintain equilibrium at various levels of sickling gene frequency and of premalarial, prepubertal mortality. This latter concept is one of logical convenience and does not correspond exactly to any of the usual mortality indices. However, as the table shows, and as pointed out by Molineaux (1985), malarial mortality is not highly sensitive to changes in prepubertal mortality.

In reviewing different aspects of malarial mortality, Molineaux (1985) considers the empirical evidence, as do Carnevale and Vaugelade (1987), while Cohen (1988) attempts to synthesize the outcome and transmission approaches in a mathematical model. Empirical data are discussed separately, but any attempt to put together the apparently conflicting evidence must take one of three broad approaches. One is to deny the validity of some of the data. This is not difficult because all the studies have methodological defects, some bristle with assumptions, and many have broad confidence limits even though the observations are correct. The data, therefore, give the author space to choose the conclusions he prefers and to explain discrepancies. This tends to be Carnevale's approach. The second way of dealing with the range of results on mortality is to assume the existence of confounding variables that affect the scale of the observed mortality ascribed to malaria. This view is adopted by Molineaux and developed by Cohen. A third view, perhaps a variant of the second, is to assume that the consequences of equally endemic malaria are heterogeneous due to interventions of other types, a position

Table 12-5. Total, and Malarial Mortality to Maintain Equilibrium at Different Levels of the Sickling Gene (S) and Premalarial Mortality (M)

Premalarial mortality	S = 0		S = 0.05		S = 0.1		S = 0.15		S = 0.2	
	Total	Malarial	Total	Malarial	Total	Malarial	Total	Malarial	Total	Malarial
0.0	0	—	51	48	100	90	151	128	200	160
0.1	100	—	145	42	190	81	236	115	300	144
0.2	200	—	241	38	280	72	321	102	360	128
0.3	300	—	335	33	370	63	405	89	440	112
Percentage heterozygous	0		9.5		18		25.2		32	

Notes: S indicates the equilibrium frequency of the sickling gene; when, for example, S = 0.15, 15 percent of the alleles are S and 85 percent are hemoglobin A. Premalarial mortality (M) indicates the proportion of children dying from a cause other than malaria before the risk of malarial death is taken into account. M = 0.1 indicates that 10 percent of children die from other causes before malarial mortality. Total mortality before puberty per thousand live births is given in each cell, followed by the malarial mortality over the same period. To get a gene frequency for S of 15 percent when there is a 10 percent nonmalarial (nonsickling) mortality, total prepubertal mortality will be 236 per thousand, of whom 115 will die of malaria. The difference between malarial mortality and total mortality in the first row is due to the mortality of persons with sickle cell anemia.

which explains some of the problems confronting Carnevale.

Molineaux (1985), in an exceptionally careful and imaginative analysis of the data on malaria mortality, confronts two problems. The first is that the reduction in mortality after malaria control operations take place is much greater than the fall in deaths ascribed specifically to malaria would suggest. This is most apparent in data from non-African countries such as Guyana and Sri Lanka, where an indirect effect of malaria control on mortality was two to four times the direct reduction of deaths from malaria. In Guyana part of this reduction was due to a fall in nephritis deaths, which are probably a late effect of *P. malariae*, but part appears to be due to falls in acute and chronic respiratory disease. This can most conveniently be explained by suggesting that for some of the respiratory mortality, both respiratory disease and malaria are necessary causes, but neither is sufficient on its own. Cohen (1988) goes further to suggest that the indirect mortality was in fact not causally related to malaria and that the fall was due to concomitant improvements in living standards during the malaria control campaigns. For Guyana this appears speculative. Respiratory infections did not steadily decline; in fact they rose when malaria increased for a few years. Moreover, changes in housing and drug availability most relevant to reducing respiratory diseases only became available after the falls in infections had occurred. The main relevance of this discussion to Africa concerns the Kisumu project where, in spite of holoendemic malaria, the crude death rate fell after insecticide spraying more than could be accounted for by infant and early childhood mortality decreases (Payne *et al.*, 1976). Experimental work on the interaction of malaria with other infections in laboratory animals certainly supports the existence of a synergistic effect on mortality under some circumstances, but the scale of that effect cannot be assessed from African data.

A converse effect appears to prevail in two West African studies where the removal or massive reduction in deaths from malaria led to a much smaller fall than expected in the mortality of infants and young children. This was seen in Garki, Nigeria (Molineaux and Gramiccia, 1980), where malaria control removed the seasonal peaks of malaria deaths but mortality remained high overall, and in the Gambia when a measles epidemic shifted the peak season of infant mortality from the malaria season without massive effects on total mortality (McGregor, 1964). The most economical hypothesis to explain these results is that of competing risks: a certain number of children are likely to die anyway, possibly with low birth weights and for other ultimate reasons, and the immediate cause of death may be malaria, if present, or some other infection, if malaria is absent. Both malaria and, say, measles may be sufficient causes, and only one is necessary. In either situation, deaths averted by malaria control are not equal in number to deaths due to malaria.

The twin explanations of indirect malarial mortality and competing risks are dangerously easy explanations for most sets of paradoxical results. In a long-term study many other variables also change, which limits the researcher's ability to refute some of these possible explanations of observed data.

Carnevale and Vaugelade (1987) are primarily concerned with African data that suggest a fall in adult as well as infantile mortality after malaria control operations and with the relatively small effects seen in some recent control projects, mainly using chemotherapy, in francophone Africa. Although they argue from the earlier campaigns forward, it is reasonable to infer that their main starting points were their own and colleagues' recent work in Burkina Faso and the Congo, which showed very little reduction in mortality among children subject to a vigorous chemoprophylactic and chemotherapy regime. Carnevale and Vaugelade (1987) criticize an earlier Senegalese study on diagnostic grounds and then attempt to undermine the conclusions of the three major control programs in Pare-Taveta, Garki, and Kisumu. They argue, first, that the decline in mortality was general, progressive, and the result of social and economic development along with a broadly based improvement of medical care and, second, that the insecticidal and chemotherapeutic programs were nonspecific, contrary to what has generally been asserted.

It is certainly true that the economy and access to health care of several of the communities improved over the periods studied and that this is likely to have produced some of the changes observed. The changes in Kisumu are difficult to explain on any grounds. But the rapidity of the effects in Pare-Taveta and Garki argue strongly that a specific antimalarial intervention was the primary determinant of the main changes observed and described above.

The argument that the effects of residual insecticiding are nonspecific is unconvincing. What other lethal vector-borne diseases are present in the communities studied? None of the communities suffered substantial levels of sleeping sickness, tick-borne relapsing fever, or kala-azar at the time of the projects. Filariasis is not responsible for significant mortality in the areas. The only possible candidate for such a role would have been shigellosis, carried by house flies, or some other fly-borne lethal disease, and no convincing evidence is put forward. That the sulfonamide component of Fansidar could have had other protective effects is more readily accepted. Once again, that this was a significant issue in Garki is hard to accept, since the key effect was to reduce mortality in the peak malarial season and "compensatory" mortality seems to have increased if anything! A more likely hypothesis to the present author is that the earlier studies did indeed demonstrate substantial malarial mortality, that the intermediate ones at Kisumu, Kenya, and Ngayok-heme, Senegal, had methodological problems that make their results difficult to interpret reliably, and that the recent studies in francophone countries showed little benefit from organized chemoprophylax-is or chemotherapy because mortality from malaria had already been reduced by various forms of progress, chiefly by individuals purchasing chemotherapy for members of their families when febrile.

The studies are all compatible with heavy infant mortality in uncontrolled holoendemic malaria greatly reduced by individual access to chemotherapy in recent years.

Trends

In spite of its epidemiologically "stable" nature, African malaria is undergoing substantial and rapid changes in its basic epidemiology, in the pattern of mortality, and in the pattern of resistance displayed by *P. falciparum* to antimalarial drugs. It is possible that in the medium term immunization methods may become available to produce a fourth and massive type of change.

Several types of changes in malarial transmission are taking place. In the Sahel and savanna areas, where lack of surface water prevents transmission for several months of each year, the development of water storage dams and irrigation, particularly for rice production, is extending the breeding season for anophelines and increasing the mosquito populations. The development of storage dams may stabilize unstable malaria along the southern edge of the Sahara Desert and change seasonal to perennial transmission in the savanna areas such as northern Nigeria and the Gambia. Few new large dams are now being planned, but small dams proliferate, often unaccompanied by health assessment. Although their effect on malaria (as distinct from schistosomiasis) should not be exaggerated, they will have some effect in the more arid areas.

Urbanization is proceeding rapidly, and up to 43 percent of the population of Africa may live in urban areas by the year 2000. The usual effect of urban development is to decrease anopheline densities substantially. Pollution of urban surface waters has led to a marked increase in the culicines, such as *Culex quinquefasciatus,* that breed in dirty water and a fall in the mosquitoes that flourish in clean water, such as the anophelines. This has been well-documented in Dar es Salaam. However, the recent surprising observations of *An. gambiae* adapting to sullage and other dirty water situations in Accra, Ghana (Chinery, 1984) will need careful follow-up. If they prove at all widespread, the findings have serious implications for urban malaria in the future.

The widespread availability of some antimalarials, chiefly chloroquine, has undoubtedly affected the childhood mortality from malaria. In some places, few fevers, whether due to malaria or not, escape partial if not complete courses of chloroquine, which has brought down the number of fatalities. Within the remaining areas that are sensitive to chloroquine, this trend will continue. It has already been argued above that this provides a better explanation of the apparently changing effects of malaria control on population mortality than do the suggestions of lack of specificity of the earlier insecticidal programs. The duration and severity of illness have also been reduced, principally by antimalarials that are readily accessible at local shops as well as at health services. Whether transmission has also been reduced is far from clear, although it probably has been in some places. The gap between malarial parasitemia and the subsequent appearance of the gametocyte stage in the peripheral blood means that early treatment could in theory greatly reduce the number of cases infectious to mosquitoes. The proportion of subclinical cases in patients, who therefore have no reason to contact the health care services, is sufficiently large in endemic areas that treating the sick may have a very limited effect on transmission. It can substantially protect the individual from developing significant immunity and thereby postpone to a later age the liability of suffering a massive initial malaria attack. McGregor (personal communication) has described the appearance of cerebral malaria in teenagers in Banjul, the Gambia, where it was previously a disease of infants. The combination of urbanization, which may reduce transmission, and frequent chemotherapy or even chemoprophylaxis, which diminishes individual duration of parasitemia, has probably been responsible for this.

If the malaria parasites had remained unchanged, the steadily increasing availability of antimalarials at health care facilities and shops, and consequently in the home, would probably have led to a progressive decrease in malarial mortality. Thus malaria would have remained a major cause of disease but would have become a less important cause of death. However, the spread of drug-resistant strains of *P. falciparum* is greatly altering this optimistic picture. Resistance to the folic acid antagonists proguanil and pyrimethamine emerges rapidly after their widespread use, and pyrimethamine resistance is common in many parts of tropical Africa. (Proguanil resistance, although more problematical, is only an issue in relation to expatriate prophylaxis rather than indigenous use and is not a curative drug.) The crucial resistance has been to chloroquine, which has dominated the treatment of malaria in Africa because it is efficacious, cheap, relatively nontoxic, and easy to administer. The rapid spread of chloroquine-resistant *P. falciparum* in Africa in the past five years has created a new situation. It is common in East and central Africa and has reached Cameroon, Ghana, and other West African states. It will probably have reached all of West Africa by 1992. The second therapeutic drug is Fansidar (a mixture of pyrimethamine and a long-acting sulfonamide), which is more toxic and much more expensive, and resistance to it has been clearly described in East Africa and part of central-southern Africa. Alternatives for treatment are also expensive, resistance emerges quickly to mefloquine, and quinine is both toxic and more difficult to administer than other antimalarials. Chloroquine resistance and Fansidar resistance will surely continue to spread, and the scanty number of new drugs that will be available in the near future suggests that mortality from malaria may cease to decline. In areas where drugs are already used, it may even begin to rise. The outlook is not good in the absence of major innovations, among which a vaccine is the item on which most hopes are based.

Given that large-scale control programs have not been a feature of efforts to deal with African malaria, the collapse of insecticiding programs in so many countries has not had a major effect in Africa. However, experiments using insecticide-impregnated bed nets and curtains or screens are taking place at multiple sites in both West and East Africa. The results, which are largely unpublished, are promising and may prove of particular value in protecting infants and young children and in reducing the human inoculation rate. The benefits to health will most likely be in areas where the biting rate for infective mosquitoes has already been reduced substantially by urbanization or the climatic pattern. The effect on areas of intense perennial transmission is unlikely to be substantial, and the characteristics that have made African malaria so resistant to efforts at control are unlikely to be overcome by attacks on the mosquito phase of transmission alone, although impregnated nets may prove to be less expensive than other approaches and effective in the highly vulnerable infant.

Given that the pattern of African malaria is largely regulated not by transmission but by human acquired immunity, the attractions of vaccination as a means of control are obvious. Vaccination reinforces rather than works against the naturally operating mechanisms. Attempts to produce malaria vaccines, which have a long history of failure, initially struggled against the lack of culture methods for the parasite. Now that this has been overcome for the three relevant stages of the *P. falciparum* life cycle, far greater advances are feasible. Work has progressed rapidly on recombinant DNA and the use of monoclonal antibodies to select potentially protective antigens. Although current trials of sporozoite vaccines have been disappointing, a vaccine might be available for large-scale use within a decade. Provided that the cost is not very high and, even more crucially, that immunity does not wane too rapidly (it takes a long time for immunity to be acquired by the inhabitants of a holoendemic area, although a vaccine could perhaps avoid components that might stimulate suppressor T-cells), a vaccine operating at either the trophozoite or the sporozoite stage, with or without an added gametocyte vaccine, could make a massive difference to the endemicity and consequences of malaria in Africa.

Methodological and Research Issues

It would be easy to complain that, in view of the vast amount of malariological research carried out in the past century, the uncertain magnitude of mortality due to malaria reflects much methodological confusion and a failure to tackle the problem of impact evaluation adequately. Only by comparison with work on the health effects of water supply and sanitation or on the impact of schistosomiasis does malariological work emerge in a favorable light. This is one view. The opposing one would point to the history of control programs and use of health services and suggest that the importance of African malaria is more than adequately known by comparison with the many unsolved health problems of Africa and that the search for more detailed definition of what is a clear and acknowledged massive health problem will merely divert effort and attention from the more urgent need to do something about controlling the disease. In fact, the two positions are not necessarily as polarized as described above, particularly because the best evidence of the effects of malaria has resulted from careful studies in parallel with pilot control programs.

It is clear with hindsight that if studies such as that at Pare-Taveta had been undertaken specifically to determine malarial mortality along with experimental transmission control, a few low-cost modifications to the study design and a more extended demographic population would have met many of the objections that can be raised to that project. Implementing a specific, rapid intervention to stop the transmission of malaria in a limited area, with concomitant observation of adjacent areas lacking the intervention, provides the best opportunity to determine the impact of malaria. Whereas scientific elegance is best achieved by subsequently stopping the intervention and observing a reversion to the status quo ante, ethical considerations rightly limit such a refinement.

The relevance of this logic for the future is clear. Malarial vaccines, if effective, will provide a highly specific antimalarial intervention that is not even open to the objections that have been raised to the specificity of residual insecticiding in East Africa. For the trials of candidate vaccines in the community to provide the type of data sought on malarial impact requires planning the study adequately and far enough in advance to include impact studies and sufficient baseline observations prior to intervention. Since trials of a successful vaccine are likely to be followed by rapid, widespread, and probably indiscriminate use of the vaccine, the opportunity for observations with simultaneous controls will probably be presented only briefly and at a few sites.

The preceding scenario depends on the optimistic view about vaccines proving correct. If it does not, chemotherapy with or without chemoprophylaxis will remain immensely important even if decreasingly effective in controlling malaria in Africa. Studies are needed of communities where chloroquine (or another effective drug) is used to treat malarial attacks and where extremely detailed longitudinal follow-up is used to define the relations between clinical state and frequency of treatment as well as the outcome for child health. Such studies would throw light on the issues of "compensatory" mortality, which remain obscure except in relation to nutritional and anthropometric risk factors. The level of intervention likely to be practiced in an ethical detailed longitudinal study is likely, however, to complicate interpretation of the results. The valuable historical longitudinal observations of McGregor in the Gambia (see chapter 20 of this volume) are unlikely to be repeatable, and methodology for field studies may have to focus on interpreting natural history where multiple interventions overlie the complex pathological processes occurring in children who have both malaria and multiple concurrent other infections.

A third methodological area requires comment, perhaps relatively unwelcome comment. Given the present preoccupation with overt processes for setting priorities, one can expect frequent elaboration of the type of procedure pioneered in Ghana (Ghana Health Assessment Project Team, 1981). The result will be calculations of the social and economic consequences of various diseases and interventions. While the malaria data are a good deal more reliable than those for most other parasitic diseases, the ranking of diseases is a relative matter and depends on the quality of data and assumptions for the more common diseases. It is easy to build economic houses of epidemiological straw, and given the inveterate habit of seizing upon and using numbers provided by other authors without carrying over their caveats and explanations, one can only plead for caution in the use of such priority-setting exercises. The welcome growth of interdisciplinary work is too easily accompanied by a fall in critical standards in this respect.

To survey Africa broadly and in a few pages requires overlooking the small-scale epidemiological heterogeneity that is increasingly being found even within the areas of intense stable malaria. This heterogeneity superficially does not appear to fit into the theoretical scheme set out above and challenges current research. Not the least challenge is that the villages concerned may have a total population of only a few hundred people and therefore pose difficult statistical problems when comparisons are made. It is remarkable that the three Gambian villages studied by McGregor, although adjacent, have maintained markedly different spleen rates in children throughout the 30 years of research. Similar microheterogeneity has been observed and studied in Papua New Guinea and Tanzania. The findings will need to be taken into epidemiological theory. As far as the impact on mortality is concerned, the small size of the communities may provide an insuperable obstacle to analysis (except by aggregating data from villages stratified by spleen or parasite rate, which begs the question). Greater attention to the spatial structure of communities and their relation to breeding sites will be necessary to understand much of this microheterogeneity (unless the prior discovery of an efficacious vaccine causes most people to lose interest).

References

Baudon, D., Roux, J., Carnevale, P., Vaugelade, J., Boudin, C., Chaize, J., Rey, J. L., Meyran, M. B. and Brandicourt, O. (1984). Étude de deux stratégies de contrôles des paludismes, la chimiothérapie systématique des accès fébriles et la chimioprophylaxie hebdomadaire dans 12 villages de Haute-Volta, en zone de savane et zone rizicole de 1980 à 1982. Document technique OCCGE, no. 8450. Organisation de Coordination et de Coopération pour la Lutte contre les Grandes Endémies.

Baudon, D., Gazin, P., Rea, D., and Carnevale, P. (1985). A study of malaria morbidity in a rural area of Burkina Faso (West Africa). *Transactions of the Royal Society of Tropical Medicine and Hygiene*, 79, 283–284.

Carnevale, P., Robert, V., Molez, J.-F., and Boudon, D. (1984). Épidémiologie générale: faciès épidémiologique des paludismes en Afrique subsaharienne. *Études médicales*, 3, 123–133.

Carnevale, P. and Vaugelade, J. (1987). *Paludismes, morbidité palustre et mortalité infantile et juvénile en Afrique sub-Saharienne.* WHO/MAL/87.1036. Geneva: World Health Organization.

Chinery, W. A. (1984). Effects of ecological changes on the malarial vectors *Anopheles funestus* and the *Anopheles gambiae* complex of mosquitoes in Accra, Ghana. *Journal of Tropical Medicine and Hygiene,* 87, 75–81.

Christophers, S. R. (1911). *Malaria in the Punjab: Scientific Memoirs by Officers of the Medical and Sanitary Departments of the Government of India.* N.S. 46. New Delhi: Medical and Sanitary Departments.

Cohen, J. E. (1988). Estimating the effect of successful malaria programmes on mortality. *Population Bulletin of the United Nations*, 25, 6–26.

Davidson, G. (1955). Further studies on the basic factors concerned in the transmission of malaria. *Transactions of the Royal Society of Tropical Medicine and Hygiene,* 49, 339–350.

Davidson, G. and Draper, C. C. (1953). Field studies of some of the basic factors concerned in the transmission of malaria. *Transactions of the Royal Society of Tropical Medicine and Hygiene*, 47, 522–535.

Fleming, A. F., Storey, J., Molineaux, L., Iroko, E. A., and Attai, E. D. I. (1979). Abnormal hemoglobins in the Sudan savanna of Nigeria: prevalence of hemoglobins and relationships between sickle cell trait, malaria, and survival. *Annals of Tropical Medicine and Parasitology*, 73, 161–172.

Garenne, M. and Vimard, P. (1984). Un cadre pour l'analyse des facteurs de mortalité des enfants. *Cahiers ORSTOM [Office de la Recherche Scientifique et Technique Outre-Mer], Sciences humaines*, 20 (2), 305–310.

Garenne, M., Cantrelle, P., and Diop, I. L. (1985). Le cas du Sénégal (1960–80). In: *La lutte contre la morte*, Vallin, J. and Lopez, A. (editors), pp. 307–330. Travaux et documents, no. 108. Paris: Presses Universitaires de France.

Ghana Health Assessment Project Team. (1981). A quantitative method of assessing the health impact of different diseases in less developed countries. *International Journal of Epidemiology*, 10 (1), 73–80.

Livingstone, F. B. (1971). Malaria and human polymorphisms. *Annual Review of Genetics*, 5, 33–64.

Macdonald, G. (1951). Community aspects of immunity to malaria. *British Medical Bulletin*, 8, 33–36.

Macdonald, G. and Chowdhuri, K. L. (1926). Malaria in the children of Freetown, Sierra Leone. *Annals of Tropical Medicine and Parasitology*, 20, 239–262.

McGregor, I. A. (1964). Measles and child mortality in the Gambia. *West African Medical Journal*, 13, 251–257.

Molineaux, L. (1985). La lutte contre les maladies parasitaires: le problème du paludisme, notamment en Afrique. In: *La lutte contre la morte*, Vallin, J. and Lopez, A. (editors), pp. 111–140. Travaux et documents, no. 108. Paris: Presses Universitaires de France.

Molineaux, L. and Gramiccia, G. (1980). *The Garki Project: Research on the Epidemiology and Control of Malaria in the Sudan Savanna of West Africa.* Geneva: World Health Organization.

Payne, D., Grab, B., Fontaine, R. E., and Hempel, J. H. G. (1976). Impact of control measures on malaria transmission and general mortality. *Bulletin of the World Health Organization*, 54, 369–377.

Prothero, R. M. (1965). *Migrants and Malaria.* London: Longmans.

Williams, E. H., Hayes, R. J., and Smith, P. G. (1986). Admissions to a rural hospital in the West Nile District of Uganda over a 27 year period. *Journal of Tropical Medicine and Hygiene*, 89 (4), 193–211.

Wilson, D. B. (1949). Malaria incidence in central and south Africa. In: *Malariology*, Boyd, M.E., pp. 8–809. Philadelphia and London: Saunders.

Wilson, D. B., Garnham, P. C. C., and Swellengrebel, N. H. (1950). A review of hyperendemic malaria. *Tropical Diseases Bulletin*, 47, 677–698.

Chapter 13

The Epidemiology and Projected Mortality of AIDS

James Chin

Acquired immunodeficiency syndrome (AIDS) emerged during the 1980s as a major health problem in Sub-Saharan Africa. After 1985 and the advent of serologic tests to detect antibodies to the human immunodeficiency virus (HIV)—the etiologic agent of AIDS—thousands of subsequent serologic surveys have confirmed that a very high prevalence of HIV infections was present among sexually active adults in many central African cities.

This chapter reviews the current HIV/AIDS epidemic in Africa and provides short-range projections (five to ten years) of its potential impact on mortality rates and demographic patterns in Sub-Saharan Africa.

Natural History and Reporting of AIDS and HIV Infections

Natural History of HIV Infections

AIDS represents the late clinical stage of infection with HIV. Within several weeks to several months after being infected with HIV, many persons develop an acute, self-limited illness resembling mononucleosis. Subsequently, infected persons may have no clinical signs or symptoms for months or even years. The severity of subsequent illness is, in general, directly correlated with the degree of immune damage caused by HIV. Onset of clinical illness is usually insidious: initial symptoms are nonspecific and may include lymphadenopathy, anorexia, chronic diarrhea, weight loss, fever, and fatigue. However, such nonspecific complaints are not ordinarily sufficient for a diagnosis of AIDS, and the clinical signs and symptoms noted above have been referred to as AIDS-related complex (ARC).

About a dozen diseases, primarily *Pneumocystis carinii* pneumonia, Kaposi's sarcoma, and other severe opportunistic infections, are considered to be sufficiently specific surrogate or indirect markers of the underlying immunodeficiency related to HIV infection to enable AIDS to be diagnosed. This clinical description and case definition apply to adult AIDS cases primarily in developed countries. The clinical manifestations of adult AIDS in developing regions, such as Sub-Saharan Africa, can be very different from those in developed countries because the background microbiological flora are different.

The clinical manifestations and case definition of AIDS in infants and young children present additional clinical and laboratory diagnostic problems. Diagnosing HIV infection in infants born to HIV-infected women is difficult because virtually all of these infants will have detectable HIV antibodies passively acquired from their mothers regardless of whether they have been infected. In addition, the frequent occurrence of other childhood infections that present signs and symptoms similar to those of the AIDS indicator diseases makes the clinical diagnosis of AIDS in infants and young children very difficult.

The proportion of HIV-infected persons who ultimately develop AIDS is not yet precisely known. Cohort studies of HIV-infected homosexual men and persons with hemophilia indicate that about 15–20 percent develop AIDS within five years and about 50 percent within ten years (Moss and Bacchetti, 1989). Beyond ten years, it is projected that the vast majority of infected persons may develop AIDS within another five to ten years. Although the data are limited, the rate at which AIDS develops is believed to be similar in Africa (Piot *et al.*, 1988). This very long incubation period differs only among infected infants, the majority of whom develop AIDS before their fifth birthday.

Surveillance of AIDS Cases

The public health surveillance of AIDS cases began in 1982 when the Centers for Disease Control (CDC), of the U.S. Public Health Service, developed an AIDS case definition for reporting purposes (Centers for Disease Control, 1982). A list of diseases was specified as surrogate indicators of the underlying immunodeficiency caused by HIV infection where other known causes of immunodeficiency had been ruled out. These diseases, if diagnosed by standard histological or culture techniques or both, were accepted as meeting the definition of AIDS. It was recognized that this strict case definition was not likely to include the full clinical spectrum of the disease syndrome but a very specific definition was needed. The definition was modified slightly in 1985 (Centers for Disease Control, 1985) and adopted by the World Health Organization (WHO) in 1986 (World Health Organization, 1986). In late 1987, this definition (CDC/WHO) was revised extensively to place greater emphasis on the status of HIV infection, to include additional indicator diseases, and to accept presumptive diagnosis of some indicator diseases (Centers for Disease Control, 1987; World Health Organization, 1988a).

The use of the CDC/WHO definition of AIDS, however, was not feasible in most developing countries, which often lack adequate laboratory facilities for undertaking the histologic or cultural diagnosis of the specified diseases in order to meet the rigid surveillance definition of AIDS. In addition, some indicator diseases in areas such as Africa appear to be different from those observed in the United States and Europe. In October 1985 an AIDS workshop was held in Bangui, Central African Republic, in which the WHO clinical definition of AIDS was developed (World Health Organization, 1985). AIDS case reports from Africa are usually based on the WHO clinical definition, although in the late 1980s some countries added a requirement that AIDS cases show evidence of HIV seropositivity in addition to the WHO clinical criteria.

AIDS case reports from Africa are generally delayed an average of nine months and are incomplete for a variety of reasons. These include the reluctance of many countries until 1987 to acknowledge officially the existence of AIDS; the general lack of laboratory and clinical expertise and facilities for diagnosing AIDS; and the limited access of large segments of the population to health care facilities where AIDS might be diagnosed. For these reasons, it is estimated that 10 percent or fewer of all AIDS cases—especially pediatric AIDS cases—that occur in Africa are reported to WHO (Chin and Mann, 1988).

HIV Seroprevalence Studies

Estimates of the prevalence of HIV infections are essential for monitoring the epidemiologic patterns and scope of the HIV/AIDS pandemic. In addition, the future numbers of HIV-related diseases, including AIDS, will depend on the numbers of persons infected with HIV. HIV seroprevalence data obtained by the majority of studies throughout the world during the 1980s must, however, be interpreted and compared with extreme caution. This is because of wide differences in survey methodology and the different populations used in these surveys and studies. Despite such problems, during the last half of the 1980s thousands of HIV serologic surveys and studies involving many millions of persons have been carried out. Collectively they have been able to describe broadly the distribution and prevalence of HIV infections in most areas of the world.

HIV infections are not randomly distributed in any human population. Relatively high prevalence rates (ranging from a few to over 50 percent) can be found among persons who have multiple sexual partners, especially men who have many male partners, or who frequently share injection equipment for intravenous (IV) drug use. The prevalence rate of HIV infections in any general population in industrial countries is very low and can range from almost zero to a high of only one per several thousand. In areas where heterosexual transmission is predominant, HIV seroprevalence levels of up to 1 percent or more of the total population and up to 30 percent of the sexually active adults in urban areas have been recorded as of 1987. Using the available data and estimates made by many countries, in 1987 WHO estimated that between five and ten million persons in the world were infected with HIV. In 1990, the cumulative total of global HIV infections was estimated to be closer to the upper end of the 1987 estimate, about eight to ten million (World Health Organization, 1990). This figure was based largely on recent estimates of HIV seroprevalence in the United States (Dondero *et al.*, 1989) and Europe (World Health Organization, 1988b) and on a detailed meta-analysis of available seroprevalence data for each country in Sub-Saharan Africa (World Health Organization, 1990).

The Epidemiology of HIV/AIDS in Africa

Three broad yet distinct epidemiologic patterns of HIV/AIDS have been described by the World Health Organization (Mann *et al.*, 1988). In pattern 1 the primary population groups affected are homosexual men and intravenous drug users. In pattern 2 HIV/AIDS is found predominantly in sexually active heterosexuals; and in pattern 3 the HIV/AIDS epidemic is fairly recent, and relatively few persons were HIV-infected during the 1980s. Important factors responsible for these patterns include:

- The probable date of HIV entry or the period when HIV began to spread extensively in the population or both;
- The relative frequency of the three documented modes of HIV transmission: through sexual intercourse (heterosexual or homosexual); by parental inoculation or administration of infected blood or blood products; and from infected women to their infants.

All three patterns are found in Africa. Patterns 1 and 2 are present in the Republic of South Africa, pattern 2 in Sub-Saharan Africa, and pattern 3 in North Africa. This chapter focuses only on the problem of pattern 2 in Sub-Saharan Africa, since the vast majority of HIVinfections and AIDS cases in Africa are found in this region.

Heterosexual Transmission of HIV in Africa

A question often asked is why HIV/AIDS in Africa affects sexually active men *and* women in almost equal proportions while in the industrial West males make up the overwhelming preponderance (the proportion of men to women ranges from 15:1 to 10:1) of AIDS cases. What accounts for these widely varying distributions of HIV, and what particular factors can explain the preponderance of heterosexual transmission in Sub-Saharan Africa? Intravenous drug use is not a significant problem in Sub-Saharan Africa, and although homosexuality exists worldwide, it has not been documented to any appreciable extent among AIDS cases or HIV-infected persons in Sub-Saharan Africa. Many epidemiologic studies have shown that transfusion of HIV-infected blood accounts for only a small proportion of HIV infections in Sub-Saharan Africa (Piot *et al.*, 1988). The use of unsterile needles or other skin-piercing instruments within the health care system or as part of traditional healing (or other) practices also accounts for only a small proportion of HIV infections in these areas. Female circumcision, another possible contributory factor in the spread of HIV in Africa, is not prevalent in the areas where HIV/AIDS is prevalent.

Evidence increasingly implicates several contributory factors (cofactors) as accounting for much of the marked difference in the heterosexual spread of HIV in Africa compared with North American or Western

European countries. The relatively high prevalence of numerous infectious diseases, including malaria and other parasitic diseases, in tropical Africa may be a contributory factor since some of these etiologic agents may activate the immune system and facilitate HIV infection. In addition, recent studies have implicated the presence of other sexually transmitted diseases, especially those associated with genital ulcers such as syphilis and chancroid, as significant cofactors in the spread of HIV (Simonsen *et al.*, 1988). Some preliminary data suggest that uncircumcised males may be more susceptible to HIV infection than those who are circumcised (Simonsen *et al.*, 1988). It is believed that the heterosexual spread of HIV in Africa can be attributed to the combination of such cofactors and the recurring social or political upheavals and very large population migration to the cities of central and East Africa during the 1970s.

Estimating the Number of HIV Infections in Sub-Saharan Africa

A relatively consistent age distribution of HIV-infected persons has been found in many central African cities. From 5 to 10 percent of infants born in these urban areas are HIV positive; very few infections are found in the 5–15 year olds, and the prevalence of HIV infection increases among sexually active young adults, with a peak at about age 35 (Rwandan HIV Seroprevalence Study Group, 1989). In 1989 up to 40 percent of the 30–34 year age group in some cities were found to be infected. The HIV seroprevalence rates were lower in persons over 35. A relatively consistent preponderance of HIV infections was noted in sexually active women 15–24 years old compared with men, but this difference was, in some instances, reversed in the older age groups. Over the entire age range, slightly more females than males were infected.

Another relatively consistent finding was the marked differential between urban and rural HIV seroprevalence rates. In most instances up to 1987, rural seroprevalence of HIV was about one-tenth the rate found in large urban areas; in a few notable exceptions rural areas located along much traveled roads had relatively high HIV rates. In most central and eastern African countries 75 percent or more of the population is rural; and in both urban and rural areas close to 50 percent or more of the population is under 15 years of age. Thus the absolute number of HIV-infected persons in Africa is not nearly as large as might at first be suspected from the very high HIV seroprevalence—20 to 30 percent—among sexually active adults in the largest urban areas.

Figure 13-1. Estimated HIV Infections, January 1990

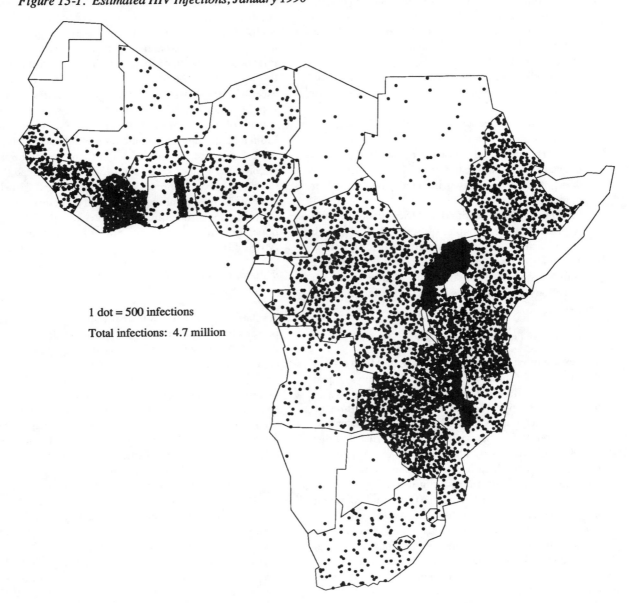

1 dot = 500 infections

Total infections: 4.7 million

Source: Generated by the author from the internal data files of the WHO Global Programme on AIDS, 1990.

The World Health Organization used the distribution from serologic surveys of HIV infection by age and urban or rural residence to estimate the prevalence of HIV infections in urban and rural areas of Sub-Saharan African countries as of 1990. Where HIV serologic data were not available for rural areas, the rural seroprevalence was assumed to be 10 to 20 percent of the urban seroprevalence. For all Sub-Saharan African countries, the total adult HIV infections were estimated to be close to 5 million as of the end of 1989 (Chin, forthcoming). Figure 13-1 presents the geographic distribution of estimated HIV infections in Sub-Saharan countries. About a dozen countries across the central belt of Africa account for over 80 percent of the estimated HIV infections.

Distribution and Trends of HIV Infection in Africa

At the end of the 1980s, the HIV/AIDS epidemic in Africa appeared to be most severe in central and eastern Africa and affected Burundi, the Central African Republic, Congo, Kenya, Rwanda, Tanzania, Uganda, Zaire, and Zambia. It also appeared to be extending to adjacent countries of southern Africa and into West Africa. Serologic studies of female prostitutes during the mid- to late 1980s in most large urban areas of central and eastern Africa generally showed that more than half, and up to 80 percent or more, were infected with HIV (Kreiss *et al.*, 1986; Piot *et al.*, 1988). Similar surveys among blood donors and pregnant women in these same cities showed HIV seroprevalence ranging from a low of about 5 percent up to 30 percent (World Health Organization, 1989).

Virtually all the results described above are for HIV-1, the virus responsible for most AIDS cases throughout the world. Another distinct type of AIDS virus, designated HIV-2, has been found primarily in West Africa and more recently in one southern African country (Lyons *et al.*, 1989). Seroprevalence studies in West African countries such as Côte d'Ivoire and Senegal have shown HIV-2 to be substantially less prevalent than HIV-1 in the urban areas of central and East Africa (Kanki *et al.*, 1987). In addition, clinical and epidemiological data suggest that HIV-2 is less pathogenic than HIV-1. Only future studies can verify this supposition.

HIV prevalence continues to rise in almost all countries where surveys or studies have been carried out during the latter half of the 1980s. In Abidjan, Côte d'Ivoire, HIV-1 prevalences increased from around 1 percent to at least 4 percent from 1986 to 1988 (Mann,

1989). The prevalence among pregnant women attending antenatal clinics in Lilongwe and Blantyre, Malawi, rose from around 3 percent in 1986 to about 18 percent in early 1989 (Liomba *et al.*, 1989), and it rose in adults in Bangui, Central African Republic, from around 2 percent in 1985 to about 7 percent in 1989 (Soms *et al.*, 1989). Preliminary data from a community-based cluster survey of HIV prevalence in 1987–88 indicate that in rural parts of the Central Region, Uganda (the most populous region of the country), the observed HIV prevalence among adults was about 12 percent (Ndumu *et al.*, 1989).

Estimating the Demographic Impact of AIDS in Africa

An AIDS Projection Model

What impact will the very high HIV infection rates documented in central African cities have on future mortality rates and population patterns? The Global Programme on AIDS (GPA) of the World Health Organization has developed an AIDS projection model that utilizes HIV serologic survey data and observed and estimated annual progression rates from HIV infection to the development of AIDS (Chin and Mann, 1989). The following assumptions or estimates are needed to operate this model.

1. *Prevalence of HIV infection in the population.* An estimate can be developed from HIV serologic survey data, when available. An extensive data base consisting of close to a thousand published (Way, 1989) and unpublished (World Health Organization, 1989) HIV serologic surveys and studies was used to estimate HIV seroprevalence in African countries.

2. *The year that HIV infection began to spread extensively in the population.* For most Sub-Saharan countries, extensive spread probably did not begin until the late 1970s or early 1980s.

3. *The number of persons infected with HIV annually (annual infected cohorts), starting the year that HIV began to spread extensively.* Available epidemiologic data suggest that the incidence of HIV infection may have been highest in the early 1980s; subsequent transmission rates, at least in some of the large urban areas, may have declined after the mid-1980s. The curve for cumulative HIV infections in Sub-Saharan Africa has been assumed to be more sigmoid in shape than exponential, and annual HIV infections for the WHO projection model were distributed in such a pattern.

4. *The annual rate of progression from HIV infec-tion to AIDS.* Progression rates were estimated from cohort studies of HIV-infected persons (homosexual men and persons with hemophilia). The adult progression rate was projected to be about 20 percent within 5 years, close to 50 percent within 10 years, 75 percent within 15 years, and 95 percent within 20 years. For HIV-infected infants, the progression rate used was 25 percent during the first year, 20 percent in the second, 15 percent in the third, and 10 percent each in the fourth and fifth years, for a cumulative rate of 80 percent by the fifth birthday.

With these estimates and assumptions, the annual incidence and prevalence of both pediatric and adult AIDS in a given population can be calculated by applying the specific (adult or pediatric) annual progression rate for the development of AIDS to each annual HIV-infected cohort. The assumptions and estimates used in this model will need to be modified when and if additional data, especially data specific to Africa, become available.

Projecting AIDS Cases and Deaths

Short-term projections (five to ten years) of AIDS cases and deaths can be reasonably derived from estimated HIV seroprevalence and the rate of progression from infection to AIDS. The median progression is about ten years. Thus, the majority of new AIDS cases during the early to mid-1990s will come from the pool of persons already infected with HIV by 1989. In Africa, it was assumed that persons with AIDS would die within the year of diagnosis.

Based on the estimate of 5 million HIV-infected adults in Sub-Saharan Africa, the WHO model estimated that by the end of 1990 a cumulative total of about 700,000 AIDS cases in adults and close to 400,000 pediatric AIDS cases had occurred. The model also projected that by 1992, the cumulative total will be about 1.5 million AIDS cases and deaths (close to a million in adults and a half million in children) in all of Sub-Saharan Africa (figure 13-2). Of the cumulative total, close to 90 percent of the cases in adults and about 80 percent of the cases in children were projected to occur between 1988 and 1992. In 1992 alone, over 400,000 new AIDS cases of all ages can be expected, which is a cumulative total greater than the number of AIDS cases in Sub-Saharan Africa up to 1988. Approximately two-thirds of the 1992 total will occur in persons between the ages of 15 and 49—the most economically productive age group—and close to 20 percent in the pediatric age group.

Figure 13-2. Estimated Cumulative Pediatric and Adult AIDS Cases in Africa

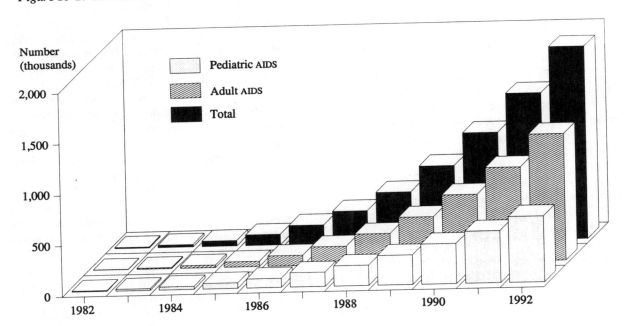

Source: Generated by the author from the internal data files of the WHO Global Programme on AIDS, 1990.

Impact of AIDS on Mortality Rates and Demographic Patterns

During the early to mid-1990s, most countries in Sub-Saharan Africa can expect large increases in mortality for children under 5 years of age and adults, particularly between the ages of 20 and 49. To illustrate these expected increases in deaths due to AIDS, the following examples of projected increases in mortality among children and adults are presented along with expected demographic changes in a hypothetical central African country during the 1990s.

Impact on Under-Five Mortality

The following example is based on the assumptions that about 25 percent of infants born to HIV-infected women will be infected and about 80 percent of the infected infants will die before their fifth birthday. In an area where the under-five mortality was 100 (that is, 100 infants or children out of 1,000 live births did not survive to their fifth birthday) before the introduction of HIV infections, the approximate contribution of pediatric AIDS to under-five mortality can be calculated from the HIV seroprevalence among pregnant women. Figure 13-3 presents the increases in under-five mortality expected for HIV seroprevalence levels of 5, 10,

20, and 30 percent. A range of 1 to 30 percent of HIV seroprevalence has been documented among pregnant women in several central African cities in the late 1980s. AIDS deaths were adjusted downward by 10 percent to take into account competing causes of death in this age group. The under-five mortality can increase by over 50 percent from 100 to over 150 when the HIV seroprevalence reaches 30 percent among pregnant women, a value recorded in some central African cities in the late 1980s.

Impact on Mortality Rates for Adults (20–49 Years of Age)

In this example, the hypothetical population is a city of one million, of which 40 percent (400,000) are adults 20–49 years old. The contribution of AIDS deaths to the adult mortality rate (AMR) in a city where the AMR in the mid-1980s was 5 per 1,000 adults per year can be calculated for different HIV seroprevalence levels by using the WHO projection model. Projected AIDS-related deaths in 1991 based on an HIV seroprevalence level of 5 percent in 1987 will be over 1,000 (table 13-1). AMRS in Sub-Saharan countries range from about 2.5 to 10 per 1,000 per year, equivalent to about 1,000 to 4,000 deaths annually in this hypothetical population. Figure

Figure 13-4. Projected Increase in Adult Mortality Attributable to AIDS, Sub-Saharan Africa, 1992

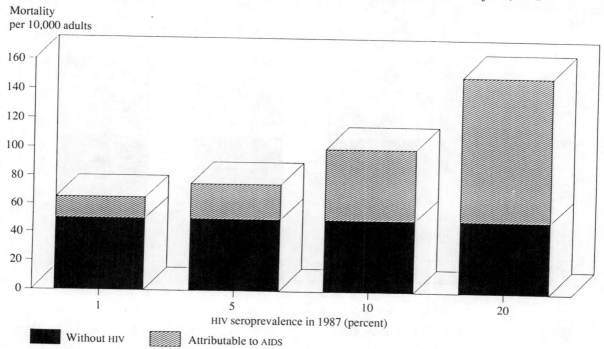

Mortality per 10,000 adults

HIV seroprevalence in 1987 (percent)

■ Without HIV   ▨ Attributable to AIDS

Table 13-1. Projected Deaths due to Aids in a Population of 400,000 Adults

Percentage HIV positive in 1987	Number of HIV-infected adults	AIDS deaths in 1991
1	4,000	More than 200
5	20,000	More than 1,000
10	40,000	More than 2,000
20	80,000	More than 4,000

13-4 shows that at the levels of HIV infection present in many central African cities during the latter half of the 1980s the AMR could double or triple by the early 1990s. Thus AIDS deaths could equal or exceed expected adult deaths from all other causes in the most severely affected Sub-Saharan African cities by the early 1990s.

Potential Demographic Changes

A hypothetical country was constructed with a geographic and age group distribution similar to that of several central African countries (Chin *et al.*, 1989). In 1987 the total population numbered just under 20 million: about 15 percent lived in urban areas (table 13-2), and over half were under the age of 15. The growth projected for this hypothetical population from 1987 to 1997 without the presence of HIV/AIDS is about 6.6 million (0.895 million in urban and 5.7 million in rural areas) for a total growth rate of over 3 percent a year. It was assumed that this hypothetical population had the prevalence and pattern of HIV infection previously described for central African countries in 1987. The accumulated deaths attributed to AIDS during the ten years from 1987 to 1997 were determined by using the WHO projection model. Pediatric AIDS deaths were adjusted downward by 10 percent to take into account competing causes of infant and child deaths, but adult deaths were not adjusted for competing causes. Total adult and pediatric AIDS cases projected for this country by 1997 are over 420,000 (table 13-2). By 1997 deaths due to AIDS are predicted to *diminish* the *expected increase* of the urban population by over 30 percent, but should have a relatively negligible effect—a 2.4 percent decrease—on the growth of the rural population.

Figure 13-3. Projected Increase in Under-Five Mortality Attributable to HIV/AIDS, Sub-Saharan Africa, 1992

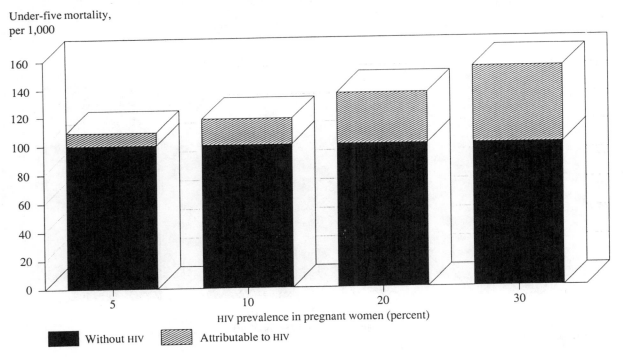

Under-five mortality, per 1,000

HIV prevalence in pregnant women (percent)

■ Without HIV   ▨ Attributable to HIV

Table 13-2. Projected Changes in Population due to AIDS in a Central African Country

Year and scenario	Urban	Rural	Total
1987 population	2,943,000	16,712,000	19,655,000
1997 population			
Without the presence of AIDS	3,838,000	22,412,000	26,250,000
Growth	895,000	5,700,000	6,595,000
With the presence of AIDS	3,556,117	22,273,202	25,829,319
Deaths due to AIDS	281,883	138,818	420,701
Percentage decrease due to AIDS	31.5	2.4	6.4

Conclusions

Epidemiologic and medical data indicate that HIV did not begin to spread extensively in central and eastern Africa until the mid- to late 1970s. One study, in a rural area of Zaire, tested blood specimens collected in 1976 and similar samples collected in 1986 for HIV antibody (Nzilambi *et al.*, 1988). This study showed that HIV infections had probably been present and were maintained at a low endemic level in this rural area for an unknown length of time prior to 1976. The authors of that study postulated that the higher prevalence of HIV infections subsequently found in large urban areas of central Africa was probably related to sexual life-style, which was more active in cities than in most rural areas. During the 1980s AIDS in Africa and throughout the world was primarily an urban problem that predominantly involved sexually active adults. The impact of AIDS on the population projected over the next decade in the most severely affected central African countries will not be strongly felt in most rural areas, where the majority of the population live. According to the AIDS projection model developed by the WHO, the total AIDS cases expected to occur over the next decade will *not* reverse the projected positive population growth rate, even for the most severely affected central African countries. Nevertheless during the next decade urban areas will, because of AIDS, experience a marked and very selective *decrease* in the *projected increase* among the very young and among the sexually active who have multiple sexual partners. The national population growth rate of between 3 and 4 percent a year for most of these countries will be reduced by 1 percent or less. For many central African countries, however, AIDS-related deaths expected by the mid-to-late-1990s among adults in their most productive years will number in the hundreds of thousands. The selective impact on young and middle-aged adults, including business and government workers, as well as members of the social, economic, and political elite, will have grave social and economic consequences well beyond the absolute number of deaths. These countries can also expect hundreds of thousands of pediatric AIDS cases, due to mother-to-fetus or infant transmission, by the late 1990s. The resulting increase in child mortality due to AIDS will more than offset any expected reduction achieved by ongoing child survival programs.

Coinfection with more than one disease agent is common in Sub-Saharan Africa, and researchers have been investigating potential interactions between HIV infection and other severe tropical disease agents (Smith *et al.*, 1988). Tuberculosis is the main endemic disease in tropical areas for which specific interaction with HIV infection has been clearly established. In Sub-Saharan African countries, more than half of adults have latent tuberculosis, which may be activated as a result of the immunosuppression caused by HIV. Tuberculosis will be an increasing public health problem in areas where the prevalence of HIV is also high. Surveillance data as of the late 1980s showed increasing numbers of tuberculosis patients in Burundi and Tanzania (Slutkin *et al.*, 1988; Standaert *et al.*, 1989), and similar increases had probably occurred in all Sub-Saharan African countries.

Beyond the 1990s, if HIV infections continue to increase in urban areas and to spread extensively in rural areas, a negative population growth rate might be possible. The long-term demographic impact of AIDS in central Africa cannot be projected with any assurance until it can be determined whether or not such a spread of HIV will occur.

AIDS will continue to be a global public health problem of immense magnitude, especially in Sub-Saharan Africa. The greatest public health challenge facing AIDS prevention programs is to reduce HIV transmission to the maximum extent possible. In the absence of vaccines or effective treatments, national AIDS programs will be unable to prevent the several million AIDS cases expected throughout the world among the eight million or more persons infected with HIV during the 1980s. At least three or four million of these cases will be in Sub-Saharan Africa. Beyond the year 2000, the eventual endemic level of HIV/AIDS will be a measure of both the commitment and the effectiveness of the AIDS prevention programs now being developed.

References

Centers for Disease Control. (1982). Update on acquired immunodeficiency syndrome (AIDS)—United States. *Morbidity and Mortality Weekly Report*, 31, 507–514.

———. (1985). Revision of the case definition of acquired immunodeficiency syndrome for national reporting—United States. *Morbidity and Mortality Weekly Report*, 34, 373–375.

———. (1987). Revision of the CDC surveillance definition for acquired immunodeficiency syndrome. *Morbidity and Mortality Weekly Report*, 36 (supplement), 1s.

Chin, J. (forthcoming). Global estimates of AIDS cases and HIV infections—1990. *AIDS*.

Chin, J. and Mann, J. M. (1988). Global patterns and prevalence of AIDS and HIV infection. *AIDS*, 2 (supplement 1), S247–S252.

———. (1989). Global surveillance and forecasting of AIDS. *Bulletin of the World Health Organization*, 67, 1–7.

Chin, J., Lwanga, S., and Mann, J. M. (1989). The global epidemiology and projected short-term demographic impact of AIDS. *Population Bulletin*, 27, 54–68.

Dondero, T. J., St. Louis, M., Anderson, J., Peterson, L., and Pappaioanou, M. (1989). Evaluation of the estimated number of HIV infections using a spreadsheet model and empirical data. Fifth International Conference on AIDS, Montreal, June 1989, abstract M.A.O. 4, 45.

Kanki, P. J., M'Boup, S., Ricard, D., Barin, F., Denis, F., Boye, C., Sangare, L., Travers, K., Albaum, M., Marlink, R., Romet-Lemonne, J., and Essex, M. (1987). Human T-lymphotropic virus type 4 and the human immunodeficiency virus in West Africa. *Science*, 236, 827–831.

Kreiss, J. K., Koech, D., Plummer, F. A., Holmes, K. K., Lightfoote, M., Piot, P., Ronald, A. R., Ndinya-Achola, J. O., D'Costa, L. J., Roberts, P., Ngugi, E. N., and Quinn, T. C. (1986). AIDS virus infection in Nairobi prostitutes. *New England Journal of Medicine*, 314, 414–418.

Liomba, N. G., Guertler, L., Eberle, J., Ntaba, H. M., Deinhardt, F., and Rehle, T. (1989). Comparison of the age distribution of anti-HIV-1 and anti-HBc in an urban population from Malawi. Fifth International Conference on AIDS, Montreal, abstract W.G.O.29, 986.

Lyons, S. F., McGillivray, G., Schaub, B. D., Smith, A. N., and Clausen, L. (1989). AIDS caused by HIV-2 in southern Africa. Fifth International Conference on AIDS, Montreal, abstract M.A.P.83, 91.

Mann, J. M. (1989). *Global AIDS into the 1990s*. WHO/GPA/DIR/89.2. Geneva: World Health Organization.

Mann, J. M., Chin, J., Piot, P., and Quinn, T. (1988). The international epidemiology of AIDS. *Scientific American*, 259, 82–89.

Moss, A. R. and Bacchetti, P. (1989). Natural history of HIV infection. *AIDS*, 3, 55–61.

Ndumu, J. R., Kengeya-Kayondo, J. F., Amaana, A., and Naamara, W. (1989). Anti-HIV seroprevalence in adult rural populations of Uganda and its implications for preventive strategies. Fifth International Conference on AIDS, Montreal, abstract T.A.P.11, 100.

Nzilambi, N., DeCock, K. M., Forthal, D. N., Francis, H., Ryder, R. W., Malebe, I., Getchell, J., Laga, M., Piot, P., and McCormick, J. B. (1988). The prevalence of infection with human immunodeficiency virus over a 10-year period in rural Zaire. *New England Journal of Medicine*, 318, 276–279.

Piot, P., Plummer, F. A., Mhalu, F. S., Lamboray, J., Chin, J., and Mann, J. M. (1988). AIDS: an international perspective. *Science*, 239, 573–579.

Rwandan HIV Seroprevalence Study Group. (1989). National community-based serological survey of HIV-1 and other human retrovirus infections in a central African country. *Lancet* 1, 941–943.

Simonsen, J. N., Cameron, D. W., Gakinya, M. N., Ndinya-Achola, J. O., D'Costa, L. J., Karasira, P., Cheang, M., Ronald, A. R., Piot, P., and Plummer, F. A. (1988). Human immunodeficiency virus infection among men with sexually transmitted diseases. *New England Journal of Medicine*, 319, 274–278.

Slutkin, G., Leowski, J., and Mann, J. M. (1988). Tuberculosis and AIDS. The effects of the AIDS epidemic on the tuberculosis programmes. *Bulletin of the International Union for Tuberculosis and Lung Diseases*, 63, 21–24.

Smith, P. G., Morrow, R. H., and Chin, J. (1988). Investigating interactions between HIV infection and tropical disease. *International Journal of Epidemiology*, 17, 705–707.

Soms, P., Georges, A. J., Siopathis, R. M., Vohito, J. A., Bouquety, J. C., and Vohito, M. D. (1989). Les aspects épidémiologiques des affections liées aux VIH1 et 2 en République Centrafricaine. Fifth International Conference on AIDS, Montreal, abstract W.G.O.28, 986.

Standaert, B., Niragira, F., Kadende, P., and Piot, P. (1989). The association of tuberculosis and HIV infection in Burundi. *AIDS Research and Human Retroviruses*, 5, 247–251.

Way, P. (1989). United States Bureau of the Census, Center for International Research, AIDS/HIV statistics database.

World Health Organization. (1985). Workshop on acquired immunodeficiency syndrome in central Africa, Bangui, Central African Republic, October.

———. (1986). Acquired immunodeficiency syndrome

WHO/CDC case definition for AIDS. *Weekly Epidemiological Record*, 10, 69–70.

———. (1988a). Acquired immunodeficiency syndrome (AIDS), 1987 revision of CDC/WHO case definition for AIDS. *Weekly Epidemiological Record*, 63, 1–7.

———. (1988b). Consultation on information support for the AIDS surveillance system, Tatry-Poprad/Strbske Pleso, Czechoslovakia, 17–19 February.

———. (1989). Surveillance, Forecasting, and Impact Assessment Unit. Unpublished data.

———. (1990). Surveillance, Forecasting, and Impact Assessment Unit. Unpublished data.

Chapter 14

AIDS and Its Demographic Impact

Roy M. Anderson

A growing body of evidence suggests that the human immunodeficiency virus type 1 (HIV-1) is spreading rapidly among heterosexuals in urban communities in Sub-Saharan Africa and South America (figure 14-1) (Quinn *et al.*, 1986; Piot and Carael, 1988; Piot *et al.*, 1988). As of September 1990, 157 countries had reported at least one case of the acquired immunodeficiency syndrome (AIDS) induced by infection with HIV-1 (table 14-1). The rapid spread of the infection has stimulated much discussion of the degree to which the pandemic of AIDS will influence population growth and age structure in developing countries over the coming decades.

Assessing this problem precisely in a defined country is difficult at present because our understanding of the epidemiology of the infection (HIV-1) and the disease (AIDS) is limited. The need for assessment, however, is urgent in order to facilitate the long-term planning of governments and international aid agencies. In this chapter a brief review is presented of recent work on the demographic impact of AIDS in Sub-Saharan Africa (Anderson *et al.*, 1988; May *et al.*, 1988). This research is based on simple mathematical models that combine the demography of populations that have positive net growth rates with the known epidemiological characteristics of the heterosexual transmission of HIV-1 and with the available data on key epidemiological processes. Studying these simple models is a preliminary step toward exploring much more complicated and realistic models when data accumulate. Their investigation also helps to focus attention on areas in which our understanding of the epidemiology of infection and disease is inadequate at present.

Demography

The key demographic parameters, such as crude birth, death, and population growth rates, for a series of

African countries in which HIV-1 is spreading rapidly are recorded in table 14-1. For comparison, data for the United Kingdom are also presented. The populations of Sub-Saharan countries are characterized by high population growth rates, low life expectancies, high dependency ratios (defined as the number of children less than 15 years old and the number of elderly 65 years or older divided by the number of adults 15 to 64 years of age) and low proportions living in urban areas (table 14-1).

Epidemiology of HIV-1

Many uncertainties surround the key epidemiological processes that determine the rate of spread of HIV-1 and the incidence of AIDS. These processes include the following: the fraction of persons infected who will develop AIDS and on what time scale; the likelihood of vertical transmission from infected mother to child in utero, during childbirth, and through breast-feeding; the importance of cofactors such as the presence or absence of other genital infections (chancroid, gonorrhea, etc.) in promoting transmission between heterosexuals; the degree to which the infectiousness of patients changes throughout the long and variable incubation period of AIDS; and the rates at which sexual partners change and the types of sexual behavior that occur in defined communities (Quinn *et al.*, 1986; May and Anderson, 1987; Piot and Carael, 1988; Piot *et al.*, 1988; Anderson *et al.*, 1988).

The mean incubation period of AIDS, estimated from transfusion-associated cases in the United States, is 8–10 years (Medley *et al.*, 1987), although this is expected to rise as the cohorts of infected persons are studied for longer periods. However, the mean may be somewhat less for persons in developing countries, who are typically exposed more frequently to a larger

Table 14-1. Demographic Statistics for Selected Sub-Saharan African Countries and the United Kingdom

Country	Dependency ratio[a]	Crude rates[b]		Instantaneous rates[c]			Population characteristics				
		Birth	Death	Birth	Death	Growth	Mid-year size, 1987 (thousands)	Percentage urban	Median age (in years)	Density (km^{-2})	Persons per physician (1980)
The Gambia	0.84	48.4	29.0	0.047	0.028	0.0192	670	18.2	18.8	59.0	n.a.
Kenya	1.19	55.1	14.0	0.054	0.014	0.040	22,397	15.5	14.1	38.0	7,890
Ruwanda	1.02	51.0	22.0	0.050	0.022	0.028	6,488	6.2	15.9	246.0	31,510
Uganda	1.02	50.3	16.8	0.049	0.017	0.033	16,018	9.5	15.9	68.0	26,810
United Kingdom	0.53	12.9	11.4	0.013	0.011	0.001	56,160	91.5	35.4	230.0	620
Zaire	0.93	44.8	14.5	0.044	0.014	0.029	31,760	36.6	17.3	13.6	14,780

n.a. Not available.

a. The dependency ratio is the number of persons less than 15 years old plus the number older than 64 divided by the number between the ages of 15 and 64.

b. Rates are births or deaths per 1,000 persons.

c. The instantaneous rates are as follows: birth, γ for yr^{-1}; death, μ for yr^{-1}; growth, r for yr^{-1}.

215

Figure 14-1. Proportion of Persons in At-Risk Groups Who Have Antibodies to the HIV-1 Antigens, Selected Countries of Sub-Saharan Africa, 1980–87

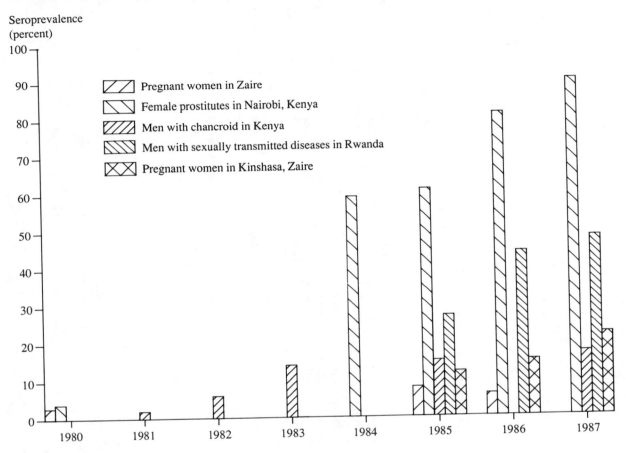

Source: Piot *et al*. (1988).

range of infectious agents than persons in the developed world.

The fraction of persons infected who will eventually develop AIDS is unknown at present, but studies of infected male homosexuals and intravenous (IV) drug abusers in North America and Europe suggest that it is likely to be high (Anderson, 1989). Disease progression in African heterosexuals appears to occur at rates of between 2 and 7 percent per year (Mann *et al.*, 1986). Limited studies in North America, Europe, and Africa suggest that between 30 and 65 percent of babies born to HIV-seropositive mothers develop the infection (Piot *et al.*, 1988). In utero infection appears to be the dominant mode of vertical transmission. The death rate among infected babies is very high (perhaps 20 times that among infants born to uninfected mothers

in the months immediately after birth). Data on the transmission probability (β) (either from men to women or the reverse) are very limited. Current evidence suggests values in the range of 0.05–0.1 per partner for female to male transmission provided cofactors (genital ulcers) are present (Piot *et al.*, 1988).

Data on rates of sexual partner change are extremely limited. Crude estimates of the parameter combination characterizing the rate of transmission, βc, where β is the transmission probability and c is the effective average rate of partner change, can be derived from the rate of increase, Λ, in the infected (that is, seropositive) population, or the incidence of AIDS, in the early stages of the epidemic (Anderson *et al.*, 1988). In this case c is not simply the mean number; it is close to the mean (m) plus the variance to mean ratio (σ^2/m) of the relevant distribution of partner change (May and Anderson, 1987; Anderson *et al.*, 1986). Some of the available data on the rise in seropositivity in defined populations in certain African countries are recorded in figure 14-1. Estimates of the time needed to double the incidence range from one to a few years in urban populations or high-risk groups (such as prostitutes or truck drivers). The spread of infection is especially fast in men and women who have multiple sexual partners, have a high rate of infection with other sexually transmitted diseases (such as chancroid), or are pros-

titutes (Quinn *et al.*, 1986). Rates of spread appear to be slower in rural than in urban areas. The observed 1:1 ratio of cases of infection (and disease) in heterosexual men and women in Africa suggests that the parameter combination $\beta_1 c_1$ that characterizes transmission from female to male and $\beta_2 c_2$ from male to female are of approximately equal magnitude.

Demographic Impact

Simple age-structured mathematical models that combine demography and epidemiology enable a crude

Figure 14-2. Predicted Population Growth in the Presence and the Absence of HIV-1 Infection

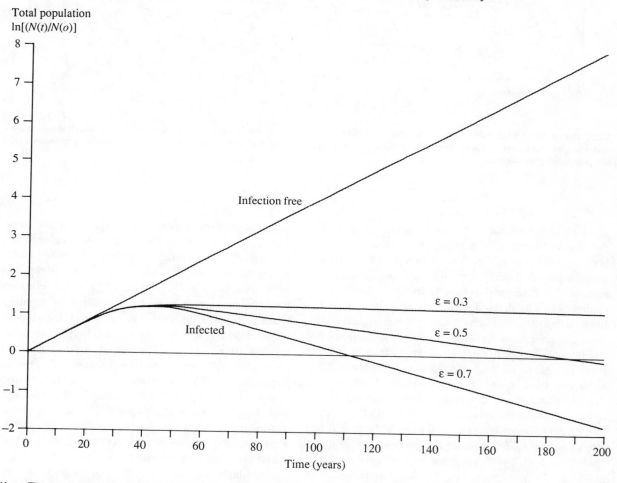

Note: The population trajectories through time are recorded as $\ln[(N(t)/N(o)]$, where $N(t)$ is population size at time t and $N(o)$ is population size at time $t = o$, as predicted by the delayed recruitment demographic model defined in Anderson *et al.* (forthcoming) and May *et al.* (forthcoming). The top curve is for an uninfected population. For the lower three trajectories, ε, the fraction of healthy babies born to infected mothers, is set at 0.3, 0.5, or 0.7 (from top to bottom); r, the population growth rate, $= 0.04yr^{-1}$, μ, the death rate of persons not infected, $= 0.019yr^{-1}$, D, the incubation period, $= 8$ years, and $\wedge$, the rate of infection in the early stage of the epidemic, $= 0.233yr^{-1}$. (See the text for a more detailed discussion.) Note that for small ε the infection is predicted to change population growth rates from positive to negative values.

Figure 14-3. Time Elapsed for Growth Rates to Change from Positive to Negative in the Presence of HIV-1 Infection

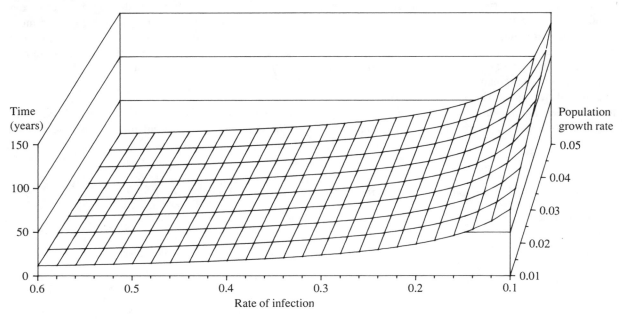

Note: The predicted relationship between the time that elapses, t_c, between the introduction of HIV-1 and the point at which the population ceases to grow exponentially is expressed as a function of the rate of infection in the early stages of the epidemic, Λ, and the population's pristine population growth rate, r.

assessment to be made of the likely impact of AIDS on the size and structure of a population as the infection spreads (May *et al.*, 1988; Anderson *et al.*, 1988). This exploration of model properties and predictions is tentative because the data base from which parameter estimates can be derived is limited. A crude guide to the possible ranges of certain key epidemiological and demographic parameters is as follows: the fraction of healthy babies born to infected mothers ε, 0.3–0.7; the mean incubation (that is, infectious) period of AIDS, D, 8–20 yrs; fraction of the persons infected who will develop AIDS, f, 0.5–1.0; human population growth rate in the absence of the infection, r, 0.01–0.04 yr^{-1}; death rate of persons not infected μ, 0.019–0.021 yr^{-1}; the rate of spread of infection in the early stages of the epidemic, Λ, 0.15–0.5 yr^{-1}; maturation delay of humans, τ, 15 yrs; birth rate of the population, γ, 0.02–0.06 yr^{-1}.

Analyses of these simple models reveal that for large areas of these parameter ranges the disease is predicted to be capable of changing positive population growth rates to negative ones within a few to many decades (Anderson *et al.*, 1988; May *et al.*, 1988). The

infection will only persist and spread if its basic reproductive rate, R_0, is greater than or equal to unity in value. R_0 is the average number of secondary cases generated by one primary case in a susceptible population ($R_0 = \beta c D$). Provided $R_0 > 1$, the infection will change growth rates from positive to negative when $\Lambda/\beta c > r/\theta$, where θ is the extra mortality linked to infection arising from vertical and horizontal transmission ($\theta = 1/D + \gamma[1 - \varepsilon]$). If $\Lambda/\beta c < r/\theta$, the population will continue to grow exponentially, but at a reduced rate, if $R_0 > 1$. In the former case the time that elapses, t_c, between the introduction of the infection and the point when the population ceases to grow exponentially and starts to decline in size is given very approximately by $t_c \sim \ln(1/\Delta)/(\Lambda - r)$, where Δ is the initial prevalence of infection.

An illustration of the potential impact of the infection and disease on population growth through time is displayed in figure 14-2. In this example, prior to the introduction of HIV-1, the population growth rate was 4 percent per year, with a life expectancy of 52 years. The incubation period of the disease was 8 years, the fraction of healthy babies born to infected mothers, ε, varied between 0.3 and 0.7, the fraction infected who developed AIDS, *f*, was 1.0, and the rate of spread of the infection in the early stages of the epidemic, Λ, was 0.233 yr^{-1}. The approximate time it would take for the population growth rates to change from positive to negative values, t_c, as a function of the rate of spread of infection, Λ, and the pristine population growth rate, *r*, is presented in figure 14-3.

The models from which these predictions are derived can also be used to assess how the dependency ratio of an infected population changes as the infection spreads (the ratio is defined as the number of children less than 15 years of age plus the number of elderly more than 64 years of age divided by the number of adults 15–65 years of age). The models suggest that the infection may induce a small but beneficial change in the ratio caused by the counteracting forces of adult deaths due to horizontal transmission and a reduction in the effective birth rate due to vertical transmission (Anderson *et al.*, 1988). Figure 14-4 displays proportional age distributions of a population prior to the introduction of HIV-1 and after the infection has spread

Figure 14-4. Proportional Age Distribution in the Presence and the Absence of HIV-1 Infection

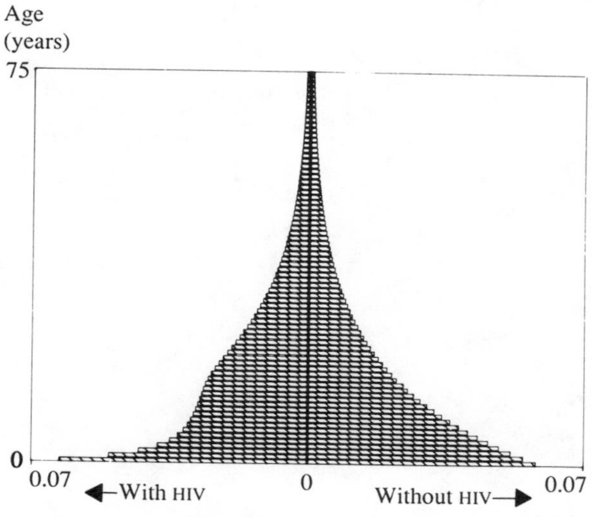

Note: In the age-structured model, the growth rate, *r*, is set at 4 percent and life expectancy at 52 years in the absence of HIV. The incubation (that is, infectious) period is set at 15 years and the fraction of healthy babies born to infected mothers, ε, at 0.3. The rate of infection in the early stages of the epidemic, Λ, is set at 0.233yr^{-1}. The dependency ratio in the infected population is less than that in the uninfected one.

Source: Anderson *et al.* (1988); May *et al.* (forthcoming).

(the asymptotic age distribution). The result of the epidemic is a small but beneficial change in the ratio.

Discussion

Analyses of simple models produce three important predictions. First, for plausible ranges of parameter values the disease AIDS is predicted to be able to reverse the sign of population growth rates. Second, the time scale of this reversal is predicted to be long, on the order of many decades for low to moderate rates of infection. Third, whether or not AIDS will decrease or increase dependency ratios depends critically on the values of the major demographic and epidemiological parameters prevailing in a community. For the plausible range of values, the models suggest little change or a small beneficial change.

The simplicity of the models that produce these predictions and the scarcity of quantitative data argue against accepting the conclusions uncritically. For precise predictive work, models must be more complex and realistic. Specifically, they should incorporate assumptions about heterogeneity in sexual activity, the importance of "who mixes with whom," the role of cofactors in transmission, the significance of prostitutes in transmission, and the difference between urban and rural areas, among others. Moreover, the data base must become much more extensive. The need clearly exists for longitudinal cohort studies of seroprevalence (stratified by, for example, age, sex, and socioeconomic status), surveys of sexual partner change rates, and work on the incubation and infectious periods and the fraction of persons infected who will eventually develop AIDS within afflicted communities in Sub-Saharan Africa. While data slowly accumulate, however, the depressing patterns predicted by very simple models that combine demographic and epidemiological processes help to focus attention on the urgent need to promote vigorously the educational campaigns that aim to change sexual behavior. This method of controlling the spread of HIV is the only option available at present and for the foreseeable future.

Acknowledgments

I thank the Overseas Development Agency and Panos for their financial support and Robert May and Angela McLean for many helpful discussions.

References

Anderson, R. M. (1989). Mathematical and statistical studies of the epidemiology of HIV. *Aids*, 3, 333–346.

220   *Roy M. Anderson*

Anderson, R. M., Medley, G. F., May, R. M., and Johnson, A. M. (1986). A preliminary study of the transmission dynamics of the human immunodeficiency virus (HIV), the causative agents of AIDS. IMA *Journal of Mathematics Applied in Medicine and Biology*, 3, 229–263.

Anderson, R. M., May, R. M., and McLean, A. R.)1099). Possible demographic consequences of AIDS in developing countries. *Nature, 332, 191–290.*

Mann, J. M., Bila, K., Colebunders, R. L., Kalenba, K., Khonde, N., Bosenge, N., Nzilambi, N., Malonga, M., Jansegers, L., Francis, H., McCormick, J. B., Piot, P., Quinn, T. C., and Curran, J. W. (1986). Natural history of human immunodeficiency virus infection in Zaire. *Lancet*, 2, 707–709.

May, R. M. and Anderson, R. M. (1987). Transmission dynamics of HIV infection. *Nature*, 326, 137–142.

May, R. M., Anderson, R. M., and McLean, A. R. (1988). Possible demographic consequences of HIV/AIDS epidemics. 2: assuming HIV infection does not necessarily lead to AIDS. *Lecture Notes in Biomathematics*, 81, 220–248.

Medley, G. F., Anderson, R. M., Cox, D. R., and Billard, L. (1987). Incubation period of AIDS in patients infected via blood transfusion. *Nature*, 328, 719–721.

Piot, P. and Carael, M. (1988). Epidemiological and sociological aspects of HIV-infection in developing countries. *British Medical Bulletin*, 44.

Piot, P., Plummer, F. A., Mhalu, F. S., Lamboray, J. L., Chin, J., and Mann, J. M. (1988). AIDS: an international perspective. *Science*, 239, 573–579.

Quinn, T. C., Mann, J. M., Curran, J. W., and Piot, P. (1986). AIDS in Africa: an epidemiologic paradigm. *Science*, 234, 955–963.

Chapter 15

Cancer and Cardiovascular Diseases

Michael S. R. Hutt

During the first fifty years of this century when the whole of Sub-Saharan Africa, with the exception of Ethiopia, was in some form of colonial relationship with one of the European nations, few medical services were available to the African populations. For this reason those services concentrated on the major epidemic diseases of bacterial, viral, or parasitic origin, many of which remain problems and are described elsewhere in this book. Textbooks written during this period suggest that tropical medicine is synonymous with specific infectious and parasitic diseases and with nutritional deficiencies.

During the second half of the century several developments emphasized that tropical medicine, as just defined, is only a part, albeit a large part, of medicine in the tropics. As the postwar wind of change swept the continent toward independence, university medical schools were established in several countries, bringing an increase in medical staff and specialization in clinical, laboratory, and community-based disciplines. This was followed by an overall improvement in doctor to patient ratios and a gradual increase in the number of African doctors. During this period basic demographic data were collected or improved, including, in some areas, censuses of national and district populations. At the same time epidemiological techniques, which had been used almost exclusively in the field of infectious diseases, were being applied to the problems of cancer and heart disease and producing new insights into their etiology.

In Sub-Saharan Africa the situation in the 1950s and 1960s was particularly favorable for developing epidemiological studies of noninfectious diseases. In localized areas, particularly around the new medical schools, there was a concentration of skilled personnel and of diagnostic facilities. There was also a comparatively static population whose way of life had not altered greatly despite increasing development and urbanization. That population was increasingly using the facilities that modern medicine was offering. As the patterns of noninfectious diseases became apparent in these areas, studies were instituted in rural areas by concentrating on specific problems that were amenable to diagnosis by the use of postal histopathology services and specific clinical surveys.

Taylor (1982) diagrams the patterns of mortality in a poor developing country and a rich Westernized country (see figure 15-1). Although reasonably accurate, this generalization hides important differences in disease patterns between rich and poor countries and between or within the latter. Moreover, it does not distinguish between mortality in different age groups or give any indication of the impact of the disease pattern on the health services. In the absence of any formal systems of disease notification or death certification, it is necessary to rely on hospital-based returns for estimates of disease frequency and mortality. Many factors influence the reasons patients are admitted to the hospital, and these vary in different geographic and sociocultural situations. Similar factors influence whether patients die in the hospital or at home and whether a necropsy is performed. However, useful information can be obtained from hospital returns. The data in table 15-1 are derived from the *1980 Annual Report* of Zambia's Ministry of Health, which analyzes admission diagnoses for all government, mission, and mine hospitals and the hospital deaths in children from 1 to 14 years of age and in adults over 14 years. Despite the difficulties in assessing their accuracy, such figures do give an idea of the importance or otherwise of diseases of the cardiovascular system and of neoplastic disease. In children under the age of 14 years, malaria and respiratory disease (mostly various forms of pneumo-

Figure 15-1. Distribution of Causes of Death in Developing and Industrial Countries

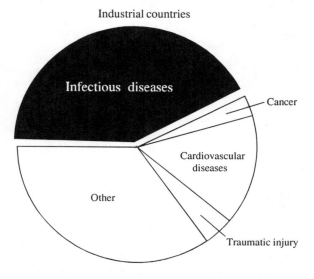

Industrial countries

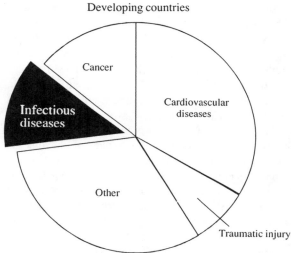

Developing countries

Source: Taylor (1982).

nia) account for over 38 percent of all admissions and 19 percent of all hospital deaths. As might be expected, cardiac and neoplastic diseases are not important, though even at this age cardiac disease accounts for 2 percent of hospital deaths. In adults, by contrast, cardiac disease and tumors account for 7 percent of all admissions and 27 percent of hospital deaths, significantly more than malaria and respiratory disease. In older age groups both cancer and heart disease are likely to account for a great proportion of both admissions and deaths.

Cancer in Sub-Saharan Africa

During the early part of this century many doctors working in Africa held the view that cancer was rare in African populations. John Gunther, in his book *Inside Africa*, wrote, "Africa has malaria, leprosy, syphilis, and yaws; cancer is however almost unknown among Africans." Some clinicians, such as Sir Albert Cook who built the first hospital for African patients in Kampala, Uganda, in 1897, recognized that malignant disease was not uncommon. An analysis of the records of his hospital, Mengo, showed that cancer as a percentage of all admissions was similar over the decades from 1897 to 1946. Moreover, the relative frequency of specific tumors was different from that found in Europe and did not change during the period of observation (Davies *et al.*, 1964).

In 1934, Smith and Elmes (1934) reported the first large series of histologically confirmed malignant tumors in Nigerians. Among their 500 cases were several with Kaposi's sarcoma and some with what we now recognize as Burkitt's lymphoma. The following year Vint (1935) analyzed a similar series of cancer patients diagnosed in the central laboratories in Nairobi, Kenya. He also drew attention to the differences in these cancer patterns from those seen in Europe. It was not until after World War II that clinicopathological and epidemiological studies in the field of cancer were formally established in several countries of Africa. The first two cancer registries were set up in Johannesburg, South Africa (Higginson and Oettlé, 1960), and in Kyadondo County near Kampala, Uganda (Davies *et al.*, 1965), in the early 1950s. Other registries were later established in Ibadan, Nigeria (Edington and MacLean, 1965), Lourenço Marques, Mozambique (Prates and Torres, 1965), and Bulawayo, Zimbabwe (Doll *et al.*, 1970). Concurrent with these efforts to establish age-standardized incidence rates in select populations, the extension of histopathological diagnostic services to the smaller district hospitals showed that patterns of cancer varied both within and between the countries of the region (Hutt and Burkitt, 1965; Cook and Burkitt, 1971). This led to setting up cancer registries in some small district hospitals (Williams, 1986) and to adding regional and district data on the relative frequencies of all or specific tumors throughout the country (Cook and Burkitt, 1971).

The first conference on cancer in Africa was held in Nairobi, Kenya, in 1967 (Clifford *et al.*, 1968). By that time the importance of epidemiological studies in Africa had been widely recognized from observations

Table 15-1. Admissions and Deaths in All Government, Mission, and Mine Hospitals in Zambia, by Age, 1980

Admissions and deaths	Age 1–14		Age 14 and older	
	Number	*Percent*	*Number*	*Percent*
Admissions				
Infectious and parasitic diseases	43,115		34,307	
Other diseases	59,660		94,853	
Total	102,775		129,213	
Malaria	22,643	22.03	20,617	15.95
Bilharziasis	934	0.02	1,451	1.12
Respiratory	16,785	16.33	16,595	12.64
Cardiac	664	0.62	5,476	4.23
Neoplastic	369	0.36	3,616	2.79
Deaths				
Infectious and parasitic diseases	1,715		997	
Other diseases	3,947		3,091	
Total	5,662		3,998	
Malaria	381	6.72	174	4.52
Bilharziasis	1	0.02	8	0.19
Respiratory	697	12.31	437	10.68
Cardiac	117	2.06	594	14.50
Neoplastic	32	0.56	514	12.57

Notes: These figures exclude accidents and trauma, obstetrics, and disorders of pregnancy. Cardiac includes diseases of the heart but not of the blood vessels. Neoplastic includes some benign and unspecified neoplasms.
Source: Extracted from Zambia (1984).

of the distribution of Burkitt's lymphoma and its implications for a viral etiology.

Detailed studies on the pathology and epidemiology of all tumors (over 10,000) in Uganda (Templeton and Hutt, 1973) added to the information being collected throughout Africa and in other developing countries throughout the world. Specific etiologic studies, such as the role of the Epstein-Barr virus in Burkitt's lymphoma in the West Nile region of Uganda, were supported by the International Agency for Cancer Research (Geser *et al.*, 1982), which also collected and collated information on the occurrence of cancer in developing countries throughout the world (Parkin, 1986).

The Frequency and Distribution of Cancer in Sub-Saharan Africa

DATA SOURCES AND QUALITY. Reliable mortality rates are not available from any part of Sub-Saharan Africa, and relying on hospital death rates, even those supported by a good necropsy rate, is problematical. Nevertheless, some useful information has been ob-

tained where satisfactory circumstances combine, as in Mulago Hospital, Kampala, from 1968 to 1971. During this period 4,271 necropsies were performed, a higher rate than in most hospitals in the United Kingdom today. Of the 373 men of 60 years or more who were examined, 19.3 percent had died of cancer, of whom 15.7 percent had hepatocellular carcinoma. In a matched group of men who were 30 years younger at the time of their death, 11.7 percent had died of cancer, of whom 24 percent had liver cancer (Drury, 1972). Mortality figures such as these inevitably tend to underestimate deaths from the more slowly growing tumors because persons with such tumors usually die at home.

POPULATION-BASED CANCER REGISTRIES. Only a few registries have been established in the region to obtain age-standardized incidence rates. They require a well-defined population with an accurate census of all individuals. Medical facilities must be of high quality and quantity and must be well used by the population. Case-finding should be thorough and involve all clinical facilities in the geographic area, and close links should exist among the cancer registrar, clinicians, pathologists, and epidemiologists. These circumstances existed in a few places in the 1960s, and although some underdiagnosis and misdiagnosis must have occurred, they provide a good basis for interpreting measures of cancer frequency, such as relative frequencies (Parkin, 1986).

Registration of cancer frequency in different regions and districts of a country may be done by the central registry, usually based in the department of pathology of the medical school or hospital in the capital city, or by individual hospitals in rural areas (Williams, 1986). Such data can be improved by organizing regular returns of cancer cases by postal questionnaires (Cook and Burkitt, 1971). Although several forms of bias occur in such data (such as a tendency to overestimate the frequency of superficial—easily biopsied—tumors as opposed to deep ones [Burkitt *et al.*, 1968]), these tend to operate in a similar way in all district hospitals. Marked differences in the relative frequency of specific common tumors usually represent a true difference in incidence (see relative frequencies, below). Interpretation of information from these sources can be enhanced by close contact among persons working in the central registry, the histopathology department, and the district hospitals, particularly when this contact is maintained for a long period of time.

STUDIES ON RELATIVE FREQUENCIES. For many countries relative frequencies are used to indicate the cancer pattern of specific tumors and to determine different cancer patterns within a country or region. The relative frequency of selected tumors in some of the major tribal groups in Uganda is shown in table 15-2 (Templeton and Hutt, 1973). Each of the tribes, at that time, lived in or came from a specific area of the country so that their environments were geographically as well as socioculturally different. Of particular interest is the very low frequency of Burkitt's lymphoma in the Kiga of the mountainous southwest as compared with the high frequency in the Lugbara of the northwest; this observation has stood the test of time. The value of such studies will be apparent in the consideration of specific tumors.

AGE-STANDARDIZED INCIDENCE RATES. All-sites age-standardized rates derived from several cancer registries in Sub-Saharan Africa show the characteristic rise in cancer with age up to 50 or 60 years. This is similar to, but at a lower level than, that of developed countries. In older age groups the incidence curves flatten or even fall, unlike the continuously rising rates seen in Europe or North America (figure 15-2); this feature is mainly due to the reluctance of older people, particularly women, to use hospital facilities or to recognize symptoms and signs of chronic disease. Most developing countries in Africa and elsewhere have lower all-sites incidence rates than countries in Europe or North America (table 15-3). This probably reflects a truly lower overall incidence of cancer, but underdiagnosis and underregistration must play a significant part. The all-sites incidence rates from Bulawayo, Zimbabwe, provide an exception to the above. This can be explained by the high rates of liver, bladder, and esophageal carcinoma (African tumors) and also the relatively high rate of lung cancer (a Western tumor). Such rates do not, however, necessarily reflect rates throughout the country, particularly in some rural areas.

Table 15-2. Relative Frequencies of Selected Tumors in Major Tribes in Uganda, by Gender

Tumor	All tribes	Ganda	Kiga	Toro	Lugbara	Teso	Rwanda/Rundi
Males							
Liver	11.0	6.2	7.7	7.8	14.8	8.1	16.3
Penis	12.0	12.0	4.2	31.2	3.0	25.1	10.7
Kaposi	8.0	6.9	12.5	12.8	14.8	3.8	5.9
Burkitt	5.0	1.4	0.0	0.7	14.8	8.9	2.8
Females							
Cervix	22.3	27.3	14.8	24.3	10.1	20.9	17.5
Skin	9.0	2.2	31.7	4.3	18.2	6.2	15.6
Burkitt	3.2	1.1	0.5	0.9	13.1	4.4	2.5

Note: Each tribe except Rwanda/Rundi lives in a different region of Uganda. Histopathology diagnostic services are freely available to all hospitals in every region.

Source: Templeton and Hutt (1973).

Figure 15-2. Incidence Rates of Cancer in Ibadan, Nigeria, and the United States, by Gender and Age

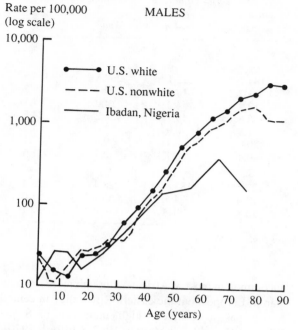

Rate per 100,000 (log scale) — MALES

— U.S. white
--- U.S. nonwhite
— Ibadan, Nigeria

Age (years)

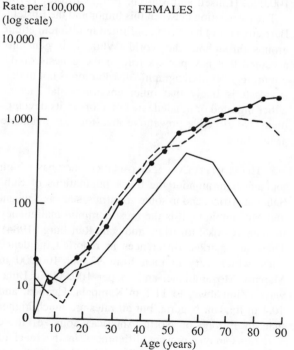

Rate per 100,000 (log scale) — FEMALES

Age (years)

Source: Edington and MacLean (1965).

DISTRIBUTION OF SPECIFIC CANCERS IN SUB-SAHARAN AFRICA. There is a group of tumors whose incidence rates are significantly lower throughout the region than in Europe or North America. These include carcinoma of the large bowel and rectum and pancreas in both sexes, the prostate in men, and breast and endometrium in women. With the exceptions of parts of Zimbabwe and South Africa, the incidence rates and frequency of lung cancer are still very low. Evidence suggests that the frequency of all these tumors is increasing, or will increase, as the urbanized and more affluent sections of the population adopt Western life-styles in relation to diet and cigarette smoking.

Throughout most of Sub-Saharan Africa carcinoma of the stomach is uncommon: the incidence rates are less than 5 per 100,000 compared with 20–30 per 100,000 in Europe. An exception to this is found in the highlands of Rwanda and in the region around Mount Kilimanjaro in Tanzania.

By contrast carcinoma of the cervix and the liver have high rates in all the populations that have been studied in the region, and overall they are the most important causes of mortality.

In certain regions carcinoma of the bladder and esophagus have a high incidence. Kaposi's sarcoma, Burkitt's lymphoma, nasopharyngeal carcinoma, and penile carcinoma are all relatively more common than in Europe or North America, but their distribution within the region is quite variable.

Specific Cancers in Africa

Those tumors that are of particular importance or interest to the region, either because of their high incidence or frequency, morbidity, or mortality or because of other unusual features, will be considered in more detail in this section.

CARCINOMA OF THE ESOPHAGUS. This tumor, which is associated with a high mortality rate, shows sharp gradients of frequency within the region, often over quite short distances, an increase in frequency over the past 50 years, and a spread from the southern regions of the continent to parts of central and East Africa (Cook, 1971). The first reports of high incidence came from Transkei in South Africa (Burrell, 1962), where the gradient of incidence ranges from 80 per 100,000 in south Transkei to 10 per 100,000 in the north (Rose and McGlashan, 1975). Esophageal carcinoma is also common in Natal, South Africa, and in Zimbabwe (63.8 per 100,000 in men) but is uncommon in Mozambique. High relative frequencies have been

Table 15-3. Standardized (Age-Adjusted) Incidence Rates for Cancer, Selected Countries, by Gender

Type of cancer	Bulawayo, Zimbabwe	Ibadan, Nigeria	Bombay, India	Miyagi, Japan	Oxford, United Kingdom	Detroit, United States	
						White	Black
Males							
All sites	345.9	79.5	141.0	184.7	222.1	267.5	318.5
Bladder	28.7	3.9	2.9	3.7	14.5	19.7	8.7
Esophagus	63.8	1.5	15.2	12.9	4.2	4.0	14.1
Large bowel	7.0	1.3	4.6	5.6	15.7	26.2	24.5
Liver	64.6	10.4	1.4	1.8	0.9	2.6	4.5
Lung	70.7	0.8	13.5	20.0	68.4	59.6	77.1
Penis	6.6	0.2	1.9	0.4	0.7	0.7	1.6
Females							
All sites	147.4	107.0	120.5	127.7	183.8	228.4	223.4
Breast	13.8	15.3	20.1	13.0	54.5	65.7	51.0
Cervix	28.4	21.6	23.2	13.8	11.4	14.0	32.1

Source: The rates were compiled by Segi (1977) from data in Waterhouse *et al.* (1976).

reported from parts of Zambia, Malawi, Tanzania, and several regions of Kenya, particularly the Nyanza district and the region around Kisumu by Lake Victoria (see figure 15-3) (Cook, 1971). By contrast, carcinoma of the esophagus is uncommon in northwestern and southwestern Uganda, in Zaire, and in West Africa. All high-incidence areas have a strong male predominance, which varies from 10:1 to 15:1, although in recent years the incidence is increasing in women in South Africa.

In Africa, and in other high-incidence areas, such as northern Iran and central China, specific dietary deficiencies appear to predispose populations to the effects of ingested carcinogens such as tobacco and alcohol. These include low intakes of vitamin C, riboflavin, and nicotinic acid and of the trace elements zinc, manganese, and molybdenum. In South Africa a high consumption of home-brewed spirits and pipe smoking are common in high-incidence areas. In East and central Africa the increasing incidence may be related to the use of maize for brewing local beers (Cook, 1971).

In the high-incidence areas carcinoma of the esophagus is an important cause of overall cancer mortality and throws a heavy strain on hospital resources to little effect. Dietary improvement and education on the use of alcohol and tobacco are the only approach in the light of present knowledge.

CARCINOMA OF THE NASOPHARYNX. This is an extremely rare tumor in Europe and North America; it is uncommon in most of Africa—although more frequent than in Europe—but the eastern Rift Valley in central Kenya has a relatively high incidence (7–8 per 100,000) (Linsell and Martyn, 1962; Clifford, 1970).

The association between this tumor and the Epstein-Barr virus (EBV) has been confirmed in different ethnic groups throughout the world. While it is generally accepted that EBV plays a role in the genesis of the tumor, its overall geographic distribution is not understood. It is likely that other environmental factors, either ingested or inhaled, are cofactors in its development. No effective preventive measures are available at this time.

HEPATOCELLULAR CARCINOMA (HCC). HCC has a high incidence throughout the black populations of Sub-Saharan Africa, and in some countries, such as Senegal and Mozambique, it is the most common malignancy in men (Cook-Mozaffari and van Rensburg, 1984). There are marked differences in reported incidence rates, which vary in men from 97 per 100,000 in Maputo, Mozambique, and 64 per 100,000 in Bulawayo, Zimbabwe, to 11.1 in Kampala, Uganda, and 10.4 in Ibadan, Nigeria, but all rates are much higher than in Europe or North America. Some of these variations may represent differences in the level of case finding or criteria for diagnosis. The tendency is for deep-seated tumors to be underrepresented in returns from developing countries (Burkitt *et al.*, 1968).

HCC is more common in men than in women, occurs

Figure 15-3. Estimated Age-Standardized Incidence Rates for Cancer of the Esophagus in Men in East and Central Africa

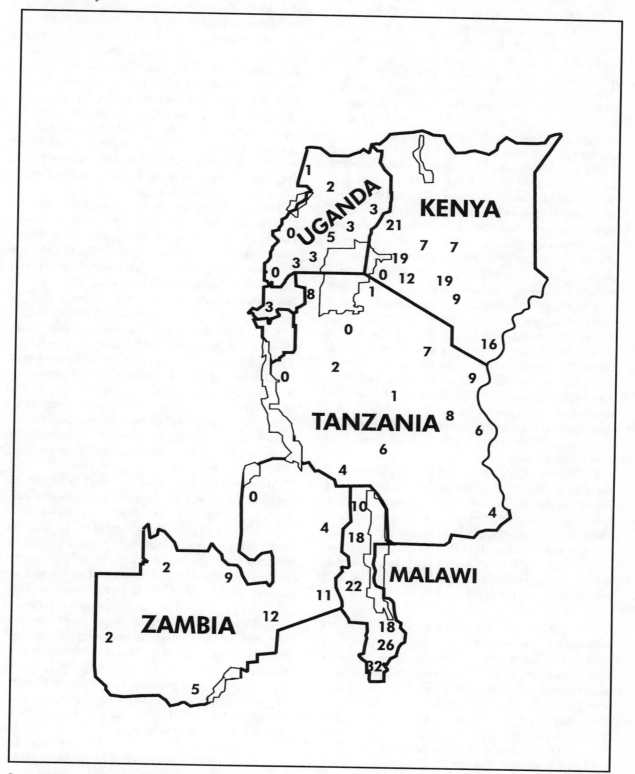

Source: Supplied by P. Cook-Mozaffari and D. P. Burkitt.

at younger ages in Africa than in the West, and is nearly always associated with a cirrhosis of the macronodular type. Urbanized South Africans have lower rates than their tribal counterparts in rural areas.

Throughout the world the prevalence of hepatitis B viral (HBV) carriers in the general population is higher where HCC is common than where it is rare. The HBSAg (hepatitis B surface antigen) carrier state in patients with HCC is 100 times higher than in matched controls. HBV infections precede the development of liver damage, and patients may pass through the sequence of chronic hepatitis→cirrhosis→HCC (Kew *et al.*, 1979). Individuals who are carriers of HBSAg followed for five years have over a hundredfold greater risk of developing HCC than non-carriers (Cook, 1988). Evidence that the virus plays a direct role in the development of the tumor comes from the finding that HBV-DNA is in tumor cells (Shafritz and Kew, 1981) and that a closely related DNA virus causes HCC in woodchucks. In parts of the world with high HCC incidence rates vertical transmission of HBV from mothers to infants may be the primary route for perpetuating the HBSAg carrier state (Maupas *et al.*, 1981).

The role of aflatoxin, a product of the fungus *Aspergillus flavus*, which is known to contaminate foodstuffs, particularly peanuts, in many parts of Africa and is a potent carcinogen, remains uncertain. Associations between the incidence of HCC and the level of aflatoxin contamination of foodstuffs have been reported from Kenya and South Africa. It may be a cofactor with HBV or may have an effect through its immunosuppressive properties.

Prevention of HCC should be a priority in cancer prevention as it accounts for a high mortality in the region, its therapy is costly, and the results are poor. Large-scale trials of immunization with hepatitis B vaccines of various types are now in progress in the Gambia and other countries (World Health Organization, 1988), but it is too soon to say how they will affect the incidence of HCC, and the costs are still prohibitive for many countries.

CARCINOMA OF THE BLADDER. There are great variations in the incidence or relative frequency of bladder carcinoma in different countries and regions of Sub-Saharan Africa. Comparing age-standardized rates (Waterhouse *et al.*, 1976) shows that the highest world rates in men and women are in Bulawayo, Zimbabwe (28.7 and 7.0 per 100,000, respectively). This contrasts with rates of 3.9 and 2.3 in Ibadan, Nigeria. The frequency of bladder carcinoma is high in northern Transvaal, coastal Mozambique, eastern Zambia, Malawi, the coastal regions of Tanzania and Kenya, and around the eastern, southern, and western shores of Lake Victoria. By contrast, rates are low in the highlands of Burundi, Kenya, Rwanda, and Tanzania. The frequency is also low in northern Uganda and adjacent Zaire, while the rates in southern Uganda are intermediate. Bladder cancer occurs in West Africa, but with a lower frequency than in countries such as Zimbabwe and Malawi. A feature of the tumor throughout this region is that the great majority are squamous or anaplastic in histological type; this contrasts with the tumors seen in the West, which are nearly all transitional in type. In high-incidence areas the tumor often appears at a young age and nearly always at a late clinical stage.

The association between *Schistosoma haematobium* and bladder cancer was first reported by Fergusson (1911) in Egypt. Case-control studies in Zimbabwe, using bladder calcification as an index of infection, have shown a significantly higher rate of infestation in patients than in controls (Gelfand *et al.*, 1967), and the association is supported by case-control studies on postmortem material in Zambia (Elem and Purobit, 1983). Further evidence of an association comes from Zambia (Bhagwandeen, 1976) and Malawi (Lucas, 1982), where eggs are found significantly more often in squamous than in transitional cell carcinomas or sarcomas. Estimated incidence rates of the tumor in many districts and regions of East and Central Africa show a close relationship between the frequency of bladder cancer and the prevalence and intensity of *S. haematobium* infection in the area (Cook-Mozaffari, 1982).

Many theories have been advanced to explain the relationship. Heavy infestation with *S. haematobium* leads to inflammation, fibrosis, and calcification of the bladder wall with gross impairment of bladder function and inadequate emptying. This predisposes the individual to recurrent, and mixed, bacterial infections. In such patients elevated levels of nitrosamines are present (Hicks *et al.*, 1977; El-Merzabani *et al.*, 1979; El-Bolkainy, 1982). The presence of these carcinogens in bladders with intense reactive epithelial hyperplasia may provide the stimulus to malignant change. This theory is consistent with the observations from Nigeria (Udeh *et al.*, 1966) and Uganda (Anthony, 1973) that the frequency of squamous cell carcinoma of the bladder is raised in patients with urethral stricture whose bladder function is also associated with repeated mixed urinary infections.

Controlling the problem of bladder cancer is dependent on improving the control of *S. haematobium* infection within the region and its widespread effect on the morbidity of affected populations. In high-incidence areas the complication of bladder cancer strains hospital resources and is an important cause of schistosomal mortality.

MALIGNANT TUMORS OF THE SKIN. Iversen and Iversen (1973) and Lewis (1973) provide a valuable discussion of malignant epithelial tumors and malignant melanomas. The great majority of malignant epithelial tumors in the black populations of Sub-Saharan Africa are squamous cell in type; basal cell carcinomas are rare except in the white races. The heavy melanin pigmentation of the African skin provides complete protection against the common solar cancers of fair-skinned races. For these reasons the incidence rates are much lower in Africans than in Europeans. However, in certain regions of some African countries skin cancer is an important clinical problem. In Uganda it accounts for 9.9 percent of all malignancies in men and 9.3 percent in women; similar frequencies are found in Malawi. Within Uganda the differences in relative frequencies between tribal groups and geographic areas are marked (see figure 15-2).

The great majority of squamous cell carcinomas of the skin in Africans arise in areas of damaged skin, particularly at the site of old tropical ulcers on the lower leg. Other less common predisposing lesions are burn scars and chronic sinuses, which may have a wide anatomical distribution. The geographic areas with a high frequency of skin cancers are usually very poor with a paucity of primary and secondary health facilities. These cancers could be reduced markedly by improving the facilities for treating the early stages of tropical ulcers and by paying attention to other chronic skin lesions.

Malignant melanoma is a relatively uncommon tumor in Africa. In contrast to the pattern common for the white races, in Africa it usually occurs on the soles of the feet or the palmar surface of the hands. The frequency on the sole of the foot may be related to trauma in individuals who go barefoot.

CARCINOMA OF THE CERVIX. This is the most important form of malignant disease in Sub-Saharan Africa. It accounts for 20–35 percent of all malignancies in women, many of whom are of child-bearing age, and is the most common overall malignancy in combined male and female relative frequencies. Incidence rates of 24.3 per 100,000 in Kyadondo County, Uganda, 28.4 in Bulawayo, Zimbabwe, and 21.6 in

Ibadan, Nigeria, have been reported. It is probable that these figures represent underestimates. Relative frequency studies show a somewhat similar picture throughout the region, although lower frequencies have been found in the West Nile region of Uganda and in the Kisii and Kerichio districts of Kenya (Cook-Mozaffari, 1982).

Carcinoma of the cervix is a sexually transmitted disease. It is most common in the sections of any population where sexual promiscuity is common, particularly if this occurs at an early age, around the time of the menarche. These strong epidemiological associations have led to the search for a sexually transmissible agent that could initiate or promote cervical neoplasia (Rotkin, 1973). A variety of organisms have been considered, but the strongest contender for a role is one of the human papillomaviruses (HPV). DNA-hybridization studies have shown that most genital cancers and cell lines harbor a specific HPV type (Gissman and Schwartz, 1986); type 16 and 18 are found in 40–70 percent of invasive cancers, and others contain other types of DNA sequences. However, there is a high prevalence of HPV in normal women, which suggests that other events are necessary to initiate the carcinogenic process.

Primary prevention of cervical cancer should be approached as part of a general attack on sexually transmitted disease that emphasizes safe sexual practices and is aimed particularly at the young. If HPV proves to be an etiologic agent, appropriate immunization programs might be developed if a suitable vaccine can be produced (McCance, 1986). There is a prima facie case for introducing a widespread cervical cytology screening program for detecting precancerous and early cancerous lesions. Unfortunately, many of the countries of this region do not have enough trained laboratory staff to fulfill basic clinical requirements, and screening on a wide scale would be beyond their personnel and material resources. Educational programs to draw attention to the early symptoms of cervical cancer, such as postcoital bleeding, should encourage women to seek assistance when therapy offers some hope of success.

CARCINOMA OF THE PENIS. This tumor is more common in Sub-Saharan Africa than in Western countries, but shows marked variations in frequency within the region (Cook-Mozaffari, 1982). The highest relative frequencies have been recorded in some regions and tribes of Uganda, varying from 20 percent of all male tumors in some places to 4 percent in others (Dodge *et al.*, 1973). Despite its disfiguring and destructive nature, the tumor spreads slowly and is not an important cause of mortality.

Carcinoma of the penis is most frequent in areas and population groups who do not circumcise. This accounts for the marked differences between Uganda (over 7.0 percent) and Kenya (1.1 percent) (Dodge *et al.*, 1973). However, within Uganda the frequencies vary between tribes who do not circumcise, which suggests that other factors are involved. As with cervical cancer, human papillomavirus (HPV) may be an etiologic agent (McCance, 1986), and sexual transmission may play a role. Evidence from several parts of the world suggests that personal hygiene is a factor in the etiology, and emphasis should be placed on this in health and sex education.

KAPOSI'S SARCOMA. Kaposi's sarcoma (KS) has long been endemic in parts of Africa (Hutt, 1984), but, in addition to the endemic variety, it is now frequently associated with AIDS. Both varieties are discussed in the paragraphs that follow.

The first ten cases in Africa were described by Smith and Elmes (1934), but Kaposi's sarcoma was not recognized as a common tumor throughout a large part of Sub-Saharan Africa until the 1950s. The first international symposium on Kaposi's sarcoma was held in Kampala, Uganda, in 1961 (Ackerman and Murray, 1962). The main clinical and epidemiological features of the tumor were then outlined and later elaborated at a second conference held in Kampala in 1980 (Olweny *et al.*, 1981). Endemic African Kaposi's sarcoma is limited to a geographic region south of the Sahara. Its epicenter of high incidence is in eastern Zaire and neighboring countries, where it accounts for over 10 percent of all malignant tumors in the black population. The tumor decreases in frequency in the countries to the south and west of this area, accounting for only 1.3 percent of malignancies in parts of South Africa and 0.8 percent in Ghana. Most patients with endemic KS present with skin lesions, often multiple, on the extremities, and the majority of these lesions run a long clinical course so that the tumor is more a cause of morbidity than mortality. In all areas there is a strong male predominance, with male to female ratios of over 10:1.

With the rapid spread of AIDS in the 1980s, AIDS-related KS was superimposed on the endemic variety. Clinically, this type is more aggressive, often affects organs such as the mouth, pharynx, palate, and other systemic sites, and is associated with a poor prognosis (Bayley, 1984). HIV antibodies are present in these cases, and the characteristic pattern of immunodepression is found (Bayley *et al.*, 1985).

The etiology of KS remains obscure, although its occurrence in AIDS cases and in patients on long-term immunosuppressive drugs indicates that this is a significant factor. There is no evidence that HIV is directly related to the development of KS, although any measures that can reduce the incidence and impact of AIDS in Africa would reduce the frequency of aggressive Kaposi's sarcoma in the region.

MALIGNANT LYMPHOMAS. Although the frequency and behavior of lymphomas of various types differ between Africa and Europe or North America (Hutt, 1987), the major difference is the high frequency of Burkitt's lymphoma in a belt across tropical Africa. This tumor was first described as a clinical entity by Burkitt (1958) and was later defined as a specific cytological entity by Wright (1970). The tumor occurs in a belt across Sub-Saharan Africa that extends down to Zimbabwe with a tail along the Mozambique coast. Within this area the tumor is rare in the highlands of west Uganda and Kenya (Burkitt, 1970). Throughout the tumor belt Burkitt's lymphoma is the most common malignancy in children, accounting for over 35 percent of all children's tumors in Uganda.

The association of the tumor with altitude, temperature, and rainfall in the region where the tumor is prevalent led to the hypothesis that it was related to endemic malaria (Dalldorf *et al.*, 1964; Burkitt, 1969). Isolation of Epstein-Barr virus from cell lines of the tumor (Epstein *et al.*, 1964), the presence of Epstein-Barr nucleic acid (EBNA) in fresh tumor cells, and the demonstration that EB infection preceded the onset of the tumor suggest a causal role of EB infection in its development. Endemic (African) Burkitt's lymphoma is the result of a nonrandom chromosomal translocation of differentiating B-cell lymphocytes, which is associated with the c-mycogene. The geographic distribution of the tumor in Africa and Papua New Guinea is best explained by the presence of endemic malaria with early and heavy infection in childhood, which may compromise immune responses. Infection by the EB virus at this stage of life may be the trigger that initiates the tumor.

There is evidence that where malaria has been controlled, as in Zanzibar, the tumor is rarely seen and that widespread malarial prophylaxis may have a similar effect. As yet no effective EB vaccine is available for use in susceptible populations.

LEUKEMIAS. Comparing the incidence of leukemia in different parts of Africa is complicated by lack of information and standardization of techniques for identifying subtypes. Studies in Kenya and Nigeria show that the acute lymphoblastic leukemia of early childhood is less common than in temperate climates, although acute myeloid leukemia in older children is often seen (Fleming, 1986; Kasili, 1981). Other forms of leukemia occur with similar frequency to that seen elsewhere, although T-cell lymphoma and leukemias appear to be more frequent (Fleming, 1986).

Cancer Prevention and Strategies for Control

All countries in Sub-Saharan Africa are faced with shortages of personnel at every level of their health services as well as with severe restrictions in health budgets and in foreign currency for purchasing drugs and equipment. Many countries do not have basic radiotherapy facilities, and in those that do the facilities are only available to a small percentage of the persons who need them.

For reasons already explained, cancer cannot be considered a top priority, compared with infectious diseases, for the persons and agencies planning health services under many limitations. Nevertheless, certain types of cancer make a significant contribution to mortality rates in all adult groups, and patients with cancer strain limited diagnostic and curative services, as hospital returns reveal. In planning a strategy for cancer prevention and control (Aoki *et al.*, 1982; Khogali *et al.*, 1986), each country must take into consideration its own circumstances. These include its overall resources (health budget, personnel, equipment, etc.), its geographic and sociocultural circumstances, and its particular cancer pattern. It is essential that all programs be directed toward objectives that are achievable in the light of the constraints mentioned above.

PRIMARY PREVENTION. The use of tobacco and increasing rates of lung carcinoma in some countries in the southern part of Africa and elsewhere in the developing world reflect the adoption of Western patterns of cigarette smoking over the past 30 years. Falling sales of tobacco products in developed countries have resulted in mounting pressure to increase sales in regions such as Africa. It is vital that educational programs be mounted, particularly for the young generations now in school, to counteract commercial advertising pressures. Such campaigns, if successful, would not only prevent an epidemic of lung cancer in the region but would also decrease other tobacco-related carcinomas, such as of the esophagus, and other noninfectious diseases, including coronary artery disease and emphysema.

Adopting certain aspects of Western diets, which is common in some affluent groups, is likely to be associated with increases in certain tumors, such as carcinoma of the large bowel, rectum, and breast, as well as other "Western" diseases, including diverticulosis, coronary artery disease, and cholelithiasis. Although dietary change is much slower than the adoption of habits such as cigarette smoking and is not yet widespread, nutritional education should emphasize the best aspects of traditional diets while pointing out the poorer aspects, such as lack of protein, vitamins, and essential minerals, that may contribute to the development of some cancers and have other effects on health.

Any measure that reduces the impact of *S. haematobium* infection in the countries of Sub-Saharan Africa will also reduce the incidence of bladder carcinoma and the morbidity from the nonneoplastic but functionally disabling bladder lesions of the infection.

The association of Burkitt's lymphoma with a high endemicity of *P. falciparum* malaria is well substantiated even though the precise relationship of this and EBV infection is still ill understood. Evidence suggests that malarial control, carried out in its own right, may lead to a decrease in the frequency of Burkitt's lymphoma.

Early and effective treatment of tropical ulcers leads to healing without sequelae. The high incidence in some areas of malignant change in poorly treated ulcers nearly always reflects poverty and lack of good primary health care facilities. Improvements in this part of the health sector should reduce the frequency of skin malignancies.

Carcinoma of the cervix, the most important cause of cancer mortality in the continent, is a sexually transmitted disease associated particularly with promiscuity in the young. Educational programs in schools that deal with sexually transmitted disease should include information on this topic.

At least six of the most common cancers in Africa are associated directly or indirectly with viruses: hepatitis B with HCC, EBV with Burkitt's lymphoma and naso pharyngeal lymphoma, HPV with carcinoma of the cervix and penis, and HIV with some forms of Kaposi's sarcoma.

The availability of highly safe and effective hepatitis B vaccines now makes programs possible that aim to eventually eliminate hepatitis B as a disease in man and to prevent the first human cancer by immunization (Maynard *et al.*, 1988). However, translating this idea into a practical policy for the whole of Sub-Saharan Africa is a formidable task, in the light of logistic and economic considerations. Current trials in various parts of the developing world will need careful evaluation over a long period before whole population immunization can be considered.

At the present time effective vaccines against the other viruses associated with human cancers are not available.

SECONDARY PREVENTION. On theoretical grounds, screening for precancerous and early cancerous lesions of the cervix should be a top priority for this important cause of cancer mortality throughout the region. The World Health Organization recommended that in low-income countries every woman should be screened at least once in her lifetime, between the ages of 35 and 40 years (World Health Organization, 1988). Effective cytological screening schemes have been established in local areas, serving limited populations, usually in capital cities. Several of these have collapsed for want of personnel or funds. The shortage of pathologists and well-trained technologists is acute in nearly every country of the region, and until this can be remedied, establishing population screening on any large scale will be difficult.

All clinical reports on specific cancers emphasize that patients present at a late stage of the disease. Educational campaigns that focus on the common and effectively treatable cancers are required. These must be adapted to the needs of each country or area.

TREATMENT. Only a few large cities have all the modern facilities for surgery, radiotherapy, and chemotherapy; even when present those facilities can only deal with a fraction of the patients requiring therapy in the country. Where facilities are limited, it is important to have a national or regional plan for determining priorities, and these priorities should take into account the realistic prospects for cure or long-term survival or for alleviating distressing symptoms. More attention should be paid to the lessons of the hospice movement, particularly about relieving pain, for treating many incurable late-stage cancers.

Cardiovascular Disease

Most studies of heart disease in Sub-Saharan Africa are based on analyses of hospital records (Vaughan, 1977, 1978). Although many factors influence the reasons for hospital admissions, a similar pattern of cardiac disease is reported from many countries. Heart disease accounts for between 8 and 12 percent of all medical admissions (Shaper and Shaper, 1958; Vaughan, 1977). The relative frequencies of cardiac diagnoses from different countries are shown in table 15-4 (Vaughan, 1977). Throughout the region the major problems are hypertensive and rheumatic heart diseases, which together account for between 40 and 60 percent of all cardiac admissions. Syphilitic heart disease features prominently in earlier reports but is now less common. Coronary heart disease is still rare in most African populations.

A necropsy study at Mulago Hospital in Kampala, Uganda, showed that 15.3 percent of 373 male Africans 60 years old or more and 13.1 percent of matched controls who were 30 years younger at the time of their death died of cardiac disease (Drury, 1972). This emphasizes the importance of cardiac disease in younger age groups in Africa. Another study, at the same hospital, revealed significant organic heart disease in 613 of 3,599 necropsies (see table 15-5; Hutt, 1975).

Traditional Patterns of Cardiovascular Disease

Direct and circumstantial evidence suggests that certain forms of heart disease have existed in the African continent for many years. These will be considered first.

RHEUMATIC HEART DISEASE (RHD). Rheumatic heart disease accounts for 10 to 35 percent of all clinical cardiac admissions to the hospitals of Sub-Saharan Africa (table 15-4) and up to 20 percent of all cardiac deaths confirmed at necropsy (table 15-5). Its importance as a cause of morbidity and mortality is amplified by the young age of the individuals afflicted.

A survey of 12,050 black children from the crèches and primary schools of Soweto, South Africa, revealed an overall prevalence of RHD of 6.9 per 1,000, with a peak prevalence of 19.2 per 1,000 in the seventh grade. The maximal incidence was from 15 to 18 years, and the prevalence was higher in large families; the majority of these children were asymptomatic (McClaren *et al.*, 1975). In Ibadan a survey of schoolchildren found only 0.03 percent to have evidence of RHD (Ogunbi *et al.*, 1976).

Children and young adults presenting with established RHD have a definitive history of extracardiac manifestations of rheumatic fever in about 25 to 50 percent of cases. The majority present with cardiac

Table 15-4. Cardiac Disease as Reported by Hospital Studies in Selected African Countries
(percentage frequency, unless otherwise specified)

Disease	Kampala, Uganda	Dar es Salaam, Tanzania	Addis Ababa, Ethiopia	Accra, Ghana	Ibadan, Nigeria	Kano, Nigeria	Blantyre, Malawi	Lusaka, Zambia	Cape Town, South Africa
Hypertension	19.5[a]	42.0	16.3	44.5	28.5[a]	34.0	16.0[a]	34.1	43.0
Rheumatic heart disease	24.7	9.7	34.8	20.6	18.1	23.0	23.0	18.2	25.0
Endomyocardial fibrosis	4.0	11.1	n.a.	n.a.	12.1	n.a.	n.a.	n.a.	n.a.
Idiopathic cardiomegaly	13.5	11.0	13.6	8.6	13.9	n.a.	5.0	21.7	9.0
Syphilitic heart disease	6.2	5.3	16.8	n.a.	2.7	16.0	4.4	n.a.	2.0
Coronary heart disease	0.7	0.5	n.a.	1.2	1.5	n.a.	n.a.	n.a.	1.4
All categories listed	75.7	72.5	81.5	74.9	76.8	73.0	48.4	74.0	80.4
Number of subjects	449	226	558	303	267	385	114	170	6,679

n.a. Not available.

a. Includes only hypertension with heart disease.

Source: Vaughan (1977). Sources for the specific studies are as follows: Kampala, D'Arbella *et al.* (1966); Dar es Salaam, Nhonoli (1968); Addis Ababa, Parry and Gordon (1968); Accra, Pobee *et al.* (1975); Ibadan, Carlisle and Ongulesi (1972); Kano, Beet (1956); Blantyre, Brown and Willis (1975); Lusaka, Bahl *et al.* (1975); and Cape Town, Schrire (1971).

Table 15-5. Organic Heart Disease Found at Necropsy in Mulago Hospital, Kampala, Uganda, 1964–68

Disease	Percentage
Hypertensive heart disease	20.5
Rheumatic heart disease	19.7
Endomyocardial fibrosis	12.9
Pericarditis	8.5
Aortic disease	8.3
Cor pulmonale	7.7
Infective endocarditis	6.1
Idiopathic cardiomegaly	4.7
Congenital heart disease	3.7
Coronary heart disease	0.5
Other	7.4

Note: These diagnoses are based on the presence of significant organic lesions diagnosed macroscopically and microscopically. Not all represent the major cause of death or the reason for clinical admission. The number of necropsies performed was 4,768, of which 637 found organic heart disease.

Source: Hutt (1975).

murmurs or evidence of carditis. A study of 80 children with RHD in Ibadan revealed evidence of mitral incompetence in 95 percent and mitral stenosis in 26 percent; many had evidence of heart failure. The cumulative mortality at six years was 20 percent attributable to cardiac failure and infective endocarditis (Jaiyesimi and Antia, 1981; Jaiyesimi and Abioye, 1982). The impact of RHD on the young is evident: 33 percent of all mitral valvotomies done in Nairobi, Kenya, were performed on patients under the age of 16 years (Knight *et al.*, 1973).

Rheumatic heart disease is a disease of poverty and is now an extreme rarity in Western countries. Its prevalence in any community can be linked to overcrowding, poor housing, and undernutrition. The etiological link between Group A beta-hemolytic streptococci and rheumatic disease is well established, and several studies have shown high carrier rates of this organism in the tropics. Lebga (1981) examined schoolchildren in Yaoundé, Cameroon, and found a prevalence of 10.5 percent carriers of Group A streptococci. Antistreptolysin (ASO) titers were positive in 92 percent of children, and 43.5 percent had high titers. Its high prevalence and impact on younger members of the population, who have considerable morbidity and mortality, suggest that RHD should be a priority for prevention. The decline of RHD in most parts of the world indicates that general social measures are most important. However, in the present state of Africa's economy changes of sufficient magnitude in the standard of living are unlikely in the next 20 years. The two proven measures that might reduce the impact of RHD are related to the predisposing streptococcal infection. Primary prevention is based on adequate treatment of all beta-hemolytic streptococcal infections, both pharyngeal and of the skin. Secondary prevention involves the long-term administration of appropriate antibiotic cover to prevent recurrent infections that lead to exacerbations of the underlying carditis. Both approaches present formidable difficulties in areas where medical personnel and supplies are scarce.

ENDOMYOCARDIAL FIBROSIS (EMF). EMF is a specific clinicopathological entity first described in detail by Davies (1948) in Uganda. The characteristic lesions occur on the inflow tracts of the right or left ventricles, or both, which are covered by dense fibrous tissue that involves the papillary muscles and chordae tendineae of the tricuspid valve and the posterior cusp of the mitral valve; the fibrosis extends into the inner portion of the ventricular wall. Functionally the lesions result in incompetence of either or both valves, and the ventricular muscle function is impaired somewhat by the restrictive effect of the fibrosis. Most patients are seen in the third or fourth decades, but the condition may also occur in the first decade of life or in old age.

EMF occurs in a belt across tropical Africa below the Sahara and rarely below the Zambezi River. In Kampala, Uganda, and Ibadan, Nigeria, it accounts for between 8 and 12 percent of clinical heart disease, and necropsy studies reveal a similar frequency. In Uganda EMF is much more common in the immigrant Rwandan population than in the indigenous Baganda (Shaper, 1974b).

In temperate climates the condition is a rarity and is associated with marked and prolonged eosinophilia (Löffler's syndrome). This has led to the suggestion that EMF in the tropics is related to eosinophilia, which is common in many populations and is often due to filariasis (Andy *et al.*, 1981; Brockington and Olsen, 1973; Davies *et al.*, 1983). It has also been suggested that tropical EMF is related to an abnormal immune response to malaria (Shaper, 1974b). Neither of these hypotheses explains the curious geographic distribution of EMF, and its etiology remains the subject of speculation. No preventive

measures can be undertaken in the present stage of our knowledge.

CONGESTIVE CARDIOMYOPATHY (IDIOPATHIC CARDIOMEGALY). The syndrome of recurrent congestive cardiac failure associated with a dilated and hypertrophied heart, in the absence of other specific lesions or extracardiac disease, occurs throughout the world. It has, however, been reported with unusual frequency in Sub-Saharan Africa and other tropical countries (table 15-4). In some regions it accounts for over 20 percent of clinically diagnosed heart disease (Ikeme, 1976). There are, however, difficulties in establishing a definite diagnosis, and necropsy studies tend to show lower figures. Congestive cardiomyopathy may represent the pathological endpoint of a number of factors that damage the cardiac muscle. Pathologically, a similar picture may be seen in beriberi and alcoholic cardiac disease, although neither is common in Africa. Recent evidence suggests that some cases may result from infections by viruses, particularly cocksackie B. Other cases are thought to be due to ventricular muscle failure in untreated hypertension, but in the absence of any prior record of hypertension in the individual or of other pathological indications of hypertensive vascular changes this diagnosis is difficult to sustain. Until specific etiologic factors can be identified with certainty, it is impossible to adopt preventive measures. Treatment of the condition follows the usual therapeutic practices for congestive cardiac failure.

Emerging Patterns of Cardiovascular Disease

Hypertension and coronary artery disease were very rare in Africans in the early part of this century. Both are now emerging in certain population groups and are likely to increase in frequency and importance as causes of morbidity and mortality.

HYPERTENSION. For many years hypertension was considered a rare condition in Africa. This observation was based on community surveys and clinical and necropsy reports (Trowell, 1981). Although we know that hypertension is now prevalent in many African communities, in several isolated rural communities blood pressure does not show the usual increase with age (Shaper, 1974a). These include tribal groups in eastern Uganda, western Kenya, the Masai, Hadza, and Mzigua tribes of Tanzania, and the bushmen of the Kalahari Desert in Botswana. Population studies in several rural, traditional African communities also show only slight rises in blood pressure with age, although the prevalence of hypertension in other rural communities is significant (Seedat and Hackland, 1984).

In a study of 4,993 rural Zulus the overall prevalence of primary hypertension was 8.4 percent. This is slightly higher than that observed in rural studies in Ghana, Nigeria, and Lesotho (Pobee *et al.*, 1977; Oviasu, 1978; Mokhobo, 1976). In urban Zulus the mean blood pressures were significantly higher than in their rural counterparts (Seedat and Hackland, 1984).

Significant differences were also found in community studies between the black Xhosa populations of South Africa living in tribal homelands and those working in Cape Town. The latter were more obese, and their blood pressure was significantly higher, than those who remained in their homelands (Sever *et al.*, 1980). Similar findings have been reported in Côte d'Ivoire (Bertrand, 1987) and Nigeria (Akinkugbe, 1976).

The rural Luo of western Kenya are a low-pressure community, and many migrate to Nairobi to work during the week. Longitudinal studies in the latter group show that the slope of linear regression of blood pressure is significantly different in the two communities. Within two months of arriving in the city both the diastolic and systolic pressures rise, and at six months the differences in blood pressure profiles, particularly in males over 45 years, are significant (Poulter, 1988).

Outpatient studies, analyses of hospital admissions, and necropsy results indicate the importance of hypertension in clinical practice in Africa. Approximately 80 percent of patients with high blood pressure seen in the clinics or wards have essential hypertension, and most of the remainder have underlying chronic renal disease, predominantly glomerulonephritis (Akinkugbe, 1976). Severe hypertension, often of the malignant variety, under the age of 40 years, is nearly always due to underlying renal disease (Hutt and Coles, 1969). Such patients die from a combination of renal and cardiac failure or from a cerebrovascular accident. Most elderly patients have essential hypertension.

Cross-sectional and longitudinal surveys of rural and urban communities indicate the importance of environmental influences on the development of "essential" hypertension. Studies by Poulter *et al.* (1984a, 1984b) and Poulter (1988) on Luo migrants to Nairobi show that increases in blood pressure in migrants to the city are associated with a marked rise in dietary sodium and a fall in dietary potassium, as demonstrated by measurements of urinary electrolytes in 12- and 24-hour urine collections. Several investigators have shown that populations with low blood pressure have a low salt intake, often less than 60 mmol per day (Tobian, 1979). This may account for the many reports that hypertension was uncommon in Africa before 1940, when salt intake was much lower than it is now (Trowell, 1981; Wilson, 1986).

It is likely that other factors such as weight increase and stress also play a role in these geographic differences. In Western countries no significant differences can be found in salt intake between persons with and without high blood pressure.

In Côte d'Ivoire adequate surveillance and treatment (by Western standards) of all hypertensives would consume about one-fifth of the national health budget (Bertrand, 1987). The disease imposes a heavy social burden: it accounts for 7 percent of all medical admissions and 9 percent of all medical deaths. Little can be done to reduce the impact of hypertension related to chronic renal disease, but early detection of high blood pressure coupled with simple regimens of low salt intake and weight control might reduce the morbidity at no great cost (Bertrand, 1987).

CEREBROVASCULAR DISEASE (STROKES). Cerebrovascular accidents are an important cause of admission to hospitals in the countries of Sub-Saharan Africa and account for 10 to 35 percent of all neurological admissions (James, 1975; Osuntokun, 1976). Strokes account for 8–10 percent of nonviolent deaths in urban black populations of South Africa (Walker, 1981) and for 4.5 percent of all registered deaths in black Zimbabweans over the age of 5 years (Matenga *et al.*, 1986). An incidence of 26 per 100,000 has been recorded by the Ibadan Stroke Registry (Osuntokun, 1976). This rate is lower than in most Western countries but may reflect the younger age structure of the population. The relative frequency of the underlying pathology of strokes in reports from the region is shown in table 15-6. The higher frequency of hemorrhage than of nonembolic infarction in the necropsy series from Uganda—in contrast to the clinical series—reflects the former's high mortality. Both clinical and necropsy observations show a higher relative frequency of intracerebral hemorrhage in Africa than in Western countries.

Hypertension is the most important cause of cerebrovascular accidents except embolic strokes. It was present in 80 percent of patients with subarachnoid and intracerebral hemorrhage and in 56.6 percent of patients with nonembolic thrombosis in Nigeria (Ibadan Stroke Registry, from Osuntokun, 1976). The importance of hypertension contrasts with the low prevalence of cerebral atherosclerosis in Africans

Table 15-6. Distribution of Clinicopathological Diagnoses in Patients with Strokes, Nigeria and Uganda

Country and source	Subarachnoid hemorrhage	Intracerebral hemorrhage	Embolic infarction	Nonembolic infarction	Acute ill-defined
Uganda					
Billinghurst (1973)	17	12	7	64	
James (1975)[a]	13	36	23	28	
Nigeria					
Osuntokun *et al.* (1969)	14	23	5	58	
Osuntokun (1976)	11	16	3	46	24

a. Necropsy series.

(Williams *et al.*, 1969), and atherosclerosis of the major extracranial cerebral vessels is almost unknown. In most clinical series the majority of patients who present with strokes had not previously been diagnosed or treated for hypertension (Osuntokun, 1976; Matenga *et al.*, 1986). Only by improved management and control of hypertension can the mortality from strokes be reduced in the region.

CORONARY ARTERY DISEASE (ISCHEMIC HEART DISEASE). Until recently coronary heart disease (CHD) with its complications of sudden death, myocardial infarction, and congestive cardiac failure was an extreme rarity in the black populations of Sub-Saharan Africa. Only 3 cases were found in over 3,500 necropsies performed in Ghana (Edington, 1954), and less than 1.0 percent of 637 cardiac diseases diagnosed at postmortem in Uganda had evidence of ischemic heart disease (Hutt, 1975). During the period 1961 to 1970 only 26 patients with CHD were admitted to University Hospital in Ibadan (Falase *et al.*, 1973); clinical studies have shown no significant increase in the prevalence of CHD in Nigerians during the past 15 years (Ogunnowo *et al.*, 1986). Reports from a number of urban centers suggest that there is a small but definite increase in the number of patients presenting with symptoms of CHD (Makene, 1976; Bertrand, 1987), particularly in the Westernized elite. Necropsy studies of black populations from East, West, and South Africa show that atheroma of the coronary arteries is quantitatively and qualitatively less than in similar age groups in the black and white populations of the United States (Florentin *et al.*, 1963; Williams, 1971; Isaacson, 1977). However, there has been a significant increase in the amount of coronary artery disease in black South Africans, as shown by necropsy studies carried out in 1959 and 1976 (Isaacson, 1977). An increase in coronary atheroma has also been reported from Ife,

Nigeria, in a study of 111 consecutive necropsies. The grossest lesions occurred in elderly, affluent, hypertensive patients exposed to Western habits and diet (Ogunnowo *et al.*, 1986).

Population studies show that the best indicator of high or low risk in a community or nation is the mean serum cholesterol level. Most Western nations have a mean level of 200 mg/ml (5.2 mmol/1) or more. Populations in Africa have much lower levels. The most important cause of these differences in serum cholesterol level is diet. Low-risk groups such as Africans eat much less animal fat and refined sugar, and much more complex carbohydrates with a high fiber content (Trowell, 1981; Hutt and Burkitt, 1986). In high-risk populations hypertension, cigarette smoking, obesity, and lack of exercise are important risk factors, but in low-risk populations these factors do not appear to lead to atheroma or its complications.

If CHD is not to become an African epidemic of the twenty-first century, public education should begin as soon as possible so that the most harmful aspects of Western life-style, in particular diet and a high consumption of tobacco, should not become the norm in Sub-Saharan Africa. Experiences in the urbanized southern part of the region indicate the urgency of developing health education on these problems.

Conclusions

The evidence presented in this chapter is, by the nature of circumstances in the vast and varied region of Sub-Saharan Africa, incomplete and lacking much of the hard data that epidemiologists and health planners in the richer, industrial countries of the world expect and are accustomed to. Nevertheless, it provides a broad picture of the problems of noninfectious diseases, particularly cancer and heart disease. With both diseases, the patterns can be divided between the conditions that have existed in Africa since before

European and Western influences arrived and those that can be related directly or indirectly to such influences. Among the former are carcinoma of the liver, bladder (in some regions), cervix, and penis, Burkitt's lymphoma and Kaposi's sarcoma of the endemic type, rheumatic heart disease, EMF, and congestive cardiomyopathy. Among the latter are carcinoma of the lung, large bowel, rectum, pancreas, prostate, breast, and endometrium, hypertension, and coronary artery disease. Some conditions, such as carcinoma of the esophagus, do not fit so neatly into this distinction.

Experience from other parts of the world suggests that these two patterns may coexist in the same country with differences in disease-specific frequencies both between rich and poor and between urban and rural populations. Marked differences in disease patterns already exist in many countries between different regions and tribes, both for infectious and non-infectious diseases. These differences depend on a mixture of environmental factors including geographic, economic, and sociocultural factors.

In planning preventive and curative services for the countries of this region, all these factors must be assessed so that some overall, uniform strategy is not applied to areas or groups for whom it is not appropriate. National atlases of disease distribution may be of value in solving these problems.

References

Ackerman, L. V. and Murray, J. F., editors. (1962). *Union Internationalis Contra Cancrum.* Symposium on Kaposi's sarcoma. Basel: Karger.

Akinkugbe, O. O. (1976). The epidemiology of hypertension in Africa. In: *Cardiovascular Disease in Africa,* Akinkugbe, O. O. (editor), pp. 91–100. Switzerland: Ciba-Geigy.

Andy, J. J., Bishara, F. F., and Soyinka, O. D. (1981). Relation of severe eosinophilia and microfilariasis to chronic African endomyocardial fibrosis. *British Heart Journal,* 45, 672–680.

Anthony, P. P. (1973). Malignant tumors of the kidney, bladder, and urethra. In: *Tumours in a Tropical Country,* Templeton, A. C. (editor), pp. 145–170. Berlin, New York: Springer-Verlag.

Aoki, K., Tominaga, S., Hirayama, T., and Hirota, Y., editors. (1982). *Cancer Prevention in Developing Countries.* Nagoya: University of Nagoya Press.

Bahl, V., Mistry, C. M., and Obineche, E. N. (1975). Pattern of cardiovascular disease in Lusaka. *Medical Journal of Zambia,* 9, 167–169.

Bayley, A. C. (1984). Aggressive Kaposi's sarcoma in Zambia, 1983. *British Medical Journal,* 2, 1318–1320.

Bayley, A. C., Downing, R. G., Tedder, R. S., Weiss, R. A., Cheingsong-Popov, R., and Dalgliesh, A. G. (1985). HTLV-III serology distinguishes atypical and endemic Kaposi's sarcoma in Africa. *Lancet,* 1, 359–361.

Beet, E. A. (1956). Rheumatic heart disease in northern Nigeria. *Transactions of the Royal Society of Tropical Medicine and Hygiene,* 50, 587–593.

Bertrand, E. (1987). Cardiovascular disease. In: *Manson's Tropical Diseases, Nineteenth Edition,* Manson-Bahr, P. E. C. and Bell, D. R. (editors), pp. 1027–1029. London: Balliere Tindall.

Bhagwandeen, S. B. (1976). Schistosomiasis and carcinoma of the bladder in Zambia. *South African Medical Journal,* 25, 1616–1620.

Billinghurst, J. R. (1973). Neurological disorders in Uganda. In: *Tropical Neurology,* Spillane, J. D. (editor), pp. 191–206. London: Oxford University Press.

Brockington, I. F. and Olsen, E. G. J. (1973). Löffler's endocarditis and Davies endomyocardial fibrosis. *American Heart Journal,* 85, 308–322.

Brown, K. G. E. and Willis, W. H. (1975). Cardiac disease in Malawi. *South African Medical Journal,* 49, 926–929.

Burkitt, D. P. (1958). A sarcoma involving the jaws in African children. *British Journal of Surgery,* 46, 218–223.

———. (1969). Etiology of Burkitt's lymphoma. An alternative hypothesis to a vectored virus. *Journal of the National Cancer Institute,* 42, 19–28.

———. (1970). Geographical distribution. In: *Burkitt's Lymphoma,* Burkitt, D. P. and Wright, D. H. (editors), pp. 186–197. Edinburgh: Livingstone.

Burkitt, D. P., Hutt, M. S. R., and Slavin, G. (1968). Clinico-pathological studies of cancer distribution in Africa. *British Journal of Cancer,* 22, 1–6.

Burrell, R. J. W. (1962). Esophageal cancer among Bantu in the Transkei. *Journal of the National Cancer Institute,* 28, 495–514.

Carlisle, R. and Ongulesi, T. O. (1972). Prospective study of adult cases, presenting at the Cardiac Unit, University College Hospital, Ibadan, 1968–1969. *African Journal of Medical Science,* 3, 13–25.

Clifford, P. (1970). On the epidemiology of nasopharyngeal carcinoma. *International Journal of Cancer,* 5, 287–303.

Clifford, P., Linsell, C. A., and Timms, G. L., editors. (1968). *Cancer in Africa.* Nairobi: East African Publishing House.

Cook, G. C. (1988). *Communicable and Tropical Diseases.* London: Heinemann.

Cook, P. J. (1971). Cancer of the oesophagus in Africa. *British Journal of Cancer,* 25, 853–880.

Cook, P. J. and Burkitt, D. P. (1971). Cancer in Africa. *British Medical Bulletin,* 27, 14–20.

Cook-Mozaffari, P. (1982). Symposium on tumours in the tropics. *Transactions of the Royal Society of Tropical Medicine and Hygiene,* 76, 157–163.

Cook-Mozaffari, P. and van Rensburg, S. (1984). Cancer of the liver. *British Medical Bulletin,* 40, 342–345.

Dalldorf, G., Linsell, C. A., Barnhart, F. E., and Martyn, R. (1964). An epidemiological approach to the lymphoma of African children and Burkitt's sarcoma of the jaws. *Perspectives in Biology and Medicine*, 74, 435–449.

D'Arbella, P. G., Kanyerezi, R. B., and Tulloch, J. A. (1966). A study of heart disease in Mulago Hospital, Kampala, Uganda. *Transactions of the Royal Society of Tropical Medicine and Hygiene*, 60, 782–790.

Davies, J. N. P. (1948). Endocardial fibrosis in Africans. *East African Medical Journal*, 25, 10.

Davies, J. N. P., Elmes, S., Hutt, M. S. R., Mtimvalye, R. A. R., Owor, R., and Shaper, L. (1964). Cancer in an African community, 1897–1956. An analysis of the records of Mengo Hospital, Kampala, Uganda. *British Medical Journal*, 1, 259–264, 336–341.

Davies, J. N. P., Knowelden, J., and Wilson, B. A. (1965). Incidence rates of cancer in Kyadondo County, Uganda (1954–1960). *Journal of the National Cancer Institute*, 35, 789–821.

Davies, J., Spry, C. J. F., Sapsford, R., Olsen, E. G. J., de Perez, G., Oakley, C. M., and Goodwin, J. F. (1983). Cardiovascular features of eleven patients with eosinophilic endomyocardial disease. *Quarterly Journal of Medicine*, 52, 23–39.

Dodge, O. G., Owor, F., and Templeton, A. C. (1973). Tumours of the male genitalia. In: *Tumours in a Tropical Country*, Templeton, A. C. (editor). Berlin, New York: Springer-Verlag.

Doll, R., Muir, C. S., and Waterhouse, J. A. H., editors. (1970). *Cancer Incidence in Five Continents*, vol. 11. Geneva: Springer, UICC.

Drury, R. A. B. (1972). The mortality of elderly Ugandans. *Tropical and Geographical Medicine*, 24, 385–392.

Edington, G. M. (1954). Cardiovascular disease as a cause of death in Gold Coast, Africa. *Transactions of the Royal Society of Tropical Medicine and Hygiene*, 48, 419–425.

Edington, G. M. and MacLean, C. M. (1965). A cancer rate survey in Ibadan, western Nigeria, 1960–63. *British Journal of Cancer*, 19, 471–481.

El-Bolkainy. (1982). Bladder cancer in Egypt. In: *Geographical Pathology in Cancer Epidemiology. Cancer Campaign*, vol. 6, Grundman, E., Clemmesen, J., and Muir, C. S. (editors). New York and Stuttgart: Gustav Fischer Verlag.

Elem, B. and Purobit, R. (1983). Carcinoma of the urinary bladder in Zambia. *British Journal of Urology*, 55, 275–278.

El-Merzabani, M. M., El-Aaser, A. A., and Zakhary, N. I. (1979). A study of the etiologic factors of bilharzial bladder cancer in Egypt-1. Nitrosamine and their precursors in urine. *European Journal of Cancer*, 15, 287–291.

Epstein, M. A., Achong, B. G., and Barr, Y. M. (1964). Virus particles in cultured lymphoblasts from Burkitt's lymphoma. *Lancet*, 1, 702–703.

Falase, A. O., Cole, T. O., and Osuntokun, B. O. (1973). Myocardial infarction in Nigerians. *Tropical and Geographical Medicine*, 25, 147–150.

Fergusson, D. R. (1911). Associated bilharziasis and primary malignant disease of the urinary bladder. *Journal of Pathology and Bacteriology*, 16, 76–79.

Fleming, A. F. (1986). Geographical variation in blood disease: Leukaemias. In: *Oxford Textbook of Medicine*, Weatherall, D. J., Ledingham, G. G., and Warrell, D. A. (editors), pp. 19, 256. Oxford: Oxford University Press.

Florentin, R. A., Lee, K. T., Daoud, A. S., Davies, J. N. P., Hall, E. W., and Goodale, F. (1963). Geographical pathology of arteriosclerosis. A study of the age of outset of significant arteriosclerosis in adult Africans and New Yorkers. *Experimental and Molecular Pathology*, 2, 103–113.

Gelfand, M., Weinberg, R. W., and Castle, W. M. (1967). Relation between carcinoma of the bladder and infestation with *Schistosoma haematobium*. *Lancet*, 1, 1249–1251.

Geser, A., de Thé, G., Lenoir, G., Day, N. E., and Williams, E. H. (1982). Final case reporting from Ugandan prospective study of the relationship between EBV and Burkitt's lymphoma. *International Journal of Cancer*, 29, 397–400.

Gissman, L. and Schwartz, E. (1986). Persistence and expression of human papillomavirus DNA in genital cancer. In: *Papilloma Viruses*, Evered, D. and Clark, S. (editors), pp. 190–207. Chichester: Ciba Foundation Symposium.

Gunther, J. (1955). *Inside Africa*. London: Hamilton.

Hicks, R. M., Walters, C. L., El-Sebai, I., El-Aaser, A., El-Merzabani, M., and Gough, T. A. (1977). Demonstration of nitrosamines in human urine. Preliminary observations on a possible etiology for bladder cancer associated with chronic urinary tract infection. *Proceedings of the Royal Society of Medicine*, 70, 413–417.

Higginson, J. and Oettlé, A. G. (1960). Cancer incidence in the Bantu and Cape coloured races of South Africa: report of a cancer survey in the Transvaal (1953–55). *Journal of the National Cancer Institute*, 24, 589–671.

Hutt, M. S. R. (1975). Cardiac pathology in the tropics. In: *The Pathology of the Heart*, Pomerance, A. and Davies, M. J. (editors). Oxford, London: Blackwells.

———. (1984). Kaposi's sarcoma. *British Medical Bulletin*, 40, 159–365.

———. (1987). Geographical variations in blood disease, lymphoma, and leukaemia. In: *Oxford Textbook of Medicine*, Weatherall, D. J., Ledingham, J. K. G., and Warrell, D. A. (editors), pp. 19, 260, 262. Oxford: Oxford University Press.

Hutt, M. S. R. and Burkitt, D. P. (1965). Geographical distribution of cancer in East Africa: a new clinicopathological approach. *British Medical Journal*, 2, 719–722.

———. (1986). *The Geography of Non-infectious Disease*. Oxford, New York, Tokyo: Oxford University Press.

Hutt, M. S. R. and Coles, R. (1969). Postmortem findings in hypertensive subjects in Kampala, Uganda. *East African Medical Journal*, 46, 342–358.

Ikeme, A. C. (1976). Idiopathic cardiomegaly in Africa. In: *Cardiovascular Disease in Africa*, Akinkugbe, O. O. (editor). Switzerland: Ciba-Geigy.

Isaacson, C. (1977). The changing pattern of heart disease in South African blacks. *South African Medical Journal*, 52, 793–798.

Iversen, U. and Iversen, O. H. (1973). Tumours of the skin. In: *Tumours in a Tropical Country*, Templeton, A. C. (editor). Berlin, New York: Springer-Verlag.

Jaiyesimi, F. and Abioye, A. A. (1982). Fatal rheumatic carditis in early life. *Cardiologic Tropicale*, 8, 7–11.

Jaiyesimi, F. and Antia, A. V. (1981). Childhood rheumatic heart disease in Nigeria. *Tropical and Geographical Medicine*, 33, 8–13.

James, P. D. (1975). Cerebrovascular disease in Uganda. *Tropical and Geographical Medicine*, 27, 125–131.

Kasili, E. G. (1981). Leukaemia in African children. *Postgraduate Doctor*, 3, 126–129.

Kew, M. C., Desmyter, J., Bradburne, A. F. and Menab, G. M. (1979). Hepatitis B virus infection in southern African blacks with hepatocellular cancer. *Journal of the National Cancer Institute*, 62, 517–520.

Khogali, M., Omar, Y. T., Gjorgo, V. A., and Ismail, A. S., editors. (1986). *Cancer Prevention in Developing Countries*. Oxford, New York: Pergamon Press.

Knight, E. O. W., Kamdar, H. H., and Chukwemeka, A. (1973). Juvenile mitral stenosis in Kenya. *East African Medical Journal*, 50, 476–479.

Lebga, J. (1981). An epidemiologic study of beta haemolytic streptococci among school children in Yaoundé (Cameroon). *Tropical Cardiology*, 7, 187–191.

Lewis, M. G. (1973). Melanoma. In: *Tumours in a Tropical Country*, Templeton, A. C. (editor). Berlin, New York: Springer-Verlag.

Linsell, C. A. and Martyn, R. (1962). The Kenya Cancer Registry. *East African Medical Journal*, 39, 642–648.

Lucas, S. B. (1982). Squamous cell carcinoma of the bladder and schistosomiasis. *East African Medical Journal*, 59, 345–355.

Makene, W. J. (1976). Ischaemic heart disease in East Africa. In: *Cardiovascular Disease in Africa*, Akinkugbe, O. O. (editor). Switzerland: Ciba-Geigy.

Matenga, J., Kitai, I., and Levy, L. (1986). Strokes among black people in Harare, Zimbabwe: results of computed tomography and associated risk factors. *British Medical Journal*, 1649–1651.

Maupas, P., Chiron, J. P., Coursaget, P., Barin, F., Goudeau, A., Perrin, F., Denis, F., and Diop Mar, I. (1981). Efficacy of hepatitis B vaccine in prevention of early HBsAg carrier state in children. Controlled trial in an epidemic area (Senegal). *Lancet*, 1, 289–292.

Maynard, J. E., Kane, M. A., Alter, M. J., and Hadler, S. C. (1988). Control of hepatitis immunization: global perspectives. In: *Hepatitis and Liver Diseases*, Zuckerman, A.J. (editor). New York: Alan R. Liss.

McCance, D. J. (1986). Human papillomaviruses and cancer. *Biochimica et Biophysica Acta*, 823, 195–205.

McClaren, M. J., Hawkins, D. M., Koornhof, H. J., Bloom, K. R., Bramwell-Jones, D. M., Cohen, E., Gale, G. E., Kanarek, K., Lachman, A. G., Lakier, J. B., Pocock, W. A., and Barlow, J. B. (1975). Epidemiology of rheumatic heart disease in black school children of Soweto, Johannesburg. *British Medical Journal*, 3, 474–478.

Mokhobo, K. P. (1976). Arterial hypertension in rural societies. *East African Medical Journal*, 52, 440–444.

Nhonoli, A. M. (1968). Heart disease in Dar es Salaam. *East African Medical Journal*, 46, 55–57.

Ogunbi, O., Fadahunsi, H. O., Ahmed, I., Animaswaun, A., Daniel, S. O., Onuoha, D. U., and Ogunbi, L. Q. O. (1976). An epidemiological study of rheumatic fever and rheumatic heart disease in Lagos. In: *Cardiovascular Disease in Africa*, Akinkugbe, O. O. (editor). Switzerland: Ciba-Geigy.

Ogunnowo, P. O., Odesanmi, W. O., and Andy, J. T. (1986). Coronary artery pathology of 111 consecutive Nigerians. *Transactions of the Royal Society of Tropical Medicine and Hygiene*, 86, 923–926.

Olweny, C. M., Hutt, M. S. R., and Owor, R., editors. (1981). Second Kaposi's sarcoma symposium, 1980. *Antibiotics and Chemotherapy*, vol. 29. Basel: Karger.

Osuntokun, B. O. (1976). Stroke in the African. In: *Cardiovascular Disease in Africa*, Akinkugbe, O. O. (editor), pp. 288–301. Switzerland: Ciba-Geigy.

Osuntokon, B. O., Odeku, E. L., and Adeloye, R. A. A. (1969). Non-embolic ischaemic cerebrovascular disease in Nigerians. *Journal of Neurological Sciences*, 9, 361–388.

Oviasu, V. O. (1978). Arterial blood pressures and hypertension in a rural Nigerian community. *African Journal of Medicine and Medical Science*, 7, 137–143.

Parkin, D. M. (1986). *Cancer Occurrence in Developing Countries*. IARC Scientific Publications, no. 75. Lyon, France: IARC.

Parry, E. H. O. and Gordon, C. G. I. (1968). Ethiopian cardiovascular studies. Case finding by mass miniature radiography. *Bulletin of the World Health Organization*, 39, 859–871.

Pobee, J. O. M., Addo, Y. A., Larbi, E. B., and Adu, J. (1975). A review of cardiovascular diseases as seen in the cardiac clinic at the Korle Bu Teaching Hospital, Accra, Ghana. *Ghana Medical Journal*, 14, 41–49.

Pobee, J. O. M., Larbi, E. B., Belcher, D. W., Wurapa, F. K., and Dodu, S. R. A. (1977). Blood pressure in a rural Ghanaian population. *Transactions of the Royal Society of Tropical Medicine and Hygiene*, 71, 66–72.

Poulter, N. R. (1988). Longitudinal study of BP among rural/urban immigrants in Kenya. In: *Ethnic Factors in Health and Disease*, Cruickshank, D. K. and Beevers, D. G. (editors). Bristol: IOP Publishing.

Poulter, N. R., Khaw, K. T., Hopwood, B. E. C., Mugambi, M., Peart, W. S., Rose, G., and Sever, P. S. (1984a). Blood pressure and associated factors in a rural Kenyan community. *Hypertension*, 6, 810–813.

————. (1984b). Blood pressure and its correlates in an African tribe in urban and rural environments. *Journal of Epidemiology and Community Health*, 38, 181–186.

Prates, M. D. and Torres, F. O. (1965). A cancer survey in Lourenço Marques, Portuguese East Africa. *Journal of the National Cancer Institute*, 35, 729–757.

Rose, E. and McGlashan, N. D. (1975). The spatial distribution of oesophageal carcinoma in the Transkei, South Africa. *British Journal of Cancer*, 31, 197–266.

Rotkin, I. D. (1973). A comparison review of key epidemiological studies in cervical cancer related to current searches for transmissible agents. *Cancer Research*, 33, 1353–1367.

Schrire, V. (1971). Heart disease in southern Africa with special reference to ischaemic heart disease in Cape Town. *South African Medical Journal*, 45, 634–644.

Seedat, Y. K. and Hackland, D. B. T. (1984). The prevalence of hypertension in 4,993 rural Zulus. *Transactions of the Royal Society of Tropical Medicine and Hygiene*, 78, 785–789.

Segi, M. (1977). Graphic presentation of cancer incidence by site and by area and by population. Nagoya, Japan: Segi Institute of Cancer Epidemiology.

Sever, P. S., Peart, W. S., Gordon, D., and Beighton, P. (1980). Blood pressure and its correlates in urban and tribal Africa. *Lancet*, 2, 60–64.

Shafritz, D. A. and Kew, M. C. (1981). Identification of integrated hepatitis B virus DNA frequencies in human hepato-cellular carcinoma. *Hepatology*, 1, 1–8.

Shaper, A. G. (1974a). Communities without hypertension. In: *Cardiovascular Disease in the Tropics*, Shaper, A. G., Hutt, M. S. R., and Fejfar, Z. (editors), pp. 77–83. London: British Medical Association.

————. (1974b). Endomyocardial fibrosis. In: *Cardiovascular Disease in the Tropics*, Shaper, A.G., Hutt, M. S. R., and Fejfar, Z. (editors), pp. 22–41. London: British Medical Association.

Shaper, A. G. and Shaper, L. (1958). An analysis of medical admissions to Mulago Hospital, 1957. *East African Medical Journal*, 35, 647–678.

Smith, E. C. and Elmes, B. G. T. (1934). Malignant diseases in natives of Nigeria: an analysis of 500 tumours. *Annals of Tropical Medical Parasitology*, 28, 461–476.

Taylor, D. (1982). *Medicine, Health, and the Poor World*. London: Office of Health Economics.

Templeton, A. C. and Hutt, M. S. R. (1973). Distribution of tumours in Uganda. In: *Tumours in a Tropical Country. Recent Results in Cancer Research*, Templeton, A. C. (editor), no. 41. Berlin, New York: Springer-Verlag.

Tobian, L. (1979). Interrelationships of sodium and hypertension. In: *Hypertension, Determinants, Complications, and Intervention*, Onesti, G. and Klimt, C. R. (editors), pp. 13–32. The fifth Hahnemann international symposium on hypertension. New York: Grune and Stratton.

Trowell, H. C. (1981). Hypertension, obesity, diabetes mellitus, and coronary heart disease. In: *Western Diseases: Their Emergence and Prevention*, Burkitt, D. P. and Trowell, H. C. (editors), pp. 3–32. London: Edward Arnold.

Udeh, F. N., Anand, S. V., and Edington, G. M. (1966). Carcinoma of the bladder in western Nigeria. *Journal of Urology*, 96, 479–482.

Vaughan, J. P. (1977). A brief review of cardiovascular disease in Africa. *Transactions of the Royal Society of Tropical Medicine and Hygiene*, 71, 226–231.

————. (1978). A review of cardiovascular diseases in developing countries. *Annals of Tropical Medicine and Parasitology*, 72, 101–109.

Vint, F. W. (1935). Malignant disease in the natives of Kenya. *Lancet*, 2, 628.

Walker, A. R. P. (1981). South African black, Indian, and coloured populations. In: *Western Diseases: Their Emergence and Prevention*, Trowell, H. C. and Burkitt, D. P. (editors), p. 293. London: Edward Arnold.

Waterhouse, J., Muir, C. S., Correa, P., and Powell, J., editors. (1976). *Cancer Incidence in Five Continents*. Vol. 3. IARC Scientific Publication, no. 42. Lyon, France.

Williams, A. O. (1971). Coronary arteriosclerosis in Nigeria. *British Heart Journal*, 33, 85–100.

Williams, A. O., Resch, J. A., and Loewenson, R. B. (1969). Cerebral arteriosclerosis: a comparative autopsy study between Nigerian Negroes and American Negroes and Caucasians. *Neurology*, 19, 205–210.

Williams, E. H. (1986). Cancer in Kuluva Hospital, Uganda. In: *Cancer Occurrence in Developing Countries*, Parkin, D. M. (editor). IARC Scientific Publication, no. 75. Lyon, France.

Wilson, T. W. (1986). History of salt supplies in West Africa and blood pressures to-day. *Lancet*, 1, 784–786.

World Health Organization. (1988). *Prevention of Liver Cancer. WHO Technical Report 1988*, no. 691, 8–9.

Wright, D. H. (1970). Microscopic features, histochemistry, histogenesis, and diagnosis. In: *Burkitt's Lymphoma*, Burkitt, D. P. and Wright, D. H. (editors), pp. 82–102. Edinburgh: Livingstone.

Zambia. Ministry of Health. (1984). *Ministry of Health Report—1980*. Lusaka: Government Printers.

Part III

Longitudinal Studies
of Small Populations

Chapter 16

Community-Based Studies in Sub-Saharan Africa: An Overview

Eleuther Tarimo

Although the vital registration and statistical systems of Sub-Saharan Africa have been improved and expanded in recent decades, only a small minority of vital events are recorded in most countries. For example, in many less than 10 percent of infant deaths are registered. Data on deployment of health resources, including the use of health services and the impact of different interventions, are also deficient. Decision-making in health matters is therefore based on guess-work and intuition about the level of health in different parts of a country. Community-based studies, in which an entire community, not individuals, is the unit of study, can potentially overcome or at least ameliorate these deficiencies.

The six studies reported in this section differ in their objectives, the size of their study population (which ranges from 710 in Keneba, the Gambia, to 200,000 in Malumfashi, Nigeria), their duration, and their timing. The Keneba and Pare-Taveta projects began in the early 1950s, Danfa in the late 1960s, Malumfashi and Machakos in the 1970s, and Kilombero in the 1980s. These six studies are included because information on them is available and accessible, not because they have earned any special merit. Other community studies, such as that of Kasongo, Zaire (Kasongo Project Team, 1981, 1983), could have been considered as well. Many such studies were initiated in the 1960s and 1970s in Africa (World Health Organization, 1972) and have been carried out in other parts of the world, such as Lampang, Thailand (Thailand, 1981), Azerbaijan, Iran (King, 1983), Matlab, Bangladesh (Phillips *et al.*, 1984), Brazil (McAuliffe *et al.*, 1985), Narangwal, India (Kielmann *et al.*, 1983), and Bohol, Philippines (Williamson *et al.*, 1983).

The information obtained through such studies can support the efforts of national health authorities to improve their health care programs. In a broader sense, their findings can benefit the entire international community. What lessons can be drawn from analyzing the potentials and pitfalls of these studies?

Some of the criteria for such an analysis are suggested below, followed by brief information on each of the studies included in this volume. Community-based health studies have been studied and have evolved over the years. Assessing past studies using present-day criteria is, therefore, not justified. Although a current assessment may not be fair to the persons and organizations involved in the studies, it will, however, indicate ways in which community-based studies in general can be improved in the future.

Criteria for Assessing Community-Based Studies

Community-based health studies should be assessed in light of five criteria: relevance, appropriate mix of factors, involvement of existing structures and the community, cost, and use of the findings.

Relevance

The purpose of community-based studies is to obtain information on health and health care that is not available or cannot be obtained from routine data and that will improve the country's ability to meet the health needs of its communities. Saying that a study will increase knowledge and that the findings may be useful to providing health care is not sufficient. Although previously unexpected use may be made of the findings, such an expectation is not an adequate reason for conducting studies. An explicit decision should be made on how the data will be analyzed and used in decisionmaking.

A number of questions, therefore, need to be raised before such studies are undertaken. Will the information being sought affect intervention strategies? Is the information sufficiently important to justify the cost of the study, both of resources for the investigators and time of community members? If the missing data were available, could officials act effectively on the findings? How do the potential benefits from the particular areas and subjects studied compare with those gained from alternative uses of resources?

Finally, are the data being sought truly unavailable? Much more information exists in developing countries than is immediately apparent. Visits to ministries of health reveal piles of data in deserted offices; sometimes the people working in the ministries are not even aware they exist! Other places to visit include the ministries of planning and the interior, local government offices, planning institutes, and relevant university departments. Calls for studies and more data are often unjustified and can be used to delay making sensitive resource decisions to improve or intensify health activities in communities.

Appropriate Mix of Factors for Study

Concurrent studies of interrelated issues concerning populations, illness, health care, and environment make sense because they maximize the basic investment in a study. Because risk factors for various diseases often interact (for example, morbidity and mortality from measles are closely related to morbidity and mortality from malnutrition and diarrhea), studying several problems together is crucial. For policymakers, obtaining a broad, comprehensive, valid understanding of different problems, their interrelationships, and what can be done about them is more useful than understanding a single disease in isolation. This implies that many specialists from various disciplines need to be involved. One problem is that when separate organizations with different concerns initiate, fund, and implement a community study, each wants to be identified with its own separate study.

Single studies run the risk of trying to obtain too much information on too many problems. The challenge of investigators, in consultation with policymakers, is to decide on a reasonable number of issues. Moreover, a narrow, detailed, in-depth study can occasionally help determine the critical role of a particular activity, such as immunization using a particular vaccine.

Another issue is whether to assess the situation before and after an intervention or at a single point in time without an intervention. Moral and ethical questions are raised by studies that measure population data, but contribute little or nothing to the health care of the community studied.

The final issue, and a key concern, is whether the study pays attention to distributional equity, which is the cornerstone of primary health care. Do the data being sought identify underserved and high-risk subgroups by collecting information on age, sex, income, race, culture, and other social and geographic attributes? Studies that look at geographically defined populations in the aggregate, without attempting to understand the health risk differentials between, for example, rich and poor members of the population, can easily overlook opportunities for policy and service intervention.

Involvement of Existing Structures and Communities

Involving existing staff, reinforced as necessary, improves their ability to carry out such studies and ensures that innovations introduced as part of the study, or as a result of it, are sustained.

Involving the community can take different forms depending on the study's purpose. Ideally, the community should participate in developing and implementing the project.

Cost

What are the costs of obtaining *and* using the information being sought? If beneficial results are obtained, is applying them on a large scale affordable? Lack of consideration of costs and resource implications is a common omission in many studies. When this occurs, decisionmakers have difficulty judging the feasibility of applying the findings. A checklist of ten questions for determining the cost and economic impact of a study (Drummond *et al.*, 1987) might be applied to planning community-based studies in the future.

Use of the Findings

The last criterion concerns the extent to which the results of the study are used and disseminated. More specifically, one must ask how the results of each study influence health policy formulation, health plans for the concerned areas and beyond, and actual program implementation.

One must also ask whether the results of the study have been disseminated in a wide range of forms so that all audiences to which they are relevant are reached. What are the effects of the results beyond the study area? The presentation and dissemination of findings influence considerably the extent of their use. The results should be as explicit and as easy for users to interpret as possible.

Six Studies

Below are some observations on how the six studies presented in chapters 17–22 satisfy the above criteria.

Pare-Taveta, Tanzania and Kenya

The Pare-Taveta project (1954–66) was conducted to assess the public health importance of malaria and whether interruption could be achieved by spraying residual insecticides (see chapter 17 of this volume). Detailed studies of morbidity and mortality before and during the intervention were carried out in two groups of villages. Enumerators recorded the name, sex, estimated age, and maternity history of villagers. Births and deaths were recorded at each six-month survey, and entomological and parasitological data were also collected. Control measures resulted in a dramatic fall in malaria levels, a fall in the crude death and infant mortality rates, and a rise in hemoglobin levels and serum proteins. Most of the anthropometric data, particularly beyond the age of five years, were not of value. Mosquito density fell dramatically following spraying, but transmission was only reduced, not stopped. Residual spraying could not be continued indefinitely. When it stopped, mosquito density rose again, and mortality reverted more or less to its former levels once transmission resumed. Chapter 17 refers to a later study by Hannan-Anderson on water supplies and women's role that, although carried out in the area, did not use the findings of the malaria project. It is rightly pointed out that the two studies could have been carried out in a complementary way. In fact, a number of other diseases (particularly those caused by parasites) and issues on the delivery of health care could have been studied concurrently.

The findings of the project have been widely disseminated in technical journals and have been useful for determining malaria control policies and strategies in the country and elsewhere. This was one of the first studies to show the impracticability of malaria eradication using the technologies available at the time.

Machakos, Kenya

This longitudinal population study (see chapter 18) had seven objectives ranging from obtaining accurate data on morbidity and mortality from measles, whooping cough, and acute respiratory and diarrheal diseases to developing a system of registering births and deaths to conducting biological studies of vaccines for measles and whooping cough. The large number of objectives probably reflects the diversity of the in-

terests and skills of its supporting institutions. The study was carried out by special teams who visited each of 4,000 households, initially every two weeks and later every month. They used registration forms similar to those used in the Keneba study. Only the vaccine component involved intervention.

The study's finding that the optimum age for measles immunization is nine months has been the basis for immunization policies on age of measles immunization in Kenya and throughout the world. For pertussis, it found that six-month vaccination campaigns were suitable in areas with poor access to health services. The data on morbidity and mortality revealed no seasonal variations, but found that the population structure and main causes of mortality were similar to those of other developing countries. The findings are published in a book and several articles.

Kilombero, Tanzania

The study has three components: analysis of routine data (from 20 dispensaries, 2 health centers, and the essential drugs program); an annual collection of morbidity and mortality data from one large village; and an assessment of interventions addressing priority problems (see chapter 19). Survey data revealed the importance of malaria, hookworm, schistosomiasis, and malnutrition. Interventions therefore included latrine campaigns, improvements in the water supply, and community-based chemotherapy for schistosomiasis. The lack of information at the district, regional, and national levels was mostly due to deficiencies in evaluating the existing data available from community health workers, dispensaries, and health centers. Also, the registration of births and deaths by community health workers revealed the same number of births and deaths as was found with an intensive vital statistics survey. Most deaths occurred in the rainy season, and the disease perception pattern (revealed by a simple questionnaire) matched parasitological and clinical findings. The project has been extensively discussed at the local level, and the findings, which have been published in technical journals, are being used to implement primary health care.

Keneba, The Gambia

In 1956 this study began to collect information on the epidemiology of communicable diseases in rural areas (see chapter 20). The study, which continues to this day, consists of annual surveys by medically qualified personnel who identify each resident and record his or her name, age, sex, dwelling, and the results of a physical examination. Births and deaths are also recorded through the reports of reliable and influential villagers. The study is broadly based rather than narrowly targeted to specific diseases and does not include any interventions. Initially this area had no organized health service, so the question of involving local structures did not arise. That situation has changed, and it is hoped that such linkages have been established. Results show that morbidity and mortality patterns are similar to those of other developing countries. Important diseases include malaria (with an overall parasite rate of 54.7 percent), hookworm (100 percent after the age of five years), trachoma, and hepatitis. With a few exceptions, such as the disappearance of trypanosomiasis, no major changes have occurred in disease patterns over the years. Other findings include the seasonal effects of morbidity and mortality, which increase during the rainy seasons. The other studies reach the same conclusion, with the exception of Machakos, where malaria is not important. The study findings have been extensively published in medical journals, which do not report how the findings have been used to improve local health activities nor the results of those efforts.

The main use of the study has been to stimulate the concept of health monitoring, specifically the possibility of using a sentinel village to furnish information on changes that could alert health authorities to parallel changes in larger geographic areas. The potential use of sentinel villages, health centers, or districts to supplement information collected routinely needs to be explored rigorously. First, more than one village or district must be selected that reflect major socioeconomic or other groupings in the country. Second, the sentinel area should include normal interventions. Finally, the additional costs required should be within the means of the community, the health services, or both. Few countries, including the Gambia, are able to support a sentinel post on the lines of Keneba.

Malumfashi, Nigeria

The objective of this study was to measure the harmful effects of chronic malaria, urinary schistosomiasis, and meningococcal infections (see chapter 21). Nutrition and diarrhea components were added to the study later. The study was built on the strong interests of researchers at Ahmadu Bello University in Zaria. No specific interventions were provided in the study area. Trained enumerators visited assigned houses monthly and recorded data on forms similar to those used in the Machakos study.

The data were analyzed in Liverpool, and the findings on population, morbidity, and mortality resembled those of other developing countries. Over 64 percent of deaths occurred in the rainy season, when morbidity was also high. The study found that meningococcus resisted sulfonamides and that chloroquine chemoprophylaxis only had a small impact on malaria. A shortage of funds halted the study and prevented the findings from being implemented locally. Perhaps closer links between the study and local health authorities might have facilitated implementation of some of the findings.

Danfa, Ghana

The Danfa Project in Ghana began in 1970 with the aim of identifying a cost-effective health and family planning strategy (see chapter 22). The project region, consisting of 300 villages and a population of 65,000, was divided into four areas. In area 1, comprehensive health services, including family planning and health education, were offered. In area 2, family planning services (through mobile units) and health education (through four health education assistants) were provided, but comprehensive services were not. In area 3 only family planning services were provided. Area 4 was the control and received no new services. The project ended in 1979, but by the end of 1975 it had already become clear that the combination of services in area 2 was the most cost-effective.

The project staff included 6 physicians, 10 nurse-midwives, 18 auxiliaries, 56 trained traditional midwives, and about 60 field research assistants temporarily employed as interviewers. The project was particularly useful because it trained Ghanaians, and a Ghanaian codirected the project. Many data, particularly demographic, were collected and sent overseas to be analyzed at the center directing the project. The project was too expensive for the country to replicate, even though some components of the research and training would not have to be carried over into other districts.

Conclusions

The six studies illustrate how data can be obtained in community-based studies and how they have been used. However, little information is available on the relevance of the studies or their cost. Governments must take a more active role if the potential of community-based studies is to be realized. Similar studies in other countries have reached the same conclusion. Community-based studies are often isolated from government efforts to improve health information systems. Several interrelated options emerge for harnessing community-based studies for an overall national effort.

One option is for governments to select a number of sentinel districts or smaller geographic areas. The selected districts should represent the major socio-economic and ecological realities of the country so that the information gathered can reflect the situation of the country as a whole. The districts are thus guards that alert decisionmakers to impending dangers. More detailed health information can be collected and monitored in a sentinel district than is possible in an entire country, and different types of community studies can be carried out as well. In addition to the ongoing measurement of levels and changes in standard demographic and epidemiological variables, studies can conduct operational and intervention activities. For example, the study can explore various ways to deliver a particular intervention and measure the cost-effectiveness of selected interventions, either singly or in combination.

References

Drummond, M. F., Stoddart, G. L., and Torrance, G. W. (1987). *Methods for the Economic Evaluation of Health Care Programmes.* Oxford: Oxford Medical Publications.

Kasongo Project Team. (1981). Le Projet Kasongo: une expérience d'organisation d'un système de soins de santé primaires. *Annales de la Société Belge de Médecine Tropicale,* 60 (supplement).

———. (1983). The Kasongo Project. *World Health Forum,* 4, 41–45.

Kielmann, A. A., Taylor, C. E., DeSweemer, C., Parker, R. L., Chernichovsky, D., Reineke, W. A., Uberoi, D. N., Kakar, N. M., and Sarma, R. S. S. (1983). *Child and Maternal Health Services in Rural India: The Narangwal Experiment.* Vol. 1: *Integrated Nutrition and Health Care.* A World Bank Research Publication. Baltimore, Md.: Johns Hopkins University Press.

King, M., editor. (1983). *An Iranian Experiment in Primary Health Care: The West Azerbaijan Project, 1983.* Oxford: Oxford University Press.

McAuliffe, J. F., Tavares, I. L., Leslie, J., Araujo, J. G., and Guerrant, R. L. (1985). Prospective studies of the illness burden in a rural community of northeast Brazil. *Bulletin of the Pan American Health Organization,* 19 (2), 139–146.

Phillips, J. F., Simmons, R., Chakraborty, J., and Chowdhury, A. I. (1984). Integrating health services into an MCH-FP program: lessons from Matlab, Bangladesh. *Studies in Family Planning,* 15, 153–161.

Thailand. Ministry of Public Health. (1981). *Summary Final Report of the Lampang Health Development Project,* 6 vols. Bangkok.

Williamson, M. E., Parado, J. P., and Maturan, E. G. (1983). Providing maternal and child health–family planning services to a large rural population: results of the Bohol project, Philippines. *American Journal of Public Health,* 73, 62–71.

World Health Organization. (1972). *Demonstration Training and Research Areas.* WHO document AFR/PHA/90. Brazzaville: WHO Regional Office for Africa.

Chapter 17

Morbidity and Mortality at Pare-Taveta, Kenya and Tanzania, 1954–66: The Effects of a Period of Malaria Control

David J. Bradley

This study of an African population living near the border between Tanzania and Kenya and subject to a period of intensive malaria control is one of the important, yet most neglected, longitudinal studies of health in an African community. It is important because both the effects of a malaria control intervention and the consequences of withdrawing control were observed, and it has been neglected partly because of where the results were published and partly for reasons that remain obscure. The study was ahead of its time in conception and execution, but typical of its period in other respects: some of the documentation lacks detail, the demographic picture is sketchy in parts, and the quality control was less rigorous than would be demanded today. However, in the continuation of observations for many years after the key intervention period, the Pare-Taveta Malaria Scheme is outstanding, and much of the information it provides is unique. For several reasons it is most unlikely that a similarly complete study can be carried out again.

Project Background: Purpose and Timing

The Pare-Taveta Malaria Scheme, which arose from discussions beginning in 1946, was initiated in 1954 with two aims. The first was to assess the public health importance of malaria, in relation to other endemic diseases, in the relatively immune community that occurs under conditions of high-intensity transmission in East Africa. The second aim was to determine whether the transmission of malaria could be stopped in that area using the residual insecticides that had recently become available. This, if even partly successful, would permit the impact of malaria to be determined more critically by observing the changes in health, morbidity, and mortality that followed control.

Transmission was greatly reduced but not stopped, and residual insecticide spraying could not be continued indefinitely. Thus a further check on the specificity of the changes in health and disease was possible by observing the extent to which the patterns of ill-health reverted toward the initial conditions once transmission had resumed its previous, high level. This later phase, although not part of the original plan, has proved valuable for considering arguments about the specificity of the changes observed in health. In most other studies in which interventions were undertaken, the causal relation of those interventions to observed changes is less securely based.

In selecting a study area emphasis was placed on finding a manageable, highly endemic area for malaria transmission that was readily accessible to the study group, but geographically isolated from other malarious areas (see figure 17-1). The two East African areas selected were contiguous, lying to the east of Mount Kilimanjaro: the Taveta subdistrict of Kenya and the Pare district of Tanzania (then called Tanganyika). Both were accessible to the East African Institute of Malaria and Vector-borne Diseases at Amani, which then served all three East African territories and was not restricted by the national boundaries dividing the study area.

The overall boundary of the scheme covered a substantial area that included approximately 132,000 people. Of these, 79,000 lived in the mountains, where malaria was not transmitted; they could, however, become infected and ill if they visited the plains. The remaining 53,000 people lived in the plains, and their 17,500 houses were subject to the residual spraying.

Two groups of villages were selected in order to study morbidity and mortality in detail before and during the intervention. One group comprised villages in the Taveta forest at the northern end of the study area; the other comprised the hillfoot and swampland villages of South Pare, which were located in the

Figure 17-1. Boundaries of the Pare-Taveta Malaria Control Scheme and Vital Statistics Survey

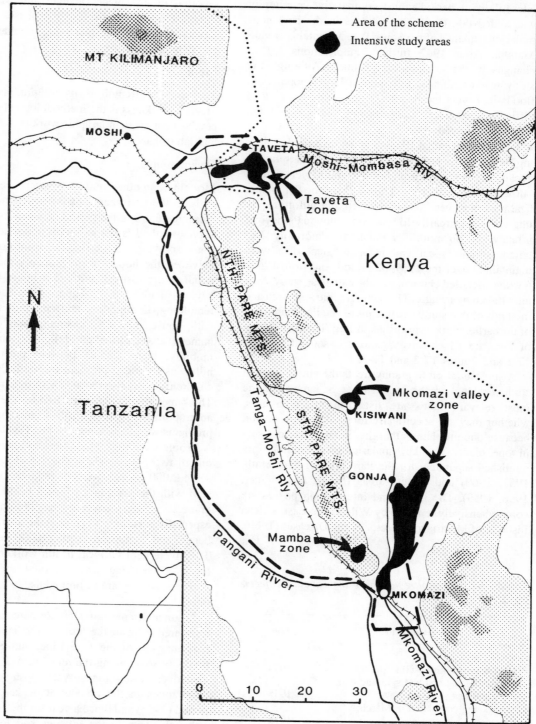

Source: Modified from Pringle (1964).

Mkomazi Valley, southeast of the sprayed area. In the later follow-up period a third, comparative community was added that comprised villages in the cool non-malarious uplands of the South Pare Mountains around Mamba. After 1962 further complications led to changes in the communities studied. Although the study was capable of following a larger population, floods in Taveta led to resettlement, which produced difficulties of access and tracing and reduced the numbers involved.

Fieldwork began in 1954, residual insecticide spraying began in the north in mid-1955, and six spraying cycles, which moved from north to south, were carried out from then until 1959. During that time the human health studies were also conducted, but unfortunately interest was primarily focused on individuals beyond infancy and on morbidity rather than mortality. Detailed entomological and parasitological data were maintained over the 1959–62 period, and from 1962–66 the detailed human vital statistics study was undertaken by Pringle. The demographic approach and methods of that study became more detailed than those of the earlier work as priorities shifted. The chronology of the Pare-Taveta investigations is set out in table 17-1 and figures 17-2 and 17-3.

A substantial bibliography treats the entomological studies related to the Pare-Taveta Scheme, and the most relevant items are listed in the references, whether they are specifically referred to here or not, because one problem is that the literature is not listed in one place. The key malariological findings are published separately for the Pare (Draper and Smith, 1957, 1960) and Taveta areas (Smith and Draper, 1958, 1959). The initial and intervention phases are comprehensively reported by Wilson and East African Institute of Malaria and Vector-borne Diseases (1960),

and the demographic work for 1962–66 is also reported in one place (Pringle and Matola, 1967). Pringle (1969) examines all the phases of the Pare-Taveta studies in one place and emphasizes malaria and demography.

Methods

The study's strength is its longitudinal nature; its greatest weakness is the methodological change in the emphasis of the demographic work between the earlier and later phases.

Demography

Mortality and other vital events were measured differently in the two phases of the scheme and were not measured at all in the period between the phases. The survey method is not explicitly reported for phase 1. Since spraying was carried out from house to house, however, the houses were probably marked and the population registered through a house-by-house survey. Difficulties in this approach arose from house rebuilding, immigration and emigration, interference with house numbers, changing spouses, changing names (between tribal and religious names), and high mobility. Transhumance between the plains and the hills was an added problem in South Pare, and some children were registered at school rather than at home. The same populations were used for the demographic, anthropometric, and medical surveys. All the mobility problems were less severe in the Taveta area.

People were registered at each village or school, at one of two grades. The grade 1 registers, comprising some 2,000 people, were maintained by the research staff with the assistance of local health workers. The grade 2 registers covered an additional population, especially persons who entered the area after the study began, and comprised another 8,000 people by 1959. They were kept by local health workers, and a lower level of checking was accepted for the grade 2 registers, so they are of limited use in calculating vital rates.

In grade 1, approximately 25 percent of the people registered were of the less mobile Taveta people, 60 percent were of the Pare tribe, and Sambaa people predominated among the remainder. The people were visited on a six-month cycle throughout the study: three times in the precontrol or very early control period (1955) and twice a year for the next three years, although visits to the villages had to be staggered. About 70–80 percent of the persons registered were seen on any one visit, and most of the anthropological and parasitological data therefore compare successive

Table 17-1. Chronology of the Pare-Taveta Projects, 1954–66

Phase and activity	Year
Phase 1	
Project begins with baseline studies	1954
Spraying begins; residual spraying every eight months	1955
Last spraying completed in March; treatment teams set up	1959
Phase 2	
Vital statistics study begins	1962
Demographic study completed	1966

Figure 17-2. Mosquito Density before and after the Dieldrin Spraying, Pare-Taveta

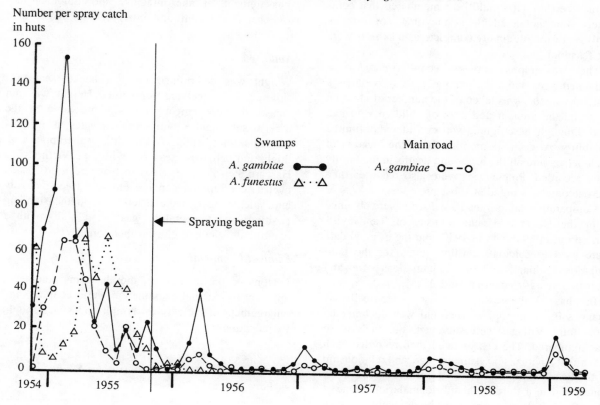

Figure 17-3. Density of A. gambiae in Huts and the Mean Sporozoite Rate after Spraying Stopped, Pare-Taveta

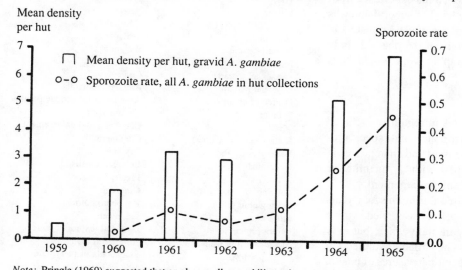

Note: Pringle (1969) suggested that an abnormally exophilic strain present in 1960–64 was gradually replaced by the original phenotype.

cross-sectional surveys with about a 75 percent overlap of membership. (It should be remembered that computers were not available at the time, so complex analyses of longitudinally complete data subsets were not feasible).

The demographic surveys recorded name, sex, estimated age, and tribe; in the case of women a maternity history was taken of the number of children born and the number and ages of children who had died, although these figures were considered of limited reliability. At each six-month survey, the location of each person and all the births and deaths in the family were recorded. Pregnancies were also recorded, and the outcome was noted at subsequent visits.

Comparative data for the Pare district were obtained from the General African Census of Tanganyika carried out in 1948 and in 1957, and the original data were used to calculate fertility ratios for the nonmalarious highlands and for the plains areas before and after two years of malaria control.

In phase 2 the research focused specifically on changes in demographic rates and was documented more fully. Villages were surveyed, and each house was numbered. The census team then recorded each inhabitant's name, sex, estimated age, and relationship to the head of the household. In the Pare and Taveta zones, and in a third highland nonmalarious zone at Mamba, 1,500 or more households were studied. Maternity histories were not taken, but the study population was revisited every four months for five years. At each visit pregnancies, live births, stillbirths, deaths, and population movements were recorded. The staff carrying out the study had gained experience from their work in phase 1, and the level of supervision was probably comparable to that of the grade 1 registers in phase 1. Moreover, the structure of the phase 2 study was simpler, and the demographic work would have required less supervision.

Morbidity

The malariometric measures taken regularly included the parasite rate, gametocyte rate, and species of malaria present, as well as the liver and spleen rates in the upright position, together with a quantitative measure of the degree of splenic enlargement.

Morbidity was only measured during the four years of phase 1. A variety of measures was tried, which made this a pioneering study in many ways, but only some were pursued in detail. The variables studied fell into several categories: nonspecific measures of health, such as childhood anthropometry; specific variables likely to be influenced by malaria, such as hemoglobin

level, blood proteins, and body temperature; and measurements of other infections and etiological factors that might confound interpretation of the data (table 17-2).

Anthropometry

Weight was determined using a basket scale for children or a steelyard for adults. Height was not measured. Subcutaneous fat was measured at the triceps, subscapular, and suprailiac sites using Harpenden skinfold calipers. The girth of the upper arm, thigh, and calf was measured with tape. A modified Harvard Step Test, timed to a metronome, used 30 step cycles over 5 minutes on a 38 cm step. Hepatomegaly and splenomegaly were determined in the standing position, and temperature was taken orally with a one-minute standard clinical thermometer.

Clinical Examination

Lesions of the skin, eyes, mouth, gums, and teeth apparent to external examination were recorded, and enlargement of the cervical lymph nodes was sought by palpation.

Table 17-2. Human Health Variables Studied in Pare-Taveta

Demographic	Anthropometric
Age	Circumference
House number	Calf
Name	Chest
Sex	Mid-arm
Tribe	Mid-thigh
Village	Height
	Sitting
Morbidity	Standing
Blood pressure	Weight
Blood smear	
Asexual malaria	*Clinical*
Sexual malaria	Angular stomatitis
Degree of enlargement	Atrophy of the tongue papillae
Liver	Carious teeth
Spleen	Cervical gland enlargement
Dietary surveys (some)	Conjunctivitis
Harvard Step Test	Dry skin
Helminths	Enlarged tonsils
Fecal	Fissured tongue
Urine	Gingivitis
Hemoglobin levels	Hypochromotrichia
Pulse rate	Leg ulcers
Serum protein levels	Loss and texture of hair
Sickle cell trait (in a few	Number of teeth
persons)	Pinguecula or pterygium
Temperature	Scabies
White cell counts	Xerosis

Hemoglobin levels were determined almost entirely by a single person who examined finger-prick blood samples, collected in the mornings, with an MRC Grey Wedge photometer.

Urine specimens for helminthological examinations were collected randomly, and 5 ml samples were preserved with formalin until they could be centrifuged and the deposit examined for schistosome ova.

Stool samples (1 ml) were preserved in a Merthiolate-formaldehyde-iodine solution until they were concentrated by an unspecified acid-ether method and the deposit examined.

Basic, unsophisticated dietary surveys were carried out in the South Pare area. The striking findings were that, apart from a clear rise in hemoglobin level following malaria control, very few changes took place in the anthropometric or clinical variables studied.

Results

Effects on Mosquitoes and Malaria

The effects of dieldrin spraying on the anopheline mosquito populations of the project area were studied in immense detail because this was the first major trial of large-scale residual insecticiding in an endemic area of East Africa. Although the anopheline mosquitoes remained susceptible to the insecticide, resistance appeared in *Culex quinquefasciatus*, fleas, lice, and bedbugs. Their reappearance distressed the inhabitants, who had become used to the initial benefits of spraying.

The densities of *Anopheles gambiae* and *An. funestus* fell dramatically following spraying, and both remained scarce throughout the project (see figure 17-2). Some outdoor-feeding anophelines of other species (and of forms resembling *An. funestus*) persisted, but they were box trapped and appeared not to feed on man. This review does not attempt to cover the mass of entomological detail that is available. When spraying ended in 1959, the anopheline population

gradually recovered much less rapidly than anticipated, and thereafter malaria endemicity rose slowly (see figure 17-3). The dramatic epidemics that some had forecast, and all had feared, did not take place, partly because dieldrin persisted and insecticidal pressure did not cease suddenly and partly, it is inferred, because of the treatment teams' activities.

The sporozoite rate in the mosquitoes fell to undetectable levels after spraying. Even before intervention the rate did not exceed 50 infective bites per person per year, a level that was only reached in the swamp villages, and *An. funestus* was a more important vector than *An. gambiae*.

Prior to intervention the malaria levels of the groups of villages in the project area were as seen in table 17-3; the effects of malaria control on the parasite rates and the degree of splenic enlargement are clearly seen in figure 17-4. A remarkable reduction in transmission was achieved, and the infant parasite rates shown in figure 17-5 illustrate the time-course of this reduction. Toward the end of the spraying period, persons were asked about the likely source of infection in infants: about half had probably been infected outside the project area. The gradual return of malaria once the control measures ended is shown in figure 17-6.

Effects on Mortality

The information from the Pare-Taveta Scheme that excites the most interest today appears almost as an afterthought in the original study, perhaps because the effect of malaria on child mortality was already accepted or because some of the planners did not wish to think about it. However, data available from the grade 1 registers (see table 17-4) show statistically significant falls in the crude death rate and infant mortality rate (1 percent and 5 percent levels, respectively) and increases in the birth rate. The grade 2 registers show rises in both the birth and the fertility rates following control, but their mortality data are unreliable.

Table 17-3. Malaria Levels Prior to Intervention, by Area

Rate and prevalence	Taveta forest	Pare mesoendemic	Hillfoot villages	Swampland villages
Calculated human inoculations per person per year	12–26	—	13–27	27–53
Prevalence of parasitemia, 5–9 years	74	40	59	73
Prevalence of palpable splenomegaly, 5–9 years	85	38	73	81

— Not applicable.

254   *David J. Bradley*

Figure 17-4. Malaria Endemicity in Pare-Taveta, by Age, 1955–59

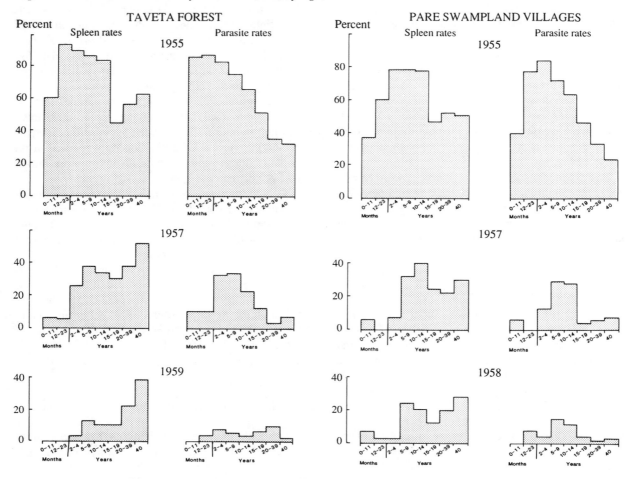

Note: Spleen rates denote the percentage of the population with an enlarged spleen; parasite rates denote the percentage of the population with any parasites in the blood.
Source: Wilson and East African Institute (1960).

Corroborative data (see figure 17-7) recorded in the postcontrol phase for deaths of infants and young children showed that the seasonal timing of mortality closely followed the risk of malarial infection in the previous month. Care must be exercised, however, in accepting such interpretations. An inverse correlation appeared to exist between the risk of malaria and the frequency of successful conception in the same month, but the graph of conceptions also closely resembled that of a nearby nonmalarious area!

The particular feature of Pare-Taveta, the cessation of the intervention and the continuation of data collection, makes the changes in mortality over time of special interest. Figure 17-8 shows the dramatic fall in infant mortality and early childhood mortality that immediately followed malaria control and the smaller falls in mortality at other ages. Childhood mortality completely reverted after transmission resumed, whereas mortality at older ages did not. Availability of treatment can readily explain the latter, but the failure of infant mortality to rise as well during this period remains difficult to explain. No good explanation has been put forward, although the transfer of maternal immunity may have been sufficient to protect infants against the much lower level of malarial challenge in the postcontrol phase. Weanlings and slightly older

Figure 17-5. Quarterly Infant Parasite Rates before and after Spraying, South Pare

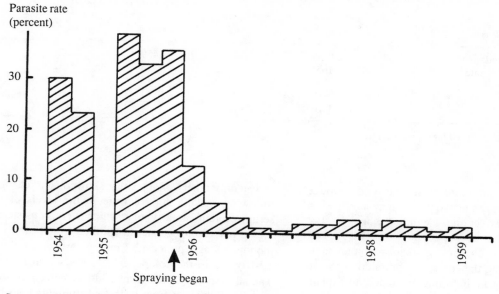

Source: Wilson and East African Institute (1960).

Figure 17-6. Parasite Rates and Estimated Malaria Risk for Children Age 5–9, Mkomazi Valley

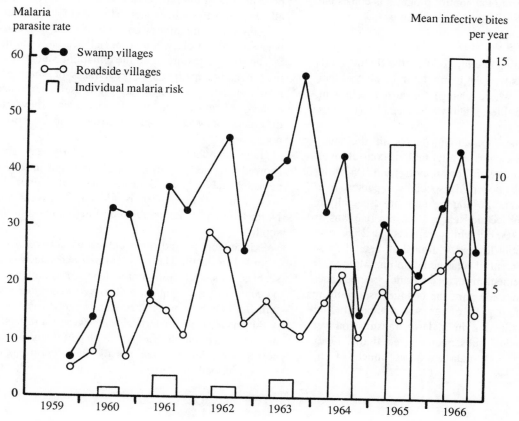

Source: Pringle (1964).

Table 17-4. Effect of Malaria Control on Vital Rates, by Phase of the Project

Rate and sample size	Before control, year 1	Early control, year 2	Effective control	
			Year 3	Year 4
Number studied	2,021	2,348	2,459	2,621
Infant mortality rate	165	260	78	132
Crude death rate	24	23	12	16
Birth rate	40	34	51	47
Fertility rate	138	122	175	163

Note: Rates are incidence per 1,000 persons per year.

children were not protected. Also, the food shortage that occurred between the two phases may have had an especially severe effect on the children who were 1–4 years old by 1962.

The concomitant changes in socioeconomic status that occurred during the control program do not seem to have been adequate in timing and extent to explain the sudden and massive fall in infant and child deaths. That fall was most likely due to malaria control, and the sustained benefits were due in part to malaria treatment. The fall of approximately 100 in the infant mortality rate during the control program is consistent with the findings of comparable programs.

Effects on Morbidity

To avoid presenting essentially negative findings, this section considers first the hemoglobin levels and then other variables where changes occurred following antimalarial activities. Finally, the negative findings are enumerated.

Studies of the hemoglobin levels in the study population show clear rises after malaria control for all age groups between 1955 (prespraying) and 1957; after 1957 smaller rises occurred, especially in persons over the age of 15 years. In infants, and more especially in children in their second year of life, the rise was as great as 2 g per 100 ml, which amounts to a 26 percent rise in hemoglobin levels. At almost all ages the rise exceeded 10 percent of total hemoglobin. Although a general improvement in socioeconomic circumstances probably played some part, the change, especially in children under four years of age, was dramatic before and after the reduction in malaria transmission yet much more gradual subsequently (see figure 17-9), which suggests that malaria caused much of the anemia.

The only other variables that showed clear changes following malaria control were in the levels of the serum proteins as a whole, which were consistently 2.25 g per 100 ml greater in children from birth to 18 months of age protected from malaria, (see figure 17-10) and in the components of the serum protein. The albumin levels fell from 58 to 49 percent of total protein in children from birth to 18 months who had been exposed to malaria and only fell 3 percent in those who had been protected; in the former group gamma globulin, as then measured, rose from 15 to 27 percent, and in the protected group it scarcely rose at all. Far more sophisticated studies of the serum proteins and their antibody contents have subsequently been carried out elsewhere, especially in the Gambia.

The striking feature of all the remaining studies was their negative nature. The great mass of anthropometric statistics, although forming a useful reference archive of growth in the project area, show no difference between the protected and the malarious populations.

Helminth infections were not particularly heavy, but showed a moderate prevalence of the major intestinal parasites (table 17-5). Schistosomes varied over the area, with *S. mansoni* preponderant in Taveta and North Pare and *S. haematobium* more common in the south.

Skin infections and other cutaneous changes were recorded in detail. The only dramatic change was in scabies, which fell from a prevalence of as high as 17 percent to 0; the frequency of *Tunga penetrans* also fell. Both changes were attributed to the insecticide.

Surprisingly, the malaria changes were not reflected in attendances at the outpatient departments of the hospitals serving the area, nor did the proportions of cases ascribed to "malaria" change, although the

Figure 17-7. Deaths in Infants and Children, Successful Conceptions, and Mean Monthly Malaria Risk, Mkomazi Valley and Mamba, 1962–66

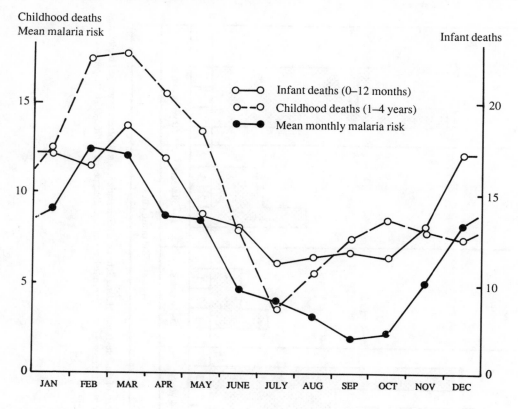

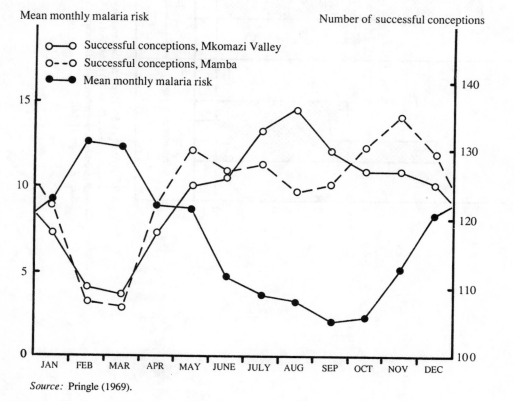

Source: Pringle (1969).

Figure 17-8. Changes in Infant Mortality Rates and Death Rates, Mkomazi Valley

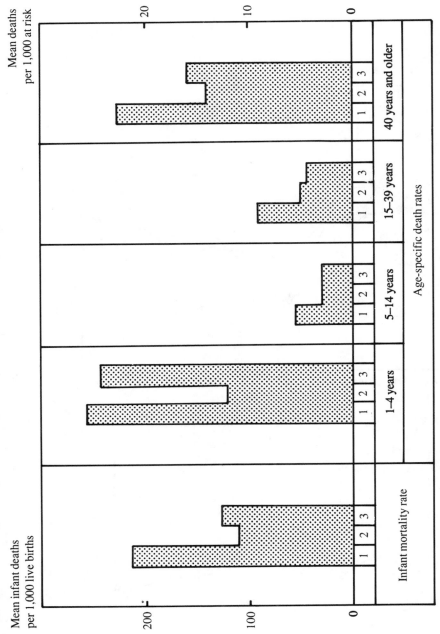

Note: Period 1 (1954–56) covers the first two years of the Pare-Taveta Malaria Scheme, when malaria was still intense or was just beginning to decline; period 2 (1956–58) is the final two years of the scheme, when transmission was negligible; period 3 (1962–66) is the period of the vital statistics survey, when transmission was resuming.
Source: Draper (1962).

258

Figure 17-9. Mean Hemoglobin Levels, by Age and Sex, before and after Malaria Control, 1955–59

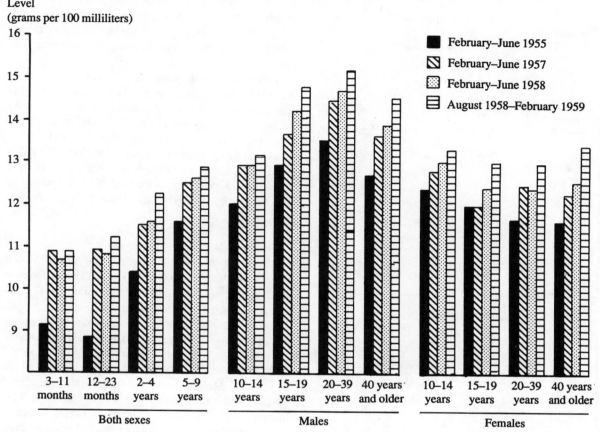

Table 17-5. Helminth Prevalence, South Pare Area
(percent, except as otherwise specified)

Age (years)	Number examined	Prevalence						
		Schistosoma haematobium	S. mansoni	Ascaris	Hookworm	Trichuris	Strongyloides	Taenia
2–4	54	6	0	2	26	13	2	0
5–9	229	11	1	10	48	25	6	1
10–14	267	14	1	12	62	36	8	0
15–19	89	24	0	8	51	24	6	2
20–39	386	17	2	3	47	21	10	1
40 and above	248	12	1	1	40	15	11	1

a. These rates are comparable to those of other areas, except Taveta, where *S. mansoni* reached 30 percent, *S. haematobium* was rare, and *Ascaris* reached 32 percent.

Figure 17-10. Serum Proteins in Treated and Untreated Areas

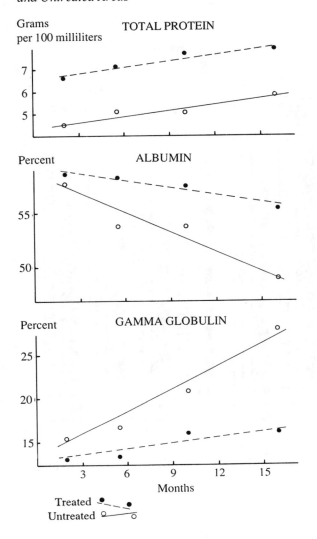

Treated ●‑‑●
Untreated ○—○

implemented or even, as in Pare-Taveta, after it has been discontinued. Sequential and simultaneous controls were both used to good effect. Conversely, the problems of years missing from the records and the great difficulties caused by changing the demographic methodology between the two phases of the project are clear.

Some more subtle points also emerge. The project did not focus on infant mortality because it was felt that enough was known about that; yet today the data on infant mortality are considered to be some of the most important data from the project. On the other hand, the large amounts of anthropometric data that were collected from persons above the age of five years proved to be uninformative, a lesson that had to be relearned by studies of other diseases in East Africa.

Other Aspects

The boundary between Kenya and Tanzania runs southeast in an almost straight line from Mount Kilimanjaro to the coast near Tanga. Taveta forms a small area on Kenya's side of the border near Kilimanjaro. Pare is a larger and more elongated part of Tanzania, running south-southeast from Kilimanjaro and including the north and south Pare Mountains (rising to 8,000 feet) and almost reaching the Usambara Mountains and Amani, where the East African Institute of Malaria (now the Tanzanian Institute of Malaria and Vector-borne Diseases) is situated. This institute was the base for the Pare-Taveta Scheme, whose spraying covered a large tract of country even though the scheme's detailed observations were confined to a few clusters of villages within the larger area.

The Amani Institute also instigated other studies of malaria in areas within or near the Pare-Taveta, both before and after the time of the project. From the literature alone it is often difficult to relate the field studies to each other or to assess how directly applicable some of the findings are to nearby areas.

Others have also worked in the Pare area. Hannan-Andersson (1982), for example, studied water supplies and women's roles in a Pare hamlet of 42 houses. This did not overlap with the Pare-Taveta villages, but did lie within the area sprayed by the scheme. Although the Hannan-Andersson study was concerned with the area's relevant health problems, it did not use any of the Amani-based studies of the area. Much could be gained by integrating the various studies more closely. This is one of the three or four best studied areas within Tanzania (and within East Africa as a whole), and integrating the studies would give a sound basis for further multidisciplinary work.

proportion of attendances at the sisal estate dispensaries attributed to malaria fell from 16.2 to 4 percent, while the annual attendances for any cause rose from 6.9 to 8.4 per person per year.

Lessons from Pare-Taveta

The epidemiological lessons of the Pare-Taveta Scheme have been applied to succeeding generations of population-based control projects for vector-borne diseases both in East Africa and in West Africa at Kankiya and Garki. The scheme illustrates the advantages of longitudinal follow-up that begins before an intervention and continues well after it has been

Acknowledgments

I would like to take this opportunity to thank Sheila Giles and Julia Mitchell, in particular, for their secretarial help, but also to remind the reader of the persons who were responsible for this pioneering study.

The Pare-Taveta study was made possible by the advocacy and determination of D. Bagster Wilson and others such as G. Macdonald and key medical advisers in the colonial office. The study took place in two phases. During the initial work and intervention phase, C. C. Draper was the epidemiologist and A. Smith, the entomologist. They were assisted by M. Butler, D. P. Thomas, J. D. Phipps, E. Hemingway, R. Smith, K. C. Draper, W. Marijani, and others. Specialist advice and help were provided by M.T . Gillies, T. E. Fletcher, J. M. Press, K. S. Hocking, and J. A. Armstrong. In the second, follow-up phase, G. Pringle led the project with the help of J. G. Matola, J. Mbelwa, and several of the previous team.

The first phase was funded for five years by the Colonial Development and Welfare Scheme of the British government and by the East African governments; the follow-up phase was made possible by a grant from the Nuffield Foundation.

The comments and help of C. C. Draper were invaluable in the preparation of this summary of their work.

Bibliography

Allison, A. C. and Clyde, D. F. (1961). Malaria in African children with deficient erythrocyte glucose-6-phosphate dehydrogenase. *British Medical Journal*, 1, 13 May, 1346–1349.

Barlow, F. and Hadaway, A. B. (1956). Effect of changes in humidity on the toxicity and distribution of insecticides sorbed by some dried soils. *Nature*, 178, 1299.

Burnett, G. F. (1956). Variation in mortality with differences in humidity among mosquitoes exposed to BHC, dieldrin, and DDT. *Nature*, 177, 664.

———. (1957). Trials of residual insecticides against anophelines in African-type huts. *Bulletin of Entomological Research*, 48, 631–668.

Clyde, D. F. (1958). Radical cure of malaria in premunes. *British Medical Journal*, 1, 1238–1239.

———. (1961). Malaria control in Tanganyika under the German administration. *East African Medical Journal*, 38, 27–42, 69–82.

———. (1962). Malaria distribution in Tanganyika. *East African Medical Journal*, 39, 528–535.

Clyde, D. F. and Msangi, A. S. (1963). Malaria distribution in Tanganyika. 2: Tanga region. *East African Medical Journal*, 40, 71–82.

Clyde, D. F., Webbe, G., and Shute, G. T. (1958). Single dose pyrimethamine treatment of Africans during a malaria epidemic in Tanganyika. *East African Medical Journal*, 35, 23–29.

Davidson, G. (1953). Experiments on the effect of residual insecticides in houses against *Anopheles gambiae* and *A. funestus*. *Bulletin of Entomological Research*, 44, 231–254.

———. (1958). Studies on insecticide resistance in anopheline mosquitoes. *Bulletin of the World Health Organization*, 18, 579–621.

Davidson, G. and Draper, C. C. (1953). Field studies of some of the basic factors concerned in the transmission of malaria. *Transactions of the Royal Society of Tropical Medicine and Hygiene*, 47, 522–535.

Draper, C. C. (1960). Effect of malaria control on haemoglobin 65 levels. *British Medical Journal*, 1, 1480–1483.

———. (1962). Studies of malaria in man in Africa. M.D. thesis, Oxford University.

Draper, C. C. and Smith, A. (1957). Malaria in the Pare area of northeast Tanganyika. 1: epidemiology. *Transactions of the Royal Society of Tropical Medicine and Hygiene*, 51, 137–151.

———. (1960). Malaria in the Pare area of Tanganyika. 2: effects of three years' spraying of huts with dieldrin. *Transactions of the Royal Society of Tropical Medicine and Hygiene*, 54, 342–357.

Draper, K. C. and Draper, C. C. (1960). Observations on the growth of African infants with special reference to the effect of malaria control. *Journal of Tropical Medicine and Hygiene*, 63, 165–171.

Fletcher, T. E., Press, J. M., and Draper, C. C. (n.d.). Effect of malaria on the serum proteins of African infants. In: *Report on the Pare-Taveta Malaria Scheme, 1954–59*, Wilson, D. B. (editor). Dar es Salaam: Government Printer.

Garnham, P. C. C. (1935). Hyperendemic malaria in a native reserve of Kenya. *Transactions of the Royal Society of Tropical Medicine and Hygiene*, 29, 167–186.

Gillies, M. T. (1954a). Studies of house leaving and outside resting of *Anopheles gambiae* Giles and *Anopheles funestus* Giles in East Africa. 1: the outside resting population. *Bulletin of Entomological Research*, 45, 361–373.

———. (1954b). Studies of house leaving and outside resting of *Anopheles gambiae* Giles and *Anopheles funestus* Giles in East Africa. 2: the exodus from houses and the house resting population. *Bulletin of Entomological Research*, 45, 375–387.

———. (1956). The problem of exophily in *A. gambiae*. *Bulletin of the World Health Organization*, 15, 437.

Gillies, M. T. and Smith, A. (1960). The effect of a residual spraying campaign in East Africa on species balance in the *Anopheles funestus* group. 1: replacement of *A. funestus* by *A. rivulorum*. *Bulletin of Entomological Research*, 51, 243–252.

Gillies, M. T. and Wilkes, T. J. (1963a). *Annual Report of the East African Institute of Malaria and Vector-borne Diseases*. Tanzania: East African Institute of Malaria and Vector-Borne Diseases.

———. (1963b). Observations on nulliparous and parous rates in a population of *Anopheles funestus* in East Africa. *Annals of Tropical Medicine and Parasitology*, 57, 204–213.

———. (1965). A study of the age-composition of populations of *Anopheles gambiae* Giles and *A. funestus* Giles in north-eastern Tanzania. *Bulletin of Entomological Research*, 56, 237–262.

Hannan-Andersson, C. (1982). *Women, Water, and Development in a Pare Settlement, Tanzania*. Bureau of Resource Assessment and Land Use Planning, Research Report, no. 52. Dar es Salaam.

Heisch, R. B. (1948). A parasitological survey of Taveta. *East African Medical Journal*, 25, 78–94.

Jordan, P. (1956). Filariasis in the Eastern Tanga and Northern Provinces of Tanganyika. *East African Medical Journal*, 33, 225–232.

Lumsden, W. H. R. (1955). Entomological studies relating to yellow fever epidemiology at Gedi and Taveta, Kenya. *Bulletin of Entomological Research*, 46, 149–183.

Maclean, G., Webbe, G., and Msangi, A. S. (1958). A report on a bilharzia molluscan survey in the Tanga District of Tanganyika. *East African Medical Journal*, 35, 7–22.

Pringle, G. (1964). Malaria and vital rates in three East African Bantu communities. 1: initial demographical survey. *British Journal of Preventive and Social Medicine*, 18, 43–51.

———. (1967). Malaria in the Pare area of Tanzania. 3: the course of malarial transmission since the suspension of an experimental programme of residual insecticide transmission. *Transactions of the Royal Society of Tropical Medicine and Hygiene*, 61, 69–79.

———. (1969). Experimental malaria control and demography in a rural East African community: a retrospect. *Transactions of the Royal Society of Tropical Medicine and Hygiene*, 63, 2–18.

Pringle, G. and Matola, Y. G. (1967). Report on the Pare Taveta vital statistics report, 1962–1966. Nairobi: East African Common Services Printer.

Pringle, G., Draper, C. C., and Clyde, D. F. (1960). A new approach to the measurement of residual transmission in a malaria control scheme in East Africa. *Transactions of the Royal Society of Tropical Medicine and Hygiene*, 54, 434–438.

Scott, R. R. (1938). Malaria research in Tanganyika. *East African Medical Journal*, 15, 2–6.

Smith, A. (1957). Outdoor cattle feeding and resting of *A. gambiae* and *A. pharoensis*. *East African Medical Journal*, 35, 559.

———. (1958). Dieldrin resistance in *Cimex hemipterus*. *Bulletin of the World Health Organization*, 19, 1124.

———. (1959a). Dieldrin resistance in *Culex pipiens fatigans*. *Indian Journal of Malariology*, 12, 341.

———. (1959b). Effect of residual house spraying in the plains on anopheline densities in huts in the Pare mountains. *Nature*, 183, 198.

———. (1959c). Results of screening *A. gambiae* for resistance to dieldrin. *Bulletin of the World Health Organization*, 21, 239.

———. (1959d). Susceptibility to dieldrin of *Pulex irritans* and *Pediculus humanus corporis*. *Bulletin of the World Health Organization*, 21, 240.

———. (1962). Malaria in the Taveta area of Kenya and Tanganyika. 3: entomological findings three years after the spraying period. *East African Medical Journal*, 39, 553–564.

———. (1966). Malaria in the Taveta area of Kenya and Tanzania. 4: entomological findings six years after the spraying period. *East African Medical Journal*, 43, 7.

Smith, A. and Draper, C. C. (1958). Malaria in the Taveta area of Kenya and Tanganyika. 1: epidemiology. *East African Medical Journal*, 36, 99–113.

———. (1959). Malaria in the Taveta area of Kenya and Tanganyika. 2: results of three and a half years' treatment with dieldrin. *East African Medical Journal*, 36, 629–643.

Smith, A. and Pringle, G. (1967). Malaria in the Taveta area of Kenya and Tanganyika. 5: transmission eight years after the spraying period. *East African Medical Journal*, 44, 469–474.

Smith, A. and Vail, J. W. (1959). Relationship between salinity and breeding of *A. gambiae* in N.E. Tanganyika. *Nature*, 183, 1203.

Smith, A. and Weitz, B. (1959). The feeding habits of *A. gambiae* with particular reference to subsidiary hosts. *Annals of Tropical Medicine and Parasitology*, 53, 414.

Webbe, G. (1959). A bilharzia and molluscan survey in the Handeni and Korogwe districts of Tanganyika. *Journal of Tropical Medicine and Hygiene*, 62, 37–42.

White, G. B. (1969). *Blood Feeding Habits of Malaria Vector Mosquitoes in the South Pare District of Tanzania 10 Years after Cessation of a Dieldrin Residual Spraying Campaign*. WHO/MAL/69.684. Geneva: World Health Organization.

Wilson, D. B. (1936a). *Report of the Malaria Unit, Tanga, 1933–1934*. Dar es Salaam: Government Printer.

———. (1936b). Rural hyperendemic malaria in Tanganyika territory. *Transactions of the Royal Society of Tropical Medicine and Hygiene*, 29, 583–618.

———. (1939). Implications of malarial endemicity in East Africa. *Transactions of the Royal Society of Tropical Medicine and Hygiene*, 32, 435–465.

———. (1946). Notes on the epidemiology of malaria in the East Africa Command. *East African Medical Journal*, 23, 258–272.

Wilson, D. B. and East African Institute of Malaria and Vector-borne Diseases. (1960). *Report on the Pare-Taveta Malaria Scheme, 1954–59*. Dar es Salaam: Government Printer.

Wilson, D. B. and Wilson, M. E. (1934). On the significance of splenic enlargement in East Africa. *East African Medical Journal*, 11, 156–165.

———. (1935). Infections with *Plasmodium ovale* in Tanganyika territory. *Transactions of the Royal Society of Tropical Medicine and Hygiene*, 28, 469–474.

———. (1937). The manifestations and measurement of immunity to malaria in different races. *Transactions of the Royal Society of Tropical Medicine and Hygiene*, 30, 431–448.

———. (1962). Rural hyperendemic malaria in Tanganyika territory. 2: *Transactions of the Royal Society of Tropical Medicine and Hygiene*, 56, 287–293.

Wilson, D. B., Garnham, P. C. C., and Swellengrebel, N. H. (1950). A review of hyperendemic malaria. *Tropical Diseases Bulletin*, 47, 677–698.

Chapter 18

Morbidity and Mortality in Machakos, Kenya, 1974–81

Alexander S. Muller and Jeroen K. van Ginneken

This chapter summarizes the major findings on morbidity and mortality of a longitudinal, population-based study carried out between 1973 and 1981 in the northwestern part of the Machakos District in Kenya. The Machakos Project produced numerous studies and reports, which the present authors, project leaders during the periods 1973–77 (Muller) and 1977–81 (van Ginneken), used extensively in preparing this account.

The major findings of the Machakos Project appear in *Maternal and Child Health in Rural Kenya: An Epidemiological Study,* edited by J. K. van Ginneken and A. S. Muller (1984), and many of the results presented here are published in that volume.

Study Design and Methodology

In 1971 a longitudinal, population-based project was initiated in Machakos District of Kenya. Its aim was to develop the means of improving maternal and child health in a rural area. The objectives of the Machakos Project were as follows:
- To obtain accurate data on morbidity and mortality caused by measles, whooping cough, other acute respiratory infections, and acute diarrheal diseases in children from birth to four years of age;
- To obtain data on nutritional status, social behavior and attitudes, socioeconomic status, and biological and physical environment and to study the influence of these factors on disease patterns;
- To obtain accurate data on maternal and perinatal morbidity and mortality in relation to the antenatal and delivery care received;
- To develop a system for registering births, deaths, and causes of death for all age groups and specifically for children 0–4 years of age from particular target diseases. The aim was to develop a system capable of producing data useful for planning,

operating, and evaluating health services and suitable for a typical district in Kenya with limited resources;
- To study and measure the influence, if any, of the presence of a medical research team on mortality.

In the course of the project two objectives were added:
- To test the impact of several health interventions under field conditions and to determine in particular the clinical efficacy of two rather than three pertussis vaccine immunizations during infancy;
- To study the relationship between the mother's nutritional status during pregnancy and her child's birth weight, lactation performance, and growth during infancy.

During the implementation of the project objectives 4 and 5 were abandoned because of methodological problems and staff constraints.

Study Design

The core of the project was the demographic and disease surveillance system whereby fieldworkers visited each of the approximately 4,000 households in the study area every two weeks until September 1978 and every month until April 1981. The fieldworkers recorded pregnancies, births, deaths, migrations, and morbidity from measles, whooping cough, other respiratory infections, and acute diarrhea among children from birth to four years of age. In practice they recorded all cases of measles and whooping cough, regardless of age.

The study design was semilongitudinal. At the start it included all children less than five years of age. Newborn babies and immigrant children under five were continuously entered into the study; when children reached their fifth birthday or permanently left the area follow-up was discontinued.

The surveillance system produced information that

supported longitudinal and cross-sectional studies. The longitudinal studies covered child growth, outcome of pregnancy, nutritional status during pregnancy and infancy, and the results of two vaccine trials. The cross-sectional surveys dealt with a number of explanatory variables in the environment.

Study Area

The area of 87 square kilometers forms part of the northern division of Machakos District and is located approximately 80 kilometers east of Nairobi (see figure 18-1). The total population was 18,583 according to the 1973 census, and the average population density was 214 persons per square kilometer (the range was 118–532). The area is divided in two by a range of hills. Coffee is an important cash crop in the western region, which is relatively fertile; subsistence farming predominates in the semiarid eastern region. The altitude ranges from 1,300 to 1,700 meters, and the mean annual rainfall is 900 millimeters. There are no villages or large, concentrated groups of homesteads, except around trading centers (see figure 18-2). The study area has one government dispensary and is located near a 50-bed government hospital, a subhealth center, a mission maternity hospital, and a small private clinic. Four field offices and one small field laboratory were established for the project. The average de jure number of household members is six. There is considerable migration; about one-quarter of all heads of households work in one of Kenya's larger towns—mostly Nairobi—and come home on weekends or once a month. Because of the shortage of land many families leave or maintain one farm within and one outside the study area, moving back and forth several times a year.

Disease and Demographic Surveillance

The disease and demographic surveillance system was established in four stages:

1. *Close links were established with the chiefs, subchiefs, and other local leaders of the area.* The chiefs organized open-air meetings in various parts of the area. During these *barazas* the project staff introduced themselves to the community and explained the aims of the project.

2. *A demographic baseline survey was conducted of the entire population, which included preparing detailed maps of every village and numbering every household.* Initially fieldworkers drew crude sketches of each village. Later these maps were improved by the use of fairly recent aerial photographs of the area. The demographic baseline and follow-up surveillance pro-

duced a register that could also be used to study groups other than infants, children less than five, and fertile women.

The project adopted a form that was slightly modified from the form designed by J. G. C. Blacker for Uganda and identical to that of the British Medical Research Council's Kano Plain Project near Kisumu, Kenya. This form was designed to include the following information on every member of a household: name, relationship to the head of the household, sex, age, presence or absence, whether father and mother were alive, and fertility information on females 12 years of age or older.

A household was defined as a group of people habitually eating and sleeping together in the same compound, and one form was used for each household. It became clear early in the project that fieldworkers were not using the same criteria to enter individuals as members of a household; therefore it was decided to register only the de facto population, that is, persons who had slept in the household during the night before the interview. Every person considered by the head of household to be a family member, whether present or not (de jure population), was added to the rolls later. This later list produced the denominator for vital events and incidence rates.

After two months of training the fieldworkers and testing the questionnaires, the project began to conduct the demographic survey. All the *utui* (villages) in one of the five sublocations were mapped. All households received a card marked with a number, which was also painted on the door after the chief and the community gave their permission at a *baraza*. The households were listed according to number, followed by the name of the head of the household. With these lists and the maps drawn by the field staff, fieldworkers were assigned 12–15 households for which they completed demographic survey forms each day. After registering all the *utui* in one sublocation, the entire staff moved to the next.

Many people did not know their age in calendar years, so the staff compiled a calendar of events listing all the important events that were known (either through experience or from hearsay) to have taken place in the area since around 1880. For infants and children under five, birth dates accurate to a month could usually be obtained from birth certificates or records of baptism kept by the parents.

As a rule fieldworkers interviewed the head of the household or his wife. If necessary, they obtained information from any member of the household over 15 years of age who was available for an interview.

Figure 18-1. Kenya, Showing the Machakos Study Area

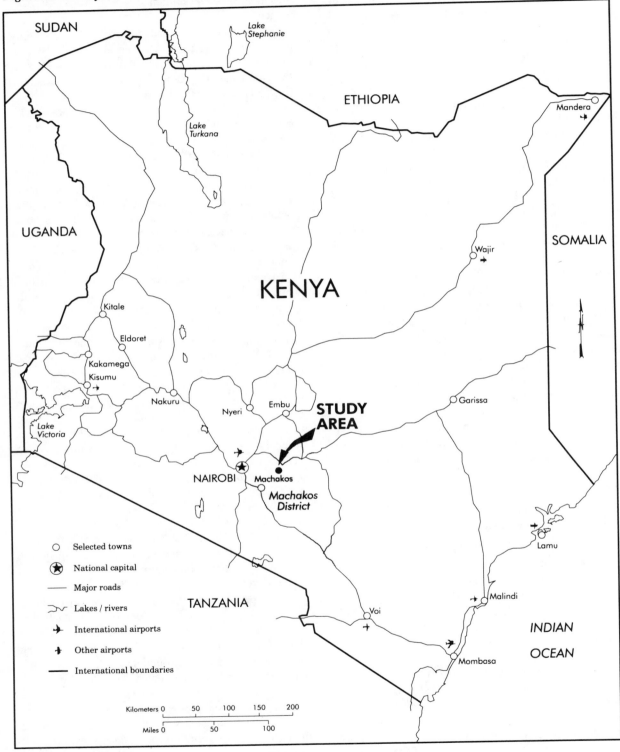

Figure 18-2. *Machakos Study Area*

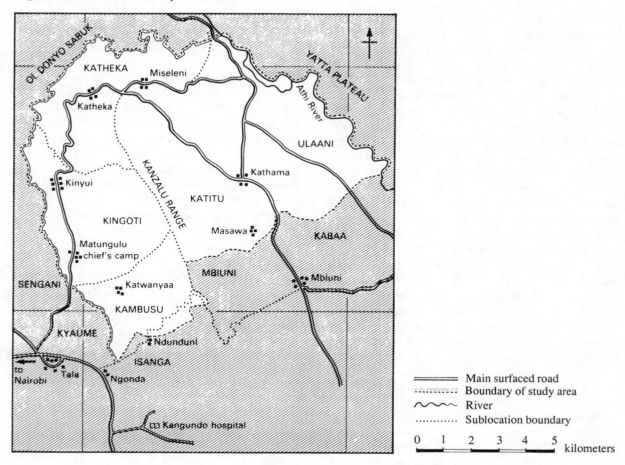

An attempt was made to assess interviewer variations. Every three to four weeks fieldworkers revisited some of the households. Discrepancies between the two interviews were discussed at regular meetings of the field and supervisory staff. Whether discrepancies were the result of interviewer errors or real differences in the information given by different respondents was often unclear. The most common discrepancies concerned the year of birth and the number of live births, especially when some of those children were no longer alive.

The demographic baseline survey, including the recruitment and training of field staff, took 10 months; at the end of this another round of household visits updated the demographic information (September and October 1973).

3. *Demographic surveillance was introduced.* In November 1973 three fieldworkers began to visit each household in a sublocation every two weeks and to collect information on births, deaths, and migration. After three months, demographic surveillance was introduced to the entire study area, which had been divided into 12 clusters of approximately 300 households. Each fieldworker was assigned to a cluster, preferably that in which he himself lived.

4. *The surveillance system was consolidated and field staff were trained to recognize specific signs and symptoms of disease in infancy and childhood.* This stage lasted five months (November 1973 to April 1974). A disease surveillance form was designed that included two screening questions: Has the child been ill since the previous visit? and Does the child look ill? If the answer to both questions was no, the fieldworker recorded only whether a child had a runny nose and cough. If the answer to either question was yes, the fieldworker asked the mother about vomiting and

268   *Alexander S. Muller and Jeroen K. van Ginneken*

diarrhea during the past two weeks, took the child's temperature, and recorded specific observations relating to measles, respiratory distress, and dehydration. The field-worker then reported every suspected case of measles or whooping cough during the doctor's regular clinic visit. The doctor verified the diagnosis according to a standardized list of clinical signs. With the mother's permission, the doctor took nose swabs for culture and finger-prick blood for determining serum antibody levels. During these clinics any child accompanying the mother was also examined and treated.

Because an increasing number of measles and pertussis cases were being seen at nearby health facilities, disease surveillance began one month ahead of schedule. As a result epidemics of these diseases were documented in their early stages. No doubt this early documentation was achieved at the expense of training, but the missed training was compensated by the considerable amount of on-the-job training provided by the medical project staff. Therefore case-identification was probably fairly accurate even during the early days of the measles and whooping cough outbreaks. Owing to the work involved in covering epidemics of measles and whooping cough at the same time, surveillance of acute diarrhea and acute respiratory illness was not sufficiently standardized to be included in the system until 1976.

Demographic surveillance continued for more than seven years, from November 1973 to April 1981, while disease surveillance was conducted from April 1974 to April 1981. Until August 1978 surveillance took place every two weeks; from September 1978 to April 1981 fieldworkers visited all households every four weeks.

Disease surveillance was also simplified in August 1979, when it was restricted to measles and whooping cough.

Population and Mortality

The distribution of the study population by age and sex resembled that of the district as a whole. Comparing the survey results with the 1979 census of the Machakos District shows, however, that the age groups between 15 and 44 years were somewhat underrepresented in the study population, while several of the older age groups were overrepresented. These differences are probably due largely to overestimation of ages by adults, particularly women.

The de facto population increased from 18,583 at the end of 1973 to 23,680 at the end of 1980. The annual natural increase was 37.4 per 1,000, while net loss from outmigration was 3.5 per 1,000 between 1974 and 1980. The rate of natural increase was fairly constant between 1974 and 1980, but the balance between migration in and out fluctuated widely in the same period. The population grew rapidly between 1974 and 1978 and only slightly in 1979 and 1980. Crude birth and death rates and the de facto rate of natural increase averaged 45.7, 6.7, and 39.0, respectively, per 1,000 each year from 1975 to 1978.

Infant and Child Mortality

Mortality rates during the first year after birth (see table 18-1) show the probability of dying to be highest within 24 hours after birth and to decline gradually until the fourth month. Death rates were somewhat elevated between six and nine months after birth. Male

Table 18-1. Probability of Dying, Machakos Study Area, Kenya, by Age below One Year and by Sex, 1975–78

Age interval	Male			Female		
	Number of infants at start of interval	Number of deaths	Probability of dying	Number of infants at start of interval	Number of deaths	Probability of dying
Less than 24 hours	2,356	29	0.0123	2,271	15	0.0066
1–6 days	2,327	25	0.0107	2,256	12	0.0053
7–27 days	2,302	15	0.0065	2,244	13	0.0058
28 days–2 months	2,287	11	0.0048	2,231	13	0.0058
3–5 months	2,276	14	0.0061	2,218	12	0.0054
6–8 months	2,262	19	0.0084	2,206	24	0.0109
0–11 months	2,243	15	0.0067	2,182	13	0.0060
Total below 1 year	2,356	128	0.0543	2,271	102	0.0449

mortality was considerably higher than that of females in the first week after birth; in later months, the differences were small. The overall infant mortality rate was 49.7 per 1,000 births.

The mortality rates for children between one and four years old (see table 18-2) were different in the five sublocations. They were generally high in the east and particularly high in Katheka.

Adult Mortality

De facto mortality rates for the major age groups between 1975 and 1978 are provided in table 18-3. Mortality declined sharply after the first year of life. In later adulthood (age 45–64) rates increased again, reaching their maximum (29 to 47 per 1,000) in the ages 65 years and older.

To assess the quality of the data on mortality by age and sex, the project compared mortality rates with model life tables. The difference in mortality by sex was small at young ages. Mortality at age 5–44 was very low in the project area; incidental nonreporting and statistical fluctuations may well have caused the slight discrepancy. The differences for persons older than 45 years were too large, however, to be acceptable and even increased with age. No realistic model can account for these large discrepancies.

Mortality by Season

Four seasons can be distinguished in Machakos District: a dry season from the middle of January to the middle of March; a wet season marked by long rains from the middle of March to the end of June; a dry season between July and the middle of October; and a

Table 18-2. Infant and Child Mortality Rates in Machakos Study Area, 1975–78

Location	Infant mortality rate[a]	Childhood mortality rate[b]	
		1–4 years	0–4 years
Western Machakos			
Kingoti	36.9	5.0	12.5
Kambusu	53.1	8.4	18.7
Eastern Machakos			
Katheka	68.6	11.1	24.9
Ulaani	61.3	6.7	19.9
Katitu	43.7	7.3	17.5
Total	49.7	7.0	17.2

a. Deaths per 1,000 live births.
b. Deaths per 1,000 registered population.

Table 18-3. Mortality Rates, Machakos Study Area, by Age and Gender, 1975–78

Age (years)	Females	Males
Less than 1	46.7	61.8
1–4	6.3	7.7
5–14	1.2	2.1
15–44	2.1	3.3
45–64	4.6	7.1
65 and above	29.6	39.1
All ages	5.9	7.7

Note: Rates are deaths per 1,000 persons.

wet season marked by short rains from the middle of October to the middle of January. Unlike many African countries, where death rates change profoundly with season, Machakos's mortality, based on infant and child mortality data, did not vary significantly by season.

Discussion of Mortality Rates

The de facto crude death rate in the study area was 6.7 per 1,000. This result can be compared with two national surveys conducted in 1973 and 1977. The first estimated the crude death rate at 13, while the second estimated 14 (Kenya Central Bureau of Statistics, 1975, 1979, respectively). Mortality in the study area was lower than in Kenya as a whole.

The study area's infant mortality of about 50 per 1,000 live births was also lower than reported in two recent national sample surveys. One obtained an infant mortality rate for Kenya of 83 per 1,000 live births; the other, 87 per 1,000 live births (Mott, 1982). The difference between the study area and Kenya as a whole appears to be genuine and not due to underreporting of infant deaths (van Vianen and van Ginneken, 1984).

The most likely reason for these low infant mortality levels is that the economic, social, and hygienic conditions were more favorable in the area than in other parts of Kenya. The adult mortality rates were too low, especially for the population 65 years and older, yet massive underreporting of deaths is unlikely. Data were collected every two weeks between 1974 and 1978, and the quality of the data was controlled in several ways (van Ginneken *et al.*, 1984). A more probable explanation is that older people systematically exaggerated their ages; another may be that, as a result of problems encountered in processing the data, the age composition of the population was less accurate for older ages than for younger ones.

Causes of Child and Adult Deaths

The Machakos Project derived information on causes of death from several sources. The first was the demographic surveillance system in which causes of death were determined retrospectively through household interviews. The fieldworker recorded the respondent's opinion of the cause or the likely cause of death. Information was collected on all deaths of children and adults in the study population. In a number of cases accurate information was not available since relatives of the deceased did not know the cause. A second source of data was a longitudinal study of morbidity and mortality related to pregnancy and delivery. One of the project physicians interviewed women who had experienced a stillbirth or whose child had died within its first year to determine the most likely cause of death. A third source of information was the death records of infants and children less than five years of age. This group was the subject of several longitudinal studies on the epidemiology of communicable childhood diseases. A fourth source was a special in-depth study of adult deaths. That study was conducted by a medical student who interviewed the relatives of 105 persons who had died. More details on sources of data and results are given in Omondi-Odhiambo *et al.* (1990).

Table 18-4 presents the 678 deaths recorded by the Machakos Project between 1975 and 1978 and the cause of death, listed by the three-digit level of classification in the ninth revision of the International Classification of Diseases, or ICD (World Health Organization, 1977). Cause-specific death rates per 100,000 persons are also shown. Because the number of reported deaths is limited, the major groups of causes of death are presented.

This table also summarizes the relative contribution of each cause of death to the total number of deaths from all causes. The leading cause of death was respiratory illness, particularly pneumonia, which accounted for 15.8 percent of all deaths (or 102 deaths for every 100,000 persons). Respiratory illness is a disease of the very young and the very old. Second in rank were congenital anomalies and conditions originating in the perinatal period (hereafter abbreviated as congenital anomalies and perinatal conditions). Such conditions caused 12.8 percent of all deaths (or 83 per 100,000). Intestinal infectious diseases (particularly diarrhea) and measles ranked third and fourth, respectively, with 10.8 and 8.1 percent of all deaths. Malaria caused relatively few (3.1 percent), probably because of the area's high altitude.

There is a clear division between the causes of death among children less than five years old and those more than five. Three classes of causes can be discerned: those affecting infants and children; those affecting the

Table 18-4. Causes of Death in the Machakos Study Area, by ICD Classification and Code, 1975–78

Cause of death	ICD rank and code[a]	Number of reported deaths	Percentage of all deaths	Death rate[b]
Diseases of the respiratory system	1: 460-519	107	15.8	102
Congenital anomalies and perinatal conditions	2: 740-779	87	12.8	83
Intestinal infectious diseases	3: 001-009	73	10.8	70
Measles	4: 055	55	8.1	53
Diseases of the circulatory system	5: 390-459	49	7.2	47
Tuberculosis	6: 010-018	48	7.1	46
Other infectious and parasitic diseases	7: rest of 001-139	45	6.6	43
External causes of injury and poisoning	8: 800-999	42	6.2	40
Nutritional and metabolic diseases	9: 240-279	30	4.4	29
Neoplasms	10: 140-239	25	3.7	24
Diseases of the digestive system	11: 520-579	24	3.5	23
Malaria	12: 084	21	3.1	20
All other		27	4.0	26
Unknown		45	6.6	43
All causes		678	100.0	648

a. The rank and codes assigned by the ninth revision of the International Classification of Diseases.
b. Deaths per 100,000 persons.

older population; and those common in both groups, such as diseases of the respiratory system. Congenital anomalies and perinatal conditions (12.8 percent), respiratory diseases (such as pneumonia and influenza) and intestinal infectious diseases, especially diarrhea (9.7 percent each), and measles (7.1 percent) were the leading causes of death among infants and children under five years of age. Diseases of the circulatory system (7.2 percent), tuberculosis (6.2 percent), diseases of the respiratory system (7.0 percent), external causes of injury and poisoning (5.6 percent), and other infectious and parasitic diseases (5.6 percent) were important causes of death for persons five years old and more. Causes related to neoplasms and diseases of the circulatory and digestive systems were only reported for persons at least five years of age. Among infants, pneumonia and influenza (15.7 percent, or 11.5 deaths per 1,000 live births) and intestinal infectious diseases, especially diarrhea (15.4 percent, or 11.2 deaths per 1,000 live births) were the major killer diseases. Among children one to four years of age, measles and nutritional deficiencies were the leading causes of death, accounting for 9.8 and 5.0 percent of all deaths, or 2.1 and 1.1 deaths per 1,000, respectively.

About 62 percent of all deaths occurred at home and 38 percent in a hospital. Deaths due to diseases of the circulatory system and malaria occurred more frequently at home than elsewhere, and those due to congenital anomalies and perinatal problems, measles, and neoplasms took place more often in a hospital.

The reported cause-of-death statistics, compiled from various sources, were of fairly good quality. The fieldworkers' lack of medical training limited their ability to diagnose causes of death, especially degenerative diseases among the older population. Further information on causes of death of adults was gathered by a supplementary study (the fourth source of information mentioned above). The present study confirmed that the cause-of-death structure in the Machakos area resembled that in a number of developing countries. A relatively high proportion of deaths was due to infectious diseases (35.6 percent) followed by diseases of the respiratory system (15.8 percent), congenital anomalies and perinatal problems (12.8 percent), diseases of the circulatory system (7.2 percent), and external causes (6.2 percent). The main difference between Machakos and many developing countries is that the death rates from these causes are relatively low in Machakos. Van Ginneken *et al.* (1984) gives a number of reasons for this.

Measles

During the surveillance visits, children whom the mother or fieldworker suspected of having measles were sent to a project physician who verified the diagnosis using carefully designed diagnostic criteria. Cases were classified as possible, probable, or definite based on these criteria. In this chapter cases or estimated cases of measles and pertussis are in fact cumulative probabilities that the disease was present (Voorhoeve *et al.*, 1977). During the first two years of the study the doctors collected nose swabs for culture and capillary blood for serology when the mothers gave their permission.

Incidence and Mortality

In 1974–81 three epidemic waves of measles occurred, and measles was also present between epidemics (see figure 18-3). At the height of the epidemics, between 80 and 170 cases were reported for each two-month period. In the first epidemic (April 1974 to April 1976) 422 cases of measles were reported, and 26 deaths attributed to measles occurred within four weeks of the onset of the measles rash; the case-fatality rate was 6.3 percent. The second epidemic (April 1976 to April 1978) produced 978 cases and 14 deaths, a case-fatality rate of 1.4 percent. In the third epidemic, up to April 1981, 734 measles cases were reported, with 8 deaths, a case-fatality rate of 1.1 percent. Of all measles cases 27 percent were in persons at least five years old: half were between five and seven, and half between seven and fifteen. Only four cases were in older persons, who were 17, 19, 23, and 35 years of age. Very few cases occurred in infants below the age of six months. In the second half of the first year of life the incidence rose considerably, to peak at nine and ten months of age. More cases occurred between six and twelve months of age than in any other six-month age group. This may occur because, apart from waning maternal antibodies, the secondary-attack rate is high (54 percent) in households where an older sibling acts as an index case or because children contract the infection while visiting a health facility for an unrelated complaint. See table 18-5 for the incidence rates by age between 1974 and 1981. Most deaths from measles occurred before the second birthday. In children under five, the case-fatality rate observed over the total seven-year period was 2.4 percent (37 out of 1,545); in persons over five, it was 1.9 percent (11 out of 589). For the first two epidemics the project compared data from the population-based surveillance

Figure 18-3. *Measles Cases and Deaths, by Two-Month Period,*
April 1974–April 1981, Machakos

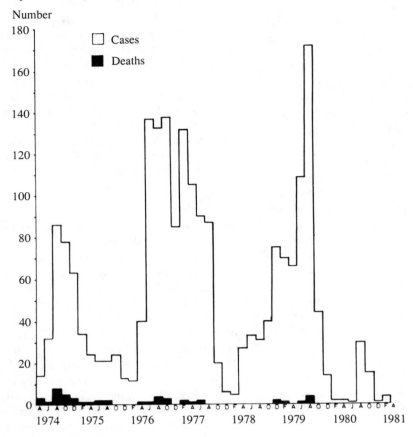

Table 18-5. *Average Annual Incidence of Measles, Machakos Study Area, April 1974–April 1981*

Age (years)	Estimated number of cases	Average population at risk[a]	Average annual incidence[b]
Less than 1	352	1,097	46 (41–51)[c]
1	455	1,081	60 (55–65)
2	295	1,030	41 (36–46)
3	255	964	38 (33–43)
4	188	928	29 (25–33)
5	150	928	23 (19–27)
6	143	896	23 (19–27)
7–14	292	5,974	7 (6–8)
15 and above	4	14,387	0.04
Total	2,134	27,285	11 (11–11)

a. At the end of 1977.
b. Per 1,000 persons.
c. 95 percent confidence limits.

study with data from the Kangundo Hospital, the referral hospital for the study area (Muller *et al.,* 1977). The case-fatality rate of persons admitted to the hospital with measles was 22 percent in both periods. This contrasts sharply with the case-fatality rates of the entire population, which were 6.2 and 1.4 percent, respectively. In 1974–78, the median age of persons hospitalized and of all persons with measles was 18 and 31 months, respectively.

Measles Mortality and Nutritional Status

The Machakos Project investigated the impact of nutritional status on the outcome of measles using the data collected on the mid-upper-arm circumference in children before they contracted measles. The surveillance system measured this circumference routinely every three months and more frequently in cases of illness. No statistically significant difference in nutritional status, as measured by arm circumference, was found between the children who died of measles and those who survived. Only children whose arm circumference had been measured within three months of the onset were included in the analysis. The survivors were selected from the definite measles cases and matched for age, date of onset of the disease, and sublocation. When the data were broken down by sex and age (those above and those below the median age of contracting measles) the measurements were no different for the deceased than for the survivors (Leeuwenburg *et al.,* 1984b).

Vaccination

Combining the age-specific incidence of measles with data from a 1975 collaborative study on seroconversion after vaccination (Kenya Ministry of Health and World Health Organization, 1977) resulted in a recommendation of the optimal age for measles immunization. In a population with the same age distribution of measles cases as Machakos, nine months is the optimal age for administering the measles vaccine (World Health Organization, 1982).

In an Attenuvax II vaccine trial only the vaccine administered by syringe and needle or dermojet evoked a significant antibody response. The other three methods (nose drops, needle-bearing cylinder, and bifurcated needle) produced titers not significantly different from those of the control group (Kok *et al.,* 1983).

Alternatives to Two-Week Surveillance

To find out whether accurate data on measles could be collected more cheaply, in 1978 the project compared

the recall of mothers with the data obtained in the project's two-week surveillance. Recall up to six months corresponded with the surveillance data in 66 percent of the cases detected by surveillance. The 7–18 month recall produced agreement in only 27 percent of the cases. For certain purposes, therefore, a six-month recall may be acceptable. Using recall after longer periods may, however, yield data of doubtful value. Based on a list of major and minor criteria the diagnosis of measles agreed closely with laboratory-supported diagnosis (Gemert *et al.,* 1977). Laboratory support for routine measles surveillance may be unnecessary, and the data obtained after the collection of laboratory data was discontinued are probably reasonably accurate.

Discussion

Measles surveillance through two-week home visits is obviously beyond the resources of health services, even when, as in Machakos, laboratory support of the diagnosis is unnecessary. Nonetheless, historical information on the occurrence of measles was deficient when the recall period exceeded six months. This may, of course, be different for other populations.

Reliable incidence data obtained through two-week disease surveillance provided a unique opportunity to determine the optimal age for measles immunization. The optimal age may, however, differ in areas with different age-specific incidence rates.

The study also compared median age of cases and case-fatality rates based on population data and hospital statistics. The comparison quantified the magnitude of the bias obtained when parameters were based on hospital returns. It is not clear why the measles case-fatality rate was substantially higher during the first epidemic than during the second and third. Case management did not change during the study period, either at the field clinics run by the project staff or at the nearby hospital. Nor could a relationship be established between measles mortality and prior malnutrition.

Pertussis

Pertussis is much more difficult than measles to diagnose in a brief household visit. Typical paroxysms may not occur during the visit, or mothers may consider any frequent cough to be whooping cough. Laboratory support is not particularly helpful: isolating *Bordetella pertussis* is only possible in the early stages of the disease, and lymphocytosis and agglutinating antibodies (the only antibodies that could be tested at the time of the study) are not always present in culture-proven cases.

In the pertussis vaccine trial the effect of two doses given six months apart was compared with the conventional schedule of three doses every three months during infancy (Muller *et al.*, 1984).

Incidence and Mortality

Figure 18-4 presents the number of cases diagnosed between April 1974 and April 1981, when two epidemic waves occurred; the small number of cases among children in the vaccine trial coincided with the second epidemic. The largest number of cases occurred in children less than one year old, and children six years of age or younger accounted for 84 percent of all cases. The median age was 3.5 years. Out of 1,465 cases, 758 were in females, giving a sex ratio of 0.93. Pertussis incidence rates are presented in table 18-6.

Between April 1974 and April 1981, 14 deaths were attributed to pertussis, a case-fatality rate of 1 percent. Half occurred in children below the age of one year (a case-fatality rate of 2.6 percent); the rest were evenly distributed among children one to four years of age. None of the children in the vaccine trial died from pertussis (Muller *et al.*, 1984).

Vaccine Trial

The project tested the titer distributions of the two- and three-dose groups. One month after the last (the second or the third) dose of DPT vaccine was administered, no difference existed in the titers. At longer postvaccination intervals antibodies waned more rapidly in the two-dose group than in the three-dose group. Differences between the groups were statistically significant after an interval of two years ($p < 0.01$). The proportion with no demonstrable titer rose in the two-dose group

Figure 18-4. Distribution of Pertussis Cases among Children in Vaccine Trial and All Children, April 1974–April 1981, Machakos

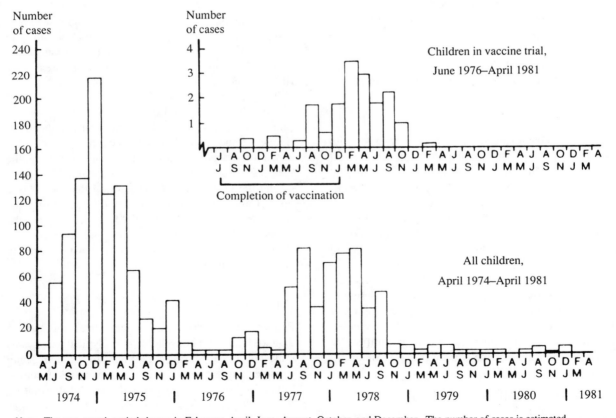

Note: The two-month periods began in February, April, June, August, October, and December. The number of cases is estimated.

Table 18-6. Average Annual Incidence of Pertussis, Machakos Study Area, April 1974–April 1981

Age (years)	Estimated number of cases	Average population at risk[a]	Incidence[b]
Less than 1	270	1,097	35 (31–39)[c]
1	150	1,081	20 (17–23)
2	171	1,030	24 (20–27)
3	189	964	28 (24–32)
4	183	928	28 (24–32)
5	168	928	26 (22–29)
6	106	896	17 (14–20)
7–14	228	5,974	6 (5–6)
Total less than 15	1,465	12,898	16 (15–17)
Total population		27,285	8 (7–8)

a. At the end of 1977.
b. Per 1,000 persons.
c. 95 percent confidence limits.

from 10 percent after one month to 38 percent after two years or more. The corresponding percentages for the three-dose group were 6 and 23 percent, respectively. The rate of pertussis cases was the same, 8.15 in the two-dose and 8.55 in the three-dose group. Compared with that of the 1,281 children of the same birth cohort who were not in the trial, the rate of pertussis cases in the vaccinated children was reduced 54 percent. The unvaccinated children were not a random control group because some had probably received DPT immunizations elsewhere. Therefore these percentages do not express actual vaccine efficacy.

Discussion

The case-fatality rate of 1 percent, although lower than that in most developing countries, is still formidable compared with that in the developed countries. It is much higher than the incidence of serious adverse reactions to the vaccine reported from, for example, the Netherlands (Hannik and Cohen, 1979) and England (Miller *et al.*, 1981).

The vaccine trial suggests that six-month mass immunization campaigns may be suitable for protecting children living in remote areas that lack access to continuous mother and child health services. Many parts of the world do not have DPT, either on a continuous basis in regular mother and child health clinics or at intervals considerably shorter than six months. A three-DPT schedule is preferable in such situations because it obviates the problem of children contracting whooping cough during the six-month interval between the first, nonprotecting DPT dose and the second one (administered before the age of nine

months). Children are vulnerable to incidence and mortality during this interval period.

Diarrhea

Two-week surveillance data are available from April 1974 to the middle of 1977 (Leeuwenburg *et al.*, 1984a). The age-specific incidence rates of diarrhea in children who were reported or observed to be ill are given in figure 18-5. The differences between age groups are striking: children 0–5 months of age had virtually the same incidence as children 12–23 months of age, while those 6–11 months old had a consistently and significantly ($p < 0.001$) higher percentage of diarrhea than the younger or older children. A marked decline in the incidence of diarrhea in all age groups was noticeable in the second half of 1975.

Comparing the incidence of diarrhea in children under five with the incidence minus that associated with measles did not produce a more stable diarrhea pattern over the years. The decline in diarrhea incidence was apparently not caused by the absence of measles during the period. The decline in all age groups in the second half of 1975 coincided with a lower frequency of reported measles cases and with a drop in the frequency of malnutrition. In the under-five population, however, cases of measles and malnutrition were present in only a small portion of the children.

From April 1976 to June 1977 diarrhea information was obtained on all children whether the mothers considered them ill or not. During that time the incidence of diarrhea, by age group, was four to seven

Figure 18-5. *Percentage of Children Reported or Observed to Be Ill with Diarrhea during Two-Week Periods, by Age, 1974–77*

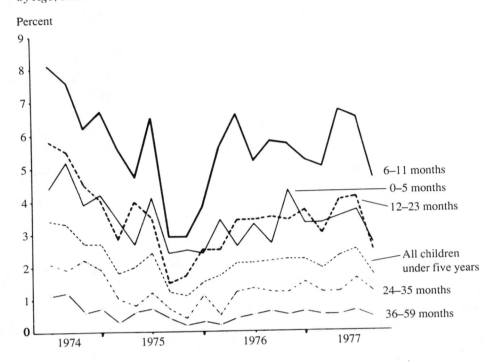

Percent

6–11 months

0–5 months

12–23 months

All children
under five years

24–35 months

36–59 months

times higher in all children than in children who were reported ill (see table 18-7).

From April 1974 to December 1977, out of 306 deaths of children under five, 46 children (22 males and 24 females) were reported to have died of diarrhea and vomiting. Of these children, 33 were under one year of age; 13 were newborn to five months of age; the median age of death was seven months, the mode was six months, and the mean was thirteen; the age at death ranged from 2 to 57 months. About half the children died in the subdistrict hospital at Kangundo.

Most diarrhea deaths (80 percent) occurred in March–July, while overall deaths in children under five were spread fairly evenly over the months. Although the pattern of rainfall shows a bimodal seasonality, the diarrhea morbidity did not follow a seasonal trend.

Over the period of observation the proportional mortality was approximately the same for measles (13 percent) as for diarrhea (15 percent). Only in the first half of the study did measles outrank diarrhea as a cause of death. During that period the case-fatality rate for measles was high.

Table 18-7. *Average Two-Week Incidence of Diarrhea in Children under Five Years of Age*
(percent, unless otherwise noted)

	Age (months)					
Item	*0–5*	*6–11*	*12–23*	*24–35*	*36–59*	*Total*
Incidence in						
Ill children, June 1974–June 1977	3.4	5.6	3.4	1.3	0.5	2.2
All children, April 1976–June 1977	15.8	24.5	15.9	7.4	3.7	10.5
Average number of children per two-week period, June 1974–June 1977	394	422	832	797	1,454	3,899

Infection and Nutrition

Anthropometric studies of preschool children showed a moderate degree of growth faltering after the first six months of life (weight-for-age was 83 percent and height-for-age was 92 percent of the Harvard standard). Energy and protein intake from birth to 18 months was adequate (Oomen *et al.*, 1984). The period of growth faltering coincided with the ages during which diarrhea incidence was highest. Infectious diseases seemed to play a larger role than nutritional inadequacy in retarding growth. In Sub-Saharan Africa immunization programs and diarrhea prevention are likely to be more effective than nutrition programs in improving the nutritional status of preschool children (Kusin and Jansen, 1984).

Determinants of Perinatal Mortality

After diagnosing a woman as pregnant, fieldworkers would fill out a questionnaire covering previous pregnancies and deliveries, where she intended to deliver, and any complaints related to the pregnancy. Height was measured with a headboard and tape measure.

After the woman gave birth, fieldworkers filled out another form with questions about the recent delivery and the care received. If a pregnancy was undetected, fieldworkers filled out both questionnaires after the delivery. During the last two years of the study the fieldworkers weighed babies born at home as soon after birth as possible. When a pregnancy ended in stillbirth or a child died within its first week of life, the project physician interviewed and examined the mother in order to establish the most likely cause of perinatal death.

The Machakos study included all women who delivered between 1 January 1975 and 31 December 1978 after a gestation of at least 28 weeks. All belonged to the study population at the time of delivery, regardless of whether delivery took place inside or outside the study area. This section will describe obstetric care in the study area.

Most women who gave birth at home were assisted by one of the thirty or so traditional midwives in the area. These were usually elderly women known for their skills and experience. Some were also herbalists. None had any medical training. Other women were assisted by a relative, usually the mother or mother-in-law, and sometimes by the husband or a neighbor. Some gave birth completely on their own.

Formally trained midwives and doctors were only found in health centers and hospitals, where midwives attended uncomplicated deliveries, and physicians or medical assistants attended difficult deliveries. For more detail on sources of data and results, see Voorhoeve *et al.* (1984) and Nordbeck *et al.* (1984).

Risk Factors

The total number of children born was 4,768, including 52 pairs of twins (1 for every 91 deliveries). The rates for perinatal and other mortality in early infancy are provided in table 18-8. In the study area perinatal mortality was 46 per 1,000 births. Perinatal rates for a number of factors are shown in table 18-9, which presents separate rates for home and hospital deliveries. The perinatal rate was 39 per 1,000 total births for home deliveries and 65 per 1,000 for hospital deliveries. Of all deliveries 73 percent took place at home and 27 percent in the hospital. Age and parity related to perinatal mortality in the usual manner: rates were highest for the children of the youngest and oldest women, of women without a previous delivery, and of women with seven or more children. Marital status was

Table 18-8. Outcome of Pregnancy, Machakos Study Area, 1975–78.

Outcome	Number	Type of rate	Annual rates
Total children born	4,768	n.a.	n.a.
Live births	4,627	Crude birth	43.6 per 1,000 persons
Late fetal deaths (stillbirths)	141	Stillbirth	29.6 per 1,000 total births
Perinatal deaths[a]	221	Perinatal mortality	46.4 per 1,000 total births
Neonatal deaths[b]	107	Neonatal mortality	23.1 per 1,000 live births
Infant deaths[c]	230	Infant mortality	49.7 per 1,000 live births
Maternal deaths	4	Maternal mortality	0.8 per 1,000 deliveries

n.a. Not applicable.
a. First-week deaths and stillbirths.
b. First-month deaths.
c. First-year deaths.

Table 18-9. Perinatal Mortality Rates for Selected Screening Criteria

Characteristic	Overall mortality		Home mortality		Hospital mortality		Hospital deliveries as percentage of all deliveries
	Rate	Number of deaths	Rate	Number of deaths	Rate	Number of deaths	
Maternal age (years)							
20 years or less	47	41	45	27	52	14	31
21–30	44	109	38	67	58	42	29
31–40	49	55	36	32	97	23	21
41 or older	55	16	48	11	82	5	21
Parity							
No births	62	59	59	36	67	23	36
1–6 births	42	120	37	80	55	40	24
7 births or more	49	42	31	21	113	21	22
Marital status							
Unmarried	62	53	55	34	82	19	28
Married	43	168	36	103	60	65	27
Maternal height (centimeters)							
150 or less	70	40	64	25	84	15	31
More than 150	44	171	35	102	76	69	25
Previous stillbirths							
None	44	191	37	122	59	69	27
1 or more	68	30	48	15	118	15	30
Previous cesarean section							
No	47	220	—	—	—	—	26
Yes	14	1	—	—	—	—	74
Previous forceps or vacuum extraction							
No	46	217	—	—	—	—	26
Yes	63	4	—	—	—	—	53
Previous postpartum hemorrhage							
No	46	212	—	—	—	—	27
Yes	49	9	—	—	—	—	32
Birth interval							
First child	60	59	59	36	72	23	36
1–6 years	42	154	37	98	63	56	20
More than 6 years	100	8	29	3	143	5	33
Mode of delivery							
Breech	569	33	719	23	385	10	45
Other	40	188	33	114	59	74	26
Multiple birth							
Yes	183	19	109	4	241	15	56
No	43	202	38	133	60	69	27

— Numbers were too small to measure.
Note: Rates are deaths per 1,000 births.

also related to perinatal mortality: the rate was higher among the babies born to unmarried than to married women. Birth interval was related to mortality as follows: a short interval between the previous and the present live birth or stillbirth was not associated with increased perinatal mortality, but after intervals of six years or more mortality increased steeply. The mother's height was another risk factor: the children of short women (less than 150 centimeters) experienced on average a higher perinatal mortality than those of taller women. The number of previous perinatal deaths was also related to subsequent mortality: mothers who had not lost a child had lower rates than mothers who had. Among 58 breech deliveries, 29 babies were stillborn and 4 died during the first week of life. The resulting perinatal death rate of 569 per 1,000 births was 14 times the rate of 40 per 1,000 for vertex deliveries. Twinning also strongly influenced mortality: the perinatal death rate was 183 per 1,000 among pairs of twins compared with 43 among single births.

Two other factors, not included in table 18-9, strongly influenced mortality: length of gestation and birth weight. Gestational age was known for a biased sample of 1,049 pregnancies. The sample was biased because women who gave birth to a low-birth-weight infant or lost their baby at birth had a higher chance of being questioned. Perinatal mortality was much higher than average for the 27 children with a gestational age of less than 34 weeks and also higher than average for the 93 children with a gestation of 42 weeks or more. Birth weights measured within the first 48 hours were available for 1,091 live-born single babies. Neonatal mortality rates were much higher among children with a low birth weight (less than 2,500 grams) than among those with a high one (2,500 grams or more; see table 18-10).

Screening Criteria and Discriminant Analysis

Using this information, the project identified four groups of pregnant women who had a significantly higher risk than other women of losing their baby at birth (see table 18-11).

1. Women who had a breech delivery ran the highest risk: two-thirds of the 46 single babies born in a breech delivery died perinatally. These women accounted for 1 percent of all women who deliv-

Table 18-10. Neonatal and Postneonatal Mortality, by Birth Weight

Birth weight (grams)	Number of children	Neonatal mortality		Postneonatal mortality	
		Number of deaths	*Rate*	*Number of deaths*	*Rate*
Less than 2,500	76	9	118	3	39
2,500 and more	1,015	9	9	18	18
Total	1,091	18	16	21	19

Note: Rates are deaths per 1,000 live births.

Table 18-11. Births and Perinatal Deaths, by Risk Group

Risk group	Births		Perinatal deaths	
	Number	*Percent*	*Number*	*Percent*
Breech (single birth)	46	1	31	14
Twins	104	2	19	9
Primigravidae				
At risk	160	3	16	7
Not at risk	774	16	33	15
Multigravidae				
At risk	372	8	24	11
Not at risk	3,312	70	98	44
Total	4,768	100	221	100

ered, but contributed 14 percent of the perinatal deaths.

2. Women who delivered twins ran the second highest risk. If the women who gave birth to twins were added to those in the first group, then 2.5 percent of the women accounted for 23 percent of the perinatal deaths.

3. At-risk primigravidae formed a third group of 160 women. These first-time mothers were less than 16 years old, more than 30 years old, or less than 151 centimeters in height. The perinatal mortality in this group was 100 per 1,000 compared with 42 among primigravidae not at risk. Adding this group to the previous two means that 5.5 percent of the women were associated with 30 percent of the perinatal deaths.

4. At-risk multigravidae formed a group of 372 women. At-risk means they had lost two or more babies to perinatal deaths (or one if they had only been pregnant once before), had given birth to more than ten children and more than six years had passed since their last delivery, or had previously had a cesarean section. Their perinatal mortality was 65 per 1,000 compared with 30 for multigravidae not at risk. Adding these women to the previous three groups associates 13 percent of the women with 41 percent of the perinatal deaths.

Table 18-12 shows the distribution of the five groups of causes of perinatal death for the six at-risk groups. Even if all perinatal deaths could be identified prospectively, not all could be prevented by specialized obstetric care. All the deaths in group 1 in table 18-12 could have been prevented by timely cesarean section, and some of the deaths in groups 2 and 3 might have been prevented by better neonatal care. Group 4 contains only obvious congenital malformations incompatible with independent life; and whether any of the deaths in group 5 could have been prevented is uncertain. Of the 85 deaths in group 1, 50 occurred among the children of women in the four high-risk groups. These 50 deaths could have been prevented if all the pregnant women had been screened and if the 13 percent at risk had received good obstetric care. This would have reduced the perinatal mortality from 46 to 36 deaths for every 1,000 births.

A discriminant analysis was performed with a number of these risk factors as the independent variables and perinatal mortality as the dependent variable. Breech delivery was by far the most discriminating variable, followed to a much lesser extent by multiple birth, maternal height, and marital status.

Discussion

Interpreting the results is complicated by whether delivery took place at home or in the hospital. Place of delivery influences the relationship between various risk factors and perinatal mortality. Analyzing perinatal mortality rates by a number of risk factors or screening criteria identified four groups of pregnant women, totaling 13 percent of all pregnant women, who were associated with 41 percent of all perinatal deaths. More than half of the perinatal deaths of the babies of these four high-risk groups could probably have been avoided if appropriate obstetric care and antenatal screening had been available. The results of the discriminant analysis were disappointing, probably because the number of perinatal deaths (221) was too small and some variables were dichotomous, which resulted in a loss of information.

Table 18-12. Causes of Perinatal Deaths, by Risk Group

Risk group	1	2	3	4	5	Total
Breech (single birth)	26	1		3	1	31
Twins	6	12		1		19
Primigravidae						
At risk	10	2		2	2	16
Not at risk	16	2	4	1	10	33
Multigravidae						
At risk	8	8	2		6	24
Not at risk	19	30	10	11	28	98
Total	85	55	16	18	47	221

Note: 1, Complications of labor in mature infants; 2, low birth weight and antepartum hemorrhage; 3, infection; 4, congenital malformations; 5, unknown and accidental.

Determinants of Child Mortality

The Machakos Project conducted a multivariate analysis with economic, social, hygienic, and demographic variables as the independent variables and mortality of children less than five as the dependent variable. Probit analysis, the statistical method used to perform this multivariate analysis, was chosen instead of multiple regression analysis because the dependent variable was dichotomous (the children studied either lived or died).

The dependent variable was the number of deaths of children under five in the study area between April 1974 and April 1976. During this period 150 children less than five died, 19 in the first month after birth. An alternative dependent variable was the number of deaths of children under five excluding neonatal deaths. A sample of 360 children from households with children under five but no deaths of children in this age group was used as a control group. In order to arrive at a proportional sample the project gave each household in the control group a weight of 5.

The independent variables were obtained from two cross-sectional surveys conducted in 1974 and 1975 and from the demographic registration system. Below we describe the variables that were statistically significant ($p < 0.10$) and a few that were not. The latter were included because their influence was different than expected.

The economic variables originated from the economic survey conducted among all households in the study area in February–March 1974. The income variable used was an index composed of data relating to subsistence income, cash income (from coffee, for example), and nonfarm income (such as remittances of migrant workers). The quality of housing variable was an index composed of several characteristics (such as the number of sleeping rooms and the quality of the walls, roof, and floor). The social variables originated from the social and hygienic survey conducted in May–August 1975 among all households. Three social variables were derived from this survey (education of the mother, marital status of the mother, and presence of the child's father) and one hygienic variable, which is a combination of data on hygienic conditions in the child's bedroom (for example, the number of persons sleeping in one room and whether food is cooked in the child's bedroom). The following demographic variables were included in the analysis: size of household, number of other children under five of the mother, and birth interval. Kuné (1980) details the methods and results of this analysis.

Results

Except for income, the results for all children under five corresponded fairly closely with those for all children under five not counting neonatal deaths. Education of the mother, presence of the father, hygienic conditions, and the number of other children under five in the household had a significant influence on mortality. The other variables appeared to be less important.

The project calculated the effect of changing one explanatory variable on the probability of finding a death in the average household. The maximum change was assumed in one explanatory variable, and all other variables were kept at their population mean. Children of mothers with the highest educational level (score 3) had, all things being equal, a 65 to 115 percent lower death risk than children of mothers with no education (the lowest score). With all else being equal, children of mothers who were married (score 2) had a 220 to 300 percent lower risk of dying than children of mothers who were never married (score 0). The importance of a stable family relationship was also sustained by the significance of two coefficients: the presence of the child's father and the aggregate of this variable and marital status. Households whose children slept in the best conditions (score 5) showed, all else being equal, a 100 to 160 percent lower probability of childhood mortality than households with the poorest conditions (score 0). Finally, a household's probability of having a child under five die increases proportionate to the number of other children that the mother has under the age of five. If the number of children increases from one to two, so does the probability of death. The increase is more than proportionate, 60 to 85 percent, when the number of children under five increases from two to three.

Discussion

These results confirm conclusively that social, hygienic, and demographic factors were important influences on child mortality in the Machakos project area. First, the mother's education had a substantial influence on child mortality. It is assumed that the level of the mother's education and her knowledge of personal hygiene, sanitation, preventive measures, and nutrition, and her willingness to use health services were positively associated. Second, stable family relationships were important to child mortality. Children whose mothers were unmarried or whose fathers were absent were more poorly fed, bathed, changed, or otherwise cared for than children of married mothers.

Consequently they were more susceptible to infectious diseases and injury. Furthermore, the hygienic condition of the child's sleeping room appeared to influence child mortality. Children who slept in good hygienic conditions had lower mortality than children who slept in poor conditions. Finally, the probability of a child under five dying increased with the number of children under five present in the household. The economic condition of the household did not have a significant influence on childhood mortality.

Conclusions

The Machakos Project produced high-quality information relevant to health care. It produced age-specific figures on the incidence of measles, which yielded a recommendation of the optimal age to immunize children for measles; it studied the adequacy of two pertussis immunizations during infancy; and it analyzed the impact of a pregnant woman's nutritional status and of the delivery care received on the outcome of pregnancy. All of these contributions were made possible by the epidemiological and demographic surveillance system, which provided regular follow-up for a number of years.

Information on the incidence of disease and the outcome of pregnancy could have been collected in a cross-sectional study using the mother's recall, but the reliability of such a study would never be known. In the case of measles—but not of pertussis—a positive or negative history could be verified by testing for antibodies, but serological surveys do not provide information on age-specific incidence or mortality.

In addition, the project's solid infrastructure, which included collecting complete demographic information on the total population rather than on the target groups alone, allowed the addition of investigations that had not been considered at the onset, but appeared useful later.

External Validity of the Studies

The extent of external validity is not known. There is no way of measuring this except to conduct similar studies in other parts of Kenya, tropical Africa, or the tropics in general.

The optimal age of measles immunization may be different where the age-specific incidence rates are different. On the other hand, the pertussis and measles vaccine trials would probably produce similar results in other parts of the world. Above all, the project developed surveillance methodologies that, if adapted to local circumstances, could be used elsewhere. It

provided a valuable population laboratory for testing hypotheses and for measuring the results of well-defined interventions that are not necessarily purely medical. The project can continue to act as such a field instrument as long as its basic surveillance system is maintained. A training ground for multidisciplinary research, it brought together local and expatriate scientists from a wide range of professional backgrounds.

Disease Surveillance

The two-week surveillance system constituted the basis of the project. Clinical manifestations of measles take about two weeks to disappear completely, which is why the two-week interval between household visits was chosen. Carefully inspecting measles cases up to two weeks after onset nearly always reveals the typical, if minimal, fine desquamation of the skin. Relying more on the mothers' history of measles over the past one to three months would have allowed the home visits to be less frequent. The accuracy of such information, however, would have been uncertain.

In cases of pertussis, two-week visits increased the likelihood of isolating *Bordetella pertussis;* the clinical manifestations of the disease usually persist at least six weeks. Collecting laboratory specimens to diagnose measles and pertussis was necessary, nonetheless, because an illness resembling measles was suspected in Kenya (Hayden, 1974). The absence of physical signs of pertussis made the use of diagnostic methods other than examinations desirable as well. Besides, whooping cough can be caused by organisms other than *B. (para) pertussis.*

For both diseases, once the causative agent was firmly established by several isolations or a rise in the antibody titer in paired sera, laboratory specimens were not systematically collected where the clinical diagnosis was certain.

As a result, in September 1978 the project began to carry out surveillance every month instead of every two weeks. An appreciable number of measles or pertussis cases do not appear to have been missed as a result.

Measles and whooping cough were defined according to careful diagnostic criteria that minimized the variations in the observations of the diagnosing physicians and—occasionally—the diagnosing fieldworkers. The original intention was to code the presence or absence of clinical signs and use a computer to produce a score according to a standard program. In practice such a program was not feasible because the study was too small, and eventually all cases were diagnosed by a physician according to the agreed criteria.

The 14-day interval between visits was arbitrary for the surveillance of other acute respiratory infections and acute diarrhea. In the case of diarrhea, the diagnosis could be based on actual observation in only a minority of cases. Limited attempts were made to relate these observations to the history given by the mother.

Although signs of lower respiratory tract infection were recorded on the disease surveillance form, their rarity made any reasonably standardized, systematic study difficult. In practice only manifestations of upper respiratory tract infection (nasal discharge, cough) were considered.

At first, the question "has the child been well since my last visit?" determined whether the fieldworker collected specific morbidity information. To ease data processing, the project redesigned the question to be "has the child been *ill* since my last visit?" Although leading, this question did not draw an unjustified number of positive answers.

Population Surveillance

Temporary migration in and out of the study area made estimating the numerators and denominators of rates difficult, as did movements within the area, which created the possibility of registering individual residents twice or missing them altogether. Migratory movements are common among the Kamba, as in many other parts of Africa.

Each individual was given a number corresponding to his or her household. The head of the household decided who belonged to it during the demographic baseline survey. This was an arbitrary decision, but project guidelines that helped fieldworkers decide whom to include based on how long the individual had been with the household before the interview yielded equally inconsistent results.

Internal migration complicated the situation: individuals who moved within the area were supposed to be assigned new numbers corresponding to their new households. Double-counting the individual in both the previous and the present household could not be avoided entirely. Some so-called emigrants did in fact return regularly to the same or a different household after a few months, while others not called emigrants were absent for years on end. Consequently, at the end of 1978, persons who had been continuously absent for more than six months (including weekends) were classified as emigrants.

For epidemiological rates the de facto population did not suffice: pregnant women belonging to the study population were included even if they delivered outside the study area; registered children returning from a temporary absence with traces of recent measles attacks were included in both the numerator and the denominator of the measles attack rate.

An alternative way of tracing migrants would have been to attach numbers to individuals rather than to households. Thus a person's identification number would remain the same regardless of his or her movements. This might have worked for individuals moving within the study area, but would not have been feasible for those moving in and out of the area.

In order to obtain reliable information on disease outcome, the project traced hospitalized patients. Individuals were supposed to show their household's numbered card on being admitted to a hospital. Most of the persons requiring hospitalization were admitted to the nearby divisional hospital in Kangundo, but their household number was rarely recorded because they—or their mother in the case of children—did not produce the card.

Usually, however, hospitalized children could be traced by fieldworkers, who knew the people of the study area and visited the hospital wards once a week. Tracing persons who used outpatient services, including maternal and child health clinics, was far less easy. Moreover, mothers often lost their children's vaccination cards, and reliable information on vaccination and illness never became available.

Data Processing

Although the need to handle data promptly was stressed from the beginning, the magnitude of the requirements of creating and maintaining an ongoing, longitudinal data base was not sufficiently recognized. The technical problems of storing a large quantity of data were much more formidable than anticipated.

A delay in analyzing the data and feeding the information back to the field meant that at times superfluous information was produced and errors were discovered after the data were computerized. Successful pilot studies in the field do not in themselves indicate that all is well. The data collected during such pilot studies should be coded, punched, and stored. Not until the computer produces useful tabulations with a minimal number of errors should the main study begin. Promptly tabulating the data by hand is useful, but does not obviate the need for pilot runs of computerized data if such computerization is essential to handling the massive amount of data anticipated.

The system used to code the demographic baseline survey was elegant and economical, but ignored a number of cross-checks built into the form. These cross-checks could easily have been incorporated into the computer program if the items had been coded according to a more straightforward system. The program for updating the demographic file proved to be inadequate. This only became apparent late in the project, when data collection in the field was already in full swing. Coding directly on the forms in the field would have saved time, but introduced an additional source of error. Direct coding was not adopted. Mark-sensing was also too vulnerable to error under the prevailing conditions. The final analysis of the demographic data required in some cases returning to the raw data and relying on the hand tabulations.

This longitudinal, population-based study in Machakos, Kenya, produced valuable information that could not have been obtained by simpler, cheaper methods. Its findings are relevant to health administrators and to the scientific community.

The project design called for the long-term, continuous commitment of a large scientific staff, adequate administrative and logistic support, and, most of all, a receptive study population. Some of these requirements could be translated into financial terms; others were a matter of motivation, mentality, or good fortune. These requirements were met most of the time.

Field research is expensive, laborious, and unglamorous. It does not produce immediate results, but is essential to understanding the health of the community rather than of the individual.

Bibliography

Gemert, W., Valkenburg, H. A., and Muller, A. S. (1977). Agents affecting health of mother and child in a rural area of Kenya. 2: the diagnosis of measles under field conditions. *Tropical Geographical Medicine*, 29, 303–313.

Hannik, C. A. and Cohen, H. (1979). Pertussis vaccine experience in the Netherlands. *Third International Symposium on Pertussis*, DHEW Publication, no. NIH 79-1830. Bethesda, Md.: National Institutes of Health.

Hayden, R. J. (1974). Measles. In: *Health and Disease in Kenya*, Vogel, L. C., Muller, A. S., Odingo, R. S., Onyango, Z., and de Geus, A. (editors), pp. 267–271. Nairobi: East African Literature Bureau.

Kenya Central Bureau of Statistics. (1975). *Demographic Baseline Survey Report 1973*. Nairobi.

———. (1979). *Economic Survey 1979*. Nairobi.

Kenya Ministry of Health and World Health Organization. (1977). Measles immunity in the first year after birth and the optimum age for vaccination in Kenyan children. *Bulletin of the World Health Organization*, 55, 21–32.

Kok, P. W., Kenya, P. R., and Ensering, H. (1983). Measles immunization with further attenuated heat stable vaccine using five different methods of administration. *Transactions of the Royal Society of Tropical Medicine and Hygiene*, 77, 171–176.

Kuné, J. (1980). Some factors influencing the mortality of under-fives in a rural area of Kenya: a multivariate analysis. *Journal of Tropical Pediatrics*, 26, 114–122.

Kusin, J. A. and Jansen, A. A. J. (1984). Overview of nutrition studies. In: *Maternal and Child Health in Rural Kenya: An Epidemiological Study*, van Ginneken, J. K. and Muller, A. S. (editors). London: Croom Helm.

Leeuwenburg, J., Gemert, W., Muller, A. S., and Patel, S. C. (1984a). The incidence of diarrhoeal disease. In: *Maternal and Child Health in Rural Kenya: An Epidemiological Study*, van Ginneken, J. K. and Muller, A. S. (editors). London: Croom Helm.

Leeuwenburg, J., Muller, A. S., Voorhoeve, A. M., Gemert, W., and Kok, P. (1984b). The epidemiology of measles In: *Maternal and Child Health in Rural Kenya: An Epidemiological Study*, van Ginneken, J. K. and Muller, A. S. (editors). London: Croom Helm.

Miller, D. L., Ross, E. M., Alderslade, R., Belleman, M. H., and Rawson, N. S. (1981). Pertussis immunisation and serious acute neurological illness in children. *British Medical Journal*, 282, 1595–1599.

Mott, F. L. (1982). *Infant Mortality in Kenya: Evidence from the Kenya Fertility Survey*. Scientific Report Series, no. 32. Voorburg, Netherlands: International Statistical Institute.

Muller, A. S., Voorhoeve, A. M., 't Mannetje, W., and Schulpen, T. W. (1977). The impact of measles in a rural area of Kenya. *East African Medical Journal*, 54, 364–372.

Muller, A. S., Leeuwenburg, J., and Voorhoeve, A. M. (1984). Pertussis in a rural area of Kenya: epidemiology and results of a vaccine trial. *Bulletin of the World Health Organization*, 62, 899–908.

Nordbeck, H. J., Voorhoeve, A. M., and van Ginneken, J. K. (1984). Use of perinatal mortality data in antenatal screening. In: *Maternal and Child Health in Rural Kenya: An Epidemiological Study*, van Ginneken, J. K. and Muller, A. S. (editors). London: Croom Helm.

Omondi-Odhiambo, van Ginneken, J. K., and Voorhoeve, A. M. (1990). Mortality by cause of death in a rural area of Machakos District, Kenya, in 1975–1978. *Journal of Biosocial Science*, 22, 63–75.

Oomen, H. A. P. C., Blankhart, D. M., and 't Mannetje, W. (1984). Growth pattern of pre-schoolchildren. In: *Maternal and Child Health in Rural Kenya: An Epidemiological Study*, van Ginneken, J. K. and Muller, A. S. (editors). London: Croom Helm.

van Ginneken, J. K. and A. S. Muller. (1984). *Maternal and Child Health in Rural Kenya: An Epidemiological Study*. London: Croom Helm.

van Ginneken, J. K., Muller, A. S., Voorhoeve, A. M., and Omondi-Odhiambo. (1984). Demographic characteristics of a rural area in Kenya in 1974–1980. *Journal of Biosocial Science,* 16, 411–423.

van Vianen, H. A. W. and van Ginneken, J. K. (1984). Analysis of demographic data collected in a rural area of Kenya. *Journal of Biosocial Science,* 16, 463–473.

Voorhoeve, A. M., Muller, A. S., Schulpen, T. W. J., Gemert, W., Valkenburg, H. A., and Ensering, H. E. (1977). Agents affecting health of mother and child in a rural area of Kenya. 3: the epidemiology of measles. *Tropical Geographical Medicine,* 29, 428–440.

Voorhoeve, A. M., Muller, A. S., Schulpen, T. W. J., 't Mannetje, W., and van Rens, M. (1978). Agents affecting health of mother and child in a rural area of Kenya. 4: the epidemiology of pertussis. *Tropical Geographical Medicine,* 30, 125–139.

Voorhoeve, A. M., Muller, A. S., and W'Oigo, H. (1984). The outcome of pregnancy. In: *Maternal and Child Health in Rural Kenya: An Epidemiological Study,* van Ginneken, J. K. and Muller, A. S. (editors). London: Croom Helm.

World Health Organization. (1977). *International Statistical Classification of Diseases, Injuries, and Causes of Death.* Vol. 1. Geneva.

World Health Organization. Expanded Programme on Immunization. (1982). The optimal age for measles immunization. *Weekly Epidemiological Record,* 57, 89–91.

Chapter 19

Morbidity and Mortality at Kilombero, Tanzania, 1982–88

Marcel Tanner, Don De Savigny, Charles Mayombana, Christoph Hatz,
Eric Burnier, Severio Tayari, and Antoine Degremont

Data on morbidity and mortality in southern Tanzania are scarce despite the economic importance of this area and the widespread activities of governmental and missionary medical services. After Tanzania's independence in 1961, an in-depth evaluation of the Kilombero and Ulanga districts within the frame of the Rufiji River Development Project also addressed medical issues relating to trypanosomiasis, malaria, and schistosomiasis (Food and Agriculture Organization, 1961). No regular health surveys were conducted, however, and information on disease, morbidity, and mortality came mainly from the data collected routinely at dispensaries, health centers, and hospitals. Heggenhougen *et al.* (1987) recently summarized the structural development of Tanzania's health sector and UNICEF (1985a) comprehensively analyzed the situation of children and their mothers. UNICEF's report lacked, however, detailed knowledge of the community's health status, particularly in remote areas such as southern and western Tanzania.

This chapter provides data on morbidity and mortality in the Kilombero District (Morogoro Region) collected mainly by the Kilombero Health Research Programme (KIHERE) initiated in 1981. KIHERE is a cooperative program of the National Institute for Medical Research, the Swiss Tropical Institute, and the Tanzania Ministry of Health. At the district level, the collaboration includes the Kilombero District Health Office, the St. Francis Designated District Hospital (SFDH), the Medical Assistants Training Centre, and the Swiss Tropical Institute Field Laboratory (STIFL, Utafiti wa Afya). A comprehensive description, and the presentation of baseline data from community-based, longitudinal studies carried out within the framework of a primary health care program were published as a special issue of the journal *Acta Tropica* (44[2]) in 1987. Because the project only began in 1982, it is too

soon to report trends in morbidity and mortality or to assess the impact on community health of the long-term interventions launched in the past three years. Thus this chapter summarizes some of the major findings on morbidity and mortality from the initial phase of the study; reviews information from the routine data collection system of the district; indicates major data deficiencies and possible measures to overcome them in our study area; and outlines how the KIHERE experience generated approaches useful for collecting data at the district level and within a primary health care framework.

The Kilombero Study Area

Figure 19-1 shows the location of the Kilombero District within the Morogoro Region of Tanzania. The district covers 14,900 square kilometers and is divided into 5 divisions, 19 wards, and 50 villages (Tanzania Bureau of Statistics, 1978; UNICEF, 1985a). Topographically, the district extends along the Usagara and Uzungwa mountains in the northwest and the Kilombero River in the south. The alluvial river plain has an average altitude of 270 meters and lies along the Kilombero River (Jatzold and Baum, 1968). The area has two seasons: the rainy season from November to May and the dry season from June to October. Annual rainfall ranges from less than 1,200 millimeters in the Kilombero plain and the extreme eastern part of the district to more than 1,800 millimeters on the western mountain range (DHV Consulting Engineers, 1983). Access to the district is relatively difficult. The trunk road from Mikumi to Ifakara is not paved and the western divisions (Mngeta, Mlimba; see figure 19-1) cannot be reached by road during much of the rainy season. The Tanzania Zambia Railway (TAZARA) passes through all the divisions of the district. The national census of 1978 reported a population of

Figure 19-1. KIHERE Program Area, Tanzania

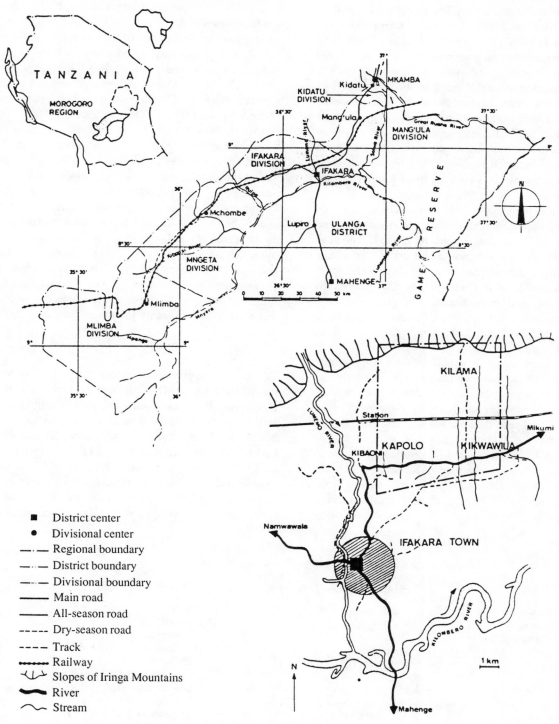

District center
Divisional center
Regional boundary
District boundary
Divisional boundary
Main road
All-season road
Dry-season road
Track
Railway
Slopes of Iringa Mountains
River
Stream

Source: Reproduced from Tanner *et al.* (1987b) with the permission of Schwabe and Company.

132,510 (9 persons per square kilometer) (Tanzania Bureau of Statistics, 1978). The projected population in 1984, based on a natural increase of 3.1 percent per year, was 159,050 (11 persons per square kilometer). Infant mortality was estimated at 140 per 1,000 (Tanzania Bureau of Statistics, 1978; UNICEF, 1985b).

An important feature of the Kilombero District is its tribal heterogeneity. More than 30 tribes are recorded and can be found even within a single village (Tanner *et al.*, 1987b). This heterogeneity is the result of traditional migration patterns (Schaer, 1985), colonial settlement policies (Kjekshus, 1977), and the villagization campaign of 1974 (International Labour Office, 1982).

The rural populace of the Kilombero District are mainly subsistence farmers (who grow rice, maize, and cassava) and fishermen. Jatzold and Baum (1968) gave a detailed account of each major tribe's economic formations. Cattle are rarely raised due to the abundance of tsetse flies. Traditional houses with walls made of mud and roofs thatched with grasses or palm leaves are the norm. Brick houses with corrugated iron roofs are mainly seen in Ifakara and settlements along the trunk road.

Rural water supply is variable. Some communities (60 percent of the total population) have gravity water supply schemes, boreholes, or shallow wells, while the remaining ones rely entirely on hand-dug wells (UNICEF, 1985b). These data are biased, however, by the urban areas of Ifakara, where 24 percent of the population lives. A detailed description of each village's water supply and proposals for improving it was compiled in 1983 during a water supply survey of the southern Morogoro Region (DHV Consulting Engineers, 1983). At that time only half to two-thirds of the households had sanitation facilities or used existing pit latrines. So far, ventilated, improved pit latrines have not been promoted.

An extensive description of the topography, demography, and agricultural production pattern of the Ifakara Division and particularly of the large rural community of Kikwawila village, where most of the reported data were collected, has been published (Tanner *et al.*, 1987b; Zehnder *et al.*, 1987). The Ifakara Division fits into the general description of the whole Kilombero District, but its proximity to the district capital creates a population density higher than that of the district as a whole: 52,800 inhabitants (40 percent of the total population) in about 1,730 square kilometers (31 persons per square kilometer); 32,000 live in the town of Ifakara. The population density in the rural area of the Ifakara Division, excluding Ifakara town, is 12 persons per square kilometer, which resembles the figure for the district as a whole (9 persons per square kilometer). These population figures are based on Tanzania's most recent official census in 1978 (Tanzania Bureau of Statistics, 1978).

The KIHERE Project

The KIHERE program was initiated in 1981 and was funded by the Swiss Development Co-Operation from 1982 onward. After extensive discussions with district authorities the program was established to focus on health problems of local importance. The district health office, the team of the St. Francis Designated District Hospital, the Medical Assistants Training Centre, and the Swiss Tropical Institute worked together to outline research priorities, which were subsequently presented to the Tanzanian national

Figure 19-2. Phases of the Kilombero Program, Tanzania, 1982–90

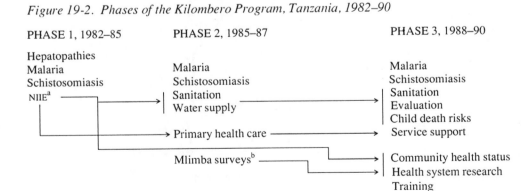

a. A community-based project on interactions among nutrition, infection, immunity, and environment in Kikwawila.
b. Conducted in the Mlimba Division of Kilombero District.

Figure 19-3. Structure of the Primary Health Care Component of the KIHERE Program

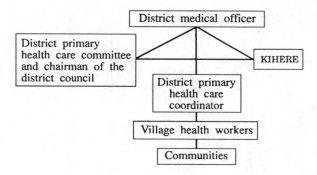

authorities and the Swiss Development Co-Operation. Figure 19-2 presents the topics, the evolution of the applied and operational field research programs, and the service support components that have been undertaken within the framework of KIHERE.

The program focused initially on applied research such as the etiology of liver disorders, the resistance of malaria to chloroquine, the transmission and control of schistosomiasis, and the interactions among nutrition, infection, and immunity. These projects gave rise to interventions (water supply, sanitation campaigns, community-based chemotherapy) followed by operational research on controlling schistosomiasis. At present, the impact of water supply and sanitation is being evaluated and health systems are being researched.

Providing service support for implementing primary health care (PHC), a major component of the program, made initiating the longitudinal projects possible. Those projects collected most of the morbidity and mortality data reported below. Figure 19-3 depicts the structure of the PHC program component at the district level. At this level, the program emphasized village health workers (VHW) and directly helped the Kilombero District to implement the national PHC program through district authorities, nongovernmental organizations, and UNICEF. It also conducted operational research on the health impact and cost-effectiveness of various elements of the program as they evolved in the district. The activities, including training schedules, diagnostic and treatment guidelines, a referral system, drug supply, community compliance, remuneration, and a first evaluation, are documented in Swiss Tropical Institute and Kilombero District Health Office (1985) and Tanner *et al.* (1987b).

The morbidity and mortality data from the large rural community of Kikwawila village, which represents many of the 50 villages of the Kilombero District, were collected within a longitudinal project on the interactions among nutrition, parasitic infections, and immunity. The special 1987 issue of *Acta Tropica* summarizes the study's design and its results from the first four years.

Morbidity

Routine Data

Table 19-1 shows the pattern of diseases and conditions reported by the 20 dispensaries and 2 health centers of the Kilombero District in 1983, 1984, and 1985. The diseases and conditions are ranked according to their frequency. The number, pattern, and frequency of diseases and conditions vary substantially from one year to the next, especially from 1983 to 1984. The number of cases reported was 2.2 times higher in 1985 than in 1983, which reflects a highly deficient reporting system. Conditions such as respiratory tract infections, for example, were only reported beginning in 1984, while tuberculosis was not reported after 1983. Whooping cough and malnutrition were not reported in 1984, while skin, eye, and ear diseases were not reported at all in 1983. Some of the differences arise because the Essential Drug Programme (EDP) and a new form for collecting routine data from health centers and dispensaries, but not from village health posts, were introduced in February 1984. The new form provided the list of diseases and conditions used in 1985. Fully functional only from around mid-1984 onward, the EDP reporting form provided the basis for the monthly drug allocation. This may partly explain the great increase in reported cases from 1983 to 1985.

To understand fully some of the problems with reporting diseases at the peripheral level requires analyzing the data routinely collected by EDP according to health center or dispensary and division. The KIHERE program is performing this analysis and monitoring how the new EDP recording and reporting systems are being introduced. The aim is to determine whether the routine data collection will be more accurate than before.

Malaria was the most frequent disease. The number of cases did not vary substantially from one year to the next, reflecting the stability of malaria endemicity in the Kilombero Valley. Clyde (1967) classified the area as holoendemic, and our studies in Kikwawila village

Table 19-1. *Principal Causes of Morbidity in the Kilombero District, Tanzania, 1983–85*

Rank	1983 Disease or condition	1983 Number of cases	1983 Percentage of all cases	1984 Disease or condition	1984 Number of cases	1984 Percentage of all cases	1985 Disease or condition	1985 Number of cases	1985 Percentage of all cases
1	Malaria	50,553	77.6	Malaria	31,540	44.3	Malaria	44,372	31.2
2	Schistosomiasis	2,876	4.4	Pneumonia and URI[a]	10,085	14.2	Pneumonia and URI[a]	18,218	12.8
3	Amebiasis	2,024	3.1	Diarrhea	7,401	10.4	Diarrhea	9,725	6.8
4	Scabies	1,864	2.9	Eye diseases	4,486	6.3	Skin diseases	9,132	6.4
5	Diarrhea	1,745	2.7	Skin diseases	4,428	6.2	Eye diseases	5,306	3.7
6	Measles	1,618	2.5	Intestinal helminths	3,917	5.5	Intestinal helminths	4,530	3.2
7	Hookworm	953	1.5	Anemia	2,965	4.2	Venereal diseases	3,290	2.3
8	Other intestinal helminths	917	1.4	Accidents	2,839	4.0	Anemia	3,239	2.3
9	Tuberculosis	681	1.0	Venereal diseases	1,749	2.5	Accidents	2,005	1.4
10	Venereal diseases	662	1.0	Measles	1,017	1.4	Ear diseases	1,373	1.0
11	Leprosy	603	0.9	Schistosomiasis	792	1.1	Schistosomiasis	1,171	0.8
12	Malnutrition	574	0.9				Nutritional disorders	967	0.7
13	Tetanus	48	0.1				Whooping cough	488	0.3
14	Filariasis	36	0.1				Pregnancy complications	354	0.2
15	Whooping cough	12	0.0				Measles	345	0.2
16							Mental disorders	316	0.2
17							Acute polio	7	0.0
18	No other diseases/conditions reported			No other diseases/conditions reported			Neonatal tetanus	5	0.0
19							Adult tetanus	0	0.0
	All other diagnoses	0	0.0	All other diagnoses		0.0	All other diagnoses	27,946	19.6
	Symptoms and ill-defined conditions	0	0.0	Symptoms and ill-defined conditions		0.0	Symptoms and ill-defined conditions	9,520	6.7
	Total	65,166	100	Total	71,219	100	Total	142,309	100

Note: A new form of routine data collection, gradually introduced by the EDP in 1984, was fully functional in 1985.

a. Upper respiratory tract infections.

Source: The 1983 and 1984 data were collected by the District Health Office from 2 health centers and 18 dispensaries; the 1985 statistics are from the records of 2 health centers and 17 dispensaries. No hospital statistics are included.

indicated a hyper- to holoendemic situation (see Tanner *et al.*, 1986a, 1987a). If 80 percent of the malaria episodes (34,000, based on the mean for 1983 to 1985) occur in children under five years of age (26,300 children in 1984; District Health Office statistics for 1984), approximately 1.3 episodes occur in the Kilombero Valley per child per year. Because the number of reported cases of diarrhea and respiratory tract infections varies greatly, no similar calculations can or should be made for these illnesses.

Table 19-2 summarizes the inpatient statistics of the St. Francis Designated District Hospital (1986), which resemble those of the periphery (table 19-1). These statistics underscore the importance of the malaria-fever-anemia complex in the Kilombero District. The

report of the St. Francis Designated District Hospital (SFDH) draws attention to the fact that the system of recording data, even within the hospital, still needs to be improved and that, therefore, the pattern of the diagnoses (table 19-2) should be interpreted with caution. Data from the outpatient department, which averages 400 contacts each day, excluding visits to the maternal and child health (MCH) clinic, are incomplete and cannot be summarized. The most reliable data are from the pediatric wards, which have been substantially reorganized in recent years. In 1986 the pediatric ward recorded 4,285 admissions. Underweight and kwashiorkor showed a significant seasonal variation, peaking in May and March, during the lean season and the rainy season before the harvest. These

Table 19-2. Morbidity Statistics from the St. Francis Designated District Hospital, Ifakara, Tanzania, 1986

Disease or diagnosis	Cases		Pediatric deaths	
	Number	Percent	Number	As percentage of all pediatric cases
All admissions	15,234	100.0		
Infectious, parasitic[a]	4,984	32.7		
Anemia	4,210	27.6		
Respiratory tract[b]	1,541	10.1		
Urogenital tract	920	6.0		
Injury, poisoning	715	4.7		
Endocrine, metabolic, marasmus[c]	711	4.7		
Skin and subcutaneous tissue	619	4.1		
Digestive system	444	2.9		
Circulatory system[d]	321	2.1		
Mental disorders	210	1.4		
Neoplasma	208	1.4		
Nervous system, sense organs	187	1.2		
Musculoskeletal system	149	1.0		
Perinatal conditions	8	0.1		
Congenital anomalies	7	0.0		
Pediatric	4,285[e]			
Anemia	2,559	60	33	1.3
Malaria	1,969	46	22	1.1
Underweight	1,624	38		
Respiratory tract	1,101	26	17	16.8
Marasmus	685	16	213	31.1
Diarrhea	503	12	6	1.2
Kwashiorkor	140	3	36	25.7
Measles	139	3	6	4.3

a. Malaria, 56 percent; gastroenteritis, 19 percent; hookworm, 10 percent.
b. Pneumonia and bronchopneumonia, 87 percent.
c. Marasmus, 96 percent.
d. Hypertension, 23 percent.
e. Because of multiple diagnoses, numbers do not sum to total cases.
Source: St. Francis Designated District Hospital (1986).

hospital-based observations correlated with our community-based studies on food consumption and production patterns, which clearly revealed seasonal nutritional deficiencies (Tanner and Lukmanji, 1987; Zehnder et al., 1987). A further significant seasonal variation occurred among cases admitted at the SFDH for malaria (which peaked toward the end of April) and for the anemia that sharply followed the malaria curve, which peaked in mid-May (St. Francis Designated District Hospital, 1986). The hospital report further listed 24 cases of tetanus (10 deaths), but contained no data on the age of those patients.

The PHC component of the KIHERE program collected routine morbidity data through the VHW register. Village health workers recorded an average of 30 attendances per working day (500–600 per month), which was affected by temporary drug shortages but not by seasonal variations. Wounds and the fever-malaria complex were the major reasons for attendance throughout the year and did not vary substantially by season (Swiss Tropical Institute and Kilombero District Health Office, 1985; Degremont et al., 1987). The statistics from the health post registers stressed the importance of malaria. Health post statistics also reflected the therapeutic possibilities available to VHWS, which could explain why they did not see or diagnose eye and nutritional problems (see table 19-5, below).

Special Surveys

Initially, the KIHERE program focused on one large community, Kikwawila village, located approximately 14 kilometers north of Ifakara town (see figure 19-1) and extending over 50 square kilometers. As outlined in the description of the study area (Tanner et al., 1987b), this community accurately represents many of the 50 villages of the Kilombero District. Table 19-3 summarizes the basic demographic data of the community and compares them with those available for the district and the country as a whole. District data are rare and are mainly extrapolations of the 1978 national census and UNICEF reviews (Tanzania Bureau of Statistics, 1978; UNICEF, 1985a, 1985b).

Community-based surveys were undertaken in Kikwawila each year beginning in 1982. The surveys took place in October, after the harvest and toward the end of the dry season. All children (one month to fifteen years of age) were invited to participate (compliance was always more than 95 percent when compared with the census) and underwent comprehensive anthropometric, parasitological, clinical, biochemical, and serological examinations (see table 19-4). The results of the surveys from 1982 to 1984 were published in *Acta Tropica* (44, 1987).

Parasitosis

The annual surveys of health status revealed the prevalence of malaria in the study area. Figure 19-4 depicts the spleen and parasite rates of children (two to nine years of age) for three consecutive years; these rates indicate a situation of hyper- to holoendemic malaria. High malaria endemicity was also evident in the answers individuals gave to a standard question

Table 19-3. Demographic Data for Tanzania, Kilombero District, and Kikwawila Village. Various Years

Demographic indicator	Tanzania		Kilombero, 1978–84	Kikwawila, 1984–85
	1967–70	1982		
Surface (square kilometers)	945,203		14,918	50
Total population	12,313,500	19,137,000	132,510	1,937
Percentage of children under age 15	44	46	43	49
Rates per 1,000				
Crude birth	47	48	n.a.	44
Crude death	19	16	n.a.	19
Natural increase (percent)	2.8	3.2	3.1	2.5
Total fertility	n.a.	7.0	n.a.	n.a.
General fertility	n.a.	n.a.	n.a.	282
Infant mortality	150	103	140	163
Maternal mortality	n.a.	n.a.	n.a.	n.a.

n.a. Not available.

Source: For Tanzania, Tanzania Bureau of Statistics (1978) and International Labour Office (1982); for Kilombero District, Tanzania Bureau of Labor Statistics, 1978, and Swiss Tropical Institute and Kilombero District Health Office (1985); for Kikwawila Village, Swiss Tropical Institute Field Laboratory (1985) and Tanner et al. (1987b).

Table 19-4. Data Collected from Children between 1 Month and 15 Years of Age by the Annual Cross-Sectional Surveys, Kikwawila Village, Tanzania, October 1982–84

Type of data	Information collected
Personal	Age, gender, household
Medical history	MCH card, health problems
Anthropometry	Weight, height, mid-upper arm circumference
Blood samples	
Smears, hematocrit	Malaria parasite rate, packed-cell volume, filarial parasites
Serum, plasma	Parasite serology, zinc and retinol determinations, serum protein electrophoresis
Stool samples	MIF, Kato, culture
Urine samples	Filtration for schistosomiasis eggs, dip sticks[a]
Clinical evaluation	General status, spleen, liver, hair, eyes, skin

Note: MCH, maternal and child health; MIF, Merthiolate-iodine-formalin fixation.

a. To test for the presence of blood, protein, and leukocytes.

Source: For a comprehensive description of these health status surveys, see Tanner *et al.* (1987a, 1987b).

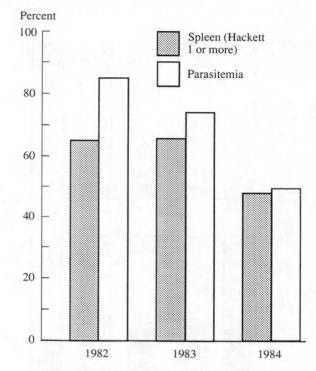

Figure 19-4. Malaria Endemicity in Children Age 2–9, Kikwawila Village, 1982–84

Note: The sample size was 85. The average enlarged spleen was 2.0, 2.2, and 1.6 in 1982, 1983, and 1984, respectively.
Source: Tanner *et al.* (1986a).

about their major health problem (figure 19-5; tables 19-5 and 19-6). More than 90 percent of the malaria infections were due to *P. falciparum* (Tanner *et al.*, 1986a).

Hookworm (*Necator americanus*) and *S. haematobium* were also prevalent and high incidences (20–40 percent) were found even among children under five years of age (see figures 19-6 and 19-7). Using stool culture techniques established a fairly high (20 percent overall) prevalence of *Strongyloides stercoralis*. Although only one stool sample was examined for each individual using MIF (Merthiolate-iodine-formalin fixation and stain), around 20 percent of the samples showed cysts of *G. lamblia*. *E. histolytica* was of minor importance. The dominance of intestinal problems in the perceived illnesses reported by individuals (figure 19-5; table 19-5) might reflect the high prevalence of intestinal helminths and giardiasis. The transient change in the pattern of perceived diseases between 1982 and 1983 (after measures to control helminths were initiated) further supported this correlation (Degremont *et al.*, 1987; Tanner and De Savigny, 1987). Figure 19-8 shows the prevalence of the major

parasitic infections, malaria, hookworm, and urinary schistosomiasis, by age group. The data are from the 1985 survey, but the curves for 1982 to 1984 are not significantly different. The age and prevalence curves indicate once again the hyperendemicity of malaria and the well-known patterns of urinary schistosomiasis and hookworm in endemic areas. No sex- or occupation-related differences existed in the prevalences and incidences by age groups.

Multiparasitism was frequent. One-third of all children harbored three or more parasites, and less than 11 percent were free of parasites each year. Not one child remained parasite-free for three consecutive years. The pattern of multiparasitism was changing in the study area, making correlations with nutritional parameters difficult; that is, the effects of single parasites or nutrients could not be unraveled (Tanner *et al.*, 1987a). Hookworm and *S. haematobium* infections and multiparasitism did not cluster within households (the analysis of household clusters allowed for age).

Figure 19-5. Perception of Health Problems of Children and Adults in Kikwawila Village, 1982 and 1985

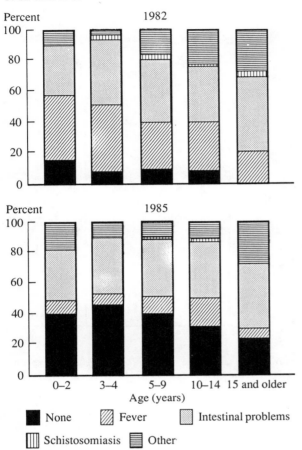

None   Fever   Intestinal problems

Schistosomiasis   Other

Note: The sample size was 636 in 1982 and 909 in 1985. Schistosomiasis includes complaints about hematuria and dysuria; fever includes the fever-malaria complex; intestinal problems include abdominal pain and diarrhea, with or without fever.

The health statistics from the periphery and the center reveal that malaria is responsible for substantial morbidity and for an unknown proportion of mortality in the Kilombero District. Malaria exerted a significant negative effect on the packed-cell volume of children (ANOVA after controlling for age and hookworm and *S. haematobium* infection). In-depth studies similar to those undertaken in the Gambia (Greenwood *et al.*, 1987) are being planned to establish more precisely the impact of malaria on the morbidity and mortality of infants, children, and adults living in the district.

S. haematobium shows a highly focal distribution in the Ifakara Division (Zumstein, 1983); the prevalence in Kikwawila village exceeds 50 percent among schoolchildren. The intensity of infection among children in three age groups (0–5, 6–10, and 11–15) was moderate, with geometric mean egg counts per 10 milliliters of urine between 7 and 30 (the proportion of children with at least 50 eggs per 10 milliliters was 14–44 percent). For all children, the mean was between 2 and 12 eggs per 10 milliliters and the proportion with at least 50 eggs was 6–29 percent after $x + 1$ transformation of egg counts. High prevalence and intensity correlated with high frequency of microhematuria and proteinuria as well as with anamnestic hematuria and dysuria (Zumstein, 1983; Tanner *et al.*, 1983). Hematuria and proteinuria were associated with infection (a positive predictive value of more than 75 percent), and sonography revealed substantial pathology in the bladders and kidneys of children and adults (Degremont *et al.*, 1985; Burki *et al.*, 1986). Community-based treatment campaigns with praziquantel (40 or 20 milligrams per kilogram given in a single oral dose) or metrifonate (10 milligrams per kilogram in three oral doses) showed that a substantial proportion of bladder and kidney lesions could be reversed in children and that the morbidity indicators such as hematuria, proteinuria, leukocyturia, and dysuria could be reversed as well (Burki, 1987; Hatz *et al.*, 1990). The correlations between morbidity indicators (hematuria, proteinuria), disease perception patterns (anamnestic hematuria and dysuria), and infection led the project to simplify its approach to establishing transmission foci in the district. Surveys that questioned schoolchildren, teachers, and village leaders about priorities, symptoms, and signs of disease were highly cost-effective and accurate. They produced information on the relative importance of urinary schistosomiasis in different rural communities and identified the major transmission sites (Tanner, 1989b).

Hookworm infection was of comparatively low intensity. Based on Kato stool examinations, geometric mean egg counts were below 200 eggs per gram of stool for infected children in all age groups (less than 100 for all children after $x + 1$ transformation of egg counts). Hookworm was not associated with anemia: that is, the effect of hookworm infection on the packed-cell volume could not be established.

A latrine campaign (which increased the number of households with simple pit latrines from 57 to 80 percent) followed by a single mass treatment against

Table 19-5. Disease Rankings: Community Perception Compared with Survey and Routine Data Collected at Village Health Posts, Tanzania 1984

Rank	Household interviews on individual health problems[a]	Village health post registers[b]		Standardized question on individual health problems[c]		Clinical examinations[c]	Parasitological examinations[c]	
		Kikwawila	Kapolo	Kikwawila	Kapolo		Diagnosis	Percent[d]
1	Fever, malaria	Fever, malaria	Headache	Abdominal problems	Abdominal problems	Splenomegaly	Malaria	77
2	Headache	Wound	Fever, malaria	Fever, malaria	Fever, malaria	Teeth caries	Hookworm	66
3	Abdominal problems	Headache	Wound	Schistoso-miasis	Headache	Skin infections	Schistoso-miasis	58
4	Other health problems	Abdominal problems	Abdominal problems	Headache	Cough	Signs of malnutrition (skin, hair)	Strongy-loidosis	25
5	Schistoso-miasis	Cough, chest	Cough	Cough	Schistoso-miasis	Eye problems	Giardiasis	17

Note: All responses are for both Kikwawila and Kapolo, unless otherwise noted.
a. Among people more than 6 years of age in Kikwawila and Kapolo.
b. Recorded by village health workers at village health posts (VHP).
c. Data from the cross-sectional health status survey of children in 1984. See also Tanner *et al.* (1987a, 1987b).
d. Percentage based on prevalence among the 588 children surveyed in 1984.
Source: Degremont *et al.* (1987).

Table 19-6. Frequency of Individual Health Problems Reported in Cross-Sectional Surveys in Kikwawila and Kapolo, Tanzania, 1982–84

(percent, unless otherwise indicated)

Symptoms and signs	1982		1983		1984	
	Kikwawila	Kapolo	Kikwawila	Kapolo	Kikwawila	Kapolo
Number	336	220	338	213	375	213
Headache	7.7	8.6	2.4	7.5	6.4	8.5
Wound	0.3	0.5	0.0	0.5	0.0	0.0
Fever, malaria	28.8	32.0	26.6	21.6	17.9	5.6
Fever and abdominal pain	5.1	5.9	2.4	9.9	0.5	1.9
Abdominal problem	36.6	35.0	27.0	22.5	31.7	24.4
Cough, chest	1.5	1.8	2.4	1.4	0.3	3.8
Schistosomiasis	1.5	2.7	18.0	14.1	13.6	2.8
Other problems	8.1	4.0	5.2	3.7	6.1	2.3
None	10.4	9.5	16.0	18.8	23.5	50.7

Note: The standardized, open-ended question was "What is your main health problem?"
Source: Degremont *et al.* (1987).

hookworm (400 milligrams of albendazole given in a single oral dose; the compliance rate was 62 percent) and/or *G. lamblia* (40 milligrams of ornidazole per kilogram given in a single oral dose) only temporarily affected the prevalence and incidence of giardiasis. The intensity of hookworm infections decreased only during the six months after the interventions. Consequently, the latrine and treatment campaigns apparently had no sustained impact on nutritional status (Tanner *et al.*, 1987a).

Nutrition

The community-based surveys also allowed the project to assess the nutritional status of children by using the Harvard standards adapted for Tanzania (Kilimanjaro Christian Medical Centre, 1978). The frequency of wasting (stages 2 and 3, in which weight-for-height is below 80 percent of the standard median and reflects current malnutrition) was 3 percent among children under five. Severe wasting (less than 70 percent of the standard median) was found among 1 percent or less. Stunting (stages 2 and 3, in which height-for-age is below 87.5 percent of the standard median) was found among two-thirds of the children under five. Severe stunting (less than 80 percent of the standard median) was seen in 10–15 percent of the children. Figure 19-9 shows the distribution of the *z*-scores for weight-for-height, weight-for-age, and height-for-age among the children of Kikwawila in 1982. The same distribution pattern was found for all three parameters in 1985.

Further anthropometric data came from a survey at the MCH clinic at SFDH during the lean (March) and postharvest (September) seasons. More than 2,000 children (in March 2,211; in September 2,097) attending the MCH clinic were measured, and a questionnaire on the family structure, situation, birth, pregnancy, and vaccination status was administered to their mothers or caretakers. Figure 19-10 shows the frequency of stunting and wasting among those children compared with data from the total community survey of Kikwawila in 1983 and 1985. The wasting and wasting plus stunting of those children are essentially the same as those of the entire community. A slightly higher proportion of stunted children was observed in the community-based surveys than in the clinic surveys. This might be due to an overestimation of age, since MCH cards were not always available in the community-based studies and age had to be asked for or estimated by the village health worker. According to census data 60–70 percent of the children under five attended the MCH clinic. Nonattendance did not appear

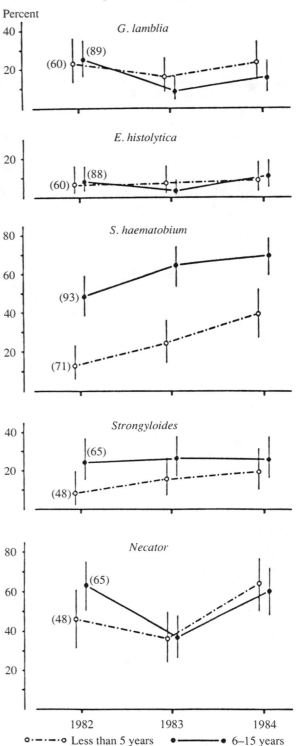

Figure 19-6. Prevalence of Parasitic Infections in Kikwawila Village, 1982–84

Note: The number of children appears in parentheses. The confidence limit is approximately 95 percent.
Source: Tanner *et al.* (1987a).

Figure 19-7. Incidence of Parasitic Infections in Kikwawila Village, 1982–84

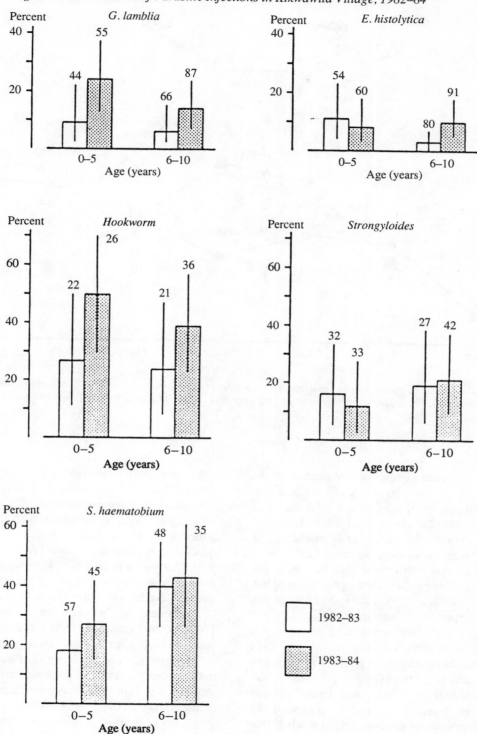

Note: Numbers on the bars represent the number of children. The confidence limit is approximately 95 percent.

Figure 19-8. Age-Specific Prevalence of the Three Major Parasitoses in Kikwawila Village, 1985

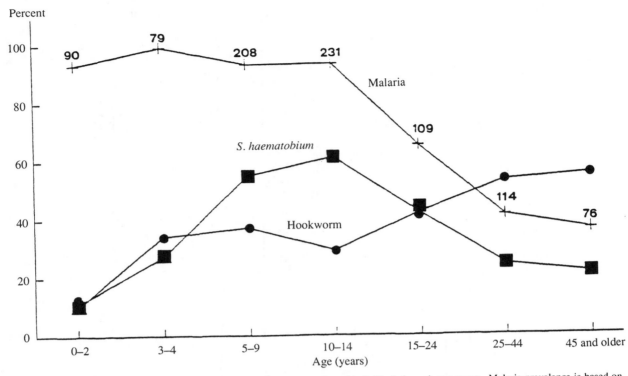

Note: Numbers on the malaria prevalence rate curve represent the number of individuals in each age group. Malaria prevalence is based on parasite rates in thick smears, hookworm prevalence on egg count per gram of stool (Kato smear), and *S. haematobium* prevalence on egg count per 10 milliliters of urine.

to cluster in particular villages or town sectors of the catchment area of the SFDH MCH clinic investigated. More than 80 percent of the children older than nine months who attended this central clinic had been vaccinated against DPT, polio, and measles. This coverage is far above the mean for many rural areas of Tanzania (Tanzania Ministry of Health, 1982). The MCH survey further revealed that the prevalence of low birth weight (less than 2,500 grams) was 17 percent in March and 16 percent in September.

Biochemical analysis of serum and plasma samples collected in Kikwawila village revealed that 3–12 percent of the children had serum retinol levels below 100 micrograms per liter in October (Sturchler *et al.*, 1987). Retinol deficiency is a public health problem when more than 5 percent of the children between six months and six years of age have retinol levels below 100 micrograms per liter (World Health Organization, 1982). This proportion existed in our study area in

1982 and 1983, although few children had conjunctival xerosis and none had severe forms of xerophthalmia (Degremont *et al.*, 1987). Surveys of food consumption and production in the study area indicated a seasonal pattern of vitamin A deficiency, which may explain these results (Tanner and Lukmanji, 1987; Zehnder *et al.*, 1987). Leafy vegetables rich in vitamin A were consumed during the lean season, but not after the harvest, when rice was abundant.

Prealbumin levels were below standard values (200–300 milligrams per liter) and reached a plateau with 130 milligrams per liter, among four-to-six-year-old children (Betschart *et al.*, 1987). Prealbumin levels did not correlate with the anthropometric parameters and thus could not be used as a biochemical indicator of nutritional problems. Plasma zinc concentrations varied markedly among individuals, even in the same age group. Zinc concentrations (a mean of 0.8–1.2 milligrams per liter) correlated well with retinol levels

Figure 19-9. Anthropometric Data for Children under 11 Years of Age, Kikwawila Village, 1982

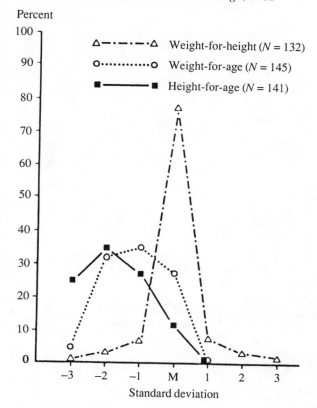

Percent

△ —·—·— △ Weight-for-height (*N* = 132)

○ ·········· ○ Weight-for-age (*N* = 145)

■ —————— ■ Height-for-age (*N* = 141)

Standard deviation

Source: Tanner *et al.* (1987a).

Disease Perception

The anthropometric, clinical, parasitological, and biochemical parameters revealed only slight changes in and a transient improvement of Kikwawila's health status during the first four years of the community-based surveys. On the other hand, the community itself provided useful information on the outcome of health interventions. Standardized open-ended questionnaires administered during the annual health status surveys or household interviews revealed patterns of disease perception that matched those of parasitological and of some clinical findings (table 19-5, figure 19-5). However, the patterns of perception did not include malnutrition and eye problems, which were only picked up by the clinical examinations.

The proportion of individuals who cited abdominal problems (including diarrhea and abdominal pain with or without fever) as their major problem did not change between 1982 and 1985 (figure 19-5). The proportion of people who had no health problem increased, while that of individuals who complained of fevers or malaria decreased in the same period. In addition, schistosomiasis (including complaints about hematuria and dysuria) was no longer mentioned after control measures were initiated in 1984. Although the methodology suffers from interview biases (discussed by Degremont *et al.*, 1987), these disease perception patterns can be used to monitor aspects of community health status and health interventions (Tanner *et al.*, 1986b; Tanner and De Savigny, 1987; Tanner, 1989a, 1989b). The villagers indicated the area in which they felt improvement had been achieved (the transient effect of mass treatment on abdominal problems in 1983), where they considered that the curative activities of the VHW satisfied some of their needs (the treatment of wounds, supply of drugs against fever and malaria), and where they were no longer conscious of disease-specific morbidity (schistosomiasis). By seeing health problems within the context of all the community's priorities, the project could also learn how the villagers ranked community development issues and where and how they were prepared to participate in addressing them. This interplay between the assessment of health problems by professionals and the perception of community health and development issues by the population has already involved the community in programs to control schistosomiasis and improve water supply and sanitation. This interplay could also efficiently direct control strategies (Tanner *et al.*, 1986b; Tanner, 1989b).

and inconsistently with prealbumin levels. They did not correlate with the prevalence and intensity of any parasitosis (Betschart *et al.*, 1987). The transient effects on the parasite load of single mass treatments with albendazole or ornidazole were not reflected in the biochemical parameters such as serum protein or retinol levels (Betschart *et al.*, 1987; Sturchler *et al.*, 1987). The nutritional status assessed by biochemical and anthropometric parameters could be related to the pattern of food consumption and production in the household. These studies are summarized by Tanner and Lukmanji (1987) and Zehnder *et al.* (1987). Seasonal food deficiencies and agricultural production patterns that impoverish the soil were major problems identified in these surveys and gave rise to specific proposals for strengthening subsistence farming, especially crop management and crop selection.

Figure 19-10. Frequency of Stunting and Wasting in Children under Five Years of Age, Ifakara Division, 1983

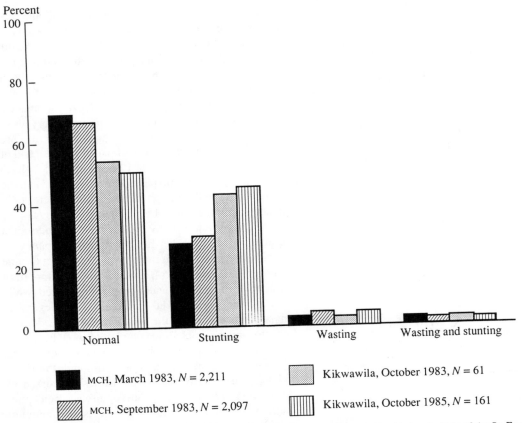

Percent

MCH, March 1983, N = 2,211   Kikwawila, October 1983, N = 61

MCH, September 1983, N = 2,097   Kikwawila, October 1985, N = 161

Note: The attendances of children under five years of age at the maternal and child health (MCH) clinic of the St. Francis Designated District Hospital took place during the lean season (March) and after the harvest (September). The Kikwawila village community-based surveys were conducted in 1983 and 1985.

Mortality

Routine Data

As shown in table 19-3, hardly any vital statistics were routinely collected for the district. Birth and death rates are not stated in the annual reports of either the district health office or the district administration, and the most common regional figures are extrapolations of the 1978 census (UNICEF, 1985a, 1985b). The 1978 census and the collection of routine morbidity data lead to a ranking of the top ten killers of children and adults in Tanzania and the districts as seen in table 19-7.

The lack of information at the district, regional, and national levels is due not only to the lack of routine data collection at the village level, but to deficiencies in evaluating the data and feeding the analysis back to

Table 19-7. Principal Causes of Death of Children and Adults, Morogoro Region, Tanzania

Rank	Children (under age 5)	Adults (age 15 and older)
1	Malaria	Malaria
2	Measles	Diarrhea
3	Pneumonia	Anemia
4	Anemia	Pneumonia
5	Diarrhea	Cardiac disease
6	Tuberculosis	Hypertension
7	Malnutrition	Poisoning
8	Intestinal helminths	Tuberculosis
9	Gastroenteritis	Peptic ulcers
10	Tetanus	Diabetes

Source: UNICEF (1985a).

Table 19-8. Results of the Vital Statistics Survey, Kikwawila Village, Tanzania, 1984–85

Parameter	Survey data (number/number surveyed)	Rate per 1,000[a]	
		Number	Range
Crude birth	86/1,937	44	35–53
Crude death	36/1,937	19	13–25
Natural increase	50/1,937	25	18–32
General fertility	88/312	282	232–332
Mortality			
Perinatal	11/88	125	64–213
Neonatal	7/86	81	33–160
Infant	14/86	163	92–258
Child deaths			
Age 1–5	6/159	38	14–80
Under age 15	24/771	31	19–43
Adult deaths (age 15 and older)	12/811	15	7–23

a. 95 percent confidence interval.
Source: Swiss Tropical Institute Field Laboratory (1985).

the relevant level. Routine data collection forms for births and deaths are part of the village registration system. This register should be completed by the village secretary and, with the village census, provide vital statistics at the village level. Completed forms are rarely collected, however, and even more rarely evaluated; in turn, the forms are no longer completed by the village authorities.

Special Surveys

This situation prompted the KIHERE program to investigate the vital statistics and the health status of mothers and children in the project community, Kikwawila, in more detail. Using a comprehensive population survey undertaken in 1982 and repeated in 1984 as a model, the program designed and conducted a vital statistics survey with household interviews. The evaluation of the survey led to the creation of a child survival fact sheet for the study community (Swiss Tropical Institute Field Laboratory, 1985). These data should not be extrapolated to the district. Table 19-8 summarizes major data and allows, together with table 19-3, the community to be compared with the nation. The high infant mortality rate, with a substantial proportion (50 percent) due to neonatal mortality, is striking when compared with the national average of 103 per 1,000 in 1982. This fits into the picture of a northeast to southwest gradient within Tanzania in which the northeastern, economically stronger regions

have the lowest rates (less than 115), and the southwestern regions account for the highest ones (more than 145) (UNICEF, 1985a). In Kikwawila village, 58 percent of all recorded deaths in 1984 occurred among children under five years of age and 69 percent among children under fifteen. At least 11 percent of all deaths among children under five occurred in the hospital. The cause of death could not be established, since the community-based vital statistics surveys had a recall period of one year. A significant seasonal trend peaked in mid-July (at the beginning of the harvest): half of the deaths in children under five occurred between June and August, and birth rates peaked at the end of June (Swiss Tropical Institute Field Laboratory, 1985).

The village health workers' register of births and deaths revealed the same number of births and deaths in a given catchment area as was found by a labor-intensive vital statistics survey (Swiss Tropical Institute and Kilombero District Health Office, 1985). These results could not be compared with the village register, which at that time was no longer being completed by the secretary of Kikwawila.

Faced with comparatively high perinatal and neonatal mortality rates (table 19-8), the project investigated the mothers in more detail, using the vital statistics survey information for 1984, the community health status survey for 1985, and the comprehensive MCH survey among more than 4,000 children and mothers in 1983. Table 19-9 summarizes basic information on the

Table 19-9. Vital Statistics of Women in Kikwawila Village, 1985

Parameter	Number	Rate per 100 (percent)
Women of childbearing age	312	73.1
Pregnancies	88	28.2
Live births	86	97.7
Births at home	57	66.3
Antenatal attendance	80	90.9
MCH attendance after delivery	67	77.9

Note: The number of women surveyed was 327.
Source: Swiss Tropical Institute Field Laboratory (1985).

women of Kikwawila. The in-depth study of parameters related to the parity of 145 mothers (with 649 births and 176 infant deaths) revealed an average age of primagravida of 19 years (the median was 18) and a median parity of 4 (the mode was 2); the range was 1 to 16. The mean was 1.2 child deaths per mother (48 percent of mothers had lost at least one child), and 22 percent of the mothers were related to three-quarters of the child deaths. An analysis of 1,061 maternal years at risk and 82 deaths showed that child death was parity dependent. The relative risk of losing a child when parity was 4–6 was 4.8 times (90 percent confidence interval; 2.5–9.5) higher than when parity was 1–3. The high-parity groups (more than 6) showed similar relative risks; when parity was 7–9, the risk was 4.7 and above 9, it was 3.9. The MCH survey at SFDH revealed that 90 percent of all mothers had a birth spacing greater than 22 months. Of the mothers 37 percent (815 of 2,204) had lost one child or more after birth and 21 percent reported at least one abortion. A survey undertaken by the Tanzania Food and Nutrition Centre in selected villages of the Morogoro Region revealed that all mothers breast-feed for the first 6 months, 91 percent from 7 to 12 months, and 63 percent from 13 to 24 months (UNICEF, 1985b).

Besides the lack of comprehensive mortality data for the Kilombero District, no study has surveyed the cause of death by age and by endemic setting. The special surveys were based on recall periods of one year, which makes reliable identification of the cause of death difficult. Oral postmortems similar to those performed in morbidity and mortality studies in the Gambia (Greenwood *et al.*, 1987) are now attempting to pinpoint the relative importance of the factors contributing to the excessively high rates (compared with the national average) of infant and child death in the Kilombero District.

Conclusions

This chapter briefly reviewed the data on morbidity and mortality in an economically important district of southeastern Tanzania. The lack of data to support decisions about allocating resources to and planning for the health sector and, more generally, for community development is substantial. The initial phase of the KIHERE program (the first five years) indicated ways to overcome this lack of information at the district level (Tanner 1988, 1989b). The program continues to assist the district authorities in collecting and evaluating data. In addition, health interventions such as PHC implementation, antihelminth treatment campaigns, sanitation and education campaigns, and schistosomiasis transmission control were launched in pilot communities.

The national Essential Drug Program (EDP) initiated in 1984 introduced a routine system of collecting morbidity data at health centers and dispensaries that promises to improve data collection. However, the evaluation and feedback at the district level are still slow, which could gradually discourage health staff from completing the forms. The village health worker statistics, which were not used in the EDP, provided vital statistics that compared favorably with those collected by specially designed, labor-intensive household surveys. In addition, the village government keeps an official birth and death register, which could, with the village census, provide essential vital statistics. This, the ongoing efforts of the VHW program extension, as well as the EDP forms for morbidity data provide a sound basis for reliable, routine collection of morbidity and mortality data in the district. Emphasizing the importance during training and on the job of keeping these district records and supporting an EDP that includes VHW posts are the most important prerequisites for sustained success.

The existing data from special surveys in a few communities representing the rural areas of the district provide only part of the morbidity pattern. Malaria's influence on child health and survival is clearly significant. Among intestinal helminths only hookworm was highly prevalent, but its influence on the community's health status was only moderate. On the other hand, urinary schistosomiasis caused substantial morbidity in the areas of high transmission. Morbidity control alone or in combination with transmission control using local plant molluscicides not only reduced the prevalence and incidence of urinary schistosomiasis, but substantially reduced bladder and kidney lesions among children. There is still little information on the importance of other, nonparasitic communicable diseases. Ongoing surveys address these diseases as well, especially the respiratory tract infections, the diarrhea complex, and the impact of AIDS.

Nutritional problems were seasonal and could be related to patterns of food production, utilization, and consumption. This connection was particularly evident in assessments of vitamin A status. Combining clinical surveys with food consumption and food production surveys is essential for collecting comprehensive baseline data and designing future intervention strategies.

The rankings that individuals gave to health problems and health priorities matched those of community-based, annual health status surveys involving clinical, anthropological, parasitological, serological, and biochemical examinations. Perception patterns also reflected the outcome of specific health interventions. These results and the recent experience with urinary schistosomiasis showed that disease perception patterns established by questionnaire surveys among village leaders, children, or randomly selected households can be cost-effective tools for routine community diagnosis and for monitoring health interventions. In addition, this approach can stimulate community participation within a PHC program.

Mortality data were scarce owing to the deficient routine data collection and the age of the KIHERE program. Recent vital statistics surveys indicated a high infant mortality rate, half of which was due to neonatal mortality. This, the equally high perinatal mortality rate, and the parity parameters pinpoint the situation of the mother as a priority area for intervention. However, comprehensive district-based demographic studies are also needed to provide sound vital statistics. In addition, household-based vital statistics surveys (combined with the VHW registers and standardized oral postmortems) of births, deaths, and causes of death will continue, as they provide a feasible method for establishing community-specific child survival fact sheets. This information can in turn help tailor interventions to each setting within existing PHC efforts. The data from Kikwawila village have already been used for this purpose.

Based on the available morbidity and mortality data, a comprehensive UNICEF program was launched in collaboration with the district authorities. KIHERE will provide evaluation support through its links with the district. Focusing on child survival, the program uses a comprehensive community development approach (UNICEF, 1985a, 1985b). The following intervention areas were developed from 1987 onward:

- Improve food security by building better storage facilities, promoting small animal husbandry and vegetable gardens, and offering education on weaning;
- Improve health and environmental sanitation by strengthening the VHW program according to the national guidelines for implementation, the immunization program, and the promotion of pit latrines, based on an appropriate standard design;
- Improve organized care of children at the village level;
- Support district infrastructure by providing transportation and maintenance of district vehicles;
- Strengthen the village information systems by training the village record keepers and providing evaluation support and training to ensure efficient feedback and exchange of data;
- Introduce appropriate technology to reduce the workload of women (provide wheelbarrows and hand milling machines) and to slow deforestation (introduce clay stoves).

The community-based activities of the KIHERE program and the cross-sectional health status, vital statistics, and food consumption and production surveys undertaken since 1982 provided essential baseline data for the district. These surveys and simplified, cost-effective adaptations for use at the district level are continuing. They provide a basis for evaluating how the long-term interventions can be consolidated to improve community health in the Kilombero District of Tanzania.

Acknowledgments

We wish to thank the villagers and their government for their excellent cooperation. We are grateful to W. L. Kilama, director general of the National Institute for Medical Research, Tanzania, and W. Moll, medical superintendent of St. Francis Designated District Hospital, 1980–85, for their support of the project. The Kilombero Health Research Programme could not have been initiated and continued without the untiring expert assistance of the laboratory and fieldworkers of the district health office of the Swiss Tropical Institute Field Laboratory (Utafiti wa Afya) in Ifakara as well as many members of the Swiss Tropical Institute in Basel, Switzerland. We wish to thank Jennifer Jenkins for reading the manuscript.

The Kilombero Health Research Programme is supported by grants from the Swiss Development

Co-Operation, and research clearance was granted by the Tanzania National Scientific Research Council.

We wish to thank Schwabe and Co. Publishers, Basel, Switzerland, for their permission to reproduce figures 1, 6, 7, and 9 and table 5 from *Acta Tropica* 44 (2, 1987).

References

Betschart, B., Rieder, H. P., Gautschi, K., De Savigny, D., Degremont, A., and Tanner, M. (1987). Serum proteins and zinc as parameters to monitor the health of children in a rural Tanzanian community. *Acta Tropica*, 44(2), 191–211.

Burki, A. (1987). Use of diagnostic ultrasound in the study of urinary schistosomiasis: a morbidity study before and after treatment. M.D. thesis, University of Basel.

Burki, A., Tanner, M., Burnier, E., Schweizer, W., Meudt, R., and Degremont, A. (1986). Comparison of ultrasonography, intravenous pyelography, and cystoscopy in detection of urinary tract lesions due to *Schistosoma haematobium*. *Acta Tropica*, 43, 139–151.

Clyde, D. F. (1967). *Malaria in Tanzania*. London: Oxford University Press.

Degremont, A., Burki, A., Burnier, E., Schweizer, W., Meudt, R., and Tanner, M. (1985). The use of ultrasonography to study *Schistosoma haematobium* related morbidity. *Lancet*, 1, 662–665.

Degremont, A., Lwihula, G. K., Mayombana, C., Burnier, E., De Savigny, D., and Tanner, M. (1987). Longitudinal study on the health status of children in a rural Tanzanian community: comparison of community-based clinical examinations, the diseases seen at village health posts, and the perception of health problems by the population. *Acta Tropica*, 44(2), 175–190.

DHV Consulting Engineers. (1983). Water supply survey, southern Morogoro region. *DHV Final Report*. Amersfoort.

Food and Agriculture Organization. (1961). *The Rufiji Basin Tanganyika*. FAO Expanded Technical Assistance Programme Report, no. 1269. Rome.

Greenwood, B. M., Bradley, A. K., Greenwood, A. M., Byass, P., Jammeh, K., Marsh, K., and Hayes, R. (1987). Mortality and morbidity from malaria among children in a rural area of the Gambia, West Africa. *Transactions of the Royal Society of Tropical Medicine and Hygiene*, 81, 478–486.

Hatz, C., Mayombana, C., De Savigny, D., Macpherson, C. N. L., Koella, J., Degremont, A., and Tanner, M. (1990). Ultrasound scanning for detecting morbidity due to *Schistosoma haematobium* and its resolution following treatment with different doses of praziquantel. *Transactions of the Royal Society of Tropical Medicine and Hygiene*, 84, 84–88.

Heggenhougen, K., Vaughan, P., Muhondwa, E. P., and Rutabanzibwa-Ngaiza, J. (1987). *Community Health Workers: The Tanzanian Experience*. Nairobi: Oxford University Press.

International Labour Office. (1982). *Basic Needs in Danger, A Basic Needs Oriented Development Strategy for Tanzania*. Addis Ababa.

Jatzold, R. and Baum, E. (1968). *The Kilombero Valley: Characteristic Features of the Economic Geography of a Semihumid East African Flood Plain and Its Margins*. London: C. Hurst and Co.

Kilimanjaro Christian Medical Centre. (1978). *Management Schedules of Paediatric Department KCMC (Kilimanjaro Christian Medical Centre): Management of Common Children's Diseases in East Africa*. 4th ed. KCMC Low-cost Booklet, no. 2. Moshi, Tanzania.

Kjekshus, H. (1977). *Ecology Control and Economic Development in East African History: The Case of Tanganyika, 1850–1950*. London: Heinemann.

Schaer, A. (1985). Kikwawila, ein Dorf in Suedost-Tansania, Aspekte der Detribalisation und Integration. Faculty of History Essay, University of Basel.

St. Francis Designated District Hospital. (1986). *Annual Report 1986*.

Sturchler, D., Tanner, M., Hanck, A., Betschart, B., Gautschi, K., Weiss, N., Burnier, E., Del Giudice, G., and Degremont, A. (1987). Longitudinal study on relations of retinol with parasitic infections and the immune response in children of Kikwawila village, Tanzania. *Acta Tropica*, 44, 213–227.

Swiss Tropical Institute and Kilombero District Health Office. (1985). *Collaborative Primary Health Care Project in Kilombero District Tanzania*. Working Document STIFL/DHO, no. 1.

Swiss Tropical Institute Field Laboratory. (1985). *Child Survival Fact Sheet Kikwawila Village*. Update, no. 1.2. Ifakara: STIFL and the Kilombero Health Research Programme.

Tanner, M. (1988). District level data collection and use. A paper prepared for the Independent International Commission on Health Research for Development, School of Public Health, Harvard University, Cambridge, Mass.

———. (1989a). Evaluation and monitoring of schistosomiasis control. *Tropical Medicine and Parasitology*, 40, 207–213.

———. (1989b). From the bench to the field: control of parasitic infections within primary health care. *Parasitology*, 99, 81–92.

Tanner, M. and De Savigny, D. (1987). Monitoring of community health status: experience from a case study in Tanzania. *Acta Tropica*, 44(2), 261–270.

Tanner, M. and Lukmanji, Z. (1987). Food consumption patterns in a rural Tanzanian community (Kikwawila village, Kilombero district, Morogoro region) during lean and post-harvest season. *Acta Tropica*, 44(2), 229–244.

Tanner, M., Holzer, B., Marti, H. P., Saladin, B., and Degremont, A. (1983). Frequency of haematuria and proteinuria among *Schistosoma haematobium* infected children of two communities from Liberia and Tanzania. *Acta Tropica*, 40, 231–237.

Tanner, M., Del Giudice, G., Betschart, B., Biro, S., Burnier, E., Degremont, A., Engers, H. D., Freyvogel, T. A., Lambert, P. H., Pessi, A., Speiser, F., Verdini, A. S., and Weiss, N. (1986a). Malaria transmission and development of anti-sporozoite antibodies in a rural African community. *Memorias Instituto Oswaldo Cruz (Rio de Janeiro)*, 81 (supplement 2), 199–205.

Tanner, M., Lwihula, G. K., Burnier, E., De Savigny, D., and Degremont, A. (1986b). Community participation within a primary health care programme. *Tropical Medicine and Parasitology*, 37, 164–167.

Tanner, M., Burnier, E., Mayombana, C., Betschart, B., De Savigny, D., Marti, H. P., Suter, R., Aellen, M., Ludin, E., and Degremont, A. (1987a). Longitudinal study on the health status of children in a rural Tanzanian community: parasitosis and nutrition following control measures against intestinal parasites. *Acta Tropica*, 44(2), 137–174.

Tanner, M., Degremont, A., De Savigny, D., Freyvogel, T. A., Mayombana, C., and Tayari, S. (1987b). Longitudinal study on the health status of children in Kikwawila village, Tanzania: study area and design. *Acta Tropica*, 44(2), 119–136.

Tanzania Bureau of Statistics. Ministry of Finance and Planning. (1978). *1978 Population Census. Preliminary Report*. Dar es Salaam.

Tanzania Ministry of Health. (1982). Evaluation of maternal and child health care programme in Tanzania, 1981. Mimeo. Dar es Salaam.

UNICEF (1985a). *Analysis of the Situation of Children and Women*. Dar es Salaam.

———. (1985b). *Programme for Child Survival and Development in Morogoro Region, 1987–1991*. Dar es Salaam.

World Health Organization. (1982). *Control of Vitamin A Deficiency and Xerophthalmia*. WHO Technical Report Series, no. 672. Geneva.

Zehnder, A., Jeje, B., Tanner, M., and Freyvogel, T. A. (1987). Agricultural production in Kikwawila village, southeastern Tanzania. *Acta Tropica*, 44(2), 245–260.

Zumstein, A. (1983). A study on some factors influencing the epidemiology of urinary schistosomiasis at Ifakara (Kilombero district, Morogoro region, Tanzania). *Acta Tropica*, 40, 187–204.

Chapter 20

Morbidity and Mortality at Keneba, The Gambia, 1950–75

Ian A. McGregor

Medical investigations in the West Kiang District of the Gambia began in late 1949 as a collaboration between the Human Nutrition Research Unit of the British Medical Research Council (MRC), which had established a research base at Fajara on the Atlantic coast in 1947, and the Health Department of the Gambia. The investigations were prompted by an increasing awareness of the dearth of information on the identity and epidemiology of communicable diseases in rural areas and of their cause of, or effect on, malnutrition. Protein deficiency malnutrition in particular was considered widespread throughout the country and, indeed, throughout all of Sub-Saharan Africa. The Human Nutrition Research Unit under the direction of Professor B. S. Platt had already studied agricultural and dietary practices in other rural areas of the Gambia. The West Kiang investigations were designed to supplement those studies and to seek relationships between zymotic, particularly parasitic, diseases and nutritional state.

West Kiang was chosen for two main reasons. First, its remote, peninsular location (see figure 20-1) and low level of development suggested a less mobile population than that of areas with better roads and lines of communication. Second, no medical facilities existed, or had ever existed, within the district. This history permitted diseases whose prevalence and effects had not been modified by prior, undocumented medical intervention to be assessed. Keneba village, in the center of the peninsula, became the principal site of operations because it reasonably represented other villages of the district and was acceptably large.

The study was designed to last several years, long enough to prepare an accurate census of village residents, establish valid vital statistics and age-specific anthropometric data, identify the principal endemic and epidemic communicable diseases, and, if possible, assess their impact on the health of residents. Medical assessments were to be made by intermittent surveys because resources did not permit medically qualified personnel to reside continuously in the area. From the beginning this deficiency, together with the impossibility of securing postmortem examinations of persons who died within the village, limited the project's ability to identify the cause of death precisely in most instances.

In practice, the study continued much longer than originally anticipated and was enlarged periodically to include special investigations such as assessing age-specific immunoresponsiveness to malaria and other endemic diseases. In 1974 the primary orientation of research returned to nutritional and dietary assessment, and these interests have been maintained by the Dunn Nutrition Research Unit of the British MRC to the present. This chapter will describe the patterns of mortality and morbidity observed in Keneba from 1950 to 1975. Observations made subsequently will be mentioned briefly where appropriate.

The Keneba Environment

Keneba village is situated in an orchard savanna roughly in the center of the West Kiang peninsula. The social environment has been described in detail by Thompson (1965). The people are Muslim and belong predominantly to the Mandinka and Jola tribes. The society is patrilineal and polygamous, permitting each man a maximum of four wives at any given time. Divorce and remarriage are frequent, and men and women may have many marriage partners throughout their lives. The belief is widely held that children must be breast-fed for at least 18 months, and sexual intercourse during lactation is discouraged. These beliefs and practices shape birth rhythms to a considerable degree. Children are highly esteemed and,

Figure 20-1. Keneba Area, The Gambia

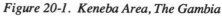

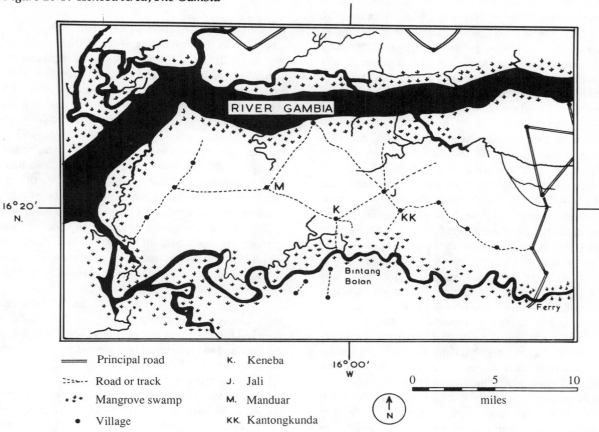

══════ Principal road	K. Keneba
╌╌╌╌ Road or track	J. Jali
✦✦✦ Mangrove swamp	M. Manduar
● Village	KK. Kantongkunda

16°20′ N.

16°00′ W

0   5   10

miles

N

because of the extended nature of the family, neither divorce nor death of the parents appears materially to affect their welfare. Age is respected, as in many Islamic countries, and old people are well cared for. Over the first 20 years of the studies in Keneba no formal educational facilities were available within West Kiang, and instruction was generally confined to knowledge of the Koran taught in Arabic script by village elders. However, in the mid-1970s the government established primary schools in select villages; as a consequence literacy in the English language was, and continues to be, greatly extended.

The climate of the area is sharply divided into wet and dry seasons, which exerts a profound influence on the lives of all village residents. The annual rainfall is variable (ranging from about 50 to 150 centimeters) and occurs entirely between late May and early November. In the first 18 years of the Keneba study, rainfall averaged about 100 centimeters per year; since 1968, however, annual precipitation has tended to be

much less. The Gambia, like other countries of the Sahel, has been experiencing a protracted drought. Daytime temperatures are highest in March to May and lowest in December to January. The variation between day and night temperatures is smaller during the rainy than during the dry season. Humidity by day is low in the dry months, but high during the wet.

The economy is essentially subsistence, being based on peasant farming, and the sale of groundnuts forms virtually the entire source of income. In 1950, the average income of the male farmer was about £25; by the late 1970s this had increased sixfold, probably as the result of inflation rather than increased prosperity.

Agriculture is dominated by the climate. During the long hot dry season the ground is too hard to be cultivated by the primitive hand tools that constitute the bulk of farming equipment. The cultivation of food and cash crops is strictly confined to the brief wet season. Because the growing season is so short, men and women are equally responsible for producing food crops, and pregnant women are not exempt. Women cultivate rice in the swamplands, while men tend the upland crops of maize, millet, sorghum, and groundnuts. Every able-bodied person participates from early morning until after dark; the young and infirm protect maturing crops from the ravages of birds and monkeys and look after very young children. The preparation of agricultural land entails the severe, sustained physical labor of both sexes.

Although the villagers keep sizable herds, cattle are rarely killed for food. Instead, they represent an important capital reserve for when crops fail and food has to be purchased from outside sources. The diet, therefore, is almost totally vegetarian, and its composition and quantity vary with the seasons. The fastest maturing crops are maize and finger millet (*Digitaria* spp.), which comprise the major source of food in September and October and are consumed almost totally at that time. Subsequently, they are replaced by rice, bullrush millet, and sorghum, which are the staple foods throughout the dry season. Some 15 percent of the groundnut harvest is retained for food; the rest is sold. Thus, during the late rains and the early dry season food stocks are abundant, but gradually diminish, reaching their lowest level between May and August, when agricultural activity is at a peak and endemic disease is frequent. Infants are entirely breastfed for the first few months after birth. Feeding children supplementary paps of rice, millet, or sorghum is introduced at 4–6 months and gradually augmented until the children are on full, mixed diets. Breast-feeding is usually terminated at 18–24 months.

Environmental hygiene is poor. Water for all domestic purposes is drawn from wells some 20 meters deep and stored in large earthenware jars placed at the entrance to houses. These jars, for superstitious reasons, are rarely cleaned and often constitute an important breeding site for *Aedes aegypti*. There is no sanitary disposal of feces. In early childhood, defecation is permitted within the house and on the adjacent land. At older ages, it takes place in designated areas on the outskirts of the village.

Many species of biting insects capable of transmitting a wide range of parasitic and viral infections exist (Bertram *et al.*, 1958a, 1958b; Murphy, 1961; Lewis and Murphy, 1965), and their prevalence fluctuates markedly with the season. During the long dry season the contact between man and mosquito is drastically reduced as the atmospheric humidity diminishes. With the return of humid conditions and the start of the rains, mosquito populations increase explosively and remain high throughout the wet months (Giglioli, 1965).

Methods

The first health assessment survey of Keneba villagers was made in the dry season of 1950 (McGregor and Smith, 1952). Each resident was identified, and the name, sex, and dwelling place were recorded. Ages were estimated by dentition and general development because residents did not know their dates of birth. These estimates were subsequently checked by reference to social grouping within the village and to precisely dated events in local history. Weight, height, and intercristal diameter were measured and recorded. Each person was then examined for signs of nutritional deficiency and clinically detectable evidence of other diseases; the findings were recorded. Blood was taken by fingerprick to estimate hemoglobin concentration and prepare thick and thin blood slides. Enlarged lymph glands were aspirated and examined for trypanosomes; lumbar punctures were performed on persons with neurological involvement.

A series of brief supplementary studies followed this general survey. They aimed to assess the prevalence of intestinal helminthiasis and of filariasis and its clinical sequelae and to identify the prevalent insects that were potential vectors of disease.

Following these initial operations an accurate census of the village was systematically compiled and gradually developed. The result was a genealogical tree to ease tracing and identifying family relationships. This tree was valuable in later years for investigating genetic polymorphisms among villagers and assessing hereditary as opposed to environmental influences as determinants of stature.

Recording births and deaths was instituted by choosing a reliable and influential village elder to record each event in Arabic script as it occurred. Each month these records were collected and, after their accuracy had been confirmed, transcribed to the project's register of births and deaths and genealogical tree. This accurate recording of births and deaths proved indispensable for assessing anthropometric data precisely and for compiling vital statistics accurately.

To meet the requirements of villagers in times of sickness, the Gambian government's health department constructed a dispensary on the outskirts of the village, stocked it with medicine, and appointed a resident dresser-dispenser. Originally it was hoped that the records of attendances and treatment kept by the dresser-dispenser would provide a useful indication of the pattern and prevalence of disease in the area. Unfortunately, this did not occur. Illnesses diagnosed during the survey periods were treated immediately by the physician leading the survey team. Patients with serious illnesses were transported to the MRC Laboratories' hospital at Fajara for follow-through and treatment.

Beginning in 1950 similar surveys of virtually all village residents were conducted at regular annual intervals, always during the dry season. Surveys of the entire population were made less frequently during the wet season because they were unpopular and interfered with essential agricultural duties. In the mid-1960s survey procedures began to monitor immunoresponsiveness to malarial antigens and to test new seroepidemiological techniques. To this end fingerprick samples of capillary blood were taken from all villagers, and small amounts of plasma (about 0.4 milliliters) were deep frozen and stored at –20°C. This plasma bank proved to be a valuable resource that permitted new serological techniques to be applied to stored, characterized material.

Population Size and Structure

In April 1951 Keneba was a village of 710 residents. In April 1975 it had grown to 915. This change corresponds to an annual increase of approximately 1.1 percent, a rate that would have been double if 176 males and 188 females had not left the area during that time.

Despite the care taken in selecting Keneba as a study site, population mobility proved to be considerable. Determining whether individual movements represented emigration or merely temporary absence was often extremely difficult. An adult man would sometimes leave suddenly, taking all or part of his family with him, to undergo religious instruction in a distant village. Such absences could last many years, after which the family would return to Keneba. Rules for establishing residence were therefore devised and are discussed in detail by Billewicz and McGregor (1981).

Table 20-1 shows the average age structure of the resident population in the first and last quinquennia of the 25 years of observation.

Endemic Infections

Malaria is one of the most prevalent and important infections in Keneba. The initial survey, conducted in the dry season of 1950, yielded an overall parasite rate of 54.7 percent. Age-specific prevalence rates conformed to a pattern of hyper- to holoendemicity. Prevalence was close to 100 percent by the second year of life, remained high throughout childhood, and fell slowly through adolescence and early adult life to attain approximately 20–25 percent in adult life (McGregor and Smith, 1952). Table 20-2 shows parasite prevalence by age from 1961 to 1975 (that for 1951–60 is not given since it was disturbed by studies involving malaria control). *P. falciparum* is the dominant parasite; *P. malariae* and *P. ovale* are much less frequent. Parasites with the morphological characteristics of *P. vivax* have been recorded in Keneba on only four occasions in 30 years. The almost total absence of this parasite is believed to be caused by the villagers' lack of the receptor sites associated with Duffy blood group antigens on the surface of red blood cells (Welch *et al.*, 1977).

Malaria transmission is negligible at the height of the dry season, increases gradually with the onset of the rains, and reaches a peak toward the end of the rains (September–November). The changes in transmission rates parallel changes in the severity of clinical

Table 20-1. Average Age Structure, Keneba, The Gambia, 1951–75
(percent)

Age (years)	1951–55		1971–75	
	Males	Females	Males	Females
0–4	9.6	8.9	9.6	9.5
5–14	12.2	11.2	12.4	12.3
15–29	12.4	15.5	9.3	12.8
30–44	8.3	8.3	7.1	8.8
45–59	4.4	5.5	4.8	7.0
60 and older	2.0	1.7	3.2	3.3
Total	48.9	51.1	46.3	53.7

Note: The population was surveyed in the first and last quinquennia of the period.

Table 20-2. Mean Prevalence of Malaria Parasitemia during the Dry Season, by Age and Sex, Keneba, The Gambia, 1961–75

(percent)

Age (years)	1961–65			1966–70			1971–75		
	Male	Female	All	Male	Female	All	Male	Female	All
Less than 1	23.9	26.3	25.1	27.5	27.7	27.6	11.6	14.3	12.7
1–4	67.6	72.0	69.6	70.7	71.2	70.9	41.7	45.3	43.6
5–9	85.8	76.6	81.6	80.7	78.9	79.8	68.1	65.8	67.0
10–14	80.4	76.5	78.2	73.1	71.6	72.4	57.8	65.6	61.8
15–29	40.9	47.4	44.4	42.7	37.0	39.1	26.5	21.4	23.2
30–44	12.0	20.5	17.7	12.7	19.9	17.2	6.3	8.0	7.3
45–59	16.3	19.4	17.7	8.8	12.1	10.5	6.0	6.1	6.0
60 and older	7.4	15.9	11.5	18.0	8.6	13.4	3.9	8.3	5.9
All ages	48.5	47.3	47.9	45.4	41.9	43.5	31.3	29.9	30.5
Number of blood smears									
Positive	807	885		826	936		554	647	
Examined	1,665	1,870		1,818	2,235		1,770	2,167	

malaria and to a lesser extent in the prevalence of parasitemia. Since prolonged malarial infection induces effective immunity, the seasonal change in clinical importance and prevalence is most marked in young children and inconspicuous in older subjects (McGregor, 1987). The ubiquity of malarial parasitemia implies that malaria often coexists with many other diseases, a feature that tends to confound accurate diagnosis and, consequently, the importance of specific diseases as causes of morbidity and mortality in an environment such as Keneba's.

Two filarial parasites, *Dipetalonema perstans* and *Wuchereria bancrofti*, were common infections in Keneba in the early 1950s. At that time age-specific prevalence of both parasites rose slowly throughout childhood to reach levels of around 60 percent in adults (McGregor et al., 1952). Following mass treatment schedules using diethylcarbamazine, the prevalence of *W. bancrofti* microfilaremia fell to very low levels, which were subsequently maintained (McGregor and Gilles, 1956). Perstans infections, however, were not affected significantly by the treatment, and prevalence levels persisted virtually unchanged.

In 1950 African trypanosomiasis (*T. gambiense*) affected some 2 percent of the Keneba population. By the 1960s the disease had disappeared from the village and, indeed, from most of the Gambia. This remains the situation, although reasons for the disappearance are a matter for conjecture.

Ascaris and hookworm infections are highly prevalent, and most are probably acquired during the wet,

humid season. Ascaris infections become evident in the second year of life, and by 3–6 years of age about half the village children carry the parasite. Prevalence then declines and remains low. Infections can be heavy at young ages, but tend to be light at older ages. Hookworm infections first appear in toddlers, but rapidly reach prevalences of 100 percent, which are maintained throughout life. Worm loads sometimes occur in association with anemia.

Among the nonparasitic infections, trachoma and infections with hepatitis B virus were common. A survey conducted in 1963 by an experienced ophthalmologist found clinical evidence of trachoma infection in 34 percent of Keneba children less than five years of age. In the age group 2–5 years, the prevalence was 51 percent. Trachoma in the Gambia seems a much less serious infection, however, than in some countries of the Middle East. Most infections clear up without causing visual impairment. Some, however, persist and, in conjunction with secondary infections, lead to entropion with subsequent trichiasis and corneal damage. Some 6 percent of adult residents of Keneba had eye lesions that were mainly trachomatous in origin (McGregor and Smith, 1952). Hepatitis B infections were also frequent. Examination of serum samples taken from all Keneba residents in 1972 showed that 17.6 percent of the children 2–4 years of age were carriers of the hepatitis B surface antigen (HBsAg); the prevalence rates were lower at older ages. The carrier state was generally prolonged, and 63 percent of the persons found positive for HBsAg in 1972 were still positive in 1980. Although the relationship between hepatitis B antigenemia and hepatoma is not fully understood, all four of the residents of the Keneba area who were diagnosed with primary hepatoma had HBSAg in their blood, and two had carried the virus for at least seven years (Whittle *et al.*, 1983).

Examining serum samples taken from the Keneba area revealed high prevalences of antibodies to arboviruses (West Nile, yellow fever, Trinidad dengue, zika, bunyamwera, Semliki Forest, and Uganda S), poliovirus types 1, 2, and 3, and diphtheria toxin (Barr and McGregor, 1962; McGregor, 1976). Despite the presence of these latter antibodies, clinical manifestations of diphtheria are very rare.

Manifestations of leprosy were identified in about 2 percent of Keneba adults, some of whom had severely deformed hands and feet. In the mid-1960s a national diagnosis and treatment campaign organized by the government health services reduced new cases, but did not improve existing deformities. No specific survey of tuberculosis was ever made in Keneba, but knowledge of its prevalence was gained from diagnoses made during annual surveys and from examining sick villagers at other times. In the period 1961–75, five cases of pulmonary tuberculosis were diagnosed and treated. On this evidence tuberculosis does not seem to be particularly common in the Keneba area.

Epidemic Infections

Epidemics of measles and whooping cough occurred in Keneba's young children from time to time. Measles, as will be described later, caused great mortality during an epidemic in 1961. Later epidemics caused less mortality, presumably because of the successful vaccination campaigns sponsored by the Gambian government in collaboration with international agencies, notably USAID. The effects of whooping cough, however, were much more difficult to assess. An epidemic that occurred in the period from October 1962 to April 1963 boosted the incidence of respiratory tract infections, but had little discernible effect on patterns of mortality (McGregor *et al.*, 1970a).

Serological studies conducted between 1968 and 1974 revealed three influenza epidemics. The Hong Kong virus became epidemic for the first time in Keneba in March 1969, followed by epidemics of it, or of an antigenic variant, in 1971, 1973, and probably also in 1974. Death records showed no evidence that mortality in the village was enhanced during any of the epidemic periods (McGregor *et al.*, 1979). Similar

serological investigations showed that two major periods of rubella transmission occurred in Keneba, one in 1963–64, and one in 1973–74. This ten-year interval is in keeping with intervals between epidemics in other parts of the world. Retrospective examination of clinical records failed to reveal evidence of a rubella-like syndrome in newborns. The absence of such a syndrome could be a consequence of the high level of immunity maintained in adolescents and adults by the ten-year cycle of epidemicity (Clarke *et al.*, 1980).

Mortality Patterns

From 1951 to 1975, 715 deaths were recorded in the Keneba population. Table 20-3 shows the distribution of these by quinquennia and, for all but two, by age. Of the 713 deaths for which age at death was known, 34.4 percent occurred in the first year of life, 37.7 percent at 1–4 years of age, 4.3 percent at 5–14 years, 9.4 percent at 15–44 years, and 14.2 percent at 45 years and older. This pattern clearly illustrates the extreme vulnerability of young children in a rural village environment. The high mortality rate recorded for children less than one year old in 1961–65 was largely due to an extremely lethal epidemic of measles that occurred in February–April 1961. Despite this, mortality patterns remained remarkably constant in each quinquennial period.

Deaths by age and gender are shown in table 20-4. There was no clear sex difference in death rates save, perhaps, in the 30–44-year-old group, where the rate for females exceeded that for males. Maternal mortality was high; 12 deaths associated with childbirth were recorded, 3 in primigravidae and 9 in multigravidae, yielding a rate of 10.5 per 1,000 live births.

The month in which death occurred was recorded for 691 deaths. Table 20-5 shows the distribution of these deaths by age and by season and also gives the annual death rates per 1,000. The mortality of children less than five years old was profoundly influenced by season; death rates peaked in the months when the rains were well established (August–October), remained high in the succeeding trimester, and fell to much lower levels in the latter part of the dry season and throughout the early rains. A similar seasonal effect was discernible for older children (5–14 years), whose mortality rates were, however, greatly reduced at all seasons. The mortality of adults showed no striking association with season, although it may have been slightly higher in the dry than in the wet months.

Table 20-3. Death Rates, by Age, Keneba, The Gambia, 1951–75

Quinquennium	0–1	1–4	5–14	15–44	45 and older	Total
1951–55						
Death rate	245.4	82.6	6.2	9.9	23.7	32.2
Number of deaths	40	39	5	15	11	110
1956–60						
Death rate	231.2	101.2	8.1	9.8	42.2	37.1
Number of deaths	40	49	7	16	22	136[a]
1961–65						
Death rate	309.3	105.6	9.3	9.3	38.5	40.9
Number of deaths	60	51	9	15	25	160
1966–70						
Death rate	298.1	124.1	3.0	6.8	35.0	40.2
Number of deaths	62	67	3	12	24	168
1971–75						
Death rate	174.8	109.2	6.6	5.5	24.2	32.6
Number of deaths	43	63	7	9	19	141

Note: Rates are deaths per 1,000 persons.
a. Includes two deaths with age not stated.

Table 20-4. Death Rates, by Age and Sex, Keneba, The Gambia, 1951–75

Sex	0–1	1–4	5–14	15–29	30–44	45–59	60 and older
Males							
Death rate	251.4	103.8	6.3	7.3	7.1	19.2	63.5
Number of deaths	126	138	15	16	10	19	33
Females							
Death rate	246.4	106.8	6.9	7.1	11.6	20.4	52.4
Number of deaths	119	131	16	19	22	22	27
Total							
Death rate	249.0	105.2	6.6	7.2	9.7	19.8	58.0
Number of deaths	245	269	31	35	32	41	60

Note: Rates are deaths per 1,000 persons.

Stillbirth, First-Week, and Neonatal Mortality

Records of stillbirths were incomplete up to 1955, but appeared adequate between 1956 and 1975. For the latter period the stillbirth rate was 63.9 per 1,000 births. This rate agrees with the 7 percent rate that Thompson (1965) directly observed over a period of two years, 1962–63.

In the 25 years from 1951 to 1975, 1,138 live births occurred in Keneba. The mortality of infants in the first week of life was 49.2 per 1,000 live births (56 deaths), and the sex-specific rates were 54.3 (32 deaths) for males and 43.7 (24 deaths) for females. The highest rate for both sexes combined occurred in the November–January quarter: 69.5 per 1,000.

Neonatal (first-month) mortality for 1951–75 was 85.2 deaths per 1,000 live births. Sex-specific rates were 95.1 per 1,000 for males and 74.7 per 1,000 for females. Mortality before the end of the first month among infants who had survived the first week was 37.9 per 1,000. The highest rate of such deaths (59 per 1,000 of first-week survivors) occurred in the August–October quarter.

Early Childhood Mortality

The details of young child mortality are best presented by cohort of live births. Table 20-6 examines survival to the age of five years of 865 children born in four five-year cohorts from 1951 to 1970. Almost exactly half failed to reach their fifth birthday. Of the deaths due to the measles epidemic of 1961, all but one occurred in the 1956–60 cohort. Epidemics notwithstanding, the different cohorts are remarkably similar in their survival patterns. Of those who died, 87 percent failed to reach the fourth year of life: nearly 48 percent died in their first year, 23.6 percent in their second, and 15.5 percent in their third.

Table 20-7 illustrates mortality in young children during the six months following their survival to a given age. The chances of dying decreased very slowly even though a large number of neonatal deaths occurred in the first age interval. The information in this table emphasizes again how common death was in children less than two years old. Moreover, mortality increased slightly between 2.5 and 3.0 years of age. This increase, also detected in earlier studies involving

smaller numbers of Keneba children, may be related to child care and nutrition more than to age-specific diseases (McGregor *et al.*, 1961).

The data presented in tables 20-6 and 20-7 suggest that age is the most important factor shaping mortality in young Keneba children. Analyzing the seasonality of death prompts a somewhat different conclusion, however. Within individual cohorts the frequency of death tended to wax and wane rhythmically, with high rates of mortality tending to coincide with the late rains and the early dry season (August–January) and low rates with the late dry season and early rains (February–July). The seasonal fluctuations were greatest in younger children and became much less noticeable as they approached their fifth birthdays. The pattern suggests that, in the Keneba environment, the causes of mortality are not uniformly present throughout the year, and their intensity changes markedly with season. Furthermore, the effect of these seasonal influences apparently diminished progressively and gradually as age advanced. Season of birth also influenced survival over the first five years of life. The chances of surviving the first five years were significantly greater for children born in the May–July period ($p < 0.01$) than for children born in either the August–October or November–January periods and were greater but not significantly ($p > 0.05$) than for children born in

Table 20-5. Death Rates, by Age and Season, Keneba, The Gambia, 1951–75

Season	Age (years)				
	0–1	*1–4*	*5–14*	*15–44*	*45 and older*
November–January					
Death rate	260.2	81.4	6.8	7.8	33.5
Number of deaths	64	52	8	16	26
February–April					
Death rate	174.8	54.8	4.3	8.3	41.2
Number of deaths	43	35	5	17	32
May–July					
Death rate	178.9	65.7	0.9	6.4	18.0
Number of deaths	44	42	1	13	14
August–October					
Death rate	378.0	216.0	11.1	6.9	27.0
Number of deaths	93	138	13	14	21
Month not stated					
Number of deaths	1	2	4	7	8
All					
Death rate	249.0	105.2	6.6	8.2	32.5
Number of deaths	245	269	31	67	101

Note: Rates are deaths per 1,000 persons.

Table 20-6. Percentage of Children Surviving to a Given Age, by Birth Cohort, Keneba, The Gambia, 1951–70

	Birth cohort				
Surviving to	1951–55	1956–60	1961–65	1966–70	All
1 week	92.9	97.6	96.3	93.9	94.1
1 month	89.1	95.6	89.5	89.1	90.8
1 year	75.5	76.7	76.8	75.3	76.1
2 years	66.3	63.1	68.9	59.5	64.3
3 years	58.7	55.3	61.4	51.4	56.5
4 years	52.2	49.5	58.3	49.0	52.3
5 years	50.0	45.2	57.5	47.4	50.1
Number of children	184	206	228	247	865

Table 20-7. Age-Specific Mortality in Children under Five, Keneba, The Gambia

Age (years)	Number alive at x years	Interval between x and (x + 0.5 years)	
		Number dying	Death rate per 1,000
0.0–0.5	865	122	141.0
0.5–1.0	743	85	114.4
1.0–1.5	658	61	92.7
1.5–2.0	597	41	68.7
2.0–2.5	556	25	45.0
2.5–3.0	531	42	79.1
3.0–3.5	489	20	40.9
3.5–4.0	469	17	36.2
4.0–4.5	452	11	24.3
4.5–5.0	441	8	18.1

February–April. The survival advantage for children born in May–July was consistently evident. The percentage of children born in May–July and in the remainder of the year who were alive at five years of age was, respectively, 56.4 and 47.6 (1951–55), 55.3 and 42.1 (1956–60), 66.7 and 45.4 (1961–65), and 61.0 and 44.7 (1966–70).

The survival advantage of being born in May–July operated only over the first year of life. In subsequent years, the chances of survival did not differ significantly between cohorts. When mortality in the first month of life was discounted, being born in May–July still gave infants a significant survival advantage for the remainder of their first year. This advantage may be because they traverse the season of greatest hazard (August–October) when their passively acquired immunity to important endemic infections is still effective.

Table 20-8 examines the relationship between young child mortality and the mother's age and the child's birth rank. No convincing differences in mortality correlated with either the age of the mother or the child's birth order. If anything, older mothers and higher birth order have lower first-week and infant mortality.

Cause-Specific Mortality

In Keneba the absence of a medically qualified scientist in residence (except for survey periods) and the impossibility of performing autopsies militated against attempts to obtain accurate data on disease-specific mortality. In two episodes, however, mortality was fairly closely observed. These are worth mentioning.

The Measles Epidemic of 1961

McGregor (1964) describes this epidemic in detail. In February 1961 measles was introduced to Keneba by a

Table 20-8. Child Mortality, by Mother's Age and Child's Birth Rank, Keneba, The Gambia

	Mortality		
Indicator	1 week	Under 1 year	Under 5 years
Maternal age (years)			
Less than 20			
Death rate	90.9	257.6	515.2
Number of deaths	132		
20–24			
Death rate	102.8	280.4	518.7
Number of deaths	214		
25–29			
Death rate	47.9	239.4	494.7
Number of deaths	188		
30–34			
Death rate	17.3	196.5	526.0
Number of deaths	173		
35 and older			
Death rate	43.5	217.4	447.2
Number of deaths	161		
Birth order			
1			
Death rate	86.1	264.9	543.0
Number of deaths	151		
2			
Death rate	43.5	287.8	546.8
Number of deaths	139		
3			
Death rate	93.0	271.3	534.9
Number of deaths	129		
4			
Death rate	46.9	203.1	476.6
Number of deaths	128		
5 and more			
Death rate	28.0	208.7	457.9
Number of deaths	321		

Note: Rates are deaths per 1,000 live births.

child returning from an area in which the disease was prevalent. The villagers, who recognized and feared the disease (known as *fusiba* in the Mandinka language), asserted that the infection had not occurred within the village during the past 12–13 years. This assertion agreed with medical observations. The infection spread rapidly, reaching an epidemic peak around mid-March and then declining slowly until it ended in April. In its course, it affected virtually every person less than 13 years of age, but only one adult, a female who had been absent from Keneba when the last epidemic of measles had occurred. In 1961, 230 children less than ten years of age lived in Keneba. Of these, 35 (15.2 percent) died, and the cause of all these deaths, except two that occurred in the neonatal period,

was diagnosed as measles. No deaths occurred at older ages. The distribution of deaths is shown in table 20-9.

The 1961 epidemic of measles was noteworthy for the following reasons:

- By causing high rates of mortality in the late dry season, it totally reversed the customary mortality patterns recorded in Keneba from 1951 to 1975.
- Although it affected virtually all children less than 13 years of age, its lethality was almost totally confined to children less than five (22 percent). In the age group 5–10, mortality was 2.2 percent.
- Bronchopneumonia was the most common complication and cause of death.
- Corneal opacity with impaired vision was a frequent sequel. Subsequent studies in other villages iden-

Table 20-9. Mortality of Children under Ten, by Age, Keneba, The Gambia, February–April 1961

Age (months)	Number of deaths	Number in cohort	Death rate per 100
0–6	5[a]	23	21.7[a]
7–12	8	21	38.1
13–24	7	29	24.1
25–36	7	22	31.8
37–48	3	25	12.0
49–60	3	21	14.3
61–72	0	19	0.0
73–84	0	24	0.0
85–96	0	15	0.0
97–108	2	17	11.8
109–120	0	14	0.0
Total	35[a]	230	15.2[a]

a. Includes two nonmeasles deaths.

tified measles as one of the most important causes of blindness in the Gambia.

Mortality Observed in Child Health Studies, 1962–63

All children less than five years of age were regularly observed and medically examined for most of 1962 and 1963 (for details on how this study operated, see the section on morbidity). During the study 35 of the 215 children died: 9 in the neonatal period, and 3 in the remainder of the first six months of life. Fifteen of the deaths occurred between the ages of 6 and 23 months, and eight at 2–4 years of age (McGregor *et al.*, 1970a).

Of the nine neonatal deaths, four were due to *tetanus neonatorum*, one to prematurity, and one probably to overlaying. No diagnoses were established for the remaining three, which occurred at 2, 3, and 19 days of age, respectively. Of the three deaths at ages 1–5 months, two were associated with whooping cough and one with diarrhea and malaria. Of the fifteen deaths at 6–23 months, two occurred in children who had emigrated from Keneba and no information was available on possible cause of their deaths. Two further deaths appeared to be due to congenital cardiac defects in children with Down's syndrome. Three deaths were sudden and unexpected; malaria was suspected as the cause of death, but no precise diagnosis was possible. Of the remaining eight deaths, two were due to fulminating *P. falciparum* malaria, one to broncho-pneumonia and multiple lung abscesses, and five to malnutrition that developed after recurrent infections

in which malaria, diarrhea, and respiratory infections were frequent. In these cases death could not be ascribed to a single cause.

Of the eight deaths occurring at 2–5 years of age, four occurred suddenly and unexpectedly after short illnesses attributed to either malaria or pneumonia. The remaining four occurred following multiple infections; the immediate cause of death could not be established in three of these; the fourth child was hospitalized with a diagnosis of prekwashiorkor, but an autopsy revealed fulminating amebic dysentery.

As noted above, some deaths occurred swiftly and suddenly in children who until then had been in good health and sound nutritional condition. Most deaths, however, took place after a series of infectious episodes lasting one to four months, and many of these children showed evidence of adverse nutritional change such as depressed growth patterns and loss of body weight. However, prolonged malnutrition was only evident in three instances. In one, maternal care was notably inadequate; in another the mother was persistently, seriously ill; and in the third the mother had leprosy and was unable to breast-feed.

Morbidity

Young Child Morbidity, 1962–63

From January 1962 to November 1963 an intensive study was made in Keneba of children less than five years of age. All children were weighed, measured, and inspected for clinical features; the results were recorded on a standard form. Children 6–24 months of age (the ages bearing the greatest burden of mortality) were seen every two weeks; other ages were seen each month. These operations were conducted by an experienced medical sociologist assisted by qualified dispensers and technicians. Children found to be ill at these examinations or who had failed to gain weight since the last examination were examined by medically qualified scientists who visited Keneba each week. Rectal temperatures were recorded, and blood films were taken when indicated. Symptomatic treatment was given freely; specific therapy, such as antimalarial and antibiotic drugs, was given only when indicated and preferably after a reliable diagnosis had been established. Severely ill children were treated at the MRC base hospital at Fajara. In addition, quarterly surveys were conducted each year: participants were weighed, measured, and medically examined, and capillary blood samples were taken for hematological assessment and determination of malaria parasitemia.

The methods used, the definition of clinical features, and the results observed are described in detail by McGregor *et al.* (1966, 1970a) and Thomson *et al.* (1968). A much abbreviated account of the prevalence of some indices of morbidity and their seasonal change will be given here.

Although the two years were not identical, illnesses in both were most prevalent during the late rains (August–October) and the early dry season (November–January).

Clinical malaria peaked in the second half of each wet season, and at the peak about one-third of all children were clinically affected. A much higher proportion of children had parasitemia without obvious symptoms, and virtually no child escaped infection. Clinical malaria was never diagnosed in infants less than three months of age, although 5 percent of the blood films taken from this group showed low levels of parasitemia. All cases of malaria in children less than six months old occurred in children between three and five months. About two-thirds of those at least six months old had clinical malaria or dense parasitemia in the period from August to October. No clear trend was evident for children over six months of age, but malarial episodes seemed to be clinically less severe in older children. Malaria was, of course, a prime cause of pyrexia, of anemia, and, to a lesser extent, of edema.

The pattern of respiratory tract infection (RTI) was influenced by an epidemic of whooping cough that occurred from October 1962 to June 1963. Except during this epidemic, RTI appeared to be more common in the wet than in the dry months. Prevalence in both years rose about May. Young infants were not exempt; three cases of pneumonia occurred in infants less than three months old and six in children between three and five months.

Diarrhea and vomiting, as a clinical entity, also tended to be more common in the wet than in the dry months. Its prevalence, associated with the whooping cough epidemic, was also high in the dry season of 1962–63. Seasonal variations in prevalence were most obvious in children 6–23 months of age. After the second year the incidence of diarrhea and vomiting was relatively low at all seasons. Studies by the Dunn Nutrition Unit between 1974 and 1980 described the high prevalence of many intestinal pathogens including viruses, bacteria, and protozoa in the Keneba environment. These may be important causes of diarrhea in young children, especially in the months following the termination of exclusive breast-feeding and the introduction of supplementary foods; that is, in

the weanling infant (Rowland *et al.*, 1978a, 1978b, 1980, 1981; Barrell and Rowland, 1979a, 1979b).

Skin sepsis also peaked during the wet months and was most marked in children between 6 and 23 months of age. The trends for abscesses and *otitis media* were similar. Skin rashes and insect bites sustained in the hot, humid months predisposed children to septic skin conditions.

Eye infections also showed peak prevalence in the rains and at 6 to 23 months of age. Worm infections showed no clear evidence of seasonal trends. Only threadworm infections were diagnosed in children less than 15 months old. Ascaris was the most common infection, and prevalence was highest, in the oldest children. Since all cases were diagnosed clinically, many infections were probably overlooked.

Wasting and edema were sometimes associated with diagnoses of marasmus, kwashiorkor, and prekwashiorkor. The term wasting was used to describe severe loss of tissue from any cause. Almost all of the children affected had experienced severe infections, and wasting occurred mainly during the second half of the rains and into the early months of the dry season. No cases of wasting occurred in children less than six months old, and only two in children older than two years. Edema followed a trend similar to that of wasting by age and season, but, unlike wasting, occurred more often in older children. Some cases were associated with the dermatoses of kwashiorkor, and some occurred in association with severe anemia (usually postmalarial). In rare cases edema may have been caused by nephrosis associated with *Plasmodium malariae*.

Overall, the pattern of morbidity suggests that communicable diseases were exceedingly common in the Keneba environment, particularly in the late wet season and the early dry season. The distribution of clinical illness in children under five suggests that in the first months following birth immunity passively acquired from their mothers protected young infants from the effects of many of these infections, that the principal brunt of infection fell at 6–23 months of age, and that acquired immunity was probably important at older ages in lessening the severity of the onslaught of communicable disease. Subsequent studies in Keneba (Rowe *et al.*, 1968; McGregor *et al.*, 1970b) described the very high concentrations of immunoglobulins that occurred in sera from all ages of the population. During the study period no child escaped at least one episode of illness, and the great majority of children had several, often simultaneously or in rapid succes-

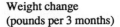

Figure 20-2. Weight Change in Keneba Children, According to Age and Season, 1962–63

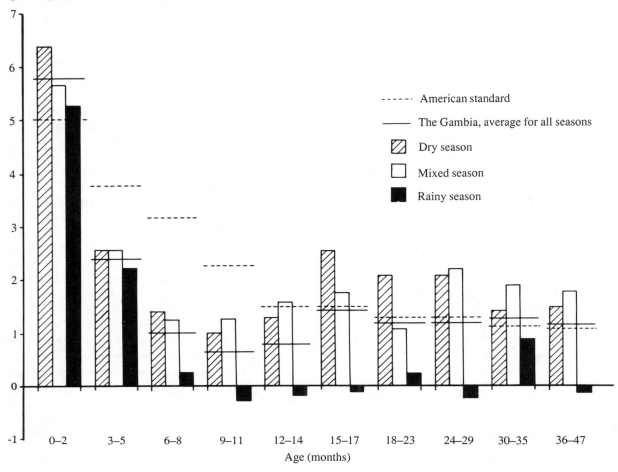

sion. Virtually all children received treatment, and 13 were admitted to the hospital for more intensive care than was available in the village.

Growth and Nutritional Status

The adult resident of Keneba is well muscled and of moderate stature and, in general, possesses a physique well-suited to the arduous agricultural activity that life demands. Males occupy an intermediate position in the range of height reported for other African populations (McGregor, 1976). They are considerably taller than inhabitants of northeastern Angola (David, 1972), slightly taller than Kikuyan farmers of Kenya (Willi-

ams, 1969) and village dwellers in Malawi (Nurse, 1968), about the same height as urban Nigerians (Johnson, 1970), and smaller than nomadic Samburu, Rendille, and Turkana tribesmen of Kenya (Shaper *et al.*, 1969). Compared with males in non-African populations, they are taller than Asians, about the same height as Greeks and Portuguese, and smaller than northern Europeans (Takahashi, 1971).

Studies assessing the contribution that genetic rather than environmental factors make to determining stature analyzed anthropometric and genealogical data collected in Keneba over a period of 26 years. Findings indicate that the heritability estimate (0.6) was lower than that reported by studies of European populations, while the environmental contribution was pronounced (Roberts *et al.*, 1978).

Records of the body weight and height of young children revealed marked seasonal environmental influences on growth. McGregor *et al.* (1968) described growth patterns in children less than five years old in 1962–63. Keneba infants 0–3 months of age grew at least as much as healthy American infants (according to the Harvard Standard for body weight). However, from 3–15 months of age the average growth of Keneba children was much lower than that of American children. At older ages, the average gains were much the same. Until about six months of age, season did not affect rates of weight gain in Keneba, but thereafter weight gain was zero or even negative during the wet months and some catch-up occurred during the dry months. After about 15 months of age rates of weight gain varied greatly with season, being well in excess of American rates in the dry season but negligible, and even negative, in the wet season. Figure 20-2 illustrates these changes.

The crown-heel (height) measurements of Keneba children showed similar seasonal changes. Keneba infants grew much faster than American infants over the first three months of life, but more slowly from then until the end of their second year. In the third and fourth years increments were similar in both groups of children. The data for Keneba also suggest that growth in children more than nine months of age slowed during the second half of the rainy season and sped up during the subsequent quarter (McGregor *et al.*, 1968).

The nutritional state of Keneba children, and thus their growth patterns, change considerably with sea-son. The prevalence of protein-energy malnutrition (PEM) within a population can be assessed by determining the proportions of children whose weight-for-age (World Health Organization, 1971) or weight-for-height (Waterlow, 1972) falls below the corresponding 50th percentile values found for healthy North American children. Values below 60 percent of the standard indicate severe and values of 60–80 percent indicate moderate PEM. Table 20-10 shows the prevalence of PEM detected by both methods in a cohort of Keneba children examined three times between November 1971 and November 1972. PEM is common in children less than 18 months old, frequent at the end of the wet season (November), and less frequent in the dry season and as age advances. The two methods also estimate the prevalence and severity of PEM differently, which emphasizes the difficulty of assessing this condition in community studies. However, direct observation has shown that the graver forms of PEM, marasmus and kwashiorkor, become most prevalent in the latter part of each wet season (Mc Gregor *et al.*, 1968).

The etiology of malnutrition, notably PEM, requires brief comment. As mentioned in the introduction, food supplies in Keneba vary markedly with season, being least abundant before the early-maturing crops are harvested in September and most abundant when the main crops are harvested in November. Although food shortage and growth depression did not coincide exactly, dietary insufficiency probably played a role in the seasonal loss of body weight in children. How great that contribution was could not be assessed with precision, although McGregor *et al.* (1970a) did not consider lack of food a dominant factor. Analysis of

Table 20-10. Prevalence of Protein-Energy Malnutrition in Children, by Age and Season, West Kiang, The Gambia
(percent)

	November 1971			May 1972			November 1972		
Nutritional class	*0–18 months*	*18–48 months*	*All*	*0–18 months*	*18–48 months*	*All*	*0–18 months*	*18–48 months*	*All*
Percentage of weight-for-height									
0–60	0.0	0.0	0.0	0.0	0.0	0.0	0.0	0.0	0.0
60–80	34.5	20.0	26.3	5.2	2.7	3.8	17.2	5.3	10.5
80 and more	65.5	80.0	73.7	94.8	97.3	96.2	82.8	94.7	89.5
Percentage of weight-for-age									
0–60	12.1	9.3	10.5	0.0	0.0	0.0	5.2	0.0	2.3
60–80	52.2	56.0	55.6	43.1	40.0	41.4	67.2	41.3	52.6
80 and more	32.7	34.7	33.8	56.9	60.0	58.6	27.6	58.7	45.1
Number	58	75	133	58	75	133	58	75	133

Note: Ages are as of November 1971.

individual records, on the other hand, frequently showed that episodes of growth faltering were preceded by episodes of clinical, usually infectious, illness (see figure 20-3). These episodes of illness and subsequent faltering were much more common in the wet than in the dry season, which reflects the high frequency of communicable diseases occurring during the rains.

The factors influencing the growth of young children are complex (McGregor *et al.*, 1961, 1968, 1970a). Inheriting passive immunity against many endemic diseases, and the prevalence of exclusive breast-feeding, probably account for the excellent growth and low rates of morbidity and mortality that the young Keneba infant exhibits in the first few months of life. Thereafter, as passive immunity wanes and supplementary feeding is introduced, clinical infections associated with anorexia become commonplace, particularly in the late wet season. Relatively low standards of child care, which are imposed by a harsh agricultural system and by dietary practices in which young children are given bulky, unappetizing, frequently infected vegetable supplements, add further nutritional stress. Between the ages of 6 and 18 months these factors combine to produce their most damaging effects in the wet months. As age progresses and immunity to many endemic infections is actively acquired, illness and the concomitant anorexia decrease, and toddlers more readily accept the prevalent diet and become less dependent on parental care. The effects of these changes are first noticeable during the dry months when, from 18 months of age onwards, catch-up growth is good; later they lead to substantial gains in growth even during the rains.

Figure 20-3. Weight Curve of a Keneba Child from Birth to Age Two Years, Illustrating the Effects of Infectious Diseases and of Season

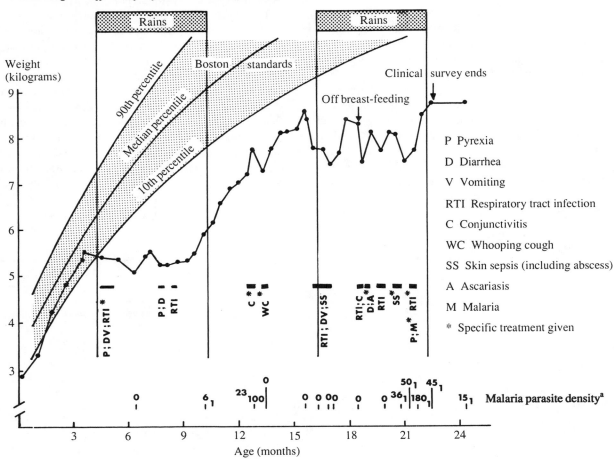

a. Malaria parasite density is expressed as parasites per oil field (for example, 6_1) or per 100 oil fields (for example, 23_{100}).

Anemia

Anemia is frequent among Keneba residents. Surveys from 1961 to 1980 studied the prevalence of hemoglobin concentrations of less than 10 grams per deciliter in males and nonpregnant females (see table 20-11). Pregnant women have been excluded from this table, since they tend to have significantly lower hemoglobin levels because of the physiological hemodilution effect that occurs in pregnancy (see table 20-12).

Anemia was exceptionally frequent at young ages and became less common at older ages. For males, the fall in frequency was progressive as age advanced; for females, the frequency was least in older children and adolescents, but increased again in persons over 15 years of age. This might reflect the persistence of stress caused by pregnancy and lactation.

At young ages malaria is perhaps the most important cause of anemia and most probably accounts for the marked seasonal variation in hematological indices that was apparent in the first five years of life (McGregor *et al.*, 1966). In the quarterly surveys conducted throughout 1962 and 1963, hemoglobin and hematocrit values clearly tended to increase during the dry season and early rains (January–July) and to fall sharply in the rains, reaching low levels in November. The pattern was cyclical, showing the same trend in 1963 as in 1962, and occurred irrespective of cohort age. A similar trend was apparent, but less clear, for values of mean corpuscular hemoglobin concentration (MCHC). The greatest falls occurred in younger children, notably those less than 18 months old; in older cohorts the falls decreased in magnitude as age advanced, perhaps reflecting the acquisition of effective malarial immunity. The overall improvement in hematological indices in the January to July period was not associated with marked and consistent falls in the

Table 20-11. Prevalence of Low Concentrations of Hemoglobin in Males and Nonpregnant Females, Keneba, The Gambia, 1961–80

Item	Age (years)			
	1–4	*5–9*	*10–14*	*15 and older*
Males				
1961–65				
Prevalence (percent)	59.2	28.3	16.4	7.2
Number in cohort	262	247	219	851
1966–70				
Prevalence (percent)	52.3	23.4	16.9	6.4
Number in cohort	287	269	219	952
1971–75				
Prevalence (percent)	42.9	11.9	14.3	5.4
Number in cohort	266	270	237	868
1976–80				
Prevalence (percent)	49.3	19.0	12.1	10.3
Number in cohort	408	358	256	910
Nonpregnant females				
1961–65				
Prevalence (percent)	50.9	13.6	12.0	15.1
Number in cohort	218	206	259	941
1966–70				
Prevalence (percent)	48.9	15.9	6.1	9.0
Number in cohort	274	270	213	1,173
1971–75				
Prevalence (percent)	43.6	8.6	5.6	7.1
Number in cohort	289	266	252	1,084
1976–80				
Prevalence (percent)	50.2	20.4	8.0	12.2
Number in cohort	408	318	249	1,177

Note: Low concentrations are defined as less than 10 grams per deciliter.

Table 20-12. Mean Hemoglobin Levels in Adult Females, by Pregnancy, Parity, and Parasitemia, Keneba, The Gambia, 1961–75

Parasitemia	Nonpregnant women	Pregnant women		
		Parity 0	Parity 1–2	Parity 3 and more
Negative				
Level	12.2	11.7	11.1	10.9
Number in cohort	1,672	27	83	253
Positive				
Level	11.6	10.6	10.6	10.8
Number in cohort	586	48	53	68
Mean difference	0.6	1.1	0.5	0.1

Note: Hemoglobin values are in grams per deciliter. Females are between 15 and 44 years of age.

prevalence of parasitemia. This discrepancy implies that the capacity of malaria to cause severe anemia is probably due to the acute, short-lived episodes of dense parasitemia sustained during the malaria transmission season, rather than to the high-prevalence, low-density parasitemias present the rest of the year.

In older children and adults, who have considerable naturally acquired immunity, malaria is a much less important cause of anemia. However, as table 20-12 shows, in females of reproductive age mean hemoglobin values tend to be consistently lower in the presence of parasitemia, and this association is most marked in women pregnant for the first time. This suggests that, even in effectively immune adults, malaria continues to cause a mild degree of anemia.

Conclusions

The medical investigations that have been maintained at Keneba for almost 40 years probably represent the oldest ongoing study of the health of a tropical community. It may, therefore, be timely to consider how these investigations differed from earlier population studies and to identify some areas in which they have significantly altered contemporary concepts of tropical health.

Investigations at Keneba differed from earlier population studies in several ways. First, they involved a population that was defined and characterized; every individual was identified, and virtually all participated in the medical investigations, irrespective of age. This meant that observations could be verified rapidly if necessary, which ensured the accuracy of recorded findings. Second, the studies were broadly based rather than narrowly targeted to specific diseases. Thus, in

addition to identifying and quantifying prevalent pathogens and their vectors, where applicable, levels of general health and nutrition in the population were repeatedly assessed, birth and death rates together with age-specific indices of growth (body weight and stature) were progressively compiled, and, where indicated, special studies were undertaken to determine how beliefs and social practices influenced health. Third, the investigations were prospective and added a longitudinal dimension to their basic cross-sectional nature. In due course the repetitive, cross-sectional studies were reinforced by specifically designed longitudinal investigations. Finally, the longitudinal studies advanced the concept of health monitoring within a sentinel village as a valid method of furnishing information on temporal changes in health and disease. This information could alert health authorities and epidemiologists to parallel changes occurring in larger areas and populations.

The Keneba studies illuminated several areas of tropical health. First, by describing the marked changes with season that occurred in the prevalence and severity of endemic infections and also in health indices, their findings emphasized the need to take seasonal effects into account in planning both health services and health assessment investigations. Prior to these studies, seasonality had received little attention in health planning. Second, in the area of child health several important features emerged. One was the compelling body of evidence that the great burden of mortality and morbidity falls on the young children of rural Gambian communities. Before long, other studies showed that this burden also fell on young children in the rural areas of many developing countries. The

Keneba studies also identified communicable diseases, notably measles, diarrheal states, respiratory infections, and malaria, as major factors in the genesis of morbidity and mortality and in the development of highly abnormal growth patterns in early life. In the Keneba environment, the clinical effects of a large number of infections with viruses, bacteria, and parasites seemed to be more important and common than simple dietary deficiency as a cause of protein-energy malnutrition. Dietary deficiency probably did, however, compound and aggravate the effects of infection. The impact of this evidence on strategies to improve the health and nutrition of young children has been profound.

A third area in which research in Keneba influenced contemporary thought concerns malaria. Over many years studies examined the demographic impact of malaria, probed the correlation between the acquisition of clinical immunity and age-specific serological changes, and explored the antigenic identity and diversity of *Plasmodium falciparum*. Together with the results of other investigations at the MRC Laboratories' main campus at Fajara, the findings of the Keneba studies had a seminal influence on concepts of the nature and effectiveness of acquired malarial immunity and stimulated wide interest in the possibility of devising vaccines for controlling this disease.

Finally, studies at Keneba were influential in demonstrating how modern serological techniques could with advantage be applied to the epidemiological monitoring and assessment of prevalent endemic and epidemic communicable diseases.

Acknowledgments

I gratefully acknowledge permission from the editor of the *Transactions of the Royal Society of Tropical Medicine and Hygiene* to republish the data contained in table 20-9 and figures 20-2 and 20-3, from the editor and publishers of *Parasitology* to republish data in table 20-12, and from the editor and publishers of the *Journal of Biosocial Science* to republish data contained in tables 20-1 and 20-3 through 20-8.

References

Barr, M. and McGregor, I. A. (1962). Diphtheria antitoxin levels in the serum of Gambian Africans. *Transactions of the Royal Society of Tropical Medicine and Hygiene*, 56, 368–370.

Barrell, R. A. E. and Rowland, M. G. M. (1979a). Infant foods as a potential source of diarrhoeal illness in rural West Africa. *Transactions of the Royal Society of Tropical Medicine and Hygiene*, 73, 85–90.

———. (1979b). The relationship between rainfall and well water pollution in a West African (Gambian) village. *Journal of Hygiene*, 83, 143–150.

Bertram, D. S., McGregor, I. A., and McFadzean, J. A. (1958a). The mosquitoes of the Colony and Protectorate of the Gambia. *Transactions of the Royal Society of Tropical Medicine and Hygiene*, 52, 135–151.

———. (1958b). Some diptera, other than mosquitoes, from the Colony and Protectorate of the Gambia. *Transactions of the Royal Society of Tropical Medicine and Hygiene*, 52, 217–222.

Billewicz, W. Z. and McGregor, I. A. (1981). The demography of two West African (Gambian) villages, 1951–75. *Journal of Biosocial Science*, 13, 219–240.

Clarke, M., Schild, G. C., Boustred, J., McGregor, I. A., and Williams, K. (1980). Epidemiological studies of rubella virus in a tropical African community. *Bulletin of the World Health Organization*, 58, 931–935.

David, J. H. S. (1972). Height growth of melanodermic natives in northeastern Luanda (Angola). *South African Journal of Medical Science*, 37, 49–60.

Giglioli, M. E. C. (1965). The age composition of *Anopheles melas* Theobald (1903) populations collected simultaneously by different methods in the Gambia, West Africa. *Cahiers ORSTOM Série Entomologie, Médicale et Parasitologie*, 3–4, 11–26.

Johnson, T. O. (1970). Height and weight patterns of an urban African population sample in Nigeria. *Tropical and Geographical Medicine*, 22, 65–76.

Lewis, D. J. and Murphy, D. H. (1965). The sandflies of the Gambia (Diptera: Phlebotominae). *Journal of Medical Entomology*, 1, 371–376.

McGregor, I. A. (1964). Measles and child mortality in the Gambia. *West African Medical Journal*, 13, 251–257.

———. (1976). Health and communicable diseases in a rural African environment. *OIKOS*, 27, 180–192.

———. (1987). The significance of parasitic infections in terms of clinical disease: a personal view. *Parasitology*, 94, S159–S178.

McGregor, I. A. and Gilles, H. M. (1956). Diethylcarbamazine control of Bancroftian filariasis: follow-up of a field trial in West Africa. *British Medical Journal*, 1, 331–332.

McGregor, I. A. and Smith, D. A. (1952). A health, nutrition, and parasitological survey in a rural village (Keneba) in West Kiang, Gambia. *Transactions of the Royal Society of Tropical Medicine and Hygiene*, 46, 403–427.

McGregor, I. A., Hawking, F., and Smith, D. A. (1952). The control of filariasis with Hetrazan: a field trial in a rural village (Keneba) in the Gambia. *British Medical Journal*, 2, 908–911.

McGregor, I. A., Billewicz, W. Z., and Thomson, A. M. (1961). Growth and mortality in children in an African village. *British Medical Journal*, 2, 1661–1666.

McGregor, I. A., Williams, K., Billewicz, W. Z., and Thomson, A. M. (1966). Haemoglobin concentration and anaemia in young West African (Gambian) children. *Transactions of the Royal Society of Tropical Medicine and Hygiene*, 60, 650–667.

McGregor, I. A., Rahman, A. K., Thompson, B., Billewicz, W. Z., and Thomson, A. M. (1968). The growth of young children in a Gambian village. *Transactions of the Royal Society of Tropical Medicine and Hygiene*, 62, 341–352.

McGregor, I. A., Rahman, A. K., Thomson, A. M., Billewicz, W. Z., and Thompson, B. (1970a). The health of children in a West African (Gambian) village. *Transactions of the Royal Society of Tropical Medicine and Hygiene*, 64, 48–77.

McGregor, I. A., Rowe, D. S., Wilson, M. E., and Billewicz, W. Z. (1970b). Plasma immunoglobulin concentrations in an African (Gambian) community in relation to season, malaria, and other infections and pregnancy. *Clinical and Experimental Immunology*, 7, 51–74.

McGregor, I. A., Schild, G. C., Billewicz, W. Z., and Williams, K. (1979). The epidemiology of influenza in a tropical (Gambian) environment. *British Medical Bulletin*, 35, 15–22.

Murphy, D. H. (1961). Biological species confused under the name *Culicoides austeni* (Carter, Ingram, and McFie). *Nature*, 192, 186–187.

Nurse, G. T. (1968). Body weight of African village men. *Central African Journal of Medicine*, 14, 94–96.

Roberts, D. F., Billewicz, W. Z., and McGregor, I. A. (1978). Heritability of stature in a West African population. *Annals of Human Genetics*, 42, 15–24.

Rowe, D. S., McGregor, I. A., Smith, S. J., Hall, P., and Williams, K. (1968). Plasma immunoglobulin concentrations in a West African (Gambian) community and in a group of healthy British adults. *Clinical and Experimental Immunology*, 3, 63–79.

Rowland, M. G. M., Barrell, R. A. E., and Whitehead, R. G. (1978a). Bacterial contamination in traditional Gambian weaning foods. *Lancet*, 1, 136–138.

Rowland, M. G. M., Davies, H., Patterson, S., Dourmashkin, R. R., Tyrrell, D. A. J., Matthews, T. H. J., Parry, J., Hall, J., and Larson, H. E. (1978b). Viruses and diarrhoea in West Africa and London: a collaborative study. *Transactions of the Royal Society of Tropical Medicine and Hygiene*, 72, 95–98.

Rowland, M. G. M., Leung, T. S. M., and Marshall, W. C. (1980). Rotavirus infection in young Gambian village children. *Transactions of the Royal Society of Tropical Medicine and Hygiene*, 74, 663–665.

Rowland, M. G. M., Cole, T. J., and McCollum, J. P. K. (1981). Weanling diarrhoea in the Gambia: implications of a jejunal intubation study. *Transactions of the Royal Society of Tropical Medicine and Hygiene*, 75, 215–218.

Shaper, A. G., Wright, D. H., and Kyobe, J. (1969). Blood pressure and body build in three nomadic tribes of northern Kenya. *East African Medical Journal*, 46, 273–281.

Takahashi, E. (1971). Geographic distribution of human stature and environmental factors: an ecological study. *Journal of the Anthropological Society*, 79, 259–286.

Thompson, B. (1965). Marriage, childbirth, and early childhood in a Gambian village: a socio-medical study. Ph.D. diss., University of Aberdeen.

Thomson, A. M., Billewicz, W. Z., Thompson, B., Illsley, R., Rahman, A. K., and McGregor, I. A. (1968). A survey of growth and health of young children in tropical Africa. *Transactions of the Royal Society of Tropical Medicine and Hygiene*, 62, 330–340.

Waterlow, J. C. (1972). Classification and definition of protein calorie malnutrition. *British Medical Journal*, 3, 566–569.

Welch, S. G., McGregor, I. A., and Williams, K. (1977). Duffy blood groups and malaria prevalence in Gambian West Africans. *Transactions of the Royal Society of Tropical Medicine and Hygiene*, 71, 295–296.

Whittle, H. C., Bradley, A. K., McLaughlan, K., Ajdukiewicz, A. J., Howard, C. R., Zuckerman, A. J., and McGregor, I. A. (1983). Hepatitis B virus infection in two Gambian villages. *Lancet*, 2, 1203–1206.

Williams, A. W. (1969). Blood pressure differences in Kikuyu and Samburu communities in Kenya. *East African Medical Journal*, 46, 262–272.

World Health Organization. (1971). Food Fortification: Protein Calorie Malnutrition. Technical Report Series, no. 477. Geneva.

Chapter 21

Morbidity and Mortality at Malumfashi, Nigeria, 1974–79: Studies of Child Health in Hausaland

Andrew Tomkins, Andrew Bradley, Alice Bradley-Moore, Brian Greenwood,
Sarah MacFarlane, and Herbert Gilles

Malumfashi District is situated 80 kilometers north of Zaria and 90 kilometers west of Kano in northern Nigeria (see figure 21-1). Established within Katsina Province for over 500 years, Malumfashi District consists of a town with a population of some 100,000 and surrounding villages with another 100,000, making a total population in excess of 200,000. Three main groups of people inhabit the area: the Hausa, the Maguzawa, and the Fulani. Although ethnically similar, the Hausa and Maguzawa have different cultural patterns (Hill, 1972). The most numerous, the Hausa live in compact villages or hamlets and adhere strongly to Islam. The Maguzawa usually live in large, isolated compounds in extended families. Unlike the Hausa, they did not embrace Islam as it spread through these parts of Africa and maintained instead their traditional beliefs. In recent years many of the Maguzawa have become Christians. (Maguzawa is sometimes interpreted as "running away from Islam.") The Maguzawa work principally in farming, whereas the Hausa are both farmers and active in commerce. The Hausa strictly seclude their females, who do not work in the fields; in the Maguzawan family both sexes are active in farming.

The third group, the Fulani, are ethnically distinct and have the typical taller, slimmer body proportions found in many African pastoral groups. Although usually Muslim, the Fulani still maintain many aspects of traditional religion. Their life-style has diversified considerably in the past fifty years. The nomadic Fulani speak Fulani as their first language and are pastoralists who build temporary shelters and move every few days or weeks. These nomadic Fulani regard themselves as the true Fulani; they do not farm, but rely instead on their cattle, goats, and sheep for their main source of food and barter or buy the cereals or other foods they need. The semisettled Fulani cultivate crops and raise cattle; they live in reasonably settled huts and farm until January or February, when local water supplies become too dry to sustain their herds and force them to move to other areas. A third group, the settled Fulani, have intermarried with the Hausa and become settled, frequently living in the town of Malumfashi. For all intents and purposes they have adopted the Hausa life-style.

The whole area is flat, and hard rocks such as granite, schist, and quartzite lie just beneath the surface. Occasional outcrops of granite inselbergs rise to several hundred feet, but nothing is higher. The terrain is crisscrossed by a series of streams that drain into the Jare River, eventually reaching Lake Chad or

Figure 21-1. Nigeria, Showing Location of Malumfashi

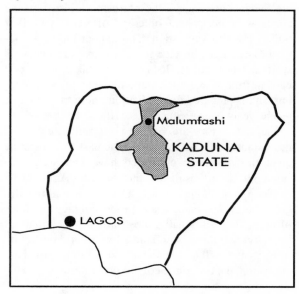

the Niger River system. The streams are essentially sand beds, only flowing during the rainy season. Wells are generally shallow (a maximum of 10 meters) because continuous layers of hard rock lie near the surface. The wells far from rivers or streams tend to dry up early in the dry season, whereas those nearer the water table supply water throughout the year. There is considerable use of surface water trapped in rock depressions, and in recent years excavations for laterite, used to surface the feeder roads by an agricultural development program, have produced a series of shallow tanks to collect rainwater throughout the area. Nobody, apart from persons living in certain areas of Malumfashi townships, has piped water.

From 1962 to 1976 the mean annual rainfall was 962 millimeters, which includes the early 1970s when a severe water shortage affected the whole area. Characteristic seasonal patterns of rainfall affect farming patterns and disease prevalence. *Domuna* is the rainy season, lasting from May to October. During this time the weather is warm, but not hot (usually less than 29° C); humidity is usually high, especially before the heavy electric rainstorms that occur between July and September. *Agazarri* is the short, hot season that follows the end of the rains. *Dorri* is the cold season associated with the harmattan, a dust-laden wind that blows from the northeast and lasts from November to February. During this time night temperatures may fall to 10° C or less. *Bazara* is the hot, humid season from March to May in which increasing temperatures and humidity are broken only by the onset of the rains.

Most of the soil is sandy with a red-brown, gravelly surface (laterite). The district is transitional between the Sudan savanna and the northern Guinea savanna zones with occasional outcrops of trees typical of Sudan savanna vegetation. Throughout the area relatively large trees provide food or important materials such as shea butter, locust bean, silk cotton, and baobab fruit. Usually left standing when the surrounding land is prepared for cultivation, these trees have in recent years been frequently sacrificed for firewood.

The main crops are Guinea corn, millet, cowpeas, groundnuts, and cotton. During the past few years the quantities of maize cultivated have increased considerably as a result of the Federal Agricultural Development Project (FADP). Cassava is traditionally grown as an insurance against food shortages in times of drought. Traditionally, most farming is carried out by individual farmers on land allocated to families by district and village leaders. The systems of land allocation, the economic conditions of farmers, and the patterns of food production are described in detail by Longhurst (1984). Most crops are grown under rainfall conditions, although some, usually vegetables such as tomatoes, peppers, and aubergines, are grown with irrigation using the shadoof. Rice production has increased in the limited areas able to control the runoff of rainwater or to increase the local water supply by building earthen dams that create small lakes. The FADP has emphasized the use of oxen for ploughing, improved seed varieties, and fertilizers. The FADP has also improved local roads considerably. Not only did this improvement affect the agricultural economy of the area, it increased the access to health facilities for persons able to obtain transport.

Data Sources

Many sources, particularly reports on research performed about ten years ago, were consulted. The most comprehensive information comes from the Endemic Diseases Research Unit (EDRU). Established following pilot surveys in 1971, the EDRU is a collaborative research activity of the Faculty of Medicine at Ahmadu Bello University (ABU) in Zaria and the Liverpool School of Tropical Medicine. The project at Malumfashi focused on chronic malaria, urinary schistosomiasis, and meningococcal infections. The stated objectives of the project were (1) to measure the possible harmful effects of chronic malaria infection on the immune system in childhood, (2) to discover the extent to which urinary schistosomiasis damages the health of the community, and (3) to identify the epidemiology of nasopharyngeal carriage of *meningococci* and to assess the value of antibiotic prophylaxis in preventing meningococcal infections.

These studies were built on the strong existing research interests of investigators at Zaria. The immune suppression associated with acute malaria in children had been well documented at ABU (Greenwood and Whittle, 1981). Similarly a large research group at ABU had done considerable work on the clinical and immunological aspects of the annual epidemics of meningococcal meningitis (Greenwood and Whittle, 1981). The FADP's development of small earthen dams as a basis for controlled irrigation in the Malumfashi District stimulated the work on schistosomiasis.

A pilot survey was carried out in 1971, and the project, funded by the Medical Research Council, began toward the end of 1974. A nutrition and diarrheal disease component, funded by the Wellcome Trust and Medical Research Council, was added to the

EDRU project, which finished as planned at the end of 1979. The Department of Community Health of Ahmadu Bello University continued to register vital events even after overseas financial support ended. Some of these data are contained in Adeleke (1983).

During the EDRU project a detailed study was conducted on the economic status and agriculture of a village adjacent to the Malumfashi area (Longhurst, 1984). This study contained some health and nutrition data. In addition, individual studies were undertaken by workers at the Malumfashi Hospital and scholars from ABU. Some anthropological studies of perceptions of illness in select villages were also performed (Last, 1972).

Demography

The EDRU collected demographic information over a number of years. After mapping the entire district, the project conducted a census and counted 43,216 persons. Educational opportunities in the area were poor, and the few individuals who had a secondary school education had no trouble obtaining employment in Malumfashi township or other towns or cities in the country. For this reason none of the project enumerators had more than a primary school education (Bradley, 1980). The problems of training, monitoring, and evaluating the performance of these staff are reviewed by Bradley *et al.* (1977). The authority structure in Malumfashi District was hierarchical, which meant that discussing the aims of the EDRU project and obtaining the cooperation of the village chiefs were relatively easy. Nonetheless, the enumerators had to spend a considerable amount of time explaining to family heads why personal information was required, and women were reluctant to allow enumerators into their compound when the family head (always male) was absent.

The census questionnaire was based on Uganda's 1969 census (Bradley *et al.*, 1982a). Each enumerator was responsible for and visited a number of households each month. Enumeration and coding occurred between October 1974 and September 1977; follow-up registration was collated in November 1977. Despite initial plans to analyze the data on the computer at Ahmadu Bello University, Zaria, that computer could not handle the quantity of data produced, and the analysis was performed in Liverpool, United Kingdom.

Several problems occurred that were anticipated, and a considerable number that were not. Bradley *et al.* (1977) sensitively described the main difficulties:

• Ages were often reported inaccurately. The ages of children were often rounded up to a six-month grouping (for example, ages of 6, 12, or 18 months were often reported even though enumerators used a local events calendar). Young men usually added several years to their age when interviewed.

• Mortality was often not reported or was hidden during the interview. Questions about cause of death were particularly unwelcome and considered irrelevant or blasphemous or both.

• Young infants were not regarded as existing until they were at least seven days old, and births were often denied until the naming ceremony, which took place 40 days later. Thus fertility data and perinatal and infant mortality figures were not always reliable.

• When the Universal Primary Education Scheme was being introduced, individuals were reluctant to report accurately the number of their children because they did not want to send children to school who could otherwise work on the farm.

• The strong tradition of *kunya* (modesty or shame) meant that persons were extremely reticent about discussing menarche, marriage, abortion, stillbirth, pregnancy, or childbirth (Bradley and Gilles, 1981).

Despite these constraints the project was able to produce data that were analyzed by a variety of techniques.

The age-sex structure of Malumfashi (see figure 21-2 and table 21-1) resembles that of other developing countries; it is broad based and tapers rapidly, with 45 percent of the population less than 15 years of age. An excess of men are between 15 and 39 years old. Few individuals were away at secondary school or working in the towns; this may be due to an artifact of males stating their age as greater than reality.

The number of childless women (see table 21-2) was small. Only 16 percent of women in the age group 20–24 years were childless. Among older women the percentage never exceeded 9 percent. During the year prior to enumeration 2,408 births produced a crude birth rate of 57 percent and a general fertility rate of 221 percent. During the registration year there were 1,264 births. Fewer individuals were registered that year, so the crude birth rate remained high at 48 percent; the general fertility rate was 191 percent. The highest number of births was in May, and the birth rate hit a high plateau in July–October. The fewest number of births occurred in February–April, because they would have been conceived in May–July when farming activities are at their peak and food stocks are low. The problems of recording pregnancy accurately were considerable, and the crude birth rate can be compared

Figure 21-2. Population Pyramid for Malumfashi, Nigeria, 1974–77

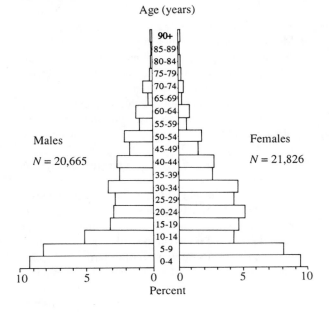

Age (years)

Males

N = 20,665

Females

N = 21,826

Percent

high. The crude death rate (divide the total number of deaths in a year by the midyear population and multiply by 1,000) was calculated on several occasions. Data obtained by recall methods for 12 months before the census produced a crude death rate (CDR) of only 13 percent. Prospective data derived from the registration period November 1977–October 1978 gave a rate of 16 percent. When the data were cleaned up to ensure that only reliable sources were included, the CDR came close to 19 percent.

Infants formed 2.8 percent of the Malumfashi population, but accounted for 26.9 percent of all registered deaths. Children under five years of age made up 60 percent of all registered deaths. When infant and child mortality rates were calculated from registration data (see table 21-3) the figures, 88 deaths per 1,000 live births for infants and 34 per 1,000 for children 1–4 years of age, were much lower than expected, emphasizing how difficult it is to rely on data from registration. Bradley *et al.* (1977) analyzed the enumeration data by the Truswell (South) equations; the infant mortality rate (IMR) was much higher using this estimate. Indeed it may have been over 200 for many years, with a tendency to fall during the years prior to the study. The excess of mortality among boys was slight but consistent, unlike the pattern reported in Asian studies (Bradley *et al.*, 1982b).

EDRU's infant and child mortality rates for Malumfashi District resemble those of other studies in the area (see table 21-4); however, the other studies were confined to small communities. The Malumfashi Hospital, for example, was just beginning to operate fully, and a number of maternal and child health (MCH) clinics were being established by local government at

with those recorded in the 1952 census of Nigeria (43 percent) and in the malaria eradication project at Garki (46–47 percent) (Molineaux and Gramiccia, 1980). The complete absence of any family planning facilities for this population might explain why the rates were so

Table 21-1. Population Structure, Malumfashi, Nigeria

Age (years)	Males	Females	Male/female ratio
0–1	3,996	3,979	1.00
5–9	3,555	3,456	1.03
10–14	2,202	1,822	1.21
15–19	1,346	2,028	0.66
20–24	1,201	2,186	0.55
25–29	1,167	1,814	0.64
30–34	1,452	1,960	0.74
35–39	1,053	1,111	0.95
40–44	1,169	1,136	1.03
45–49	765	653	1.17
50 and older	2,759	1,681	1.64
Total	20,665	21,826	0.95

Source: Bradley (1980).

Table 21-2. Women without Children, Malumfashi, Nigeria

Age (years)	Number of women[a]	Number of women without children	Percentage of women without children
15–19	1,976	1,036	52.4
20–24	2,080	336	16.1
25–29	1,775	147	8.1
30–34	1,901	117	6.1
35–39	1,090	56	5.1
40–44	1,117	77	6.9
45–49	645	47	7.3

a. Excludes 304 women with impossible fertility histories.
Source: Bradley *et al.* (1982a).

Table 21-3. Mortality Rates for Infants and Young Children, Malumfashi, Nigeria

Type of mortality rate	Number of deaths	Number in population category	Rate
Neonatal	51	1,264 live births	39.3[a]
Infant	111	1,264 live births	87.8[a]
Child	137	4,019 children age 1–4	34.1[b]

a. Per 1,000 live births.
b. Per 1,000 children age 1–4.
Source: Bradley *et al.* (1982b).

Table 21-4. Infant and Child Mortality Rates, Hausaland, by Area

Location	Reference	Mortality Infant[a]	Child[b]
Malumfashi (enumeration)	Bradley *et al.* (1982b)	170	182
Ruwan Sanyi (a Malumfashi study village)	Launiala (1975)	170	210
Dayi (25 km north of Malumfashi)	Launiala (1975)	160	190
Dayi	Longhurst (1980)	163	133
Gamzago (a Malumfashi study village)	Bradley-Moore *et al.* (1985a)	93[c]	n.a.
Garki (100 km north of Kano)	Molineaux and Gramiccia (1980)	Various	154

n.a. Not available.
a. Per 1,000 live births.
b. Per 1,000 children age 1–4.
c. Based on a cohort of children followed from one week to one year.

that time. In addition, clinics were being run by ABU's Department of Community Medicine with support from the Finnish Malumfashi Project Team. Perhaps the most consistent activity, however, was the EDRU project's offer of immunizations, simple medical treatment for certain illnesses, and assistance with transport to the Malumfashi Hospital.

Of all the deaths in Malumfashi 64 percent occurred between May and September, during the rainy season. This seasonal influence was even more marked among infants. Establishing the cause or causes of death at Malumfashi was no easier than elsewhere. The poor level of medical services available prior to the EDRU project meant that death was an expected event that happened to many people rather than unexpected and, therefore, needing an explanation. A limited but detailed anthropological study of perception of illness and health among the Maguzawa revealed a general classification of symptoms, signs, and causes (Last,

1972). However, these bore little relation to the more commonly recognized biological causes of death; therefore, diseases were classified and causes of death determined by the symptoms that the enumerators recorded on their monthly visits.

Several problems occurred. First, an entire month could elapse between the visit and an interview. Second, some enumerators favored certain causes of death over others. Third, Hausa did not always translate smoothly into English. For instance, the Hausa have one word for both measles and chicken pox.

Nevertheless, by limiting the analysis to 25 symptoms thought to be the most important part of any illness, the project was able to group deaths into well-defined conditions, loosely defined conditions, and accidents or poisoning (see tables 21-5 and 21-6, Bradley *et al.*, 1982b). The selectivity of meningococcal deaths during the dry season and the increase in

Table 21-5. Symptoms Present before Death, by Age, Malumfashi, Nigeria, 1977–78
(number, unless otherwise specified)

Symptom	Age in years				Total	Percentage of all deaths
	0–4	*5–14*	*15–44*	*45 and above*		
Infective diseases						
Meningococcal infection	4			1	5	2.2
Measles	30	4			34	14.9
Ill-defined conditions						
Cough with and without pyrexia, diarrhea	2			3	5	2.2
Jaundice with and without pyrexia, swelling	5			1	6	2.6
Pyrexia of unknown origin with and without diarrhea, vomiting, headache, swelling	59	11	12	4	86	37.7
Diarrhea with and without vomiting, swelling, headache, labored breathing	37	7	5	6	55	24.1
Swelling with and without cough, headache	3	1	3	8	15	6.6
Accidents and poisoning	2		1	2	5	2.2
Other	9	2	3	3	17	7.5
Total	151	25	24	28	228	100.0

Source: Bradley *et al.* (1982b).

Table 21-6. Symptoms Present before Death, by Season, Malumfashi, Nigeria, 1977–78

Symptom	Number of deaths		
	Wet season	*Dry season*	*Total*
Infective diseases			
Meningococcal infections	0	5	5
Measles	21	13	34
Ill-defined conditions			
Cough with and without pyrexia, diarrhea	2	3	5
Jaundice with and without pyrexia, swelling	4	2	6
Pyrexia of unknown origin with and without diarrhea, vomiting, headache, swelling	46	40	86
Diarrhea with and without vomiting, swelling, headache, labored breathing	34	21	55
Swelling with and without cough, headache	8	7	15
Accidents and poisoning	2	3	5
Other	10	7	17
Total	127	101	228

Source: Bradley *et al.* (1982b).

measles-associated deaths in the wet season support somewhat the accuracy of the enumerators' diagnoses.

Table 21-7 shows the seasonal pattern of 126 deaths among children from birth to four years of age. Regardless of cause, deaths increased in the rainy season. The deaths from measles were probably due to the combination of pneumonia, persistent diarrhea, and protein-energy malnutrition that occur in the months following an attack of measles. Measles was a major precipitating cause of protein-energy malnutrition at the pediatric ward of Malumfashi Hospital, and the deaths recorded in table 21-8 include children who died despite energetic medical treatment. The deaths from pyrexia might have been due to malaria, but probably included pneumonia and other infections that cause high fevers. The inclusion of deaths attributable to diarrhea is probably the least satisfactory of all. It

was not possible to determine if this was acute watery diarrhea with rapid progression to severe dehydration and death, dysentery, or persistent diarrhea (of more than 14 days' duration). Persistent diarrhea may have been the end stage of an illness that began as a specific infection, such as measles or malaria.

Many lessons were learned about methodology, and these studies discuss them painfully and honestly. Perhaps the most important lesson was that populations with minimal medical care and high rates of mortality and morbidity are likely to view detailed demographic and medical questionnaires with cynicism, mistrust, conservatism, or frank rebuttal. Throughout the EDRU project, in which a consistent level of simple medical assistance and caring was given, such conservatism thawed slowly but steadily. Producing sophisticated longitudinal demographic

Table 21-7. Deaths of Children Age 0–4 Attributed to Measles, Pyrexia, and Diarrhea, by Two-Month Intervals, Malumfashi, Nigeria, 1977–78

Interval	Measles deaths		Pyrexia deaths		Diarrhea deaths	
	Number	Percent	Number	Percent	Number	Percent
January–February	2	6.7	8	13.6	2	5.4
March–April	6	20.0	4	6.8	4	10.8
May–June	9	30.0	18	30.5	11	29.7
July–August	8	26.7	11	18.6	13	35.1
September–October	2	6.7	13	22.0	4	10.8
November–December	3	10.0	5	8.5	3	8.1
Total	30	100.1	59	100.0	37	99.9

Note: Numbers may not sum to 100.0 because of rounding.
Source: Bradley *et al.* (1982b).

Table 21-8. Deaths in Children Age 0–4 Attributed to Measles, Pyrexia, and Diarrhea, by Age, Malumfashi, Nigeria, 1977–78

Age (months)	Measles deaths		Pyrexia deaths		Diarrhea deaths	
	Number	Percent	Number	Percent	Number	Percent
Less than 1	0	0.0	13	22.0	6	16.2
1–5	3	10.0	8	13.5	4	10.8
6–11	10	33.3	5	8.5	4	10.8
12–23	10	33.3	19	32.2	9	24.3
24–35	4	13.3	11	18.6	9	24.3
36–47	3	10.0	2	3.4	2	5.4
48–59	0	0.0	1	1.7	3	5.4
Total	30	99.9	59	99.9	37	97.2

Note: Numbers may not sum to 100.0 because of rounding.
Source: Bradley *et al.* (1982b).

data was not the prime purpose of the EDRU, but the project established a rapport with the community that became a major resource for the individuals who continued to collect demographic data after the project had ended.

A series of options exist, therefore, for developing population laboratories. Perhaps the first prerequisite is a climate of trust between researcher and community. Such a climate takes time to develop, which has financial implications for those who may be asked to support researchers in the field for years rather than months. Second, moral and ethical questions are raised by researchers who measure population data, but contribute little or nothing to the health care of the community they study. The problem, of course, is that the interaction between the researcher and the community may affect the very indicators of interest: mortality and morbidity.

In practice, these considerations tend to divide the indicators that can be obtained by rapid, relatively noninvasive techniques (such as determining child survivorship indirectly) from those that require a greater relationship between researcher and respondent (such as determining the symptoms, signs, and possible cause of a child's death).

Malaria

The problem of malaria in young children was selected for a major study within the EDRU. Recognized as an important cause of child death, malaria also contributed to morbidity, anemia, and impaired growth. An important finding of the Medical Research Council

and the Immunology Group at the Department of Medicine, ABU, Zaria, was that severe suppression of the immune response occurs in acute malaria (Greenwood and Whittle, 1981). Yet, even where malaria is prevalent, acute episodes of clinical malaria are relatively uncommon. Asymptomatic parasitemia, however, might still depress the immune response, and could therefore affect the response to other protozoal, bacterial, or viral infections. It could also have important implications for immunization policy. To study these effects, the project placed 185 infants in a control group and gave 198 infants weekly chemoprophylaxis with chloroquine from shortly after birth until one or two years of age. Because the level of supervision was high, the level of compliance was remarkable; the children received on average 95 percent of the doses that they should have. The survival curves for children in the two groups are given in figure 21-3. All deaths among the study children during chemoprophylaxis and during a further six-month period were investigated. Of the 198, 21 (10.6 percent) died while receiving chemoprophylaxis; a similar proportion (23 of 185, or 12.4 percent) of the unprotected children died. Since children who were protected might not develop immunity and might die after stopping the chloroquine, the children were followed for six months after chemoprophylaxis was stopped. Only one death was reported during that time.

An intense follow-up was conducted in which enumerators visited households regularly when they heard that a child was sick; thus the study obtained reasonable cause of death data (see table 21-9; Brad-

Figure 21-3. Survival Curves for Infants and Children in a Protected and a Control Group, Malumfashi

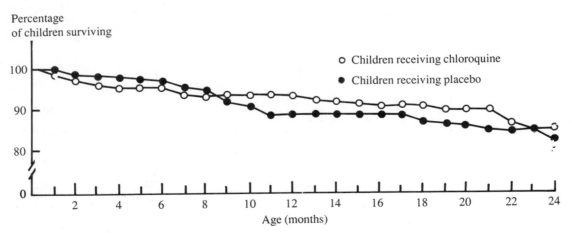

Percentage
of children surviving

○ Children receiving chloroquine
● Children receiving placebo

Age (months)

Source: Bradley-Moore *et al.* (1985c).

Table 21-9. Suspected Cause of Death among Children Receiving Malaria Chemoprophylaxis with Chloroquine and Control Group, Malumfashi, Nigeria

	Number of deaths	
Cause of death[a]	Protected children	Control children
Malaria	1	5
Fever (probably not malaria)[b]	6	7
Malnutrition	1	6
Anemia	1	1
Hemoglobinopathy	1	2
Chest infection	2	1
Measles	1	0
Poliomyelitis	0	1
Other	2	0
Unknown	10	5
Number of children in group	21	23

a. When more than one serious condition was present at the time of death, both diagnoses were recorded.

b. Blood films negative for malaria or not taken.

Source: Bradley-Moore *et al.* (1985c).

ley-Moore *et al.*, 1985c). All sick persons were encouraged to attend a clinic held at the study village on regular days. Those who received chemoprophylaxis had significantly fewer attendances than those who did not (see table 21-10). Routine blood films taken from unprotected children were positive for sexual and asexual forms of *P. falciparum* and

asexual forms of *P. malariae* significantly more often than films taken from children taking chloroquine. However, the protection was far from complete, and the prevalence of positive blood films increased with age (Bradley-Moore *et al.*, 1985c). Nevertheless, the prevalence of parasitemia was always less in the protected groups. As expected, the levels of malaria antibodies were high in the unprotected children, but, especially in the second year of life, they were considerably higher than in the children taking chemoprophylaxis.

The immune response of these children to immunization with triple antigen (diphtheria, tetanus, and pertussis), poliomyelitis, measles, typhoid, and meningococcal vaccines was then assessed. The unprotected and protected groups responded similarly to all vaccines, except meningococcal polysaccharide antigen; the protected children had higher antibody titers against both the group A and group C antigen than the unprotected children (Bradley-Moore *et al.*, 1985b).

During the study, anthropometric and biochemical indices of nutritional status were taken regularly. Protected children tended to be taller and heavier than unprotected children and to have a larger mid-upper-arm circumference (see table 21-11). Mean serum albumin and prealbumin levels were higher in protected than in unprotected children. However, none of these differences was very striking (Bradley-Moore *et al.*, 1985d).

More impressive was the improvement in hemoglobin in the protected children (see figure 21-4), who also had higher packed-cell volumes. Serum ferritin, often used as a measure of iron status, was greater

Table 21-10. Attendances at Routine Clinics by Children Receiving Malaria Chemoprophylaxis with Chloroquine and of Control Group, Malumfashi, Nigeria

	Protected children			Control children			
Reason for visit	Number	Percent	Number of visits	Number	Percent	Number of visits	Significance[a]
Any illness	129	65.2	398	140	75.7	442	$p < 0.05$
Suspected malaria[b]	15	7.6	35	44	23.8	104	$p < 0.001$
Proven malaria[c]	12	6.1	15	43	23.2	78	$p < 0.001$

Note: The protected group contained 198 children, the control group, 185.

a. Difference between proportions of protected and of control children visiting clinics.

b. Clinical diagnosis of malaria, but blood film not taken.

c. Clinical diagnosis of malaria confirmed by a positive blood film.

Source: Bradley-Moore *et al.* (1985c).

Table 21-11. Anthropometric Measures of Protected Children Receiving Malaria Chemoprophylaxis with Chloroquine and of Control Group, Malumfashi, Nigeria

Age and group	Number of children	Height-for-age Percentage of mean	Variance	Weight-for-age Percentage of mean	Variance	Weight-for-height Percentage of mean	Variance	Arm circumference Percentage of mean	Variance
0–5 months									
Protected	149	97.6 ±	5.0	95.4 ±	17.8	101.7 ±	13.6	12.5 ±	1.1
Control	143	98.2 ±	5.3	97.6 ±	16.1	102.3 ±	10.0	12.5 ±	1.2
6–11 months									
Protected	146	96.2 ±	4.7	83.6 ±	12.9	91.7 ±	10.1	13.3 ±	1.3
Control	142	95.8 ±	4.2	81.9 ±	11.7	90.8 ±	9.2	13.1 ±	1.1
12–17 months									
Protected	91	95.0 ±	4.4[a]	80.0 ±	10.1	88.5 ±	8.1	13.8 ±	1.1[b]
Control	88	93.7 ±	4.4	78.0 ±	11.0	88.5 ±	8.1	13.4 ±	1.1
18–23 months									
Protected	87	93.2 ±	4.8[a]	88.5 ±	8.3	88.5 ±	8.3	13.9 ±	1.0
Control	80	91.7 ±	5.1	76.5 ±	10.5	88.1 ±	8.8	13.6 ±	1.2

Note: Means are expressed as percentage of the National Child Health Statistics standard.

a. $p < 0.05$.

b. $p < 0.01$.

Source: Bradley-Moore *et al.* (1985d).

among those with parasitemia than among those without (Bradley-Moore *et al.*, 1985a). This is in keeping with the general finding that ferritin levels rise in inflammatory conditions. This assay cannot be recommended unreservedly for assessing iron stores in communities susceptible to infection.

Overall, therefore, the addition of chloroquine to the preventive health regime these children received appeared to have rather a small impact. Does this mean that malaria is unimportant as a cause of morbidity and mortality? Probably not. Studies, such as this, that offer immunization and simple medical care do not allow malaria to have its most detrimental effect. Thus, although some children may die from pure malaria with acute convulsions or anemia and rapid death, many more probably start to suffer an attack of malaria and proceed, as a result of immune suppression, to develop pneumonia or another infection. Septicemia especially from *Salmonella* sp. is not uncommon in children with malaria. An attack of measles might be worse in an immune-suppressed child. Diarrhea in malaria, though recognized clinically, has received little attention. All these multiplier effects may turn an attack of malaria into a fatal illness.

Figure 21-4. Hemoglobin Levels in Children in a Protected and a Control Group, Malumfashi

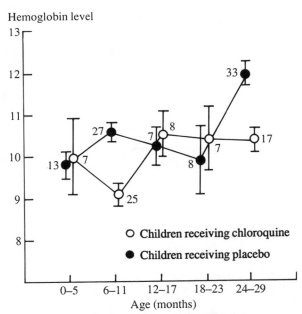

Note: The level is measured as grams per deciliter plus or minus SEM.

Source: Bradley-Moore *et al.* (1985a).

Schistosomiasis

Hematuria is common in Malumfashi since the majority of villagers, especially young males, are heavily infected with *Schistosoma haematobium* (Pugh and Gilles, 1976). A pilot study in 1971 showed a prevalence of 59.3 percent among boys 5 to 15 years of age. However, after five years of drought the prevalence declined considerably. The overall prevalence was four times greater in boys than in girls and the transmission of *S. haematobium* varied markedly. In general the villages with considerable opportunity for man-water contact had the higher prevalence. Dependence on surface water and the existence of swamps for cultivating sugar cane and convenient pools for boys and men seeking to cool off were important factors. A severe drought affected the area in 1973, and informal questioning revealed its effects. Nearly all middle-aged males remembered hematuria in their youth, when water was abundant. Since the drought, the prevalence was generally thought to have declined.

The EDRU studied the effects of the construction of 16 earthen dams on the transmission of schistosomiasis. Initial studies showed large populations of *Bulinus (P.) globosus* snails and smaller numbers of *B. forskalii* and *Biomphalaria pfeifferi*. The concentration of these snails was reduced while the dams were being built, but, remarkably, within a month of the dams' completion all three species of snail recovered (Tayo and Jewsbury, 1978).

In order to assess the human risk of these findings, EDRU observed in detail how man came into contact with water (Tayo *et al.*, 1980). The females remained secluded in their households and waited for the men to bring them water for cooking, washing, etc. In fact males were responsible for over 98 percent of the activity involving contamination from and exposure to water. Even clothes washing, a female task in many societies, was performed by men so that the women could remain secluded in their compounds. Washing clothes, utensils, and vegetables (28 percent), fishing (25 percent), and bathing and playing (14 percent) were the most common water-contact activities in the dry season. Swimming (65 percent) was the most common in the rainy season. The 10–14 and 15–24 year age groups were exposed to water longer and more often than others.

The prevalence and intensity of *Schistosoma haematobium* infection are shown in figure 21-5. The cercarial shedding period is maximal during the early afternoon and minimal in the evening and at night. The occasional woman who did venture to a pool nearly always did so at night, when onlookers were infrequent and cercarial shedding rates were low. Limited studies showed a beneficial effect of metrifonate on the radiological urographic examinations.

Eye Disease

A single cross-sectional survey, using specially trained nurses with experience in ophthalmic disorders, was conducted among 8,254 persons (Bhar *et al.*, 1982). Overall the blindness rate was 1.0 percent; in persons with impaired vision, it was 2–3 percent (see tables 21-12 and 21-13). The variety of eye pathology was considerable among the 125 individuals with less than one-third of the normal visual acuity or with unilateral blindness (table 21-13). This survey failed to identify a single case of xerophthalmia, confirming previous impressions that vitamin A deficiency is not an overt

Figure 21-5. Prevalence of Schistosoma haematobium, by Gender, Malumfashi

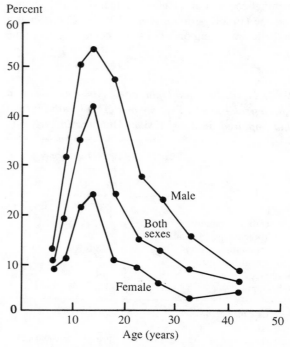

Note: Curves indicate the percentage of persons with egg counts exceeding 50 per 10 milliliters of urine.

public health problem in the area. Nevertheless, xerophthalmia was seen in children with severe protein-energy malnutrition in the pediatric ward of the Malumfashi Hospital. Furthermore, the prevalence of marginal vitamin A deficiency has not been documented in this community. Access to effective medical treatment for eye disorders appeared to be limited, and a high proportion of persons needing treatment had received only local, traditional remedies.

Meningococcal Meningitis

The cool, dry season of *Dorri* (November to February) and the early hot season of *Bazara* (March to May) provide an ideal environment for spreading meningococcal meningitis. Considerable experience in the clinical management of many hundreds of adults and children with this disease had been gained at ABU, Zaria, where several trials of chemotherapeutic regimes had been conducted (Whittle *et al.*, 1973). The most important finding, perhaps, was the resistance of *meningococci* to the sulfonamides being prescribed at government hospitals and health centers. Several vaccines were introduced and tested on 206 children between the ages of 3 and 18 months who were immunized with a combined group A and group C meningococcal polysaccharide, measles, and tetanus vaccine (Bradley-Moore *et al.*, 1985b). The response to the tetanus component of the vaccine was good; the

Table 21-13. Ophthalmic Disorders Detected in 125 Persons with Unilateral Blindness or Less Than One-Third Normal Visual Acuity, Malumfashi, Nigeria

Disorder	Number of persons diagnosed
Trachoma[a]	20[b]
Pterygium	14
Pingueculum	2
Corneal nebulae and opacities	13
Adherent leukoma (other than trachoma)	6[b]
Anterior uveitis	5
Iris atrophy	4
Hypermature cataract	9
Immature cataract	27
Myopia	24
Hypermetropia	3
Macular degeneration	10[b]
Choroidoretinitis	6
Retinal arteriosclerosis	6
Opting atrophy	4
Divergent squint	6
Convergent squint	2
Miscellaneous[b]	11
Total	172

a. Includes eight with entropion.

b. Includes two with bilateral blindness.

c. Includes one each of the following: blocked lacrimal duct, central corneal leukoma, keratoconus, phthisis bulbi, buphthalmos, secondary glaucoma, congenital cataract, vitreous floaters, asteroid hyalosis, and physiological cupping.

Source: Bhar *et al.* (1982).

Table 21-12. External Ophthalmic Abnormalities and Etiological Factors Present in Persons with Normal and Impaired Bilateral Vision, Malumfashi, Nigeria

Condition	Visual acuity	
	Impaired[a]	Normal[b]
Total	180	7,909
Detected abnormalities (percentage of total)		
Conjunctival lesions	18.5	3.3
Corneal lesions[c]	19.4	1.0
Cataract	14.4	0.2
Glaucoma	2.2	n.a.

a. Less than 6/18.

b. 6/6.

c. Keratoconjunctival lesions, 37.9 percent; trachoma, 17.8 percent; nonspecific keratitis, 9.8 percent; measles, 3.3 percent; trauma, 2.2 percent; smallpox, 2.0 percent; onchocerciasis, 1.7 percent; leprosy, 1.1 percent.

Source: Bhar *et al.* (1982).

response to the measles vaccine was reasonable. The serological response to the meningococcal polysaccharide components of the vaccine was poor, however, even when the antigenic stimulus was enhanced by a further booster dose of group A and group C meningococcal polysaccharide one month after the first injection.

The epidemiology of the spread of *Neisseria meningitidis* and *Neisseria lactamica* was carefully studied in longitudinal microbiological studies performed by Blakeborough *et al.* (1982). The complexities of the spread of these organisms and their carriage may explain why effective development of herd immunity is difficult. For instance, Greenwood and Wali (1980) found that many of the villagers who were not vaccinated with group A and group C meningococci polysaccharide antigen, because they were away from home when the vaccination team visited, were at considerable risk of meningococcal disease even when up to 80 percent of their neighbors had been immunized.

The annual epidemics of meningococcal infection (mostly meningitis, but also severe systemic illness) continue to affect adults and children. The studies suggest that effective vaccines exist, but that unless the coverage rate is very high many will still develop the infection.

Diarrheal Diseases

Diarrheal disease was not a component of the original EDRU project, but during its last year, the project evaluated the epidemiology of diarrhea and its relation to preexisting nutritional states. The nursing and medical staff in Malumfashi Hospital recognized the prevalence of diarrhea during the rainy season. A study was initiated in which, during the months of the rainy season, enumerators made weekly visits to households with young children to assess the number of days in which diarrhea occurred. Measuring weight and height at the beginning of the study enabled EDRU to examine the relation between shortness, underweight or thinness, the subsequent attack rate of diarrhea, and the duration of time spent with symptoms. There was no obvious link between stunting or underweight and the subsequent attack rate, although children who were wasted (less than 80 percent of the expected weight for their height) had more frequent episodes of diarrhea than those who were not. Subsequent analysis revealed that a number of the thin children had experienced an

attack of measles in the hot, dry months before the diarrhea study began. The wasted children might have been recovering from measles and were in fact suffering from postmeasles diarrhea rather than episodes of diarrhea. In other words, underlying nutrition has relatively little effect on attack rate (Tomkins, 1981). Short stature, underweight, and wasting were, however, clearly associated with a significantly greater duration of diarrhea (see table 21-14).

Unfortunately, detailed microbiological studies to detect the pathogens responsible were not possible. However, diarrhea was generally characteristic of the acute watery type, and dysentery was rare. The prevalence of *Salmonella* sp. was high and that of *Campylobacter* was low in both healthy and undernourished children from the area (see table 21-15; Lloyd Evans et al., 1983). These studies were performed among the Maguzawa and Hausa; the continued mobility of the Fulani was a major constraint on longitudinal studies. The considerable differences in housing density, type of water supply, local environment, and exposure to cattle and fomites would have made a study of the morbidity patterns of ethnic groups interesting. The opportunity to ingest diarrheal pathogens was ample, given the amount of bacterial contamination of food and water (see figure 21-6; Tomkins et al., 1978).

Because metabolites produced by the resident intestinal flora provide effective protection against certain diarrheal pathogens, EDRU observed the concentrations of intestinal bacteria in the three major ethnic groups. The meat-eating and-milk-drinking Fulani had

Table 21-14. Relation of Diarrhea and Nutritional Status, Malumfashi, Nigeria

Nutritional status	Number of children	Episodes per child in a three-month period	Percentage of time with diarrhea
Weight-for-age			
More than 75%	220	1.25	8.5
Less than 75% (underweight)	123	1.52	11.3[a]
Height-for-age			
More than 90%	245	1.37	7.9
Less than 90% (stunting)	98	1.45	10.8[a]
Weight-for-height			
More than 80%	302	1.29	7.6
Less than 80% (wasting)	41	1.90[b]	13.6[c]

a. Significance of comparison within group, $p < 0.01$.
b. Significance of comparison within group, $p < 0.05$.
c. Significance of comparison within group, $p < 0.001$.
Source: Tomkins (1981).

Table 21-15. Proportions of Malnourished and Well-Nourished Children in Whom Fecal Bacterial Pathogens Were Isolated, The Gambia and Nigeria

Pathogen and group	The Gambia		Nigeria		Significance of comparison between groups
	Number	Percent	Number	Percent	
Campylobacter					
Well-nourished	4	6.8	1	2.6	*p* < 0.05
Malnourished	6	10.2	1	2.6	
Salmonellae					
Well-nourished	3	5.1	2	5.3	*p* < 0.01
Malnourished	2	3.4	11	28.9	
Shigellae					
Well-nourished	3	5.1	0	0.0	n.s.
Malnourished	1	1.7	3	7.9	

n.s. Not significant.
Note: The total number of children was 59 in the Gambia and 38 in Nigeria.
Source: Tomkins *et al.* (1981).

high levels of *Bacteroides* sp. and of fecal bile acids, which imply that their patterns of dietary intake might, to some degree, protect them against diarrheal disease (Tomkins *et al.*, 1981). This hypothesis is as yet unproven.

Despite the lack of detailed community-based data on diarrheal morbidity at Malumfashi, the single longitudinal study and the survey of causes of admission to Malumfashi Hospital indicate that diarrhea is a major problem. The community did not seem to resist the use of sugar-salt, but packets of oral rehydration salts were almost unobtainable. Several local remedies for diarrhea, including cereal-based remedies and drinks prepared from tree bark and leaves, would be interesting to evaluate.

Malnutrition

Although nutritional studies were not a major part of the original EDRU project, results are available. Bradley-Moore *et al.* (1985c; table 21-11) and Tomkins *et al.* (1978; table 21-16) measured the height and weight of two groups of children. Their studies showed a steady decline in stature, compared with international standards, during the first three years of life and some catch-up of height thereafter. During the second and third years the rates of weight gain faltered considerably. During the second year of life, wasting was prevalent. The impact of infection, especially measles, was striking at this time, as clinical studies at Malumfashi Hospital demonstrated (Tomkins *et al.*, 1983).

Oomen (1979) described the difference in the body stature of older children and adults in the Fulani and Maguzawa/Hausa groups. Despite the lack of opportunity to conduct longitudinal studies of nutritional status, other than the chloroquine chemoprophylaxis study (Bradley-Moore *et al.*, 1985d), a series of cross-sectional measurements showed that over several years the nutritional status of the Hausa children improved much more than that of the Maguzawa

Figure 21-6. Level of Coliform Contamination in the Supply of Food and Water, Malumfashi

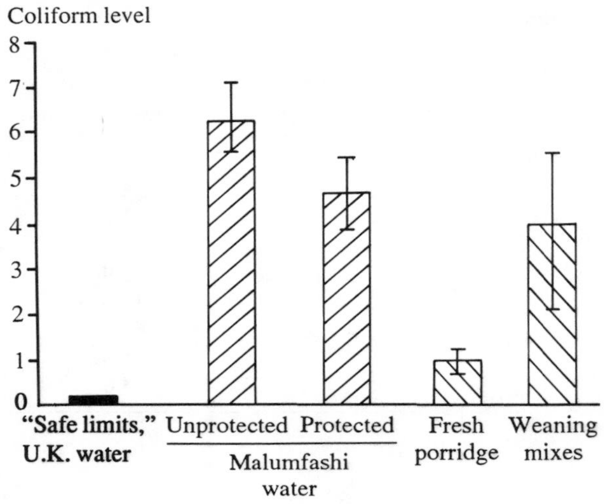

Note: The level is measured as $\log_{10}$ per 100 milliliters plus or minus SEM.

Table 21-16. Wasting and Stunting in Preschool Children, by Age, Malumfashi, Nigeria

	Age (months)				
Anthropometric index[a]	3.0–5.9	6.0–11.9	12.0–23.9	24.0–35.6	36.0–47.9
Weight-for-age	94.8 ± 7.8	80.3 ± 11.4	73.4 ± 9.5	77.3 ± 12.3	77.4 ± 10.8
Height-for-age	98.2 ± 2.9	97.5 ± 5.4	92.5 ± 4.9	90.2 ± 5.6	90.3 ± 5.1
Weight-for-height	94.3 ± 7.6	84.3 ± 9.2	82.4 ± 8.6	89.8 ± 8.5	94.4 ± 10.3

a. Mean given as a percentage plus or minus the standard deviation (National Child Health Statistics standard).
Source: Tomkins *et al.* (1978).

children (see table 21-17; Tomkins, unpublished). This improvement occurred during the intensive activities of the FADP, which had a favorable impact on food production and cash availability. The Hausa families, being at the center of commercial and political activities, probably benefited more from the FADP than the Maguzawa, which in turn affected the nutritional state of their children.

Maternal Morbidity and Mortality

Because no research was conducted on the health of mothers in Malumfashi District, data collected among mothers in Zaria are presented. Harrison (1985) and an editorial in the *Lancet* (Maternal health, 1987) summarize some of the problems affecting maternal health. An analysis of 22,774 consecutive hospital records showed 238 maternal and 2,718 perinatal deaths. Interviews of mothers suggested that maternal mor-

Table 21-17. Proportions of Children Age 6–36 Months Who Are Malnourished
(percent)

Index and tribe	1976	1978
Height-for-age[a]		
Hausa	19.8	17.2
Maguzawa	43.2	35.2
Weight-for-age[b]		
Hausa	42.7	37.3
Maguzawa	74.5	57.0
Weight-for-height[b]		
Hausa	10.9	13.5
Maguzawa	25.5	20.5

Note: The sample size was 183 for 1976 and 196 for 1978.
a. Less than 90 percent of the National Child Health Statistics standard.
b. Less than 80 percent of the National Child Health Statistics standard.

tality overall (including those who delivered at home) may have been as high as 40 per 1,000 deliveries, although accurate community-based figures are not available. The risks are highest in the young. Indeed, 6 percent of the women who delivered in Zaria were less than 15 years of age. The problems they faced include anemia, postpartum hemorrhage, preeclamptic toxemia, obstructed labor, and vesicovaginal fistula. The complications and mortality rates were reduced by adequate antenatal care, including malaria chemoprophylaxis and iron therapy. However, Harrison emphasizes that universal, formal education to eliminate mass illiteracy is essential for improving maternal health.

Conclusions

It would be pleasing to report that these findings were followed by a program of primary health care, especially one treating vaccine-preventable diseases. However, the resources necessary for such a follow-up have not been consistently forthcoming. This review only included data published in readily available journals. It may well be that, despite our failure to procure them, more recent reports of health and nutrition status are available locally. One of the most striking findings of the EDRU project was that fathers, mothers, and children were steadily becoming more interested in health. Their enthusiasm was, however, underutilized in the programs reviewed in this paper. It is to be hoped that future reports will be written on programs of primary health care that arise from participatory activity.

Acknowledgments

We are grateful for the assistance of many of the research groups working in Malumfashi during our residence. We have included all the published data that we could, but apologize to anyone whose work we may have omitted.

References

Adeleke, A. M. (1983). Fertility and mortality in Malumfashi, Kaduna State, Nigeria. M.S. thesis, Department of Medical Demography, London School of Hygiene and Tropical Medicine.

Bhar, I. S., Kasin, S., Gall, J., Pugh, R. N. H., Bradley, A. K., Moody, J. B., and Gilles, H. M. (1982). Malumfashi Endemic Diseases Research Project. 18: the programme for blindness and ophthalmic disease. *Annals of Tropical Medicine and Parasitology*, 76, 243–245.

Blakeborough, I. S., Greenwood, B. M., Whittle, H. C., Bradley, A. K., and Gilles, H. M. (1982). The epidemiology of *Neisseria meningitidis* and *Neisseria lactamica* in a northern Nigerian community. *Journal of Infectious Diseases*, 146, 626–637.

Bradley, A. K. (1980). *Population Studies in Part of Malumfashi, Kodura State, Nigeria*. Liverpool: Liverpool School of Tropical Medicine.

Bradley, A. K. and Gilles, H. M. (1981). Malumfashi Endemic Diseases Research Project. 17: a knowledge-attitude-practice survey on perception of disease and fertility. *Annals of Tropical Medicine and Parasitology*, 75(6), 581–590.

———. (1984). Malumfashi Endemic Diseases Research Project. 21: pointers to causes of death in the Malumfashi area, northern Nigeria. *Annals of Tropical Medicine and Parasitology*, 78, 265–271.

Bradley, A. K., Gilles, H. M., and Shehu, U. (1977). Malumfashi Endemic Diseases Research Project. 1: some ecological and demographic considerations. *Annals of Tropical Medicine and Parasitology*, 71(4), 443–449.

Bradley, A. K., MacFarlane, S. B. J., Moody, J. B., and Gilles, H. M. (1982a). Malumfashi Endemic Diseases Research Project. 19: demographic findings, population structure and fertility. *Annals of Tropical Medicine and Parasitology*, 76(4), 381–391.

Bradley, A. K., MacFarlane, S. B. J., Moody, J. B., Gilles, H. M., Blacker, J. G. C., and Musa, B. D. (1982b). Malumfashi Endemic Diseases Research Project. 20: demographic findings, mortality. *Annals of Tropical Medicine and Parasitology*, 76(4), 393–404.

Bradley-Moore, A. M., Greenwood, B. M., Bradley, A. K., Akintunde, A., Attai, E. D. E., Fleming, A. F., Flynn, F. V., Kirkwood, B., and Gilles, H. M. (1985a). Malaria chemoprophylaxis with chloroquine in young Nigerian children. 4: its effect on haematological measurements. *Annals of Tropical Medicine and Parasitology*, 79(6), 585–595.

Bradley-Moore, A. M., Greenwood, B. M., Bradley, A. K., Bartlett, A., Bidwell, D. E., Voller, A., Craske, J., Kirkwood, B. R., and Gilles, H. M. (1985b). Malaria chemoprophylaxis in young Nigerian children. 2: its effect on the immune response to vaccination. *Annals of Tropical Medicine and Parasitology*, 79(6), 563–572.

Bradley-Moore, A. M., Greenwood, B. M., Bradley, A. K., Bartlett, A., Bidwell, D. E., Voller, A., Kirkwood, B. R., and Gilles, H. M. (1985c). Malaria chemoprophylaxis with chloroquine in young Nigerian children.

1: its effect on mortality, morbidity, and the prevalence of malaria. *Annals of Tropical Medicine and Parasitology*, 79(6), 549–562.

Bradley-Moore, A. M., Greenwood, B. M., Bradley, A. K., Kirkwood, B. R., and Gilles, H. M. (1985d). Malaria chemoprophylaxis with chloroquine and young Nigerian children. 3: its effect on nutrition. *Annals of Tropical Medicine and Parasitology*, 79(6), 575–584.

Greenwood, B. M. and Wali, S. S. (1980). Control of meningococcal meningitis in the African meningitis belt by selective vaccination. *Lancet*, 1, 729–732.

Greenwood, B. M. and Whittle, H. C. (1981). *Immunology of Medicine in the Tropics*. London: Edward Arnold.

Harrison, K. A. (1985). Childbearing, health, and social priorities: a survey of 22,774 consecutive hospital births in Zaria, northern Nigeria. *British Journal of Obstetrics and Gynaecology*, 92 (supplement 5), 1–119.

Hill, P. (1972). *Rural Hausa: A Village and Setting*. Cambridge: Cambridge University Press.

Last, M. (1972). The presentation of sickness in a community of pagan Hausa (Nigeria). Paper presented at the Association of Social Anthropologists conference on social anthropology and medicine, University of Kent, 5–8 April.

Launiala, K. (1975). Paediatric Field Training Unit in Malumfashi. *Journal of Tropical Pediatrics and Environmental Child Health*, 21, 74, 1B.

Lloyd Evans, N., Drasar, B. S., and Tomkins, A. M. (1983). A comparison of the prevalence of Campylobacter, Shigellae, and Salmonellae in faeces of malnourished and well nourished children in the Gambia and northern Nigeria. *Transactions of the Royal Society of Tropical Medicine and Hygiene*, 77, 245–247.

Longhurst, R. W. (1980). Work, nutrition, and child malnutrition in a northern Nigerian village. Ph.D. diss., University of Sussex.

———. (1984). *The Energy Trap: Work, Nutrition, and Child Malnutrition in Northern Nigeria*. Cornell International Nutrition Monograph Series, no. 13. Ithaca, N.Y.: Cornell University Press.

Maternal health in sub-Saharan Africa. Editorial. (1987). *Lancet*, 1, 255–256.

Molineaux, L. and Gramiccia, G. (1980). *The Garki Project*. Geneva: World Health Organization.

Oomen, J. M. V. (1979). Body build and nutritional status of three ethnic groups inhabiting the same locality in northern Nigeria. *Tropical and Geographical Medicine*, 31, 395–403.

Pugh, R. N. H. and Gilles, H. M. (1976). Malumfashi Endemic Diseases Research Project. 3: urinary schistosomiasis, a longitudinal study. *Annals of Tropical Medicine and Parasitology*, 72, 471–482.

Tayo, M. and Jewsbury, J. M. (1978). Changes in snail population following the construction of a small dam. *Annals of Tropical Medicine and Parasitology*, 72, 483–487.

Tayo, M., Pugh, R. N. H., and Bradley, A. K. (1980). Water contact activities in the schistosomiasis study area. *Annals of Tropical Medicine and Parasitology*, 74, 347–354.

Tomkins, A. M. (1981). Nutritional status and severity of diarrhoea among pre-school children in rural Nigeria. *Lancet*, 1, 504–505.

Tomkins, A. M., Drasar, B. S., Bradley, A. K., and Williamson, W. A. (1978). Water supply and nutritional status in rural northern Nigeria. *Transactions of the Royal Society of Tropical Medicine and Hygiene*, 72, 239–243.

Tomkins, A. M., Bradley, A. K., Oswald, S., and Drasar, B. S. (1981). Diet and the faecal microflora of infants, children, and adults in rural Nigeria and urban UK. *Journal of Hygiene*, 86, 285–293.

Tomkins, A. M., Garlick, P. J., Schofield, W. H. N., and Waterlow, J. C. (1983). The combined effect of infection and malnutrition on protein metabolism in children. *Clinical Science*, 65, 313–324.

Whittle, H. C., Greenwood, B. M., Davidson, N., Tomkins, A. M., Tugwell, P., Warrell, D. A., Zalin, A., Bryceson, A. D. M., Parry, E. H. O., Brueton, M., Duggan, M., Oomen, J. M. V., and Rajkovic, A. D. (1973). Trial of chloramphenicol for meningitis in northern savanna of Africa. *British Medical Journal*, 3, 379–381.

Chapter 22

The Danfa Comprehensive Rural Health Project, Ghana, 1969–79: Health Sector Teaching, Service, and Research

Alfred K. Neumann, Frederick T. Sai, and Samuel Ofosu-Amaah

The Danfa Comprehensive Rural Health Project (1969–79) was a service, research, and training project designed to find solutions to health problems and to demonstrate feasible methods of delivering effective health and family planning services in rural Ghana.

The Danfa Project, although primarily a Ghanaian enterprise, is a dramatic example of the positive results that international collaboration can produce. This chapter summarizes material from the many studies carried out in Ghana by the University of Ghana Medical School (UGMS) Department of Community Health, and the Ministry of Health's Danfa Project, in collaboration with the University of California, Los Angeles (UCLA). The discussion will briefly review the Danfa Project's research design, organization and management, objectives, methods, and findings. It will focus particularly on the results of the epidemiological investigation carried out as one of the four project objectives.

National Background

At the time of this project, the pattern of health problems in Ghana was similar to that of most other West African countries and had an especially important impact on maternal and child health. Maternal health problems included mortality and morbidity from hemorrhage, infection, and toxemia associated with pregnancy. Child health was especially diminished by the interaction of malnutrition and infectious diseases, many of which were partially or wholly preventable.

Compared with most other countries in the region, Ghana's economic position was relatively strong due to substantial export earnings from cocoa, timber, gold, and diamonds. Yet, in the 1960s the government of Ghana recognized that the delivery of effective health care to the majority of rural Ghanaians was inadequate. Plans to expand rural health services were impeded by

funding problems. Funding was limited, partially because decelerating growth of real national income per capita accompanied the political and economic instability of the previous 15 years, and resources were highly concentrated in urban hospital facilities.

In 1969, the government recognized the consequences of Ghana's rapid population growth and developed an official population policy. A year later it established the Ghana National Family Planning Programme, with the objective of making family planning services accessible to all Ghanaians.

History and Design of the Danfa Project

In 1964, the University of Ghana Medical School (UGMS) decided to train general medical officers to supervise rural health teams. To do this, it needed a demonstration rural district close to the capital of Accra, where the Department of Community Health could conduct research, training, and service activities (see figure 22-1). In 1967 the Danfa District was selected as a field research and training area for the Medical School, and in 1970 the Danfa Health Center was opened. Thus, the UGMS/UCLA collaboration was added to the existing activities.

In order to allocate scarce resources rationally to the entire country, the Department of Community Health needed more systematic collection and analysis of rural health information. Furthermore, research was required to help determine how the family planning services, mandated by the national population policy, could best be implemented in rural Ghana. As a result, the Danfa Project was created.

External assistance funding to develop the research component of the Danfa Project was obtained from the United States Agency for International Development (USAID). The University of California, Los Angeles (UCLA), School of Public Health was identified to collaborate in the project. A feasibility study was

Figure 22-1. Danfa Project: Research and Service Areas

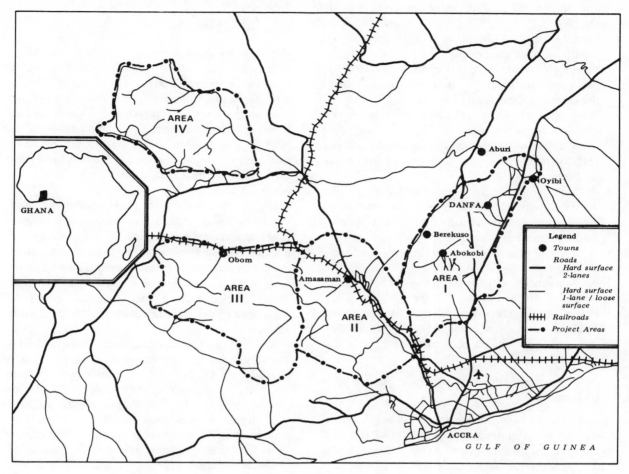

initiated in 1969, and the project agreement between the University of Ghana Medical School and the USAID mission to Ghana was signed in April 1970. The agreement indicated that four UCLA staff members were to be assigned to Ghana: a chief of party responsible for management, an epidemiologist, a family planning/maternal and child health (MCH) specialist, and a health educator. A health systems analyst was added to the staff in 1973. The Ghana Medical School was fully responsible for the service components of the project; UCLA was responsible for providing research assistance and also participated in some of the project's planning and teaching activities.

Goals and Objectives

The goal of the Danfa Project was to assist in initiating a demonstration family health program to improve the health and welfare of the people, especially in rural areas.

The objectives of the project were the following:

1. *Institutional development and training.* To strengthen the institutional capability of the Ghana Medical School to conduct research and to train doctors and other health workers in the delivery of rural health and family planning services.
2. *Information transfer.* To transfer information derived from the project activities to relevant government agencies on an ongoing basis.

Organization and Management

To foster harmonious working relationships, and to recognize the directive role of Ghanaian principals, the cooperating parties agreed to several conditions. These are mentioned here because observing the letter and the spirit of these preconditions, in retrospect, was key to the success of the collaboration over the ten-year period:

- Project goals and objectives would be developed jointly by UGMS and UCLA .
- The project would have two codirectors, one Ghanaian and one from UCLA. In case of disagreement, the Ghanaian view would prevail.
- Prospective staff for the UCLA team would have to be approved by both codirectors.
- Every effort would be made to promote genuine collaboration through joint UGMS-UCLA staffing of the project committees.
- A UGMS project budget provided by USAID and separate from UCLA would give the medical school the authority to hire requisite Ghanaian staff under local personnel practices.
- UGMS would bear nearly all service costs and most training costs.
- All data generated by the project would be available both in Ghana and at UCLA.
- Published materials would generally be coauthored by at least one Ghanaian and one UCLA staff member.
- A formal project review conference would be held at least once a year.

Health Status and Objectives of Health Status Measurement

One of the goals of the Danfa Project was to learn about the factors influencing the health of the rural population. Information generated by studies of health status was used to focus the Danfa health services delivery program and to enhance its effectiveness and efficiency.

- *Operational research in health and family planning.* To demonstrate several health care models that include family planning as an integrated component suitable to the Ghanaian context.
- *Epidemiological investigation.* To investigate a rural Ghanaian community by concentrating on factors associated with health and family planning behavior.

Initial Research Design

When the project was designed, controversy existed, both within Ghana and in international circles, over the most cost-effective way to deliver family planning services. Many thought that the most effective program would combine comprehensive health care and family planning services. This combination would produce a synergistic effect on fertility reduction, partly as a result of increased child survival and partly as a result of increased contact with women who needed family planning.

One of the major research efforts of the Danfa family planning program was to implement a quasi-experimental research design to help resolve this controversy and to evaluate four arguments regarding the implementation of national family planning policy. Four research areas were identified in the Danfa Project district, and each received services corresponding to one of the four arguments presented (see table 22-1).

The four-cell research design was deemphasized by 1976 because the government of Ghana decided (partially on the basis of the Danfa experience) to integrate family planning with basic health services (the area 1 approach). This decision also related to the high degree of population mobility and the socioeconomic differences existing among the four research areas over time. Epidemiologic studies, training, and research continued to be carried out.

Health status is not a self-evident concept. At the time of the project, consensus had only recently been reached that the definition of health should include physical, mental, and social well-being. Unfortunately, it was not possible, in the rural areas where the project district was located, to measure mental and social well-being. Our investigations into the health of the rural community concentrated primarily on the status

Table 22-1. Health Services Provided in Four Project Areas of the Danfa Project, Ghana, 1972–75

Area	Comprehensive health care	Health education	Family planning	Standard Ministry of Health services
1	Yes	Yes	Yes	Yes
2	No	Yes	Yes	Yes
3	No	No	Yes	Yes
4	No	No	No	Yes

of physical health and the sociodemographic and environmental factors related to it. The major objectives of these investigations were the following:

• To determine the sociodemographic characteristics of the population.
• To assess the prevalence of health problems and their impact on the population.
• To define the relation between sociodemographic and environmental factors and health status.

Phase 1: Assessment and Measurement

Sociodemographic data collected in a 1971 baseline census included information on the ethnic group, religion, occupation, and educational level of the respondents. A survey was conducted annually to identify movement into and out of the Danfa Project's district, and the same sociological data were recorded for immigrants. In 1975, a one-time socioeconomic survey was conducted to characterize the population by type of housing, material possessions, and source and quantity of income.

Health Status Measurement

The health problems of the Danfa District population were assessed by monitoring the records of the Danfa Rural Health Center, by conducting a Village Health Survey, special epidemiological surveys, and mortality assessments, and by analyzing regional and national health records.

HEALTH CENTER RECORDS. Each visit to the Danfa Rural Health Center was recorded on patient encounter cards specially designed for electronic data processing. From these data files, monthly and annual summaries were compiled of the diagnoses made at the Health Center.

VILLAGE HEALTH SURVEY. The Village Health Survey (VHS) comprised a physical and laboratory examination of a sample of about 4,000 persons in each of three years: 1973, 1975, and 1977. In the physical examination, physicians evaluated both acute and chronic problems and recorded the anthropometric measurements of children. In addition, data were obtained on activities that were restricted due to illness or injury in the previous two weeks.

SPECIAL EPIDEMIOLOGICAL SURVEYS. Special epidemiological surveys were conducted to assess the prevalence of malaria, poliomyelitis, and guinea worm. In addition, medical students carried out less elaborate surveys.

• *Malaria prevalence surveys.* Spleen and blood smear surveys were conducted before and during the malaria prophylaxis program in area 1, the treatment area, and in area 2, the control area, where no special malaria program was implemented. Children 0–5 years and schoolchildren 6–10 years of age were examined, and spleen, parasite, and parasite density rates were determined.
• *Poliomyelitis survey.* While the immunization program was being planned, the scarcity of reliable epidemiological data about the importance of poliomyelitis in tropical developing countries became obvious. In fact, most textbooks and reports suggested that poliomyelitis was infrequent because epidemics rarely occurred. The significance of poliomyelitis as an endemic disease had not been carefully studied. Schoolchildren, who were past the period of exposure to the widely prevalent virus, were examined to determine the prevalence of residual lameness attributable to poliomyelitis. Surprising results were obtained, and the polio survey became one of the project's most important investigations, having worldwide policy significance for polio vaccination.
• *Guinea worm survey.* In 1973, a reported outbreak of guinea worm led to a survey of the villages in the Danfa Project district. Prevalence rates were obtained, and the epidemiology of guinea worm in this part of Ghana, along with its social and economic consequences, was studied.

Mortality

Mortality data, especially on infant and child mortality rates, were derived from the census, from the annual resurvey of the population, and from the continuous registration of vital events. An attempt was also made to obtain cause-of-death data through the vital events registration program, but this proved futile because relatives, as a rule, could only vaguely describe the deceased's condition at the time of death.

Health Knowledge, Attitudes, and Practices

To assess health knowledge, attitudes, and practices the Danfa Project examined the records of health centers and conducted maternal and child health KAP surveys, health practice surveys (formerly referred to as the Household Health Related Behavior Survey), and other special surveys.

MCH KAP SURVEY. In 1972, 1975, and 1977 longitudinal surveys were carried out to examine changes in knowledge, attitudes, and practices concerning pregnancy and delivery as well as the cause and treatment of some specific problems of infancy and childhood. Data were collected on a group of 900 women in the four research areas.

HEALTH PRACTICES SURVEY. A survey was initiated to obtain information on behavioral patterns related to maternal and child health, nutrition, participation in well-child clinics, preventive care (such as immunization) programs, and village-level sanitation projects. The baseline data from this survey were used to focus the health education component of the project. Conducted initially in 1973, the survey was repeated in 1974 and 1975 to evaluate and refine the health education effort.

Results: Health Status at the Baseline

The greatest proportion of preventable morbidity and mortality occurs in mothers and children, who also use ambulatory health care services more than any other group. Infectious disease is important to both at all ages.

Maternal Health

At the time of this study, pregnancy-related deaths represented at least 4 percent of all deaths in Ghana (Kouznetsovir, 1977). No accurate records were kept of maternal mortality, but the rate in Ghana was estimated to be between 5 and 15 deaths per 1,000 live births. The leading causes of maternal death in Ghana were hemorrhage (65 percent), infection (7 percent), and toxemia (15 percent).

Maternal mortality is difficult to estimate in a small rural population because of mobility, inaccurate recording of cause of death (if a death certificate is completed at all), lack of pregnancy status information on the death certificate, and variability in number of deaths from year to year. A special attempt to estimate maternal mortality midway through the project produced an estimate of 4 per 1,000 live births, but the confidence intervals were wide.

Analysis of the frequency of pregnancy-related complaints seen during the Health Center's first year of operation suggested that only a small percentage of maternal problems were reported at the Health Center and its satellites in 1972. Based on incidence rates in the United States, less than 20 percent of the expected annual number of cases of bleeding, infection, toxemia, or prolonged labor in area 1 were being seen. Given the observed conditions of delivery in the village and the estimated maternal mortality rate,

maternal mortality and morbidity must have been an important problem. In that case, the low incidence of pregnancy-related problems reported at the Health Center could have been due to poor diagnosis and record keeping by the Health Center staff, poor referral practices by untrained traditional birth attendants (TBAS), or use of regional hospitals instead of the Health Center for maternal complications.

The Health Center's records of referrals to regional hospitals showed a somewhat higher incidence of pregnancy-related complications than the hospitals' own records did. This suggests that patient encounter cards may not have been filled out completely for all referrals. Still, it is likely that many complications were not seen at the Health Center, but were taken care of in the village or directly at a regional hospital. The patient thus by-passed the Health Center.

Child Health

The following are baseline indices of certain child health problems in area 1. They refer to 1972, unless otherwise noted. Infant mortality rate (less than 1 year): 54 per 1,000 (midyear population); preschool mortality rate (1–4 years): 16 per 1,000; child mortality rate (0–4 years): 25 per 1,000; percent of children 6–35 months below 80 percent of the standard weight-for-age: 33 percent; mean hemoglobin (0–4 years): 10.3; malaria mean parasite rate (0–10 years, 1973–74): 41 percent; measles incidence: 7.6 per 1,000 persons; pertussis incidence: 1.8 per 1,000 persons; *Ascaris* prevalence (0–4 years): 33 percent; hookworm prevalence (0–4 years): 22 percent; poliomyelitis lameness prevalence (schoolchildren, 1974): 7 per 1,000 children; diarrhea prevalence (0–4 years): 7 percent; skin infection prevalence (0–14 years): 22 percent.

Child mortality was serious, but not as severe as in less developed African countries or in other parts of Ghana at the time of this project. The baseline mortality rates were probably underestimated by as much as 30 percent, but still indicate that at least 12 percent of all children died before reaching age five even in this area, which had better medical services than most.

Nationally, *neonatal deaths* accounted for about 9 percent of all deaths. Many were due to prematurity, which is difficult to prevent or treat, especially in rural areas. The prematurity rate was 13 percent at the Danfa Health Center from 1970 to 1973. Neonatal tetanus was, however, an important cause of neonatal mortality and preventable either by immunization of the mother or by proper care of the cord. Although neonatal tetanus was not uncommon in the Greater Accra Region and 78 percent of the TBAS in the Danfa Project district reported having seen a condition resembling neonatal tetanus, the Health Center staff reported that they had not seen any cases. A baseline survey discovered that 59 percent of the TBAS used clean razor blades to cut the cord, which may have resulted in a lower rate of neonatal tetanus than in areas of Ghana where less clean objects (such as scissors or machetes) were often used.

Malnutrition

Mean birth weight for infants born at or near term (38–40 weeks gestation) and delivered at the Danfa Health Center from 1970 to 1973 was 3.3 kilograms, or 97 percent of the U.S. standard of 3.4. Only 6 percent could be classified as small for their gestational age, about the same percentage as in the United States. Although the sample was small (only 81 births) and the midwives' estimation of gestational age perhaps not wholly reliable, infants in area 1 of the Danfa District apparently began their lives in a normal nutritional state.

The first Village Health Survey showed, however, that nutritional status declined in early childhood. In the 5–35 months age group, 33 percent of the children's weights fell below 80 percent of the standard (normally only 3 percent of international reference groups fall below 80 percent of the standard weight-for-age), and 23 percent of their heights fell below 90 percent of the standard. An even larger percentage of children fell below standard in the 11–17 year age group. Arm circumference-for-age was similar to weight-for-age, with 37 percent of children 6–35 months of age falling below the standard.

Birth weights at the Danfa Health Center appeared to be near normal. The mean weights and heights dropped compared with standards during the period 12–35 months in males and 18–35 months in females. There was some catch-up from 3 to 10 years and then a further falling off during the usual period of adolescent growth (11 to 17 years). Rapid catch-up occurred again between 18 and 25 years, but the mean weights and heights never reached 100 percent of the standard.

Mean weight for mean height was below normal from 1 to 17 years. The departure of these growth patterns from international standards could have several explanations:

• It was a normal genetic variant unrelated to malnutrition.

• It represented a permanent reduction in growth related to intrauterine growth retardation and a permanent reduction in the number of body cells.

• It was due to suboptimal nutrition during childhood and adolescence and insufficient catch-up, which caused a degree of permanent reduction in final growth.

• A combination of the above.

Mild to moderate malnutrition may be important for two reasons:

• Diminished nutritional status seems to reduce immunologic competence and to cause more severe infections. Even if death does not ensue, nutritional status may deteriorate still further during the course of infection because of anorexia, vomiting, diarrhea, and increased metabolic demands. This can set up a vicious circle. At the time of the Danfa Project, case-fatality rates of diseases such as measles and whooping cough increased.

• Final growth attainment may be below the genetic potential of some children. This may compromise both their intellectual and their motor performance.

Infections

At the time of the project, the infectious diseases that affected mothers and children in Ghana the most were malaria, measles, pertussis, diarrhea, respiratory infection, helminths, poliomyelitis, tuberculosis, schistosomiasis, guinea worm, tetanus, and skin infections. Each is discussed in the following subsections.

MALARIA. In Ghana, 8 percent of all deaths were attributed to malaria, or about 16,000 deaths per year (Ghana Ministry of Health, 1967). Malaria also accounted for 30 percent of outpatient visits and 9 percent of hospital admissions.

Malaria had long been recognized as a problem in the Accra Plains. As is true today, the vectors *Anopheles gambiae* and *Anopheles funestus* were present all year, but their number increased, as did malaria transmission, during the rainy season. The Village Health Survey and the special malaria surveys provided epidemiological data on malaria prevalence, which are shown in table 22-2. The special malaria surveys conducted at various seasonal points from 1973 to 1975 showed that in area 2, where no malaria control was instituted, the mean enlarged spleen rate (for children 2–9 years old) was 46 percent, with a seasonal range of 33 to 58 percent. The Village Health Survey first showed, and the special surveys later confirmed, that malaria was an important problem, not

Table 22-2. Malaria Indices in Areas 1 and 2 of the Danfa Project, Ghana, 1973–75

Age and index	Baseline values (June 1973)[a]		Mean values (1973–75)[b]	
	Area 1	Area 2	Area 1	Area 2
0–5 years				
Spleen rate (percent)	16	43	14	41
Parasite rate (percent)	40	30	30	41
Parasite density[c]	—	—	60	109
6–10 years[d]				
Spleen rate (percent)	22	46	23	35
Parasite rate (percent)	34	41	28	40
Parasite density[c]	—	—	42	67

— Not examined.

a. Start of the rainy season.

b. Various seasons after the baseline in June 1973.

c. Geometric mean parasite density per cubic millimeter.

d. Schoolchildren only.

only among preschool children, but also among school-age children. The mean parasite rate in the 0–1 age group was 24 percent, in the 1–4 age group 45 percent, and in the 5–9 age group 44 percent. The mean parasite density (per cubic millimeter of blood) over a three-year period in area 2 was 145 in the 0–5 age group and 95 in the 6–10 age group. The lower density in the latter suggests that, although their parasite rates are similar, the 6–10 age group had a higher degree of immunity. In 88 percent of the cases the infections were single infections of *P. falciparum,* the most dangerous form of malaria. In the other cases the infections were either single or mixtures of *P. malariae* or *P. ovale,* with or without *P. falciparum.*

By strict World Health Organization definition, malaria in the Accra Plains (where most of the research areas were located) would be called mesoendemic since the spleen rate in the 2–9 year age group was not consistently over 50 percent. However, the age-specific spleen rates, parasite rates, and lack of marked seasonal change presented an epidemiological picture more consistent with hyperendemic malaria. This is supported by spleen rates over 45 percent in five of seven monthly observations, a low spleen rate in adults, parasite rates in the 1–4 year age group over 30 percent throughout the year, and inconsistent seasonal changes. Stable malaria is characterized by a high density of the vector, a vector with a frequent man-biting habit, and a temperature favorable to a rapid sporogenic cycle. In Danfa, malaria manifested many of the characteristics usually associated with stable malaria: hyperendemicity, *A. gambiae* vector, *P.*

falciparum predominating type, and high degree of immunity in adults. For these reasons, controlling the disease was difficult in the Accra Plains.

Malaria was the single most frequent diagnosis made at the Danfa Rural Health Center and its satellites (area 1) in 1972, accounting for 31 percent of all patient visits. However, 1972 was a relatively light year for malaria: the mean malaria diagnosis at the Health Center satellites for the five years 1972–76 was 43 percent. Of all infant visits, 13 percent were diagnosed as having malaria, as were 50 percent of 3–4-year-olds, 59 percent of 5–14-year-olds, and 33 percent of persons over 14. The monthly distribution of visits tended to follow the pattern of the rainy season, with 33 percent of malaria cases visiting the center and its satellites in May, June, and July, the wet period in this part of Ghana.

MEASLES. In Ghana, 5 percent of all deaths were attributed to measles. In fact, measles may have contributed to even more deaths since this disease frequently precedes kwashiorkor. While the cause of death may have been listed as kwashiorkor, the precipitating disease was often measles. The result was an underreporting of mortality due to measles (Ghana Ministry of Health, 1967).

During the first Village Health Survey, 44 percent of the mothers in area 1 said that their children under five had had measles; this may not be a reliable estimate, however, since other viral exanthems are often confused with measles. Baseline serological studies conducted as part of the VHS showed that by age five, 87 percent of children had positive measles antibody titers, which indicate either natural infection or vaccination.

The measles and smallpox eradication program, which had been operating prior to 1972, may have greatly reduced the usually high incidence of measles. In 1972 the Danfa Health Center and its satellites reported only 101 new cases, about 40 percent of the expected number. These cases accounted for only 1.3 percent of all diagnoses in children under five, but measles still ranked as a priority disease to hold under control.

PERTUSSIS. At the time of the project, accurate data about pertussis were difficult to obtain in most African countries, including Ghana. David Morley's studies in Nigeria suggested, however, that pertussis was a problem on the same order of magnitude as measles (see Morley, 1973).

The Village Health Survey serological studies showed that 27 percent of children 0–5 years of age had positive pertussis antibodies, although the reliability of using serological studies as an indicator of pertussis immunity is questionable. Still, since only 8 percent of mothers reported that their children had DPT immunization, as many as 19 percent may have had the illness. Only 24 new pertussis cases were reported at the Danfa clinics in 1972. This low figure could mean that pertussis was between epidemics at that time or that the disease was not being accurately diagnosed by Health Center staff.

DIARRHEA. The primary indicator of acute gastrointestinal infection is diarrhea. Despite water sources that are often impotable and a significant amount of mild to moderate malnutrition, severe diarrhea with dehydration (and severe malnutrition) was rarely diagnosed in children. The reasons are not clear.

At the Health Center, diarrhea constituted 21 percent of the complaints and diagnoses registered for 0–4 year-olds, with a peak clearly occurring in the 6–24 month age group. In the Village Health Survey, diarrhea was found in 7 percent of the children under 5 years of age, in 3 percent of those 5–14, and in 2 percent of those 15 or older. In a subsample, only 2 percent of the specimens from children under five contained *Salmonella* or *Shigella,* a considerably lower level than had been expected based on other studies of the region. Enteroviruses were isolated from 28 percent of the sample, including polioviruses types I and II, coxsackievirus groups A and B, and several types of ECHO virus, but these may not have been etiologic. As in other countries, enteropathogenic and enterotoxigenic *E. coli* or rotaviruses are probably responsible for a large majority of cases.

RESPIRATORY INFECTION. Respiratory complaints and diagnoses were second only to malaria in frequency at the Health Center. Upper respiratory infection (URI) was the most common respiratory complaint, accounting for 11 percent of all visits to Danfa clinics in 1972. Bronchitis and other lower respiratory disease accounted for another 3 percent of all visits. Children 0–4 years of age had an even higher rate; 17 percent of visits were due to respiratory disease.

HELMINTHS. At the time of the project the primary helminth problems in the Danfa District were *Ascaris* and *Necator.* Infections were acquired early and persisted, probably intermittently. Stool samples examined at the baseline Village Health Survey in area 1 showed positive rates for *Ascaris* (roundworm): 33 percent for children under 5 years of age, 51 percent for those 5–17, and 42 percent for persons 15 and older. The corresponding, positive rates for *Necator* (hookworm) were 22, 43, and 38 percent. By contrast, other intestinal parasites were much less frequent: *Strongyloides,* 4 percent overall; *Trichuris,* 1 percent overall; and *Giardia, Taenia,* and *E. histolytica*, not at all. No significant association existed between hookworm infections and anemia, which suggests that most of the hookworm loads were light.

A diagnosis of worms was the third most frequent diagnosis at the Health Center and its satellites in 1972, nearly 8 percent overall. Fewer than 1 percent of infants were diagnosed as having worms. Of children 1–4 (crawlers and toddlers), 11 percent were so diagnosed, as were 13 percent of 5–14-year-olds. But only 4 percent of persons 15 and older were diagnosed as having worms. The considerable difference between the levels seen by examining stools and diagnoses made by the Health Center staff was probably due to the large number of asymptomatic carriers, as well as the community's acceptance of mild worm infection as a relatively unimportant, self-limiting problem.

POLIOMYELITIS. Serological studies during the first VHS showed that the poliovirus was endemic. By five years of age, 65 percent of the children had antibodies to all three types of poliovirus; only 7 percent were triple negative.

Children were examined for lameness to assess the impact of endemic poliomyelitis and to test a widely held hypothesis that paralytic poliomyelitis was relatively rare (less than 1 case of lameness per 1,000 children affected) in the Danfa Project district. The observed prevalence of lameness attributable to poliomyelitis was 7 per 1,000 school-age children, and the annual incidence was at least 28 per 100,000 persons (Nicholas *et al.*, 1977). Although no evidence of an epidemic was found, these rates were comparable to those in the United States and Europe during severe epidemics and indicated the high price being paid in the Danfa District for the natural acquisition of immunity. As a result, immunization against poliomyelitis was given high priority in the Danfa Project. A teacher questionnaire, tested for use in postal surveys, was a rapid means of estimating the prevalence of lameness attributable to poliomyelitis in countries with a reasonable network of primary schools. This survey was administered by project staff to teachers in a sample of schools throughout Ghana, producing similar results (Ofosu-Amaah *et al.*, 1977).

The Danfa Project suggests that mean annual incidence rates in tropical endemic countries had always been as great as, if not greater than, those experienced by temperate countries in the twentieth century during epidemic periods. Moreover, the annual number of cases of paralytic poliomyelitis occurring in the world at the time of this study had been reduced only 25 percent since the advent of the polio vaccine. Partly as a result of this study, poliomyelitis immunization was given renewed emphasis in Ghana and helped stimulate polio-related work in other developing countries.

TUBERCULOSIS. A tuberculin skin test, which excluded persons showing a BCG scar, was included in the Village Health Survey. Conversion to a positive reaction rose with age. Only 3 percent of children under 5 were positive, but 15 percent of 5–14-year-olds and 42 percent of persons over 14 were positive. The Health Center staff diagnosed only four cases of tuberculosis in the entire year, although some of the cases in which a cough was diagnosed may actually have been tuberculosis. The Health Center staff, working with limited training and equipment, found diagnosing tuberculosis to be very difficult in all but its latest stages.

In any case, the skin test results indicated that tuberculosis was only a moderate problem (compared with areas of the world where as many as 90 percent of children have positive tuberculin reactions by age five) and that the greatest danger of infection existed during adolescence.

SCHISTOSOMIASIS. An important problem in other parts of Ghana, schistosomiasis was not significantly prevalent in area 1 of the Danfa Project district.

GUINEA WORM. At the time of the project, guinea worm was highly prevalent in northern Ghana, but much less so in southern Ghana, including area 1 of the Danfa Project district. In the Village Health Survey, only 1 of 957 people examined was diagnosed with guinea worm. The Health Center recorded 33 visits by 22 people with guinea worm in 1972. However, an outbreak in area 2 in 1973 led the project to conduct a special epidemiologic survey of 159 villages in areas 1, 2, and 3. Most of the problem was confined to area 2, where attack rates as high as 80 percent were found in some villages (among males 25–44 years old). This was the first outbreak of guinea worm in many of these villages, which suggests that the disease was spreading. The study documented particularly important economic implications. The average work loss in untreated adults was more than five weeks, and guinea worm disease, which is seasonal, coincides with peak agricultural activities. Because few alternative labor sources were available for incapacitated farmers, agricultural output was markedly reduced (Belcher *et al.*, 1975).

TETANUS. Tetanus accounted for 3 percent of all deaths in Ghana (Ghana Ministry of Health, 1967); about half were neonatal. Only one case of tetanus was diagnosed at the Danfa Health Center in 1972.

SKIN INFECTIONS. Severe skin infections were primarily pyoderma and tropical ulcer. Pyoderma was the most common and showed a pronounced age-related distribution. The first Village Health Survey found 22 percent of children under 15 in area 1 suffering from one or more pyodermal foci, but only 6 percent of those who were older. Young children seem to be more prone to dermal injury and subsequent infection. Among older ages, farmers and laborers were more likely than teachers and traders to have pyoderma. Tropical ulcers were seen in 5 percent of the persons examined in the Village Health Survey and were concentrated in people over five years of age, especially in the 5–14 year age group.

Immunizations

For a number of years before the Danfa Project began, the Regional Medical Field Unit carried out BCG, measles, and smallpox vaccinations as part of the West African campaign to eradicate smallpox. In the first

Village Health Survey, mothers were asked about prior immunizations of their children under five. In area 1, 44 percent reported prior smallpox vaccination (60 percent actually had a smallpox vaccination scar), 23 percent reported measles vaccination, 8 percent pertussis vaccination, and only 7 percent BCG vaccination against tuberculosis (although 10 percent had BCG scars). Prior measles vaccination might actually have been higher because it was usually given with smallpox vaccination. Of children 5–14, 11 percent had BCG scars; of persons over five, 90 percent had smallpox scars.

These results showed that smallpox immunization levels were diminishing, but the significance was questionable since the disease appeared to have been eradicated from West Africa at that time. Measles, pertussis, and BCG immunization levels were far too low.

Chronic Disabilities and Other Health Problems

Chronic disabilities and chronic health problems included hernia, hypertension, leprosy, anemia, loss of visual acuity, hearing loss, amputation, and diseases associated with smoking.

HERNIA. The Village Health Survey found that 34 percent of children under one in area 1 had umbilical hernias, as did 19 percent in the 5–14 year age group. In persons over 14, umbilical hernias were present in only 8 percent of the cases. This is a self-limiting condition that decreases with age and does not usually require surgery. However, indirect inguinal hernias were present in 7 percent of the males over 20, a problem that creates great surgical demand in Africa.

HYPERTENSION. Of the 16–55-year-old adults in the project district screened for hypertension, only 2.5 percent had diastolic pressures equal to or greater than 95.

LEPROSY. The prevalence of leprosy measured in the Village Health Survey was about 2 per 1,000. This prevalence was lower than that in some African countries where rates of 10 to 20 per 1,000 had been observed and where prevalence was even higher in certain highly endemic pockets.

ANEMIA. Only 1.7 percent of the pregnant women seen at the Danfa Health Center from 1970 to 1973 had a hemoglobin count below 7.1 grams. The first Village Health Survey also showed that severe anemia was uncommon in the project district. However, one-fourth

of the children 0–4 years and one-tenth of those 5–9 years had a hemoglobin of 7–10 grams.

VISUAL ACUITY. Of the persons under 45, 84 percent had normal vision; of those 45 and older, 51 percent were suffering moderate to severe loss of acuity.

HEARING LOSS. Significant reduction in hearing was evident in fewer than 1 percent of the persons 15–44 years but in 8 percent of those 45 or older.

AMPUTATIONS. Only 2 of 961 people examined had lost an arm or a leg.

SMOKING HABITS. Only men smoked in the Danfa Project area: 7 percent of the adult males were pipe smokers, and 41 percent smoked cigarettes, as reported in the first VHS. Only 16 percent of the adult male population smoked 10 or more cigarettes per day. Smoking by women was virtually nonexistent.

Functional Impairment

As part of the early effort to assess morbidity in the Danfa District, the baseline longitudinal survey included a section on illnesses and related sequelae in the two weeks before the interview. Respondents were asked to describe their symptoms and to indicate the number of days they had been forced to restrict their activities either entirely or in part during the past two weeks. Of the persons surveyed, 24 percent had been ill at some time in the previous two weeks, and of these, 39 percent had had to restrict some of their activity. Thus, of the total sample, 9 percent had restricted their activities due to illness in the preceding 14-day period. To a slight but statistically significant degree, women were restricted more days than men. Of the schoolchildren, 7 percent had lost at least one day of school due to illness, and the average loss for all schoolchildren was 0.2 days in the two-week period. Of the individuals who were economically active, 10 percent had lost at least one day of work due to illness. The average loss of productive time per member of the working population in the project district was 0.6 days in the two-week period, or roughly 5 percent of a six-day work week.

Mortality Rates

Table 22-3 shows mortality rates in the four research areas observed in 1971–72. The variation among the areas was considerable. Most impressive is the infant mortality rate, which ranged from a low of 54 per

Table 22-3. Baseline Mortality Rates in Four Project Areas of the Danfa Project, Ghana, First Vital Events Registration Period, 1971–72

Rate	Area 1	Area 2	Area 3	Area 4
Infant mortality rate[a]	54	79	99	59
Preschool mortality rate[b]	16	17	23	16
Childhood mortality rate[c]	25	31	41	24
Crude death rate[d]	12	14	15	10

a. Per 1,000 children under age 1 at midyear (used instead of live births because of high inmigration).
b. Per 1,000 children age 1–4 years.
c. Per 1,000 children age 0–4 years.
d. Per 1,000 persons.

1,000 in area 1 to 99 per 1,000 in area 3. Areas 1 and 4 were closely matched in many respects, including mortality rates. Areas 2 and 3 were similar in many respects, and this can be seen in the infant mortality rates.

Phase 2: Malaria Prevention

At the time of the Danfa Project, malaria required attention in all MCH programs in West Africa. It was prevalent and serious, and Africans were susceptible to attack. In Africa 87 percent of the people were exposed to malaria, most in areas without any control measures. Malaria was probably the number one killer in Africa, causing approximately 600,000 deaths annually in children under five. Malaria caused 10–20 percent of all deaths in this age group.

The Danfa Project provided a good opportunity to study the effects of chemoprophylaxis as a control measure in rural Ghana. Pyrimethamine, trade-named Daraprim, was used as the suppressant rather than chloroquine for several reasons:

- Pyrimethamine is tasteless—a major advantage in ensuring that small children will take the medication without fuss.
- It has a lower toxicity than chloroquine if an overdose is accidentally taken.
- Pyrimethamine had been used by David Morley, whose approach was being widely applied in many African clinics for children under five. Further evaluation of the effectiveness of this drug in monthly prophylaxis was desirable.

One 25 milligram tablet was given each month to children under six years and two tablets to schoolchildren six to ten years of age. Infants under three months received one-half tablet. Schoolchildren were included because project surveys showed high parasite rates persisting until 10 years of age. The tablet was given monthly rather than weekly to reduce parasite density in the blood and prevent severe attacks. It was hypothesized that in this way the development of naturally acquired immunity to malaria would not be suppressed. To reduce the likelihood of severe attacks further, mothers were given a chloroquine tablet to use if their child developed fever during the month.

The crucial task was to reach at least 80 percent of the children. Initially, children under five who lived in villages within one mile of the Health Center or its satellite clinics came to an under-five clinic to receive their tablet. In other villages, volunteers were recruited and trained to organize monthly tablet distributions. In schools, the head teachers usually accepted responsibility for distribution. An important policy was that the tablet had to be swallowed in the presence of the volunteer distributor. During the first year of the program, 56 percent of the children under five received tablets each month in the volunteer villages, but only 35 percent in the Health Center villages. For this reason, a completely volunteer system was subsequently used. The Health Center's sanitarian supervised the field program as one of his many responsibilities.

The impact of the study was assessed in area 1, the treatment area, by periodic malaria surveys during the first two years and for comparison in area 2, where no control program was carried out.

Based on blood surveys of a sample of both participants and nonparticipants at the Danfa Health Center and on a mathematical analysis of differences in parasitemia rates in areas 1 and 2, the risk of parasitemia was apparently reduced by as much as 78 percent in the month after the tablet was taken.

A major objection to the use of pyrimethamine in mass chemoprophylaxis was the development of resistance. After the first five program months, no pyrimethamine resistance was found, but after two years 38 percent of parasitemia in area 1 was found to be resistant. Most of these resistances were mild, and parasite densities were reduced markedly after the drug was administered. Only 7 percent were fully resistant, and resistance to pyrimethamine usually disappeared rapidly after the drug was withdrawn. The pyrimethamine-resistant parasite seemed to be at a natural disadvantage in the usual ecological state.

Family Planning

The family planning component of the Danfa Project was considerable, and no attempt will be made to do it justice here. The appendix contains references to the appropriate articles and the *Danfa Final Report*. Suffice it to say that the highest acceptance and best continuity rates were attained in the presence of a good MCH program, a community health education program, and trained TBAS. The results were so good, in fact, that if the same acceptance and continuity rates had continued for 25 years, an absolute decline would have taken place in the population. The Danfa Project demonstrated the practicality of a viable, affordable, low-cost family planning program offering rural southern Ghana no cash incentives and no giveaways, just a good service and educational program.

Although this chapter is primarily devoted to epidemiological considerations, the fact must be underscored that a major portion of the Danfa effort and expenditure was devoted to seeking effective, realistic, and affordable ways of implementing a national family planning program along with maternal and child health services. That the very positive and practical recommendations from this aspect of the research were largely not implemented is unfortunate. The full analysis of the dynamics explaining this requires more space than is available here. Prominent factors include a general and severe economic decline through most of the 1970s and into the 1980s, political instability, and the apparent absence of forceful, effective Ghanaian health and family planning leadership at critical junctures.

Conclusions and Recommendations

Feachem and Jamison, in chapter 1 of this volume, indicate that "at the time of independence for most African nations, inadequate data sharply limited the capacity of the new African governments to form an adequate picture of the demographic and epidemiological status of the populations for which they were responsible." In the last quarter century, many African countries have taken great strides toward remedying this situation.

One of the major objectives of the Danfa Project was to gather accurate demographic and epidemiologic data. One of its major accomplishments was to demonstrate that Ghana had the planning and managerial talent and the personnel necessary to conceptualize and carry out a complex undertaking.

What, if any, is the role of external assistance and collaborators? Their role must be limited, and perhaps catalytic; most of the work and financing of research must be done by the host country.

A handful of hardworking, dedicated individuals are at the heart of every successful effort, and these individuals work most efficiently away from the demands and pressures of routine chores and family. This is even more true in developing countries, where the demands that the extended family makes on the successful person are awesome and not to be ignored. Shortages and equipment breakdowns, relatively minor annoyances in industrialized countries, often frustrate even the most dedicated worker. One of the implicit objectives of this volume is to help strengthen existing and create new "islands of national and international demographic and epidemiologic excellence" in Africa. The following observations from the Danfa experience might help explain the productivity of its staff and suggest useful ideas for others:

1. A core of computer equipment and logistic support was already in place in Ghana.
2. Additional equipment and vehicular support were provided through external funding sources.
3. When an equipment breakdown or supply shortage occurred, the Danfa team had foreign exchange resources and could quickly secure the needed items or services.
4. Expert consultants could be brought in quickly.
5. Statistical, editorial, and manuscript preparation services were available through UCLA.
6. At critical junctures at which concentrated periods of activity and collegial discussion were required, senior Ghanaians could be brought to a university setting outside of Ghana.
7. The UCLA collaborators in Ghana often served as extra pairs of hands at critical junctures.
8. Long-term (10 year) funding was assured.

In the future, we can use the experiences of the Danfa and other projects to expand and facilitate further the collection and analysis of the high-quality demographic and epidemiologic data so important to planning. One approach might be to foster a series of at least five-year, but preferably ten-year, collaborative grants involving clusters of African countries and external institutions working under multilateral agency auspices.

The legacy of the Danfa Project is multifaceted and continues. The immediate objectives of the Danfa project were met. There was disappointment that more of the research findings and recommendations were not implemented, as was mentioned in "Family Planning," above. But much of the work initiated during the years of active collaboration between the UGMS and UCLA continues as ongoing activities of the Department of Community Health of the University of Ghana Medical School. "Danfa alumni" are in key educational, administrative, research, and policymaking positions in Ghana and in key positions in organizations in many other parts of the world. Concepts and ideas evolved during the "Danfa years" continue to be refined and applied. Rural focused teaching and practical experience for UGMS medical students initiated during the UGMS/UCLA collaboration continues and has increased the pool of Ghanaian physicians with a good understanding of rural health problems. The organizers of the current national Ghanaian Traditional Birth Attendant (TBA) training program utilized the Danfa TBA materials, the experience of the UGMS staff—who continue to work with TBSS in the Danfa area to this day—and the experience of Danfa alumni to build a solid national program. As Ghana prepares a new national MCH/family planning program, it is anticipated that the Danfa experience will make a significant contribution.

Thus, the Danfa legacy is far-reaching, evolving, and enduring. It is planned to reevaluate this project in the 1990s.

Acknowledgment

Silas R. A. Dodu, while dean of the University of Ghana Medical School, served as project co-director of the Danfa Project from 1972 through 1975 to emphasize the importance the Medical School attached to the project and to the UGMS/UCLA collaboration. In this capacity he helped ensure financial and administrative continuity and provided critical intellectual input to the project at a time of administrative transition. Both this contribution to the project and his comments on an earlier draft of this chapter are gratefully acknowledged.

Appendix. Danfa Project Publications and Reports

This appendix consists of a chronological list of published papers, monographs, and training manuals dealing with the Danfa Project.

Published Papers

1972

Ashitey, G. A., Wurapa, F. K., and Belcher, D. W. Danfa Rural Health Centre: its patients and services, 1970–71. *Ghana Medical Journal*, 11(3), 266–273.

Kpedekpo, C. M. K. The planning and design of sampling surveys with particular reference to the epidemiological survey of the Danfa Project in Ghana. *Ghana Medical Journal*, 11(4), 377–382.

Kwansa, E. V. G., Cannon, J. A., Belcher, D. W., and Hosu-Porbley, M. Perception and comprehension of health education visual aids by rural Ghanaian villagers. *Ghana Medical Journal*, 11(4), 387–396.

Neumann, A. K., Prince, J., Gilbert, E. F., and Lourie, I. M. The Danfa/Ghana Comprehensive Rural Health and Family Planning Project: preliminary report. *Ghana Medical Journal*, 11(1), 18–24.

Sai, F. T., Wurapa, F. K., and Quartey-Papafio, E. The Danfa/Ghana Comprehensive Rural Health and Family Planning Project: a community approach. *Ghana Medical Journal*, 11(1), 9–17.

1973

Neumann, A. K., Sai, F. T., Lourie, I. M., and Wurapa, F. K. A new trend in international health work: the Danfa Project. *Focus: Technical Cooperation, International Development Review*, 2, 11–12.

1974

Neumann, A. K., Ampofo, D. A., Nicholas, D. D., Ofosu-Amaah, S., and Wurapa, F. K. Traditional birth attendants: a key to rural maternal and child health and family planning services. *Journal of Tropical Pediatrics and Environmental Child Health* 20(1), 21–27.

Neumann, A. K. and Dodu, S. R. A. Danfa Project. Letter. *Lancet*, 1(7857), 570.

Neumann, A. K., Sai, F. T., and Dodu, S. R. A. Danfa Comprehensive Rural Health and Family Planning Project: Ghana, research design. *Journal of Tropical Pediatrics and Environmental Child Health*, 20(1), 39–54.

Wurapa, F. K., Belcher, D. W., Neumann, A. K., and Lourie, I. M. An approach to illness measurement in a rural community: a questionnaire sample survey of households in the population of the Danfa Comprehensive Rural Health and Family Planning Project in Ghana. *Ghana Medical Journal*, 13, 98–105.

1975

Belcher, D. W., Afoakwa, S. N., Osei-Tutu, E., Wurapa, F. K., and Osei, L. Non-group-A streptococci in Ghanaian patients with pyoderma. *Lancet*, 2(7943), 1032.

Belcher, D. W., Neumann, A. K., Wurapa, F. K., Nicholas, D. D., and Ofosu-Amaah, S. The role of health survey research in maternal and child health/family planning programs: Danfa Project, Ghana. *Journal of Tropical Pediatrics and Environmental Child Health*, 21(4), 173–177.

Belcher, D. W., Nicholas, D. D., Ofosu-Amaah, S., Wurapa, F. K., and Blumenfeld, S. N. Factors influencing utilization of a malaria prophylaxis programme in Ghana. *Social Science and Medicine*, 9, 241–248.

Belcher, D. W., Wurapa, F. K., and Ward, W. B. Failure of thiabendazole and metronidazole in the treatment and suppression of guinea worm disease. *American Journal of Tropical Medicine and Hygiene*, 24(3), 444–446.

Belcher, D. W., Wurapa, F. K., Ward, W. B., and Lourie, I. M. Guinea worm in southern Ghana: its epidemiology and impact on agricultural productivity. *American Journal of Tropical Medicine and Hygiene*, 24(2), 243–249.

Kpedekpo, G. M. K., Wurapa, F. K., Lourie, I. M., Belcher, D. W., and Neumann, A. K. A modified Myburgh's formula for estimating the expectation of life at birth from survival data derived from vital registration records. *Sankhya: The Indian Journal of Statistics*, 37(series B, part 1), 106–113.

Wurapa, F. K., Belcher, D. W., and Ward, W. B. A clinical picture of guinea worm disease in southern Ghana. *Ghana Medical Journal*, 14, 10–15.

Wurapa, F. K., Derban, L. K. A., Belcher, D. W., Chinery, W. A., and Asante, R. O. A survey of parasitic infections in rural Ghana. *Ghana Medical Journal*, 14(4), 282–288.

1976

Ampofo, D., Nicholas, D. D., Ofosu-Amaah, S., and Neumann, A. K. The Danfa family planning program in rural Ghana. *Studies in Family Planning*, 7(10), 266–274.

Belcher, D. W., Neumann, A. K., Wurapa, F. K., and Lourie, I. M. Comparison of morbidity interviews with health examination survey in rural Africa. *American Journal of Tropical Medicine and Hygiene*, 25(5), 751–758.

Belcher, D. W., Pobee, J. O. M., Larbi, E. O., Occran, K., and Wurapa, F. K. A rural health examination survey in Ghana—non-response factors. *Public Health Reports*, 91(4), 368–372.

Belcher, D. W., Wurapa, F. K., and Atuora, N. Endemic rabies in Ghana: epidemiology and control measures. *American Journal of Tropical Medicine and Hygiene*, 25(5), 724–729.

Belcher, D. W., Wurapa, F. K., Neumann, A. K., and Lourie, I. M. A household morbidity survey in rural Africa. *International Journal of Epidemiology*, 5(2), 113–120.

Belcher, D. W., Wurapa, F. K., Nicholas, D. D., and Ofosu-Amaah, S. The role of health examination surveys in planning rural medical services. 1: planning and conducting rural health surveys. *Ghana Medical Journal*, 15, 86–92.

Johnson, O. G., Neumann, A. K., and Ofosu-Amaah, A. Health information system installation: principles and problems. *Medical Care*, 3, 210–222.

Neumann, A. K., Ofosu-Amaah, S., Ampofo, D. A., Nicholas, D. D., and Asante, R. O. Integration of family planning and MCH in rural West Africa. *Journal of Biosocial Science*, 8, 161–173.

Neumann, A. K., Ward, W. B., Pappoe, M., and Boyd, D. Education and evaluation in an integrated MCH/FP project in rural Ghana: the Danfa Project. *International Journal of Health Education*, 18(4), 233–244.

Nicholas, D. D., Ampofo, D. A., Ofosu-Amaah, S., Asante, R. O., and Neumann, A. K. Attitudes and practices of traditional birth attendants in rural Ghana: implications for training in Africa. *WHO Bulletin*, 54, 343–348.

Wurapa, F. K. and Belcher, D. W. A tuberculin skin test survey in a rural Ghanaian population. *Tropical and Geographical Medicine*, 28, 291–296.

Wurapa, F. K., Belcher, D. W., Afoakwa, S. N., Mingle, J. A. A., Kelemen, G., and Voros, S. Gastrointestinal infections in preschool children in the Danfa Project area. *Ghana Medical Journal*, 15, 158–162.

1977

Ampofo, D. A., Nicholas, D. D., Amonoo-Acquah, M. B., Ofosu-Amaah, S., and Neumann, A. K. The training of traditional birth attendants in Ghana: experience of the Danfa rural health project. *Tropical and Geographical Medicine*, 29, 197–203.

Belcher, D. W., Afoakwa, S. N., Osei-Tutu, E., Wurapa, F. K., and Osei, L. Endemic pyoderma in Ghana: a survey in rural villages. *Transactions of the Royal Society of Tropical Medicine and Hygiene*, 71(3), 204–209.

Bruce-Tagoe, A., Belcher, D. W., Wurapa, F. K., Turkson, P., Nicholas, D., and Ofosu-Amaah, S. Haematological values in a rural Ghanaian population. *Journal of Tropical and Geographical Medicine*, 29, 237–244.

Nicholas, D. D., Kratzer, J. H., Ofosu-Amaah, S., and Belcher, D. W. Is poliomyelitis a serious problem in developing countries? 1: the Danfa experience. *British Medical Journal*, 1, 1009–1012.

Ofosu-Amaah, S., Kratzer, J. H., and Nicholas, D. D. Is poliomyelitis a serious problem in developing countries? 2: lameness in Ghanaian schools. *British Medical Journal*, 1, 1012–1014.

Pobee, J. O. M., Larbi, E. B., Belcher, D. W., Wurapa, F. K., and Dodu, S. R. A. Blood pressure distribution in a rural Ghanaian population. *Transactions of the Royal Society of Tropical Medicine and Hygiene*, 71(1), 66–77.

1978

Belcher, D. W., Neumann, A. K., Ofosu-Amaah, S., Nicholas, D. D., and Blumenfeld, S. N. Attitudes toward family size and family planning in rural Ghana. *Journal of Biosocial Science*, 1Q, 59–79.

Belcher, D. W., Nicholas, D. D., Ofosu-Amaah, S., and Wurapa, F. K. A mass immunization campaign in rural Ghana: factors affecting participation. *Public Health Reports*, 93(2), 170–176.

Belcher, D. W., Nyame, P. K., and Wurapa, F. K. The prevalence of inguinal hernia in adult males. *Tropical and Geographical Medicine*, 30, 39–43.

Lamptey, P., Nicholas, D. D., Ofosu-Amaah, S., and Lourie, I. An evaluation of male contraceptive acceptance in rural Ghana. *Studies in Family Planning*, 9(8), 222–226.

Ward, W. B., Sam, M., Nicholas, D., and Pappoe, M. E. Impact of family planning information on acceptance at a Ghanaian rural health post. *International Journal of Health Education*, 21(4), 266–274.

1979

Belcher, D. W., Nicholas, D. D., Ofosu-Amaah, S., and Kratzer, J. A comparison of methods for estimating the frequency of paralytic poliomyelitis in developing countries. *WHO Bulletin*, 57(2), 301–307.

Neumann, A. K., Wurapa, F. K., Lourie, I. M., and Ofosu-Amaah, S. Strategies for strengthening health service infrastructure. *Social Science and Medicine*, 13C(2), 129–135.

Monographs (published by the University of California at Los Angeles)

1975

Belcher, D. W., Wurapa, F. K., Nicholas, D. D., Kpedekpo, G. M. K., Ofosu-Amaah, S., Derban, L. K., and Asante, R. O. *Conducting a Rural Health Survey: Experience from the Village Health Survey, Danfa Project, Ghana.* Monograph Series, no. 9.

Kpedekpo, G. M. K., Asuming, K., Blumenfeld, S. N., Wurapa, F. K., and Belcher, D. W. *An Analysis of the Characteristics of Households.* Demography 3, Monograph Series, no. 8.

Kpedekpo, G. M. K., Belcher, D. W., Wurapa, F. K., Neumann, A. K., and Lourie, I. M. *Results of the Analysis and Evaluation of Vital Registration Data from the Four Project Areas.* Vital Events 1, Monograph Series, no. 1.

Kpedekpo, G. M. K., Lourie, I. M., Wurapa, F. K., Belcher, D. W., and Neumann, A. K. *The Basic Demographic Characteristics of the Danfa Project Areas: An Analysis of the Population Size, Age/Sex Distribution.* Demography 1, Monograph Series, no. 6.

Kpedekpo, G. M. K., Nicholas, D. D., Ofosu-Amaah, S., Wurapa, F. K., and Belcher, D. W. *Estimates of Indices of Fertility from Registration Data.* Vital Events 3, Monograph Series, no. 3.

Kpedekpo, G. M. K., Wurapa, F. K., Belcher, D. W., Neumann, A. K., and Lourie, I. M. *The Basic Demographic Characteristics of the Danfa Project Areas: An Analysis of Marital Status, Education, Ethnic, Religious, and Occupational Composition.* Demography 2, Monograph Series, no. 7.

Kpedekpo, G. M. K., Wurapa, F. K., Lourie, I. M., Belcher, D. W., and Neumann, A. K. *Estimates of Indices of Mortality from Registration Data.* Vital Events 2, Monograph Series, no. 2.

Kpedekpo, G. M. K., Wurapa, F. K., Lourie, I. M., Neumann, A. K., and Belcher, D. W. *Some Results and Problems on the Estimation of Vital Rates in a Rural African Setting via Multiple Methods.* Vital Events 4, Monograph Series, no. 4.

———. *Migration Patterns, Population Growth, and Change in the Project Areas of Danfa.* Vital Events 5, Monograph Series, no. 5.

1976

Belcher, D. W., Kpedekpo, G. M. K., Wurapa, F. K., and Lourie, I. M. *Mapping and House Numbering Methods in a Rural Health Project.* Monograph Series, no. 10.

Belcher, D. W., Wurapa, F. K., Lourie, I. M., Kwabia, K., and Avle, S. *Experience in Selecting Training and Supervising Interviewers in a Rural Health Project.* Monograph Series, no. 11.

1979

Danfa Project. *Final Report.* Accra and Los Angeles: University of Ghana and UCLA.

Training Manuals

1977

Manual A and B for Health Workers and Serving Personnel, March.

A Programme Manual for Traditional Birth Attendants: Organization, Training, and Evaluation, December.

1978

Danfa Comprehensive Rural Health and Family Planning Project: Ghana—Preliminary Manual for Trainers of Village Health Workers, Phase I and Phase II.

References

Belcher, D. W., Wurapa, F. W., Ward, W. B., and Lourie, I. M. (1975). Guinea worm in southern Ghana: its epidemiology and impact on agricultural productivity. *American Journal of Tropical Medicine and Hygiene*, 24(2), 243–249.

Ghana Ministry of Health. (1967). *Medical Statistics Report 1.* Accra.

Kouznetsovir, L. (1977). Malaria control. *WHO Chronicle*, 31, 98–101.

Morley, D. (1973). *Paediatric Priorities in the Developing World.* London: Butterworth's.

Nicholas, D. D., Kratzer, J. H., Ofosu-Amaah, S., and Belcher, D. W. (1977). Is poliomyelitis a serious problem in developing countries? 1: the Danfa experience. *British Medical Journal*, 1, 1009–1012.

Ofosu-Amaah, S., Kratzer, J. H., and Nicholas, D. D. (1977). Is poliomyelitis a serious problem in developing countries? 2: lameness in Ghanaian schools. *British Medical Journal*, 1, 1012–1014.